HANDBOOK ON THE POLITICS AND GOVERNANCE OF BIG DATA AND ARTIFICIAL INTELLIGENCE

ELGAR HANDBOOKS IN POLITICAL SCIENCE

Elgar Handbooks in Political Science provide an overview of recent research in all areas relating to the study of political science including comparative politics, international relations, political economy, political theory and research methods, ensuring a comprehensive and overarching guide to the field. The constituent volumes, edited by leading international scholars within the field, are high quality works of lasting significance, often interdisciplinary in approach. The Handbooks discuss both established and new research areas, expanding current debates within the field, as well as signposting how research may advance in the future. The series will form an essential reference point for all academics, researchers and students of political science.

For a full list of Edward Elgar published titles, including the titles in this series, visit our website at www.e-elgar.com.

Handbook on the Politics and Governance of Big Data and Artificial Intelligence

Edited by

Andrej Zwitter

Professor of Governance and Innovation and Dean of Faculty, Campus Fryslân, University of Groningen, the Netherlands

Oskar J. Gstrein

Programme Director of BSc Data Science and Society, Assistant Professor of Governance and Innovation, Member, Data Research Centre, Campus Fryslân, University of Groningen, the Netherlands

ELGAR HANDBOOKS IN POLITICAL SCIENCE

Edward **Elgar**
PUBLISHING

Cheltenham, UK • Northampton, MA, USA

Published by
Edward Elgar Publishing Limited
The Lypiatts
15 Lansdown Road
Cheltenham
Glos GL50 2JA
UK

Edward Elgar Publishing, Inc.
William Pratt House
9 Dewey Court
Northampton
Massachusetts 01060
USA

A catalogue record for this book
is available from the British Library

Library of Congress Control Number: 2023935407

This book is available electronically in the **Elgar**online
Political Science and Public Policy subject collection
http://dx.doi.org/10.4337/9781800887374

ISBN 978 1 80088 736 7 (cased)
ISBN 978 1 80088 737 4 (eBook)

Typeset by Cheshire Typesetting Ltd, Cuddington, Cheshire
Printed and bound by CPI Group (UK) Ltd, Croydon, CR0 4YY

Contents

Figures

Tables

Contributors

Halefom H. Abraha – University of Malta

Javier Argota Sánchez-Vaquerizo – Researcher, Computational Social Science Department at ETH Zurich, Switzerland

Taís Fernanda Blauth – Doctoral Researcher at the Department of Governance and Innovation, Campus Fryslân – University of Groningen, The Netherlands

Malcolm Campbell-Verduyn – Assistant Professor, Faculty of Arts, University of Groningen; Associate Fellow, Käte Hamburger Kolleg Centre for Global Cooperation, Research University of Duisburg-Essen, Germany

Elizabeth Coombs – Affiliated Associate Professor, University of Malta

Caroline L. Davey – Design Against Crime Solution Centre, University of Salford, UK

Daniel Feitosa – Assistant Professor Faculty of Science and Engineering, University of Groningen, The Netherlands

Nikolaus Forgó – Professor, Department of Innovation and Digitalisation in Law, University of Vienna, Austria

Joshua C. Gellers – Associate Professor and Director of the MA in International Affairs program in the Department of Political Science and Public Administration at the University of North Florida, USA

Oskar J. Gstrein – Programme Director, BSc Data Science & Society; Assistant Professor, Governance and Innovation, Member, Data Research Centre, Campus Fryslân, University of Groningen, The Netherlands

David J. Gunkel – Presidential Teaching Professor of Communication Studies at Northern Illinois University, USA

Amelia Hadfield – Dean International, Head of Department of Politics, Founder and Former Co-Director of the Centre for Britain and Europe (CBE), University of Surrey, UK

Dagmar Heinrich – Design Against Crime Solution Centre, University of Salford, UK

Dirk Helbing – Professor, Computational Social Science at ETH Zurich, Switzerland; Complexity Science Hub Vienna, Austria

Theresa Henne – Research Associate at the Department of Innovation and Digitalisation in Law, University of Vienna, Austria

Catherine Jasserand – Marie Curie postdoctoral researcher at KU Leuven (CiTiP-imec), Belgium

Emily Johnson – Department of Innovation and Digitalisation in Law, University of Vienna, Austria

Iana Kazeeva – Department of Innovation and Digitalisation in Law, University of Vienna, Austria

Christopher K. Lamont – Associate Professor of International Relations, Tokyo International University, Japan

Alex Leveringhaus – Lecturer in Political Theory; Co-Director, Centre for International Intervention, University of Surrey, UK

Medlir Mema – Associate Professor of International Relations, Tokyo International University, Japan

Paul Nemitz – Professor at the College of Europe and Principal Advisor at the European Commission

Lukasz Olejnik – Independent researcher and consultant; Fellow of the Geneva Academy of International Humanitarian Law and Human Rights, Switzerland

Maximilian Querbach – Federal Ministry of the Interior and Community, Germany

Eko Rahmadian – Doctoral Researcher at the Department of Governance and Innovation, Campus Fryslân – University of Groningen, The Netherlands

Susanne Schmuck – Department of International Relations and International Organisation (IRIO), University of Groningen, The Netherlands

Elisabeth Steindl – Research Associate, Department of Innovation and Digitalisation in Law, University of Vienna, Austria

Linnet Taylor – Professor of International Data Governance at the Tilburg Institute for Law, Technology, and Society (TILT), The Netherlands

Nynke E. Vellinga – Postdoctoral researcher at the Faculty of Law, University of Groningen, The Netherlands, involved in the Cybersecurity

Noord-Nederland project, and international research fellow at the Information Society Law Center (ISLC), University of Milan, Italy

Andrew B. Wootton – Design Against Crime Solution Centre, University of Salford, UK

Andrej Zwitter – Professor at the Department of Governance and Innovation and Dean of the Faculty, Campus Fryslân, University of Groningen, The Netherlands

Foreword

This handbook scrutinizes the real and potential societal impacts of Big Data and AI Systems and the discourse around these systems. We learn not only how far AI has moved into or has impacts on crucial questions of Justice and Equality, Peace and War, Education and Health in our societies; we also realize how important the contribution of independent thinking is in a technized world, in which an increasing share of the discourse around technology is produced and controlled by those who produce and control technology.

None of the contributions in this volume could have been written by AI because, as Stuart Russell tells us in his seminal book *Human Compatible: Artificial Intelligence and the Problem of Control* (Viking 2019), AI cannot apply general principles. And I would add, as AI is based on past empirics, on the data of yesterday, as it learns only from the past, it lacks the critical mindset, the discontent with the present, the vision of a better future, the unfulfilled dream, the imagination of the non-existing and the questioning attitude that characterize humans in free societies.

It is the political scientist's quest for a just society, for peace- and rule-based international relations, for functioning democracy, which ensures the delivery of essential services to its citizens and allows citizens to participate in the shaping of their daily lives that drives the investigation in this volume. This handbook thus contributes to the promise of independent science, insofar as the latter is a counterpower that scrutinizes power, the systems of power, the claims of power, be they economic power, political power or, increasingly relevant, technological power.

Hans Jonas in his 1979 *Principle of Responsibility* (University of Chicago Press), the bible of philosophy of technology and the birthplace of the precautionary principle, worried that the combined power of capitalism and technology could wipe out all other legitimate interests in free societies. His book was a wakeup call with long-lasting impacts in the primary law of the European Union and in the politics of today. It created a basis for the democratic shaping of technologies and the development of tools for this purpose such as the technology impact assessment and the precautionary principle. It legitimized a critical view on technology, informed by multidisciplinary and independent scientific contributions such as those in this volume.

It is important to strengthen this tradition of critical studies of technology in all sciences in a time of an increasing concentration of the combined power of technology and wealth. If it is true that 'Software eats it all', that 'Data is the oil of the future' and that AI is omnipresent, it becomes increasingly important to inject into the democratic process the knowledge of impacts and the willingness to act to shape these technologies, systems and infrastructures through democratic process in such a way that they serve and not undermine the good functioning of democracies and the delivery of individual rights and well-being to people. And as we are talking about the potential future impacts of technology, it is significant that we are allowing the space for theory and reflection that is necessary to understand and assess potential impacts of technology on complex systems of society and the longer future. Empirics alone do not do justice to the openness of the future and the ability of humans to innovate and analyse. Restricted also by its capacity to learn based only on past data, AI is severely limited in its usefulness for free societies, just as the usefulness of science would be limited if it were merely 'evidence based' and without theory and critical reflections. To conclude, a merit of this volume is that it is able to demonstrate, with a focus on concepts and sectors, the value of political sciences that integrate facts and evidence into a critical theory of AI and big data. The technology and technologists of today and of the future need such a critical theory to give them direction and to enable them to act responsibly. Legislators of today and of the future need such a critical theory of technology to ensure that the output of democracy serves the people and is based on well-informed considered choices for policy making, underpinned by independent science.

Paul Nemitz
Professor at the College of Europe and Principal Advisor
at the European Commission
1 September 2022

PART I

INTRODUCTION

Introduction to the *Handbook on the Politics and Governance of Big Data and Artificial Intelligence*
Andrej Zwitter and Oskar J. Gstrein

THE OMNIPRESENCE OF BIG DATA AND ARTIFICIAL INTELLIGENCE

Big Data and Artificial Intelligence (AI) have pervaded all aspects of modern life. For decades, popular culture and science fiction literature have frequently featured autonomous systems, robots, algorithms and other manifestations—or imaginations—of what data-driven lives could look like. Asimov's three laws of robotics or Philip K. Dick's question whether androids dream of electric sheep have inspired not only Hollywood but scientific research too. With the turn to the new millennium, Big Data infrastructures and methods using some form of machine learning gained permanent foothold in scientific debates across all disciplines.[1] They reshape the way scientific success is measured, established and communicated. In a similar manner, politics and governance are heavily influenced and shaped by Big Data and AI. The control over Big Data infrastructures and the 'possession' of the most advanced AI—in whichever form available—is a strategic priority for political leaders in the East and the West.[2] At the same time, leaders in the global south and less wealthy countries of the world fear being dominated by those who master the new technologies. In those countries able to afford it, the application of techniques related to the collection, cleaning and analysis of Big Data and its further processing through different algorithmic models (broadly labelled AI) can be found in many domains of the administrative and

---

[1] Viktor Mayer-Schönberger and Kenneth Cukier, *Big Data: A Revolution That Will Transform How We Live, Work, and Think* (Houghton Mifflin Harcourt 2013); Andrej Zwitter, 'Big Data Ethics' (2014) 1 Big Data & Society 205395171455925.

[2] Cecilia Rikap and Bengt-Åke Lundvall, *The Digital Innovation Race: Conceptualizing the Emerging New World Order* (Springer International Publishing 2021) <https://link.springer.com/10.1007/978-3-030-89443-6> accessed 24 August 2022.

security sector.[3] We find it in health, education, tourism, law enforcement, cybercrime, as well as the military.

This opens rich business opportunities for those private companies able to swiftly provide and deploy technology at scale. As such, Big Data infrastructures and the AI systems leveraging their potential emerged into a new form of general-purpose technology. Similar to inventions such as the steam engine or the internal combustion engine, they fundamentally transform the way in which we approach and shape politics, governance and societal interaction more broadly. This new sort of general-purpose technology has quickly become an indispensable aspect of knowledge generation and efficiency. When discussing the effects of AI and Big Data on society, one is too easily tempted to understand the terms themselves not as metaphors or broad themes, but as denoting actual processes. Looking at these technologies through the perspective of Data Science allows digging deeper into the toolbox and investigating the dynamics between the technical aspects, societal dynamics and governance implications of Big Data and AI.

Taking the term 'artificial intelligence' as an example, popular science debates abound with notions of the self-aware AI, malicious killer robots, and 'the singularity' where machines can form an independent and self-sustaining 'civilization' that will bring an end to all humanity—or at least to the relevance of humanity as 'the rulers' of the world as we know it. Such simplified stories are the result of taking the terms too literally. The metaphorical use of the term 'intelligence' could be interpreted as some sort of autonomous self-aware agency. In truth, the term 'intelligence' is a misnomer describing the algorithmic (i.e. mathematical) process of coming from data to certain conclusions in a logical sense, which are in themselves not to be confused with decisions or intent. There is nothing intelligent in the sense of autonomous agency taking place, nor is there a will, self-reflection or consciousness. Hence, taking these metaphors too literally has often led to serious academic and policy debates on the rights of AI—or robo-rights—which are falsely understood as being equivalent to human rights.[4] A sound understanding of the underlying principles of the technology is a precondition for a fruitful debate in political science, law and governance, lest one run the risk of adopting conclusions based on metaphors that might not actually represent reality.[5]

---

[3] 'Automating Society Report 2020' (*Automating Society Report 2020*) <https://automatingsociety.algorithmwatch.org> accessed 24 August 2022.

[4] See Chapter 14, this volume, Gellers and Gunkel.

[5] Zoë Corbyn, 'Microsoft's Kate Crawford: "AI Is Neither Artificial nor Intelligent"' *The Observer* (6 June 2021) <https://www.theguardian.com/

When we refer to Big Data and AI, it is worthwhile to note that these terms, while not being metaphors, are still placeholders for a wide variety of techniques for data collection, processing and analysis. The exact definition and meaning of either of the terms is still subject to debate, which is somewhat surprising given their broad application and rapid implementation.[6] While it is essential for any normative and regulatory treatment of the subject matter to have a firm grasp of the underlying ideas in order to avoid a metaphorical or superficial treatment of the subject, it is of little use to the non-technical reader to introduce fundamental techniques such as pattern recognition, data mining, natural language processing and Bayesian estimation in detail. What is important to consider, though, is that different sectors make use of slightly different techniques and different datasets—or a combination of these—to achieve objectives. Whether these objectives are always commonly or well understood seems one of the aspects where the design and engineering of the technologies frequently clash with 'real-life' needs. But in essence, there are common societal properties that lend themselves to a more generic treatment from the perspective of politics and governance, which is central to this handbook. One concrete example is the networked nature of Big Data and AI, which paves the way towards power shifts.[7] This and similar general themes (or properties) relate to all important sectors of social life, such as education, health, security and warfare, humanitarian aid, as well as other industry and government activities, many of which are covered in the chapters of this volume. There are also more principled issues that require reconsideration, such as the impact of Big Data and AI on social justice (especially in transitional and economic settings), how AI and Big Data relate to or shape the perception and expression of gender, the profiling of users online, as well as how the design of security applications should evolve taking the availability of these emerging technologies into account. Finally, to gain a more comprehensive understanding, we can also pivot and ask ourselves what society does to these technologies themselves.

---

technology/2021/jun/06/microsofts-kate-crawford-ai-is-neither-artificial-nor-intell igent> accessed 24 August 2022.

6   Anne Beaulieu and Sabina Leonelli, *Data and Society: A Critical Introduction* (SAGE Publications Ltd 2022); Tom Taulli, *Artificial Intelligence Basics: A Non-Technical Introduction* (2019) <https://link.springer.com/epdf/10.1007/978-1-4842-5028-0_1> accessed 24 August 2022.

7   Zwitter (n 1); Andrej Zwitter and Jilles Hazenberg, 'Decentralized Network Governance: Blockchain Technology and the Future of Regulation' (2020) 3 Frontiers in Blockchain <https://www.frontiersin.org/articles/10.3389/fbloc.2020.00012/full> accessed 13 May 2020.

Some might argue that there should be a separate category of rights for AI and autonomous systems, that liability of autonomous systems needs careful consideration,[8] and that AI in the context where it could 'kill' humans autonomously requires meaningful human control.[9]

PURPOSE AND AIM OF THE HANDBOOK

The purpose of the present handbook is to highlight the mutual effects of Big Data and AI on society. The contributions focus on governance aspects, political implications, the impact of Big Data and AI on international relations, as well as emerging initiatives for legal regulation. When it comes to the last in the list, particularly initiatives on the level of the United Nations (UN) are covered, as well as ongoing developments in regional organizations such as the European Union (EU, e.g. the currently discussed proposal for an AI Act).[10] Where it makes sense and has a broader relevance for the subject also, perspectives from specific nation states are the point of departure of the analysis and discussion in the individual contributions.

The present handbook aims to consolidate the current state of the debate on the political role, the policy implications, and the regulation and governance of Big Data and AI as its main method of value extraction and knowledge generation. To attempt to map a topic as revolutionary to modern economy, industry and society as Big Data and AI in one single handbook is quite a challenge, one that is bound to result in an incomplete coverage and necessary omissions of concepts and debates. At the same time, it is a great opportunity to gather experts in the field of politics and governance of Big Data and AI, a field that has gained immense traction since the 2010s, producing a very substantial body of literature in a relatively short period of time. As a result, the present handbook cannot be more than the beginning of a consolidation process that is very necessary for identifying the key debates and core theories that guide this field. Such topics include, but are not limited to, AI in warfare, AI as liable actor in law and the quantified human being. While certainly interesting, it would have exceeded the bounds of this volume to include emergent debates in sufficient detail to do them justice, matters

---

[8] See Chapter 15, this volume, Vellinga.
[9] See Chapter 16, this volume, Blauth.
[10] 'A European Approach to Artificial Intelligence | Shaping Europe's Digital Future' <https://digital-strategy.ec.europa.eu/en/policies/european-approach-artificial-intelligence> accessed 24 August 2022.

such as digital identity,[11] data ownership, the normative function of data infrastructures,[12] blockchain governance and AI as moral agents. Nevertheless, we wish to flag that a holistic consideration of the emergence of these technologies is desirable, since their effects on society seem interrelated and partially co-dependent.

CONTEXT, CONSEQUENCES AND IMPACT

With the emergence of AI as general-purpose technology comes a variety of consequences. For example, a direct effect of the societal transformation that happens through the adoption of AI can be witnessed on the job market, where recruitment practices change, and job candidates increasingly face automated sorting, profiling and selection mechanisms.[13] At the same time, the replacement of skilled labour through the automation of processes (sometimes also called 'de-skilling') can be witnessed, and a strong tendency towards more comprehensive surveillance at work manifests.[14] Unfortunately, it seems that the trend towards more work from home and similar measures to prohibit the spread of SARS-CoV-2, its variants and other pandemics in the future will only further exacerbate such developments.[15] But other recent crises also can be understood through the lens of Big Data and AI. The utility of AI in cybercrime is increasing and causes an arms race between criminals and IT security

---

[11]   Andrej J Zwitter, Oskar J Gstrein and Evan Yap, 'Digital Identity and the Blockchain: Universal Identity Management and the Concept of the "Self-Sovereign" Individual' (2020) 3 Frontiers in Blockchain <https://www.frontiersin.org/articles/10.3389/fbloc.2020.00026/full> accessed 11 November 2020.

[12]   Andrej Zwitter and Jilles Hazenberg, 'Cyberspace, Blockchain, Governance: How Technology Implies Normative Power and Regulation' in Benedetta Cappiello and Gherardo Carullo (eds), *Blockchain, Law and Governance* (Springer International Publishing 2020).

[13]   'Auditors Are Testing Hiring Algorithms for Bias, but There's No Easy Fix' (*MIT Technology Review*) <https://www.technologyreview.com/2021/02/11/1017955/auditors-testing-ai-hiring-algorithms-bias-big-questions-remain/> accessed 24 August 2022.

[14]   Jeremias Adams-Prassl, 'Regulating Algorithms at Work: Lessons for a "European Approach to Artificial Intelligence"' (2022) 13 European Labour Law Journal 30.

[15]   Oskar J Gstrein, Dimitry V Kochenov and Andrej Zwitter, 'A Terrible Great Idea? COVID-19 "Vaccination Passports" in the Spotlight' [2021] Centre on Migration, Policy and Society Working Papers 28.

service providers as well as amongst states.[16] For example, the emergence of toolkits such as GPT-3 and DALL-E 2 by OpenAI has sparked concerns about the potential for malicious (ab)use.[17] Luckily, most deepfake videos featuring politicians or public figures were created by comedians, or geeks experimenting with the technology. However, the fake videocalls in June 2022 of a system that presented itself as the mayor of the Ukrainian capital Kiev—Vitali Klitschko—with his respective 'real' counterparts in the cities of Berlin, Madrid and Vienna demonstrate the potentially severe impact of use of such and similar toolkits with malicious intent. It remains unclear who exactly the persons and motives behind setting up these fake video encounters were and which combinations of technologies they exactly used. It also seems unlikely that sustainable harms emerged from the attempt to mislead the mayors and their administrations. Nevertheless, the negative potential of such an application of the technology is very clear by now.[18]

Such debates on the emerging risks of Big Data and AI add to the more established debate on the risks of misinformation and 'Big Nudging', as well as the risk of political manipulation based on psychometric analysis and auto-generated targeted based on individuals' psychological profiles. While the early days of data-driven businesses such as Facebook were characterized by the 'data is the new oil' paradigm (originally moulded by British mathematician Clive Humby in 2006),[19] the end of the previous decade saw Zuckerberg's data empire under heavy pressure stemming from the political and legal aftermath of the Cambridge Analytica scandal (covert illegal profiling/surveillance of parts of the US electorate through a private company with access to Facebook, yet knowingly neglected by

---

[16] Andrej Zwitter, 'The Artificial Intelligence Arms Race' (*Policy Forum*, 27 July 2017) <https://www.policyforum.net/artificial-intelligence-arms-race/> accessed 3 September 2017.

[17] Taís Fernanda Blauth, Oskar Josef Gstrein and Andrej Zwitter, 'Artificial Intelligence Crime: An Overview of Malicious Use and Abuse of AI' (2022) 10 IEEE Access 77110.

[18] Philip Oltermann, 'European Politicians Duped into Deepfake Video Calls with Mayor of Kyiv' *The Guardian* (25 June 2022) <https://www.theguardian.com/world/2022/jun/25/european-leaders-deepfake-video-calls-mayor-of-kyiv-vitali-klitschko> accessed 24 August 2022.

[19] Charles Arthur, 'Tech Giants May Be Huge, but Nothing Matches Big Data' *The Guardian* (23 August 2013) <http://www.theguardian.com/technology/2013/aug/23/tech-giants-data> accessed 25 January 2022; The Economist, 'The World's Most Valuable Resource Is No Longer Oil, but Data' [2017] *The Economist* <https://www.economist.com/leaders/2017/05/06/the-worlds-most-valuable-resource-is-no-longer-oil-but-data> accessed 10 December 2019.

Facebook's leadership),[20] which first became public on 17 March 2018.[21] While formal investigations and a \$5 billion fine levied against Facebook by the US Federal Trade Commission followed in 2019,[22] the unleashed rage of the 'post-truth politics' movements ultimately culminated in an insurrection at the US Capitol on 6 January 2021. The role of social media – including Meta Platforms/Facebook – is still debated at the time of writing of this text in 2022.[23] Regardless, these developments would have been impossible without Big Data infrastructures and AI technologies.

Another important aspect that should be mentioned is the datafication of society, which these general-purpose technologies support.[24] Datafication is a concept that currently emerges in the social sciences (e.g. Science and Technology Studies) and that goes beyond traditional concepts (e.g. 'digitalization') that describe the critical role of data in society and politics. Datafication captures the turning of objects and processes into data, while also considering the role of the associated data community and the care that is put into data, as well as data-related infrastructural capacities.[25] Much attention has recently been paid to reconsidering how privacy as a proxy for individual autonomy transforms in the light of datafication.[26] On the one hand, privacy is still needed as a right that protects individual autonomy and the potential of societies to develop freely.[27] This is only possible with clearly stipulated rights and obligations for companies and public institutions.[28] On the

---

20   Ryan Mac and Cecilia Kang, 'Whistle-Blower Says Facebook "Chooses Profits Over Safety"' *The New York Times* (3 October 2021) <https://www.nytimes.com/2021/10/03/technology/whistle-blower-facebook-frances-haugen.html> accessed 26 January 2022.

21   Margaret Hu, 'Cambridge Analytica's Black Box' (2020) 7 Big Data & Society 2053951720938091, 1.

22   ibid 3.

23   Greyson K Young, 'How Much Is Too Much: The Difficulties of Social Media Content Moderation' (2022) 31 Information & Communications Technology Law 1, 1–5.

24   Ulises A Mejias and Nick Couldry, 'Datafication' (2019) 8 Internet Policy Review <https://policyreview.info/concepts/datafication> accessed 24 August 2022.

25   Beaulieu and Leonelli (n 6) 6–10.

26   For an overview see Oskar J Gstrein and Anne Beaulieu, 'How to Protect Privacy in a Datafied Society? A Presentation of Multiple Legal and Conceptual Approaches' (2022) 35 Philosophy & Technology 3.

27   Luciano Floridi, 'On Human Dignity as a Foundation for the Right to Privacy' (2016) 29 Philosophy & Technology 307, 311–312.

28   See e.g. Gloria González Fuster, 'The Right to the Protection of Personal Data and EU Law' in Gloria González Fuster (ed), *The Emergence of Personal*

other hand, the increasing use of data-driven infrastructures, products and services comes with benefits and opportunities that are sometimes too easily taken for granted in the 2020s, as they will inevitably become more restricted with the limitation of (international) data flows and information sharing.[29] In light of all of this, it does not come as a surprise that regional regulators such as the EU increasingly pay attention to the various emerging problems and respond with legal regulations such as the 2016 EU General Data Protection Regulation, the draft EU-AI Act, and similar initiatives such as constantly updated cybercrime policies, the Digital Services Act and the Digital Markets Act.[30] These regulations and policies, which we see in similar fashion established in many parts of the world,[31] in turn have effects on the potential use of data and AI applications and the safeguards commercial and governmental actors must observe.

In an attempt to point more specifically to the problematic issues and potential harms that Big Data and AI directly or indirectly bring about, a variety of problems emerges, such as:

- biases embedded in algorithms and the calibration of AI systems, which are the result of a narrow training data sample of oversimplified consideration of the underlying societal reality;
- reproducing societal inequality and manifesting its effects further by replacing analogue mechanisms to 'discipline and punish' with fully automated and autonomous means;[32]
- eliminating unmonitored spaces online or offline, where new types of personalities and lifestyles can be explored—this is a particular

---

Data Protection as a Fundamental Right of the EU (Springer International Publishing 2014) <https://doi.org/10.1007/978-3-319-05023-2_7>.

[29] Oskar Josef Gstrein and Andrej Janko Zwitter, 'Extraterritorial Application of the GDPR: Promoting European Values or Power?' (2021) 10 Internet Policy Review 20–22 <https://policyreview.info/articles/analysis/extraterritorial-applica tion-gdpr-promoting-european-values-or-power> accessed 26 January 2022.

[30] 'A Europe Fit for the Digital Age' (*European Commission – European Commission*) <https://ec.europa.eu/info/strategy/priorities-2019-2024/europe-fit-digital-age_en> accessed 24 August 2022.

[31] Graham Greenleaf, 'Now 157 Countries: Twelve Data Privacy Laws in 2021/22' (Social Science Research Network 2022) SSRN Scholarly Paper 4137418 <https://papers.ssrn.com/abstract=4137418> accessed 24 August 2022; 'ZhōngHuá Mundus | A Regulatory Iron Fist for Chinese Big Tech' <https://mailchi.mp/92448ff21d57/bruegel-china-newsletter-november-2021> accessed 24 August 2022.

[32] Michel Foucault, *Discipline & Punish: The Birth of the Prison* (Vintage 1995).

problem for minorities, special groups and people who identify with gender types that are not accepted by mainstream society;

- black boxes of AI systems that are the result of a cybernetic approach to information management purely focused on input signals and output results, and therefore disregard the importance of the process through which the final output was produced—this problem was prominently discussed in the case of using AI to assessing recidivism probabilities in parole judgements in the COMPAS system in some states in the United States;[33]
- dehumanizing effects of the use of algorithms to manage human affairs (see the use of algorithmic decision-making in medical triage,[34] or the use of digital twinning of social structures);[35]
- removal of human agency by automatised decision-making, such as in automated target detection of drones and killer robots in AI assisted warfare;[36]
- problems for decision-making that are the result of a lack of awareness or a lack of considering the dynamics of fruitful human–machine interaction;
- incursions into the private sphere through invasive data collection practices such as data scraping from the web, strategic de-anonymization through linking databases and other data practices of software and hardware providers (see Facebook, Angry Birds);[37]
- inability of the technology to perform in unstructured or unforeseen environments due to a lack of flexibility or a misconception of social realities and contexts.

While this is an extensive list, it is certainly not comprehensive. For example, new data practices in humanitarian action and development aid showed how demographic groups could be just as vulnerable as

---

[33]   Julia Angwin and others, 'Machine Bias' (*ProPublica*, 23 May 2016) <https://www.propublica.org/article/machine-bias-risk-assessments-in-criminal-sentencing?token=MJx_BFsEFMNT2bSeAG2YZISppjWRS64u> accessed 21 September 2020.

[34]   Dirk Helbing and others, 'Triage 4.0: On Death Algorithms and Technological Selection. Is Today's Data-Driven Medical System Still Compatible with the Constitution?' (2021) 10 Journal of European CME <https://doi.org/10.1080/21614083.2021.1989243> accessed 20 December 2021.

[35]   See Chapter 3, this volume, Helbing and Argota Sánchez-Vaquerizo.

[36]   See Chapter 16, this volume, Blauth.

[37]   Sarah Coble, 'Angry Birds Developer Accused of Illegal Data Collection' (*Infosecurity Magazine*, 26 August 2021) <https://www.infosecurity-magazine.com/news/angry-birds-alleged-illegal-data/> accessed 24 August 2022; Hu (n 21).

individuals.[38] Concepts such as group privacy thereby marked a shift from personally identifiable information to demographically identifiable information.[39] Further automatization processes that would use real-time data to gain insights in and eventually steer industrial, medical, and ultimately environmental and social processes gave rise to the term of digital twins.[40] The questions emerge as to how humans can still scrutinize the suggestions provided by immensely complex algorithmic models, how they can perform a meaningful and comprehensive review of automated decisions, and whether the human perception and reasoning might not become a limiting factor to the potential of the technologies. In other words, while AI might lack moral agency, the extensive use of and reliance/dependency on it reduces the moral agency of human actors. Furthermore, new concepts such as digital or artificial agency also result in concrete legal consequences. Artificial agency, for example, denotes autonomous actions without direct input from human agents as for example in self-driving cars. These autonomous systems cause tremendous legal conundrums when it comes to liability regimes and create a distance between moral agency of human actors and its results.[41] Who is to blame when a self-driving car causes an accident with damage to people and property? The owner, the software engineer, the car producer, the sensor developer, and so on? The possibilities seem entirely endless, and society needs to approach this question with an overarching strategy and governance approach.

THE ROLE OF POLITICS AND GOVERNANCE IN MANAGING TECHNOLOGY

Big Data and AI have ushered in the fourth industrial revolution.[42] The first two industrial revolutions refer to the steam engine and electricity

---

[38]   Siddique Latif and others, 'Caveat Emptor: The Risks of Using Big Data for Human Development' (2019) 38 IEEE Technology and Society Magazine 82.

[39]   Linnet Taylor, Luciano Floridi and Bart van der Sloot (eds), *Group Privacy: New Challenges of Data Technologies* (Springer International Publishing 2017) <https://www.springer.com/gp/book/9783319466064> accessed 30 March 2020; Nathaniel A Raymond, 'Beyond "Do No Harm" and Individual Consent: Reckoning with the Emerging Ethical Challenges of Civil Society's Use of Data', *Group Privacy* (Springer 2017) <http://link.springer.com/chapter/10.1007/978-3-319-46608-8_4> accessed 3 September 2017.

[40]   See also Chapter 4, this volume, Rahmadian, Feitosa and Zwitter; Chapter 3, this volume, Helbing and Argota Sánchez-Vaquerizo.

[41]   See Chapter 15, this volume, Vellinga.

[42]   Klaus Schwab, *The Fourth Industrial Revolution* (Crown 2017).

respectively, whereas the third might be termed the digital revolution. The fourth revolution adds an automation component through AI, which only became possible with the emergence of high-speed data transmission, large-scale data processing and related features that are typically expressed through the concept of Big Data. Since this approach to data management and processing has become so fundamental to industry and government, it also causes shifts in power balances between those who deploy the tools and those who create them, as well as between those who produce data (often without their intent or awareness—'data exhaust') and those who collect, process and use them. Such power shifts are always accompanied by ethical problems.[43] These result from an emergence of new economies that still require regulation (e.g. the data economy) and the emergence of new monopolies such as social media giants (e.g. Meta, TikTok, Twitter).

New technologies of the kind that cause such shifts in power relations require new social compacts between those who hold the means of data collection, information production and distribution and those who are affected by it. Such agreements on how to ensure that this power will not be misused and that negative ethical consequences for individuals, groups and the governance institutions are averted are yet to be made. We are in the very beginning of the formation process of regulatory frameworks for Big Data and AI. And there are still many open questions, many problems yet to be discovered, and many governance and regulatory holes to be plugged.

Additionally, the questions on how to engage with Big Data infrastructures and AI are also projected in the regulatory domain, with bodies such as the Council of Europe and the EU working on regulatory frameworks. This also happens with the aspiration either to become standard-setting organizations on the international level ('the Brussels effect'), or at least to start a movement towards more international political cooperation that focuses not purely on power-based pursuit of short-term interest.[44] Besides such regional developments, discussions are also ongoing on the level of the UN. These cover topics such as how to regulate Lethal Autonomous Weapons Systems, or how to reach an international agreement on cybercrime.[45] The question is, however, how influential such regulatory frameworks can become in light of factual developments and the development of technology largely controlled by a few massive

---

[43] Zwitter (n 1).
[44] Gstrein and Zwitter (n 29).
[45] 'Council of Europe Convention on Cybercrime: A Future-Proof International Benchmark?' (*IPPI*, 30 June 2022) <https://www.ippi.org.il/council-of-europe-convention-on-cybercrime/> accessed 24 August 2022.

corporations, and the seeming unwillingness of states to commit to constructive multilateral cooperation.[46]

STRUCTURE OF THE HANDBOOK

This research handbook consists of five parts, covering the topic of the governance and politics of Big Data and AI from different perspectives. The parts are designed in a way to logically flow from conceptual perspectives to principle-based approaches, before considering specific sectors in more detail. The last part is dedicated to a point of departure that is more technology-centric and approaches the subject of autonomous systems, rights and duties from different perspectives that complement each other.

Following Part I, 'Introduction', we continue with Part II, 'Conceptual Perspectives', covering topics such as group privacy and abnormal justice (Chapter 1), emergent data-sharing practices in the humanitarian sector (Chapter 2), and the conceptual development, application and ethical considerations surrounding digital twins (chapters 3 and 4). Part III presents 'Principle-based Approaches to the Governance of Big Data and AI' and addresses some fundamental categories such as justice, peace and conflict (Chapter 5), a principle-oriented perspective on how to approach autonomous weaponry from the perspective of international relations (Chapter 6), the role of these emerging technologies for shifting power relations in the international economy (Chapter 7), as well as the impact of AI on the perception and representations of gender (Chapter 8). Part IV ('Sectoral Approaches to Big Data and AI Governance') deals with the way different sectors have approached the regulation of the harmful effects of data collection and processing in different fields. It covers privacy preservation in cyberspace (Chapter 10), as well as in the real world in the case of facial recognition (Chapter 11). It also addresses the question of how security applications should be designed when taking the possibilities of the new technologies into account, while keeping the outcomes focused on the human agents (Chapter 9). Furthermore, this part discusses the national, regional and international legal frameworks pertaining to health data (Chapter 12); and it deals with the implications of using AI in the education sector (Chapter 13).

In the concluding Part V ('Autonomous Systems, Rights and Duties'), the insights from the previous parts in different forms converge when

---

[46] See Chapter 16, this volume, Blauth.

authors discuss, for example, whether AI and autonomous systems should have rights (Chapter 14). The types of rights the authors argue for are different from human rights and should not be confused with them. Furthermore, the part provides normative guidance on questions such as how to design liability regimes and security systems that can cope with the implications of AI while keeping human dignity in mind (Chapter 15). In addition, the question of what is left of meaningful human control when weapons become autonomous challenges fundamental ideas of moral agency in an era of automation and smart machines (Chapter 16).

This handbook and its thematic parts can by no means cover all relevant aspects pertaining to the subject of politics and governance of AI and Big Data. However, it provides novel insights into existing debates and opens spaces for insights into new subject areas that have up until now received only limited attention. We hope the readers of the handbook have as much joy exploring the contents as we had during putting it together. Finally, we wish to sincerely thank all authors who contributed to this volume.

NOTE

REFERENCES

'A Europe Fit for the Digital Age' (*European Commission – European Commission*) <https://ec.europa.eu/info/strategy/priorities-2019-2024/europe-fit-digital-age_en> accessed 24 August 2022.
'A European Approach to Artificial Intelligence | Shaping Europe's Digital Future' <https://digital-strategy.ec.europa.eu/en/policies/european-approach-artificial-intelligence> accessed 24 August 2022.
Adams-Prassl J, 'Regulating Algorithms at Work: Lessons for a "European Approach to Artificial Intelligence"' (2022) 13 European Labour Law Journal 30.

Angwin J and others, 'Machine Bias' (*ProPublica*, 23 May 2016) <https://www.propublica.org/article/machine-bias-risk-assessments-in-criminal-sentencing?token=MJx_BFsEFMNT2bSeAG2YZISppjWRS64u> accessed 21 September 2020.

Arthur C, 'Tech Giants May Be Huge, but Nothing Matches Big Data' (*The Guardian*, 23 August 2013) <http://www.theguardian.com/technology/2013/aug/23/tech-giants-data> accessed 25 January 2022.

'Auditors Are Testing Hiring Algorithms for Bias, but There's No Easy Fix' (*MIT Technology Review*) <https://www.technologyreview.com/2021/02/11/1017955/auditors-testing-ai-hiring-algorithms-bias-big-questions-remain/> accessed 24 August 2022.

'Automating Society Report 2020' (*Automating Society Report 2020*) <https://automatingsociety.algorithmwatch.org> accessed 24 August 2022.

Beaulieu A and Leonelli S, *Data and Society: A Critical Introduction* (SAGE Publications Ltd 2022).

Blauth TF, Gstrein OJ and Zwitter A, 'Artificial Intelligence Crime: An Overview of Malicious Use and Abuse of AI' (2022) 10 IEEE Access 77110.

Coble S, 'Angry Birds Developer Accused of Illegal Data Collection' (*Infosecurity Magazine*, 26 August 2021) <https://www.infosecurity-magazine.com/news/angry-birds-alleged-illegal-data/> accessed 24 August 2022.

Corbyn Z, 'Microsoft's Kate Crawford: "AI Is Neither Artificial nor Intelligent"' *The Observer* (6 June 2021) <https://www.theguardian.com/technology/2021/jun/06/microsofts-kate-crawford-ai-is-neither-artificial-nor-intelligent> accessed 24 August 2022.

'Council of Europe Convention on Cybercrime: A Future-Proof International Benchmark?' (*IPPI*, 30 June 2022) <https://www.ippi.org.il/council-of-europe-convention-on-cybercrime/> accessed 24 August 2022.

Floridi L, 'On Human Dignity as a Foundation for the Right to Privacy' (2016) 29 Philosophy & Technology 307.

Foucault M, *Discipline & Punish: The Birth of the Prison* (Vintage 1995).

González Fuster G, 'The Right to the Protection of Personal Data and EU Law' in Gloria González Fuster (ed.), *The Emergence of Personal Data Protection as a Fundamental Right of the EU* (Springer International Publishing 2014) <https://doi.org/10.1007/978-3-319-05023-2_7>.

Greenleaf G, 'Now 157 Countries: Twelve Data Privacy Laws in 2021/22' (Social Science Research Network 2022) SSRN Scholarly Paper 4137418 <https://papers.ssrn.com/abstract=4137418> accessed 24 August 2022.

Gstrein OJ and Beaulieu A, 'How to Protect Privacy in a Datafied Society? A Presentation of Multiple Legal and Conceptual Approaches' (2022) 35 Philosophy & Technology 3.

Gstrein OJ, Kochenov DV and Zwitter A, 'A Terrible Great Idea? COVID-19 "Vaccination Passports" in the Spotlight' [2021] Centre on Migration, Policy and Society Working Papers 28.

Gstrein OJ and Zwitter AJ, 'Extraterritorial Application of the GDPR: Promoting European Values or Power?' (2021) 10 Internet Policy Review <https://policyreview.info/articles/analysis/extraterritorial-application-gdpr-promoting-european-values-or-power> accessed 26 January 2022.

Helbing D and others, 'Triage 4.0: On Death Algorithms and Technological Selection. Is Today's Data-Driven Medical System Still Compatible with the Constitution?' (2021) 10 Journal of European CME <https://doi.org/10.1080/21614083.2021.1989243> accessed 20 December 2021.

Hu M, 'Cambridge Analytica's Black Box' (2020) 7 Big Data & Society 2053951720938091.

Latif S and others, 'Caveat Emptor: The Risks of Using Big Data for Human Development' (2019) 38 IEEE Technology and Society Magazine 82.

Mac R and Kang C, 'Whistle-Blower Says Facebook "Chooses Profits Over Safety"' *The New York Times* (3 October 2021) <https://www.nytimes.com/021/10/03/technology/whistle-blower-facebook-frances-haugen.html> accessed 26 January 2022.

Mayer-Schönberger V and Cukier K, *Big Data: A Revolution That Will Transform How We Live, Work, and Think* (Houghton Mifflin Harcourt 2013).

Mejias UA and Couldry N, 'Datafication' (2019) 8 Internet Policy Review <https://policyreview.info/concepts/datafication> accessed 24 August 2022.

Oltermann P, 'European Politicians Duped into Deepfake Video Calls with Mayor of Kyiv' *The Guardian* (25 June 2022) <https://www.theguardian.com/world/2022/jun/25/european-leaders-deepfake-video-calls-mayor-of-kyiv-vitali-klitschko> accessed 24 August 2022.

Raymond NA, 'Beyond "Do No Harm" and Individual Consent: Reckoning with the Emerging Ethical Challenges of Civil Society's Use of Data', *Group Privacy* (Springer 2017) <http://link.springer.com/chapter/10.1007/978-3-319-46608-8_4> accessed 3 September 2017.

Rikap C and Lundvall B-Å, *The Digital Innovation Race: Conceptualizing the Emerging New World Order* (Springer International Publishing 2021) <https://link.springer.com/10.1007/978-3-030-89443-6> accessed 24 August 2022.

Schwab K, *The Fourth Industrial Revolution* (Crown 2017).

Taulli T, *Artificial Intelligence Basics: A Non-Technical Introduction* (2019) <https://link.springer.com/epdf/10.1007/978-1-4842-5028-0_1> accessed 24 August 2022.

Taylor L, Floridi L and Sloot B van der (eds), *Group Privacy: New Challenges of Data Technologies* (Springer International Publishing 2017) <https://www.springer.com/gp/book/9783319466064> accessed 30 March 2020.

The Economist, 'The World's Most Valuable Resource Is No Longer Oil, but Data' [2017] *The Economist* <https://www.economist.com/leaders/2017/05/06/the-worlds-most-valuable-resource-is-no-longer-oil-but-data> accessed 10 December 2019.

Young GK, 'How Much Is Too Much: The Difficulties of Social Media Content Moderation' (2022) 31 Information & Communications Technology Law 1.

'ZhōngHuá Mundus | A Regulatory Iron Fist for Chinese Big Tech' <https://mailchi.mp/92448ff21d57/bruegel-china-newsletter-november-2021> accessed 24 August 2022.

Zwitter A, 'Big Data Ethics' (2014) 1 Big Data & Society 205395171455925.

Zwitter A, 'The Artificial Intelligence Arms Race' (*Policy Forum*, 27 July 2017) <https://www.policyforum.net/artificial-intelligence-arms-race/> accessed 3 September 2017.

Zwitter A and Hazenberg J, 'Cyberspace, Blockchain, Governance: How Technology Implies Normative Power and Regulation' in Benedetta Cappiello and Gherardo Carullo (eds), *Blockchain, Law and Governance* (Springer International Publishing 2020).

Zwitter A and Hazenberg J, 'Decentralized Network Governance: Blockchain Technology and the Future of Regulation' (2020) 3 Frontiers in Blockchain

<https://www.frontiersin.org/articles/10.3389/fbloc.2020.00012/full> accessed 13 May 2020.

Zwitter AJ, Gstrein OJ and Yap E, 'Digital Identity and the Blockchain: Universal Identity Management and the Concept of the "Self-Sovereign" Individual' (2020) 3 Frontiers in Blockchain <https://www.frontiersin.org/articles/10.3389/fbloc.2020.00026/full> accessed 11 November 2020.

PART II

CONCEPTUAL PERSPECTIVES

1. Can AI governance be progressive? Group interests, group privacy and abnormal justice[1]

Linnet Taylor

1. INTRODUCTION: THE PROBLEM OF ACCOUNTABILITY IN RELATION TO AI

Over the 2000s, sharing and trade in commercial proprietary big data began to grow both within the private sector and between corporations and other spheres such as government and international organisations. Over the 2010s, these processes forked and took two different paths. One was internal to the private sector, where the data sources fed an already-thriving data market and expanded the possibilities for credit-scoring models, consumer profiling and optimising business processes. In the public sector, and amongst research institutions and international organisations, big data raised the profile of computational social science and machine learning in relation to shaping and optimising social phenomena.[2] Networks of more and less formal trade and sharing emerged to link the companies providing data with the security and law enforcement sectors (which already had access to many commercial forms of data), and with the government, academic and civil society actors who also wanted to apply it in policy and social analysis. This evolution of big data into a policy tool was made possible mainly by the presence of new social sources of data such as social media platforms, mobile phone records and e-commerce.[3]

---

[1]   In this chapter I refer to AI as an umbrella term used by those involved in governing and regulating the use of this class of technologies. More precisely, the analysis of systems and models refers to machine learning, but also to the born-digital data that feed such systems and models. This chapter therefore deals with the idea of AI as it circulates in the public sphere and in governance discussions, but with the concrete processes and demands of machine learning.

[2]   Bram Klievink and others, 'Big Data in the Public Sector: Uncertainties and Readiness' (2017) 19 Information Systems Frontiers 267.

[3]   Linnet Taylor, 'The Ethics of Big Data as a Public Good: Which Public? Whose Good?' (2016) 374 Philosophical Transactions of the Royal Society A: Mathematical, Physical and Engineering Sciences 20160126.

This evolution and broadening of the uses of digital records in the public sphere gave rise in turn to concerns about the ways in which populations and their activities could be influenced and optimised,[4] and the fact that it was no longer clear who oversaw regulating activities in the public sphere. Besides the classic formulation of the public–private partnership, other configurations emerged where firms acted in relation to the population on the mass scale. These were either hybrid, where the government contracted with them to share its data for mutually relevant goals but gained no control over their activities in return, or purely commercial, where companies took over activities in the public sphere that had previously been governed by public authorities. Examples of the latter include the way in which Facebook (now Meta) became a platform for electoral politics over the 2010s, and the adoption of its subsidiary WhatsApp as the official global public health messaging tool of the World Health Organization (WHO) during the ongoing Covid-19 pandemic, due to its widespread reach.[5]

These developments made it clear that Edward Snowden's concerns about the sharing of data between commercial entities and government security services, and the corresponding erosion of the assumption of privacy in the online world, were only the tip of the iceberg. Where individuals consciously share particular information about themselves with specific organisations such as banks and hospitals, data could be expected to remain traceable and within the organisation in question. In contrast, a model developed where data would be given and initially used for one purpose, but then shared onward and used for many more, often in de-identified form where privacy and data protection laws no longer applied. The established threat model in relation to surveillance and privacy had for decades related to identifiability: if people could be identified, they could be harmed. Provisions for protecting people from this kind of harm revolved around data security and permission for data use, either given directly in the form of consent or assumed due to the declared purposes of an organisation.

In the 2010s, this model broke down irretrievably. Instead of bits and bytes of data that people could make claims over, the challenge became for them, and the organisations handling data, to conceptualise how data might be used in the future and what this might mean for the individuals

---

    [4]   Bogdan Kulynych and others, 'POTs: Protective Optimization Technologies', *ACM FAT* 2019* (ACM Press 2020).
    [5]   For an extended analysis of these dynamics, see Linnet Taylor, 'Public Actors Without Public Values: Legitimacy, Domination and the Regulation of the Technology Sector' [2021] Philosophy & Technology.

the data related to. In another challenge to established modes of protection, data might end up relating to different individuals from those at whom the data originally pointed. For example, mobile phone records collected for billing purposes in relation to a customer in Senegal might become urban planning data or epidemiological data used and shared by local authorities in combination with international organisations (see Chapter 2 on humanitarian data sharing).[6] The data might next be compared with satellite photos of group mobility and become migration control data for the European Union,[7] and if the customer entered the EU, might then become shared within law enforcement and national security networks to scan for suspicious patterns of movement, or to compare with money transfer records, given that many of the European Union's uses of data in relation to international mobility are conceptualised in relation to security concerns.[8] As the European Data Protection Supervisor stated in a warning to the European Asylum Support office in 2019,

> The EDPS has already stressed that the concern of using data from profiles for different purposes through algorithms is that the data [lose their] original context. Repurposing of data is likely to affect a person's information self-determination, further reduc[ing] the control of [the] data subject's over their data, thus affecting the trust in digital environments and services. Indeed, the diminution of intimate space available to people, as a result of unavoidable surveillance by companies and governments, has a chilling effect on people's ability and willingness to express themselves and form relationships freely, including in the civic sphere so essential to the health of democracy.[9]

This breakdown of classic conceptualisations of the relationship between data and privacy was accurately predicted by researchers, who starting in 2014 reformulated the already-existing notion of 'group privacy'[10] to

---

[6] Yves-Alexandre de Montjoye and others, 'D4D-Senegal: The Second Mobile Phone Data for Development Challenge' [2014] arXiv:1407.4885 [physics] <http://arxiv.org/abs/1407.4885> accessed 19 June 2019.

[7] M Vespe and others, *Migration Data Using Social Media: A European Perspective.* (Publications Office of the EU 2018) <https://op.europa.eu/en/publi cation-detail/-/publication/a7ed9f5e-7ead-11e8-ac6a-01aa75ed71a1/language-en> accessed 22 February 2023.

[8] Linnet Taylor and Fran Meissner, 'A Crisis of Opportunity: Market-making, Big Data, and the Consolidation of Migration as Risk' (2020) 52 Antipode 270.

[9] EDPS, 'European Data Protection Supervisor, Communication to European Asylum Support Office: Formal Consultation on EASO's Social Media Monitoring Reports (Case 2018-1083)' <https://edps.europa.eu/sites/edp/files/ publication/19-11-12_reply_easo_ssm_final_reply_en.pdf> accessed 19 July 2021.

[10] Linnet Taylor, Luciano Floridi and Bart van der Sloot, *Group Privacy: New Challenges of Data Technologies* (Springer International Publishing 2017).

fit with the new challenges raised by big data and AI. This reformulation moved from the idea of each member of a group requiring their own privacy, to the idea that, where that group is algorithmically defined ('the people who move from A to B more than once per week' or 'the people who have visited location X in the last week'), it merits its own collective privacy concern, i.e. switching the lens from 'their privacy' to 'its privacy'. Once the activities and movement signature of the hypothetical Senegalese mobile phone user are de-identified, they become a 'type', not a 'token'.[11] The resulting data may journey through many uses, eventually becoming open data in some form so that it is no longer possible to even track the (e.g. analytical/predictive) models they inform. This conceptualisation of group privacy was cited by the EDPS in its warning about the risks of social media analysis of potential migrants in the Sahel:

> This is connected to the risk of group discrimination, i.e. a situation in which inferences drawn from [social media monitoring] can conceivably put a group, as group, at risk, in a way that cannot be covered by ensuring each member's control over their individual data.[12]

These algorithmically generated profiles and their ever-expanding forms of use have implications for many, indeed most, spheres of life. They bring with them new degrees of influence that perhaps are most recognisable from counter-terrorism and law enforcement-related surveillance in the past. They present evident possibilities for political domination, rather than merely identification and manipulation on the individual level.[13] They have brought with them, however, very little in the way of governance intervention. In the case of the EU, it took legislators until 2021 to come up with either a draft AI governance bill, or a proposal for a data governance bill that conceptualises the movement of data between sectors and beyond its original purpose.

In the meantime, digital monitoring and influence, automation and optimisation have become central tools of policy and of almost every sector, ranging from health and education to humanitarian action and migration control. Despite the EDPS' use of a group privacy logic to push back against algorithmic harms, the lack of formal governance through the 2010s left an unmanageable gap in relation to the use of big data and AI on the population level. It is due to this gap that 'responsible AI', 'fair,

---

[11]   Luciano Floridi, 'Open Data, Data Protection, and Group Privacy' (2014) 27 Philosophy & Technology 1.

[12]   EDPS (n 9).

[13]   Taylor (n 5).

accountable and transparent machine learning', 'responsible data' and other manifestations of informal governance took form.

We can therefore distinguish two ways in which 'responsibility' is used in respect to AI. First, there is a thick conceptualisation, where the researcher or deployer of the technology engages with its effects across the social and political spheres and finds ways to understand the possible unintended consequences of a system or application. Second, there is a thin conceptualisation, which focuses on process and compliance. This second interpretation has become central to governance models for AI around the world. I will argue that this serves two objectives. First, that of providing ways to identify and weigh possible harms, and thus offering guidelines for researchers and developers from technical and often commercially oriented disciplines that have, until now, not offered training in ethics or socio-political aspects of technology.[14] Second, a more political goal of grouping actors and concerns in ways that mimic effective control over the inputs, processes and outputs of AI, without actually placing limits on them in reality. This fiction of governance, I will argue, works to anchor and consolidate the economic and political power these technologies afford and to define regulation as something that reflects, rather than disrupts, established configurations of economic and geopolitical power. One possible response to this, rather than expanding the reach of thin definitions of responsibility to cover an ever-increasing set of problems, would be to adopt an alternative frame of analysis that can take in the kinds of challenges that AI technologies create. Fraser's notion of 'abnormal justice', I will argue, might serve this aim.

2. THE RISE AND FALTER OF 'RESPONSIBLE AI'

The notion of responsible data and responsible AI took shape over the 2010s in relation to the emerging epistemological disjunctures where classic thinking on privacy and discrimination started to break down. By 2019 Mittelstadt was able to review 84 different sets of principles relating to AI technologies,[15] observing that none of these constituted a meaningful governance intervention because the machine-learning community lacked, variously, '(1) common aims and fiduciary duties, (2) professional history and norms, (3) proven methods to translate principles into practice,

---

[14]   Brent Mittelstadt, 'Principles Alone Cannot Guarantee Ethical AI' (2019) 1 Nature Machine Intelligence 501.
[15]   Mittelstadt (n 14).

and (4) robust legal and professional accountability mechanisms', in the absence of which consensus on high-level principles would only continue to mask 'deep political and normative disagreement'.[16]

These high-level principles gradually came together during the 2010s around a set of principles which, as Mittelstadt explains, 'resemble the four classic principles of medical ethics': respect for autonomy, prevention of harm, fairness and explicability.[17] These were reflected across domains ranging from the humanitarian sector to banking, and were also taken up by the EU's High-level Expert Group on AI Ethics (HLEG), which published its findings in 2019.[18] For a few years during the mid-2010s, this form of soft governance through ethical principles and expert-led deliberation, dominated in policy discussions mainly by corporate representatives and academic business experts,[19] and in academia by primarily technical researchers engaged in developing AI.[20] In the latter, the core concerns centred on the FAIR and FACT principles, the first of which pointed toward the accessibility and reusability of data, while the second denoted concerns of fairness, accountability, confidentiality and transparency. Similarly to the HLEG process, the core principles mingled a concern with robust AI (automated systems that are predictable and stable) and non-harmful AI, producing from these two, essentially unrelated, concerns a claim that AI could be trustworthy so that the public could engage with the digital economy and society without concern.

One of the features that makes the soft governance of AI through 'responsibility' convincing in the absence of specific rules, monitoring or enforcement is the focus on how to turn much-debated concepts – such as, for example, fairness[21] – into requirements that can be used as parameters for machine learning models. Formalising fairness in this way provides a target for the creation of standards and requirements, which in itself is an important precursor to the regulation of algorithmic systems. It also forces both computer scientists and those developing guidelines to search

---

[16]   Mittelstadt (n 14) 1.

[17]   Mittelstadt (n 14).

[18]   AI HLEG, 'Building Trust in Human-Centric AI' (*FUTURIUM – European Commission*, 3 April 2019) <https://ec.europa.eu/futurium/en/ai-alliance-consultation/guidelines> accessed 12 March 2020.

[19]   Thomas Metzinger, 'EU Guidelines: Ethics Washing Made in Europe' (*Tagesspiegel.de*, 2019) <https://www.tagesspiegel.de/politik/eu-guidelines-ethics-washing-made-in-europe/24195496.html> accessed 25 June 2019.

[20]   VSNU, 'Responsible Data Science' (*Digital Society*, 2018) <https://www.thedigitalsociety.info/themes/responsible-data-science/> accessed 19 July 2021.

[21]   Melissa Hamilton, 'Debating Algorithmic Fairness' (2018) 52 UC Davis Law Review Online 261.

for conceptual clarity on difficult issues. This makes the discussion more inclusive of the technical disciplines and applied legal perspectives, which are in turn germane to understanding problems arising from the use of AI. However, this push to clarify and formalise is perhaps necessary but insufficient. The formalisable versions of fairness currently in play tell us nothing about whether a particular application should be deployed at all. This is because they tend to be distributional in their aims, and leave out concerns of equity that determine the playing field for distributional calculations. If we start from the assumption that the playing field for those affected by AI is equal, we miss that people are often affected by historical or structural injustice, and that ensuring equity requires a different approach from ensuring equality.[22] As such, this means that we can ask all the 'right' questions of an application and those deploying it, and still remain within a framing that is unjust overall.[23] Furthermore, the formalisation of a concept such as fairness into standards and requirements can sometimes be used strategically to distract society and legislators from more fundamental issues. This occurred during much of the 2010s, where various communities came together on the quest for standards and guidelines that would help corporations and government bodies using AI to self-regulate. While this happened, the development and deployment of AI were occurring in ways that, as Eubanks has demonstrated, have the effect of 'automating inequality'.[24] For instance, Eubanks explores how automated systems have been developed to determine eligibility for social benefits and healthcare, and to determine who is most in need of public assistance in cases of homelessness, and how the application of algorithms to problems such as these is inherently problematic because they will always require human judgement in order to be legitimate, let alone correct.

The dam started to spring leaks mid-decade, with the publication of first O'Neil's,[25] and then Eubanks' exposés of the problems caused by the

---

[22] Andrew D Selbst and others, 'Fairness and Abstraction in Sociotechnical Systems', *Proceedings of the Conference on Fairness, Accountability, and Transparency – FAT* '19* (ACM Press 2019) <http://dl.acm.org/citation.cfm?doid=3287560.3287598> accessed 18 June 2019.

[23] Os Keyes, Jevan Hutson and Meredith Durbin, 'A Mulching Proposal: Analysing and Improving an Algorithmic System for Turning the Elderly into High-Nutrient Slurry', *Extended Abstracts of the 2019 CHI Conference on Human Factors in Computing Systems - CHI EA '19* (ACM Press 2019) <http://dl.acm.org/citation.cfm?doid=3290607.3310433> accessed 18 June 2019.

[24] Virginia Eubanks, *Automating Inequality: How High-Tech Tools Profile, Police, and Punish the Poor* (St Martin's Press 2018).

[25] Cathy O'Neil, *Weapons of Math Destruction: How Big Data Increases Inequality and Threatens Democracy* (Crown 2016).

unthinking or unwitting deployment of algorithms on the general public. It burst in 2019 when big tech firms were overtaken by employee protests over, variously, women's rights,[26] firms' collaboration with the Trump administration's family separation policy,[27] firms' (lack of) climate policy,[28] and their development of automated weapon targeting systems (see Chapter 16, this volume).[29] By 2021, the Black Lives Matter protests were driving a new consciousness of the role of technology in structural racism and new protests arose that linked many of these issues around more fundamental claims. One prominent example was the claim relating to the sustainability of large language models being developed by Google and how the harms created by their unsustainability were distributed. This claim was made by Timnit Gebru, a leading researcher in Google's AI ethics group, and her coauthors.[30] The large language models the firm was developing raised serious issues around the global distribution of the costs and benefits of automation, in two forms: The first of these was the way in which large-scale computing created climate change impacts, which impacted hardest on the countries with the least access to technology and the least likelihood of benefiting from large language models. The second was the amplification of discrimination against marginalised groups by feeding huge linguistic corpora based on current public speech – inevitably reflecting the racism and discrimination present in the public sphere – into the models. The attempted publication of this paper, blocked by Google, ended with the firing of Gebru from Google's ethical Artificial Intelligence team.[31]

---

[26]   The Guardian, 'Microsoft Employees Confront CEO over Company's Treatment of Women' (4 April 2019) <http://www.theguardian.com/technology/2019/apr/04/microsoft-employees-protest-satya-nadella> accessed 19 July 2021.

[27]   Geekwire.com, 'Microsoft and GitHub Workers Protest ICE Contracts in Latest Demonstration of Employee Activism' (*GeekWire*, 10 October 2019) <https://www.geekwire.com/2019/microsoft-github-workers-protest-ice-contracts-latest-demonstration-employee-activism/> accessed 19 July 2021.

[28]   Colin Lecher, 'Microsoft Employees Are Protesting the Company's "Complicity in the Climate Crisis"' (*The Verge*, 19 September 2019) <https://www.theverge.com/2019/9/19/20874081/microsoft-employees-climate-change-letter-protest> accessed 19 July 2021.

[29]   Olivia Solon, '"We Did Not Sign up to Develop Weapons": Microsoft Workers Protest $480m HoloLens Military Deal' (*NBC News*, 23 February 2019) <https://www.nbcnews.com/tech/tech-news/we-did-not-sign-develop-weapons-microsoft-workers-protest-480m-n974761> accessed 19 July 2021.

[30]   Emily M Bender and others, 'On the Dangers of Stochastic Parrots: Can Language Models Be Too Big?🦜', *Proceedings of the 2021 ACM Conference on Fairness, Accountability, and Transparency* (2021).

[31]   Cade Metz and Daisuke Wakabayashi, 'Google Researcher Says She Was Fired Over Paper Highlighting Bias in A.I.' *The New York Times* (3 December

These protests coincided with big technology firms' exploration of self-regulation measures. In 2019 Google set up an 'Advanced Technology External Advisory Council' of eight eminent experts from technology fields, ethics and law, and nine days later disbanded it due to both public and internal employee pressure. This pressure related primarily to Google's decision to include the president of the right-wing Heritage Foundation who had a history of expressing intolerance toward some of the minorities whose interests the council was charged with protecting. In 2020 Facebook set up an oversight board for its content moderation processes, referred to by itself and the press as a 'supreme court' to which controversial decisions could be appealed.[32] The board received substantial press attention, which in turn deflected some attention from looming regulatory action due to the amount of misinformation being spread on its platform during the pandemic, and the company's decision not to moderate political content for misinformation or other potential harms.[33]

The governance of AI as is currently in place – a mixture of soft law in the form of ethics, responsibility and guidelines, and slowly developing legislation in most regions – can be seen as a stop–start series of responses to particular challenges. First, there are privacy and compliance, as it became clear that a free pass from data protection provisions would not be given to AI in some regional markets, the EU in particular. More recently, there have been broader ethics and social justice concerns to do with marginalisation, power and domination. Each of these stages has proceeded in relation to the surfacing of particular challenges, legal and social. Radu argues that this has resulted in hybrid public–private governance of AI whose chief feature is purposeful lack of clarity as to exactly what should be governed, or by whom, under what circumstances (a trait she calls 'functional indetermination').[34] In line with her logic, the next section looks at what gaps are left by this hybrid model, and what we can learn from their nature.

2020) <https://www.nytimes.com/2020/12/03/technology/google-researcher-timn it-gebru.html> accessed 23 March 2022.

[32] Evelyn Douek, 'What Kind of Oversight Board Have You given Us?' [2020] The University of Chicago Law Review Online 1.

[33] Sam Levin, 'Google Scraps AI Ethics Council after Backlash: "Back to the Drawing Board"' *The Guardian* (5 April 2019) <https://www.theguardian.com/techn ology/2019/apr/04/google-ai-ethics-council-backlash> accessed 23 March 2022.

[34] Roxana Radu, 'Steering the Governance of Artificial Intelligence: National Strategies in Perspective' (2021) 40 Policy and Society 178.

2.1   The Gaps in the Responsibility Framework

All these contestations suggest two things. First, the existing soft regulatory framework based on responsibility and ethical principles is necessary but insufficient to ensure that technology firms reliably act in the public interest. Second, new forms of contestation are arising, spurred either by the rise in AI technologies aimed at affecting elements of public life, or by the rise in public awareness of social justice issues that are in turn made visible and amplified by AI technologies.

In this section I will deal with the first suggestion, starting with an example. During the 1930s, IBM's German subsidiary was contracted by the Nazi Third Reich to conduct an analysis of the country's census data and determine which of its citizens were Jewish. The contribution of IBM was to cross-tabulate the census data in a way that could not be done without its machines (censuses requiring big data analytics, both then and now), and to search for individuals who not only reported being Jewish but who were related to ancestors who had also been classified as Jewish. The effect of this was to raise the number of Jewish people identified from between 400 and 600 thousand to two million, with consequent effects for that population in the ensuing Holocaust.[35] This account illustrates Kranzberg's first law: that 'technology is neither good nor bad, nor is it neutral':[36] IBM's subsidiary was applying a census-analysis system that was used in other countries to beneficent effect. It also, however, illustrates the problem with the value-sensitive design tradition,[37] which frequently goes together with 'responsible AI' thinking. Technology does not exist in isolation from the world: when applied to social analysis it is deeply political because it is necessarily created for, and applied by, those with more resources and power, upon those with less resources and power. It would have been possible at the time for IBM to pass muster according to today's responsibility or fairness criteria, at least at the depth in which they are currently applied to technology development and application today. IBM could have argued that its technology was 'responsible' in the sense of

---

[35]   Edwin Black, *IBM and the Holocaust: The Strategic Alliance Between Nazi Germany and America's Most Powerful Corporation – Expanded Edition* (Crown 2001).

[36]   Melvin Kranzberg, 'Technology and History: "Kranzberg's Laws"' (1986) 27 Technology and Culture 544.

[37]   Jeroen van den Hoven, 'ICT and Value Sensitive Design' in Philippe Goujon and others (eds), *The Information Society: Innovation, Legitimacy, Ethics and Democracy in Honor of Professor Jacques Berleur s.j.*, vol 233 (Springer US 2007) <http://link.springer.com/10.1007/978-0-387-72381-5_8> accessed 20 June 2019.

being legitimate and clearly regulated, because the German subsidiary was contracted by a democratically elected government to conduct an analysis of a census, an apparently legitimate activity. Its analysis was 'fair' in the bald sense of statistical parity: it took a given question and applied it to the entire population, not selectively upon particular groups. It was transparent and accountable, at least to the government that procured it. And that government – and a substantial portion of the population – openly espoused the values that the technology ended up reflecting: that Jews were a threat and needed to be identified and dealt with. It is only if we look at the bigger picture and apply a more political ethics of technology that we find the entire engagement from start to finish was unconscionable and should never have been countenanced by IBM or any of the participants.[38] It is also revealing that the technological component of this problem was not at the time visible due to the enormity of the injustice it underpinned, so that IBM's choices were not subjected to claims by the victims of genocide until more than 60 years later.[39] This case demonstrates why claims in relation to technologies that are both hidden from public view and yet have an immense effect on the public are particularly hard to make, and may require an 'abnormal' framing to update the process envisaged by the framers of human rights law (see section 3 below).

The same disjuncture is visible in the contemporary computing sciences with regard to fairness. After a decade of conferences on Fairness, Accountability and Transparency in Machine Learning, which created a forum (the FAT*, later known as FAccT, conference series) in which the US computer science community could work together with those specialising in anti-discrimination law, the discussion finally became too qualitative. In 2020 there was a split in the community between those interested in understanding how machine learning processes could be made compatible with conceptions of substantive fairness,[40] and those who felt that statistical concepts of fairness presented enough of a research and requirements engineering challenge already, and had not been sufficiently addressed. The latter began their own conference series, Foundation of Responsible Computing, which held its first meeting in 2021. This split can be traced to

---

[38]   I am indebted to Os Keyes and their coauthors for their parable on 'fair, accountable and transparent machine learning' for the spirit of this analysis: see Keyes, Hutson and Durbin (n 23).

[39]   business-humanrights.org, 'IBM Lawsuit (Holocaust Claim by Gypsies)' (*Business & Human Rights Resource Centre*, undated) <https://www.business-humanrights.org/en/latest-news/ibm-lawsuit-holocaust-claim-by-gypsies/> accessed 23 March 2022.

[40]   Selbst and others (n 22).

the inclusion of social scientific and philosophical researchers in the conference's community, who identified the problem of a too-narrow framing of fairness as being both a social justice and a research challenge. It is telling that the two perspectives require extraordinary efforts on the part of both sides if they are to be tackled as part of the same research agenda, particularly where industry, the most important sponsor both of the conference series and of the research and applications it examines, supports the statistical view of fairness.

This question of the effectiveness of principles is a very real consideration when it comes to judging what constitutes responsible AI, or for that matter fairness in an AI context. Trustworthiness is not per se connected to beneficence, unless this value is explicitly articulated as a requirement – AI can be both robust and trusted to do what it promises, and can still have negative effects on society.[41] Similarly, a quantitatively derived notion of fairness is different from one derived from principles of justice. The former asks, does this model treat like people similarly, and non-alike people differently? Does it have a high accuracy rate in terms of matching real-world instances of a phenomenon to labelled training data? Does it achieve statistical parity, or strategic affirmative bias, according to established legal rules? These questions do not map onto an idea of fairness derived from principles of justice, which may require both an understanding of the historical dimensions of a given situation, and an ability to understand different narratives and interpretations of the same situation.[42]

None of the principles and standards currently in use guarantees a normative alignment with particular values, only with the values espoused by those procuring and deploying a particular system. In IBM's case, everyone involved could justify what they were doing according to a set of values that were internally coherent. It was external coherence that was lacking, because contestation was either missing (in the US business environment) or systematically repressed (in the case of German society). This once again raises the question of politics: whose values get adopted? What is the broader reference point for what is in the public interest, or morally permissible? And how is that determined? Where technological advances are unconnected to (or purposely disconnected from) politics and effective contestation, the link between the technology and the public interest is not made.

---

[41]   Os Keyes, 'Standard Evasions' (*Real Life*, 30 August 2021) <https://real lifemag.com/standard-evasions/> accessed 23 March 2022.

[42]   For a comprehensive explanation of the difference between machine-learning-based understandings of fairness and justice and social scientific or social-justice-based understandings, see Momin M Malik, 'A Hierarchy of Limitations in Machine Learning' [2020] arXiv preprint arXiv:2002.05193.

3.   AI GOVERNANCE AS ABNORMAL JUSTICE

There is much debate about how to govern AI technologies. General and principle-based laws aiming at all applications of these technologies, sector-specific regulation, human rights frameworks, and soft law in the shape of self-regulation and guidelines deriving from medical ethics are all proposed, and are in play to different extents in different regions of the world. What nearly all lack, however, is a connection to politics and con-testation that renders these productive and generative, rather than framing them as obstacles to innovation, the public good and economic necessity. All this suggests that the politics of responsible AI have not yet been suf-ficiently conceptualised by those in charge of developing and deploying AI technologies, and unless this is achieved AI governance will remain an expert-led, hegemonic process incapable of incorporating substantive con-cerns that are not purely economic or business-related. What if, instead of responsibility, those developing and deploying AI systems in relation to the public were required to be democratically accountable? If instead of having to make systems explainable (here, tellingly, there is no agreement on to whom they should be explainable, or what kind of accountability explainability should make possible), they had to make them aligned with the public interest and politically legitimate? These demands, which cur-rently sound both unworkable and irrelevant to the stated aims of govern-ments in fostering their AI economies, evoke an entirely different world of public-interest technology, which is only imaginable if we also re-imagine the relationship between people and economic development. What might this look like, and what would its effects be if we managed to enact it?

The philosopher Nancy Fraser claims that we are living in a time of 'abnormal justice'.[43] She argues that, post-globalisation, the framing of justice claims has been disrupted so that they do not fit with established perceptions of how those claims should be made. Fraser points to several dimensions of disruption: geography, where claims and the agency for redress often now extend beyond the territorial state; the subjects of justice claims, which can now be both individuals and collectives; who should determine what is just, and whose interests should be considered (local versus broader publics); and the nature of redistribution and redress that is relevant to justice claims (beyond economic justice, cultural and political forms of justice have also entered the picture). Finally, Fraser also points to a change in which social cleavages can be the site of injustice: national-ity, class, ethnicity, race, gender, sexuality, (dis)ability and more are in

---

[43]   Nancy Fraser, 'Abnormal Justice' (2008) 34 Critical inquiry 393.

play, creating a much more diverse landscape than either philosophers or those involved in dealing with justice claims are accustomed to.

There is a deep mismatch between most discourses and practices of responsibility and accountability in AI technologies and the claims to justice that for the last decade have been arising around their use in society. This is not necessarily because AI is an exceptionally disruptive set of technologies – in fact, it has been under development for more than half a century, and has been gradually encroaching on social life for almost as long.[44] Instead, new claims in relation to AI started arising during the 2010s because the decade also saw the rise of global movements on racial, gender, political and climate justice, to name only a few, making marginalisation and oppression visible to a broader public. Advocacy organisations and individual critics of technologically enabled injustice also gained more of a voice during that decade, which began with the privacy claims of Snowden but ended with the much broader claims of Black Lives Matter, MeToo and Extinction Rebellion. Technology is no longer contested based on privacy alone, but also on its effects on labour markets, gender ideologies, racial justice and climate change. These effects are not due to individual instances and applications, but to the inexorable expansion of commercial cloud and computing infrastructures, which underpin almost all AI and big data applications and have become essential infrastructure for business and the public sector worldwide.[45] Thus making sense of technology and rights through a lens of individual applications and related harms makes very limited sense, and we now require a vocabulary and an imaginary that can make sense of the relationship of systematic technologies to systematic problems.

The kinds of claims described by Fraser in 2008 as abnormal are becoming commonplace, and the connections of technological development to fundamental issues of recognition and representation such as decolonisation, feminism and geopolitical equity are also becoming widely accepted. 'Responsibility', developed as a concept before the shift that occurred with the rise of many of these social movements, was not built to take the strain, and in fact often has the effect of actively deflecting this type of fundamental claim rather than addressing it.[46] The question, 'Is this system just in its

---

[44]   Stephen Muggleton, 'Alan Turing and the Development of Artificial Intelligence' (2014) 27 AI Communications 3.

[45]   Tobias Fiebig and others, 'Heads in the Clouds: Measuring the Implications of Universities Migrating to Public Clouds' [2021] arXiv preprint arXiv:2104.09462; Seda Gürses and Joris van Hoboken, 'Privacy After the Agile Turn' <https://osf.io/27x3q/>.

[46]   Keyes, Hutson and Durbin (n 23).

effects on the world?', versus the questions, 'Is this system legal?' or 'Does this system comply with statistical standards of fairness specified by its designers?', often produce radically different answers.

This problem of abnormal justice goes to the heart of the debates outlined in this chapter. The current notions of responsibility, accountability, trustworthiness, fairness and all the terminology in play in AI governance are thin and apolitical compared with the challenges AI actually raises. Fraser's theory – but also events in the world around us – demonstrate that it is not enough for technology to reflect the world as it is, and so to enrich and optimise the status quo. By doing so, we render the current state of affairs more efficient, more stable and more resilient. This is not, however, the direction that the world is heading. Instead, there are crowds in the streets calling for political attention to injustice, and for the recognition of interests that have been building in power and visibility for generations. The world AI reflects in its current incarnation is one where gender is stable, whiteness and wealth are sources of power, the poor are largely undeserving, the marginalised are in the minority, and our established legal and ethical frameworks are sufficient. This is not, however, the world we see around us. A set of seismic shifts are going on that are (more or less) global and that reflect a reprioritisation of interests in line with abnormal justice.

AI, in its many manifestations, has become a buzzword in relation to this current fracture and potential realignment of social, economic and political visions around issues of social justice – not because it is per se a cause or cure. AI is being debated because it epitomises both the power to preserve the status quo, and to change it. Without an informed political debate, however, the latter cannot be achieved. The current debate on AI focuses on how to do more of it, with the assumption that this will create innovation and economic growth. While this may be true, using AI as an economic engine promises to come with all the costs that using oil to fuel the global economy has done over the last century and a half. Clearly this politics of AI is insufficient and – as can be seen from current controversies – has the power to increase the negative impacts of this social fracture. The normative insight our current state of affairs offers is that political processes to do with technology, and their corresponding governance architectures, need to aim at shaping technology toward the world as it should be, and that increased pluralism in those processes is an essential starting point for doing so.

Importantly, this means that the answer to any of the questions about how to govern AI cannot be 'more AI' or 'more innovation'. Instead, every political system is challenged with finding how AI can be governed using the political and administrative tools at its disposal, some of which will need to be international. Just as with other game-changing scientific developments – such as nuclear science or cloning – a structured hierarchy of governance is needed where it is assumed that any red lines declared at the local or national level have the potential to drive undesirable developments elsewhere in the world.[47] Hence, the politics of AI must be an international as well as a national politics. Taking account of Fraser's call for equality of participation,[48] parity of participation ('the "who" of justice', as she puts it) in this case must encompass the recognition of plural interests and their corresponding participation in the political dialogue both within and between nation states. There is no 'far from here' anymore: just as nuclear testing in the Pacific can no longer be justified on the basis that it affects smaller, less powerful states, AI that amplifies injustice for groups outside the European Union, for example, cannot be justified by states within the Union. This is a genuine problem for the politics of technology, which have until now been conducted with a nation-state tunnel vision except where international cooperation is warranted to make training data flow more freely and create more freedom for technology giants.[49] Creating a more equal playing field for political discussions around technology and AI requires as a precondition that those leading such debates are able to decentre the technology,[50] and address the underlying injustices that technology – unless differently produced and governed – amplifies. Unless discussion can proceed on both fronts, there is no possibility for a just politics of AI because the only input tolerated is about the AI, not about justice. When the question instead becomes, 'What injustices need remedying, and how can technology play a positive role in a more just world?', rather than 'How can we automate democracy?' or 'How can AI's benefits be shared more widely?', the premise changes and it becomes possible for a plural politics to emerge.

---

[47]   For an outline of this dynamic with regard to data technologies, see: Linnet Taylor and others, '(Re)Making Data Markets: An Exploration of the Regulatory Challenges' <https://osf.io/preprints/socarxiv/pv98s/> accessed 25 November 2021.

[48]   Fraser (n 43).

[49]   'WTO | Trade Dialogues Lecture Series' (2021) <https://www.wto.org/english/res_e/reser_e/tradedialogueslseries_e.htm> accessed 25 November 2021; World Economic Forum, '4 Ways Regulators Must Keep up with the Global Digital Economy' (*World Economic Forum*, 2021) <https://www.weforum.org/agenda/2021/07/4-ways-regulators-global-digital-economy/> accessed 25 November 2021.

[50]   Seeta Peña Gangadharan and Jędrzej Niklas, 'Decentering Technology in Discourse on Discrimination' (2019) 22 Information, Communication & Society 882.

4. POSSIBILITIES AND ALTERNATIVE VISIONS

The question that confronts those interested in the political questions brought up by this shift toward abnormal justice in relation to AI, is how this can be resolved as a problem of governance. Will new laws be enough, or is there a need to find ways to reconcile more fundamental disagreements on what AI should do in the world, and who should be in charge of determining it? There seem to be two possibilities. One is that the current protests relating to AI and the AI economy worldwide become linked and organised over time, so that they create an insuperable obstacle to the economic status quo and lead to 'inoperativity'[51] in different sectors and regions through walkouts, obfuscation and the subversion of AI systems.[52] Alternatively, it may be possible to mobilise protest toward dialogue, in ways that are currently not clear but would need to be developed.

Mouffe has suggested that there are some situations where contestation is irresolvable and both conceptual and procedural change is required in order to include it in the political order.[53] This is the case with AI governance currently, where 'responsibility' constitutes the inner circle of governance, increasingly in company with law that focuses on keeping the AI economy moving forward at all costs, and a huge variety of protests are on what Derrida has termed the 'constitutive outside', viewed as enemies by those attempting to keep AI on the rails. Mouffe calls for an 'agonistic politics',[54] where,

> A pluralist perspective informed by the agonistic approach [...] recognizes that divergences can be at the origin of conflicts, but it asserts that those conflicts should not necessarily lead to a 'clash of civilisations'. It suggests that the best way to avoid such a situation is the establishment of a multipolar institutional framework that would create the conditions for those conditions to manifest themselves as agonistic confrontations between adversaries, instead of taking the form of antagonistic struggles between enemies.

The challenge for governance and regulation research, in this case, is to help frame the argument for an inclusive understanding of the democratic governance of AI technologies, so that engagement becomes possible.

---

[51] Bonnie Honig, *A Feminist Theory of Refusal* (Harvard University Press 2021).

[52] Kulynych and others (n 4).

[53] Chantal Mouffe, *Agonistics: Thinking the World Politically* (Verso Books 2013).

[54] Mouffe (n 53), 41.

Some of the solution may lie in decentring the technology itself,[55] to focus on the injustice that is being amplified by it, as this brings into play many societal actors who have not been conceptualised as potential contributors to technology governance. If civil society organisations involved in advocacy on the issues that come up in relation to AI, such as those of equal access to healthcare, housing and social protection (as highlighted by Eubanks), were included in discussions on how to formulate instruments and processes for governing AI, their insights might provide a very different orientation than the current, mainly economic, imperative present in all AI governance around the world.

The global landscape of AI governance requires the same shift in focus if justice claims are to be adequately heard. Organisations involved in proposing governance measures for data and AI on the international level such as the WTO, UNCTAD and the G20 all accept the premise that data must flow and AI be deployed untrammelled, so that the challenge becomes to add in considerations of rights and justice, rather than beginning with these at the centre. This has the result that calls for recentring basic principles of justice are side-lined as optional extras, and the global scale promises to see the same insider/outsider conflicts around AI as the local one. Alternative visions can be seen in the proposals of organisations such as Research ICT Africa, which has offered an agenda for reform based on the entitlement of low- and middle-income countries to the same benefits from the global flows of data and use of AI technologies as high-income nations;[56] the work of IT for Change, an organisation based in India that is proposing a feminist, structural justice approach to the global technology economy,[57] and many other groups worldwide engaged in actively attempting to reframe and reform what otherwise promises to be a governance project dominated exclusively by high-income countries' interests.

5.   CONCLUSION: A POLITICS OF JUSTICE IN RELATION TO AI

A more plural approach to AI governance will necessarily present a challenge in terms of governing transnational and global AI systems, if and

---

[55]   Gangadharan and Niklas (n 50).

[56]   See, for example: <https://researchictafrica.net/project/ai-policy-research-centre/> accessed 21 February 2023.

[57]   See: <https://itforchange.net/> accessed 21 February 2023.

when those come to exist in greater numbers. One current example is social media platforms, but the extent of infrastructural investment in systems and computing power with transnational and global reach suggests that, in the end, we will need a global approach to governing AI as well as national and regional ones. To bring together a plural world of AI governance does not necessarily mean aligning everyone's objectives and deciding on single authorities to arbitrate between them. Instead, it could be addressed through the existing structures that translate decision-making power up and down between states, regions and the global level. However, this would necessitate political will, and the commitment on the part of states to themselves represent a plurality of needs and perspectives – something that is a central challenge for the international human rights system, international civil society, and all those involved in constructing alternative visions of representation and power.

It remains to be seen what kind of power these alternative visions can achieve, but if the national scale is indicative of the future challenges of governing AI, it seems probable that 'responsibility' on the part of either sectors or countries will be insufficient to meet the justice claims being made around the world regarding the new economy of AI. The lessons of the last decade suggest that change in styles and models of governance toward a more progressive set of assumptions and goals will be painful but may be inevitable. There may even be advantages to learning from the national struggles over AI so that authorities do not need to repeat the learning process in relation to other governance challenges such as migration, trade and public health. It is likely, however, given the geopolitical power ranged behind the economic approach to AI, this will not happen.

What we should expect to see instead of an acknowledgement of the need for a pluralist approach and the evolution of architectures that can achieve that, is most probably a long path to the adoption of a more plural vision. This will happen both on the national and the international level, and the difficulty of adopting it is likely to lead us not toward active cooperation, but toward an agonistic pluralism that can take into account different views of what AI may, and should, do in the world.

NOTE

clearly credited as the rights holder for publication of the original work. Any translation or adaptation of the original content requires the written authorisation of Edward Elgar Publishing Ltd.

REFERENCES

AI HLEG, 'Building Trust in Human-Centric AI' (*FUTURIUM – European Commission*, 3 April 2019) <https://ec.europa.eu/futurium/en/ai-alliance-consul tation/guidelines> accessed 12 March 2020.

Bender EM and others, 'On the Dangers of Stochastic Parrots: Can Language Models Be Too Big? ', *Proceedings of the 2021 ACM Conference on Fairness, Accountability, and Transparency* (2021).

Black E, *IBM and the Holocaust: The Strategic Alliance between Nazi Germany and America's Most Powerful Corporation – Expanded Edition* (Crown 2001).

business-humanrights.org, 'IBM Lawsuit (Holocaust Claim by Gypsies)' (*Business & Human Rights Resource Centre*, undated) <https://www.business-human rights.org/en/latest-news/ibm-lawsuit-holocaust-claim-by-gypsies/> accessed 23 March 2022.

de Montjoye Y-A and others, 'D4D-Senegal: The Second Mobile Phone Data for Development Challenge' [2014] arXiv:1407.4885 [physics] <http://arxiv.org/abs/1407.4885> accessed 19 June 2019.

Douek E, 'What Kind of Oversight Board Have You Given Us?' [2020] University of Chicago Law Review Online 1.

EDPS, 'European Data Protection Supervisor, Communication to European Asylum Support Office: Formal Consultation on EASO's Social Media Monitoring Reports (Case 2018-1083)' <https://edps.europa.eu/sites/edp/files/pu blication/19-11-12_reply_easo_ssm_final_reply_en.pdf> accessed 19 July 2021.

Eubanks V, *Automating Inequality: How High-Tech Tools Profile, Police, and Punish the Poor* (St Martin's Press 2018).

Fiebig T and others, 'Heads in the Clouds: Measuring the Implications of Universities Migrating to Public Clouds' [2021] arXiv preprint arXiv:2104.09462.

Floridi L, 'Open Data, Data Protection, and Group Privacy' (2014) 27 Philosophy & Technology 1.

Fraser N, 'Abnormal Justice' (2008) 34 Critical Inquiry 393.

Gangadharan SP and Niklas J, 'Decentering Technology in Discourse on Discrimination' (2019) 22 Information, Communication & Society 882.

Geekwire.com, 'Microsoft and GitHub Workers Protest ICE Contracts in Latest Demonstration of Employee Activism' (*GeekWire*, 10 October 2019) <https://www.geekwire.com/2019/microsoft-github-workers-protest-ice-contracts-latest-demonstration-employee-activism/> accessed 19 July 2021.

Guardian, 'Microsoft Employees Confront CEO over Company's Treatment of Women' (*The Guardian*, 4 April 2019) <http://www.theguardian.com/technol ogy/2019/apr/04/microsoft-employees-protest-satya-nadella> accessed 19 July 2021.

Gürses S and van Hoboken J, 'Privacy After the Agile Turn' <https://osf.io/27x3q/> accessed 19 July 2021.

Hamilton M, 'Debating Algorithmic Fairness' (2018) 52 UC Davis Law Review Online 261.

Honig B, *A Feminist Theory of Refusal* (Harvard University Press 2021).

Keyes O, 'Standard Evasions' (*Real Life*, 30 August 2021) <https://reallifemag.com/standard-evasions/> accessed 23 March 2022.

Keyes O, Hutson J and Durbin M, 'A Mulching Proposal: Analysing and Improving an Algorithmic System for Turning the Elderly into High-Nutrient Slurry', *Extended Abstracts of the 2019 CHI Conference on Human Factors in Computing Systems – CHI EA '19* (ACM Press 2019) <http://dl.acm.org/citation.cfm?doid=3290607.3310433> accessed 18 June 2019.

Klievink B and others, 'Big Data in the Public Sector: Uncertainties and Readiness' (2017) 19 Information Systems Frontiers 267.

Kranzberg M, 'Technology and History: "Kranzberg's Laws"' (1986) 27 Technology and Culture 544.

Kulynych B and others, 'POTs: Protective Optimization Technologies', *ACM FAT* 2019* (ACM Press 2020).

Lecher C, 'Microsoft Employees Are Protesting the Company's "Complicity in the Climate Crisis"' (*The Verge*, 19 September 2019) <https://www.theverge.com/2019/9/19/20874081/microsoft-employees-climate-change-letter-protest> accessed 19 July 2021.

Levin S, 'Google Scraps AI Ethics Council after Backlash: "Back to the Drawing Board"' *The Guardian* (5 April 2019) <https://www.theguardian.com/technology/2019/apr/04/google-ai-ethics-council-backlash> accessed 23 March 2022.

Malik MM, 'A Hierarchy of Limitations in Machine Learning' [2020] arXiv preprint arXiv:2002.05193.

Metz C and Wakabayashi D, 'Google Researcher Says She Was Fired Over Paper Highlighting Bias in A.I.' *The New York Times* (3 December 2020) <https://www.nytimes.com/2020/12/03/technology/google-researcher-timnit-gebru.html> accessed 23 March 2022.

Metzinger T, 'EU Guidelines: Ethics Washing Made in Europe' (*Tagesspiegel.de*, 2019) <https://www.tagesspiegel.de/politik/eu-guidelines-ethics-washing-made-in-europe/24195496.html> accessed 25 June 2019.

Mittelstadt B, 'Principles Alone Cannot Guarantee Ethical AI' (2019) 1 Nature Machine Intelligence 501.

Mouffe C, *Agonistics: Thinking the World Politically* (Verso Books 2013).

Muggleton S, 'Alan Turing and the Development of Artificial Intelligence' (2014) 27 AI Communications 3.

O'Neil C, *Weapons of Math Destruction: How Big Data Increases Inequality and Threatens Democracy* (Crown 2016).

Radu R, 'Steering the Governance of Artificial Intelligence: National Strategies in Perspective' (2021) 40 Policy and Society 178.

Selbst AD and others, 'Fairness and Abstraction in Sociotechnical Systems', *Proceedings of the Conference on Fairness, Accountability, and Transparency - FAT* '19* (ACM Press 2019) <http://dl.acm.org/citation.cfm?doid=3287560.3287598> accessed 18 June 2019.

Solon O, '"We Did Not Sign up to Develop Weapons": Microsoft Workers Protest $480m HoloLens Military Deal' (*NBC News*, 23 February 2019) <https://www.nbcnews.com/tech/tech-news/we-did-not-sign-develop-weapons-microsoft-workers-protest-480m-n974761> accessed 19 July 2021.

Taylor L, 'The Ethics of Big Data as a Public Good: Which Public? Whose Good?' (2016) 374 Philosophical Transactions of the Royal Society A: Mathematical, Physical and Engineering Sciences 20160126.

Taylor L, 'Public Actors Without Public Values: Legitimacy, Domination and the Regulation of the Technology Sector' (2021) 34 Philosophy & Technology 897.

Taylor L, '(Re)Making Data Markets: An Exploration of the Regulatory Challenges' <https://osf.io/preprints/socarxiv/pv98s/> accessed 25 November 2021.

Taylor L, Floridi L and van der Sloot B, *Group Privacy: New Challenges of Data Technologies* (Springer International Publishing 2017).

Taylor L and Meissner F, 'A Crisis of Opportunity: Market-making, Big Data, and the Consolidation of Migration as Risk' (2020) 52 Antipode 270.

van den Hoven J, 'ICT and Value Sensitive Design' in Philippe Goujon and others (eds), *The Information Society: Innovation, Legitimacy, Ethics and Democracy In honor of Professor Jacques Berleur s.j.*, vol 233 (Springer US 2007) <http://link.springer.com/10.1007/978-0-387-72381-5_8> accessed 20 June 2019.

Vespe M and others, *Migration Data Using Social Media: A European Perspective.* (Publications Office of the EU 2018) <https://op.europa.eu/en/publication-detail/-/publication/a7ed9f5e-7ead-11e8-ac6a-01aa75ed71a1/language-en> accessed 22 February 2023.

VSNU, 'Responsible Data Science' (*Digital Society*, 2018) <https://www.thedigitalsociety.info/themes/responsible-data-science/> accessed 19 July 2021.

World Economic Forum, '4 Ways Regulators Must Keep up with the Global Digital Economy' (*World Economic Forum*, 2021) <https://www.weforum.org/agenda/2021/07/4-ways-regulators-global-digital-economy/> accessed 25 November 2021.

'WTO | Trade Dialogues Lecture Series' (2021) <https://www.wto.org/english/res_e/reser_e/tradedialogueslseries_e.htm> accessed 25 November 2021.

2. Big Data and the humanitarian sector: emerging trends and persistent challenges
Susanne Schmuck, Andrej Zwitter and Oskar J. Gstrein

INTRODUCTION

As of November 2020, there were around 5.2 billion unique mobile subscribers and 4 billion internet users worldwide. Their online activities produce an unprecedented amount of digital data that are instantly collected, processed, analysed and stored.[1] At the same time, it was estimated that there are 44 zettabytes of data overall. This figure is projected to become four to five times bigger by 2025.[2] This seemingly ever-growing amount of data comes with benefits and challenges. However, when we take a step back and put them in perspective, they are hardly new.

In this chapter we use the example of humanitarian action as a sector that can benefit from the growing amount of data. Humanitarian action has been using Big Data for years and dealt with its challenges in various guidelines and handbooks. Still, the humanitarian community often struggles with gaining access to Big Data owned by private companies. While possible incentives can path the way to lasting data-sharing partnerships, it might come at a high price. A dependency on data from the private sector opens crucial ethical questions and can jeopardise the core humanitarian principles. The following findings and arguments are based on research reviewing relevant literature and data that was collected between December 2020 and February 2021. This data collection was carried out in the form of semi-structured interviews with six selected academic experts and practitioners in the field of data sharing for humanitarian purposes.

---

[1] GSMA, 'GSMA Intelligence' (*GSMA Intelligence*, 2020) <https://www.gsmaintelligence.com/data/> accessed 23 November 2020.

[2] Jacquelyn Bulao, 'How Much Data Is Created Every Day in 2021?' (*TechJury*, 24 June 2021) <https://techjury.net/blog/how-much-data-is-created-every-day/> accessed 15 August 2021; Vuleta, 'How Much Data Is Created Every Day? [27 Powerful Stats]' (*SeedScientific*, 28 January 2021) <https://seedscientific.com/how-much-data-is-created-every-day/> accessed 17 August 2021.

This chapter will begin by outlining emerging trends and how they intersect with the humanitarian sector. Subsequently, we discuss the difficulties that humanitarian organisations face in accessing valuable data from the private sector. By doing so, we analyse two different understandings of data and how they lead to an impeding data-sharing environment between private and public entities. We further outline an emergent environment for data sharing in the humanitarian domain that increasingly requires regulation. In a next step, we provide possible incentives for sustainable data-sharing partnerships with the private sector. The chapter concludes with a critical examination of the value of data for humanitarian organisations. Thereby, we highlight the ethical challenges of unequal data-sharing relations with the private sector, especially considering the core principles of humanitarian action. It discusses the core barriers for humanitarian data sharing and determines why it remains important to instil the value of the humanitarian principles into the emerging actors of the data economy.

EMERGING TRENDS AND THE HUMANITARIAN SECTOR

While the science and technology behind data collection and analysis have developed tremendously over the last two decades, the ethical, legal and social concerns regarding the use of Big Data and algorithms that are trained on them remain largely unresolved.[3] Questions on the legitimacy of collection and use of data, transparency, accountability, rectification, redress, data protection, data exhaust, data security, data agency, as well as the ultimate deletion of data require detailed and practicable answers. This is not only applicable to personally identifiable data relating to individuals, but also to group and large-scale statistical/demographic data.[4] With the dawn of a new golden age for artificial intelligence (AI) the need for answers is particularly urgent,[5] and in the last few years the COVID-19

---

[3]   Pankaj Sharma and Ashutosh Joshi, 'Challenges of Using Big Data for Humanitarian Relief: Lessons from the Literature' (2019) 10 Journal of Humanitarian Logistics and Supply Chain Management; Kate Crawford, *Atlas of AI: Power, Politics, and the Planetary Costs of Artificial Intelligence* (Yale University Press 2021) <https://www.degruyter.com/document/doi/10.12987/9780300252392/html> accessed 24 September 2021.

[4]   Linnet Taylor, Luciano Floridi and Bart van der Sloot (eds), *Group Privacy: New Challenges of Data Technologies* (Springer International Publishing 2017) <http://link.springer.com/10.1007/978-3-319-46608-8> accessed 21 July 2020.

[5]   Emmanuel Letouzé, 'Big Data for Development: Challenges & Opportunities' (UN Global Pulse 2012) <https://www.unglobalpulse.org/

pandemic exacerbated risks of data abuse beyond what was imaginable during the 'old normal'. Location data of mobile phone companies or voluntarily shared datasets on whereabouts and social contacts are used by governments and other actors to understand the spread of a virus that affects the lives of all people on the planet. This raises particular concern in less-developed areas of the world.[6] While the impact of a global pandemic might require and justify increased data use to understand the health threat and legal regimes such as the European Convention on Human Rights (ECHR) legally permit the derogation from certain rights in times of an emergency threatening the life of the nation (see Article 15), every derogation from data protection comes with undesirable consequences. At the same time, the question arises whether and to which extent new digital infrastructures – such as contact tracing apps or digital COVID certificates – change the data landscape for good.[7]

---

document/big-data-for-development-opportunities-and-challenges-white-paper/> accessed 21 July 2020; Gisli Olafsson, 'Humanitarian Response in the Age of Mass Collaboration and Networked Intelligence', *ISCRAM 2012 Conference Proceedings* (2012) <https://gislio.com/2012/09/19/humanitarian-response-in-tim es-of-mass-collaboration-and-networked-intelligence/> accessed 21 July 2020; Patrick Vinck, 'World Disasters Report: Focus on Technology and the Future of Humanitarian Action' (International Federation of Red Cross and Red Crescent Societies 2013) <https://www.ifrc.org/PageFiles/134658/WDR%20 2013%20complete.pdf> accessed 9 July 2020; Kristin Bergtora Sandvik and others, 'Humanitarian Technology: A Critical Research Agenda' (2014) 96 International Review of the Red Cross 219; Nathaniel Raymond and others, 'Building Data Responsibility into Humanitarian Action' (OCHA Policy Development and Studies Branch & Harvard Humanitarian Initiative 2016) <https://www.unocha.org/pub lication/policy-briefs-studies/building-data-responsibility-humanitarian-action> accessed 21 July 2020; Oskar J Gstrein and Andrej Zwitter, 'Een transparant debat over algoritmen' (2020) 29 Bestuurskunde 30; Andrej Zwitter, 'International Humanitarian and Development Aid and Big Data Governance' in B Schippers, *The Routledge Handbook to Rethinking Ethics in International Relations* (1st edn, Routledge 2020) <https://www.taylorfrancis.com/books/9781317041771> accessed 15 July 2020.

[6] Anwaar Ali and others, 'Big Data for Development: Applications and Techniques' (2016) 1 Big Data Analytics 1; Andrej Zwitter and Oskar J Gstrein, 'Big Data, Privacy and COVID-19 – Learning from Humanitarian Expertise in Data Protection' (2020) 5 Journal of International Humanitarian Action 2; Taís Fernanda Blauth and Oskar Josef Gstrein, 'Data-Driven Measures to Mitigate the Impact of COVID-19 in South America: How Do Regional Programmes Compare to Best Practice?' (2021) 11 International Data Privacy Law 18.

[7] Oskar Josef Gstrein, Dimitry Kochenov and Andrej Zwitter, 'A Terrible Great Idea? COVID-19 "Vaccination Passports" in the Spotlight' (The Centre on Migration, Policy & Society University of Oxford 2021) 153 <10.2139/ ssrn.3802154> accessed 24 September 2021.

A sector that has been using Big Data for over a decade now and has faced these exact challenges, is the field of humanitarian action. The first-time social media data and SMS technologies played a crucial role was during the 2010 earthquake in Haiti.[8] Data were used to gather real-time information and insights on the situation on the ground. This included social media data, a dedicated short message service number for Haitians to request help, the use of online platforms (such as the Kenyan Ushahidi) and an army of so-called digital volunteers that collected, aggregated, translated and mapped data. Proponents of new technologies were inspired by the positive use of data in Haiti and believed in a new area of humanitarian aid with more efficient interventions and responses due to data.[9] However, this initial optimism has quickly been halted by several scholars and experts referring to negative consequences of increased data usage.[10] Yet, it is undeniable that this decade of use revealed the potential of phone records and the growing importance of access to private sector data, as humanitarian organisations increasingly aim at leveraging the potential of Big Data. Especially the data held by network operators and telecommunication companies is of interest to humanitarian organisations.[11]

A pioneering initiative in the field of data collaboratives with the private sector was the 'Data for Development Challenge' (D4D), which was established by the French telecommunication multinational Orange. The goal of D4D was to find innovative practices leveraging the potential of Big Data to address development problems in Ivory Coast and Senegal. Teams of researchers could apply via submitting proposals that were scrutinised

---

[8]   Harvard Humanitarian Initiative, 'Disaster Relief 2.0: The Future of Information Sharing in Humanitarian Emergencies' (UN Foundation & Vodafone Foundation Technology Partnership 2011) <https://www.alnap.org/help-library/disaster-relief-20-the-future-of-information-sharing-in-humanitarian-emergencies> accessed 21 July 2020; Robert Munro, 'Crowdsourcing and the Crisis-Affected Community: Lessons Learned and Looking Forward from Mission 4636' (2013) 16 Information Retrieval 210; Sandvik and others (n 5); Sharma and Joshi (n 3).

[9]   Harvard Humanitarian Initiative (n 8).

[10]   Munro (n 8); Sandvik and others (n 5); Kate Crawford and Megan Finn, 'The Limits of Crisis Data: Analytical and Ethical Challenges of Using Social and Mobile Data to Understand Disasters' (2015) 80 GeoJournal 491; Mark Duffield, 'The Resilience of the Ruins: Towards a Critique of Digital Humanitarianism' (2016) 4 Resilience 147.

[11]   Róisín Read, Bertrand Taithe and Roger MacGinty, 'Data Hubris? Humanitarian Information Systems and the Mirage of Technology' (2016) 37 Third World Quarterly 1314.

for their viability and ethical risks by a committee of experts.[12] Orange shared 'anonymised' Call Detail Records (CDR) including logs of calls and SMS exchanges with the successful teams. The successful applications represented research in different fields, from electrification planning to millet prices to the spread of waterborne parasites.[13] Similar projects have also been implemented in different sectors, such as Health, Environment, Education and Economic Development. The Governance Lab (GovLab), a research centre based at New York University's Tandon School of Economics, has collected such data collaboratives to better depict the potential of data and their influence on solutions to a wider range of societal problems.[14] Big Data can fill current data gaps and provide decision-makers with useful information for addressing urgent problems in a crisis. Not only can Big Data help design targeted and efficient responses, but they can also enable predictive capabilities that promise to mitigate and avert crises. Lastly, Big Data can help with insightful assessments and evaluations of crisis responses.[15]

Since the humanitarian community has used and dealt with data during emergencies, it has also dealt with associated challenges and developed guidance notes and handbooks on the responsible use of data. For instance, in 2017 the International Committee of the Red Cross and Red Crescent published a handbook on data protection in humanitarian action. These handbooks discuss general considerations relating to data processing, sharing and protection as well as specific types of data and technologies such as remote sensing, biometrics, cash transfers, cloud services, blockchain, artificial intelligence (AI), as well as social media and data from instant messaging services.[16] Also in 2017, the Harvard Humanitarian

---

[12]   Stefaan G Verhulst and others, 'Leveraging Private Data for Public Good. A Descriptive Analysis and Typology of Existing Practices' (GovLab 2019) <https://datacollaboratives.org/existing-practices.html> accessed 1 October 2020.

[13]   Yves-Alexandre de Montjoye and others, 'D4D-Senegal: The Second Mobile Phone Data for Development Challenge' (30 July 2014) <https://arxiv.org/abs/1407.4885> accessed 27 November 2020; GovernanceLab, 'Orange Telecom Data for Development Challenge (D4D)' (n.d.) <http://datacollaboratives.org/cases/orange-telecom-data-for-development-challenge-d4d.html> accessed 20 November 2020.

[14]   GovernanceLab, 'Data Collaboratives Explorer' (n.d.) <http://datacollaboratives.org/explorer.html> accessed 28 September 2021.

[15]   Stefaan Verhulst, Andrew Young and Prianka Srinivasan, 'An Introduction to Data Collaboratives. Creating Public Value by Exchanging Data' (GovLab, UNICEF, Omidyar Network, n.d.) <https://datacollaboratives.org/static/files/data-collaboratives-intro.pdf> accessed 24 November 2020.

[16]   Christopher Kuner and Massimo Marelli, 'Handbook on Data Protection in Humanitarian Action' (ICRC, Brussels Privacy Hub, Vrije Universiteit Brussel

Initiative published *The Signal Code: A Human Rights Approach to Information during Crisis.* According to the authors of the Signal Code, every humanitarian information activity must not only be consistent with the fundamental principles of humanitarian action, but also respect the fundamental human rights regarding data access, collection, generation, processing, use, treatment and transmission of data during crises. This includes the right to information, the right to protection, the right to privacy and security, the right to data agency, and the right to rectification and redress.[17] In 2020, the OCHA Centre for Humanitarian Data launched a guidance note series on data responsibility in different areas. This includes donor reporting, cash and voucher assistance, private-sector data sharing, incident management, and humanitarian data ethics.[18] In February 2021, the Inter-Agency Standing Committee has published an operational guidance on *Data Responsibility in Humanitarian Action* with recommendations for responsible data management on the system-wide level, the cluster level and the organisation level.[19]

Two Ways to See Data

While the humanitarian community permanently creates and revises guidelines on principles of data responsibility, protection and rights – and is thus well prepared to process Big Data responsibly – humanitarian actors often lack one crucial aspect of data management: the access to data themselves. Frequently, it is the private sector that collects and holds valuable datasets, which are not publicly accessible. In this context, it is useful to reiterate that these data often relate to the situation in less-developed countries where good public infrastructure and sound governance structures are too often absent and public data are not available. Despite the growing evidence of the efficiency and potential of Big Data for the public

---

2020) 2 <https://www.icrc.org/en/data-protection-humanitarian-action-handbook> accessed 30 September 2020.

[17]   Faine Greenwood and others, 'The Signal Code: A Human Rights Approach to Information During Crisis' (Harvard Humanitarian Initiative 2017) <https://hhi.harvard.edu/files/humanitarianinitiative/files/signalcode_final.pdf?m=1607469621> accessed 20 September 2020.

[18]   The Centre For Humanitarian Data, 'Guidance Note Series' (2020) <https://centre.humdata.org/tag/guidance-note/> accessed 20 August 2021.

[19]   Inter-Agency Standing Committee, 'Operational Guidance: Data Responsibility in Humanitarian Action' (Inter-Agency Standing Committee 2020) <https://interagencystandingcommittee.org/system/files/2021-02/IASC%20Operational%20Guidance%20on%20Data%20Responsibility%20in%20Humanitarian%20Action-%20February%202021.pdf> accessed 20 August 2021.

good and humanitarian action, access to valuable data remains limited.[20] A chorus of ethical, legal and social barriers relating to issues such as data protection and commercial interests impede cooperation in data sharing between the private and the humanitarian sectors.

Humanitarian organisations frequently collect and share data between organisations and third parties as the characteristics of a crisis necessitate this for efficient intervention. The already-mentioned Signal Code and the *Handbook on Data Protection* by the ICRC both intensively discuss secure data sharing with other entities by elaborating on precautions regarding data security, legal bases for data sharing, mitigation measures to mini-mise risks to the individual and the question of accountability to the data subjects.[21] While the humanitarian community is prepared to responsibly share data cross-border, it seems that the private sector is more cautious when it comes to sharing data. A detailed explanation why companies hesitate to share their data will be discussed below. In summary, there are two major differences in how the humanitarian community and the private sector see and understand data that explain the overall difficulties in data sharing.

First, humanitarian organisations use data as a source of information to better understand a crisis and design interventions accordingly. Data have a public and humanitarian value to them, regardless of their origin. Private companies, in contrast, understand data as a commercial asset and a source of income.[22] Some businesses even go as far as to consider their datasets their core business product. Even though private companies also use data as a source of information, the commercial value of data and their protection prevails in their thinking.

Secondly, since humanitarian actors understand data as a source of information, they also see the increased benefit in sharing data.[23] Through sharing, they are not only saving costs and time by not duplicating data collection, but also acknowledging the benefit shared data can bring to emergency interventions.[24] The more organisations have data access and process these data responsibly and efficiently, the better they can use it to

---

[20]   Verhulst and others (n 12).

[21]   Greenwood and others (n 17); Kuner and Marelli (n 16).

[22]   Thilo Klein and Stefaan Verhulst, 'Access to New Data Sources for Statistics: Business Models and Incentives for the Corporate Sector' (Paris 21 2017) 10 <https://papers.ssrn.com/abstract=3141446> accessed 4 October 2020; Alberto Alemanno, 'Big Data for Good: Unlocking Privately-Held Data to the Benefit of the Many' (2018) 9 European Journal of Risk Regulation 183.

[23]   Kuner and Marelli (n 16).

[24]   Klein and Verhulst (n 22).

coordinate interventions with other organisations. The private sector, on the contrary, can only see little benefit in data sharing. If data are seen as a stream of income, sharing data can only be justified with a commercial incentive, in the form of a business opportunity or financial compensation. Hence, sharing data for free is considered a loss in value and thus inconsistent with basic business sense of companies.[25] Therefore, there is little to no incentive for companies to share their data or donate them. Finally, sharing data might also be seen as losing a competitive advantage and market shares.[26]

These fundamental differences, which lead to the described dynamics, result in limited data sharing from the private sector. However, the limited dataflows between humanitarian organisations and the private sector cannot only be explained through these two major differences.

An Impeding Environment for Data Sharing

The different understandings of data result in several worries private companies typically express when sharing or donating datasets. The literature mentions legal concerns as one of the primary barriers, specifically when it comes to the lack of international regulatory frameworks and the differences between national legislations on data sharing, data ownership and privacy.[27] Despite the lack of international regulations, the mere

---

[25]   Alemanno (n 22).

[26]   ibid.

[27]   Patrick L Taylor and Kenneth D Mandl, 'Leaping the Data Chasm: Structuring Donation of Clinical Data for Healthcare Innovation and Modeling' (2015) 14 Harvard Health Policy Review 18; World Economic Forum, 'Data-Driven Development: Pathway for Progress' (World Economic Forum 2015) <http://www3.weforum.org/docs/WEFUSA_DataDrivenDevelopment_Report2015.pdf> accessed 7 October 2020; Nicholas Robin, Thilo Klein and Johannes Jütting, 'Public-Private Partnerships for Statistics: Lessons Learned, Future Steps: A Focus on the Use of Non-Official Data Sources for National Statistics and Public Policy' (OECD 2016) OECD Development Co-operation Working Papers 27 <https://www.oecd-ilibrary.org/development/public-private-partnerships-for-statistics-lessons-learned-future-steps_5jm3nqp1g8wf-en> accessed 16 November 2020; Yafit Lev-Aretz, 'Data Philanthropy' (2019) 70 Hastings Law Journal 1491; Iryna Susha, Åke Grönlund and Rob Van Tulder, 'Data Driven Social Partnerships: Exploring an Emergent Trend in Search of Research Challenges and Questions' (2019) 36 Government Information Quarterly 112; Hayden Dahmm, 'Laying the Foundation for Effective Partnerships: An Examination of Data Sharing Agreements' (UN Sustainable Development Solutions Network's Thematic Research Network on Data and Statistic 2020) <https://www.sdsntrends.org/research/dsainsightsreport?locale=en> accessed 30 September 2020.

absence of national laws on data protection in some countries – especially low-income and developing countries in Africa, Asia, the Caribbean, the Middle East, the Pacific islands and South America – are a barrier too.[28] However, even where advanced data governance regimes exist, specific and detailed guidance is missing. For instance, the vivid debate around adequate standards for the sharing of personal data in compliance with the European Union General Data Protection Regulation (GDPR) hardly addresses the needs of international organisations and humanitarian actors.[29]

One can also observe a certain degree of scepticism from the private sector towards humanitarian organisations. Companies fear the low guarantees of legal liability that humanitarian organisations can offer and want to avoid costly and time-consuming legal proceedings in case of data breaches or misuse.[30] This is especially problematic if information from business partners could be involved and where data sharing might result in repercussions such as tort claims against the private companies themselves, due to disclosure of business secrets and other confidential information. It seems as if guidelines such as the ICRC handbook and the Signal Code still need time to achieve the aim of establishing an environment of confidence and trust. Along these lines, it is also crucial for companies to get national security authorities and governments on board. Some countries have already intervened in data-sharing processes and even blocked organisations that focus on data sharing for humanitarian purposes. Contrary to the claim that the possibility of establishing influential relations with the government represents an incentive for the private sector,[31] it seems as if companies fear negative repercussions from governments and national security authorities if they share data without prior authorisation.

Related to legal barriers and the sensitivity of personal data are ethical concerns and social constraints. Companies refer to the lack of consent from their customers for their data to be shared for different humanitarian purposes.[32] Therefore, they fear negative reactions from their customers

---

[28] Graham Greenleaf, 'Global Data Privacy Laws 2021: Despite COVID Delays, 145 Laws Show GDPR Dominance' (UNSW Law Research 2021) 3 <https://papers.ssrn.com/abstract=3836348> accessed 28 September 2021.

[29] Pieter Aertgeerts and Zuzanna Gulczynska, 'The GDPR and International Organisations: Issues of EU Law and Public International Law (26 February 2021)' <http://hdl.handle.net/1854/LU-8701253> accessed 28 September 2021.

[30] World Economic Forum (n 27).

[31] Klein and Verhulst (n 22).

[32] Taylor and Mandl (n 27).

or the general public. In the context of data security, increased attention is also given to the emerging discussion around 'group privacy', which addresses the risks of the use of data-based insights to curtail collective autonomy.[33] This potential for misuse is frequently the result of the contextual nature of data. For instance, during the COVID-19 pandemic, location data of individuals and groups have been used to track the spread of the virus, which is helpful from an epidemiological point of view. The same data, however, in a political context can lead to discrimination or political prosecution of individuals and groups.[34] This underlines how important a well-defined purpose for data sharing is. Hence, it is not surprising to see that the issue of clearly defining the purpose of data sharing receives increased attention. Companies wish to ensure that their data are used only for intended and ethical purposes in a humanitarian context. This should also avoid the possibility that sets of data might be combined with other data sources. Such a combination can lead to a more revealing analysis, which not only infringes the legal principle of purpose limitation, but also makes the concerned individuals and groups immediately more vulnerable.[35] Related to this risk is the fear of providing biased datasets or results that lead to negative publicity.[36]

As already mentioned above, the definition of data as a source of income is hampering data flows from the private to the humanitarian or public sector in general. Sharing data or donating data appears to be against business logic and inconsistent with business objectives.[37] The sharing of data is related to costs and resources that companies might not be willing to spend if they cannot generate profit or any other benefit from it. Companies that use data for their core business activities have little to no interest in data sharing.[38] This hesitation is related not only to the value of data themselves, but also to the risks and potential losses that come with data sharing. Companies fear data breaches or unauthorised

---

[33]   Robin, Klein and Jütting (n 27); Taylor, Floridi and van der Sloot (n 4); William Hoffman and others, 'Collaborating for the Common Good: Navigating Public- Private Data Partnerships' (McKinsey Analytics 2019) <https://www.mckinsey.com/business-functions/mckinsey-analytics/our-insights/collaborating-for-the-common-good> accessed 1 October 2020; Zwitter and Gstrein (n 6).

[34]   Zwitter and Gstrein (n 6); Blauth and Gstrein (n 6).

[35]   Joseph A Cannataci, 'Report of the Special Rapporteur of the Human Rights Council on the Right to Privacy' (United Nations Secretary General, 2017) <https://documents-dds-ny.un.org/doc/UNDOC/GEN/N17/335/64/PDF/N1733564.pdf?OpenElement>.

[36]   Lev-Aretz (n 27).

[37]   Alemanno (n 22).

[38]   ibid.

access to their data by competitors, criminals or unfriendly governments. This can undermine their market position, which can lead to detrimental commercial losses for a company.[39] The risks vary depending on the corporate activities. For instance, telecommunication companies fear negative reactions from their customers and losses in their customer base in case data are leaked, breached or misused. Telecommunication companies with an international profile also fear negative publicity related to data sharing in developing countries, which might also affect their business in markets such as Europe and Northern America.

Incentives for the Private Sector

Despite the – partially legitimate – concerns of the private sector when it comes to sharing data, not all actors remain opposed to data sharing in principle and in practice. Companies face an internal trade-off between the risks they take when sharing their data versus the benefit and gains they might receive from sharing or donating data. Exactly this trade-off can be positively influenced by humanitarian organisations. For instance, long-term partnerships can be established that are mutually beneficial. The humanitarian community can offer several incentives such as increased legal liability for data donors through detailed legal agreements, increased public attention to the success the organisations achieved through the donated data, or specific protective measures for the private sector. A more disputed – yet probably strong – incentive comes in the form of financial compensation for data access. Lastly, technical support can also be an incentive for data sharing. However, this might only be interesting for smaller and less-developed companies.

Legal, ethical and social concerns on data sharing reveal that companies desire mechanisms guaranteeing legal indemnification. Companies will most likely only share their data under clear legal agreements, such as End User License Agreements (EULAs). These must clarify the purposes of data sharing and outline what can be done with the shared data. They must also contain rules on legitimate use of the data-based analytics and insights. Furthermore, they should include clauses that protect business partners and mitigate the impact of data breaches or misuse and provide the required level of legal certainty for parties indirectly involved in the data sharing. As the risks involved are high, it is crucial to establish relations of trust and mutual understanding between the sharing and the

---

[39]   ibid; Hoffman and others (n 33); Lev-Aretz (n 27).

receiving party.[40] If standardised EULAs fulfilling these criteria are in place before a crisis becomes urgent, they can help to avoid time-consuming and costly negotiations. The existing handbooks and guidelines that have been introduced above could serve as guidance for standardised EULAs. It is also important for the humanitarian actors themselves that the usage will not have a negative impact on their own public image. Hence, clearly defined frameworks can help to predict and mitigate the consequences and risks of the data-sharing project for all actors involved.

More recently the concept of 'data philanthropy' receives increased attention. A prominent example is the UN Global Pulse Initiative that relies on donated data to innovatively apply analytics for humanitarian and development purposes. Examples include 'Data for Climate Action', which uses Big Data from the private sector to identify new approaches to mitigate climate changes, or Global Pulse's cooperation with the Spanish bank BBVA using their financial data to measure economic resilience to disasters.[41] Despite this recent popularity of data philanthropy, some scholars such as Lev-Aretz and Daryl Koehn voice critique and scepticism about the praising of companies for sharing their data. From a legal perspective, it is not always clear if companies are allowed to pass on the data they collect. For instance, if data are collected from users of a social network or instant messaging app (e.g. WhatsApp) the question arises whether the companies providing the service (e.g. Facebook/Meta) have a licence to use the data only for the purposes indicated in their policies. Hence, such user data could not be passed on and used in the context of humanitarian work.[42]

Following this line of thinking, in these and similar scenarios companies would have nothing to donate or share in the first place, since the data

---

[40]   Willem G van Panhuis and others, 'A Systematic Review of Barriers to Data Sharing in Public Health' (2014) 14 BMC Public Health <https://doi.org/10.1186/1471-2458-14-1144> accessed 13 October 2020; Marino L Eyerkaufer, Fabiana S Lima and Mirian B Gonçalves, 'Public and Private Partnership in Disaster Risk Management' (2016) 8 Jàmbá : Journal of Disaster Risk Studies <https://www.ncbi.nlm.nih.gov/pmc/articles/PMC6014036/> accessed 2 October 2020.

[41]   Banco Bilbao Vizcaya Argentaria, 'UN Global Pulse, BBVA Announce Partnership and New Project Measuring Economic Resilience to Disasters with Financial Data' (*NEWS BBVA*, 13 September 2016) <https://www.bbva.com/en/un-global-pulse-bbva-announce-partnership-new-project-measuring-economic-re silience-disasters-financial-data/> accessed 28 September 2021; UN Global Pulse, 'Data For Climate Action Challenge' (*Data For Climate Action*, 2017) <http://www.dataforclimateaction.org/> accessed 28 September 2021.

[42]   Lev-Aretz (n 27).

collected are not 'owned' by them and since the purposes they are allowed to use the data for do not include humanitarian work.

Lev-Aretz argues that, due to the non-rivalry characteristic of data, the labelling of data sharing as an act of philanthropy remains questionable.[43] Traditionally, philanthropy meant the donation of money or tangible assets that are an actual loss for the company. Data, in contrast, can be shared at a minimal cost and still be used for commercial objectives, and are thus not donated or lost. If privacy concerns are mitigated (e.g. use of techniques such as anonymisation or differential privacy), datasets could be made available for general public use at minimal cost, while the data could also still be used for business objectives.[44]

Many experts and scholars in the privacy and data protection community are very sceptical towards the concept of data philanthropy and data ownership as such, since it is unclear whether data will ever be non-personal in times of increasing datafication.[45] Particularly in Europe, the protection of personal data is seen as a human right that cannot be waived or licensed by the data subject.[46] At the same time, new frameworks such as the European Union's Data Governance Act are being discussed by policymakers, which come with the objective of facilitating data sharing in safe environments.[47] In a global context there is an emerging discussion about the status of indigenous data governance and data sovereignty.[48] Hence, the question and desirability of data ownership needs much more attention in the context of humanitarian work.[49]

Since companies see data as a source of income, pure altruistic motivations to share data are rare. Businesses often decide to share their data when the right commercial opportunity appears that, in the best case, has a social impact as well. For instance, if a project will have a positive influence on the market, the respective company is operating in or can achieve

---

[43]   ibid.

[44]   ibid.

[45]   Michèle Finck and Frank Pallas, 'They Who Must Not Be Identified—Distinguishing Personal from Non-Personal Data under the GDPR' (2020) 10 International Data Privacy Law 11.

[46]   Oskar Josef Gstrein and Anne Beaulieu, 'How to Protect Privacy in a Datafied Society?' [2022] Philosophy & Technology.

[47]   Mahsa Shabani, 'The Data Governance Act and the EU's Move towards Facilitating Data Sharing' (2021) 17 Molecular Systems Biology <https://onlineli brary.wiley.com/doi/10.15252/msb.202110229> accessed 12 January 2022.

[48]   Stephanie Russo Carroll, Desi Rodriguez-Lonebear and Andrew Martinez, 'Indigenous Data Governance: Strategies from United States Native Nations' (2019) 18 Data Science Journal 31.

[49]   Gstrein and Zwitter (n 5).

high levels of positive media coverage. Organisers of D4D believed that the results of the research would be more innovative and engaged if participants knew (or at least believed) that they contribute to a social cause.[50] While a social impact is useful in overcoming some commercial risks, it is not enough to lead to permanent data sharing. The social value of sharing data has not yet been fully embedded in corporate culture.[51]

As most companies do not have a clear policy that outlines when and under which circumstances they share data, decisions are often spontaneous and depend on the context, as well as the type of data, the defined problem, and the organisational and legal culture.[52] Private-sector companies will engage in data collaboratives if they recognise an overall benefit through a business advantage and social impact, especially in the long run. For example, sharing their data to improve a situation in a specific country can have positive impacts for the market they are in and thus bring an economic benefit for themselves.[53] Even if companies share their data out of philanthropic motives, they at least expect an improved public image in return. However, receiving organisations often fail in providing the desired public attention. Many data-sharing projects do not receive the expected attention and positive reaction. Therefore, data sharing for the public good seems unlikely, although private companies increasingly realise the public value and utility of their data.[54]

While public image and reputation are relatively weak incentives, commercial gains are more likely to convince private companies to share. This is especially the case if the company has an economic interest in data and realises the financial value in a humanitarian context. Nevertheless, data sharing can be costly and time-consuming for companies, especially if technical infrastructures need to be installed. Hence, financial compensations can help balance this calculation or in some cases provide the only benefit that companies can gain from data sharing. The amount of the financial compensation could be based on the volume, frequency and

---

[50]   Linnet Taylor, 'The Ethics of Big Data as a Public Good: Which Public? Whose Good?' (2016) 374 Philosophical Transactions of the Royal Society A: Mathematical, Physical and Engineering Sciences <http://royalsocietypublishing.org/doi/full/10.1098/rsta.2016.0126> accessed 4 October 2020.
[51]   Alemanno (n 22).
[52]   Lev-Aretz (n 27).
[53]   Taylor (n 50).
[54]   Future for Privacy Forum, 'Understanding Corporate Data Sharing Decisions: Practices, Challenges, and Opportunities for Sharing Corporate Data with Researchers' (Future for Privacy Forum 2017) <https://fpf.org/wp-content/uploads/2017/11/FPF_Data_Sharing_Report_FINAL.pdf> accessed 8 February 2021.

veracity of the data. In any case, clear agreements need to be in place to manage expectations on both sides. However, financial compensation and its significance differ from case to case and company to company. Specifically, smaller companies often do not have the financial means to extract big datasets or analyse data internally. Financial compensation can support their efforts and make the extraction of data even possible. For bigger companies with an international profile, financial compensations are more a form of appreciation for their effort and can help cover some of the costs related to data sharing. Still, the monetisation of data can be problematic. While the market for data is regulated and clearly defined in certain countries, this is not the case in developing or lower-income countries. Without educated and appropriate estimations for the price of data from developing countries, companies might tend to overprice their data or develop new business models through selling data for the public good.

Another form of commercial incentives results from the potential to combine data sharing with internal research. The analytics of shared data can be useful for the company, too.[55] Especially an external analysis can provide relatively cheap insights into potential new markets, emerging trends, and targeted customer groups that might not have been discovered through an internal analysis.[56] However, humanitarian organisations should be careful with providing market analytics to private companies. There remains a risk that the results are used for non-intended purposes that can have a negative impact.

If commercial incentives are not an option for the humanitarian organisation, technical incentives provide a feasible alternative. Private companies differ in their technical capacities. Some are very advanced, while others do not have the infrastructure and skills required for efficient data sharing or internal analysis. This poses an increased barrier for some companies to share data, which can be mitigated by offering support in data extraction and the anonymisation processes of personal data that might enable sharing. Even more incentivising is the option of receiving technical training and capacity-strengthening activities. Companies can use those acquired skills to analyse their data internally for the public good but also their business interest. However, this also implies that the humanitarian organisation has the required capacities to provide such technical incentives (which they often lack themselves).

---

[55]   Klein and Verhulst (n 22).

[56]   Brice McKeever and others, 'Data Philanthropy: Unlocking the Power of Private Data for Public Good' (Urban Institute 2018) <https://www.urban.org/sites/default/files/publication/98810/data_philanthropy_unlocking_the_power_of_private_data_for_public_good_0.pdf> accessed 1 October 2020.

As mentioned above, every data-sharing partnership is different and comes with its own challenges. However, especially legal concerns can be mitigated by using legal agreements that include provisions comprehensively addressing essential principles such as purpose limitation. Financial compensation and in some cases technical support can incentivise companies to share their data. There are ways and methods to positively influence the internal trade-off between risks taken by a company and the benefits that can be expected.

Reconsidering the Value of Data

With the emergence of the Big Data narrative, data was often touted as the 'new oil'.[57] Certainly, the humanitarian community and the private sector can agree that there is some added value of the use of data. But how valuable are they really? Valuable enough to use money that could benefit other humanitarian activities? Valuable enough to ignore the fact that private companies might use shared data for their own business interests? Valuable enough to enter in a relation of dependency? Worth so much that humanitarian principles can be jeopardised? These are just some of the trade-offs the humanitarian community is facing today.

Data cannot only improve humanitarian action, it can also improve access to new customer groups, open new markets in developing countries and show the demand for services a company can provide.[58] Let us imagine that a company is offering a valuable dataset to a humanitarian organisation without asking for financial compensation, but under the condition that the resulting data analytics are shared back with the company. Just like any company balances risks and benefits, the humanitarian organisation must now make its own assessment. Can the improved humanitarian intervention that results from the data analysis also justify a commercial benefit for the company? When considering the core humanitarian principle of independence, it seems that it clearly cannot. By accepting the

---

[57]   Charles Arthur, 'Tech Giants May Be Huge, but Nothing Matches Big Data' (*The Guardian*, 23 August 2013) <http://www.theguardian.com/technology/2013/aug/23/tech-giants-data> accessed 2 June 2021; The Economist, 'The World's Most Valuable Resource Is No Longer Oil, but Data, The World's Most Valuable Resource Is No Longer Oil, but Data' [2017] *The Economist* <https://www.economist.com/leaders/2017/05/06/the-worlds-most-valuable-resource-is-no-longer-oil-but-data> accessed 10 December 2019.

[58]   Linnet Taylor and Dennis Broeders, 'In the Name of Development: Power, Profit and the Datafication of the Global South' (2015) 64 Geoforum 229; Gstrein and Zwitter (n 5).

condition of data usage by the company in the example, a humanitarian organisation would also pursue the economic objectives of private companies. While corporate actors see no incompatibility between humanitarian action and their own economic benefit, humanitarian principles are quite adamant that human suffering shall not be a commodity as this quickly results in perverse incentive structures. The same applies when financial compensation is paid for the dataset that leads to a profit, especially since the monetisation of data in developing countries is not well defined, and the private sector will be the one to set the price. Hence, for humanitarian organisations such cooperation might result in a higher level of dependency, particularly concerning supply–demand relationships in humanitarian action constellations, where demand defined as the need for survival leads to a one-sided dependency of beneficiaries, donors and implementing partners on private industry partners who control the data. If companies only share data once the opportunity is right for them, humanitarian organisations cannot rely on sustainable data-sharing partnerships. While not denying that companies might share their data for pure altruistic reasons in some instances, it seems that in most cases they do so when they see an opportunity. In other words, typically the social good aligns with or even strengthens a business advantage.[59] It might therefore be prudent to expect that data donations are indeed donations and not covert data sales. To incentivise corporate actors to contribute to humanitarian causes, regulators might apply tax deductions for data donations.

Will efficient and sustainable aid then depend on business opportunities and not on need alone, as the principle of impartiality demands from humanitarian organisations? The principle of impartiality also prescribes that humanitarian action must not make any differences based on nationality, race, gender, age, religious beliefs, class or political opinions.[60] Humanitarian organisations should thus be careful with data from private actors – especially data from telecommunication companies or social media platforms – as these data only represent relationships with mere consumers. Rather, data for humanitarian purposes should represent the needs of beneficiaries and not only reflect their access to mobile phones and the internet.[61] The risk of biased outcomes of data analytics applies not only to the private sector, but also to humanitarian

---

[59] Taylor (n 50).

[60] OCHA, 'What Are Humanitarian Principles?' (2012) <https://www.un ocha.org/sites/dms/Documents/OOM-humanitarianprinciples_eng_June12.pdf> accessed 21 August 2021.

[61] Gstrein and Zwitter (n 5).

organisations. Biased data can enhance vulnerabilities by further marginalising already-excluded groups or endangering minorities facing discrimination.

CONCLUSION

Most likely, Big Data will continue to play an increasingly crucial role in the future of humanitarian action, especially as more and more useful applications based on AI emerge. The humanitarian community is prepared to responsibly process data with full respect for human rights such as privacy, ethical principles such as 'do no harm' and while taking social realities on the ground into account. This is demonstrated by the large number of guidelines and handbooks that are frequently produced and revised. However, the actual challenges might not lie in mitigating these ethical, legal and social risks.

Rather, access to data remains the biggest problem. Data are not easily available and humanitarian organisations often lack the capacities and time to collect it. Frequently, the private sector holds valuable datasets and is hesitant to share or donate them for humanitarian work.[62] In this chapter, we have outlined the barriers for data-sharing partnerships with the private sector and corresponding incentives might contribute to a more flexible and sustainable data-sharing environment. Acknowledging that every data-sharing project has its own specific challenges, which depend on the kind of data shared, the level of sensitivity of data, the value of data to the private organisation, the method of sharing and the parties involved, our findings suggest that a set of recurring ethical, legal and commercial concerns appear in practically all data-sharing projects.

Still, both sectors have a fundamentally different understanding of data and their value. Companies have an interest in the commercial and economic value of data, while humanitarians see data as a source of valuable information that can improve their work substantially and sustainably. In more simple terms: companies see data as their private good while humanitarians understand data as a public good.

The question of the legitimacy of this ownership with a view to humanitarian work remains unanswered. Even worse, the current legal systems and governance mechanisms might not be capable of delivering useful answers. Specifically, the question of data ownership is only indirectly addressed through complex contract law or the terms and

---

[62]   Verhulst and others (n 12).

Table 2.1   Challenges for private-sector data sharing

Challenge	Description
Legal barriers	The lack of international and national regulatory frameworks, the low guarantees of legal liability from the humanitarian sector, and national security concerns and political tensions create legal insecurities.
Ethical barriers	These include the question of informed consent from data subjects, individual and group privacy, the need for a clear purpose for successful data sharing, and the threat of combination of datasets.
Commercial barriers	Data sharing appears to be against business logic as it is costly, time-consuming and involves high levels of risk. A data breach can lead to commercial losses, undermine the company's market position, and give competitors access to the data.

conditions that are accepted by data subjects when consenting to the collection of private data.[63] Besides, there exists a constant struggle for power over the control of the digital domain.[64] Especially large companies hold the power over their data and are aware of their political influence. If data become a public good in humanitarian contexts, these companies would not only lose some control over their datasets. This would also result in a powershift to their disadvantage.

While the current situation and restrictions for humanitarian action might potentially be interpreted as a call for the development of an international framework to regulate data ownership, access to data and usage of data for humanitarian action in the long term, the short-term question is how much the humanitarian community is willing to pay for data access. A dependency on the private sector is endangering humanitarian principles and leads to an unequal power-relation between the humanitarian community and the private sector. This suggests that, with the emergence of new corporate actors in the humanitarian domain, it is more important than ever to instil in them an understanding of the role and importance of the humanitarian principles. Otherwise, data philanthropy becomes just a tool of ethical whitewashing, while data corporations see humanitarian battlefields as emerging markets of opportunity and human suffering as a form of demand.

---

[63]   Zwitter and Gstrein (n 6).
[64]   Taylor (n 50).

BIBLIOGRAPHY

Aertgeerts P and Gulczynska Z, 'The GDPR and International Organisations: Issues of EU Law and Public International Law (26 February 2021)' <http://hdl.handle.net/1854/LU-8701253> accessed 28 September 2021.

Alemanno A, 'Big Data for Good: Unlocking Privately-Held Data to the Benefit of the Many' (2018) 9 European Journal of Risk Regulation 183.

Ali A and others, 'Big Data for Development: Applications and Techniques' (2016) 1 Big Data Analytics 1.

Arthur C, 'Tech Giants May Be Huge, but Nothing Matches Big Data' (*The Guardian*, 23 August 2013) <http://www.theguardian.com/technology/2013/aug/23/tech-giants-data> accessed 2 June 2021.

Banco Bilbao Vizcaya Argentaria, 'UN Global Pulse, BBVA Announce Partnership and New Project Measuring Economic Resilience to Disasters with Financial Data' (*NEWS BBVA*, 13 September 2016) <https://www.bbva.com/en/un-global-pulse-bbva-announce-partnership-new-project-measuring-econo mic-resilience-disasters-financial-data/> accessed 28 September 2021.

Blauth TF and Gstrein OJ, 'Data-Driven Measures to Mitigate the Impact of COVID-19 in South America: How Do Regional Programmes Compare to Best Practice?' (2021) 11 International Data Privacy Law 18.

Bulao J, 'How Much Data Is Created Every Day in 2021?' (*TechJury*, 24 June 2021) <https://techjury.net/blog/how-much-data-is-created-every-day/> accessed 15 August 2021.

Cannataci JA, 'Report of the Special Rapporteur of the Human Rights Council on the Right to Privacy' (United Nations Secretary General, 2017) <https://documents-dds-ny.un.org/doc/UNDOC/GEN/N17/335/64/PDF/N1733564. pdf?OpenElement>.

Carroll SR, Rodriguez-Lonebear D and Martinez A, 'Indigenous Data Governance: Strategies from United States Native Nations' (2019) 18 Data Science Journal 31.

Crawford K, *Atlas of AI: Power, Politics, and the Planetary Costs of Artificial Intelligence* (Yale University Press 2021) <https://www.degruyter.com/document/doi/10.12987/9780300252392/html> accessed 24 September 2021.

Crawford K and Finn M, 'The Limits of Crisis Data: Analytical and Ethical Challenges of Using Social and Mobile Data to Understand Disasters' (2015) 80 GeoJournal 491.

Dahmm H, 'Laying the Foundation for Effective Partnerships: An Examination of Data Sharing Agreements' (UN Sustainable Development Solutions Network's Thematic Research Network on Data and Statistic 2020) <https://www.sdsntrends.org/research/dsainsightsreport?locale=en> accessed 30 September 2020.

de Montjoye Y-A and others, 'D4D-Senegal: The Second Mobile Phone Data for Development Challenge' (30 July 2014) <https://arxiv.org/abs/1407.4885> accessed 27 November 2020.

Duffield M, 'The Resilience of the Ruins: Towards a Critique of Digital Humanitarianism' (2016) 4 Resilience 147.

Eyerkaufer ML, Lima FS and Gonçalves MB, 'Public and Private Partnership in Disaster Risk Management' (2016) 8 Jàmbá : Journal of Disaster Risk Studies <https://www.ncbi.nlm.nih.gov/pmc/articles/PMC6014036/> accessed 2 October 2020.

Finck M and Pallas F, 'They Who Must Not Be Identified—Distinguishing Personal from Non-Personal Data under the GDPR' (2020) 10 International Data Privacy Law 11.

Future for Privacy Forum, 'Understanding Corporate Data Sharing Decisions: Practices, Challenges, and Opportunities for Sharing Corporate Data with Researchers' (Future for Privacy Forum 2017) <https://fpf.org/wp-content/uploa ds/2017/11/FPF_Data_Sharing_Report_FINAL.pdf> accessed 8 February 2021.

GovernanceLab, 'Data Collaboratives Explorer' (n.d.) <http://datacollaboratives. org/explorer.html> accessed 28 September 2021.

GovernanceLab, 'Orange Telecom Data for Development Challenge (D4D)' (n.d.) <http://datacollaboratives.org/cases/orange-telecom-data-for-development-cha llenge-d4d.html> accessed 20 November 2020.

Greenleaf G, 'Global Data Privacy Laws 2021: Despite COVID Delays, 145 Laws Show GDPR Dominance' (UNSW Law Research 2021) 3 <https://papers.ssrn. com/abstract=3836348> accessed 28 September 2021.

Greenwood F and others, 'The Signal Code: A Human Rights Approach to Information During Crisis' (Harvard Humanitarian Initiative 2017) <https://hhi.harvard.edu/files/humanitarianinitiative/files/signalcode_final. pdf?m=1607469621> accessed 20 September 2020.

GSMA, 'GSMA Intelligence' (*GSMA Intelligence*, 2020) <https://www.gsmaintel ligence.com/data/> accessed 23 November 2020.

Gstrein OJ and Beaulieu A, 'How to Protect Privacy in a Datafied Society?' [2022] Philosophy & Technology.

Gstrein OJ, Kochenov D and Zwitter A, 'A Terrible Great Idea? COVID-19 "Vaccination Passports" in the Spotlight' (The Centre on Migration, Policy & Society University of Oxford 2021) 153 <10.2139/ssrn.3802154> accessed 24 September 2021.

Gstrein OJ and Zwitter A, 'Een transparant debat over algoritmen' (2020) 29 Bestuurskunde 30.

Harvard Humanitarian Initiative, 'Disaster Relief 2.0: The Future of Information Sharing in Humanitarian Emergencies' (UN Foundation & Vodafone Foundation Technology Partnership 2011) <https://www.alnap.org/help-libr ary/disaster-relief-20-the-future-of-information-sharing-in-humanitarian-emerg encies> accessed 21 July 2020.

Hoffman W and others, 'Collaborating for the Common Good: Navigating Public–Private Data Partnerships' (McKinsey Analytics 2019) <https://www. mckinsey.com/business-functions/mckinsey-analytics/our-insights/collaborat ing-for-the-common-good> accessed 1 October 2020.

Inter-Agency Standing Committee, 'Operational Guidance: Data Responsibility in Humanitarian Action' (Inter-Agency Standing Committee 2020) <https://inter agencystandingcommittee.org/system/files/2021-02/IASC%20Operational%20 Guidance%20on%20Data%20Responsibility%20in%20Humanitarian%20Acti on-%20February%202021.pdf> accessed 20 August 2021.

Klein T and Verhulst S, 'Access to New Data Sources for Statistics: Business Models and Incentives for the Corporate Sector' (Paris 21 2017) 10 <https:// papers.ssrn.com/abstract=3141446> accessed 4 October 2020.

Kuner C and Marelli M, 'Handbook on Data Protection in Humanitarian Action' (ICRC, Brussels Privacy Hub, Vrije Universiteit Brussel 2020) 2 <https:// www.icrc.org/en/data-protection-humanitarian-action-handbook> accessed 30 September 2020.

Letouzé E, 'Big Data for Development: Challenges & Opportunities' (UN Global Pulse 2012) <https://www.unglobalpulse.org/document/big-data-for-develop ment-opportunities-and-challenges-white-paper/> accessed 21 July 2020.

Lev-Aretz Y, 'Data Philanthropy' (2019) 70 Hastings Law Journal 1491.

McKeever B and others, 'Data Philanthropy: Unlocking the Power of Private Data for Public Good' (Urban Institute 2018) <https://www.urban.org/sites/ default/files/publication/98810/data_philanthropy_unlocking_the_power_of_pr ivate_data_for_public_good_0.pdf> accessed 1 October 2020.

Munro R, 'Crowdsourcing and the Crisis-Affected Community: Lessons Learned and Looking Forward from Mission 4636' (2013) 16 Information Retrieval 210.

OCHA, 'What Are Humanitarian Principles?' (2012) <https://www.unocha.org/si tes/dms/Documents/OOM-humanitarianprinciples_eng_June12.pdf> accessed 21 August 2021.

Olafsson G, 'Humanitarian Response in the Age of Mass Collaboration and Networked Intelligence', *ISCRAM 2012 Conference Proceedings* (2012) <https:// gislio.com/2012/09/19/humanitarian-response-in-times-of-mass-collaboration- and-networked-intelligence/> accessed 21 July 2020.

Raymond N and others, 'Building Data Responsibility into Humanitarian Action' (OCHA Policy Development and Studies Branch & Harvard Humanitarian Initiative 2016) <https://www.unocha.org/publication/policy-briefs-studies/ building-data-responsibility-humanitarian-action> accessed 21 July 2020.

Read R, Taithe B and MacGinty R, 'Data Hubris? Humanitarian Information Systems and the Mirage of Technology' (2016) 37 Third World Quarterly 1314.

Robin N, Klein T and Jütting J, 'Public–Private Partnerships for Statistics: Lessons Learned, Future Steps: A Focus on the Use of Non-Official Data Sources for National Statistics and Public Policy' (OECD 2016) OECD Development Co-operation Working Papers 27 <https://www.oecd-ilibrary.org/ development/public-private-partnerships-for-statistics-lessons-learned-future-st eps_5jm3nqp1g8wf-en> accessed 16 November 2020.

Sandvik KB and others, 'Humanitarian Technology: A Critical Research Agenda' (2014) 96 International Review of the Red Cross 219.

Shabani M, 'The Data Governance Act and the EU's Move towards Facilitating Data Sharing' (2021) 17 Molecular Systems Biology <https://onlinelibrary. wiley.com/doi/10.15252/msb.202110229> accessed 12 January 2022.

Sharma P and Joshi A, 'Challenges of Using Big Data for Humanitarian Relief: Lessons from the Literature' (2019) 10 Journal of Humanitarian Logistics and Supply Chain Management.

Susha I, Grönlund Å and Van Tulder R, 'Data Driven Social Partnerships: Exploring an Emergent Trend in Search of Research Challenges and Questions' (2019) 36 Government Information Quarterly 112.

Taylor L, 'The Ethics of Big Data as a Public Good: Which Public? Whose Good?' (2016) 374 Philosophical Transactions of the Royal Society A: Mathematical, Physical and Engineering Sciences <http://royalsocietypublishing.org/doi/ full/10.1098/rsta.2016.0126> accessed 4 October 2020.

Taylor L and Broeders D, 'In the Name of Development: Power, Profit and the Datafication of the Global South' (2015) 64 Geoforum 229.

Taylor L, Floridi L and van der Sloot B (eds), *Group Privacy: New Challenges of Data Technologies* (Springer International Publishing 2017) <http://link. springer.com/10.1007/978-3-319-46608-8> accessed 21 July 2020.

Taylor PL and Mandl KD, 'Leaping the Data Chasm: Structuring Donation of Clinical Data for Healthcare Innovation and Modeling' (2015) 14 Harvard Health Policy Review 18.

The Centre For Humanitarian Data, 'Guidance Note Series' (2020) <https://centre.humdata.org/tag/guidance-note/> accessed 20 August 2021.

The Economist, 'The World's Most Valuable Resource Is No Longer Oil, but Data' (2017) *The Economist* <https://www.economist.com/leaders/2017/05/06/the-worlds-most-valuable-resource-is-no-longer-oil-but-data> accessed 10 December 2019.

UN Global Pulse, 'Data For Climate Action Challenge' (*Data For Climate Action*, 2017) <http://www.dataforclimateaction.org/> accessed 28 September 2021.

van Panhuis WG and others, 'A Systematic Review of Barriers to Data Sharing in Public Health' (2014) 14 BMC Public Health <https://doi.org/10.1186/1471-2458-14-1144> accessed 13 October 2020.

Verhulst S, Young A and Srinivasan P, 'An Introduction to Data Collaboratives. Creating Public Value by Exchanging Data' (GovLab, UNICEF, Omidyar Network, n.d.) <https://datacollaboratives.org/static/files/data-collaboratives-intro.pdf> accessed 24 November 2020.

Verhulst SG and others, 'Leveraging Private Data for Public Good. A Descriptive Analysis and Typology of Existing Practices' (GovLab 2019) <https://datacollaboratives.org/existing-practices.html> accessed 1 October 2020.

Vinck P, 'World Disasters Report: Focus on Technology and the Future of Humanitarian Action' (International Federation of Red Cross and Red Crescent Societies 2013) <https://www.ifrc.org/PageFiles/134658/WDR%202013%20complete.pdf> accessed 9 July 2020.

Vuleta, 'How Much Data Is Created Every Day? [27 Powerful Stats]' (*SeedScientific*, 28 January 2021) <https://seedscientific.com/how-much-data-is-created-every-day/> accessed 17 August 2021.

World Economic Forum, 'Data-Driven Development: Pathway for Progress' (World Economic Forum 2015) <http://www3.weforum.org/docs/WEFUSA_DataDrivenDevelopment_Report2015.pdf> accessed 7 October 2020.

Zwitter A, 'International Humanitarian and Development Aid and Big Data Governance' in B Schippers, *The Routledge Handbook to Rethinking Ethics in International Relations* (1st edn, Routledge 2020) <https://www.taylorfrancis.com/books/9781317041771> accessed 15 July 2020.

Zwitter A and Gstrein OJ, 'Big Data, Privacy and COVID-19 – Learning from Humanitarian Expertise in Data Protection' (2020) 5 Journal of International Humanitarian Action 2.

3. Digital twins: potentials, ethical issues and limitations

Dirk Helbing and Javier Argota Sánchez-Vaquerizo

POTENTIALS

Just a few years ago, producing digital twins of dynamical, perhaps even living systems, would have been considered science fiction, and an impossibility from the point of view of science. However, some people believe this situation has recently changed,[1] and will do so even more in the future, particularly in view of the incredible amounts of data producible by the Internet of Things (IoT), transmittable by light (Li-Fi) or other low-latency communication systems, processible by Quantum Computers and learnable by powerful AI systems. This data collection may be global in scale, but detailed up to the level of individuals and their bodies, using profiling techniques such as those known from social media[2] or even more advanced ones. The upcoming technologies are expanding current personalized services, goods and devices to the areas of decision-making, behaviour and health. Due to miniaturization, some components will reach the sub-micrometre scale, as in the case of nanotechnology. Potentially, this enables an Internet of (Bio-)Nano-Things[3] and Internet of Bodies,[4]

---

[1] D Jones and others, 'Characterising the Digital Twin: A Systematic Literature Review' (2020) 29 CIRP Journal of Manufacturing Science and Technology; M Liu and others, 'Review of Digital Twin about Concepts, Technologies, and Industrial Applications' (2021) 58 Journal of Manufacturing Systems.

[2] B-C Han, *Psychopolitics: Neoliberalism and New Technologies of Power* (Verso Books 2017).

[3] F Al-Turjman, *Internet of Nano-Things and Wireless Body Area Networks (WBAN)* (CRC Press/Taylor & Francis Group 2019).

[4] M Gardner, 'The Internet of Bodies Will Change Everything, for Better or Worse' (*RAND Corporation*, 2020) <https://www.rand.org/blog/articles/2020/10/the-internet-of-bodies-will-change-everything-for-better-or-worse.html> accessed 11 July 2022, as all other URLs in references of this chapter; X Liu, 'Tracking How Our Bodies Work Could Change Our Lives' (*World Economic Forum*, 2020) <https://www.weforum.org/agenda/2020/06/internet-of-bodies-covid19-recovery-governance-health-data/>; X Liu, J Merritt and KK Tiscareno, 'Shaping the Future of the Internet of Bodies: New Challenges of Technology Governance'

allowing one to (1) uniquely identify and track everybody via an e-ID, (2) read out data of body functions, and (3) manipulate body functions, supposedly to improve the health of people. It is even conceivable that such powerful digital systems would be used in attempts to maximize 'planetary health',[5] considering also the natural resources and ecosystems of Planet Earth, while changing human behaviour and civilization as desired by those who control this system.[6]

In the following part of the chapter, we will focus on the limitations and ethical issues of using Digital Twins, while not claiming completeness. Before we do this, however, we want to stress that digital twin technology has certainly uncountable possible applications ranging from production to health, from climate change to sustainability, and from management to politics. It is also often suggested that digital twins will allow one to *predict the future* and *implement optimal control.*[7]

Even though we will question the predictability and controllability of complex dynamical systems, we do not deny the potential benefits of digital twins. They are valuable for their exploratory and prospective power, as they can give an advanced idea of 'what-if' scenarios,[8] even when their outcomes are uncertain due to randomness and possible feedback, side and cascading effects.[9] More importantly, digital twins allow performing otherwise unfeasible experiments. This does not mean, however, that safety precautions are not needed to avoid unethical experiments that would be incompatible with the principles of responsible

---

(2020) World Economic Forum <http://www3.weforum.org/docs/WEF_IoB_briefing_paper_2020.pdf>.

[5]   S Whitmee and others, 'Safeguarding Human Health in the Anthropocene Epoch: Report of the Rockefeller Foundation – Lancet Commission on Planetary Health' (Lancet Publishing Group, 14 November 2015) 1973; 'Nanotechnology, Sustainability and Society: First International Conference on Technologies for Smart Green Connected Society 2021 – ICTSGS-1' (*Frontiers in Nanotechnology*) <https://www.frontiersin.org/research-topics/34645/nanotechnology-sustainability-and-society-first-international-conference-on-technologies-for-smart-g#overview>.

[6]   For a manuscript version dated February 2022 discussing also potential issues of using Digital Twins in the area of Planetary Health, see <https://www.researchgate.net/publication/358571489>.

[7]   P Tucker, 'Can the Military Make a Prediction Machine?' (*Defense One*, 2015) <https://www.defenseone.com/technology/2015/04/can-military-make-prediction-machine/109561/>.

[8]   R Conte and others, 'Manifesto of Computational Social Science' (2012) 214(11) The European Physical Journal Special Topics.

[9]   D Helbing, 'Globally Networked Risks and How to Respond' (2013) 497 Nature.

innovation and engineering. In particular, possible risks for individuals and their environment should be evaluated, including whether they are below an acceptable threshold.

This chapter will discuss digital twins concerning simple to increasingly complex tasks, highlighting challenges and limitations. We will start with infrastructures and geography, continue with production plants, following up with the environment. After that, we turn to people, and phenomena resulting when many people interact, such as traffic flows or stock markets, or cities and societies. Finally, we provide a summary, discussion and outlook.

INFRASTRUCTURES AND GEOGRAPHY

Representing *infrastructures* has a long tradition. Starting in previous millennia with sketches and paintings, the age of information technology has brought revolutionary advances, namely in the form of helpful software tools for architects, planners and engineers. Computer Assisted Design (CAD) programs[10] were used widely, and have enabled ever more detailed three-dimensional *visualizations* of planned buildings, allowing for advanced impressions and modifications before they were actually built. These tools enabled the comparison of various building variants, to assess how a certain building would look like if one did this or that. The concept of *'what-if' scenarios* was widely used, with great success. In the meantime, such software tools have been extended into whole Building- and City Information Models (BIM and CIM) to *plan* costs, *order* materials just in time and *manage* the entire construction process, which is becoming more and more complex.[11]

---

[10]   SA Coons, 'An Outline of the Requirements for a Computer-Aided Design System', *Proceedings of the May 21–23, 1963, Spring Joint Computer Conference, AFIPS '63 (Spring)* (ACM Press 1963); IE Sutherland, 'Sketchpad a Man-Machine Graphical Communication System' (1964) 2 Simulation R; GN Harper, 'BOP: An Approach to Building Optimization', *Proceedings of the 1968 23rd ACM National Conference* (ACM Press 1968); WJ Mitchell, *Computer-Aided Architectural Design* (Petrocelli/Charter 1977); D Cardoso Llach, *Builders of the Vision* (Routledge 2015).

[11]   EUBIM Taskgroup, *Handbook for the Introduction of Building Information Modelling by the European Public Sector Strategic Action for Construction Sector Performance: Driving Value, Innovation and Growth* (EUBIM Taskgroup 2017); H Gao, C Koch and Y Wu, 'Building Information Modelling Based Building Energy Modelling: A Review' (Elsevier, 15 March 2019) 320; J Beetz and others, 'Building Information Modelling (BIM)' in Ludger Hovestadt, Urs Hirschberg

Thus, there is little doubt that digital twins of infrastructures are extremely helpful for planning, construction and management. A similar thing applies to representations of *geography*. While maps and globes have been used to depict geography for thousands of years, new ubiquitous multi-spectral sensing methods based on *satellite imagery* and pictures taken by unmanned aerial vehicles, often combined with IoT and crowd-sourced data,[12] have elevated the field to entirely new levels of detail.[13]

Compared with the systems discussed in the next sections, these applications of digital twins are relatively simple for the following reasons:

- Infrastructures and geographies change very little over time, if at all.
- The underlying structures are material and typically very *well measurable*.
- More measurements will deliver better data (at least, better averages), if there is not a systematic measurement bias.

Issues arising when other data sets, for example regarding weather, population, and so on, are overlaid, will be discussed in the following sections.

What is still often missed out in digital twins of infrastructures and geographies are *usage patterns*. However, people frequently occupy space, act, interact and move around in ways that were not well anticipated when solutions were designed and implemented. This typically makes infrastructures work differently than expected, creating various challenges.[14] We will come back to some of these problems later. Here, we just highlight the ethical problem that infrastructures allow certain people to do certain things, but may exclude others, especially with regard to *ownership, access, and agency*. This implies *competition* and sometimes *conflict*, but also

---

and Oliver Fritz (eds), *Atlas of Digital Architecture: Terminology, Concepts, Methods, Tools, Examples, Phenomena* (Birkhäuser 2020); D Cardoso Llach and J Argota Sánchez-Vaquerizo, 'An Ecology of Conflicts', *Communications in Computer and Information Science*, vol 1028 (Springer 2019).

[12] M Haklay, 'Citizen Science and Volunteered Geographic Information: Overview and Typology of Participation', *Crowdsourcing Geographic Knowledge* (Springer Netherlands 2013).

[13] S Langevin and others, 'Useable Machine Learning for Sentinel-2 Multispectral Satellite Imagery', *Image and Signal Processing for Remote Sensing XXVII; 118620F (2021)* (SPIE 2021); AC Rodriguez and JD Wegner, 'Counting the Uncountable: Deep Semantic Density Estimation from Space', *Lecture Notes in Computer Science (including subseries Lecture Notes in Artificial Intelligence and Lecture Notes in Bioinformatics)* (Springer Verlag 2019); Y Ban (ed.), *Multitemporal Remote Sensing* (Springer International Publishing 2016).

[14] J Hill, *Actions of Architecture* (Routledge 2003).

inequality and sometimes *injustice*.[15] Therefore, it is desirable to create *inclusive* spaces, goods and services (such as public transport, schools, museums and parks).

From the perspective of architects, engineers and planners, digital twins may enable true *multi-functional* infrastructures (such as reconfigurable event halls). These allow for *flexible use and adaptation*, which can make usage patterns *less predictable*. While recent technology allows one to measure usage patterns with increasing accuracy, applying 'industry 4.0' technologies such as IoT-based *sensing* to run 'smart buildings', 'smart spaces' or 'smart cities' implies *privacy* and *security* issues. However, there are further ethical issues. For example, it is conceivable that the *social or medical status* of people would be measured and used to determine access rights to services, care, jobs or facilities. This could obviously cause new kinds of discrimination.

PRODUCTION PLANTS

Production plants are particular infrastructures in which spatio-temporal processes take place, often involving people. Nevertheless, they are typically organized in a *well-predictable and -controllable* way. *Planning and optimization* are the tools of choice. In fact, this application area was one of the first to use digital twins. Hence, operations research and related disciplines have created a wide range of powerful tools.[16] The *goal (function) underlying the optimization and control of production* is usually clear (classically, it is to maximize profit), and the underlying *utilitarian approach* (which aggregates everything that matters into a one-dimensional index, *score* or goal function to decide what solution is better or worse) often works reasonably well.

Therefore, digital twins have shown themselves to be very useful for the well-defined tasks of planning, implementation and management of

---

15   P Reinbold, 'Facing Discrimination: Choosing Equality over Technology' [2021] SSRN Electronic Journal 1.
16   M Grieves, 'Digital Twin: Manufacturing Excellence through Virtual Factory Replication' [2014] 1 White Paper; E Negri, L Fumagalli and M Macchi, 'A Review of the Roles of Digital Twin in CPS-Based Production Systems' (2017) 11 Procedia Manufacturing; THJ Uhlemann and others, 'The Digital Twin: Demonstrating the Potential of Real Time Data Acquisition in Production Systems' (2017) 9 Procedia Manufacturing.

production.[17] Nevertheless, a detailed representation of *all* relevant processes implies challenges, particularly as production processes may be pretty sophisticated and complicated. This includes the following:

- Some optimization and control problems are *NP-hard* (non-deterministic polynomial-time hard, i.e., computationally complex, requiring a lot of computational resources).[18] Therefore, the optimal solution cannot be found and implemented in real-time. It must be determined offline, or *simplifications* must be made, which might reduce the system performance (see also the section on traffic control).
- *Delays* between requiring to make adjustments (e.g., of the quantity produced to meet market demands), taking the related decisions, implementing them and becoming effective, may cause *instabilities*. This may imply *limited predictability and control*.[19]
- Elements of a production plant may fail, machines may break down or supplies may fall short (see, e.g., the recent chip crisis). There may also be blackouts of electricity or communication or cyberattacks. All of this further reduces predictability and control.
- It may be difficult to break down costs and estimate or measure *side effects (externalities)*, which may imply unexpected costs (such as bankruptcies of suppliers, economic crises, lockdowns or legal cases).

The last point raises particular ethical concerns, as the neglect of *externalities* in the past has caused relentless resource exploitation and serious environmental damage, climate emergency, as well as social and health issues, to mention just a few problems. Therefore, carbon taxes shall now be introduced in order to 'price in' the damages caused by CO_2 and to incentivize carbon reduction. Overall, however, it has been concluded that measuring economic success by one index such as profit or gross domestic

---

[17] F Tao and others, 'Digital Twin in Industry: State-of-the-Art' (2019) 15 IEEE Transactions on Industrial Informatics; W Kritzinger and others, 'Digital Twin in Manufacturing: A Categorical Literature Review and Classification', *IFAC-PapersOnLine* (Elsevier 2018).

[18] V Blondel and JN Tsitsiklis, 'NP-Hardness of Some Linear Control Design Problems' (1997) 35 SIAM Journal on Control and Optimization.

[19] D Helbing and S Lämmer, 'Supply and Production Networks: From the Bullwhip Effect to Business Cycles', *Networks of Interacting Machines: Production Organization in Complex Industrial Systems and Biological Cells* (World Scientific Publishing Co 2005).

product per capita, is insufficient, such that multiple indices are needed to measure success.[20] This, however, questions the suitability of the utilitarian approach and related optimization methods based on it, particularly when a societal perspective is taken, or nature is considered.[21]

ENVIRONMENT (CLIMATE, WEATHER, ECOSYSTEMS, NATURE)

Recently, it has been proposed to build digital twins also of environmental and climate systems.[22] As the climate depends on consumption and emission patterns, such a digital twin would probably consider – at least to some extent – models of the world economy and societies on our planet. Some experts, therefore, demand that such digital twins should consider the effects of production and human activities on nature, and the effects of the environment on humans, society, and production.[23] This implies further challenges (we will first focus on the environment, here, while the challenges of capturing and simulating socio-economic dynamics will be addressed later):

- The accurate representation of the environment requires a massive amount of data. *Remote sensing* (e.g., by means of satellites) may not be enough to get the best possible representation. Therefore, *ubiquitous sensing*,[24] using the IoT, has been proposed, which would involve millions or billions of sensors, or even a lot more, if nanotechnology or 'smart dust'[25] were used as well.

---

[20]   JE Stiglitz, A Sen and J-P Fitoussi, 'Report by the Commission on the Measurement of Economic Performance and Social Progress' (2009) <https://ec.europa.eu/eurostat/documents/8131721/8131772/Stiglitz-Sen-Fitoussi-Commission-report.pdf>.

[21]   MM Dapp, D Helbing and S Klauser (eds), *Finance 4.0 – Towards a Socio-Ecological Finance System* (Springer International Publishing 2021).

[22]   N Davies and others, 'Simulating Social–Ecological Systems: The Island Digital Ecosystem Avatars (IDEA) Consortium' (2016) 5(1) GigaScience; S Nativi, P Mazzetti and M Craglia, 'Digital Ecosystems for Developing Digital Twins of the Earth: The Destination Earth Case' (2021) 13 Remote Sensing; European Commission, 'Destination Earth. Shaping Europe's Digital Future' (2021) <https://digital-strategy.ec.europa.eu/en/policies/destination-earth>.

[23]   J Mathias and others, 'Grounding Social Foundations for Integrated Assessment Models of Climate Change' (2020) 8 Earth's Future.

[24]   D Puccinelli and M Haenggi, 'Wireless Sensor Networks: Applications and Challenges of Ubiquitous Sensing' (September 2005) 19.

[25]   R Anderson, H Chan and A Perrig, 'Key Infection: Smart Trust for Smart Dust', *Proceedings – International Conference on Network Protocols, ICNP*

- Measurements are never exact. There is always a finite *confidence interval. Context* and *interpretation* may matter.
- There are many *issues with Big Data analytics.* These include sensitivity, false positives/negatives, biases and discrimination effects, overfitting, spurious correlations, difficulties to distinguish causation from correlations, etc.[26]
- Random, *probabilistic effects* (sometimes called 'noise') may also play an important role.
- There are *fundamental limits* to predictability due to 'chaos' and 'turbulence' (see the example of weather forecasts[27]), undecidability (see the theorem of Kurt Gödel[28]), and computability (NP-hard problems), plus fundamental physical limits (e.g., due to the uncertainty relation).
- The *convergence* of 'black box' learning algorithms (e.g., neural networks, or deep learning) implies additional issues:[29] machine learning is an iterative process, which takes time and assumes convergence to the truth. However, reality might change more quickly than it takes to learn. This problem is amplified by the next points.
- In contrast to simple, linearly interacting systems, environmental systems often display *complex dynamics.*[30] This implies, for example, emergent properties and phenomena (and often counter-intuitive, surprising behaviours),[31] unexpected sudden phase transitions at

---

(2004); M Ilyas and I Mahgoub, *Smart Dust* (CRC Press 2018); Nano Magazine, 'Nanosensor and Digital Twin Technologies Come Together at COP26 to Help Deliver a Circular Economy as Part of the Race to Zero' (*Nano Magazine*, 2021) <https://nano-magazine.com/news/2021/11/1/nanosensor-and-digital-twin-technologies-come-together-at-cop26-to-help-deliver-a-circular-economy-as-part-of-the-race-to-zero>.

[26] V Vasiliauskaite, N Antulov-Fantulin and D Helbing, 'Supplementary Information (SI) of the Manuscript "On Some Fundamental Challenges in Monitoring Epidemics"' (202AD) 38 Philosophical Transactions of the Royal Society A: Mathematical, Physical and Engineering Sciences.

[27] E Aurell and others, 'Predictability in Systems with Many Characteristic Times: The Case of Turbulence' (1996) 53 Physical Review E – Statistical Physics, Plasmas, Fluids, and Related Interdisciplinary Topics.

[28] K Gödel, *On Formally Undecidable Propositions of Principia Mathematica and Related Systems* (Dover Publications, Inc 1992).

[29] MJ Kaur, VP Mishra and P Maheshwari, 'The Convergence of Digital Twin, IoT, and Machine Learning: Transforming Data into Action', *Digital Twin Technologies and Smart Cities: Internet of Things* (Springer 2020).

[30] P Turchin and AD Taylor, 'Complex Dynamics in Ecological Time Series' (1992) 73 Ecology.

[31] D Helbing (ed.), *Social Self-Organization* (Springer 2012).

'tipping points'[32] (often called 'catastrophes'[33]), power laws implying extremely fluctuating statistics,[34] and overall, limited predictability[35] and controllability,[36] even if a lot of accurate measurement data are available.

- *Network interactions* may further increase the previous issues and add undesired *side, feedback and/or cascading effects*. Combined with probabilistic effects, this may cause *uncertainty*, vulnerabilities and systemic risks.[37]

- Many *wicked problems*, where measures taken to solve a problem produce even bigger problems, are a result of complex dynamics in networked systems.[38] Nevertheless, complex dynamical systems should not be considered a bad thing. They are not. However, a successful understanding and management of complex dynamical systems requires a paradigm change, namely a shift of the focus from the (material) system components to their (typically immaterial, invisible and hardly measurable) interactions.

Overall, when it comes to complex dynamical environmental phenomena such as weather, climate or ecosystems, the representation accuracy of digital twins is limited, not just by the amount of data one can measure, process and transmit. On top of this problem comes the fact that the *data volume* grows faster than the *processing power*. Moreover, a *data-driven approach* based on Big Data analytics often does not fulfil the requirements of solid *data science*, which typically requires domain knowledge and experimental tests using proper statistical methods. That is, 'data-based' must be distinguished from 'fact-based' (as the latter requires the use of *verification and falsification* measures).

---

[32]   C Folke and others, 'Regime Shifts, Resilience, and Biodiversity in Ecosystem Management' (2004) 35 Annual Review of Ecology, Evolution, and Systematics, 557.

[33]   EC Zeeman, 'Catastrophe Theory' (1976) 234 Scientific American, 65.

[34]   HE Stanley, *Introduction to Phase Transitions and Critical Phenomena* ([reprint], Oxford University Press 1987); Y Malevergne and D Sornette, *Extreme Financial Risks*, 1st edn (Springer-Verlag 2006); RN Mantegna and HE Stanley, *An Introduction to Econophysics: Correlations and Complexity in Finance* (Cambridge University Press 2000).

[35]   YA Kravtsov (ed.), *Limits of Predictability* (Springer 1993).

[36]   YY Liu and AL Barabási, 'Control Principles of Complex Systems' (2016) 88 Reviews of Modern Physics.

[37]   Helbing, 'Globally Networked Risks and How to Respond' (n 9).

[38]   D Dörner, *The Logic of Failure: Recognizing and Avoiding Error in Complex Situations* (Basic Books 1997).

All of this can lead to errors and misrepresentations as well as wrong courses of action.[39] As a consequence, a new approach called 'global systems science' has been proposed.[40] While the term 'evidence-based' has mostly been used for 'fact-based' in the past, it is now increasingly being used for 'data-based', which is confusing and problematic, exactly because there are fundamental limits to the accuracy of digital twins in environmental complex systems (and others discussed in the following). The problem is further amplified if policies are taken in response to extrapolated or inferred data, or in response to *predicted* futures, which may never materialize. In addition, there is often a gap between scientifically suggested responses and policy responses, and a gap between intended and actual solutions.

Of course, from an ethical point of view, there may be further issues. For example, the *surveillance* of consumption or other behaviours implies *privacy* issues. A *scoring* of people may imply discrimination, and *targeting* them may undermine their freedom rights, particularly when behavioural manipulation is involved.[41] All of this can be in conflict with *human dignity*.

TRAFFIC FLOWS AND MARKETS

Traffic flows and financial markets constitute two other kinds of complex dynamical systems, this time involving large numbers of people. Let us start with traffic flows.[42] Here, one can find a range of diverse congestion patterns, which depend on the traffic volume and inhomogeneities along the road (such as on- and off-ramps, gradients or changes in the number of lanes).[43] Interestingly, due to the interactions of many vehicles, traffic flows are multi-stable; that is, even for identical traffic conditions, there

---

[39]   ibid.

[40]   Helbing, 'Globally Networked Risks and How to Respond' (n 9); C Jaegar and others, 'GSS: Towards a Research Program for Global Systems Science', *Second Open Global Systems Science Conference* (2013).

[41]   D Helbing, P Seele and T Beschorner, 'Humans Degraded to Data Points' (English translation of 'Der Mensch Wird Zum Datenpunkt', published in Schweizer Monat, May 2022) <https://www.researchgate.net/publication/360620579_Humans_Degraded_to_Data_Points >.

[42]   J Argota Sánchez-Vaquerizo, 'Getting Real: The Challenge of Building and Validating a Large-Scale Digital Twin of Barcelona's Traffic with Empirical Data' (2021) 11(1) ISPRS International Journal of Geo-Information.

[43]   D Helbing and others, 'Theoretical vs. Empirical Classification and Prediction of Congested Traffic States' (2009) 69 European Physical Journal B,

can be different outcomes, depending on local fluctuations in the density. In other words, traffic flows display the feature of history dependence (*hysteresis*), and there are *counter-intuitive* phenomena such as 'faster-is-slower effects' (i.e., trying to go faster may trigger a breakdown of the traffic flow, which slows down traffic).[44]

These congestion patterns are a consequence of *systemic instability*:[45] above a certain critical density, random variations in the traffic flow are being amplified, causing a *domino effect*. It is striking that particular kinds of adaptive cruise control systems can dissolve undesirable collective effects such as traffic jams without the need for centralized control, just based on local self-organization.[46] Here, the real-time measurement of the distance and relative speed of the vehicle ahead is used by a particular adaptive cruise control system for real-time feedback to slightly change the acceleration or deceleration of a vehicle. Based on such '*distributed control*',[47] traffic jams can be dissolved by changing vehicle interactions in a minimally invasive way as compared with what drivers would do. The digitally assisted, local self-organization leads to another, desirable, collective outcome: free traffic. So, real-time feedback and coordination approaches do not only work in complex systems with many dynamically changing variables – they may even be more successful than classical control approaches. A similar finding has been made for traffic light control.[48]

Financial markets are another interesting example to discuss. Here, one important finding is that *markets would not work, if everyone decided and behaved according to the same deterministic rules.* Surprisingly, markets get more efficient, if some degree of *heterogeneity* or '*noise*' is involved; that is, if the actors decide in diverse ways. A model to illustrate some underlying

---

[44]   D Helbing, 'Traffic and Related Self-Driven Many-Particle Systems' (2001) 73 Reviews of Modern Physics; C Gershenson and D Helbing, 'When Slower Is Faster' (2015) 21 Complexity.

[45]   D Helbing and AF Johansson, 'On the Controversy around Daganzo's Requiem for and Aw-Rascle's Resurrection of Second-Order Traffic Flow Models' (2009) 69 European Physical Journal B.

[46]   A Kesting and others, 'Adaptive Cruise Control Design for Active Congestion Avoidance' (2008) 16 Transportation Research Part C: Emerging Technologies.

[47]   C Gershenson, 'Guiding the Self-Organization of Cyber-Physical Systems' (2020) 7 Frontiers in Robotics and AI, 41.

[48]   S Lämmer and D Helbing, 'Self-Control of Traffic Lights and Vehicle Flows in Urban Road Networks' (2008) 2008 Journal of Statistical Mechanics: Theory and Experiment.

principles is the so-called 'minority game'.[49] In this game, majority deci-sions tend to be less profitable than minority decisions. That is, better results can be achieved by betting against the majority.

Both examples, traffic flows and markets, illustrate that self-organization in complex systems should not be considered a problem, but can be a good *solution*. For this, having the right kinds of interactions among the system components (here, drivers or traders) is more important than the indi-vidual properties of the system components.

Finding suitable interactions, which will automatically and efficiently produce desirable outcomes based on self-organization, is a matter of *'mechanism design'*[50] and *'complexity science'*.[51] A favourable side effect of such self-organization is that the resulting collective behaviour of the system is typically robust to reasonably small perturbations ('disrup-tions'), which implies systemic *resilience*.[52] However, lack of transpar-ency and required real-time data, wrong feedback and incentives, or lack of accountability and coordination might lead to *systemic failures*,[53] as urban gridlock or financial crashes illustrate. Therefore, self-organization (sometimes also called the 'invisible hand'[54]) does not *always* deliver desirable outcomes, if everyone just does whatever they like.[55] As pointed out before, one needs suitable interactions. Importantly, however, self-organization allows for some degree of *freedom* (usually without much loss of functionality or efficiency), which does not usually apply to centralized control.[56]

---

[49] D Challet, M Marsili and Y-C Zhang, *Minority Games: Interacting Agents in Financial Markets* (Oxford University Press 2004); A Chakraborti and others, 'Statistical Mechanics of Competitive Resource Allocation Using Agent-Based Models' (2015) 552 Physics Reports.

[50] S Baliga and E Maskin, 'Mechanism Design for the Environment', *Handbook of Environmental Economics*, vol. 1 (Elsevier 2003).

[51] S Thumer, RA Hanel and P Klimek, *Introduction to the Theory of Complex Systems* (Oxford University Press 2019).

[52] L Fraccascia, I Giannoccaro and V Albino, 'Resilience of Complex Systems: State of the Art and Directions for Future Research' [2018] Complexity.

[53] D Helbing and P Mukerji, 'Crowd Disasters as Systemic Failures: Analysis of the Love Parade Disaster' (2012) 1 EPJ Data Science; D Helbing, 'Systemic Risks in Society and Economics' in Dirk Helbing (ed.), *Social Self-Organization* (Springer 2012).

[54] A Smith, *The Theory of Moral Sentiments* (printed for Andrew Millar, in the Strand; and Alexander Kincaid and J Bell, in Edinburgh 1759).

[55] T Roughgarden, *Selfish Routing and the Price of Anarchy* (MIT Press 2005).

[56] D Helbing, *Next Civilization* (Springer International Publishing 2021).

Faced with undesirable *'misbehaviour'*[57] of complex systems, one often calls for more control of their system components. Accordingly, everybody should show a certain, desired behaviour. However, above we learned that this can be counterproductive. *Diversity* is frequently needed for techno-socio-economic systems to work well[58] and, accordingly, digital twins need to be diverse (not only in terms of individual parameter specifications but also with regard to their inner working, i.e. their underlying algorithm).

Moreover, centralized control attempts tend to perform poorly or fail in systems, which are characterized by randomness, variability, heterogeneity, network effects and complex dynamics, where internal interactions typically prevail and predictability is often limited. In these systems, a flexible and prompt adaptation to the respective local conditions and needs is a promising approach to promote coordination and favourable self-organization in the system, while the possibility of optimal control is often an illusion.

Despite the specificity of traffic flows and markets, similar complexity-related challenges are abundant in many cities around the world.[59]

---

[57]   RH Thaler, *Misbehaving : The Making of Behavioral Economics* (W. W. Norton & Company 2015).

[58]   SE Page, *The Difference: How the Power of Diversity Creates Better Groups, Firms, Schools, and Societies* (Princeton University Press 2007); CA Hidalgo and others, 'The Product Space Conditions the Development of Nations' (2007) 317 Science; AW Woolley and others, 'Evidence for a Collective Intelligence Factor in the Performance of Human Groups' (2010) 330 Science.

[59]   J Hourdos and P Michalopoulos, 'Twin Cities Metro-Wide Traffic Micro-Simulation Feasibility Investigation' (2008) Report # 5 in the series Access to Destinations Study, Report # 2008-15 <https://www.lrrb.org/pdf/200815.pdf>; Ayuntamiento de Madrid, 'Madrid Actualiza Su Simulador de Movilidad e Incluye Todos Los Sistemas de Transporte Para Reducir Las Afecciones Al Tráfico' (*Diario de Madrid*, 4 March 2021) <https://diario.madrid.es/blog/notas-de-prensa/madrid-actualiza-su-simulador-de-movilidad-e-incluye-todos-los-siste mas-de-transporte-para-reducir-las-afecciones-al-trafico/>; PTV Group, 'PTV Group Successfully Integrates the UK's First Real-Time Transport Model with City of York Council (UK)' (*PTV Newsroom*, 2021) <https://company.ptvgr oup.com/en/resources/newsroom/ptv-group-successfully-integrates-the-uks-first-real-time-transport-model-with-city-of-york-council-uk>; IMEC, 'Imec and TNO Launch Digital Twin of the City of Antwerp' (2018) <https://www.im ec-int.com/en/articles/imec-and-tno-launch-digital-twin-of-the-city-of-antwerp>; SmartCitiesWorld, 'Digital Twin Created for New Indian Smart City – Smart Cities World' (*SmartCitiesWorld*, 2018) <https://www.smartcitiesworld.net/news/news/ digital-twin-created-for-new-indian-smart-city-3674>; I Kosonen, K Koskinen and J Kostiainen, 'Real-Time Traffic Data Applications in the Mobility Lab of Helsinki – Case Smart Junction', *ITS World Congress* (2021).

To accomplish fully functional, real-time, and bidirectional physical–virtual frameworks able to manage mobility and other complexity challenges effectively,[60] further research is required.[61] Recent research focuses, for example, on connecting mobility with heterogeneous socio-economic interactions and urban logistics.[62] Reflecting the diversity of actions and preferences in reality precisely is one of the goals of digital twins that increasingly aim to mirror entire economic systems.[63] Starting from operations for business intelligence,[64] they ultimately strive to optimize markets and financial ecosystems for more sustainable development[65] or other goals.

PRECISION HEALTH

Digital twins have been proposed also for use in medicine and health care.[66] For example, they have been applied to prepare for difficult surgeries.[67] Eventually, digital twins are expected to capture body structures, functions and processes not only on a macro-scale – that is, for organs[68] or entire

---

[60] Liu and others (n 1).

[61] A Fuller and others, 'Digital Twin: Enabling Technologies, Challenges and Open Research' (2020) 8 IEEE Access.

[62] LP Consortium, 'Lead Project' <https://www.leadproject.eu/>.

[63] P Pobuda, 'The Digital Twin of the Economy' [2020] Real-World Economics Review.

[64] M Anshari, MN Almunawar and M Masri, 'Digital Twin: Financial Technology's Next Frontier of Robo-Advisor' (2022) 15 Journal of Risk and Financial Management; A Bolton, M Coates and P El Hajj, 'How Finance and Digital Twins Can Shape a Better Future for the Planet' (2022).

[65] Nativi, Mazzetti and Craglia (n 22); A Preut, JP Kopka and U Clausen, 'Digital Twins for the Circular Economy' (2021) 13 Sustainability (Switzerland).

[66] K Bruynseels, F Santoni de Sio and J van den Hoven, 'Digital Twins in Health Care: Ethical Implications of an Emerging Engineering Paradigm' (2018) 9 Frontiers in Genetics; A Ricci, A Croatti and S Montagna, 'Pervasive and Connected Digital Twins – A Vision for Digital Health' [2021] IEEE Internet Computing; EO Popa and others, 'The Use of Digital Twins in Healthcare: Socio-Ethical Benefits and Socio-Ethical Risks' (2021) 17 Life Sciences, Society and Policy.

[67] H Laaki, Y Miche and K Tammi, 'Prototyping a Digital Twin for Real Time Remote Control Over Mobile Networks: Application of Remote Surgery' (2019) 7 IEEE Access; H Ahmed and L Devoto, 'The Potential of a Digital Twin in Surgery' (2021) 28 Surgical Innovation.

[68] R Martinez-Velazquez, R Gamez and A El Saddik, 'Cardio Twin: A Digital Twin of the Human Heart Running on the Edge', *2019 IEEE International Symposium on Medical Measurements and Applications (MeMeA)* (IEEE 2019);

bodies[69] – but also on a micro-scale, on a cellular level or below.[70] This requires entirely new measurement methods. Nanotechnology has been proposed to offer novel solutions: exposing the body to nanoparticles or nanobots may allow one to read out activity patterns and realize new approaches to health care.[71] Relevant technologies have become known under names such as 'Internet of (Bio-)Nano-Things',[72] 'Internet of Bodies'[73] or 'Internet of Humans'.[74] The harvested data may be used

---

NK Chakshu, I Sazonov and P Nithiarasu, 'Towards Enabling a Cardiovascular Digital Twin for Human Systemic Circulation Using Inverse Analysis' (2021) 20 Biomechanics and Modeling in Mechanobiology; G Browne, 'The Quest to Make a Digital Replica of Your Brain' [2022] *Wired*.

[69]   Bruynseels, Santoni de Sio and van den Hoven (n 66); BR Barricelli, E Casiraghi and D Fogli, 'A Survey on Digital Twin: Definitions, Characteristics, Applications, and Design Implications' (2019) 7 IEEE Access; W Shengli, 'Is Human Digital Twin Possible?' (2021) 1 Computer Methods and Programs in Biomedicine Update.

[70]   M Di Filippo and others, 'Single-Cell Digital Twins for Cancer Preclinical Investigation', *Methods in Molecular Biology*, vol. 2088 (Methods Mol Biol 2020); DeepLife, 'How Digital Twins of Human Cells Are Accelerating Drug Discovery' [2022] Nature Biopharma Dealmakers (advertisement feature).

[71]   Y Liu and others, 'A Novel Cloud-Based Framework for the Elderly Healthcare Services Using Digital Twin' (2019) 7 IEEE Access; BR Barricelli and others, 'Human Digital Twin for Fitness Management' (2020) 8 IEEE Access.

[72]   F Dressler and S Fischer, 'Connecting In-Body Nano Communication with Body Area Networks: Challenges and Opportunities of the Internet of Nano Things' (2015) 6 Nano Communication Networks; J Jarmakiewicz, K Parobczak and K Maslanka, 'On the Internet of Nano Things in Healthcare Network', *2016 International Conference on Military Communications and Information Systems (ICMCIS)* (IEEE 2016); NMM AbdElnapi and others, 'A Survey of Internet of Things Technologies and Projects for Healthcare Services', *2018 International Conference on Innovative Trends in Computer Engineering (ITCE)* (IEEE 2018); IF Akyildiz and others, 'PANACEA: An Internet of Bio-NanoThings Application for Early Detection and Mitigation of Infectious Diseases' (2020) 8 IEEE Access; Murat Kuscu and Bige Deniz Unluturk, 'Internet of Bio-Nano Things: A Review of Applications, Enabling Technologies and Key Challenges' (2021) 2 ITU Journal on Future and Evolving Technologies.

[73]   M Lee and others, *The Internet of Bodies: Opportunities, Risks, and Governance* (RAND Corporation 2020); A Maxwell, 'A Living, Breathing Internet of Things All Around You' (*Now. Powered by Northrop Grumman*, 2020) <https://now.northropgrumman.com/a-living-breathing-internet-of-bodies-all-around-you/>; G Boddington, 'The Internet of Bodies—Alive, Connected and Collective: The Virtual Physical Future of Our Bodies and Our Senses' (2021) 1 AI and Society; A Celik, KN Salama and AM Eltawil, 'The Internet of Bodies: A Systematic Survey on Propagation Characterization and Channel Modeling' (2022) 9 IEEE Internet of Things Journal.

[74]   H Lehrach and A Ionescu, 'The Future of Health Care: Deep Data, Smart Sensors, Virtual Patients and the Internet-of-Humans' (2016) 1 <https://ec.europa.

for 'personalized medicine' or 'precision health'.[75] Proposed applications might range from fighting cancer to brain activity mapping.[76] Ray Kurzweil and others even suggest we might be able to overcome death and, thereby, live forever.[77]

However, new challenges arise, such as the following: (1) Is life extension in an 'over-populated world with limited resources' ethical, or would it amplify inequality and shorten the lives of some people for the benefit of others? (2) How do we avoid technological, social, behavioural or eugenic selection,[78] which could mean bias, discrimination and population control violating the right to life? (3) What about the health threats resulting from the limited accuracy of 'read' and 'write' operations in the sub-millimetre range? (4) How do we avoid dual-use, when it becomes possible to read minds remotely and to engineer thoughts, emotions, values, decisions and behaviours?[79] (5) How do we protect ourselves from theft or manipulation of our highly sensitive health data in view of cybersecurity issues and hacking threats?[80] (6) How dangerous for our well-being would it be, if two operating systems were to interfere with each other: the natural operating system of our body and a digital, data-driven, AI-controlled one?

---

eu/futurium/en/system/files/ged/futurehealth_white_paper.pdf>; H Lehrach and A Ionescu, 'Discussion: The Future of Health Care: Deep Data, Smart Sensors, Virtual Patients and the Internet-of-Humans' (*European Commission. Futurium. Digital4Science*, 2016) <https://ec.europa.eu/futurium/en/content/future-health-care-deep-data-smart-sensors-virtual-patients-and-internet-humans-0.html>.

[75] B Björnsson and others, 'Digital Twins to Personalize Medicine' (2020) 12(4) Genome Medicine; LF Rivera and others, 'Towards Continuous Monitoring in Personalized Healthcare through Digital Twins', *CASCON 2019 Proceedings: Conference of the Centre for Advanced Studies on Collaborative Research – Proceedings of the 29th Annual International Conference on Computer Science and Software Engineering* (2020).

[76] AP Alivisatos and others, 'Nanotools for Neuroscience and Brain Activity Mapping' (2013) 7 ACS Nano.

[77] R Kurzweil and T Grossman, *Fantastic Voyage: Live Long Enough to Live Forever* (Rodale 2005).

[78] D Helbing and others, 'Triage 4.0: On Death Algorithms and Technological Selection. Is Today's Data-Driven Medical System Still Compatible with the Constitution?' (2021) 10 Journal of European CME.

[79] SA Wirdatmadja and others, 'Wireless Optogenetic Neural Dust for Deep Brain Stimulation', *2016 IEEE 18th International Conference on e-Health Networking, Applications and Services (Healthcom)* (IEEE 2016); K Nixdorff and others, 'Dual-Use Nano-Neurotechnology' (2018) 37 Politics and the Life Sciences; SR Patel and CM Lieber, 'Precision Electronic Medicine in the Brain' (2019) 37 Nature Biotechnology.

[80] S Zafar and others, 'A Systematic Review of Bio-Cyber Interface Technologies and Security Issues for Internet of Bio-Nano Things' (2021) 9 IEEE Access.

A discussion of these and further issues of a Planetary Health agenda is available elsewhere.[81]

HUMANS (VS. ROBOTS)

Traffic and stock markets are not where complexity ends. People are (to a large extent) complex self-organizing systems themselves: many body functions, including brain functions, are complex and adaptive to a changing environment.[82] The fact that people have a brain implies a number of additional challenges that make it even more difficult to produce highly accurate digital twins:

- *Information processing* comes into play and has a dominating role in the resulting individual behaviour.
- *Decision-making* becomes important. While companies may strive to choose the best-performing solution, which often narrows down the number of relevant options to one, people care about having *alternatives and freedom of choice.* Typically, decisions are not based on strict optimization, but on heuristics,[83] for example, simple decision rules such as the principle of 'satisficing'[84] (i.e., choosing an option that is considered to be 'good enough').
- People *learn*, such that their way of decision-making changes over time.
- People exchange information, for example, by using *languages.* In this connection, it is important to know that languages are not fixed and given for all times, but complex, adaptive and evolving systems themselves.[85]

---

[81]   D Helbing, 'The Planetary Health Agenda – A Global Political Problem' (*FuturICT Blog*, 2021) <http://futurict.blogspot.com/2021/09/the-planetary-health-agenda-global.html>; D Helbing and M Perc, 'Nanowars Can Cause Epidemic Resurgence and Fail to Promote Cooperation' (2022) arXiv Physics and Society <https://arxiv.org/abs/2201.04747>.

[82]   S Nativi, M Craglia and L Sciullo, 'MyDigitalTwin: Exploratory Research Report' (Publications Office of the European Union 2022).

[83]   G Gigerenzer, R Hertwig and T Pachur, *Heuristics: The Foundations of Adaptive Behavior* (Oxford University Press 2011).

[84]   HA Simon, 'Rational Choice and the Structure of the Environment.' (1956) 63 Psychological Review 129.

[85]   L Steels (ed.), *Experiments in Cultural Language Evolution* (John Benjamins Publishing Company 2012).

- People can give things a *meaning*. In fact, all words become meanings by shared usage patterns, called 'conventions'.[86]
- Language is often *ambiguous* and only fully understandable in context.
- People have *consciousness*, which until today has been conceptualized and understood only to a limited extent.
- People often act according to individual *intentions*.
- People's *goals change* over time (e.g., if they are hungry, they will look for food, but after eating, they will turn their *attention* to something else). Accordingly, their behaviour cannot be well understood by means of one utility function, particularly one that does not change.
- People act in many different contexts that are characterized by different *norms* (i.e., commonly expected behaviours). Accordingly, they play many different *roles*, which are to be modelled by different *personas*.
- People have a *self-image*, which guides their own behaviour, and *images* of others, which determine their expectations and actions.
- Most people have *empathy*, which may trigger other-regarding behaviour.
- People have *emotions*, which change their consideration and valuation of options, among which they may decide.
- People may *feel pain*.
- People are *playful*; that is, they do things that do not have an immediate purpose apart from having fun.

The above findings pose particular challenges for creating digital twins. The discipline of *cognitive computing* is trying to account for (some of) these features, but it requires a massive amount of sensitive personal data to create increasingly detailed digital twins,[87] which obviously raises *privacy* issues. However, no matter how much data is available, it is highly doubtful that one could ever create an identical digital twin. Many of the relevant variables are not directly measurable or measured – and must, therefore, be *inferred* from other observations.[88] For example, diseases are

---

[86] RXD Hawkins, ND Goodman and RL Goldstone, 'The Emergence of Social Norms and Conventions' (2019) 23 Trends in Cognitive Sciences.

[87] J Hurwitz, M Kaufman and A Bowles, *Cognitive Computing and Big Data Analytics* (John Wiley & Sons, Inc 2015).

[88] Chul Min Lee and SS Narayanan, 'Toward Detecting Emotions in Spoken Dialogs' (2005) 13 IEEE Transactions on Speech and Audio Processing; H Lin and others, 'Detecting Stress Based on Social Interactions in Social Networks' (2017) 29 IEEE Transactions on Knowledge and Data Engineering.

often inferred from symptoms, intentions from actions and meanings from context. This implies the risk of *misinterpretations*, as it is also known from AI-based emotion classifications using facial expressions.[89] The possibility of ambiguity and mimicry or deception must be considered as well.

It must further be stressed that modelling humans, their thinking, feeling, decisions and actions concerns not only the area of brain science, but also the social sciences and humanities, which tend to doubt that all of the above concepts can be quantified and measured well, or operationalized in a way that could be translated into algorithms. For example, people particularly care about non-material qualities such as *consciousness*, *dignity*, *creativity*, *friendship*, *trust* and *love*, which are not well measurable (or even hard to define), and will perhaps never be quantifiable in an adequate way. There is certainly a danger to ignore human features that are not represented by numbers, or perhaps not even representable by numbers at all. Accordingly, a data-driven society may easily neglect important qualities, which would possibly produce an *inhumane society*.

From the point of view of the social sciences, humanities and law, treating people just like things or robots (that may be reset, replaced, used or changed in arbitrary ways, or thrown away) would be considered highly inappropriate and *unethical*. It would violate their *human dignity*. It would also undermine their ability to self-organize. It would further affect their *autonomy* and *freedom*. We would like to underline, here, that freedom is not primarily a matter of allowing for selfish behaviour. It is a precondition for experimentation, learning and innovation. It is also important to enable the variability needed to make the many different roles compatible, which people are trying to fulfil every day.

(SMART) CITIES AND SOCIETIES

A further level of complexity (implying additional challenges to produce accurate digital twins) is expected for cities and societies, particularly 'smart cities' and 'smart nations'.[90]

---

[89]   JI Durán and J-M Fernández-Dols, 'Do Emotions Result in Their Predicted Facial Expressions? A Meta-Analysis of Studies on the Co-Occurrence of Expression and Emotion' (2021) 21 Emotion.

[90]   M Batty, 'Digital Twins' (2018) 45 Environment and Planning B: Urban Analytics and City Science; G Schrotter and C Hürzeler, 'The Digital Twin of the City of Zurich for Urban Planning' (2020) 88 PFG – Journal of Photogrammetry, Remote Sensing and Geoinformation Science; A Hudson-Smith and others, 'Urban IoT: Advances, Challenges, and Opportunities for Mass Data Collection,

- While smart cities and smart nations are delivering a lot more data than was ever imagined in the past, with the increasing amount of networking and interconnectivity, *the level of complexity is growing even faster than the volume of data* (namely, in a combinatorial, i.e. factorial rather than exponential way).[91] Paradoxically, this can cause an increasing loss of (centralized) control, even though we have more data and better technology than ever (which calls for distributed control approaches that can support a favourable self-organization of the system).

- Social systems are *multi-level complex systems*. People, for example, who are complex systems themselves, create complex social systems based on self-organization and emergence. Group formation, for instance, will come with an emergent *group identity*, which will change the behaviour of the group members.[92] Note that this is very different from atoms that form molecules (which will usually not change the properties of the atoms in a significant way).

- Given the many different social contexts people are part of – and the associated different roles expected from them – people have multiple and changing goals. Therefore, cities and societies are faced with a *plurality of goals* that need to be met. Accordingly, they should not be run like production plants or companies, which traditionally serve one goal, such as profit maximization. Politics is needed to bring the many different goals into a suitable balance, which may, of course, change over time. Accordingly, the diverse goals of a city are typically not well represented by a utility function.

- The network interactions of people create *social capital* such as trust, reputation or solidarity.[93] While this is of great value for the economy and society, it has been difficult so far to operationalize and measure social capital.

- To a much greater extent, the same quantification problem exists for *culture*. Defining culture as a collection of social norms and

---

Analysis, and Visualization' in W Shi and others (eds), *Urban Informatics: The Urban Book Series* (Springer 2021).

[91] M Hagner and others, 'Will Democracy Survive Big Data and Artificial Intelligence?' [2017] Scientific American.

[92] IS Lustick, 'Agent-Based Modelling of Collective Identity: Testing Constructivist Theory' (2000) 3 Journal of Artificial Societies and Social Simulation (JASSS); P Smaldino and others, 'An Agent-Based Model of Social Identity Dynamics' (2012) 15 Journal of Artificial Societies and Social Simulation (JASSS).

[93] N Lin, K Cook and RS Burt (eds), *Social Capital: Theory and Research* (Aldine de Gruyter 2001).

routines or success principles seems to capture only some of its essence. For example, culture also has to do with the playful nature of humans, with the exploration of uncharted waters, with learning and innovation.

- Societal decisions are not just about optimization and control. They trigger the exploration of new solutions and result from interactions in many parts of the system. Therefore, *co-evolution* is a much more adequate description of what characterizes cities and societies.[94]

It is questionable whether all of the above is already being considered, or even *can* be considered, by digital twins. Attempts to build digital twins of entire societies have existed at least since the Sentient World Project.[95] Promoted by the US Department of Defense and various Fortune 500 companies,[96] this simulation platform has also been used for planning wars and population-scale psychological operations (PsyOps).[97] It is not far-fetched to assume that this or a similar platform has been developed further in order to create a digital twin of the world, based on mass surveillance data.[98]

Recently, it has even been proposed that considering detailed knowledge about everyone's opinions and preferences would allow one to create a democratic post-choice, post-voting society.[99] Mass surveillance could create entirely new opportunities here. The underlying *technocracy* would automatically aggregate opinions, while politicians would no longer be

---

94   IN Dubina, EG Carayannis and DFJ Campbell, 'Creativity Economy and a Crisis of the Economy? Coevolution of Knowledge, Innovation, and Creativity, and of the Knowledge Economy and Knowledge Society' (2012) 3(1) Journal of the Knowledge Economy.

95   T Cerri and A Chaturvedi, 'Sentient World Simulation (SWS): A Continuously Running Model of the Real World' (2006).

96   J Cupp, 'USJFCOM Teams with Purdue University to Add the Human Factor to War Game Simulations' (*News from USJFCOM*, 2004) <https://web.archive.org/web/20070206184414/http://www.mgmt.purdue.edu/centers/perc/html/Media/USJFCOM.htm>.

97   S Strife, 'Sentient World: War Games on the Grandest Scale' (*The Register*, 2007) <https://www.theregister.com/2007/06/23/sentient_worlds/>.

98   DJ Watts, 'Computational Social Science: Exciting Progress and Future Directions' (2013) 43 The Bridge; D Fagella, 'Sentient World Simulation and NSA Surveillance: Exploiting Privacy to Predict the Future? (*Emerj. Artifical Intelligence Research*, 2017) <https://emerj.com/ai-future-outlook/nsa-surveillance-and-sentient-world-simulation-exploiting-privacy-to-predict-the-future/>.

99   Bundesinstitut für Bau- Stadt- und Raumforschung (BBSR) im Bundesamt für Bauwesen und Raumordnung (BBR) and B und R (BMUB) Bundesministerium für Umwelt, Naturschutz, 'Smart City Charta' (2018) 43.

needed to figure out and implement what people want and need.[100] Rather than an upgraded democracy, however, such a society could become a novel kind of *digital populism*, in which the will of majorities might be relentlessly imposed on everyone, thereby undermining the protection of minorities and diversity.

As it is more efficient to deal with data rather than people, there is also the danger that our digital twins would be given *greater authority* than us, even though the representation of our will and us by our digital twin could be *inaccurate, biased, manipulated*, or *hacked*.[101] That is, if there is a disagreement between a person and the corresponding digital twin, the system would assume the data of the digital twin and ignore the opinion of the human it should represent.

Therefore, rather than replacing individual choices with automated machine decisions, we recommend going for the digital assistance of decision-making, offering people individually and systemically good opportunities. That is, instead of identifying, taking, and implementing *one* optimal solution to a given goal (e.g., taking the shortest route), the decision-support system should offer a number of high-performance solutions, and for each of them, it should indicate a diverse set of qualities relating to various relevant goals. For example, if I need to go from A to B, and one route takes 102 minutes, while the other takes 103 minutes, there is no reason to force me to take the faster route. If the other route is more scenic and I am not in a rush, it would make sense to take the slightly longer route. This would probably have positive side effects that are well known, but hardly quantifiable, such as having a better mood when I arrive, which will lead to more agreeable decisions, a better team spirit at work, and higher creativity from everyone. The longer route might also come with fewer CO_2 emissions (if used at a lower speed), or it may allow me to do some shopping along the way, which will save time and emissions later during the week. Therefore, 'scenic', 'shopping' and 'fewer emissions' would be some of the relevant qualities of high-performance solutions, when it comes to choosing optimal routes. While offering such choices would make the system perhaps less predictable in detail, it is likely that it will improve the state of the world in many hardly quantifiable aspects, which will cause further combinatorial benefits to society.

---

[100]   CA Hidalgo, 'A Bold Idea to Replace Politicians' (*TED*, 2018) <https://www.ted.com/talks/cesar_hidalgo_a_bold_idea_to_replace_politicians>.
[101]   D Helbing, 'Who Is Messing with Your Digital Twin? Body, Mind, and Soul for Sale?' (*TEDxIHEID*, 2022) <https://www.tedxiheid.com/dirk-helbing>.

In contrast, running a society based on a digital twin can have undesired side effects, if not done wisely. It might cause *lock-in effects* in potentially outdated operation principles of the past. It might also promote a society that is too much oriented toward control rather than creating opportunities. Moreover, a digital twin of society, which includes detailed digital twins of its people, could be easily abused. For example, by knowing the strengths and weaknesses of everyone, one could trick or manipulate everybody more effectively,[102] or mob them with hate speech on social media. Furthermore, a digital twin of society would also make it possible to determine how much one can pressure people without triggering a revolution, or figure out how to overcome majorities, how to break the will of people and how to impose policies on them, which do not represent their will. Such applications of mass surveillance might be considered to be highly *parasitic* and *undermine human rights*.

Even if it would not come this bad, with the growing power of information technology, there is certainly a risk that methods originally developed for the management of supply chains, companies or theme parks would be transferred to cities and societies, without realizing the *categorical mistakes* made by this. Moreover, such an approach may be even ignorant about the many (over-)simplifications made, neglecting details and hardly measurable aspects (such as human dignity), which would be treated like 'noise'. Such an approach could destroy the main strengths of social systems: their ability to innovate and adapt, to self-organize, and to (co-)evolve. In fact, it might even *destroy societies* as we know them, just for the sake of more control.

It is to be expected that, for many people, this would not end well. There is definitely a danger that running societies in a data-driven and AI-controlled way could lead to an inhumane organization of people, which some people would characterize as '*technological totalitarianism*'. But what should we run society for, if not for the people?

SUMMARY

We would like to summarize this chapter with 12 statements on digital twins:[103]

---

102 V Bell, 'Britain's "Twitter Troops" Have Ways of Making You Think ...' *The Guardian* (London, 16 August 2015); J Isaak and MJ Hanna, 'User Data Privacy: Facebook, Cambridge Analytica, and Privacy Protection' (2018) 51 Computer.
103 E Arcaute and others, 'Future Cities: Why Digital Twins Need to Take Complexity Science on Board', Research Gate <https://www.researchgate.net/

1. **On Data:** It has become an attractive idea to create digital twins of everything, including the Earth, its climate, human bodies and their health. While this approach may have many benefits, there are limits. All in all, one must realize that a data science rather than a merely data-driven approach is needed, which requires sharing a lot more data with a lot more people.

2. **On Complexity:** Creating an accurate digital twin for infrastructures, which change little over time, is easy. However, it will probably never be possible to produce an *exact* digital twin of life on Earth, even if nanotechnology is being used for ubiquitous sensor measurements. One is faced with fundamental challenges and measurement limits when models of complex dynamical systems are being built, for example, of weather, climate or life, of brains, behaviours or health. Thus, one needs to be prepared for uncertainty.

3. **On Machine Learning:** The biggest publicly known modern machine learning models try to learn a trillion parameters or so. Unpublished corporate, governmental or military models may contain even more parameters. While this is impressive, more predictive power is often achieved by simpler models (think of 'over-fitting'). Surprisingly, noisy or little data can sometimes generate better models.[104] But no matter how many variables are being considered, there are many orders of magnitudes of interaction effects that are not captured, hence neglected. This can produce a wrong picture and bad forecasts, which can be dangerous.

4. **On Artificial Intelligence:** So far, Big Data has not been able to replace science, in contrast to what Chris Anderson had envisioned,[105] nor do we have a universal AI/Artificial General Intelligence (AGI), according to what is publicly known. Even if we had one, this could still be

---

publication/354446988_Future_Cities_Why_Digital_Twins_Need_to_Take_Com plexity_Science_on_Board> (for a later manuscript version see G Caldarelli and others (n 125)); Helbing D, '12 Statements on Digital Twins i.e. detailed digital models of the world (or parts of it)' (2021) Talk for GESDA 2021 (Geneva Science and Diplomacy Anticipator) <https://www.researchgate.net/publicati on/355202057_12_STATEMENTS_ON_DIGITAL_TWINS_ie_detailed_digital_ models_of_the_world_or_parts_of_it>.

[104]   D Brockmann and D Helbing, 'The Hidden Geometry of Complex, Network-Driven Contagion Phenomena' (2013) 342 Science; M Mäs and D Helbing, 'Random Deviations Improve Micro–Macro Predictions: An Empirical Test' (2017) 49 Sociological Methods & Research.

[105]   C Anderson, 'The End of Theory: The Data Deluge Makes the Scientific Method Obsolete' (2008) 16 Wired.

dangerous, particularly if not retaining meaningful human control.[106] Suppose, for example, one would task an intelligent system to solve the sustainability problems of the Earth or to maximize planetary health. This might result in depopulation and trigger an 'apocalyptic' scenario, even though a better future for everyone might exist. Moreover, as many of today's AI systems operate like 'black boxes', one might not even realize some of the harmful effects AI systems are causing.

5. **On Optimization:** The concept of 'optimizing the world' is highly problematic because there is no science that could tell us what is the right goal function to choose: should it be GDP per capita or sustainability, life expectancy, health or quality of life? The problem is that optimization tries to map the complexity of the world to a one-dimensional function. This leads to gross oversimplifications and to the neglect of secondary goals, which is likely to cause other problems in the future. Using (co-)evolutionary approaches would probably be better than optimizing for one goal function. Coordination approaches may be more successful than control approaches.

6. **On Qualities:** A largely data-driven society is expected to perform poorly with regard to many hardly measurable qualities that humans care about. This includes freedom, love, creativity, friendship, meaning, dignity and culture, in short: quality of life.

7. **On Innovation:** Something like a 'digital crystal ball' is unlikely to see disruptive innovations, which are not included in the data of the past. Hence, predictions could be too pessimistic and misleading. For example, consider the forecast of the world population. According to some future projections, about one-third of the world's population is sometimes claimed to be 'overpopulation'. Consequently, these people may get in trouble when managing the world via a digital twin, as its projections do not consider better ways of running our economy that may be invented. Probably, 'overpopulation' is not the main problem, but lack of economic (re-)organization.

8. **Humans vs. Things:** In a highly networked, complex world, where almost everything has feedback, side or cascading effects, ethical challenges abound. For example, people should *not* be managed like things. In times when many argue about 'trolley problems' and 'lesser evils', if there is just a big enough disaster, problem or threat, any ethical principle or law may be overruled, including human

---

[106] S Russell, D Dewey and M Tegmark, 'Research Priorities for Robust and Beneficial Artificial Intelligence' (2015) 36 AI Magazine.

rights and even the right to life. Such developments can end with crimes against humanity.

9. **On Dual Use:** A powerful tool, particularly when applied on a global scale, may cause serious, large-scale damage. It is, therefore, necessary to map out undesired side effects of technologies and their use. Effective measures must be taken to prevent large-scale accidents and dual-use. Among others, this calls for decentralized data storage, distributed control and quality standards. Moreover, transparency of and accountability for the use of data and algorithms must be dramatically improved, and participatory governance should be enabled.

10. **On Alternatives:** We should carefully consider alternative uses of technology. Here, we would just like to mention the idea of creating a *socio-ecological finance system*, a finance system that would use the IoT to measure externalities that decisions of people and companies cause.[107] The measurement of externalities would define multiple new currencies, which could locally incentivize positive behavioural change. This novel real-time feedback and coordination system is inspired by nature. Nature has already managed to develop a circular economy based on self-organization and distributed control. Hence, introducing real-time feedback into our socio-economic system could create forces promoting a sustainable re-organization. A *sustainable circular and sharing economy* would result through a co-evolutionary process. If designed in a value-sensitive way, it could be a system consistent with freedom, privacy and self-determination, with creativity and innovation, with human rights and democracy. This would probably be the best path to sustainability currently known.

11. **On Governance:** As people are increasingly an integral part of socio-technical systems, a technology-driven approach and technological innovation are not enough. We first and foremost need *social innovation* to unlock the benefits of the digital age for everyone. A platform supporting true informational self-determination is urgently needed. Moreover, the classical *war room* approach needs to be replaced by a *peace room* approach, which requires, among others, an inter-disciplinary, ethical, multi-perspective approach; in other words, a new multi-stakeholder approach to achieve better insights and participatory resilience.[108]

---

[107] Dapp, Helbing and Klauser (n 21).

[108] D Helbing and P Seele, 'We Need Peace Rooms, Not War Rooms' (*The Globalist*, 2017) <https://www.theglobalist.com/technology-big-data-artificial-intelligence-future-peace-rooms/>.

12. **In Conclusion:** Societies are not machines, and an optimization approach is too narrow to manage them.[109] It is, therefore, important to recognize that complexity is an opportunity for new kinds of solutions, not 'the enemy'. Planning should be increasingly replaced by flexible adaptation, optimization by co-evolution, and control by coordination. Obviously, all of this can be supported by *digital assistance*, if used wisely and well.[110]

OUTLOOK: FROM THE METAVERSE TO 'THE MATRIX'?

Many readers may have noticed the re-birth and extension of the cyber-punks' virtual world, advocating a 'Second Life', in the recently rebranded 'metaverse'. The massive investments imply bigger plans. The metaverse is not just a 'parallel world'. It likes to offer more than opportunities to create accurate mirrors of real, physical systems, using privacy-invasive techniques such as tracking, profiling or scanning humans (including, for example, hand gestures, iris movements and dilation),[111] or even applying nanotechnology. Going a step further, the metaverse even wants to enable real-time feedback between the digital and physical realms.[112]

What we are seeing now is just the beginning. As long as real bidirectional interactions are lacking, it could be argued that digital twins are not yet fully functional. To accomplish the full vision of digital twins, they must be able to actuate and modify the physical environment they are mirroring, but that could sometimes go wrong.

In any case, progress is quick. Imagine, for example, that it will become cheap and common to use augmented reality glasses, or to get a more realistic embodiment experience, or to project digital twins into our physical environment (by means of hologram technology) or our minds (by means of neurotechnology), or even to materialize our avatars in form of robots (if not androids). This would make digital twins – and the people using them – a lot more powerful. For example, people could interact with others remotely, without requiring transportation. This could reduce the severe

---

[109]   D Helbing, 'Society Is Not A Machine, Optimization Not The Right Paradigm!' (*Edge*, 2016) <https://www.edge.org/response-detail/26795>.

[110]   D Helbing, 'Digitally Assisted Self-Organization', *Next Civilization* (Springer International Publishing 2021).

[111]   D Virgilio, 'What Comparisons between Second Life and the Metaverse Miss' [2022] *Slate*.

[112]   Liu and others (n 1).

environmental impact of transportation, enable access to dangerous environments, and expand the capacity to interact with people without spatial limitations, allowing them to work, study and play together without the constraints of our physical world.

Yet, new ethical questions would arise. For instance, one might try to commodify digital twins and assets in metaverse-like virtual environments,[113] enabled by pervasive monitoring of individual behaviour at a level of detail that is inconceivable in the physical world, but completely feasible in immersive worlds.[114] Also, new forms of identity theft, abuse and deception would be possible. For example, how do we reach a fair society, when rich people can 'multiply' themselves, being represented in parallel by multiple avatars or robots? Furthermore, how do we make sure that the limited resources of planet Earth will not be wasted on unnecessary technology that tempts people to live in an illusionary virtual world, escaping the real problems of the physical world,[115] rather than using them in favour of humans and nature? Last but not least, how do we make sure we will not end up in 'The Matrix', a world where people would be bounded by digital technologies? And how do we prevent people from being entirely replaced by digital twins in an extreme form of transhumanism?[116] The list of potential issues could certainly be expanded.

CONCLUSIONS

Digital twins of all sorts of systems are now becoming very popular. While many successful applications are already known in architecture, geography, manufacturing and logistics, applications to traffic and smart cities are on the way. There are also attempts to build digital twins of human bodies and health, of people and society. However, they are faced with measurement and big data challenges, extreme levels of complexity, and ethical issues. Applications that interfere with individual thoughts, decisions, behaviours and bodies are particularly problematic. Therefore, it

---

[113] S Voshmgir, *Token Economy: How the Web3 Reinvents the Internet*, 2nd edn (Token Kitchen 2020); G Edelman, 'The Father of Web3 Wants You to Trust Less' [2021] *Wired*.

[114] Virgilio (n 111).

[115] M Kim, 'The Good and the Bad of Escaping to Virtual Reality' [2015] *The Atlantic*.

[116] RM Geraci, *Apocalyptic AI: Visions of Heaven in Robotics, Artificial Intelligence, and Virtual Reality* (Oxford University Press 2010).

is concerning that many strategy papers do not stress human rights and human dignity, or do ignore them altogether.

It is conceivable, for example, that digital twins would be built, using a nanoparticle-based measurement of body functions ('in-body surveillance').[117] While this may create opportunities for entirely new health services, it may also enable body hacking and the stealing of highly sensitive personal health data. Hence, besides many new opportunities, new kinds of cybercrime may arise, including forms of identity theft that are probably hard to uncover and defend against. This development is dangerous. It could potentially lead to a 'militarization' of everything from food, air and medicine to bodies and minds.[118] Therefore, apart from technological innovations, social innovations are required to manage them. To unlock the full potential of new technologies, novel participatory governance frameworks are required, which give particular weight to a scientific approach and to the individuals affected by any (potential) measures taken, considering relevant alternatives. In order to make sure applications will be beneficial and benevolent, a particular focus on the most vulnerable is recommended. Most likely, we will need a *new social contract*. This would have to include the possibility of self-managing sensitive personal data. It is still to be seen whether Web 3.0 will deliver an appropriate and well-working solution for this.

If these problems are not solved soon, however, politics and citizens may lose their birthright to co-create their future. Currently, we seem to lack sufficient protection mechanisms to prevent that, for example, pervasive mass surveillance, repressive opinion control, a restrictive cashless society and/or neurocapitalism[119] could be put in place at some point in time, even without the full and well-informed consent of people.[120]

---

[117]   Liu and Merritt (n 4); Liu (n 4).

[118]   JD Moreno, *Mind Wars: Brain Science and the Military in the 21st Century* (Bellevue Literary Press 2012); A Krishnan, *Military Neuroscience and the Coming Age of Neurowarfare* (Routledge 2017); JJ Peltz, 'The Algorithm of You: Your Profile of Preference or an Agent for Evil?' (Naval War College 2017); VF Popescu, 'From Human Body Digitization to Internet of Bodies toward a New Dimension of Military Operations' (2019) 24 Land Forces Academy Review; UK Ministry of Defence and Bundeswehr, Office for Defence Planning, 'Human Augmentation: The Dawn of a New Paradigm – A Strategic Implications Project' (2021).

[119]   J Pykett, 'Neurocapitalism and the New Neuros: Using Neuroeconomics, Behavioural Economics and Picoeconomics for Public Policy' (2013) 13 Journal of Economic Geography.

[120]   D Helbing, 'A Planetary-Scale Threat', *Next Civilization* (Springer International Publishing 2021); D Helbing, 'Digital Threats to Humans and

It further appears that we do not have enough protection to prevent the use of sensitive personal data (particularly behavioural and health data) against us. This is a serious threat that calls for novel participatory governance approaches[121] that can minimize the misuse of powerful digital technologies while maximizing benefits for everyone.[122]

There are better ways to use technologies for a more sustainable and healthier world, in harmony with nature,[123] than creating something like a technocracy, run from a war room that lacks sufficient consideration of privacy, ethics, transparency, participation, democracy and human rights.[124] Planetary health and human well-being cannot be reduced to a problem of optimization, supply chain control or resource management. Doing so would dramatically oversimplify the world and fall short in view of complex systems, their various interaction effects and emergent properties.[125] It will also miss out on the opportunities that complexity offers, such as self-organization, emergence and co-evolution.

Rather than aiming for perfect digital twins, a predictable future and total control, one should use computer simulation technology to create better opportunities for everybody, for example for digital assistance with regard to creativity, innovation, self-organization, coordination, cooperation and co-evolution. The metaverse, for instance, if used well, could provide a helpful experimental playground that would allow the user to try out alternative organizations of cities and societies. In this connection, participatory formats inspired by the classical *agora*

Society' (June 2022) <https://www.researchgate.net/publication/361600988_Digital_Threats_to_Humans_and_Society>.

[121] D Helbing, 'Innovative Governance Needed: Some Thoughts on How to Master Our Future Using Big Data (also "Avatars", "Digital Twins") with a New Kind of Multi-Lateralism' (*FuturICT Blog*, 2021) <http://futurict.blogspot.com/2021/09/innovative-governance-approaches-needed.html>.

[122] R Kitchin, *The Data Revolution* (SAGE Publications Ltd 2014); D Helbing, 'Partial List of Possible Dual Uses of Big Data Cyber-Infrastructures' (*FuturICT Blog*, 2021) <http://futurict.blogspot.com/2021/07/>.

[123] D Helbing and others, 'Ethics of Smart Cities: Towards Value-Sensitive Design and Co-Evolving City Life' (2021) 13 Sustainability.

[124] D Helbing and P Seele, 'Turn War Rooms into Peace Rooms' (2017) 549 Nature.

[125] G. Caldarelli, E. Arcaute and M. Barthelemy et al., 'The Role of Complexity for Digital Twins of Cities' (2023) Nature Computational Science <https://doi.org/10.1038/s43588-023-00431-4>. For an earlier manuscript version see this preprint: Elsa Arcaute and others (n 103).

are particularly appealing.[126] They are also promising for developing participatory approaches to achieve higher resilience.[127]

Last but not least, digital technology allows us now to develop entirely new solutions that are based on a distributed flexible adaptation to local needs, on digitally assisted self-organization, and co-evolution. This may come with less predictability and control, but it is expected to improve the sustainability and carrying capacity of our world, while promoting quality of life, prosperity and peace.[128]

ACKNOWLEDGEMENTS

JASV is grateful for partial financial support from the Future Cities Lab Global at the Singapore-ETH Centre, which was established collaboratively between ETH Zurich and the National Research Foundation Singapore.

DH acknowledges the excellent research opportunities within the project 'CoCi: Co-Evolving City Life', which receives funding from the European Research Council (ERC) under the European Union's Horizon 2020 research and innovation programme under grant agreement no. 833168.

NOTE

---

[126]   D Helbing, 'Economics 2.0: The Natural Step towards a Self-Regulating, Participatory Market Society' (2013) 10 Evolutionary and Institutional Economics Review; D Helbing and E Pournaras, 'Society: Build Digital Democracy' (2015) 527 Nature; YT Hsiao and others, 'VTaiwan: An Empirical Study of Open Consultation Process in Taiwan'; D Helbing, 'Social Mirror: More Success through Awareness and Coordination', *Towards Digital Enlightenment* (Springer International Publishing 2019); 'Pol.Is' (*Participedia*) <https://participedia.net/method/4682>.

[127]   S Mahajan and others, 'Participatory Resilience: Surviving, Recovering and Improving Together' (2022) 83 Sustainable Cities and Society.

[128]   Helbing, *Next Civilization* (n 56).

BIBLIOGRAPHY

AbdElnapi NMM and others, 'A Survey of Internet of Things Technologies and Projects for Healthcare Services', *2018 International Conference on Innovative Trends in Computer Engineering (ITCE)* (IEEE 2018).

Ahmed H and Devoto L, 'The Potential of a Digital Twin in Surgery' (2021) 28 Surgical Innovation.

Akyildiz IF and others, 'PANACEA: An Internet of Bio-NanoThings Application for Early Detection and Mitigation of Infectious Diseases' (2020) 8 IEEE Access.

Al-Turjman F, *Internet of Nano-Things and Wireless Body Area Networks (WBAN)* (CRC Press/Taylor & Francis Group 2019).

Alivisatos AP and others, 'Nanotools for Neuroscience and Brain Activity Mapping' (2013) 7 ACS Nano.

Anderson C, 'The End of Theory: The Data Deluge Makes the Scientific Method Obsolete' (2008) 16 Wired.

Anderson R, Chan H and Perrig A, 'Key Infection: Smart Trust for Smart Dust', *Proceedings – International Conference on Network Protocols, ICNP* (2004).

Anshari M, Almunawar MN and Masri M, 'Digital Twin: Financial Technology's Next Frontier of Robo-Advisor' (2022) 15 Journal of Risk and Financial Management.

Arcaute E and others, 'Future Cities: Why Digital Twins Need to Take Complexity Science on Board' (2021) ResearchGate <https://www.researchgate.net/publication/354446988_Future_Cities_Why_Digital_Twins_Need_to_Take_Complexity_Science_on_Board>.

Argota Sánchez-Vaquerizo J, 'Getting Real: The Challenge of Building and Validating a Large-Scale Digital Twin of Barcelona's Traffic with Empirical Data' (2021) 11(1) ISPRS International Journal of Geo-Information.

Aurell E and others, 'Predictability in Systems with Many Characteristic Times: The Case of Turbulence' (1996) 53 Physical Review E – Statistical Physics, Plasmas, Fluids, and Related Interdisciplinary Topics.

Ayuntamiento de Madrid, 'Madrid Actualiza Su Simulador de Movilidad e Incluye Todos Los Sistemas de Transporte Para Reducir Las Afecciones Al Tráfico' (*Diario de Madrid*, 4 March 2021) <https://diario.madrid.es/blog/notas-de-prensa/madrid-actualiza-su-simulador-de-movilidad-e-incluye-todos-los-sistemas-de-transporte-para-reducir-las-afecciones-al-trafico/>.

Baliga S and Maskin E, 'Chapter 7 - Mechanism Design for the Environment', *Handbook of Environmental Economics*, vol 1 (Elsevier 2003).

Ban Y (ed.), *Multitemporal Remote Sensing* (Springer International Publishing 2016).

Barricelli BR and others, 'Human Digital Twin for Fitness Management' (2020) 8 IEEE Access.

Barricelli BR, Casiraghi E and Fogli D, 'A Survey on Digital Twin: Definitions, Characteristics, Applications, and Design Implications' (2019) 7 IEEE Access.

Batty M, 'Digital Twins' (2018) 45 Environment and Planning B: Urban Analytics and City Science.

Beetz J and others, 'Building Information Modelling (BIM)' in Ludger Hovestadt, Urs Hirschberg and Oliver Fritz (eds), *Atlas of Digital Architecture: Terminology, Concepts, Methods, Tools, Examples, Phenomena* (Birkhäuser 2020).

Bell V, 'Britain's "Twitter Troops" Have Ways of Making You Think ...' *The Guardian* (London, 16 August 2015).

Björnsson B and others, 'Digital Twins to Personalize Medicine' (2020) 12(4) Genome Medicine.

Blondel V and Tsitsiklis JN, 'NP-Hardness of Some Linear Control Design Problems' (1997) 35 SIAM Journal on Control and Optimization.

Boddington G, 'The Internet of Bodies—Alive, Connected and Collective: The Virtual Physical Future of Our Bodies and Our Senses' (2021) 1 AI and Society.

Bolton A, Coates M and El Hajj P, 'How Finance and Digital Twins Can Shape a Better Future for the Planet' (2022) Centre for Digital Built Britain <https://www.cdbb.cam.ac.uk/files/finance_whitepaper.pdf>.

Brockmann D and Helbing D, 'The Hidden Geometry of Complex, Network-Driven Contagion Phenomena' (2013) 342 Science.

Browne G, 'The Quest to Make a Digital Replica of Your Brain' [2022] *Wired*.

Bruynseels K, Santoni de Sio F and van den Hoven J, 'Digital Twins in Health Care: Ethical Implications of an Emerging Engineering Paradigm' (2018) 9 Frontiers in Genetics.

Bundesinstitut für Bau- Stadt- und Raumforschung (BBSR) im Bundesamt für Bauwesen und Raumordnung (BBR) und Bundesministerium für Umwelt, Naturschutz B und R (BMUB), 'Smart City Charta' (2018).

Caldarelli, G, Arcaute, E and Barthelemy, M et al., 'The Role of Complexity for Digital Twins of Cities' (2023) Nature Computational Science <https://doi.org/10.1038/s43588-023-00431-4>.

Cardoso Llach D, *Builders of the Vision* (Routledge 2015).

Cardoso Llach D and Argota Sánchez-Vaquerizo J, 'An Ecology of Conflicts', *Communications in Computer and Information Science*, vol. 1028 (Springer 2019).

Celik A, Salama KN and Eltawil AM, 'The Internet of Bodies: A Systematic Survey on Propagation Characterization and Channel Modeling' (2022) 9 IEEE Internet of Things Journal.

Cerri T and Chaturvedi A, 'Sentient World Simulation (SWS): A Continuously Running Model of the Real World: A Concept Paper for Comment. Version 2.0' (2006) <https://web.archive.org/web/20220205091124/https://www.kran nert.purdue.edu/academics/mis/workshop/ac2_100606.pdf>.

Chakraborti A and others, 'Statistical Mechanics of Competitive Resource Allocation Using Agent-Based Models' (2015) 552 Physics Reports.

Chakshu NK, Sazonov I and Nithiarasu P, 'Towards Enabling a Cardiovascular Digital Twin for Human Systemic Circulation Using Inverse Analysis' (2021) 20 Biomechanics and Modeling in Mechanobiology.

Challet D, Marsili M and Zhang Y-C, *Minority Games: Interacting Agents in Financial Markets* (Oxford University Press 2004).

Chul Min Lee and Narayanan SS, 'Toward Detecting Emotions in Spoken Dialogs' (2005) 13 IEEE Transactions on Speech and Audio Processing.

Consortium LP, 'Lead Project' <https://www.leadproject.eu/>.

Conte R and others, 'Manifesto of Computational Social Science' (2012) 214(11) The European Physical Journal Special Topics.

Coons SA, 'An Outline of the Requirements for a Computer-Aided Design System', *Proceedings of the May 21–23, 1963, Spring Joint Computer Conference, AFIPS '63 (Spring)* (ACM Press 1963).

Cupp J, 'USJFCOM Teams with Purdue University to Add the Human Factor to War Game Simulations' (*News from USJFCOM*, 2004) <https://web.archive.org/web/20070206184414/http://www.mgmt.purdue.edu/centers/perc/html/Med ia/USJFCOM.htm>.

Dapp MM, Helbing D and Klauser S (eds), *Finance 4.0 – Towards a Socio-Ecological Finance System* (Springer International Publishing 2021).

Davies N and others, 'Simulating Social–Ecological Systems: The Island Digital Ecosystem Avatars (IDEA) Consortium' (2016) 5(1) GigaScience.

DeepLife, 'How Digital Twins of Human Cells Are Accelerating Drug Discovery' [2022] Nature Biopharma Dealmakers (advertisement feature).

Dörner D, *The Logic of Failure: Recognizing and Avoiding Error in Complex Situations* (Basic Books 1997).

Dressler F and Fischer S, 'Connecting In-Body Nano Communication with Body Area Networks: Challenges and Opportunities of the Internet of Nano Things' (2015) 6 Nano Communication Networks.

Dubina IN, Carayannis EG and Campbell DFJ, 'Creativity Economy and a Crisis of the Economy? Coevolution of Knowledge, Innovation, and Creativity, and of the Knowledge Economy and Knowledge Society' (2012) 3(1) Journal of the Knowledge Economy.

Durán JI and Fernández-Dols J-M, 'Do Emotions Result in Their Predicted Facial Expressions? A Meta-Analysis of Studies on the Co-Occurrence of Expression and Emotion' (2021) 21 Emotion.

Edelman G, 'The Father of Web3 Wants You to Trust Less' [2021] *Wired*.

EUBIM Taskgroup, *Handbook for the Introduction of Building Information Modelling by the European Public Sector Strategic Action for Construction Sector Performance: Driving Value, Innovation and Growth* (EUBIM Taskgroup 2017).

European Commission, 'Destination Eart: Shaping Europe's Digital Future' (2021) <https://digital-strategy.ec.europa.eu/en/policies/destination-earth>.

Fagella D, 'Sentient World Simulation and NSA Surveillance – Exploiting Privacy to Predict the Future?' (*Emerj. Artifical Intelligence Research*, 2017) <https://emerj.com/ai-future-outlook/nsa-surveillance-and-sentient-world-simulation-exploiting-privacy-to-predict-the-future/>.

Filippo M Di and others, 'Single-Cell Digital Twins for Cancer Preclinical Investigation', *Methods in Molecular Biology*, vol. 2088 (Methods Mol Biol 2020).

Folke C and others, 'Regime Shifts, Resilience, and Biodiversity in Ecosystem Management' (2004) 35 Annual Review of Ecology, Evolution, and Systematics.

Fraccascia L, Giannoccaro I and Albino V, 'Resilience of Complex Systems: State of the Art and Directions for Future Research' [2018] Complexity.

Fuller A and others, 'Digital Twin: Enabling Technologies, Challenges and Open Research' (2020) 8 IEEE Access.

Gao H, Koch C and Wu Y, 'Building Information Modelling Based Building Energy Modelling: A Review' (Elsevier, 15 March 2019) 320.

Gardner M, 'The Internet of Bodies Will Change Everything, for Better or Worse' (*RAND Corporation*, 2020) <https://www.rand.org/blog/articles/2020/10/the-internet-of-bodies-will-change-everything-for-better-or-worse.html>.

Geraci RM, *Apocalyptic AI: Visions of Heaven in Robotics, Artificial Intelligence, and Virtual Reality* (Oxford University Press 2010).

Gershenson C, 'Guiding the Self-Organization of Cyber-Physical Systems' (2020) 7 Frontiers in Robotics and AI.

Gershenson C and Helbing D, 'When Slower Is Faster' (2015) 21 Complexity.

Gigerenzer G, Hertwig R and Pachur T, *Heuristics: The Foundations of Adaptive Behavior* (Oxford University Press 2011).

Gödel K, *On Formally Undecidable Propositions of Principia Mathematica and Related Systems* (Dover Publications, Inc 1992).

Grieves M, 'Digital Twin : Manufacturing Excellence through Virtual Factory Replication' [2014] 1 White Paper.

Hagner M and others, 'Will Democracy Survive Big Data and Artificial Intelligence?' [2017] Scientific American.

Haklay M, 'Citizen Science and Volunteered Geographic Information: Overview and Typology of Participation', *Crowdsourcing Geographic Knowledge* (Springer 2013).

Han B-C, *Psychopolitics: Neoliberalism and New Technologies of Power* (Verso Books 2017).

Harper GN, 'BOP: An Approach to Building Optimization', *Proceedings of the 1968 23rd ACM National Conference* (ACM Press 1968).

Hawkins RXD, Goodman ND and Goldstone RL, 'The Emergence of Social Norms and Conventions' (2019) 23 Trends in Cognitive Sciences.

Helbing D, 'Traffic and Related Self-Driven Many-Particle Systems' (2001) 73 Reviews of Modern Physics.

Helbing D (ed.), *Social Self-Organization* (Springer 2012).

Helbing D, 'Systemic Risks in Society and Economics' in Dirk Helbing (ed.), *Social Self-Organization* (Springer 2012).

Helbing D, 'Globally Networked Risks and How to Respond' (2013) 497 Nature.

Helbing D, 'Economics 2.0: The Natural Step towards a Self-Regulating, Participatory Market Society' (2013) 10 Evolutionary and Institutional Economics Review.

Helbing D, 'Society Is Not A Machine, Optimization Not The Right Paradigm!' (*Edge*, 2016) <https://www.edge.org/response-detail/26795>.

Helbing D, 'Social Mirror: More Success through Awareness and Coordination', *Towards Digital Enlightenment* (Springer International Publishing 2019).

Helbing D, '12 Statements on Digital Twins i.e. detailed digital models of the world (or parts of it)' (2021) Talk for GESDA 2021 (Geneva Science and Diplomacy Anticipator) <https://www.researchgate.net/publication/355202057_12_STAT EMENTS_ON_DIGITAL_TWINS_ie_detailed_digital_models_of_the_world _or_parts_of_it>.

Helbing D, 'A Planetary-Scale Threat', *Next Civilization* (Springer International Publishing 2021).

Helbing D, 'Digitally Assisted Self-Organization', *Next Civilization* (Springer International Publishing 2021).

Helbing D, 'Innovative Governance Needed: Some Thoughts on How to Master Our Future Using Big Data (Also "Avatars", "Digital Twins") with a New Kind of Multi-Lateralism' (*FuturICT Blog*, 2021) <http://futurict.blogspot. com/2021/09/innovative-governance-approaches-needed.html>.

Helbing D, *Next Civilization* (Springer International Publishing 2021).

Helbing D, 'Partial List of Possible Dual Uses of Big Data Cyber-Infrastructures' (*FuturICT Blog*, 2021) <http://futurict.blogspot.com/2021/07/>.

Helbing D, 'The Planetary Health Agenda – A Global Political Problem' (*FuturICT Blog*, 2021) <http://futurict.blogspot.com/2021/09/the-planetary-health-agenda- global.html>.

Helbing D, 'Digital Threats to Humans and Society' (2022) ResearchGate <https://www.researchgate.net/publication/361600988_Digital_Threats_to_Hu mans_and_Society>.

Helbing D, 'Who Is Messing with Your Digital Twin? Body, Mind, and Soul for Sale?' (*TEDxIHEID*, 2022) <https://www.tedxiheid.com/dirk-helbing>.

Helbing D and others, 'Theoretical vs. Empirical Classification and Prediction of Congested Traffic States' (2009) 69 European Physical Journal B.

Helbing D and others, 'Triage 4.0: On Death Algorithms and Technological Selection. Is Today's Data-Driven Medical System Still Compatible with the Constitution?' (2021) 10 Journal of European CME https://www.tandfonline.com/doi/full/10.1080/21614083.2021.1989243.

Helbing D and others, 'Ethics of Smart Cities: Towards Value-Sensitive Design and Co-Evolving City Life' (2021) 13 Sustainability.

Helbing D and Johansson AF, 'On the Controversy around Daganzo's Requiem for and Aw-Rascle's Resurrection of Second-Order Traffic Flow Models' (2009) 69 European Physical Journal B.

Helbing D and Lämmer S, 'Supply and Production Networks: From the Bullwhip Effect to Business Cycles', *Networks of Interacting Machines: Production Organization in Complex Industrial Systems and Biological Cells* (World Scientific Publishing Co 2005).

Helbing D and Mukerji P, 'Crowd Disasters as Systemic Failures: Analysis of the Love Parade Disaster' (2012) 1 EPJ Data Science.

Helbing D and Perc M, 'Nanowars Can Cause Epidemic Resurgence and Fail to Promote Cooperation' (2022) arXiv Physics and Society <https://arxiv.org/abs/2201.04747>.

Helbing D and Pournaras E, 'Society: Build Digital Democracy' (2015) 527 Nature.

Helbing D and Seele P, 'We Need Peace Rooms, Not War Rooms' (*The Globalist*, 2017) <https://www.theglobalist.com/technology-big-data-artificial-intelligence-future-peace-rooms/>.

Helbing D and Seele P, 'Turn War Rooms into Peace Rooms' (2017) 549 Nature.

Helbing D, Seele P and Beschorner T, 'Humans Degraded to Data Points (English Translation of "Der Mensch Wird Zum Datenpunkt" Published on Schweizer Monat of May 2022)' (2022) <https://www.researchgate.net/publication/360620579_Humans_Degraded_to_Data_Points>.

Hidalgo CA, 'A Bold Idea to Replace Politicians' (*TED*, 2018) <https://www.ted.com/talks/cesar_hidalgo_a_bold_idea_to_replace_politicians>.

Hidalgo CA and others, 'The Product Space Conditions the Development of Nations' (2007) 317 Science.

Hill J, *Actions of Architecture* (Routledge 2003).

Hourdos J and Michalopoulos P, 'Twin Cities Metro-Wide Traffic Micro-Simulation Feasibility Investigation' (2008) Report # 5 in the series Access to Destinations Study, Report # 2008-15 <https://www.lrrb.org/pdf/200815.pdf>.

Hsiao YT and others, 'VTaiwan: An Empirical Study of Open Consultation Process in Taiwan' (2018) <osf.io/preprints/socarxiv/xyhft>.

Hudson-Smith A and others, 'Urban IoT: Advances, Challenges, and Opportunities for Mass Data Collection, Analysis, and Visualization' in W Shi and others (eds), *Urban Informatics: The Urban Book Series* (Springer 2021).

Hurwitz J, Kaufman M and Bowles A, *Cognitive Computing and Big Data Analytics* (John Wiley & Sons, Inc 2015).

Ilyas M and Mahgoub I, *Smart Dust* (CRC Press 2018).

IMEC, 'Imec and TNO Launch Digital Twin of the City of Antwerp' (2018) <https://www.imec-int.com/en/articles/imec-and-tno-launch-digital-twin-of-the-city-of-antwerp>.

Isaak J and Hanna MJ, 'User Data Privacy: Facebook, Cambridge Analytica, and Privacy Protection' (2018) 51 Computer.

Jaegar C and others, 'GSS: Towards a Research Program for Global Systems Science', *Second Open Global Systems Science Conference* (2013).

Jarmakiewicz J, Parobczak K and Maslanka K, 'On the Internet of Nano Things in Healthcare Network', *2016 International Conference on Military Communications and Information Systems (ICMCIS)* (IEEE 2016).

Jones D and others, 'Characterising the Digital Twin: A Systematic Literature Review' (2020) 29 CIRP Journal of Manufacturing Science and Technology.

Kaur MJ, Mishra VP and Maheshwari P, 'The Convergence of Digital Twin, IoT, and Machine Learning: Transforming Data into Action', *Digital Twin Technologies and Smart Cities, Internet of Things* (Springer 2020).

Kesting A and others, 'Adaptive Cruise Control Design for Active Congestion Avoidance' (2008) 16 Transportation Research Part C: Emerging Technologies 668.

Kim M, 'The Good and the Bad of Escaping to Virtual Reality' [2015] *The Atlantic*.

Kitchin R, *The Data Revolution* (SAGE Publications Ltd 2014).

Kosonen I, Koskinen K and Kostiainen J, 'Real-Time Traffic Data Applications in the Mobility Lab of Helsinki – Case Smart Junction', *ITS World Congress* (2021).

Kravtsov YA (ed), *Limits of Predictability* (Springer 1993).

Krishnan A, *Military Neuroscience and the Coming Age of Neurowarfare* (Routledge 2017).

Kritzinger W and others, 'Digital Twin in Manufacturing: A Categorical Literature Review and Classification', *IFAC-PapersOnLine* (Elsevier 2018).

Kurzweil R and Grossman T, *Fantastic Voyage: Live Long Enough to Live Forever* (Rodale 2005).

Laaki H, Miche Y and Tammi K, 'Prototyping a Digital Twin for Real Time Remote Control Over Mobile Networks: Application of Remote Surgery' (2019) 7 IEEE Access.

Lämmer S and Helbing D, 'Self-Control of Traffic Lights and Vehicle Flows in Urban Road Networks' [2008] Journal of Statistical Mechanics: Theory and Experiment.

Langevin S and others, 'Useable Machine Learning for Sentinel-2 Multispectral Satellite Imagery', *Image and Signal Processing for Remote Sensing XXVII; 118620F (2021)* (SPIE 2021).

Lee M and others, *The Internet of Bodies: Opportunities, Risks, and Governance* (RAND Corporation 2020).

Lehrach H and Ionescu A, 'Discussion: The Future of Health Care: Deep Data, Smart Sensors, Virtual Patients and the Internet-of-Humans' (*European Commission, Futurium, Digital4Science*, 2016) <https://ec.europa.eu/futurium/en/content/future-health-care-deep-data-smart-sensors-virtual-patients-and-internet-humans-0.html>.

Lehrach H and Ionescu A, 'The Future of Health Care: Deep Data, Smart Sensors, Virtual Patients and the Internet-of-Humans' (2016) 1 <https://ec.europa.eu/futurium/en/system/files/ged/futurehealth_white_paper.pdf>.

Lin H and others, 'Detecting Stress Based on Social Interactions in Social Networks' (2017) 29 IEEE Transactions on Knowledge and Data Engineering.

Lin N, Cook K and Burt RS (eds), *Social Capital: Theory and Research* (Aldine de Gruyter 2001).

Liu M and others, 'Review of Digital Twin about Concepts, Technologies, and Industrial Applications' (2021) 58 Journal of Manufacturing Systems.

Liu X, 'Tracking How Our Bodies Work Could Change Our Lives' (*World Economic Forum*, 2020) <https://www.weforum.org/agenda/2020/06/internet-of-bodies-covid19-recovery-governance-health-data/>.

Liu X, Merritt J and Tiscareno KK, 'Shaping the Future of the Internet of Bodies: New Challenges of Technology Governance' (2020) World Economic Forum <http://www3.weforum.org/docs/WEF_IoB_briefing_paper_2020.pdf>.

Liu Y and others, 'A Novel Cloud-Based Framework for the Elderly Healthcare Services Using Digital Twin' (2019) 7 IEEE Access.

Liu YY and Barabási AL, 'Control Principles of Complex Systems' (2016) 88 Reviews of Modern Physics.

Lustick IS, 'Agent-Based Modelling of Collective Identity: Testing Constructivist Theory' (2000) 3 Journal of Artificial Societies and Social Simulation (JASSS).

Mahajan S and others, 'Participatory Resilience: Surviving, Recovering and Improving Together' (2022) 83 Sustainable Cities and Society.

Malevergne Y and Sornette D, *Extreme Financial Risks*, 1st edn (Springer-Verlag 2006).

Mantegna RN and Stanley HE, *An Introduction to Econophysics: Correlations and Complexity in Finance* (Cambridge University Press 2000).

Martinez-Velazquez R, Gamez R and El Saddik A, 'Cardio Twin: A Digital Twin of the Human Heart Running on the Edge', *2019 IEEE International Symposium on Medical Measurements and Applications (MeMeA)* (IEEE 2019).

Mäs M and Helbing D, 'Random Deviations Improve Micro–Macro Predictions: An Empirical Test' (2017) 49 Sociological Methods & Research.

Mathias J and others, 'Grounding Social Foundations for Integrated Assessment Models of Climate Change' (2020) 8 Earth's Future.

Maxwell A, 'A Living, Breathing Internet of Things All Around You' (*Now. Powered by Northrop Grumman*, 2020) <https://now.northropgrumman.com/a-living-breathing-internet-of-bodies-all-around-you/>.

Mitchell WJ, *Computer-Aided Architectural Design* (Petrocelli/Charter 1977).

Moreno JD, *Mind Wars: Brain Science and the Military in the 21st Century* (Bellevue Literary Press 2012).

Murat Kuscu and Bige Deniz Unluturk, 'Internet of Bio-Nano Things: A Review of Applications, Enabling Technologies and Key Challenges' (2021) 2 ITU Journal on Future and Evolving Technologies.

Nano Magazine, 'Nanosensor and Digital Twin Technologies Come Together at COP26 to Help Deliver a Circular Economy as Part of the Race to Zero' (*Nano Magazine*, 2021) <https://nano-magazine.com/news/2021/11/1/nanosensor-and-digital-twin-technologies-come-together-at-cop26-to-help-deliver-a-circular-econ omy-as-part-of-the-race-to-zero>.

'Nanotechnology, Sustainability and Society: First International Conference on Technologies for Smart Green Connected Society 2021 – ICTSGS-1' (*Frontiers in Nanotechnology*) <https://www.frontiersin.org/research-topics/34645/nano technology-sustainability-and-society-first-international-conference-on-techno logies-for-smart-g#overview>.

Nativi S, Craglia M and Sciullo L, 'MyDigitalTwin: Exploratory Research Report' (Publications Office of the European Union 2022).

Nativi S, Mazzetti P and Craglia M, 'Digital Ecosystems for Developing Digital Twins of the Earth: The Destination Earth Case' (2021) 13 Remote Sensing.

Negri E, Fumagalli L and Macchi M, 'A Review of the Roles of Digital Twin in CPS-Based Production Systems' (2017) 11 Procedia Manufacturing.

Nixdorff K and others, 'Dual-Use Nano-Neurotechnology' (2018) 37 Politics and the Life Sciences.

Page SE, *The Difference: How the Power of Diversity Creates Better Groups, Firms, Schools, and Societies* (Princeton University Press 2007).

Patel SR and Lieber CM, 'Precision Electronic Medicine in the Brain' (2019) 37 Nature Biotechnology.

Peltz JJ, 'The Algorithm of You: Your Profile of Preference or an Agent for Evil?' (Naval War College 2017).

Pobuda P, 'The Digital Twin of the Economy' [2020] Real-World Economics Review.

'Pol.Is' (*Participedia*) <https://participedia.net/method/4682>.

Popa EO and others, 'The Use of Digital Twins in Healthcare: Socio-Ethical Benefits and Socio-Ethical Risks' (2021) 17 Life Sciences, Society and Policy.

Popescu VF, 'From Human Body Digitization to Internet of Bodies toward a New Dimension of Military Operations' (2019) 24 Land Forces Academy Review.

Preut A, Kopka JP and Clausen U, 'Digital Twins for the Circular Economy' (2021) 13 Sustainability (Switzerland).

PTV Group, 'PTV Group Successfully Integrates the UK's First Real-Time Transport Model with City of York Council (UK)' (*PTV Newsroom*, 2021) <https://company.ptvgroup.com/en/resources/newsroom/ptv-group-succes sfully-integrates-the-uks-first-real-time-transport-model-with-city-of-york-council-uk>.

Puccinelli D and Haenggi M, 'Wireless Sensor Networks: Applications and Challenges of Ubiquitous Sensing' (September 2005) 19.

Pykett J, 'Neurocapitalism and the New Neuros: Using Neuroeconomics, Behavioural Economics and Picoeconomics for Public Policy' (2013) 13 Journal of Economic Geography.

Reinbold P, 'Facing Discrimination: Choosing Equality over Technology' [2021] SSRN Electronic Journal 1.

Ricci A, Croatti A and Montagna S, 'Pervasive and Connected Digital Twins – A Vision for Digital Health' [2021] IEEE Internet Computing 1.

Rivera LF and others, 'Towards Continuous Monitoring in Personalized Healthcare through Digital Twins', *CASCON 2019 Proceedings: Conference of the Centre for Advanced Studies on Collaborative Research – Proceedings of the 29th Annual International Conference on Computer Science and Software Engineering* (2020).

Rodriguez AC and Wegner JD, 'Counting the Uncountable: Deep Semantic Density Estimation from Space', *Lecture Notes in Computer Science (including subseries Lecture Notes in Artificial Intelligence and Lecture Notes in Bioinformatics)* (Springer Verlag 2019).

Roughgarden T, *Selfish Routing and the Price of Anarchy* (MIT Press 2005).

Russell S, Dewey D and Tegmark M, 'Research Priorities for Robust and Beneficial Artificial Intelligence' (2015) 36 AI Magazine.

Schrotter G and Hürzeler C, 'The Digital Twin of the City of Zurich for Urban Planning' (2020) 88 PFG – Journal of Photogrammetry, Remote Sensing and Geoinformation Science 99.

Shengli W, 'Is Human Digital Twin Possible?' (2021) 1 Computer Methods and Programs in Biomedicine Update.

Simon HA, 'Rational Choice and the Structure of the Environment' (1956) 63 Psychological Review.

Smaldino P and others, 'An Agent-Based Model of Social Identity Dynamics' (2012) 15 Journal of Artificial Societies and Social Simulation (JASSS).

SmartCitiesWorld, 'Digital Twin Created for New Indian Smart City – Smart Cities World' (*SmartCitiesWorld*, 2018) <https://www.smartcitiesworld.net/news/news/digital-twin-created-for-new-indian-smart-city-3674>.

Smith A, *The Theory of Moral Sentiments* (printed for Andrew Millar, in the Strand; and Alexander Kincaid and J Bell, in Edinburgh 1759).

Stanley HE, *Introduction to Phase Transitions and Critical Phenomena* ([Reprint], Oxford University Press 1987).

Steels L (ed.), *Experiments in Cultural Language Evolution* (John Benjamins Publishing Company 2012).

Stiglitz JE, Sen A and Fitoussi J-P, 'Report by the Commission on the Measurement of Economic Performance and Social Progress' (2009) <https://ec.europa.eu/eurostat/documents/8131721/8131772/Stiglitz-Sen-Fitoussi-Commission-report.pdf>.

Strife S, 'Sentient World: War Games on the Grandest Scale' (*The Register*, 2007) <https://www.theregister.com/2007/06/23/sentient_worlds/>.

Sutherland IE, 'Sketchpad a Man-Machine Graphical Communication System' (1964) 2 Simulation R.

Tao F and others, 'Digital Twin in Industry: State-of-the-Art' (2019) 15 IEEE Transactions on Industrial Informatics.

Thaler RH, *Misbehaving: The Making of Behavioral Economics* (W. W. Norton & Company 2015).

Thumer S, Hanel RA and Klimek P, *Introduction to the Theory of Complex Systems* (Oxford University Press 2019).

Tucker P, 'Can the Military Make a Prediction Machine?' (*Defense One*, 2015) <https://www.defenseone.com/technology/2015/04/can-military-make-prediction-machine/109561/>.

Turchin P and Taylor AD, 'Complex Dynamics in Ecological Time Series' (1992) 73 Ecology.

Uhlemann THJ and others, 'The Digital Twin: Demonstrating the Potential of Real Time Data Acquisition in Production Systems' (2017) 9 Procedia Manufacturing.

UK Ministry of Defence and Bundeswehr. Office for Defence Planning, 'Human Augmentation: The Dawn of a New Paradigm – A Strategic Implications Project' (2021).

Vasiliauskaite V, Antulov-Fantulin N and Helbing D, 'Supplementary Information (SI) of the Manuscript "On Some Fundamental Challenges in Monitoring Epidemics"' (202AD) 380 Philosophical Transactions of the Royal Society A: Mathematical, Physical and Engineering Sciences.

Virgilio D, 'What Comparisons between Second Life and the Metaverse Miss' [2022] *Slate*.

Voshmgir S, *Token Economy: How the Web3 Reinvents the Internet* (2nd edn, Token Kitchen 2020).

Watts DJ, 'Computational Social Science: Exciting Progress and Future Directions' (2013) 43 The Bridge.

Whitmee S and others, 'Safeguarding Human Health in the Anthropocene Epoch: Report of the Rockefeller Foundation–Lancet Commission on Planetary Health' (Lancet Publishing Group, 14 November 2015) 1973.

Wirdatmadja SA and others, 'Wireless Optogenetic Neural Dust for Deep Brain Stimulation', *2016 IEEE 18th International Conference on e-Health Networking, Applications and Services (Healthcom)* (IEEE 2016).

Woolley AW and others, 'Evidence for a Collective Intelligence Factor in the Performance of Human Groups' (2010) 330 Science.

Zafar S and others, 'A Systematic Review of Bio-Cyber Interface Technologies and Security Issues for Internet of Bio-Nano Things' (2021) 9 IEEE Access.

Zeeman EC, 'Catastrophe Theory' (1976) 234 Scientific American.

4. Governing Digital Twin technology for smart and sustainable tourism: a case study in applying a documentation framework for architecture decisions

Eko Rahmadian, Daniel Feitosa and Andrej Zwitter

1. INTRODUCTION

Applications leveraging the potential of technologies such as Big Data, Artificial Intelligence (AI), Machine Learning (ML) and the Internet of Things (IoT) have recently emerged to support decision-making processes.[1] Operations have become more digital, including the applicability of Big Data analysis where the high volume of data could be transmitted to the 'cloud' in real-time.[2] The tourism industry is no exception to this development. In the last few years, technological developments related to Big Data are further promoting the transformation and rapid innovation within the tourism sector.[3] These developments also support the rapid processing, visualisation and analysis of Big Data, as well as facilitate decision-making and strategy formulation in daily operations. In general, Big Data requires technological advances in storage and computation methods, data capture applications and visualisation.[4] In the tourism sector, Big Data analytics have been used in smart tourism applications

---

[1]   Itxaro Errandonea, Sergio Beltrán and Saioa Arrizabalaga, 'Digital Twin for Maintenance: A Literature Review' (2020) 123 Computers in Industry.

[2]   Maninder Jeet Kaur, Ved P Mishra and Piyush Maheshwari, 'The Convergence of Digital Twin, IoT, and Machine Learning: Transforming Data into Action', *Digital Twin Technologies and Smart Cities* (Springer 2020).

[3]   Jacques Bulchand-Gidumal, 'M. Sigala, R. Rahimi, M. Thelwall (Eds.): "Big Data and Innovation in Tourism, Travel, and Hospitality. Managerial Approaches, Techniques, and Applications"' (2021) 13 Zeitschrift für Tourismuswissenschaft.

[4]   Amir Gandomi and Murtaza Haider, 'Beyond the Hype: Big Data Concepts, Methods, and Analytics' (2015) 35 International Journal of Information Management.

such as the smart museum,[5] smart beach[6] and Augmented Reality (AR) tours for agritourism.[7] Big Data analytics also have been implemented for various purposes, such as ecotourism, destination and attraction imaging, nature preservation, or analysis of tourist behaviour.[8] In light of this, Big Data in combination with the aforementioned technologies can help the tourism sector to operate more efficiently and sustainably.[9]

An emerging concept that requires particular attention in this field is the Digital Twin (DT).[10] A DT is usually defined as an integrated multi-physics, multi-scale, probabilistic simulation of a system (e.g., a machine), which uses the best available physical models, sensor updates, data history and so forth to reflect the life of its twin.[11] A more recent definition describes DT as a virtual image that defines the comprehensive physical and functional characteristics of the entire life cycle of a product, and which can transmit and receive information from this product.[12] One of the primary functions of a DT is to predict the response of a system before it takes place in reality.[13] This type of prediction is created by

---

5   Giuseppe Del Fiore and others, 'A Location-Aware Architecture for an IoT-Based Smart Museum' (2016) 12 International Journal of Electronic Government Research.

6   Roberto Girau and others, 'Be Right Beach: A Social IoT System for Sustainable Tourism Based on Beach Overcrowding Avoidance', *2018 IEEE International Conference on Internet of Things (iThings) and IEEE Green Computing and Communications (GreenCom) and IEEE Cyber, Physical and Social Computing (CPSCom) and IEEE Smart Data (SmartData)* (IEEE 2018) <https://ieeexplore.ieee.org/document/8726793/> accessed 11 July 2022.

7   Juan Garzón and others, 'ARtour: Augmented Reality-Based Game to Promote Agritourism', *Augmented Reality, Virtual Reality, and Computer Graphics* (Springer Nature Switzerland AG) <https://doi.org/10.1007/978-3-319-95270-3>.

8   E Rahmadian, D Feitosa and A Zwitter, 'A Systematic Literature Review on the Use of Big Data for Sustainable Tourism' (2022) 25 Current Issues in Tourism.

9   Jingjing Li and others, 'Big Data in Tourism Research: A Literature Review' (2018) 68 Tourism Management.

10   Fei Tao and others, 'Digital Twin-Driven Product Design Framework' (2019) 57 International Journal of Production Research.

11   Edward Glaessgen and David Stargel, 'The Digital Twin Paradigm for Future NASA and U.S. Air Force Vehicles', *53rd AIAA/ASME/ASCE/AHS/ASC Structures, Structural Dynamics and Materials Conference* (American Institute of Aeronautics and Astronautics 2012).

12   Rajeeth Tharma, Roland Winter and Martin Eigner, 'An Approach for the Implementation of the Digital Twin in the Automotive Wiring Harness Field' (2018) <https://www.designsociety.org/publication/40688/AN+APPROACH+FOR+THE+IMPLEMENTATION+OF+THE+DIGITAL+TWIN+IN+THE+AUTOMOTIVE+WIRING+HARNESS+FIELD> accessed 11 July 2022.

13   Benjamin Schleich and others, 'Shaping the Digital Twin for Design and Production Engineering' (2017) 66 CIRP Annals.

comparing the analyses of the presents, and the system's current reactions with behaviour predictions as DT includes an interface between the digital model and actual object to send and receive data in real-time.[14] The possibility of creating/obtaining a DT sufficiently complete to make accurate predictions depends on the integrity of the data collection, its exchange capabilities, and its simulations.[15] Considering that DTs have been implemented in many sectors and industries, including smart cities,[16] and given the rapid growth of new ICT and IoT applications in the tourism industry, we suggest that the implementation of DT can be potential in smart and sustainable tourism. By deploying cyber-physical systems and the IoT, data become both a critical asset and a competitive advantage for multiple purposes, including DT applications.[17]

However, for the data to become a competitive advantage, it must be managed and governed like any other strategic asset. This digital realm requires regulation and governance to establish more legal and balanced power among the stakeholders.[18] In addition, software engineers must deal with the complexities of laws and regulations, which need to be interpreted according to software requirements, especially those related to privacy and security.[19] Therefore, technological aspects are not the only important aspect at hand, as governance is also crucial to ensure that DT can be a potential tool for solving sustainable tourism issues based on Big Data, AI and the IoT.

This chapter aims to draw up a theoretical inspiration for ways to implement decentralisation governance power in the digital domain

---

[14]   L Wan, T Nochta and JM Schooling, 'Developing a City-Level Digital Twin: Propositions and a Case Study', *International Conference on Smart Infrastructure and Construction 2019 (ICSIC)* (ICE Publishing 2019) <https://www.icevirtual library.com/doi/10.1680/icsic.64669.187> accessed 11 July 2022.

[15]   Chao Fan and others, 'Disaster City Digital Twin: A Vision for Integrating Artificial and Human Intelligence for Disaster Management' (2021) 56 International Journal of Information Management.

[16]   Maryam Farsi and others (eds), *Digital Twin Technologies and Smart Cities* (Springer International Publishing 2020) <http://link.springer.com/10.1007/978-3-030-18732-3> accessed 11 July 2022.

[17]   Juan Yebenes Serrano and Marta Zorrilla, 'A Data Governance Framework for Industry 4.0' (2021) 19 IEEE Latin America Transactions.

[18]   Luis Felipe Luna-Reyes, 'Opportunities and Challenges for Digital Governance in a World of Digital Participation' (2017) 22 Information Polity.

[19]   Amin Rabinia and Sepideh Ghanavati, 'FOL-Based Approach for Improving Legal–GRL Modeling Framework: A Case for Requirements Engineering of Legal Regulations of Social Media', *2017 IEEE 25th International Requirements Engineering Conference Workshops (REW)* (IEEE 2017) <http://ieeexplore.ieee.org/document/8054856/> accessed 11 July 2022.

through a case study on DT geared towards sustainable tourism. We then formulate two research questions. First, what is the potential use of DT for smart and sustainable tourism? And second, how should a DT be governed to ensure its operations on smart and sustainable tourism?

To address the first research question, the main contribution of this chapter is to introduce a conceptual framework and architectural synthesis method of DT for smart and sustainable tourism. And to address the second research question, we introduce several documentation templates of a documentation framework on architecture decisions that act as navigational tools and encompass non-technical regulation within the software system. This documentation framework also advocates the importance of a governance system, bridges the gap between technical and non-technical stakeholders, and brings more transparency to the decision-making process at various stages.

To demonstrate the applicability of our work, we apply both the conceptual framework and the documentation framework to a theoretical case study and three real-world-based scenarios to propose a design of DT for smart and sustainable tourism in Indonesia. Since 2016, Indonesia has been using Big Data analysis for tourism statistics, in which mobile positioning data (MPD) has been utilised as the source. This statistical process has involved multiple stakeholders in the decision-making process. By leveraging the use of MPD to DT applications and applying our framework to govern the system, we aim to provide better insights and procedures for a data-driven policy-making process regarding sustainable tourism in Indonesia.

This chapter is structured as follows: in the subsequent section, we present the conceptual framework of the potential use of Digital Twin for smart and sustainable tourism. Section 3 proceeds to introduce relevant notions of governance and technology. Section 4 analyses the documentation framework to govern DT for smart and sustainable tourism, and illustrates three scenarios for implementation. Finally, we present conclusions and recommendations for future work.

2.   DIGITAL TWINS FOR SMART AND SUSTAINABLE TOURISM

2.1   The Evolution towards Digital Twins

The collection of tourism statistics is essential to measure the volume, scale, impact and value of tourist activities at different geographic scales. This ranges from the global to the national level and includes the smallest regions and destinations.[20] Most tourism statistics are traditionally collected using official surveys completed by a sample of households or individuals, such as on the number of tourists, expenditures and travel-related characteristics. According to the International Tourism Statistics Recommendation 2008 and Eurostat's *Methodological Manual for Tourism Statistics*, surveys are perceived as the primary data source for domestic and outbound tourism statistics.[21]

However, in recent decades, the essence of tourism and travel behaviours have changed due to rapid changes in ICT. As a result, new ICT-based data sources ('Big Data') have also increased, providing researchers with new ways to analyse the tourism industry. In contrast to traditional data, such Big Data is continuously generated to strive for exhaustive, flexible and scalable production in scope.[22] Regarding the traditional challenges of Big Data analysis, such as quantity, speed and diversity, Kitchin argued that it is too complicated and difficult to overcome other challenges of analysing Big Data (such as timeliness and dynamics, confusion, and uncertainty).[23] Recently, however, the increase of computational power, ML, IoT and new analytical techniques have made this possible.

As one of the emerging concepts in AI, ML and IoT, the DT concept has the potential to be implemented as part of the development of a smart city in a 'smart tourism' context. A DT is a digital representation of something physical.[24] By using Big Data and other supporting resources, the stakeholder will be able to simulate a virtual reality of the region by analysing the flow of activities of tourists and determining the impact of their geographic and temporal patterns on other aspects and policies, such as the provision of facilities and infrastructure, mitigation of over-tourism, mitigation and reduction of tourism risks to the environment, and tourism destination strategies (marketing, branding, competitiveness). Hence, to answer the first research question, this section proposes a conceptual framework of DT design for smart and

---

[20]   C Michael Hall, 'A Typology of Governance and Its Implications for Tourism Policy Analysis' (2011) 19 Journal of Sustainable Tourism.

[21]   UNWTO, 'International Recommendations for Tourism Statistics 2008'; Eurostat, Methodological Manual for Tourism Statistics.

[22]   Rob Kitchin, 'Big Data, New Epistemologies and Paradigm Shifts' (2014) 1 Big Data & Society.

[23]   ibid.

[24]   Fan and others (n 15); Sebastian Haag and Reiner Anderl, 'Digital Twin – Proof of Concept' (2018) 15 Manufacturing Letters.

sustainable tourism, which presents the sequence of processes and the elements required for the architecture.

The conventional approach to design and predict the life cycle of a physical system is based on computer-aided simulation and engineering tools, also to perform various methods of physical testing. The design is being optimised accordingly to maximise performance and cut costs.[25] This approach has limitations in terms of tolerances, strategies, relationships between the configurations, planning, etc. However, with the recent development in the field of AI, enhanced algorithms and increasing computational power, real-time control and digitisation capabilities have become possible.[26] With the help of DT, it is now possible to represent physical objects, processes or systems by combining data and intelligence, which allow for the monitoring of past and present operations to predict future outcomes.[27]

In order to operate, a DT requires three components: a physical product, a virtual product and the interaction/connection between them.[28] DT enables, (1) a comprehensive data exchange, which can include models, simulations and algorithms that describe its counterpart, including characteristics and behaviour in the real world, (2) enhancement of real-life perception, which can be used in virtual reality (VR), and (3) linking and combining data from various models, analyses and simulations, as well as implement social data from citizens.

---

[25] Kaur, Mishra and Maheshwari (n 2).

[26] Michael Grieves, 'Digital Twin: Manufacturing Excellence through Virtual Factory Replication' (2014); Chiara Cimino, Elisa Negri and Luca Fumagalli, 'Review of Digital Twin Applications in Manufacturing' (2019) 113 Computers in Industry.

[27] Yu Zheng, Sen Yang and Huanchong Cheng, 'An Application Framework of Digital Twin and Its Case Study' (2019) 10 Journal of Ambient Intelligence and Humanized Computing; Peyman Moghadam, Thomas Lowe and Everard J Edwards, 'Digital Twin for the Future of Orchard Production Systems', *The Third International Tropical Agriculture Conference (TROPAG 2019)* (MDPI 2020) <https://www.mdpi.com/2504-3900/36/1/92> accessed 11 July 2022.

[28] Peyman Moghadam, Thomas Lowe and Everard J Edwards, 'Digital Twin for the Future of Orchard Production Systems', *The Third International Tropical Agriculture Conference (TROPAG 2019)* (MDPI 2020) <https://www.mdpi.com/2504-3900/36/1/92> accessed 11 July 2022.

DT applications have been implemented in various sectors: manufacturing,[29] logistics,[30] energy,[31] construction,[32] healthcare,[33] and farming.[34] Furthermore, the use and potential of DT in smart cities has been rapidly increasing in recent years, with an increasing number of projects being developed such as 3D energy mapping, wind farm and infrastructure analysis.[35] Also, DT technology is being used for urban planning to tackle climate-related issues,[36] support preventive strategies to protect heritage places,[37] and support decision-making processes to create a smart and sustainable city with citizen participation.[38] The UK National Infrastructure Commission (NIC)'s report 'Data for Public Good', in 2017, pointed to the big potential of using data and digital technology to support more informed decision-making, and subsequently proposed a national DT framework for smart cities.[39] Applying these technologies will improve the performance, service quality and value of assets, processes and systems in the built environment.[40] The use of DT in virtual reality also has

---

[29] Cimino, Negri and Fumagalli (n 26).

[30] Janusz Szpytko and Yorlandys Salgado Duarte, 'Digital Twins Model for Cranes Operating in Container Terminal' (2019) 52 IFAC-PapersOnLine.

[31] Shervin Shokooh and Geir Nordvik, 'A Model-Driven Approach for Situational Intelligence & Operational Awareness', *2019 Petroleum and Chemical Industry Conference Europe (PCIC EUROPE)* (IEEE 2019) <https://ieeexplore.ieee.org/document/9011632/> accessed 11 July 2022.

[32] Chang-Su Shim and others, 'Development of a Bridge Maintenance System for Prestressed Concrete Bridges Using 3D Digital Twin Model' (2019) 15 Structure and Infrastructure Engineering.

[33] Koen Bruynseels, Filippo Santoni de Sio and Jeroen van den Hoven, 'Digital Twins in Health Care: Ethical Implications of an Emerging Engineering Paradigm' (2018) 9 Frontiers in Genetics.

[34] TR Sreedevi and MB Santosh Kumar, 'Digital Twin in Smart Farming: A Categorical Literature Review and Exploring Possibilities in Hydroponics', *2020 Advanced Computing and Communication Technologies for High Performance Applications (ACCTHPA)* (IEEE 2020) <https://ieeexplore.ieee.org/document/9213235/> accessed 11 July 2022.

[35] Aidan Fuller and others, 'Digital Twin: Enabling Technologies, Challenges and Open Research' (2020) 8 IEEE Access; Farsi and others (n 16).

[36] Gerhard Schrotter and Christian Hürzeler, 'The Digital Twin of the City of Zurich for Urban Planning' (2020) 88 PFG – Journal of Photogrammetry, Remote Sensing and Geoinformation Science.

[37] Pierre Jouan and Pierre Hallot, 'Digital Twin: Research Framework to Support Preventive Conservation Policies' (2020) 9 ISPRS International Journal of Geo-Information.

[38] Fabian Dembski and others, 'Urban Digital Twins for Smart Cities and Citizens: The Case Study of Herrenberg, Germany' (2020) 12 Sustainability.

[39] Wan, Nochta and Schooling (n 14).

[40] ibid.

the potential to address the complexity of cities through models, spatial analysis and numerical simulations, and to involve citizens in the urban planning process.[41] In 2020, the Digital Twin (DT) Hub was launched by the Centre and for Digital Build Britain as part of the UK government-mandated National Digital Twin programme. which aims to deliver the key recommendations of NIC's report 'Data for Public Good'.[42]

2.2   Conceptual Framework and Synthesis of DTs for Smart Sustainable Tourism

Accordingly, we propose that an approach of the DT concept has the potential to be implemented within the smart tourism initiative as a part of developing smart cities. By utilising Big Data and other supporting resources, the stakeholders will be able to create a virtual reality of the region by analysing the flow of activities of tourists and by determining the impact of their geographic and temporal patterns on other aspects and policies, such as the provision of facilities and infrastructure, the mitigation of over-tourism, the mitigation and reduction of tourism risks to the environment, and tourism destination strategies (marketing, branding, competitiveness). Eurostat advocated that the taxonomy of potential big data sources for tourism are: communication systems data (such as mobile network operator data, smart mobile devices, social media posts) and world wide web data, as well as data created by business processes (such as flight booking system, financial transactions), sensors (such as traffic counting, smart energy meter, satellite images) and crowdsourcing (such as open street map, Wikipedia content, picture collections).[43]

Here, we formulate a conceptual framework of DT for smart and sustainable tourism (Figure 4.1) that is inspired by Wan et al., in 2019, consisting of the process and elements needed for the architecture of a DT.[44] A DT requires a sound information management framework to guide the

---

[41]   Fabian Dembski, Uwe Wössner and Mike Letzgus, 'The Digital Twin Tackling Urban Challenges with Models, Spatial Analysis and Numerical Simulations in Immersive Virtual Environments', *Blucher Design Proceedings* (Editora Blucher 2019) <http://www.proceedings.blucher.com.br/article-details/34238> accessed 11 July 2022.

[42]   Angela Walters, 'National Digital Twin Programme' (7 September 2019) <https://www.cdbb.cam.ac.uk/what-we-do/national-digital-twin-programme> accessed 20 July 2022.

[43]   Christophe Demunter, European Commission, and Statistical Office of the European Union, *Tourism Statistics: Early Adopters of Big Data?: 2017 Edition* (2017) <http://dx.publications.europa.eu/10.2785/762729> accessed 11 July 2022.

[44]   Wan, Nochta and Schooling (n 14).

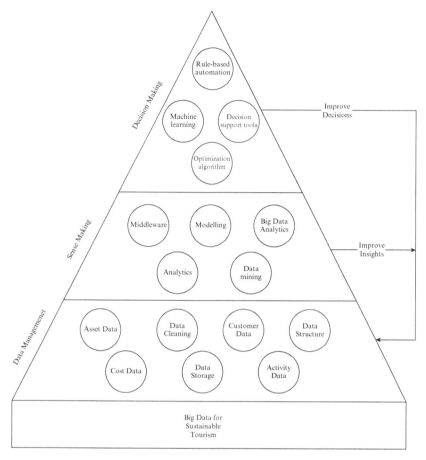

Figure 4.1   Conceptual framework of Digital Twins (DT) for smart and sustainable tourism

design of its data architecture. Figure 4.1 presents both the overview and four steps towards implementing DT for smart and sustainable tourism. Firstly, we need to define the Big Data source for the system. Secondly, defining the approach to data management is necessary in order to collect, store and use data efficiently and securely. Thirdly, we need to establish sensemaking (data exploration), in order to determine where Big Data analysis will be deployed, including modelling and data mining. The final step is decision-making, where DT is applied to improve smart and sustainable tourism. We believe that a feedback loop is critical to developing the system. In practice, this involves a post-implementation evaluation. The insights will support policy-making processes as data-driven informed decisions.

We reflect the typical steps involved in creating a DT and apply it in the context of DTs for smart and sustainable tourism (Figure 4.2). This consists of physical entities, virtual models and connected data that tie physical entities with virtual models, as a complement of our proposed conceptual framework (Figure 4.1). Firstly, a physical entity is the real product that is controlled and commanded by the users. For example, in manufacturing, this could be raw material or part of machinery, assembly and other processes.[45] In smart tourism, a physical entity can be a city environment or infrastructure plan. Secondly, a virtual model is the duplication of the physical entity that is designated a virtual space. This can mirror activities of physical entities, lifecycles and behaviours.[46] The purpose of developing a virtual model is to use it to simulate, monitor, predict and control physical entities. Thirdly, connected data contains subsets of physical and virtual entities, as well as new data required for the integrated fusion process between physical and virtual entities.[47]

Since confidential information is stored in software systems or digital devices, data security on this digital platform becomes critical. We must consider several elements that may affect the security aspects. They include the related stakeholders and users, as well as compliance with relevant laws and regulations. These elements enable the connectivity and networking of digital technologies, the so-called 'digitalisation'. Unfortunately, in many cases, the relevant stakeholders do not communicate optimally with one another, resulting in the failure of technology to ensure security. Therefore, to guarantee the reliability and security of digital technology, we need a strategy to govern the different aspects, and to address the relevant issues, so that platform security lives up to the requirements of society and regulation of the place where it is situated. To address this challenge, we combine a political science perspective when it comes to governing the digital system, as it relates to governance, power, systems of activity or behaviour, and associated constitutions and laws.[48] Furthermore, an approach to documenting architecture decisions is necessary to provide insight into the rationale behind the process and record design choices.[49]

---

[45]   Tao and others (n 10).
[46]   ibid.
[47]   ibid.
[48]   Vivian Lowndes, David Marsh and Gerry Stoker (eds), *Theory and Methods in Political Science*, 4th edn (Palgrave Macmillan 2018).
[49]   U van Heesch, P Avgeriou and R Hilliard, 'A Documentation Framework for Architecture Decisions' (2012) 85 Journal of Systems and Software.

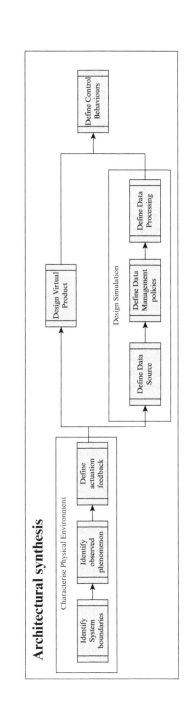

Figure 4.2   Architectural synthesis

3.   NOTIONS OF GOVERNANCE

This section discusses the modes of governance and their further implementation in digital technology or cyber-governance. As one of the final outcomes of this chapter, we aim to propose a documentation framework to support the governing process of digital architecture, which involves multiple stakeholders with diverse technological and non-technological backgrounds. To do so, we should understand the concept of governance and how it can be applied to digital technologies.

What is governance? There is no single definition of the term. Rhodes explains the term 'governance' as referring to 'self-organising and inter-organisational network.'[50] These networks complement market and hierarchical systems, and serve as the authority to allocate resources, implement control and coordinate. It is characterised by interdependence, the exchange of resources, rules and significant national autonomy. There are at least six separate uses of the term governance.[51] First, the minimal state, which redefines the scope and form of public interventions and the use of markets to deliver public services. Second, corporate governance, to describe the system for directing and controlling an organisation. Third, New Public Management, which introduces the private-sector management to the public sector. Fourth, socio-cybernetics, where the government should enable socio-political interactions in which the central government is no longer supreme. Fifth, governance as a self-organising network, which means that an organisation should be autonomous and self-governing, implying a high level of freedom and self-responsibility. Sixth, good governance, which shows efficiency, accountability and decentralised administration.

In an article in 2007, Rhodes re-emphasises that the meaning of governance is due to the latest situation.[52] Rhodes highlights the term governance as a new governing process or a new method for governing a society. Governance is considered broader than the activity of governments, in which the perspectives of public administration and public policy, and covering non-state actors, are combined.[53] This enhanced governance concept includes the changes in the group of participants in the process of formulation, implementation and coordination within the network.

---

[50]   Rod AW Rhodes, *Understanding Governance: Policy Networks, Governance, Reflexivity, and Accountability* (Open University 1997).
[51]   RAW Rhodes, 'The New Governance: Governing without Government' (1996) 44 Political Studies.
[52]   RAW Rhodes, 'Understanding Governance: Ten Years On' (2007) 28 Organization Studies.
[53]   ibid.

Similarly, Treib defined governance as a change in the status of a state, denoting a process of governing that departs from the traditional model where decisions are taken by elected representatives and implemented by an administrative official.[54] Governance also considers a change in actor composition during formulation and implementation, and a process of coordination within networks.[55] In addition, governance is described as multi-level or intergovernmental government.[56] It is called network governance when it encompasses a network of public and non-public actors, which includes the interaction between these groups.[57] Although these governance concepts are quite different, they have common elements emphasising the process of governance and the limitations of governmental power, in which power relationships are strongly associated with governance. In addition, Van Kersbergen and Van Warden mention that actors, roles, policy formulation and execution are involved in governance.[58]

In the following, we will make a distinction between traditional governance and contrast this with an approach to cyber-governance. The following table indicates the main characteristics, which are further outlined below.[59]

3.1 Traditional Governance

From the perspective of political science, where the study of political systems is central, 'old' governance, or Mode 1 governance, refers to authority mainly through the hierarchical command and control structure at the state and other public levels.[60] It relies on traditional institutions

---

[54] Oliver Treib, Holger Bähr and Gerda Falkner, 'Modes of Governance: Towards a Conceptual Clarification' (2007) 14 Journal of European Public Policy.

[55] Jan Kooiman, *Governing as Governance* (SAGE Publications Ltd 2003) <https://sk.sagepub.com/books/governing-as-governance> accessed 11 July 2022.

[56] Ian Bache and Matthew Flinders, 'Multi-Level Governance and the Study of the British State' (2004) 19 Public Policy and Administration.

[57] Erik-Hans Klijn, 'Governance and Governance Networks in Europe: An Assessment of Ten Years of Research on the Theme' (2008) 10 Public Management Review.

[58] Kees Van Kersbergen and Frans Van Waarden, '"Governance" as a Bridge between Disciplines: Cross-Disciplinary Inspiration Regarding Shifts in Governance and Problems of Governability, Accountability and Legitimacy' (2004) 43 European Journal of Political Research.

[59] Andrej Zwitter and Jilles Hazenberg, 'Decentralized Network Governance: Blockchain Technology and the Future of Regulation' (2020) 3 Frontiers in Blockchain.

[60] Rhodes, *Understanding Governance: Policy Networks, Governance, Reflexivity, and Accountability* (n 50); Zwitter and Hazenberg (n 59).

Table 4.1 *The difference between traditional governance and cyber-governance*

	Traditional governance	Cyber-governance
Entities	● States ● Companies ● IOs ● NGOs and civil society.	● Tech companies ● Online interest groups ● Hackers, hacktivists ● Cyber-criminals ● Digital entities.
Resources	● Raw materials ● Money ● Territory ● Extraction: productivity.	● Data (oil) ● Attention space (territory) ● Extraction method: AI.
Regulation	● Law ● Contracts ● Enforcement.	● Terms of use ● Code ● Bot.

to make policies through hard law enforcement. This governance model is rooted in the Westphalian concept of a nation-state and is usually constituted by a legitimate strategy based on public sovereignty and input in political decision-making.[61] Zwitter and Hazenberg interpreted this model as identity-based governance, where roles and power are assigned to, and/or executed by actors based on their identities and on a structure of governance mechanism.[62] Mode 1 governance is more hierarchical and clearly defined by the structures. The power is static, where the states have the authority to assign power to actors such as organisations, corporations and individuals.

The key criterion to distinguishing different types of governance is the relationship between public and private actors in the decision-making process.[63] In contrast, Mode 2 governance, or 'new' governance, represents a shift from the state's vertical command and control structure to a more horizontal decision-making process. This shift creates a more level playing field between private and public social participants in

---

[61] Fritz W Scharpf, *Governing in Europe: Effective and Democratic* (Oxford University Press 1999).
[62] Zwitter and Hazenberg (n 59).
[63] Treib, Bähr and Falkner (n 54).

terms of coordination and self-government, especially regarding network relationships.[64] Public–private partnerships, policy networks and private governance are examples where the state is no longer a central authority. As governance can be seen as a decision-making system, which stipulates the participation of different actors, authority is acquired through identity, performance, knowledge and expertise.[65]

The Mode 2 model is also known as role-based governance. Governance tasks and mechanisms are assigned to and/or performed by participants because they can play a role in achieving the needs of specific areas or strategic goals.[66] In recent years, old governance mechanisms have become destabilised and new governance mechanisms have been emerging. This transformation of governance to be more horizontal occurs in the private and public spheres at local, regional, national, and international levels, including the mechanism, capacities and styles of governance.[67]

While Mode 1 governance focuses on hard law as an instrument, Mode 2 governance instruments are broader and include soft law, negotiation, codes of conduct and other company sector agreements regarding specific standards. However, in practice, the difference between Mode 1 and Mode 2 governance is not always clear. Many hybrid forms have elements that borrow from both modes.[68] Furthermore, both of these forms come with certain challenges regarding implementation in digital technologies, as the relationships among various actors are fluid, and neither solely vertical nor horizontal.[69]

3.2 Digital Governance

While governance is usually defined as a system of authoritative norms, rules, procedures and practices, digital governance refers to the impact of information technology on the rules and practice systems.[70] The transition from printing technology to electronic information technology, for

---

[64] Zwitter and Hazenberg (n 59); Scharpf (n 61).

[65] Rhodes, 'The New Governance' (n 51); Kersbergen and Waarden (n 58).

[66] Zwitter and Hazenberg (n 59).

[67] Kersbergen and Waarden (n 58); Stephen P Osborne, *Public–Private Partnerships: Theory and Practice in International Perspective*, vol. 19 (Routledge 2000); Graeme A Hodge and Carsten Greve, *The Challenge of Public–Private Partnerships: Learning from International Experience* (Edward Elgar Publishing 2005).

[68] Zwitter and Hazenberg (n 59).

[69] Scharpf (n 61).

[70] Luna-Reyes (n 18).

example, provides a new environment for the law, which is less tangible, less fixed, less structured, less stable and more flexible.[71] In addition, new technologies that make information flow, and which enable social connections such as the internet, have created new opportunities for citizens to participate and organise themselves through the creation and distribution of content.

Thus, to some extent, digital technology has possibly changed the flow of information, altered vital structures within society, and triggered radical social, economic and cultural changes. Many different forms of digital participation have emerged, promoted by governmental and non-governmental institutions, covering a full range of expressions, diverse interests and values through technology platforms in order to improve policy-making.[72]

However, there are some challenges in regulating the digital realm compared with the 'real world'. Firstly, there are challenges regarding cyber threats and other risks related to digitisation efforts.[73] Cyber vulnerabilities arise from the risk of using storage facilities, supercomputers, internet exposures, and the misuse of private or sensitive data for harmful purposes. Prevention strategies are important, but these do not suffice against such attacks. Therefore, governance strategies must be designed to mitigate and recover from potential shocks posed by intrusion or a loss in system functionalities.[74]

Secondly, there are challenges to interpreting law and regulation with regards to requirements in software systems, as the law is becoming an increasingly important consideration in the engineering community.[75] Research in this area has addressed various issues, including extraction of legal requirements, ambiguity detection and resolution, and compliance determination. Legal experts for large companies will handle these challenges, but in small companies, individuals with little or no legal training might be responsible for compliance.[76]

---

[71]   M Ethan Katsh, *Law in a Digital World* (Oxford University Press 1995).
[72]   Luna-Reyes (n 18).
[73]   Igor Linkov and others, 'Governance Strategies for a Sustainable Digital World' (2018) 10 Sustainability.
[74]   'OECD Science, Technology and Innovation Outlook 2016' (Organisation for Economic Co-Operation and Development (OECD) 2016).
[75]   David G Gordon and Travis D Breaux, 'The Role of Legal Expertise in Interpretation of Legal Requirements and Definitions', *2014 IEEE 22nd International Requirements Engineering Conference (RE)* (IEEE 2014) <http://ieeexplore.ieee.org/document/6912269/> accessed 11 July 2022.
[76]   ibid.

Thirdly, there are issues related to privacy, territoriality, networking and power attributes in digital governance, especially addressing the norms and roles of each act, which are more fluid than traditional governance.[77] Regarding implementing traditional governance models into digital governance, overregulation may not match technological solutions, leading to unfavourable results such as diminishing the expected advantages of applying such a technology.[78] The roles and power relationships in the digital domain are dynamics, neither vertical nor horizontal, and often appear in a single and or anonymous actor. This concept is called Decentralised Network Governance (DNG) or Mode 3 governance, where the state has limited powers within the digital domain, and new actors emerge.[79] These new actors use network construction and network power to direct others in numerous changing relationships instead of allocating tasks based on identity and roles, whereas rules digital domain are utilised to regulate the actors and stakeholders. From a contemporary perspective, digital government, together with business and political decision-making aspects, is regarded as part of the digital governance concept. In other words, although the digital government is a structure made up of governmental practices, digital government is more of a process involving multiple interacting stakeholders using ICT.[80]

4.   GOVERNING DIGITAL TWINS FOR SMART AND SUSTAINABLE TOURISM

Motivated by the challenges of governing a digital technology, in this study, we also aim to raise awareness of each actor in both technological (e.g., data engineers and data scientists) and non-technological positions (high-level managers, data analyst, legal person) about the importance of understanding rules and regulations. This chapter provides broader perspective of both sides, and how to address them in the system through a strategic and systematic way. Compliance with regulation is becoming more and more important in developing software systems that process and manage sensitive information. In addition, identifying

---

[77]   Zwitter and Hazenberg (n 59); Neal Kumar Katyal, 'Digital Architecture as Crime Control' (2003) 112 Yale Law Journal.
[78]   Zwitter and Hazenberg (n 59).
[79]   ibid.
[80]   Burak Erkut, 'From Digital Government to Digital Governance: Are We There Yet?' (2020) 12 Sustainability.

and analysing relevant legal regulations and aligning them with security requirements becomes necessary to develop secure software systems.[81]

In this section we will introduce our approach to govern DT for smart and sustainable tourism, validated by presenting a case study, as well as three case scenarios, to answer the second research question. As a complex system, DT involves many interrelated stakeholders, who play a synergistic role in maintaining the goal throughout its life cycle. Hence, it faces many issues during the decision-making process, from planning to implementation and to evaluation. It is suggested to formulate a set of documentation frameworks in order to support the governing process of secure software systems with legal compliance. These frameworks are also beneficial for tackling technical knowledge loss due to a lack of documentation. In an agile and global team, technical or architectural knowledge is challenging due to personal interaction over documentation.[82]

4.1   Research Context: Digital Twin in Smart and Sustainable Tourism in Indonesia

To illustrate our frameworks, we use a theoretical case study of designing DTs for smart and sustainable tourism in Indonesia. The National Statistics Office of Indonesia (Statistics Indonesia, or locally known as BPS) will develop this DT design in collaboration with related stakeholders. As a new approach in the tourism industry, this project will use Mobile Positioning Data (MPD) as the Big Data source, which is provided by a major mobile network operator (MNO) in Indonesia. The country has been using MPD since 2016 for several statistical purposes, such as measuring international tourists in border areas and analysis of mobility in metropolitan areas. The institutions involved in the projects are Statistics Indonesia, the Ministry of Tourism, the Ministry of Planning, the data communication provider and Positium Estonia as the technical expert on MPD analysis.

By leveraging the use of MPD to the DT application and applying our frameworks to govern the system, we aim to provide better insights and

---

[81]   Shareeful Islam, Haralambos Mouratidis and Jan Jürjens, 'A Framework to Support Alignment of Secure Software Engineering with Legal Regulations' (2011) 10 Software & Systems Modeling.

[82]   Gilberto Borrego, Alberto L Moran and Ramon Palacio, 'Preliminary Evaluation of a Tag-Based Knowledge Condensation Tool in Agile and Distributed Teams', *2017 IEEE 12th International Conference on Global Software Engineering (ICGSE)* (IEEE 2017) <http://ieeexplore.ieee.org/document/7976687/> accessed 11 July 2022.

procedures for a data-driven policy-making process regarding sustainable tourism in Indonesia. As a statistics product, we must ensure that all statistical activities comply with the Generic Statistical Business Process Model (GSBPM) to produce official statistics,[83] as shown below in Figure 4.4.

4.2   Procedures

To govern the DT, we formulate several documentation templates based on the concept of DNG and documentation framework for architecture decisions.[84] To that aim, we propose the following overarching procedures:

1. identification of stakeholders
2. identification of laws and regulations
3. documentation frameworks for architecture decisions.

4.2.1   Step 1: Identification of stakeholders

Successful software engineering projects occur when stakeholders know the potential issues and recognise that their ideas, opinions and contributions are valued. Therefore, the projects should involve stakeholders in the decision-making process throughout the various stages of the project.[85] To identify the stakeholders, and their roles and contributions to this project, we need to understand the conceptual model of the architecture framework (Figure 4.3) and project life cycle based on GSBPM (Figure 4.4).[86]

Based on figures 4.3 and 4.4, we then identify the stakeholders based on their roles, their institutions and the life cycle of the project at hand (Table 4.2). There are five institutions involved in the project: Statistics

---

[83]   European Commission, 'Handbook on Methodology of Modern Business Statistics', Collaboration in Research and Methodology for Official Statistics (2014).

[84]   Zwitter and Hazenberg (n 59); van Heesch, Avgeriou and Hilliard (n 49); 'ISO/IEC/IEEE Systems and Software Engineering – Architecture Description' (IEEE) <http://ieeexplore.ieee.org/document/6129467/> accessed 11 July 2022.

[85]   J McManus, 'A Stakeholder Perspective within Software Engineering Projects', *2004 IEEE International Engineering Management Conference (IEEE Cat. No.04CH37574)* (IEEE 2004) <http://ieeexplore.ieee.org/document/1407508/> accessed 11 July 2022; H Sharp, A Finkelstein and G Galal, 'Stakeholder Identification in the Requirements Engineering Process', *Proceedings: Tenth International Workshop on Database and Expert Systems Applications. DEXA 99* (IEEE 1999) <http://ieeexplore.ieee.org/document/795198/> accessed 11 July 2022.

[86]   'ISO/IEC/IEEE Systems and Software Engineering – Architecture Description' (n 84); European Commission (n 83).

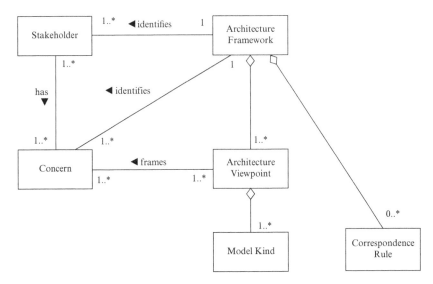

Figure 4.3   Conceptual model of the architecture framework

Indonesia, the MNO, the Ministry of Tourism, the Ministry of Planning, and Positium Estonia. Each institution has its actors, whose roles are different at various stages. For instance, at stage 1 (specify needs) and stage 8 (evaluation), all institutions are involved, and the actors are the high-level managers who function as decision-makers. At this stage, the actors have several concerns: system purposes, data accessibility, reliability, functionality, autonomy, business goals and strategies, and cost.

In contrast to this, at stage 2 (design), all institutions will be involved, but the actors are different. More actors contribute from Statistics Indonesia, such as data engineers, data scientists, data analysts and business intelligence analysts who will communicate with data engineers and data scientists from the MNO, data users from the Ministry of Tourism and the Ministry of Planning, and technical assistants from Positium Estonia. At this stage, there are slightly different concerns compared with stage 1, namely: system features, system properties, structure, limitations, performance, resource utilisation, maintainability, modifiability, security, privacy, data accessibility and customer experience. The actors at stage 2 mostly are technological people, who will communicate through the architecture system.

Meanwhile, due to data privacy and security, only two institutions will be involved at stages 3 (building) and 4 (collection): Statistics Indonesia and the MNO. The processes will be deployed by the data engineers in the MNO environment. At stage 5 (process), where the data extraction is completed and ready for further processing, the data scientists of Statistics

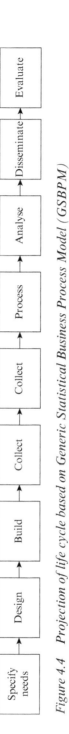

Figure 4.4   Projection of life cycle based on Generic Statistical Business Process Model (GSBPM)

Table 4.2   *Stakeholders/actors based on institutions and GSBPM activities/stages*

Activities GSBPM and conceptual framework	Statistics Indonesia	The Mobile Network Operator (MNO)	The Ministry of Tourism	The Ministry of Planning	Technical expert
Specify needs	High-level manager	High-level manager	High-level manager	High-level manager	High-level manager
Design	Data scientist Data analyst Legal person	Data engineer Data scientist Legal person	Data user	Data user	Data engineer
Build	Data engineer	Data engineer			
Collect	Data engineer	Data engineer			
Process	Data scientist	Data scientist			Data scientist
Analyse	Data scientist Data analyst	Data scientist	Data analyst	Data analyst	Data scientist Data analyst
Disseminate	Business intelligence analyst Data analyst		Data user	Data user	
Evaluate	High-level manager	High-level manager	High-level manager	High-level manager	High-level manager

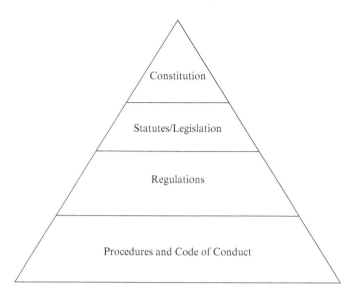

Figure 4.5   General hierarchy of law in most countries

Indonesia and the MNO will collaborate with technical assistance from the data scientist of Positium Estonia.

At stage 6 (analyses), all institutions will be involved with different roles and responsibilities. The actors from Statistics Indonesia and the MNO will have responsibilities on data modelling, digital twin deployment, analysis, as well as evaluation, whereas actors from the Ministry of Tourism, the Ministry of Planning and Positium Estonia will have roles in data analysis. Following this, at stage 7 (dissemination), only three institutions will be involved: Statistics Indonesia, Ministry of Tourism and Ministry of Planning.

4.2.2   Step 2: Identification of laws and regulations
After the identification of relevant stakeholders, we identify the rules and regulations to be implemented in the project. We differentiate between two categories of rules and regulations: technological and non-technological. Before doing so, however, we should understand the hierarchy of law, which determines the ranking in authority and how the authority and scope of each level are derived from the constitution.[87] Figure 4.5 shows

---

[87]   Michael Clegg and others, 'The Hierarchy of Laws: Understanding and Implementing the Legal Frameworks that Govern Elections' (2016) International Foundation for Electoral Systems, Arlington, VA.

Table 4.3   Laws and regulations for DT on smart and sustainable tourism

Non-technological (traditional governance regulation)	Technological (cyber-governance regulation)
● National Code of Good Practice on Official Statistics: United Nation Statistics Division ● Indonesia Law of Statistics: Act 16/ 1997 ● GDPR ● Personal data privacy regulations in Indonesia: Act 19/2016 on the amendment of Act 11/2008 on Information and Electronic Transactions (ITE), and Act 27/2022 on Personal Data Protection ● Regulation of The Minister of Communication and Information Republic of Indonesia, Number 5 the Year 2020: Electronic System Operator Private Scope ● MoU between BPS and Ministry of Tourism and MNO ● The contract between BPS and Technical Expert ● Project/program life cycle management ● Standard Operating Procedures.	● Terms of use ● Code ● Digital twin architecture framework ● Architecture viewpoint (model kinds, correspondence rules, modelling method, analysis technique, language, notations).

a general hierarchy of law in most countries, which helps us to determine the hierarchy of regulations to comply in our project.[88] It specifies how the different levels of law are applied in practice. Based on Figure 4.5, we identified a following list of laws and regulations to be implemented in order to govern DT for Smart and Sustainable Tourism (Table 4.3).

4.2.3   Step 3: Documentation framework for architecture decisions
Finally, we introduce a documentation framework for architecture decisions consisting of a set of documentation templates to govern DT on smart and sustainable tourism. The goal is to have a broader perspective on the decision-making process that involves each actor at various stages

---

[88]   ibid.

Table 4.4   Decision details viewpoint

- **Name**: A short name of the decision
- **Activities on GSBPM**: A state of the decision on GSBPM
- **Activities on DT**: A state of the decision on the DT framework
- **Problem/Issue**: The issue addressed by the decision
- **Decision**: The outcome of the decision or solution
- **Alternatives**: The alternative solutions considered when deciding
- **Arguments**: The reason behind the decision
- **Related decisions**: All decisions that have a relationship to the decision.
- **Governing system**: Laws and regulations governing the actors, both technological and non-technological
- **Decision-makes/actors**: The actors involved in the decision-making process.

---

of the project, address the governing system of each actor based on roles and responsibilities, ensure security requirements and align them with relevant regulations. To that end, we propose the tools as follows:

1. documentation framework for architecture decisions, which is modified from the conventions of ISO/IEC/IEEE 42010, the international standard for the description of system and software architectures.[89] This documentation framework consists of a decision details viewpoint (Table 4.4) and a relationship viewpoint (Figure 4.6).
2. standard operating procedure (SOP, Figure 4.7), which is modified from the SOP of the Statistics Office.

The first part of the documentation framework is a decision details viewpoint (Table 4.4). It gives detailed information about single architecture decisions, which consists of major information in architecture (e.g., decision outcome, options and arguments), and minor but useful information (e.g., issue, state, related decisions and actors).[90] We modified the existing template by selecting the elements, and added a governing system as an important element to manage the interaction of each actor. We also added activities on DT and GSBPM to give a comprehensive overview of the decisions.

The second part of the documentation framework is a decision relationship viewpoint (Figure 4.6), which shows the current state of architecture

---

[89]   van Heesch, Avgeriou and Hilliard (n 49); 'ISO/IEC/IEEE Systems and Software Engineering – Architecture Description' (n 84).

[90]   van Heesch, Avgeriou and Hilliard (n 49).

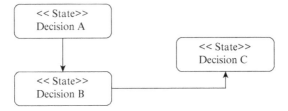

Figure 4.6   Relationship viewpoint

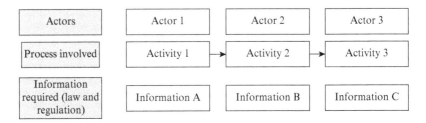

Figure 4.7   Standard operating procedure

decisions, and how they relate to other decisions. This template enables transparency and makes the relationships between architectural design decisions explicit and traceable. The final part of the documentation framework we use is the SOP (Figure 4.7), adapted and modified from the SOP of BPS-Statistics Indonesia. This template allows the project more systematic and cohesive by showing detailed procedures and flows of each activity.

4.3   Work Validation

Throughout the process of designing the architecture, we determined 24 decisions that would be implemented. In this section, to validate our work, we apply our frameworks to three scenarios or decisions as examples. Full tables and graphs of each scenario are provided in the Supplementary Materials, available on the following companion website: https://doi.org/10.5281/zenodo.5946878.

4.3.1   Scenario 1: Data collection of MPD for smart and sustainable tourism

Table 4.6 shows the decision details viewpoint of decision 1 (data collection) and Figure 4.8 describes the flow of activities, or SOP, of decision 1. This decision is related to two other decisions: decision 0 (decision on the use of MPD for tourism statistics) and decision 4 (data cleaning and structure). As we have already decided to use MPD for tourism statistics, this stage should address the issues of privacy and security during the data collection process. To solve these problems, the decision has been made to extract and process the raw data at the MNO, involving Statistics Indonesia. As the microdata are sensitive, circulating the microdata outside the MNO environment is not allowed, and the MNO will apply a sandbox mechanism during the data collection process. To ensure this process will comply with all related regulations, we will involve the legal person during the decision-making process.

4.3.2 Scenario 2: Data cleaning and validation

Table 4.7 shows the decision details viewpoint of decision 5 (data cleaning and structure), and Figure 4.9 describes the flow of activities or the SOP of decision 5. The critical problem is deciding what is allowed and not allowed during data processing and analysis. It is crucial to ensure data quality and confidentiality. Hence, we have decided to generate Tier 2 data at this stage, which is initial raw and aggregated data with no personally identifiable information. These data include the time period and geographical location at provincial and municipality levels. However, we have an alternative to generate Tier 2 data only at the provincial level, in order to anticipate unavailability of data at the municipality level. To ensure data quality, this decision is related to other decisions, for instance: decision 5 (removing duplicates), decision 7 (detecting missing data) and decision 8 (removing technical subscribers and machines), while the flow of detailed activities and related stakeholders is described by Figure 4.9.

4.3.3 Scenario 3: Designing Digital Twin virtual environment

Table 4.8 shows the decision details viewpoint of decision 13 (designing the virtual environment of the digital twin). This decision is also crucial given the data sensitivity and privacy. Therefore, this decision is related to five other decisions, such as decision 11 (big data analysis to analyse tourism granularity), decision 15 (creating user-interface platform), and decision 16 (ensuring cybersecurity by authentication). At this stage, we decided to deploy a virtual environment using the software at the MNO territory. However, there is also an alternative: to use a web application with authentication. Figure 4.10 shows the detailed activities among related stakeholders, where data scientists of the MNO and Statistics Indonesia will communicate through the architectural system, and the supervisors ensure that the virtual environment is reliable and compliant with security and privacy concerns.

5.   CONCLUSIONS

DTs can predict system responses before they occur. A DT can be described as a virtual simulation, allowing us to understand the comprehensive physical and functional characteristics of the product life cycle ex ante. DTs have been implemented in many sectors, including smart cities. With the rapid growth of new IT applications in tourism, including digitisation via the use of IoT, we believe that DTs have the potential to be implemented in smart and sustainable tourism. By utilising Big Data and other supporting resources, stakeholders will be able to create a virtual reality of the region by analysing the flow of activities of tourists and determining the impact of their geographic and temporal pattern on other aspects and policies, such as the provision of facilities and infrastructure, mitigation of over-tourism, mitigation and reduction of tourism risks to the environment, and tourism destination strategies.

5.1   Implications for Practitioners and Researchers

The main contribution of our work is to propose a conceptual framework and architectural synthesis method for DT design on smart and sustainable tourism. On the one hand, we expect the implementation of DT technology to be an alternative regarding various potential big data sources and technologies to support decision-making in the tourism industry. On the other hand, we are aware that governing the system and compliance with regulations is equally crucial. Our approach addresses this dynamic by introducing a documentation framework consisting of three templates for architectural decisions that offer several benefits. First, this provides a complete picture of the requirements of a software engineering process, both technological and non-technological. Furthermore, it supports the analysis of comprehensive requirements that align with legal issues, from the planning until the evaluation stage of the software development process. Secondly, the framework provides a complete picture of the interactions between stakeholders and how to govern them with technological and non-technological tools, such as law and regulations, terms of use, code, and architectural viewpoints within the various stages of the project. Lastly, the framework also supports design development, which enables each actor to trace back specific decisions and solutions to the relevant security and legal requirements, datafication, confidentiality, and software engineering processes.

5.2 Future Work

This chapter is an introduction to propose the use of DT technology on smart and sustainable tourism. After coming up with the idea of our architecture and documentation framework, we hope to do further investigation on the potential big data source and framework improvement and validation through a field study. We also aspire to conduct other studies implementing DT for sustainable tourism, using different big data sources and potential technologies.

ACKNOWLEDGEMENTS

The authors extend their gratitude to the editors for their valuable comments and insights on the manuscript.

REFERENCES

Bache I and Flinders M, 'Multi-Level Governance and the Study of the British State' (2004) 19 Public Policy and Administration.

Borrego G, Moran AL and Palacio R, 'Preliminary Evaluation of a Tag-Based Knowledge Condensation Tool in Agile and Distributed Teams', *2017 IEEE 12th International Conference on Global Software Engineering (ICGSE)* (IEEE 2017) <http://ieeexplore.ieee.org/document/7976687/> accessed 11 July 2022.

Bruynseels K, Santoni de Sio F and van den Hoven J, 'Digital Twins in Health Care: Ethical Implications of an Emerging Engineering Paradigm' (2018) 9 Frontiers in Genetics 31.

Bulchand-Gidumal J, 'M. Sigala, R. Rahimi, M. Thelwall (Eds.): "Big Data and Innovation in Tourism, Travel, and Hospitality. Managerial Approaches, Techniques, and Applications"' (2021) 13 Zeitschrift für Tourismuswissenschaft.

Cimino C, Negri E and Fumagalli L, 'Review of Digital Twin Applications in Manufacturing' (2019) 113 Computers in Industry.

Clegg M and others, 'The Hierarchy of Laws: Understanding and Implementing the Legal Frameworks that Govern Elections' (2016) International Foundation for Electoral Systems, Arlington, VA.

Del Fiore G and others, 'A Location-Aware Architecture for an IoT-Based Smart Museum' (2016) 12 International Journal of Electronic Government Research.

Dembski F and others, 'Urban Digital Twins for Smart Cities and Citizens: The Case Study of Herrenberg, Germany' (2020) 12 Sustainability.

Dembski F, Wössner U and Letzgus M, 'The Digital Twin Tackling Urban Challenges with Models, Spatial Analysis and Numerical Simulations in Immersive Virtual Environments', *Blucher Design Proceedings* (Editora Blucher 2019) <http://www.proceedings.blucher.com.br/article-details/34238> accessed 11 July 2022.

Demunter C, European Commission and Statistical Office of the European Union, *Tourism Statistics: Early Adopters of Big Data? 2017 Edition* (2017) <http://dx.publications.europa.eu/10.2785/762729> accessed 11 July 2022.

Erkut B, 'From Digital Government to Digital Governance: Are We There Yet?' (2020) 12 Sustainability 860.

Errandonea I, Beltrán S and Arrizabalaga S, 'Digital Twin for Maintenance: A Literature Review' (2020) 123 Computers in Industry.

European Commission, 'Handbook on Methodology of Modern Business Statistics', Collaboration in Research and Methodology for Official Statistics (2014).

Eurostat, Methodological Manual for Tourism Statistics <https://ec.europa.eu/eurostat/web/products-manuals-and-guidelines/-/ks-gq-14-013> accessed 24 February 2023.

Fan C and others, 'Disaster City Digital Twin: A Vision for Integrating Artificial and Human Intelligence for Disaster Management' (2021) 56 International Journal of Information Management.

Farsi M and others (eds), *Digital Twin Technologies and Smart Cities* (Springer International Publishing 2020) <http://link.springer.com/10.1007/978-3-030-18732-3> accessed 11 July 2022.

Fuller A and others, 'Digital Twin: Enabling Technologies, Challenges and Open Research' (2020) 8 IEEE Access.

Gandomi A and Haider M, 'Beyond the Hype: Big Data Concepts, Methods, and Analytics' (2015) 35 International Journal of Information Management.

Garzón J and others, 'ARtour: Augmented Reality-Based Game to Promote Agritourism', *Augmented Reality, Virtual Reality, and Computer Graphics* (Springer Nature Switzerland AG) <https://doi.org/10.1007/978-3-319-952 70-3>.

Girau R and others, 'Be Right Beach: A Social IoT System for Sustainable Tourism Based on Beach Overcrowding Avoidance', *2018 IEEE International Conference on Internet of Things (iThings) and IEEE Green Computing and Communications (GreenCom) and IEEE Cyber, Physical and Social Computing (CPSCom) and IEEE Smart Data (SmartData)* (IEEE 2018) <https://ieeexplore.ieee.org/document/8726793/> accessed 11 July 2022.

Glaessgen E and Stargel D, 'The Digital Twin Paradigm for Future NASA and U.S. Air Force Vehicles', *53rd AIAA/ASME/ASCE/AHS/ASC Structures, Structural Dynamics and Materials Conference
20th AIAA/ASME/AHS Adaptive Structures Conference
14th AIAA* (American Institute of Aeronautics and Astronautics 2012) <http://arc.aiaa.org/doi/abs/10.2514/6.2012-1818> accessed 11 July 2022.

Gordon DG and Breaux TD, 'The Role of Legal Expertise in Interpretation of Legal Requirements and Definitions', *2014 IEEE 22nd International Requirements Engineering Conference (RE)* (IEEE 2014) <http://ieeexplore.ieee.org/document/6912269/> accessed 11 July 2022.

Grieves M, 'Digital Twin: Manufacturing Excellence through Virtual Factory Replication' (2014) 1 White Paper.

Haag S and Anderl R, 'Digital Twin – Proof of Concept' (2018) 15 Manufacturing Letters.

Hall CM, 'A Typology of Governance and Its Implications for Tourism Policy Analysis' (2011) 19 Journal of Sustainable Tourism.

Hodge GA and Greve C, *The Challenge of Public–Private Partnerships: Learning from International Experience* (Edward Elgar Publishing 2005).

Islam S, Mouratidis H and Jürjens J, 'A Framework to Support Alignment of Secure Software Engineering with Legal Regulations' (2011) 10 Software & Systems Modeling.

'ISO/IEC/IEEE Systems and Software Engineering – Architecture Description' (IEEE) <http://ieeexplore.ieee.org/document/6129467/> accessed 11 July 2022.

Jouan P and Hallot P, 'Digital Twin: Research Framework to Support Preventive Conservation Policies' (2020) 9 ISPRS International Journal of Geo-Information.

Katsh ME, *Law in a Digital World* (Oxford University Press 1995).

Katyal NK, 'Digital Architecture as Crime Control' (2003) 112 Yale Law Journal.

Kaur MJ, Mishra VP and Maheshwari P, 'The Convergence of Digital Twin, IoT, and Machine Learning: Transforming Data into Action', *Digital Twin Technologies and Smart Cities* (Springer 2020).

Kersbergen KV and Waarden FV, '"Governance" as a Bridge between Disciplines: Cross-Disciplinary Inspiration Regarding Shifts in Governance and Problems of Governability, Accountability and Legitimacy' (2004) 43 European Journal of Political Research.

Kitchin R, 'Big Data, New Epistemologies and Paradigm Shifts' (2014) 1 Big Data & Society.

Klijn E-H, 'Governance and Governance Networks in Europe: An Assessment of Ten Years of Research on the Theme' (2008) 10 Public Management Review.

Kooiman J, *Governing as Governance* (SAGE Publications Ltd 2003) <https://sk.sagepub.com/books/governing-as-governance> accessed 11 July 2022.

Li J and others, 'Big Data in Tourism Research: A Literature Review' (2018) 68 Tourism Management.

Linkov I and others, 'Governance Strategies for a Sustainable Digital World' (2018) 10 Sustainability.

Lowndes V, Marsh D and Stoker G (eds), *Theory and Methods in Political Science*, 4th edn (Palgrave Macmillan 2018).

Luna-Reyes LF, 'Opportunities and Challenges for Digital Governance in a World of Digital Participation' (2017) 22 Information Polity.

McManus J, 'A Stakeholder Perspective within Software Engineering Projects', *2004 IEEE International Engineering Management Conference (IEEE Cat. No.04CH37574)* (IEEE 2004) <http://ieeexplore.ieee.org/document/1407508/> accessed 11 July 2022.

Moghadam P, Lowe T and Edwards EJ, 'Digital Twin for the Future of Orchard Production Systems', *The Third International Tropical Agriculture Conference (TROPAG 2019)* (MDPI 2020) <https://www.mdpi.com/2504-3900/36/1/92> accessed 11 July 2022.

'OECD Science, Technology and Innovation Outlook 2016' (Organisation for Economic Co-operation and Development (OECD) 2016).

Osborne SP, *Public–Private Partnerships: Theory and Practice in International Perspective*, vol. 19 (Routledge 2000).

Rabinia A and Ghanavati S, 'FOL-Based Approach for Improving Legal-GRL Modeling Framework: A Case for Requirements Engineering of Legal Regulations of Social Media', *2017 IEEE 25th International Requirements Engineering Conference Workshops (REW)* (IEEE 2017) <http://ieeexplore.ieee.org/document/8054856/> accessed 11 July 2022.

Rahmadian E, Feitosa D and Zwitter A, 'A Systematic Literature Review on the Use of Big Data for Sustainable Tourism' (2022) 25 Current Issues in Tourism

Rhodes RA, *Understanding Governance: Policy Networks, Governance, Reflexivity, and Accountability* (Open University 1997).

Rhodes RAW, 'The New Governance: Governing without Government' (1996) 44 Political Studies.

Rhodes RAW, 'Understanding Governance: Ten Years On' (2007) 28 Organization Studies.

Scharpf FW, *Governing in Europe: Effective and Democratic* (Oxford University Press 1999).

Schleich B and others, 'Shaping the Digital Twin for Design and Production Engineering' (2017) 66 CIRP Annals.

Schrotter G and Hürzeler C, 'The Digital Twin of the City of Zurich for Urban Planning' (2020) 88 PFG – Journal of Photogrammetry, Remote Sensing and Geoinformation Science.

Sharp H, Finkelstein A and Galal G, 'Stakeholder Identification in the Requirements Engineering Process', *Proceedings. Tenth International Workshop on Database and Expert Systems Applications. DEXA 99* (IEEE 1999) <http://ieeexplore.ieee.org/document/795198/> accessed 11 July 2022.

Shim C-S and others, 'Development of a Bridge Maintenance System for Prestressed Concrete Bridges Using 3D Digital Twin Model' (2019) 15 Structure and Infrastructure Engineering.

Shokooh S and Nordvik G, 'A Model-Driven Approach for Situational Intelligence & Operational Awareness', *2019 Petroleum and Chemical Industry Conference Europe (PCIC EUROPE)* (IEEE 2019) <https://ieeexplore.ieee.org/document/9011632/> accessed 11 July 2022.

Sreedevi TR and Santosh Kumar MB, 'Digital Twin in Smart Farming: A Categorical Literature Review and Exploring Possibilities in Hydroponics', *2020 Advanced Computing and Communication Technologies for High Performance Applications (ACCTHPA)* (IEEE 2020) <https://ieeexplore.ieee.org/document/9213235/> accessed 11 July 2022.

Szpytko J and Duarte YS, 'Digital Twins Model for Cranes Operating in Container Terminal' (2019) 52 IFAC-PapersOnLine.

Tao F and others, 'Digital Twin-Driven Product Design Framework' (2019) 57 International Journal of Production Research.

Tharma R, Winter R and Eigner M, 'An Approach for the Implementation of the Digital Twin in the Automotive Wiring Harness Field' (2018) <https://www.designsociety.org/publication/40688/AN+APPROACH+FOR+THE+IMPLEMENTATION+OF+THE+DIGITAL+TWIN+IN+THE+AUTOMOTIVE+WIRING+HARNESS+FIELD> accessed 11 July 2022.

Treib O, Bähr H and Falkner G, 'Modes of Governance: Towards a Conceptual Clarification' (2007) 14 Journal of European Public Policy 1.

UNWTO, 'International Recommendations for Tourism Statistics 2008'.

van Heesch U, Avgeriou P and Hilliard R, 'A Documentation Framework for Architecture Decisions' (2012) 85 Journal of Systems and Software 795.

Walters A, 'National Digital Twin Programme' (7 September 2019) <https://www.cdbb.cam.ac.uk/what-we-do/national-digital-twin-programme> accessed 20 July 2022.

Wan L, Nochta T and Schooling JM, 'Developing a City-Level Digital Twin – Propositions and a Case Study', *International Conference on Smart Infrastructure and Construction 2019 (ICSIC)* (ICE Publishing 2019) <https://www.icevirtuallibrary.com/doi/10.1680/icsic.64669.187> accessed 11 July 2022.

Yebenes Serrano J and Zorrilla M, 'A Data Governance Framework for Industry 4.0' (2021) 19 IEEE Latin America Transactions 2130.

Zheng Y, Yang S and Cheng H, 'An Application Framework of Digital Twin and Its Case Study' (2019) 10 Journal of Ambient Intelligence and Humanized Computing 1141.

Zwitter A and Hazenberg J, 'Decentralized Network Governance: Blockchain Technology and the Future of Regulation' (2020) 3 Frontiers in Blockchain 12.

PART III

PRINCIPLE-BASED APPROACHES TO THE GOVERNANCE OF BIG DATA AND AI

5.   Digital transitional justice: unpacking the black box
Christopher K. Lamont and Medlir Mema

INTRODUCTION

Among transitional justice practitioners, Artificial Intelligence (AI) tools are now ubiquitous in truth- and accountability-seeking processes. From the use of forensic analysis in the process of gathering of evidence to the utilization of textual content analysis in and out of the courtroom, advances in machine learning (ML) and AI have arguably increased the number of tools available to governments and the international community for addressing the impunity gap that often bedevils the demands for justice. While there is a growing interest in how technology and digital tools will impact transitional justice in a more general sense,[1] there has been comparatively little work that engages with the specific dilemmas that AI-enabled tools pose for transitional justice, a field that grapples with the legacies of authoritarianism and conflict.

AI tools have transformed governance across many sectors of public policy, and generated a vibrant debate on the ethics and utility of AI for the public good.[2] Yet, when it comes to transitional justice, defined as judicial and non-judicial mechanisms to deal with the legacy of past human rights abuse, there has been relatively little engagement with the digital nexus that produces human rights violations and atrocities, but also opens new spaces for accountability and truth-seeking processes.

Pham and Aronson tell us, 'the proliferation of technologies in transitional justice is inevitable and holds tremendous potential, but also a great deal of risk, for the field.'[3] While Pham and Aronson's special issue on technology and transitional justice in the *International Journal*

---

[1]   Jean-Marie Chenou, Lina P. Chaparro-Martínez and Ana María Mora Rubio, 'Broadening Conceptualizations of Transitional Justice through Using Technology: ICTs in the Context of Justicia Y Paz in Colombia' (2019) 13(1) International Journal of Transitional Justice.

[2]   Andrej Zwitter, 'Big Data Ethics' (2014) 1(2) Big Data & Society.

[3]   Phuong N Pham and Jay D. Aronson, 'Technology and Transitional Justice' (2019) 13 International Journal of Transitional Justice 1, 4.

of Transitional Justice highlighted how digital tools and platforms have proven valuable for practitioners in information gathering, truth seeking and accountability process,[4] the risks of relying on AI tools for decision-making remains to be explored in greater depth. Indeed, many of the significant risks that have been well documented in adjacent literatures, such as in criminal justice scholarship,[5] must also be examined in the context of transitional justice. For example, when it comes to AI tools used for DNA mixture analysis, Karen McGregor Richmond highlights how algorithmic opacity challenges basic due process norms. This is because how a particular tool arrived at an outcome cannot be disclosed in court.[6]

In this chapter it is argued that a growing reliance on AI and ML tools in public policy and governance will dramatically reshape transitional justice practice. The impact of e-governance, digital surveillance, and a wider integration of AI and ML tools into every facet of human life from driverless cars to criminal justice will have on truth seeking and accountability processes is hard to overstate. The digitalization of governance and everyday lives has brought about a dramatic growth in data about us that has outstripped our ability to analyse data using traditional analytic tools.[7] Moreover, transitional justice processes will, out of necessity, engage with a wider range of stakeholders who are involved in the collection and dissemination of Open Source Information (OSI) and will grapple with new questions and dilemmas in already complex post-conflict truth-seeking processes.

---

[4]   Chenou, Chaparro-Martinez and Rubio (n 1); Oriana Bernasconi, Elizabeth Lira and Marcela Ruiz, 'Political Technologies of Memory: Uses and Appropriations of Artefacts that Register and Denounce State Violence' (2019) 13(1) International Journal of Transitional Justice; Michelle E Anderson, 'Community-Based Transitional Justice via the Creation and Consumption of Digitalized Storytelling Archives: A Case Study of Belfast's Prisons Memory Archive' (2019) 13(1) International Journal of Transitional Justice; Tamy Guberek, Velia Muralles and Hannah Alpert-Abrams, '"Irreversible": The Role of Digitization to Repurpose State Records of Repression' (2019) 13(1) International Journal of Transitional Justice.

[5]   Karen McGregor Richmond, 'AI, Machine Learning, and International Criminal Investigations: The Lessons from Forensic Science' (10 November 2020) iCourts Working Paper Series, no. 222.

[6]   ibid. A similar concern is raised by Vyacheslav Polonski, who points out, 'Even small irregularities and biases can produce a measurable difference in the final risk-assessment. The critical issue is that problems like racial bias and structural discrimination are baked into the world around us.' See Vyacheslav Polonski, 'AI is Convicting Criminals and Determining Jail Time, But Is It Fair?' *WEF* (19 November 2018) <https://www.weforum.org/agenda/2018/11/algorithms-court-criminals-jail-time-fair/> accessed 13 April 2022.

[7]   Zwitter (n 2).

The principal question that will be asked here is, how significant are these developments in AI and ML for transitional justice practice? Beyond the practical aspects on the limits and possibilities of big data analysis, early literature on digital technologies emphasized the emancipatory potential of a new digital realm. However, in the past years the emergence of digital norms of 'cyber sovereignty or 'network sovereignty' illustrates how states have proven effective in imposing state control over digital spaces,[8] and have also weaponized digital technologies to surveil populations in a manner that would not have been possible with analogue technologies.

Therefore, before turning to how AI will influence the field of transitional justice, let us explore how a digital spaces framework, drawing upon the ontological spaces introduced by the editors of this volume,[9] can help elucidate some of the challenges AI presents for transitional justice. Following this, there will be an exploration of how an explosion of data and digital governance tools have also shifted how states engage in serious human rights abuses in order to set the stage for a discussion of AI and transitional justice. While it will be acknowledged that AI tools can prove powerful in providing a means to analyse large datasets, it is also the case that algorithmic opacity, and the reproduction in digital spaces of inequalities present in non-digital spaces highlight how there is an urgent need for a growing awareness of the limitations and risks of relying upon AI tools in transitional justice practice.

UNDERSTANDING THE DIGITAL SPACE, DIGITAL GOVERNANCE AND CYBER SOVEREIGNTY

Are digital spaces fundamentally new spaces where social relations negotiated through positions, agencies and scales, are reconstituted in a manner that is detached from physical space? While more emancipatory readings of digital spaces imply greater social agency, a relational understanding of space helps elucidate the complexities of digital spaces,[10] while also providing a means to better understand how AI tools cannot escape social norms in which they are embedded. In short, they can never be neutral. Thus, despite digital spaces being dynamic, these spaces are interwoven with physical spaces in a manner that blurs the line between the public and

---

[8] Oliver P Richmond, 'Peace in Analogue/Digital International Relations' (2020) 32(3) *Global Change, Peace & Security.*

[9] See Introduction.

[10] Yongxuan Fu, 'Towards Relational Spatiality: Space, Relation and Simmel's Modernity' (2021) 56(3) Sociology.

the private, as illustrated by the ubiquity of cell phones, which record their users' physical locations and activities.[11]

Social spaces and dispositions are reconstituted in these digital social spaces where there exists a tension between emancipatory agents that harness digital spaces to unsettle existing power relations, and agents that aim to reproduce within the digital space existing social power relations and inequalities. In regard to the latter, state regulation of internet content, the creation of statist closed digital networks, and governance of intellectual property, are all examples of a move towards digital governmentality, in which algorithmic nudging and digital surveillance mediate governance digital spaces.[12] From this perspective, China's drive for 'cyber sovereignty',[13] *wangluo zhuquan*, which it continues to promote not just domestically but also within international regulatory bodies, can be seen as reproducing analogue social spaces and relations in the digital realm. This should not be confused with digital sovereignty as espoused in the context of the European Union, which seeks to capture both the cyber dimensions' privacy protections and security, and also explores the implications of a broader digital transformation.[14]

Others, both state and non-state actors, are also wrestling with the question of how to apply a fundamental organizing principle of interstate relations such as sovereignty to cyberspace, a 'reality' less conducive to Westphalian dictates. Of particular interest for government officials and international lawyers is whether and how one goes about applying 'the sovereignty and non-intervention principles in relation to states' cyber operations in another state below the threshold of the use of force.'[15] While the answer to the first part of that question was answered in the affirmative by the United Nations Group of Governmental Experts

---

[11]   Aminreza Iranmanesh, and Resmiye Alpar Atun, 'Restricted Spatiality and the Inflation of Digital Space, an Urban Perspective' (2020) 23 Space and Culture 3.

[12]   Romain Badouard, Clément Mabi and Guillaume Sire, 'Beyond "Points of Control": Logics of Digital Governmentality' (2016) 5(3) Internet Policy Review.

[13]   Veni Markovski and Alexey Trepykhalin (2022) Country Focus Report: China Internet-Related Policy Initiatives and Laws, ICANN <https://itp.cdn.icann.org/en/files/government-engagement-ge/ge-010-31jan22-en.pdf> accessed 11 July 2022.

[14]   Julia Pohle and Thorsten Thiel, 'Digital Sovereignty' (2020) 9 Internet Policy Review: Journal of Internet Regulation 4; Justin Sherman 'How Much Cyber Sovereignty is Too Much Cyber Sovereignty?' Council on Foreign Relations (30 October 2019).

[15]   Harriet Moynihan 'The Application of International Law to State Cyberattacks' Chatham House Research Paper (2 December 2019), 5.

in 2013 and 2015,[16] there remains much disagreement and intentional ambiguity regarding the latter.[17]

What is not in question, however, is the fact that states have the capacity to control digital spaces. States, for example, are adopting legislative frameworks that criminalize specific conduct in the digital realm and investing in capabilities that allow for state agencies to exercise greater surveillance of this digital geography, all the while arguing that they are acting in its defence.[18] And, as Gstrein and Zwitter point out, the European Union's General Data Protection Regulation (GDPR) raises troubling questions as to the sustainability of efforts by states to promote their values in respect to human rights in the wider digital space.[19]

Judging by the announcement of plans for e-embassies, e-residence schemes,[20] as well as the interest expressed by local and central governments to monetize their presence in the metaverse, it is unlikely a government-free cyberspace is possible.[21] On the other hand, Kessler and Lenget argue that digital technologies have unsettled understandings of core economic and governance concepts.[22] Here it is argued that a spatial framework provides a means to explore how complex social processes and social relations are reproduced in digital spaces. This in turn helps us better understand how and why states have proven resilient in harnessing digital spaces to reinforce authority, hierarchies, and relationality in the face of algorithmic decision-making. Rather than unsettling governance, digital technologies provide state administrations with vast amounts of data, and the tools to analyse this data. As a result, AI and ML tools are deeply entangled in human rights abuse, truth seeking, and accountability.

---

[16]   ibid.

[17]   See Dan Efrony and Yuval Shany, 'A Rule Book on the Shelf? Tallinn Manual 2.0 on Cyberoperations and Subsequent State Practice' (2018) 112 American Journal of International Law 4, cited in Moynihan (n 15).

[18]   'Foreign Ministers' Communique' G7 Germany 2022 (14 May 2022).

[19]   Oskar Josef Gstrein and Andrej Janko Zwitter, 'Extraterritorial Application of the GDPR: Promoting European Values or Power?' (2021) 10(3) Internet Policy Review: Journal of Internet Regulation <https://policyreview.info/articles/analysis/extraterritorial-application-gdpr-promoting-european-values-or-power> accessed 23 February 2023.

[20]   Oskar Josef Gstrein and Dmitri Kochenov, 'Blockchain and Citizenship: Uneasy Bedfellows' in Oreste Pollicino and Giovanni De Gregorio (eds), *Blockchain and Public Law: Global Challenges in the Era of Decentralisation* (Edward Elgar Publishing 2021).

[21]   Zeyi Yang, 'China's Cities Are Going to the Metaverse—Before They Even Know What It Is' *Protocol* (15 February 2022).

[22]   Oliver Kessler and Marc Lenglet, 'Between Concepts and Thought: Digital Technologies and Temporal Relationality' (2020) 34(3) International Relations.

The Return of the State: Technological Innovation and Digital Harm

Indeed, Dragu and Lupu caution that technological innovation, far from unsettling state control, will lead to greater levels of surveillance and human rights abuse.[23] To be sure, there are multiple ways in which state control can be asserted through the digital space. The first is the periodic shut down of internet services. Often this requires the compliance or co-optation of private internet service providers, as witnessed in Zimbabwe,[24] or Kazakhstan.[25] Alternatively, this could also be achieved through the physical destruction of digital infrastructure, as witnessed in Yemen.[26] However, internet shutdowns are also a rather blunt instrument.

The second pathway for exerting state control over digital spaces is through the governance, regulation and criminalization of undesirable behaviour. While early scholarship on digital international relations emphasized the disruptive and potentially emancipatory aspects of an emergent digital space, more recently we have witnessed states invest significant capabilities in internet governance.[27] The Cyberspace Administration of China (CAC) presides over a vast bureaucratic network that surveys internet content and security.[28] China's long-term and expansive view of the role of technology at home has been laid out in a series of government reports, including its 2017 State Council Notice on the Issuance of the Next Generation Artificial Intelligence Development Plan, which makes clear China's determination to benefit from 'first-mover advantage in the development of AI' with an eye to applying 'innovative AI throughout education, health care, pension, and other urgent needs involving people's livelihood' to ostensibly 'provide for the public personalized, diversified, high-quality services.'[29]

---

[23]   Tiberiu Dragu and Yonatan Lupu, 'Digital Authoritarianism and the Future of Human Rights' (2021) 75(4) International Organization.

[24]   Admire Mare, 'Internet Shutdowns in Africa State-Ordered Internet Shutdowns and Digital Authoritarianism in Zimbabwe' (2020) 14 International Journal of Communication.

[25]   Pavlina Pavlova, 'How Kazakhstan's Control of Information Can Turn into a Regime Weakness', *Open Global Rights* (31 January 2022) <https://www.openglobalrights.org/how-kazakhstans-control-of-information-can-turn-into-a-regime-weakness/index.cfm> accessed 10 March 2022.

[26]   'Internet Returns to Yemen after Air Raid Caused Four-Day Outage', *Al Jazeera* (25 January 2022).

[27]   Richmond, 'Peace in Analogue/Digital International Relations' (n 8).

[28]   Xia Qiang, 'Chinese Digital Authoritarianism and Its Global Impact' (2021) Digital Activism and Authoritarian Adaptation in the Middle East, 35.

[29]   China State Council Notice on the Issuance of the Next Generation Artificial Intelligence Development Plan (8 July 2017) <https://digichina.

Moreover, AI technologies have significantly increased state capacity for surveillance and are widely used across both liberal democracies and non-democratic regimes.[30] Moreover, AI technologies have significantly increased state capacity for surveillance and are widely used across both liberal democracies and non-democratic regimes.[31] There is now evidence that the speed and scope of this increased state capacity have greatly accelerated since 2020[32] as governments around the world have used the threat of Covid-19 to adapt new technologies leading to a retrenchment of data privacy protections.[33] These developments come against concerns regarding possible government abuse of this data or data breaches, and also about mounting evidence that, as governments employ more technology-based solutions, large segments of populations risk being denied access to health-saving information and products due to tech-related failures or biases embedded in technologies such as facial recognition.[34]

Third, as discussed earlier, there is the emergent concept, or norm, of cyber sovereignty, which applies norms of state sovereignty to the digital space and sees the digital realm that is one which is divided among, and governed by, national state authorities.[35] Far from being transnational and freewheeling, the digital space is one that is increasingly tamed by the state.

---

stanford.edu/work/full-translation-chinas-new-generation-artificial-intelligence-development-plan-2017/> accessed 23 February 2023.

[30]   Steven Feldstein, 'The Global Expansion of AI Surveillance', *CEIP* (17 September 2019) <https://carnegieendowment.org/2019/09/17/global-expansion-of-ai-surveillance-pub-79847> accessed 24 January 2022.

[31]   ibid.

[32]   Irene Poetranto and Lotus Ruan, 'Intrusive Surveillance after the Coronavirus Pandemic' *CEIP* (19 October 2021).

[33]   Sharifah Sekalala and others, 'Big Data, Technology, Artificial Intelligence, and the Right to Health' (2020) 22(2) Health and Human Rights Journal.

[34]   Deborah Brown and Amos Toh, 'Technology is Enabling Surveillance, Inequality During the Pandemic', Human Rights Watch (4 March 2021) <https://www.hrw.org/news/2021/03/04/technology-enabling-surveillance-inequality-during-pandemic> accessed 11 July 2022.

[35]   Michael Schmitt, *Tallinn Manual 2.0 on the International Law Applicable to Cyber Operations* (2nd edn) (Cambridge University Press 2020). For a more in-depth discussion on this issue, Moynihan (2019) recommends GP Corn, 'Cyber National Security: Navigating Gray-Zone Challenges in and through Cyberspace' in WS Williams and CM Ford (eds), *Complex Battlespaces: The Law of Armed Conflict and the Dynamics of Modern Warfare* (Oxford University Press 2019). The AJIL Symposium on 'Sovereignty, Cyberspace and Tallinn Manual 2.0', *AJIL Unbound* (2017), contains several articles debating the normative character of sovereignty in the cyber context.

The latter two ways in which the state can harness the digital space to harm human rights are particularly concerning as they demonstrate how AI and ML tools have made possible state surveillance and governance of a vast digital space. They also highlight how norms of network sovereignty or cyber sovereignty, which aim to create a digital world that is divided into administrative units controlled by nation-states, in a manner analogous to territorial sovereignty, have gained increasing acceptance.

AI-enabled systems are crucial to imposing governance on the vast digital spaces that have emerged in the past decades. The sheer amount of data generated by internet users would make it impossible to conduct any meaningful surveillance in a purely analogue form. AI surveillance systems are deployed in 75 countries, according to data compiled from 2017 to 2019, yet little is understood as to the human rights consequences of AI-enabled decision-making in the realm of governance or criminal justice.[36]

In fact, there are two distinct pathways to human rights violations that AI-enabled tools open:

1. *Deliberate acts* in which policymakers use AI-enabled systems, such as facial recognition tools or the 'kill cloud',[37] to carry out an act targeting a specific individual or individuals.
2. *Unintentional acts* in which AI-enabled systems produce unintended, or unexpected, outputs that result in harm. An example of this would be racial, gender or socio-economic biases in AI decision-making.

Finally, Richmond argues that algorithmic opacity has raised the question of courts being left unable to access answers to questions such as why and how a specific AI tool arrived at a specific outcome.[38] This has the potential to loosen due process and human rights protections within liberal democratic states. Indeed, United Nations Human Rights Commissioner Michelle Bachelet observed the following in relation to predictive policing:

> In many cases, artificial intelligence-based predictions appear arbitrary and unjust, in addition to exacerbating the systemic discrimination embedded in society. These outcomes are not inevitable, but they are already occurring—and their incidence and severity will grow, unless we act.[39]

---

[36] Feldstein (n 30).
[37] For more information on the 'kill cloud' see <https://www.disruptionlab.org/the-kill-cloud> accessed 23 February 2023.
[38] Richmond, 'AI, Machine Learning, and International Criminal Investigations' (n 5).
[39] Michelle Bachelet, 'Human Rights in a New Era', United Nations High Commission for Human Rights (NYC, 14 November 2018) <https://www.ohc

As digital spaces continue to grow and become increasingly intertwined with AI-enabled tools that facilitate decision-making in almost every aspect of governance, the analytic challenge posed to future human rights investigations, truth commissions and criminal justice trial processes is also likely to grow.

HOW DIGITAL SPACES MATTER FOR TRANSITIONAL JUSTICE

As digital spaces continue to generate ever more massive amounts of data, or 'big data', AI-enabled systems have become increasingly important for both analysing data and making decisions based on this data. In short, AI governance involves machines recognizing and solving problems that are often too complex for humans to address. As the previous sections have demonstrated, governance, public policy and criminal justice are all being impacted by advancements in AI. Transitional justice is no different.

To be sure, AI decision-making and machine learning raises dual questions of *autonomy* and *transparency*. Autonomy from AI refers to the extent to which human decision-makers will delegate problem solving to AI systems. The question here is not whether there is a human in the loop of decision-making, as so often debates over lethal autonomous weapons systems (LAWS) have at their focus.[40] Rather, the question is what human decision-making means in a context where AI systems are providing decision-makers with information that points them in the direction of a specific decision, a decision that decision-makers are unlikely to question on the basis of the information that is provided.

In the United States, the use of AI among legal professionals is ubiquitous. In 2018, the *National Law Journal* identified more than fifty companies selling AI tools to the legal industry.[41] Indeed, common research platforms

---

hr.org/FR/NewsEvents/Pages/DisplayNews.aspx?NewsID=23874&LangID=E> accessed 8 March 2022.

[40] Steven C. Roach and Amy E. Eckert, *Moral Responsibility in Twenty-First-Century Warfare: Just War Theory and the Ethical Challenges of Autonomous Weapons Systems* (SUNY Press 2020); see also, Jai Galliott, Duncan MacIntosh and Jens David Ohlin, *Lethal Autonomous Weapons: Re-Examining the Law and Ethics of Robotic Warfare* (Oxford University Press 2021). Also see Chapter 16 in this volume.

[41] Keith Mullen, 'Artificial Intelligence: Shiny Object? Speeding Train?' American Bar Association (2018) <https://www.americanbar.org/groups/real_property_trust_estate/publications/ereport/rpte-ereport-fall-2018/artificial-intelligence/> accessed 18 June 2022.

used by lawyers, such as *Westlaw* and *LexisNexis*, have built-in AI tools to provide users with results that are most relevant to a given search, litigation analytics and answers to legal questions, among other applications.[42]

In 2021, the G7 issued a joint statement recognizing the centrality of the legal profession to upholding the rule of law and issued the following recommendations:

1. Where legal technology is implemented, incentivize the adoption of technology in their jurisdictions where it guarantees an anthropocentric approach and leads to better legal services for the public and more effective access to justice.
2. Require that legal technology used be in full compliance with fundamental rights, such as the rights to the protection of personal data, to a fair trial and to an effective remedy, and the principles of proportionality and subsidiarity and by adopting specific measures for the needs of the disadvantages groups, underpinned by the principles of compliance, transparency, lawfulness, competence and capability.
3. Guarantee the neutrality of data gathered and processed, as well as of algorithms and artificial intelligence used in all legal technology and data processing.[43]

The first recommendation seeks to guarantee an anthropocentric approach to judicial processes, a perennial concern that predates the latest AI-related developments. As Karpen and Senova (2021) suggest, 'the experience of courts can be confusing, intimidating or even aggravating. Court users are often overwhelmed because their needs are secondary to procedural or organizational needs. This perception is even more acute for court users with special or additional needs, such as those with past trauma, cognitive impairment or socio-cultural barriers.'[44] Given these circumstances, the G7's statement, albeit vaguely articulated and even though it does not take into account adversarial interests of different actors within the justice system, is an important reminder that the implementation of technologies should be human- rather than technology-centric.

The second recommendation notes that the technology must reinforce fundamental rights and should pay greater attention to privacy, personal

---

[42]   ibid.
[43]   'G7 Bar Leaders Call upon Governments to Take Action on Lawyers at Risk, Lawtech and Climate Change' The Law Society (11 June 2021).
[44]   IO Karpen and M Senova, 'Designing for Trust: Role and Benefits of Human-Centered Design in the Legal System' (2021) 12(3) International Journal of Court Admin, 1.

data and the right to a fair trial. This recommendation is in line with a series of recent official statements and white papers, released often in conjunction with pleas for a more ethical use of technology in ensuring the efficiency of the court. In 2018, for example, the European Council adopted the *European Ethical Charter on the Use of Artificial Intelligence in Judicial Systems*, insisting among others that, 'the design and implementation of artificial intelligence tools and services are compatible with fundamental rights', and that, in the interest of transparency, impartiality and fairness, courts should '[m]ake data processing methods accessible and understandable, authorise external audit.'[45]

The third point addresses algorithmic bias, which has been observed to discriminate individuals based on race, gender and other socio-economic factors, and which, unfortunately, is unlikely to be resolved satisfactorily soon.[46] At the heart of the matter is a two-fold and inter-related concern. First, the more we learn about the concept of algorithmic bias or 'set-up' bias, as we refer to it later in the chapter, the more we understand that there are serious systemic and societal obstacles that must be overcome, in order to ensure a bias free algorithm.

And second, even if states establish the necessary safeguards, it is important to note that states are not the only actors that collect, process and use personal data. Private actors too engage in practices analogous to mass state surveillance in digital authoritarian societies for the purpose of extracting and selling data collected from individuals.[47]

Despite these risks, transitional justice practice has been quick to adopt AI and ML tools in truth-seeking and accountability processes. The next section will explore how AI and ML have become integrated into transitional justice work in recent years.

AI: A TRANSITIONAL JUSTICE PRACTITIONER'S TOOL?

Dubberley and others demonstrate how human rights researchers can access a wide range of digital technologies and sources to collect evidence

---

[45]   'European Ethical Charter on the Use of Artificial Intelligence in Judicial Systems and their environment', adopted at the 31st plenary meeting of the European Commission for The Efficiency of Justice (CEPEJ) (Strasbourg, 3–4 December 2018).

[46]   Megan Garcia, 'Racist in the Machine' (2016) 33(4) World Policy Journal.

[47]   Shoshana Zuboff, *The Age of Surveillance Capitalism: The Fight for a Human Future at the New Frontier of Power* (Profile Books 2019).

of human rights abuse through OSI.[48] Indeed, in recent conflicts, from Myanmar to Nagorno-Karabakh and Ukraine, OSI has provided a powerful means of documenting events transpiring on the ground in real-time.[49] Moreover, in the context of the war in Ukraine, a US-based tech company offered Kyiv facial recognition services that utilize images on social networking sites to provide a means to identify individuals through image recognition in a manner claimed to be easier than using fingerprints.[50]

These developments have raised concerns over the veracity of information collected from digital sources, and the accuracy of AI-enabled decision-making. However, there is an additional challenge that relates to the amount of information that is now accessible to researchers. As the volume of digital media accessible to researchers has increased, AI and ML tools have proven critically important to allow researchers to unlock this data. AI and ML tools have been identified as tools that can aid truth commissions in analysing large amounts of data that would require significant investment and cost to do in an analogue manner. Gavshon's exploration of the potential for AI to make a positive contribution to transitional justice processes emphasizes that there is simply more content relating to human rights abuses than can be analysed for judicial or policy purposes.[51] According to Gavshon, the promise of AI in transitional justice lies in providing a set of tools that would allow us to analyse, visualise and put to use, a vast amount of data that otherwise would be lost.[52] In a similar vein, Aronson argues that AI can assist human rights groups in analysing large amounts of video data, but only if those working in technology understand the context in which human rights practitioners work and are attuned to their needs.[53]

---

[48]   Sam Dubberley, Alexa Koenig and Daragh Murray, *Digital Witness: Using Open Source Information for Human Rights Investigation, Documentation, and Accountability* (Oxford University Press 2020).

[49]   Sebastien Roblin, 'What Open Source Evidence Tells Us about the Nagorno–Karabakh War' *Forbes Magazine* (23 October 2020) <https://www.forbes.com/sites/sebastienroblin/2020/10/23/what-open-source-evidence-tells-us-about-the-nagorno-karabakh-war/> accessed 13 March 2022.

[50]   'Exclusive: Ukraine Has Started Using Clearview AI's Facial Recognition during War', *Reuters* (13 March 2022) <https://www.reuters.com/technology/exclusive-ukraine-has-started-using-clearview-ais-facial-recognition-during-war-2022-03-13/> accessed 8 March 2022.

[51]   Daniela Gavshon and Erol Gorur, 'Information Overload: How Technology Can Help Convert Raw Data into Rich Information for Transitional Justice Processes' (2019) 13(1) International Journal of Transitional Justice.

[52]   ibid.

[53]   Jay D. Aronson 'Computer Vision and Machine Learning for Human Rights Video Analysis: Case Studies, Possibilities, Concerns, and Limitations: Human Rights Video Analysis' (2018) 43(4) Law & Social Inquiry.

More specifically, AI-enabled tools are used by transitional justice practitioners for:

- forensic analysis
- analysis and identification of content on digital media
- visual content and facial recognition
- textual content analysis.

In the following sections, AI and ML tools for transitional justice applications will be explored in more detail in the context of forensic analysis and digital content analysis, which will include both visual and textual analysis.

Forensic Analysis

Transitional justice processes often require the reconstruction of material evidence based on partial physical and DNA traces. Often coming years after violence has taken place, such fragmentary evidence can be very difficult, if not impossible to obtain. According to Thurzo and others, recent ground-breaking developments in AI-enabled technology such as three-dimensional convolutional neural networks (3D CNN)—a Deep Learning algorithm that 'can take in an input image, assign importance (learnable weights and biases) to various aspects/objects in the image, and differentiate one from the other'[54]—hold out the promise of revolutionizing medical forensic analysis.

By applying these new technologies to traditional areas of interest in forensic analysis, including '(1) sex determination, (2) biological age estimation, (3) 3D cephalometric landmark annotation, (4) growth vectors prediction, and (5) facial soft-tissue estimation from the skull and vice versa', Thurzo and his co-authors conclude, '3D CNN application can be a watershed moment in forensic medicine, leading to unprecedented improvement of forensic analysis workflows based on 3D neural networks.'[55]

Another recent advancement in forensic medicine allows investigators to detect small traces of DNA. However, these highly sensitive tools often detect batches of DNA from multiple individuals that require DNA

---

[54] Andrej Thurzo and others, 'Use of Advanced Artificial Intelligence in Forensic Medicine, Forensic Anthropology and Clinical Anatomy' (2021) 9(11) Healthcare, 1545.

[55] ibid 1546.

mixture interpretation. Here, AI tools have been developed to provide ML-based methods to 'deconvolute' DNA mixtures that would not be possible to do in analogue. However, often these highly sensitive tools detect batches of DNA from multiple individuals that require DNA mixture interpretation. This is perhaps one of the more controversial applications of AI tools. As Richmond points out,

> The software makes its changes incredibly rapidly according to its own indecipherable logic. It can derive fantastically efficient results, but we can't say how it did so. It acts like a black box that takes inputs and gives outputs, but whose inner workings are invisible.[56]

As a result, it is impossible in many cases to interrogate how an AI arrived at a specific conclusion. These concerns, of course, are not unique to AI application in forensic analysis, but they do raise important questions about the wisdom of relying on opaque algorithmic reasoning to make important decisions about accountability and culpability with respect to crimes that may have been committed in the past.

The concern with 'algorithmic opacity' has spurred others to focus on finding ways to explain the reasoning or decision-making process.[57] Approaches such as the 'expert system', for example, 'follow a predefined rule base' that allow them to 'provide an explanation of the reasoning for the conclusions obtained. This enables an outside entity to criticize the reasoning process and to highlight any flaws there might be with the reasoning used.'[58] The drawback to such systems, in the context of an ongoing conflict or the immediate aftermath of violence, is that they don't do well with an open set, where 'if–then' propositions are difficult to construct fully and with reasonable certainty, nor do they perform well in circumstances where data aggregation continues to rise and new variables are introduced into the model.

'Algorithmic opacity', however, is not the only concern when it comes to large data processing, including data derived by way of medical forensics. Set-up bias or bias in algorithmic decision-making has become a topic of intense debate about the likely risks it may pose

---

[56]   Karen McGregor Richmond, 'AI Could Revolutionise DNA Evidence – but Right Now We Can't Trust the Machines' *The Conversation* (29 January 2020) <http://theconversation.com/ai-could-revolutionise-dna-evidence-but-right-now-we-cant-trust-the-machines-129927> accessed 17 January 2022.

[57]   Faye Mitchell, 'The use of Artificial Intelligence in digital forensics: An introduction' (2014) Digital Evidence and Electronic Signature Law Review 7.

[58]   ibid 36–37.

for criminal justice.[59] Numerous studies have revealed how 'flawed, racially fraught and sometimes unlawful practices ... will lead to flawed, biased, and unlawful predictions'[60] that only serve to further perpetuate systemic inequalities and harmful behaviour. Furthermore, as Milaninia points out, biased ML models may lead to 'devaluing under-reported crimes, especially [sexual and gender-based crimes] SGBC. Models that are based on that data set carry over those biases and have the potential to hinder the Prosecutor's ability to detect, investigate and "seek the truth" for marginalized crimes.'[61]

However, advocates of AI use in forensic analysis caution that the alternative to AI is not any less suspect to both bias as well as related limitations. If anything, given the inherent limitations in processing power and the deleterious effects that fatigue and subjectivity have on human judgement, it is not surprising that some believe '[i]mplementation of artificial intelligence can limit all these mentioned sources of possible bias. Machine learning works based on models that mimic neurons in the brain and can learn from experiences and solve complex problems.' One simple but important illustration of this limitation is the challenge associated with training 'forensic experts ... on thousands of skulls of all possible ethnicities',[62] a task that would present little difficulty for a deep learning algorithm.

Digital Media, and Audio-Visual Content Analysis

AI and machine learning tools can play an important role in the identification, processing and analysis of digital audio-visual media content.[63] The growth in the impact of AI-enabled technology in this area is commensurate with the growth in the availability of digital technologies and devices, which by virtue of their ubiquity have become extremely valuable sources

---

[59] Richmond, 'AI, Machine Learning, and International Criminal Investigations' (n 5). See also Nema Milaninia, 'Biases in Machine Learning Models and Big Data Analytics: The International Criminal and Humanitarian Law Implications' (28 January 2021) International Review of the Red Cross.

[60] Rashida Richardson, Jason M. Schultz and Kate Crawford, 'Dirty Data, Bad Predictions: How Civil Rights Violations Impact Police Data, Predictive Policing Systems, and Justice' (2019) 94 New York University Law Review, 192.

[61] Milaninia (n 59).

[62] Thurzo and others (n 54) 1549.

[63] Esther Shein, 'Machine Learning, Biased Models, and Finding the Truth' *The Linux Foundation* (27 November 2018) <https://www.linuxfoundation.jp/blog/2018/11/machine-learning-biased-models-and-finding-the-truth/> accessed 15 May 2022.

of information and evidence related to the commission of various international crimes. AI-enabled 'digital technologies provide new openings for human rights advocates, including non-governmental organizations (NGOs) such as Amnesty International and Human Rights Watch, to identify, expose, verify and document human rights violations.'[64]

While much of this technology is in its incipient stage, transitional justice processes stand to benefit immensely by 'the application of AI and machine learning tools for specific tasks. For example, there is interest in technologies that could improve identification of missing persons, such as AI-based facial recognition and natural language processing for name matching.'[65] These tools can be used at all stages of a conflict to 'assess damage to civilian infrastructure, patterns of population displacement, viability of food crops, or the degree of weapon contamination (unexploded ordnance).'[66]

Civil society groups with limited direct on the ground access have also been able to identify and document cluster munitions in conflicts in Syria, Yemen and Ukraine to mention just a few, by turning to crowd-sourced photographs and videos sourced from social media to document alleged atrocities. In the case of Yemen, the Global Legal Action Network (GLAN) sought to establish that illegal cluster munitions, or more specifically BLU-63, were being used by the Saudi-led coalition in the conflict. In this context, a machine learning tool was able to sift through vast amounts of video footage (5.9 billion frames of video) to retrieve images that contained cluster munitions.[67]

Similarly, AI is playing a crucial role in gathering evidence of the illicit use of cluster munitions in the war in Syria.[68] Through 3-D printed models of cluster munitions, algorithms are being trained to sort through

---

[64]   Grigorios Kalliatakis and others, 'Exploring Object-Centric and Scene-Centric CNN Features and Their Complementarity for Human Rights Violations Recognition in Images' (2019) IEEE Access PP 99.

[65]   'Digital Technologies and War: Artificial Intelligence and Machine Learning in Armed Conflict: A Human-Centered Approach' (2020) 102(913) International Review of the Red Cross, 463.

[66]   ibid.

[67]   Karen Hao, 'Human Rights Activists Want to Use AI to Help Prove War Crimes in Court' *MIT Technology Review* (25 June 2020) <https://www.techno logyreview.com/2020/06/25/1004466/ai-could-help-human-rights-activists-prove-war-crimes/> accessed 25 January 2022.

[68]   Raja Abdulrahim 'AI Emerges as Crucial Tool for Groups Seeking Justice for Syria War Crimes' *WSJ Online* (13 February 2021) <www.wsj. com/articles/ai-emerges-as-crucial-tool-for-groups-seeking-justice-for-syria-war-crimes-11613228401> accessed 22 June 2022.

massive amounts of photograph and video data to extract instances of cluster munition use.[69] Companies like Benetech now provide AI tools for the United Nations International, Impartial, and Independent Mechanism on Syrian Accountability to analyse an estimated 4 million videos for evidence of war crimes.[70]

Following the onset of the conflict between Russia and Ukraine, Bellingcat—'an independent international collective of researchers, investigators and citizen journalists using open-source and social media investigation to probe a variety of subjects'—began mapping and documenting any available evidence connecting Russian soldiers to harm against Ukrainian civilians.[71] While Bellingcat utilizes an army of open-source volunteer researchers as part of their Global Authentication Project, both the underlying technology used to produce the TimeMap as well as any future attempts to process that information will rely on machine learning tools to sift through the evidence.[72]

Finally, the ability to analyse audio from gunshot recordings can be of great assistance in criminal investigations when little other evidence is available. By training on a variety of audio recordings, ML tools under development have shown promising signs in terms of identifying both the weapon type used in a crime as well as its usage patterns.[73] Raponi and others, for example, have been able to experiment with a new technique that is able to 'identify the category, calibre, and model of the gun.'[74] In another study, Morehead and others, using Raspberry Pi 3 Model B+ to train one-dimensional and two-dimensional convolutional neural networks on a sound database, achieved an even higher success rate than Raponi, with the

---

[69]   ibid.

[70]   'JusticeAI: Turning Conflict Data into Actionable Evidence' *Benetech* (2021) <https://benetech.org/lab/ethical-ai-to-promote-justice/> accessed 25 May 2022.

[71]   'About' *Bellingcat* (2022) <https://www.bellingcat.com/about/> accessed 23 June 2022.

[72]   'Hospitals Bombed and Apartments Destroyed: Mapping Incidents of Civilian Harm in Ukraine' *Bellingcat* (2022) <https://www.bellingcat.com/news/2022/03/17/hospitals-bombed-and-apartments-destroyed-mapping-incidents-of-civilian-harm-in-ukraine/> accessed 20 March 2022.

[73]   Mohamed Elhoseny, Mohamed Abdel-Basset and K Shankar, 'Artificial Intelligence Applications for Smart Societies' in Mohamed Elhoseny, K Shankar and Mohamed Abdel-Basset (eds), *Artificial Intelligence Applications for Smart Societies: Recent Advances* (Springer Nature 2021). See also, Rajesh Baliram Singh, Hanqi Zhuang and Jeet Kiran Pawani, 'Data Collection, Modelling, and Classification for Gunshot and Gunshot-like Audio Events: A Case Study' Sensors (2021).

[74]   Simone Raponi, Gabriele Oligeri and Isra M. Ali, 'Sound of Guns: Digital Forensics of Gun Audio Samples Meets Artificial Intelligence' (2022) 81 Multimedia Tools and Applications.

added benefit of designing 'a scalable gunshot detection system that is low in cost and high in accuracy.'[75]

Still, despite significant progress across several areas, concerns remain about the ability of these tools to deliver reliable results outside the lab, as well as the ethical and practical dilemmas associated with their implementation. While one expects concerns associated with the former to abate over time, progress on the latter is likely to prove slower and more challenging in the long term. In fact, some of these challenges, as discussed previously, are just as likely to prove disruptive for societal cohesion or further entrench gender, racial, religious or ethnic discriminatory practices.

For example, AI has played a role in both the creation and detection of media disinformation, digitally altered images, and digital hate speech.[76] While AI offers powerful tools for big data analysis and to 'map local attitudes toward conflict and analyse emerging tensions, alliances, and divisions',[77] the identification and removal of hate speech from social media platforms has proven to be a more difficult task. Perhaps the best-known example from a conflict setting is that of Myanmar, where Facebook's social media platform was used to disseminate hate speech.[78] While this has raised the question of corporate liability for tech companies that allow their platforms to be used to incite crimes against humanity,[79] AI tools to automate censorship have proven largely unable to effectively remove such content.[80]

---

[75]   Alex Morehead and others, 'Low-Cost Gunshot Detection using Deep Learning on the Raspberry Pi' (2019) IEEE International Conference on Big Data (Big Data), 3038.

[76]   Michael Yankoski, Walter Scheirer and Tim Weninger, 'Meme Warfare: AI Countermeasures to Disinformation Should Focus on Popular, Not Perfect, Fakes' *Bulletin of the Atomic Scientists* (13 May 2021) <https://thebulletin.org/premium/2021-05/meme-warfare-ai-countermeasures-to-disinformation-should-focus-on-popular-not-perfect-fakes/> accessed 23 April 2022.

[77]   Eleonore Pauwels, 'Artificial Intelligence and Data Capture Technologies in Violence and Conflict Prevention' *Global Center on Cooperative Security* (September 2020), 7.

[78]   Christina Fink, 'Dangerous Speech, Anti-Muslim Violence, and Facebook in Myanmar' (2018) 71(15) Journal of International Affairs; Jenifer Whitten-Woodring and others, 'Poison If You Don't Know How to Use It: Facebook, Democracy, and Human Rights in Myanmar' (2020) 25(3) The International Journal of Press/Politics 407.

[79]   Neriah Yu, 'The "Weaponization" of Facebook in Myanmar: A Case for Corporate Criminal Liability' (2019) 71 Hastings Law Journal 3.

[80]   Will Knight, 'Three Problems with Facebook's Plan to Kill Hate Speech Using AI' *MIT Technology Review* (12 April 2018) <https://www.technologyreview.com/2018/04/12/143927/three-problems-with-facebooks-plan-to-kill-hate-speech-using-ai/> accessed 17 February 2022.

The dual nature of challenges and risks associated with recent techno-logical innovation is also evident in the discussion surrounding deep fakes or the ever-increasing ubiquity and sophistication of false content, most of it driven by advances in the same kind of technology that holds the promise of documenting and analysing large amounts of data that may prove vital for holding perpetrators of crime accountable. The fear is that, '[d]emanded by the public, content hosts and digital platforms will engage in a spiralling arms race between ever more sophisticated misinformation techniques and content moderation, with investigators left behind.'[81]

In fact, misinformation, disinformation and hate speech (MDH) has become a source of great concern for international non-governmental organizations (INGOs) and international organizations (IOs). While the term MDH may refer to more general categories, ICRC, for example, has expressed grave concerns about MDH's impact on 'such as internally displaced persons, migrants, detainees and minority groups, as well as humanitarian staff and volunteers', who now find themselves at 'a new or increased risk of humanitarian consequences.'[82]

Then there are the legal and ethical risks associated with collection and processing of large amounts of data generally required for AI and machine learning tools to make a difference on the ground. Some of these, including 'data protection, privacy, human rights, accountability and ensuring human involvement in decisions with significant consequences for people's lives and livelihoods',[83] have already been discussed previ-ously, and, in effect, go beyond questions related to transitional justice processes. Nevertheless, one could argue that, given the sensitivity of the circumstances surrounding a conflict and/or post-conflict situation, these considerations become more acute.

Textual Content Analysis

One of the most widely used applications of AI has been in the field of textual content analysis. Increasingly, due to advances in natural language processing (NLP), textual analysis has moved beyond merely describ-ing and analysing a text, to also understanding and interpreting content

---

[81] Scott Edwards, 'Open Source Investigations for Human Rights: Current in Future Challenges' in Sam Dubberley and others (eds), *Digital Witness: Using Open Source Information for Human Rights Investigation, Documentation, and Accountability* (Oxford University Press 2020), 104.

[82] 'Humanitarian operations, the spread of harmful information and data pro-tection' (2020) 102 International Review of the Red Cross 913, 28.

[83] 'Digital technologies and war' (n 65) 470.

expressed in natural language. As Lee and others point out, 'Deep NLP, which comes with AI systems such as IBM Watson, Amazon AWS Lex and Salesforce Einstein, uses both sentence structure and context of the text to provide a deeper understanding of the language. This allows such AI systems to correctly interpret 'my nose is running' as a symptom of an illness.'[84]

Textual content analysis predates the advent of AI-enabled content analysis systems, with researchers turning to both manual and 'computer-aided approach[es] ... to automate, at least partially, the coding analysis.'[85] However, ever-increasing digitization and the use of various algorithmic tools, including 'traditional statistical models, indices, or scoring systems that are used as decision tools', have set the stage for the deployment of machine learning algorithms that 'essentially work on their own to process data and discover optimal mathematical relationships between them.'[86]

To deliver such nuanced results, AI-enabled textual analysis makes use of a variety of approaches, including a rule-based approach or the expert system, which was described earlier, as well as a more sophisticated data analysis approach.[87] According to Campbell, the data analysis approach, '[which] involves a subset of machine learning, looks for patterns in large bodies of data. It finds relationships and correlations, from which it can draw conclusions and provide services. This is the kind of AI that underlies products such as translation software, natural language processing, autonomous vehicles, and some document review software.'[88]

There are a number of advantages offered by a data analysis approach. This is especially the case for a number of tasks related to the gathering, processing and evaluation of evidence, which are of particular utility for the legal profession. One aspect of law where the impact of AI is visible, is online dispute resolution. Here, AI tools enable interested parties to fill out online forms associated with a given legal procedure. Finally, and somewhat controversially, AI has been used in courtrooms to assist judges to determine the likelihood of recidivistic behaviour of a

---

[84]   Linda Lee and others, 'Making Sense of Text: Artificial Intelligence-Enabled Content Analysis' (2020) 54 European Journal of Marketing 3, 619.

[85]   ibid 616.

[86]   Cary Coglianese, Ben Dor, and Lavi M, 'AI in Adjudication and Administration' (2021) 86 Brooklyn Law Review 3, 795–796.

[87]   Ray W Campbell, 'Artificial Intelligence in the Courtroom: The Delivery of Justice in the Age of Machine Learning' (2020) 18 Colorado Technology Law Journal 2.

[88]   Campbell (n 87) 327.

particular defendant. Given the large number of documents accompanying any trial procedure whether at a domestic, hybrid or international tribunal, the need for 'analys[ing], manipulat[ing] and understand[ing] complex content such as natural language' will only increase.[89]

As in other cases, the track record of AI-enabled textual content analysis is mixed. Several studies have shown, for example, that, 'where AI has proven useful is the field of legal research.'[90] Among the benefits of letting AI perform this task include its ability to process a large amount of data, at a faster rate, without needing rest. And yet, there are concerns about the over-reliance of AI on the size and content of previously collected data, as well as the ability of AI-enabled data-processing software to produce consistent results, with researchers in some cases pointing out that at times, 'the search results were relevant but different; in other instances, the software returned irrelevant or incorrect results.'[91]

Due to such limitations, some have suggested that a better method going forward is one that combines 'computational and manual methods throughout the content analysis process.'[92] Lee and others turn that argument on its head by suggesting that advances in AI in the field of NLP, allow us to 'offer the benefits of both manual and computer-aided approaches', with the implication being that AI fuses both approaches, rather than being found only in the latter.[93]

And yet, few would disagree with Campbell, who sees emerging technologies as enhancing human capacity and capabilities, and who, nonetheless, considers unthinkable the prospect of granting 'legal rights and responsibilities to impersonal artificial questions.'[94] Until such questions are resolved, researchers and policy makers will continue to tap into the seemingly endless applications of textual content analysis, including the use of natural language processing as well as image recognition software to make the case for the admissibility of handwritten (court) documents during legal proceedings.[95]

---

[89] Lee and others (n 84) 616.

[90] Campbell (n 87).

[91] ibid.

[92] Seth C. Lewis, Rodrigo Zamith and Alfred Hermida, 'Content Analysis in an Era of Big Data: A Hybrid Approach to Computational and Manual Methods' (2013) 57 Journal of Broadcasting & Electronic Media 1, 34.

[93] Lee and others (n 77).

[94] Campbell (n 87) 327.

[95] Sargur N Srihari, 'Individuality of Handwriting' (2002) 47 Journal of Forensic Sciences 4.

CONCLUSIONS

This chapter has demonstrated how AI is both transforming governance and justice practice. On the one hand, the impact of AI on governance has been clearly transformative. It has opened up new possibilities for digital governance, but also digital authoritarianism. On the other hand, AI offers a set of tools that can contribute to accountability efforts and potentially unlock new tools for data analysis. Yet, at the same time, these tools are plagued by problems of opacity and algorithmic bias. What then does this mean for digital transitional justice going forward?

Part of the reason why there has not been a sustained discussion on this pivotal question among transitional justice practitioners is that there has been a tendency to bundle AI into broader discussions of technology or digital transformations in the field. To be sure, these transformations are immense and go far beyond the scope of paradigmatic transitions. As noted earlier in this chapter, concepts such as cyber sovereignty, digital sovereignty and distinct visions of governance of digital spaces are now being advanced by actors such as China, the United States and the European Union, to name a few examples.

Another reason for a relative absence of engagement with the question of what these digital transformations mean for transitional justice is that the pace and scope of technological innovation has been both rapid and broad. Advancements in AI, such as deep neural networks, have transformed AI systems from systems that once required significant human input, as seen in earlier generations of AI, to systems that rely on evolutionary optimization to create more sophisticated deep learning architectures that are achieved without any direct human input. This deep learning creates a black box around decision-making because it is designed to solve problems without human input. As deep learning is non-linear, there are limits to explaining an AI's output decision. Although the work is ongoing on increasing the transparency of these more sophisticated deep learning architectures, a high degree of transparency, or insight into how the system works is likely to only become more difficult to achieve as these systems become more complex and less human-dependent. This will only amplify the challenge of algorithmic opacity.

Indeed, as we have illustrated, algorithmic opacity is already posing significant challenges in relation to criminal justice proceedings as AI and ML-enabled forensic analysis tools are more frequently relied upon in criminal trials. Moreover, Open Source Information and the dramatic expansion of digital media spaces also pose emerging dilemmas regarding disinformation in digital spaces, and the reliance on AI and ML tools in collecting information from such spaces raises questions about how much power these tools will wield over these digital spaces. In addition to this, states have also proven resilient in governance of digital spaces as AI and ML tools open doors to new means of surveillance that were hitherto impossible to conceive of in analogue. All of the above highlight how digital spaces are dramatically reconfiguring not just transitional justice practices, but also governance more broadly.

AI and ML-enabled systems are now used across a variety of fields from software development and engineering to strategic decision-making in business and public policy, to criminal justice, policing and armed conflict. From safe-city initiatives that deploy AI to monitor human movement through facial recognition technology and the use of AI in marketing, to the use of facial recognition technology in lethal autonomous weapons, AI is increasingly central to everyday social interactions, governance and conflict.[96] A greater awareness of the increasingly central role of these technologies in governance, and their applications in the justice sector, will serve to help transitional justice practice adapt to the need for truth commissions, and other transitional justice mechanisms, to untangle webs of digital harm and algorithmic decision-making in truth-seeking and accountability processes.

BIBLIOGRAPHY

Abdulrahim R, 'AI Emerges as Crucial Tool for Groups Seeking Justice for Syria War Crimes' *WSJ Online* (13 February 2021) <www.wsj.com/articles/ai-emerges-as-crucial-tool-for-groups-seeking-justice-for-syria-war-crimes-11613228401> accessed 22 June 2022.

'About' *Bellingcat* (2022) <https://www.bellingcat.com/about/> accessed 23 June 2022.

'AJIL Symposium on "Sovereignty, Cyberspace and Tallinn Manual 2.0"' *AJIL Unbound* (2017).

Akselrod Olga, 'ACLU News & Commentary' *ACLU* (NYC, 13 July 2021) https://www.aclu.org/news/privacy-technology/how-artificial-intelligence-can-deepen-racial-and-economic-inequities/> accessed 8 March 2022.

Anderson ME, 'Community-Based Transitional Justice via the Creation and Consumption of Digitalized Storytelling Archives: A Case Study of Belfast's Prisons Memory Archive' (2019) 13(1) International Journal of Transitional Justice.

Aronson JD, 'Computer Vision and Machine Learning for Human Rights Video Analysis: Case Studies, Possibilities, Concerns, and Limitations: Human Rights Video Analysis' (2018) 43(4) Law & Social Inquiry: Journal of the American Bar Foundation.

---

[96] Zwitter (n 2).

Bachelet M, 'Human Rights in a New Era' *United Nations High Commission for Human Rights* (14 November 2018) <https://www.ohchr.org/FR/NewsEvents/Pages/DisplayNews.aspx?NewsID=23874&LangID=E> accessed 8 March 2022.

Badouard R, Clément M and Guillaume S, 'Beyond "Points of Control": Logics of Digital Governmentality' (2016) 5(3) Internet Policy Review.

Bernasconi O, Elizabeth L and Marcela R, 'Political Technologies of Memory: Uses and Appropriations of Artefacts that Register and Denounce State Violence' (2019) 13(1) International Journal of Transitional Justice.

Brown D and Amos T, 'Technology is Enabling Surveillance, Inequality during the Pandemic' Human Rights Watch (4 March 2021) <https://www.hrw.org/news/2021/03/04/technology-enabling-surveillance-inequality-during-pandemic> accessed 11 July 2022.

Campbell RW, 'Artificial Intelligence in the Courtroom: The Delivery of Justice in the Age of Machine Learning' (2020) 18 Colorado Technology Law Journal 2.

Chenou JM, Chaparro-Martínez LP and Rubio AMM, 'Broadening Conceptualizations of Transitional Justice through Using Technology: ICTs in the Context of Justicia Y Paz in Colombia' (2019) 13(1) International Journal of Transitional Justice.

China State Council Notice on the Issuance of the Next Generation Artificial Intelligence Development Plan (8 July 2017), translated and adapted into English from the original by Graham Webster and others, *New America* <https://www.newamerica.org/cybersecurity-initiative/digichina/blog/full-translation-chinas-new-generation-artificial-intelligence-development-plan-2017/> accessed 11 July 2022.

Coglianese C, Dor B and Lavi M, 'AI in Adjudication and Administration' (2021) 86 Brooklyn Law Review 3.

Corn GP, 'Cyber National Security: Navigating Gray-Zone Challenges in and through Cyberspace' in WS Williams and CM Ford (eds), *Complex Battlespaces: The Law of Armed Conflict and the Dynamics of Modern Warfare* (Oxford University Press 2019).

'Digital Technologies and War: Artificial Intelligence and Machine Learning in Armed Conflict: A Human-Centered Approach' (2020) 102 International Review of the Red Cross.

Dragu T and Lupu Y, 'Digital Authoritarianism and the Future of Human Rights' (2021) 75(4) International Organization.

Dubberley S, Koenig A and Murray D, *Digital Witness: Using Open Source Information for Human Rights Investigation, Documentation, and Accountability* (Oxford University Press 2020).

Edwards S, 'Open Source Investigations for Human Rights: Current in Future Challenges' in Sam Dubberley and others (eds), *Digital Witness: Using Open Source Information for Human Rights Investigation, Documentation, and Accountability* (Oxford University Press 2020).

Efrony D and Shany Y, 'A Rule Book on the Shelf? Tallinn Manual 2.0 on Cyberoperations and Subsequent State Practice' (2018) 112 American Journal of International Law 4.

Elhoseny M, Abdel-Basset M and Shankar K, 'Artificial Intelligence Applications for Smart Societies' in Mohamed Elhoseny and others (eds), *Artificial Intelligence Applications for Smart Societies: Recent Advances* (Springer Nature 2021).

'European Ethical Charter on the Use of Artificial Intelligence in Judicial Systems and their environment' Adopted at the 31st plenary meeting of the

European Commission for The Efficiency of Justice (CEPEJ) (Strasbourg, 3–4 December 2018) <https://rm.coe.int/ethical-charter-en-for-publication-4-decem ber-2018/16808f699c> accessed 15 June 2022.

'Exclusive: Ukraine Has Started Using Clearview AI's Facial Recognition during War', *Reuters* (13 March 2022) <https://www.reuters.com/technology/exclusive-ukraine-has-started-using-clearview-ais-facial-recognition-during-war-2022-03-13/> accessed 8 March 2022.

Feldstein S, 'The Global Expansion of AI Surveillance', *CEIP* (17 September 2019) <https://carnegieendowment.org/2019/09/17/global-expansion-of-ai-sur veillance-pub-79847> accessed 24 January 2022.

Fink C, 'Dangerous Speech, Anti-Muslim Violence, and Facebook in Myanmar' (2018) 71(15) Journal of International Affairs.

'Foreign Ministers' Communique' G7 Germany 2022 (14 May 2022) <https://www.mofa.go.jp/mofaj/files/100344183.pdf> accessed 13 June 2022.

Fu Y, 'Towards Relational Spatiality: Space, Relation and Simmel's Modernity' (2021) 56(3) Sociology.

'G7 Bar Leaders Call upon Governments to Take Action on Lawyers at Risk, Lawtech and Climate Change' *The Law Society* (11 June 2021) <https://www.lawsociety.org.uk/en/topics/international/g7-bar-leaders-call-on-governments-to-take-action-on-lawyers-at-risk-lawtech-and-climate-change> accessed 12 June 2022).

Galliott J, MacIntosh D and Ohlin JD, *Lethal Autonomous Weapons: Re-Examining the Law and Ethics of Robotic Warfare* (Oxford University Press 2021).

Garcia M, 'Racist in the Machine' (2016) 33(4) World Policy Journal.

Gavshon D, 'How New Technology Can Help Advocates Pursue Transitional Justice' (1 July 2019) <https://blog.oup.com/2019/07/how-new-technology-help-advocates-pursue-transitional-justice/> accessed 10 March 2022.

Gavshon D and Gorur E, 'Information Overload: How Technology Can Help Convert Raw Data into Rich Information for Transitional Justice Processes' (2019) 13(1) International Journal of Transitional Justice.

Gstrein OJ and Kochenov D, 'Blockchain and Citizenship: Uneasy Bedfellows' in O Pollicino and G De Gregorio (eds), *Blockchain and Public Law: Global Challenges in the Era of Decentralisation* (Edward Elgar Publishing 2021).

Gstrein OJ and Zwitter AJ, 'Extraterritorial Application of the GDPR: Promoting European Values or Power?' (2021) 10(3) Internet Policy Review: Journal of Internet Regulation <https://policyreview.info/articles/analysis/extraterritorial-application-gdpr-promoting-european-values-or-power> accessed 23 February 2023.

Guberek T, Velia M and Hannah A, '"Irreversible": The Role of Digitization to Repurpose State Records of Repression' (2019) 13(1) International Journal of Transitional Justice.

Hao K, 'Human Rights Activists Want To Use AI to Help Prove War Crimes in Court' *MIT Technology Review* (25 June 2020) https://www.technologyrevi ew.com/2020/06/25/1004466/ai-could-help-human-rights-activists-prove-war-crimes/> accessed 25 January 2022.

Helbing D and others, 'Will Democracy Survive Big Data and Artificial Intelligence?' *Scientific American* (25 February 2017) https://www.scientificamerican.com/article/will-democracy-survive-big-data-and-artificial-intelligence/> accessed 25 January 2022.

'Hospitals Bombed and Apartments Destroyed: Mapping Incidents of Civilian Harm in Ukraine' *Bellingcat* (2022) <https://www.bellingcat.com/news/2022/03/17/hospitals-bombed-and-apartments-destroyed-mapping-incide nts-of-civilian-harm-in-ukraine/> accessed 20 March 2022.

'Humanitarian Operations, the Spread of Harmful Information and Data Protection' (2020) 102 International Review of the Red Cross 913.

'Internet Returns to Yemen after Air Raid Caused Four-Day Outage' *Al Jazeera* (25 January 2022) <www.aljazeera.com/news/2022/1/25/yemens-internet-returns-after-airstrike-causes-4-day-blackout> accessed 5 March 2022.

Iranmanesh A and Resmiye A, 'Restricted Spatiality and the Inflation of Digital Space, an Urban Perspective' (2020) 23(3) Space and Culture.

'JusticeAI: Turning Conflict Data into Actionable Evidence' *Benetech* (2021) <https://benetech.org/lab/ethical-ai-to-promote-justice/> accessed 25 May 2022.

Kalliatakis G and others, 'Exploring Object-Centric and Scene-Centric CNN Features and Their Complementarity for Human Rights Violations Recognition in Images' (2019) IEEE Access PP 99.

Karpen IO and Senova M, 'Designing for Trust: Role and Benefits of Human-Centered Design in the Legal System' (2021) 12(3) International Journal of Court Admin.

Kessler O and Lenglet M, 'Between Concepts and Thought: Digital Technologies and Temporal Relationality' (2020) 34(3) International Relations.

Knight W, 'Three Problems with Facebook's Plan to Kill Hate Speech Using AI' *MIT Technology Review* (12 April 2018) <https://www.technologyreview.com/2018/04/12/143927/three-problems-with-facebooks-plan-to-kill-hate-spee ch-using-ai/> accessed 17 February 2022.

Lee L and others, 'Making Sense of Text: Artificial Intelligence-Enabled Content Analysis' (2020) 54 European Journal of Marketing 3.

Lewis SC, Rodrigo Z and Hermida A, 'Content Analysis in an Era of Big Data: A Hybrid Approach to Computational and Manual Methods' (2013) 57 Journal of Broadcasting & Electronic Media 1.

Mare A, 'Internet Shutdowns in Africa: State-Ordered Internet Shutdowns and Digital Authoritarianism in Zimbabwe' (2020) 14 International Journal of Communication.

Markovski V and Trepykhalin A, Country Focus Report: China Internet-Related Policy Initiatives and Laws (2022) ICANN <https://itp.cdn.icann.org/en/files/government-engagement-ge/ge-010-31jan22-en.pdf> accessed 11 July 2022.

Miikkulainen R and others, 'Evolving Deep Neural Networks' in R Kozma and others (eds), *Artificial Intelligence in the Age of Neural Networks and Brain Computing* (AP 2019).

Milaninia N, 'Biases in Machine Learning Models and Big Data Analytics: The International Criminal and Humanitarian Law Implications' (28 January 2021) International Review of the Red Cross.

Mitchell F, 'The Use of Artificial Intelligence in Digital Forensics: An Introduction' (2014) Digital Evidence and Electronic Signature Law Review 7.

Montavon G, Samek W and Müller KR, 'Methods for Interpreting and Understanding Deep Neural Networks' (2018) 73 Digital Signal Processing.

Morehead A and others, 'Low-Cost Gunshot Detection Using Deep Learning on the Raspberry Pi' (2019) IEEE International Conference on Big Data.

Moynihan H 'The Application of International Law to State Cyberattacks' Chatham House Research Paper (2 December 2019) <https://www.chathamhouse.

org/2019/12/application-international-law-state-cyberattacks/2-application-so vereignty-cyberspace> accessed 19 June 2022.

Mullen K, 'Artificial Intelligence: Shiny Object? Speeding Train?' American Bar Association (2018) <https://www.americanbar.org/groups/real_property_trust_ estate/publications/ereport/rpte-ereport-fall-2018/artificial-intelligence/> acc-essed 18 June 2022.

'OSI-Supported Website Promotes Burma Rights and Democracy' OSI (2005) *Open Society Foundations* <https://www.opensocietyfoundations.org/news room/osi-supported-website-promotes-burma-rights-and-democracy> accessed 8 March 2022.

Pauwels E, 'Artificial Intelligence and Data Capture Technologies in Violence and Conflict Prevention' *Global Centre on Cooperative Security* (September 2020).

Pavlova P, 'How Kazakhstan's Control of Information Can Turn into a Regime Weakness' *OpenGlobalRights* (31 January 2022) <https://www.openglobal rights.org/how-kazakhstans-control-of-information-can-turn-into-a-regime-weakness/index.cfm> accessed 10 March 2022.

Pham PN and Aronson JD, 'Technology and Transitional Justice' (2019) 13(1) International Journal of Transitional Justice.

Poetranto I and Ruan L, 'Intrusive Surveillance after the Coronavirus Pandemic' *Carnegie Endowment for International Peace* (19 October 2021) <https://carne gieendowment.org/2021/10/19/intrusive-surveillance-after-coronavirus-pandem ic-pub-85509> accessed 11 July 2022.

Pohle J and Thiel T, 'Digital Sovereignty' (2020) 9 Internet Policy Review: Journal of Internet Regulation 4.

Polonski V, 'AI is Convicting Criminals and Determining Jail Time, But Is It Fair?' *WEF* (19 November 2018) <https://www.weforum.org/agenda/2018/11/ algorithms-court-criminals-jail-time-fair/> accessed 13 April 2022.

Qiang X, 'Chinese Digital Authoritarianism and Its Global Impact' (2021) *Digital Activism and Authoritarian Adaptation in the Middle East*.

Raponi S, Oligeri G and Ali IM, 'Sound of guns: digital forensics of gun audio samples meets artificial intelligence' (2022) 81 Multimedia Tools and Applications.

Richardson R, Schultz JM and Crawford K, 'Dirty Data, Bad Predictions: How Civil Rights Violations Impact Police Data, Predictive Policing Systems, and Justice' (2019) 94 New York University Law Review 192.

Richmond KM, 'AI Could Revolutionise DNA Evidence – but Right Now We Can't Trust the Machines' *The Conversation* (29 January 2020) <http://thecon versation.com/ai-could-revolutionise-dna-evidence-but-right-now-we-cant-trust-the-machines-129927> accessed 17 January 2022.

Richmond KM, 'AI, Machine Learning, and International Criminal Investigations: The Lessons from Forensic Science' (10 November 2020) iCourts Working Paper Series, no. 222.

Richmond OP, 'Peace in Analogue/Digital International Relations' (2020) 32(3) Global Change, Peace & Security.

Roach SC and Eckert AE, *Moral Responsibility in Twenty-First-Century Warfare: Just War Theory and the Ethical Challenges of Autonomous Weapons Systems* (SUNY Press 2020).

Roblin S, 'What Open Source Evidence Tells Us about the Nagorno–Karabakh War' *Forbes Magazine* (23 October 2020) <https://www.forbes.com/sites/

sebastienroblin/2020/10/23/what-open-source-evidence-tells-us-about-the-nagorno-karabakh-war/> accessed 13 March 2022.

Schmitt M, *Tallinn Manual 2.0 on the International Law Applicable to Cyber Operations* (2nd edn) (Cambridge University Press 2020).

Sekalala S and others, 'Big Data, Technology, Artificial Intelligence, and the Right to Health' (2020) 22(2) Health and Human Rights Journal.

Shein E, 'Machine Learning, Biased Models, and Finding the Truth' *The Linux Foundation* (27 November 2018) <https://www.linuxfoundation.jp/blog/2018/11/machine-learning-biased-models-and-finding-the-truth/> accessed 15 May 2022.

Sherman J, 'How Much Cyber Sovereignty is Too Much Cyber Sovereignty?' *Council on Foreign Relations* (30 October 2019) <https://www.cfr.org/blog/how-much-cyber-sovereignty-too-much-cyber-sovereignty> accessed 7 July 2022.

Singh BR, Zhuang H and Pawani JK, 'Data Collection, Modelling, and Classification for Gunshot and Gunshot-like Audio Events: A Case Study' *Sensors* (2021).

Srihari SN, 'Individuality of Handwriting' (2002) 47 Journal of Forensic Sciences 4.

Thurzo A and others, 'Use of Advanced Artificial Intelligence in Forensic Medicine, Forensic Anthropology and Clinical Anatomy' (2021) 9(11) Healthcare.

Veda, 'Are AI Algorithms Misogynist? Will Tech Go Against Women?' *Analytics Insight* (24 February 2022) <https://www.analyticsinsight.net/are-ai-algorithms-misogynist-will-tech-go-against-women/> 13 March 2022.

Whitten-Woodring J, and others, 'Poison If You Don't Know How To Use It: Facebook, Democracy, and Human Rights in Myanmar' (2020) 25 The International Journal of Press/Politics 407.

Wise J, 'The DIY Intelligence Analysts Feasting on Ukraine' *New Yorker* (8 March 2022) <https://nymag.com/intelligencer/2022/03/the-osint-analysts-feasting-on-ukraine.html> accessed 10 March 2022.

Yang Z, 'China's Cities Are Going to the Metaverse—Before They Even Know What It Is' *Protocol* (15 February 2022) <https://www.protocol.com/china/metaverse-chinese-local-government> accessed 20 June 2022.

Yankoski M, Scheirer W and Weninger T, 'Meme Warfare: AI Countermeasures to Disinformation Should Focus on Popular, Not Perfect, Fakes' *Bulletin of the Atomic Scientists* (13 May 2021) <https://thebulletin.org/premium/2021-05/meme-warfare-ai-countermeasures-to-disinformation-should-focus-on-popular-not-perfect-fakes/> accessed 23 April 2022.

Yue N, 'The "Weaponization" of Facebook in Myanmar: A Case for Corporate Criminal Liability' (2019) 71 Hastings Law Journal 3.

Zuboff S, *The Age of Surveillance Capitalism: The Fight for a Human Future at the New Frontier of Power* (Profile Books 2019).

Zwitter A, 'Big Data Ethics' (2014) 1(2) Big Data & Society.

6. Autonomous weaponry and IR theory: conflict and cooperation in the Age of AI
Amelia Hadfield and Alex Leveringhaus

I. INTRODUCTION

For the past decade or so, academia has witnessed a remarkable level of interest in the topic of 'lethal autonomous weapons systems' (LAWS).[1] It is not always clear how LAWS are to be defined, and how they may – or may not – differ from existing weapons systems. In most discussions, the lowest common denominator is that LAWS have the capacity to engage targets by producing a kinetic effect without the direct supervision by a human operator. Their ability to navigate within their overall operating environment, increasingly depends on existing and emerging AI-programming techniques. The systems, their environments, and indeed the nature and consequences of achieving their intended target raise intriguing and challenging questions regarding the nature of machine autonomy, and the definition of AI.

In defining LAWS, a clear distinction first needs to be draw between these and other types of automated weaponry, which have existed for a while and have generally not been deemed overly problematic.[2] In addition to issues of classification, it is worthwhile noting that LAWS have thus far been studied for the most part from an ethical and legal angle in the social sciences. Arguments in favour of LAWS usually contain a strong ethical component, namely that the automation of kill chains via existing or emerging AI-programming techniques (i.e., the specific processes that lead to the application of force to a target) can, under certain circumstances, reduce the overall number of casualties within a given

---

[1] For a state-of-the-art overview of how this field has developed, see J Gailliot, D MacIntosh and JD Ohlin (eds), *Lethal Autonomous Weapons: Re-Examining the Law and Ethics of Robotic Warfare* (Oxford University Press 2021).

[2] As the existence of automated weapons systems, such as missile defence systems, attests, the automation of weaponry is currently not illegal in and of itself. For a comprehensive overview of the treatment of weaponry in the law of armed conflict, see WA Boothby, *Weapons and the Law of Armed Conflict*, 2nd edn (Oxford University Press 2016).

conflict situation, as well as reduce the prospect of war crimes.[3] Indeed, some contributors appear to suggest that mere automation does not go far enough, and that machines should be given some decision-making to make kill decisions.[4] Equally, arguments against LAWS often maintain that machines should not, insofar as their kinetic effect (i.e., the form of energy arising from an object by reason of its own motion) materially impacts humans, have the capacity to make decisions over life and death. Further, the automation of kill chains – that is, the procedural steps that underpin an attack on a target (at the most basic level, identify the target, track it, engage it, destroy it – see below) – is incompatible with a concern for human dignity.[5] For some contributors to the debate, legal and ethical questions intersect with issues including a proposed legal ban, or at least a moratorium, on the further development of LAWS.[6] There is, for instance, a vibrant discussion among international lawyers within the UN system on whether LAWS could be banned outright under the Convention on Certain Conventional Weapons (CCW), or merely limited, or indeed left to develop on the basis of technology and political imperatives.

Notwithstanding the importance of these trenchant ethical and legal issues in the discussion of any emerging form of weapons technology, this chapter employs a slightly different lens regarding LAWS – a lens that, in our view, has not yet been sufficiently explored in relation to the topic. Setting aside ethical and legal concerns, this chapter gauges the implications of IR theory (IRT) on the understanding of the potential impact of LAWS on armed conflict, and the relations between states.[7] Conversely, we also ask what the emergence of technologically sophisticated weapons systems such as LAWS tell us about IRT itself. In particular we are interested in the capacity of different schools within IRT to adequately

---

3   R Arkin, *Governing Behaviour in Lethal Autonomous Robots* (Taylor & Francis 2009).

4   R Arkin, 'The Case for Ethical Autonomy in Unmanned Systems' (2010) 9 *Journal of Military Ethics*.

5   See A Leveringhaus, 'Morally Repugnant Weaponry? Ethical Responses to the Prospect of Autonomous Weapons' in S Voeneky and others (eds), *The Cambridge Handbook of Responsible Artificial Intelligence* (Cambridge University Press 2022).

6   New York Times, 'U.N. Expert Calls for Halt in Military Robot Development', <https://www.nytimes.com/2013/05/31/world/europe/united-natio ns-armed-robots.html> accessed 20 October 2022.

7   For an attempt to assess the impact of LAWS on armed conflict, see A Leveringhaus, 'Autonomous Weapons and the Future of Armed Conflict' in Gailliot and others (eds) (n 1). This chapter, however, has little to say about relations between states as such.

theorise the potential impact of LAWS on armed conflict. Moreover, we seek to interrogate the overall use and consequences of LAWS against the backdrop of some seminal IRT principles, including power, anarchy and state-based cooperation.

Naturally, IRT is a broad subject area, and we cannot do justice to all its nuances within the confines of a single chapter; our contribution is designed to augment the various conceptual and experiential themes arising from the text as a whole. Accordingly, we focus on three mainstream IRTs: realism, liberalism, and the range of ideational and critique-bearing modes inherent in constructivism. At their core, these theories – each of which represents a broad church of outlooks – seek to understand and explain how states interact with each other under conditions of anarchy. The term 'anarchy' merely denotes that there is no world government that either enforces legislation against states or acts to preserve the peace among them. Different IRTs therefore aim to explain to what extent conflict and cooperation between states is possible under these circumstances. As explored in more detail below, Realists typically argue that the prospect for cooperation is generally limited, though not impossible, and that conflict remains an ever-present reality for states. The degree to which LAWS contribute to the ability of states to contribute to – and possibly benefit from – the conditioning effects of anarchy, as well as the resulting systemic impacts is the chief question here. Liberals are more optimistic and believe that cooperation between states, communities and individuals is both possible and – in the interest of states – preferable to keep transaction costs low. Constructivists, by contrast, do not believe that the conditions of anarchy are endogenously set in international affairs. Rather, anarchy, as the famous phrase goes, is what states make of it. Taken together, a brief survey of how each of these theories would approach LAWS will give us a good indication of how LAWS are likely to facilitate conflict or cooperation under conditions of anarchy.

Before applying the theoretical lens of key IRT schools and principles to LAWS, however, we must first tackle some conceptual and definitional issues regarding LAWS itself. It depends on the definition of LAWS whether one views their existence as either giving rise to new international challenges or merely highlighting already-existing dilemmas. This includes a consideration of the interface between *automation and autonomy* (in terms of specific types of weaponry, the implications of end-to-end kill chains) on the one side, and *automation and adaptation* (reviewing forms of adaptive capacity) on the other side. We turn now to these issues before tackling the interface of IRT and LAWS in detail.

II.   FROM AUTOMATION TO AUTONOMY: JUST WHAT IS NEW ABOUT LAWS?

A.   Means to Harm: Defining Weaponry

As noted earlier, LAWS can carry out certain tasks without direct supervision by a human operator. However, this capacity does not appear sufficient to conceptually separate them from automated weapons. To use a crude example, a landmine, an utterly primitive device, also destroys a 'target' without a human operator having to do anything else apart from placing it somewhere in the ground. So, the capacity to function without a human operator cannot be the only distinguishing feature of LAWS. But what other features are relevant here? And how do these features relate to existing systems that are not classified as LAWS, notwithstanding their capacity to operate independently?[8]

To answer these two questions, it is useful to begin with some brief reflections on weaponry as such. After all, the concept of 'machine autonomy' also features in many debates on emerging technologies that do not directly relate to the military or armed conflict, such as – perhaps most prominently – the debate on autonomous driving for civilian purposes.[9] To be categorised as a weapon, we argue that an artefact needs to be *specifically designed* to have a purposefully harmful effect.[10] Many things can have harmful effects. Cars can cause horrible accidents, for example. The point about weapons, however, is that they have been explicitly designed to be harmful, and thus either to deter potential opponents by signalling a state's military strength, and especially the state's capacity to threaten extremely harmful retaliation if aggressed, or to directly inflict harm upon another party in case of an actual conflict. Cars, meanwhile, are primarily designed as a means of transportation, not as a means to harm others. In this respect, we are agnostic about wider debates on the concept of harm and the ethicality of harming. Harm can be morally justified or morally prohibited, depending on the circumstances. Likewise, we argue that a variety of actors can be harmed, most obviously human individuals. But reasoning analogically, we also contend that states as entities can be materially harmed in terms of their territorial integrity, political sovereignty and

---

[8]   For more detailed versions of the arguments in this part of the chapter, see A Leveringhaus, *Ethics and Autonomous Weapons* (Palgrave 2016), chapter 2.

[9]   See M Maurer and others (eds), *Autonomous Driving: Technical, Legal, and Social Aspects* (Springer Nature 2016).

[10]   See J Forge, *Designed to Kill: The Case against Weapons Research* (Springer 2013).

financial capacity. Regardless of how these issues are resolved in detail, weapons, for the purpose of this chapter, are defined by their (primarily?) intended capacity to cause harm to individuals, communities and states.

The weapons under examination here are designed to inflict harm upon other parties through the creation of a specific kinetic effect. Two brief points regarding kinetic effects are in order. First, there are concerns about the emergence of weapons that inflict harm *without* the creation of a kinetic effect and are thus harder to grasp conceptually. Cyber weapons seem to fall into this category. But given that the cyber domain is quite different from other domains of defence (air, land, sea, space), we will set the issue of cyber weaponry aside here.

Second, kinetic harm can either be intended or come about as a side-effect of another act. For example, a robot specifically programmed to shoot at enemy combatants would cause a kinetic effect that is intended by its programmer. That being said, LAWS can also be lethal in the sense that their main kinetic effect has lethal side-effects within the weapon's overall operating environment. In such cases, the main effect of LAWS is harmful yet non-lethal, while side-effects are lethal. The distinction between lethal kinetic effects and lethal kinetic side-effects is commonly overlooked in discussions of LAWS. As such, the category itself widens, with LAWS used for a wide range of objectives, and solely to cause loss of life directly and intentionally via a kinetic effect. Sometimes loss of life is incidental, or unintentional, or even apposite to LAWS' main task. As a result, the analysis below can be applied to a range of types of LAWS, rather than only a specific type, with important repercussions for both conflictual and cooperative relations between states, regardless of the nature of the lethality of their effects.

B.   Automating Kill Chains

What separates LAWS from other types of weaponry is their ability to inflict harm on another party without supervision or further guidance by a human operator. In the literature, a common distinction is drawn between *in-the-loop systems* (where a human operator directs the weapon), *on-the-loop systems* (where a human operator is on standby and can interact with the weapon or interfere in its performance of a task, for example by stopping it) and *out-of-the-loop systems* (where the weapon operates independently of an operator, once it has been deployed).[11] LAWS are mostly

---

[11]   P Sharre, *Army of None: Autonomous Weapons and the Future of War* (W. W. Norton 2019).

likely to be *out-of-the-loop systems* or *on-the-loop systems*. (Naturally, an *in-the-loop* system cannot be autonomous, by definition. This is because the operator remotely controls the system in real time.) But even after distinguishing between *in-*, *on-* and *out*-of-the-loop systems, further considerations need to be brought into play to make sense of LAWS. For example, even an *out-of-the-loop system* still requires mission programming by a human programmer. Machines do not simply 'do' things. Usually they 'do' things humans assign them to do. This is especially true in the context of the military, where the weapon will have to be programmed with a particular task and deployed on a specific mission. Why would any military have an interest in simply deploying a LAWS without assigning a mission to it? More broadly, any autonomous system – weapon or not – depends on governing software, which is written by human programmers.[12] Without it, the system could not function.[13]

This fact also explains why it is useful to speak of an autonomous weapons *system*, rather than just an autonomous weapon. The concept of a system has two main connotations in the context of LAWS, namely, (1) that various functions and parts of the weapon are integrated and work cumulatively towards the fulfilment of a specific task, and (2) that the fulfilment of that same task occurs within certain parameters, commonly set by the governing software. The activity of LAWS and their behaviour within their operating environment are therefore not random. Rather, they are intentionally directed towards the fulfilment of an assigned task, usually (though not always) the application of force to a target, implemented via kinetic effect.[14]

---

[12]   To clarify, for the purpose of this chapter, a governing software is simply a software programme that contains the necessary commands for the system to function. The technical question in the debate on LAWS is whether the software programme can be written in such a way that the deployment of LAWS, (1) is legal under the laws of armed conflict, and (2) meets minimal ethical standards. Further, there are at least two categories of programmers in the case of LAWS: (1) those who write the governing software (engineers), and (2) those who use the existing software to programme the weapon with its specific mission parameters (mission programmers). For a strong argument that the engineers are not responsible for the 'doings' of LAWS, see R Sparrow, 'Killer Robots' (2007) 24 *Journal of Applied Philosophy*. Controversially, Sparrow seems to think that mission programmers cannot be held responsible, either.

[13]   See A Whitfield, *Robotics: A Very Short Introduction* (Oxford University Press 2012).

[14]   Autonomous weaponry can potentially have non-kinetic effects. Autonomous devices could be used to inflict psychological harms or spread disinformation. We leave these non-kinetic harms aside here because they are unlikely to be intentionally lethal. That said, non-kinetic harms could have unintended lethal side-effects.

Once the focus shifts towards systems and their constituent functions, it becomes possible to narrow down the concept of LAWS even further. Within the LAWS debate, the critical issue is the automatisation of kill chains – that is, the processes that lead to the application of force to a target:

1. identification of the target,
2. fixing the location of the target,
3. tracking the target,
4. targeting via the appropriate payload,
5. engaging the target, and
6. evaluating the effects of the application of kinetic force.

Some or all stages of such a kill chain might be automated, but this does not mean that all functions of LAWS are necessarily automated or that their automation is always morally or legally problematic. To illustrate this point, one could image an Unmanned Aerial Vehicle (UAV) where a human pilot controls the flight functions that are crucial to the initial stages of the kill chain while an automated process carries out the final stages. Similarly, one could imagine that an UAV has an automated sensor suite that collects weather data to optimise flight performance. Automation of this function is surely not as controversial as the automation of a kill chain. The challenge is that this analysis could also be applied to already-existing automated systems, such as missile defence systems. Identifying the dividing line between automation and autonomy is not a simple task; some views maintain that machine autonomy consists in the intrinsic ability of a machine to make decisions.[15] Others query the nature of the decisions themselves, and the parameters within which they take place.[16] After all, the kinds of decision that a machine can possibly make are thus far not wholly devoid of human direction and thus not truly autonomous. Rather, machine decision-making is *heteronomous* – that is, determined by the governing software itself programmed by a human programmer. At least in the context of LAWS, this is true of the overall mission programming, which is determined by the programmer. In the actual performance of the task forming part of the mission, LAWS might exhibit behaviour that is not determined by a programmer but emerges from within the system.

Arguably, the current focus on the lethality in the debate on autonomous weapons obscures the variety of tasks and effects these weapons might have.

[15] N Sharkey, 'Saying "no" to lethal autonomous targeting' (2010) 9 Journal of Military Ethics.

[16] Leveringhaus (n 8).

C.   Automation and Adaptation

With the dividing line between automation and machine autonomy still vague, we argue that it is best to view LAWS as possessing more adaptive responses to changes within their operating environment than conventional automated weaponry. This could be the result of machine learning, for example allowing LAWS to operate in open and less structured environments than the closed (and thus predictable) environments suitable for automated machines. From a purely technological perspective, it is unclear whether such a degree of machine autonomy can really be achieved. But at least theoretically, it is not unreasonable to imagine a weapon operating with significant adaptive capacity.

The adaptive capacity of LAWS has important repercussions for their predictability. Possibly counter-intuitively, *autonomous* machines are usually *less predictable* in their responses than their *automated* counterparts. True, we can expect them to operate within the parameters set by their programming. But these will be much looser than in the case of automated weapons. To illustrate the point, suppose an autonomous UAV is programmed to destroy enemy helicopters. While the UAV will destroy enemy helicopters, we do not know when and how it does so. Nor will we necessarily know which helicopter (if it encounters several) it might engage. This is because as an autonomous machine the UAV can adapt its behaviour to often highly particular circumstances. Having learned from previous missions, it might 'decide' that enemy helicopter$_{Green}$ is too hard to reach, and thus move to a different area, where it targets enemy helicopter$_{Blue}$. An automated UAV, by contrast, may only engage enemy helicopters according to more rigid criteria: if they fly within certain geographical coordinates, at a certain speed and at a certain time. Hence, it would likely target enemy helicopter$_{Green}$, even if doing so was unlikely to be successful. Automation in the more conservative sense leads to a more predictable response, though it does little to successfully intercept enemy helicopters that do not meet the programming criteria, such as enemy helicopter$_{Blue}$: for example, operating just outside the assigned coordinates, or at a higher speed, or at night. Depending on its programming, an autonomous UAV might not have any problems in adjusting to these changed parameters, and in this case, track and engage enemy helicopters wherever and whenever necessary.

This partly illustrates the potential attractiveness of LAWS to militaries. Despite less overall predictability, autonomous machines are more capable of adaptation than automated ones. This is particularly key as the ability to sustain a military campaign or successfully complete a specific mission usually requires some degree of adaptability. What use is an automated system if the enemy, as in the above example, simply changes the flight parameters of its helicopters? In addition, machine autonomy might afford quicker reaction times. Human cognitive abilities are sometimes too slow to keep up with some areas of armed conflict. LAWS, however, could not only react more quickly than both humans and their automated counterparts, but operate in more complex and open environments than automated weaponry. Further, fully autonomous systems are likely to improve the stealth capability of an army. Without the need for a communications link between a human operator and the weapon, LAWS have higher chances of avoiding detection by the enemy. Travelling at greater speed and with quicker reaction times than other weaponry, as well as the crucial ability to adapt to changes in their operating environment, LAWS are more likely to penetrate enemy territory more deeply and quickly than other weapons, retaining an element of surprise in their attack.

The above sets out the general background against which to consider the issue of both conflict and cooperation in international affairs, and how different IRTs view the impact of LAWS on state behaviour. How would the availability of LAWS affect states' willingness to engage in uses of military force? How does it impact on their potential for more cooperative behaviour? How does it impact on the role of values and ethics in international order? We seek to answer these questions in the remainder of this chapter.

III.   REALIST AND LIBERAL PERSPECTIVES ON LAWS

The IRT and AI/LAWS interface has yet to be explored in more detail. IRT itself rests on a wide, sometime unwieldy heritage of classical, historical and contemporary outlooks blending conceptual and hypothetical with experiential and evidential. It is therefore a wide church of approaches to international behaviour by which to add an issue like LAWS, with all its inherent complexity; equally, its very variety affords the broadest and indeed richest of available conceptual spectrums by which to explore possible applications of both AI and LAWS. What follows are broad observations on emerging themes rather than a forensic application of the spectrum of IRT to the body of LAWS. What IRT, AI and LAWS have in common is a key axiom – namely that those states and national communities in possession of technology, and capable of advancing that technology exponentially have control over a key source of power. This helps to underwrite the central analytical starting point for IRT and LAWS, namely the tension between technological autonomy and adaptation, which set up interesting counterbalances for approaching AI and LAWS.

Realist approaches begin with an anarchic environment, whose permissive conditions are likely to be better suited not only to the material advantages offered by LAWS in general, but the ability to accelerate from basic automation to advanced autonomy.

Realists are likely to spot enhanced opportunities to defend (and possibly expand) their territorial sovereignty by moving along the spectrum from 'in-', 'on-' and 'out-'-of-loop options, adding new and emerging kill chain philosophies to the arsenal of state power. The salient question for IRT, therefore, is how to define and locate LAWS within the realist school of thought. Doing so requires establishing a clear interface between the current canon of IR theory and the emerging body of work on LAWS, to provide insights into both relations between states, and the more specific character of armed conflict between antagonists. In doing so, the scope is conceptually appetising indeed. LAWS could, for example, add to the realist trifecta of groupism, egoism and power-centrism in several ways. Groupism is likely to be reworked based on the ever-vague concept of what physically defines a state; borders, boundaries, zones become increasingly difficult with technology that is space-agnostic, challenging physical and material concepts of territoriality in relation to land, sea, air and even space. As outlined below, and echoed by authors within this same collection, the political cohesion provided by nation-state solidarity could either inhere or attenuate, depending on the sheer prevalence and acceptance of LAWS. Equally possession of LAWS – particularly in breach of emerging codes of conduct – is likely to reinforce views of offensive realists in supporting egoism as a key motive of political behaviour, and those of defensive realists in ensuring a judicious approach to power-centrism, particularly in terms of control and resources.

Within realism, there are various key modes that offer scope for a deeper interface with LAWS, including the supervening impact of systemic over national forces, balance of power, the security dilemma and the offence–defence balance. All modes assume some measure of anarchic pre-condition goading states into pugnacious behaviour rather than necessarily encouraging measured, long-term relations or the multilateral modes needed to build and maintain workable common values. Confusingly for realists, whose approach favours a *de minimus*, parsimonious appraisal of political behaviour driven by the essentials of power, the concomitant technological developments of the 21st century will certainly not revolve around a single definition of LAWS nor a unitary form of AI. Instead, realist-oriented LAWS will evolve and indeed reflect a veritable cornucopia of systems, each utilising wholly different – and quite possibly initially apposite – AI-programming techniques. The challenge therefore will be to reconcile the singularity power-based objectives embedded in realist approaches with the myriad uses of technology by which to attain these objectives.

Nor will LAWS likely replace other forms of weaponry wholesale, but merely add a complex new option that is ironically as wide in scope as it is limited in use. Contemporary balances of power are likely to retain nuclear weapons states, while shifting the LAWS-based pedigree of international actors, with some surprising additions to both the 'haves' and 'have nots' categories. This in turn will complicate both the type and trajectory of competition between states. Clearly, LAWS will have strategic advantages for states: the ability to strike faster, penetrate enemy territory more quickly and deeply, evade detection more easily, avoid (in certain circumstances) attributability (and thus potentially legal liability), and further militarise and colonise inaccessible or hostile spaces – often but not exclusively with important resources (deep sea, polar regions and outer space). The LAWS 'haves' will access (and possibly dominate) these environments by virtue of the systems that can operate therein, and not find themselves any further up the international pecking order. Indeed, the technological 'have nots' may simply not be able to compete in the long term, rendering the balance of power-considerations applicable to those actors with sufficient resources to invest in AI research more broadly, and to develop specific LAWS applications simultaneously with necessary defensive capabilities *against* the LAWS of an adversary.

While the balance of power regards LAWS for its additionalities to force, concepts of the balance of threat are likely to view LAWS in two different, possibly apposite ways. One is the distinct retention of fear arising from the sheer range of applicability and consequent harm on offer by both the mainstreamed and the unregulated used of AI-driven technology, including LAWS. A sense of threat, itself motivated by fear, will continue a primal form of anxiety in intra-state behaviour, accentuated by the bleak prospect of a spectrum in which outright anarchy on end is now counterbalanced by full-scale automation on the other, with decreasing amounts of heteronomous constraints. The other is the absence of fear, and even emotional response, arising from the hyper-mechanisation entailed in AI and utilised in forms of LAWS. This will demand a wholesale shift of seminal principles by Jervis and others regarding the balance of threat, predicated as they are on emotional response including the fear of retaliation (MAD, NUTS, etc.). In travelling along the in-, on-, out-of-loop options, do LAWS herald operating conditions in which programmes themselves are absent feelings and fear, and therefore operating upon an entirely different index of risk? Much depends on the degree of human direction and choice, as well as remembering that AI mechanisms will themselves always be integrated into the governing software of particular military systems. Taken together, this suggests that AI is not an actor in and of itself, and that human fears and the appreciation of risk will continue to shape what any AI-based weapon is allowed to do.

IV.   SKILLS, PROGRESS AND LIBERALISM

As outlined, crucial to these developments will be the highly educated skill-sets capable of designing, programming and advancing LAWs (whether domestic or imported) in which to provide a state with its subsequently comparative advantage over states with less developed technology. That being said, programming a governing software with AI techniques is one thing; it is quite another to integrate that software into a functioning weapons system that can withstand extreme environments (temperatures, pressure). As various commentators have recently argued, 'despite the best efforts of researchers and engineers, even our most advanced AI systems remain too brittle, biased, insecure and opaque to be relied upon in high-stake use cases', a problem particularly chronic in terms of both trust and predictability of governing software systems.[17] The consequences are difficult to predict, but not impossible. If, for example, there was an arms race, AI is unlikely to be the only decisive factor. AI-programming techniques themselves, rather than the standard (replicable) software, will be the prime area over which states will fiercely compete. Here too is an area in which subsequent developments of LAWS sees realist and liberal logic interestingly aligned, though for different reasons: the latter viewing technological and programming progress as comparatively advantageous, the latter as a *sign of progress* in the service of collective gain overall.

Liberal viewpoints of cooperative behaviour suggest innate limits on the use of AI for power-based reasons and LAWS for bellicose objectives. And yet, as witnessed many times in recent history, the liberal community of states is entirely able to support hard-power, realist-oriented means in order to guarantee liberal ends. This is particularly the case in terms of effecting liberal foreign policy aims associated with the rules-based system and the democratic credentials of leading states. The hope therefore is that LAWS and its 21st-century development would not be unthinkingly added to the liberal arsenal of hard-power tools merely to ensure soft-power outcomes. History, however, has rather undone this ambition, as illustrated by a series of large- and small-scale wars in the past few hundred years.

---

[17]   IISS, 'International competition over artificial intelligence', Strategic Comment, May 2022.

The best that liberal stalwarts can hope for is ensuring that LAWS gradually come to work in their favour, by mitigating trade-offs between persistently illiberal threats on the one side, and the overarching need to maintain and increase global governance on the other. Several points offer themselves for consideration in this context.

First, there is the role of humans in directing, rather than being directed by, the range of programme-specific systems utilising AI-programming techniques. Liberalism is generally reliably robust in asserting human agency, and the range of rights and obligations that ensure agency is progressively enabled and supported constitutionally at the domestic level, and institutionally in the international sphere. Accordingly, the liberal world view is key to how human developers are likely to perceive the world as conflictual or cooperative. Liberals are every bit as transactionalist as realists in determining international antagonists as well as supporting their chosen protagonists. These perceptions in turn account for the programming choices made, including target, interactions and consequences.

Second, the truer challenge is the contextual and comparative knowledge it takes to understand what constitutes an actual international 'antagonist' in terms of their active defiance, tacit opposition or merely anomalous existence relative to the prevailing liberal world view. How, therefore, does AI-based programming, including LAWS perimeters, learn what combatants are without contextual knowledge? Clearly, humans are required to programme a specific weapon with parameters as to what constitutes a combatant. The challenge is that any AI-based weapon cannot itself make the *qualitative* distinction between non-combatants and combatants. Machine vision can easily distinguish human beings from other entities located in a specific environment. But machine vision does not, and cannot, establish what the legal status of a human is. Significant drawbacks in reliably distinguishing between and categorising the whole range of possible actions carried out by antagonists vs protagonists is fraught with difficulty. Constructing and rolling out the 'large language models' that predict words, syntax and phrases is one thing. The sheer complexity of what is effectively 'fill-in-the-blank' technology applied to identifying – and subsequently acting on – protagonists and antagonists (be they individuals, groups, systems or structures) is still at the mercy of the persistent problem in that 'deep learning systems are not trustworthy enough' and are still more than likely to be plagued by their 'bias, brittleness, transparency'.[18]

On the one hand, this provides liberals with a real challenge in ensuring that the programmatic link between human and autonomous weaponry

---

[18]   ibid.

does not fail, ensuring human agency retains the ability to take account of humans generically, and protagonists and antagonists more specifically, with all the rights and obligations patiently accrued by liberal philosophy itself. On the other, there is scope for autonomous weaponry deployed in theatres where the interaction with humans is not a risk, providing liberal states and the rules-based system itself with cutting-edge technology by which to oversee both global zones (the high deep seas, high seas, atmosphere, space, polar regions) and adversarial political uses without human direction (e.g., drones programmed to intercept other drones, etc.).

The suggestion here is that realists are likely to perceive LAWS as an opportunity to streamline the use of autonomy within areas of technology and weaponry, but to do so in a structured way, largely coterminous to their understanding of the limits of state power itself. While accepting some of the rationalist precepts in this outlook, liberals however are likely to be drawn to the same capacity for adaptation and change that they value in individuals and society, working instead to ensure that advancements underwrite progress rather than harm, leveraging (and quite possibly limiting) collective capacity rather than relative gains. Like constructivists, liberals are likely also to concentrate on the connective tissue linking human content with autonomy, by emphasising and exploring the full scope of heteronomous options on offer.

V.   MACHINE AUTONOMY IS WHAT STATES MAKE OF IT: CONSTRUCTIVIST PERSPECTIVES

Realists consider the condition of anarchy as a fixed feature of international affairs, while liberals provide cooperation-based counterpoints to suggest forms of progress and development. In relation to LAWS, both sides provide modes of engagement recognisable to constructivists. Constructivism (best thought of as an approach rather than a theory set) revolves around identities, ideas, interests and the practices that methodically institutionalise and socialise them to produce a given set of behaviours. These behaviours may still contain large amounts of conflictual assumptions or cooperative options. However, it is the mobility, change and variety afforded by understanding that large parts of reality are socially constructed that suggests the ideational aspects of LAWS are just as important as its material aspects. There are two overriding areas in which LAWS is likely to have an impact. First, there is the way in which the possession of LAWS will highly complicate the overlap – or more properly the mutual constitutiveness – of states (as actors) and the international structure in which they operate. As suggested above,

LAWS are highly likely to complicate – by rendering ambiguous – defining contours between local, national, regional and international areas of engagement, in territorial and thus political terms. LAWS technology is likely to rely on highly intra-state-based supply chains in which ownership and responsibility is fragmented; further, the use of LAWS-related software and hardware is likely to be acquired by state actors (helping to mainstream it) and non-state actors (helping to deregulate it), some of whom will demand limited usage, and others utilising it in increasingly widespread and unpredictable ways. Therefore, the social and political relationships that construct the current set of national actors and international frameworks – and which display high degrees of self-reinforcement – are likely to be uniquely complicated, even compromised in their composition, purpose and preferred behavioural logics.

Second, different perspectives are used in constructing one identity in opposition to, or in relation to, another identity. In simple terms, oppositional identities can lead to antagonistic relations, relational identities lead to nested or overlapping identities, and identities held in common generally establish clear senses of being part of a given 'in group'. As outlined above, a huge amount of contextual knowledge is needed to establish and distinguish between protagonist and antagonist identity sets (quite apart from the range of options found in between). These are just as likely to be fluid and contested, as they are static and unchanging. Constructivists approach the world on the basis that nothing is set in stone, that ideas can shift, identities transform, interests change. In consequence, the purpose and tools of foreign policy, including LAWS, are likely to be interrogated on a case-by-case basis for their various ability, to tackling international problems. Specifically at issue is their goodness of fit in determining both the initial positioning of a given national community vis-à-vis a potential conflict, and after that, the range of options they offer their users in helping to reinforce a preferred behaviour or norm. This is bound to be a highly pluralist undertaking, entailing clashing viewpoints, legacies and expectations regarding the challenge at hand, and the envisaged contribution of adding LAWS to the issue. Both are modes of effecting change in the social makeup of a given national community. The use of LAWS may over time be designated as a given 'logic of action', with a range of available outcomes, not dissimilar to the use of hard and soft power in directing sanctions against targets. Equally, depending on the way in which LAWS are regulated (as explored below), and their subsequent placement within or beyond the bounds of acceptable global governance, constructivism may help highlight the way in which self-interested states construct a series of identities to support or undermine the use of LAWS as acceptable, or unacceptable.

VI. CONTROL, FEAR AND REGULATION: HOW IS IRT USEFUL IN THE DEBATE ON LAWS?

As above, there are key behavioural principles that drive and inhibit state behaviour, producing conflict and cooperation. The two that predominate in relation to the use of LAWS are control (authority or lack of it) and fear (arising from loss of authority, lack of control, etc.). Set against anarchic conditions favoured by realists, the lack of authority is less important than the lack of control. With no supervening global authority, much rests on states' ability to deploy fear of external anarchy while retaining domestic control. Liberals suggest that cooperation reduces the sheer costs of dealing with anarchy by linking domestic with international agreements, reducing fear via a more controlled environment. Constructivism is directed meanwhile by a logic of appropriateness in which value-based behaviour and core identities help modulate domestic and international behaviour with a variety of intervening variables. With LAWS, however, IRT faces something of a reset over the use of control and fear. LAWS and AI collapse state and individual identities, leaving instead software, hardware and programmes on the protagonist side and targets on the antagonist side. What remains is the planning preceding and following potential kill chains, and the kill chains themselves. In the initial stage of design and development, the programmer is in control because LAWS will need to be programmed. They cannot function without basic mission programming. With the interface between software and programming in place, and once the weapon is deployed, the programmer necessarily cedes control over it. The governing software then assumes control. The idea of an AI-governed weapons system is that it acts *independently* of a human operator; the idea of ceding control upon deployment is thus inherent in the concept of LAWS. Two issues arise from ceding control to the governing software.

First, to what extent does the software itself translate the programmer's intentions into exclusively machine behaviour? Second, to what extent does an AI-based system begin to exhibit behaviour that is neither foreseen nor anticipated by the programmer? This is particularly pertinent given the adaptive ability of the response of the system to its environment, in which case the system will simply carry out the objectives that the programmer could not have entirely foreseen. Hence, ceding control over the weapons upon deployment necessitates the acceptance of the risk of unforeseen machine behaviour. This raises the question, first, of the scope of state-based control of LAWS exercised by a given national community, and second, the problem of the lack of control over the use of LAWS within the international environment absent a supervening authority. It is also not clear how control, once ceded, can be re-established, especially if the weapon has adapted its behaviour. Indeed, human knowledge itself of this behaviour – whether at the programme or software level – may struggle to identify the source of this change. This in turn may well promote a range of anxiety regarding both the general lack of wider state authority and specific operator control. In determining state and civil society responses to LAWS, fear is likely to operate in a way that on the one hand attempts to limit, alter or prohibit the use of LAWS within the international rules of engagement, and on the other serves to gain access to, control of and dominance over LAWS to ensure a competitive international advantage. It is tempting to divide the different IRT schools along the categories in which realists would likely support utilising fear and control to ensure dominance. Liberals would attempt to find cooperative ways to reduce the transaction costs and lack of control over LAWS' use and development, while constructivism could variously affect and reject the ideational use of LAWS in terms of substantive and procedural behaviour. However, this is likely too rudimentary a series of assumptions about both IRT itself and the various applications of LAWS to given national and international targets.

Rather than an explicit interface in which realists apply LAWS largely in one way, liberals another, the intervening mechanism of categorisation, and regulation, is more likely to explain the long-term impact of LAWS on IRT and vice versa. Here, the wider question of *global governance* – in which realism, liberalism and constructivism are all invested in different ways – requires a confluence of multilateral political institutions, international law and robust oversight of LAWS' development to answer how LAWS are used in a mode recognisable by IRT (e.g., categorically 'realist'). A key question here is how to promote communication and indeed regulation of AI, and LAWS, without regulating human-based content – both creative and programmatic – under the broader framework of rules, regulations and emergent canons of applicable law. Indeed, the question is now not how to regulate AI as such but how to standardise and regulate the development and implementation of its governing software pursuant to its intended use.

At this point, it is doubtful whether the AI itself exists independently of its application in specific artefacts or systems (e.g., self-driving cars, specific software products utilised by banks, etc.). Instead, the international community is likely to witness the emergence of weapons systems (i.e., LAWS) whose governing software draws directly upon AI-programming techniques. Insofar as these weapons are in the possession of states, there are two views on their regulatory relationship with international law. The first is that LAWS are at present so unique that the current body of international law is incapable of regulating their material development and their deployment.[19] Indeed, it is not yet clear on what grounds those claims are made. Is it because such systems can operate without supervision by a human within the context of a given state? Or is it because they may exhibit unforeseen behaviour and render unclear the distinction between intent and outcome? While automated weaponry, for example, can operate without human supervision and is legal, the question of unforeseen behaviour arising from autonomous weaponry remains unclear.

If, for instance, LAWS entailed a weapon capable of engaging random targets (i.e., targets that have not been authorised by the human programmer in the system's governing software), one could argue that it is unlikely LAWS could ever be legally deployed. 'Shoot at anything that moves' is also clearly incompatible with the requirements of distinction and proportionality (in the case of collateral damage) as found in international human rights law. Equally, while the system's emerging behaviour *does* fall within acceptable mission parameters (i.e., only engages targets authorised by the human programmer even if it is unclear precisely when and how), there is reason neither to declare LAWS inherently illegal nor to consider international law inapplicable. While realism may contribute to this analysis on points of both promulgating and attenuating state authority via the regulation of LAWS through forms of international law, liberalism and constructivism are likely to provide helpful in terms of the political economy, use of non-state actors and identity-bearing modes that are likely to complicate the application of LAWS. The question is not the possession of LAWS by non-state actors, but whether *non-state* actors have an ambiguous relationship with a *state*-centric international legal order, and their ensuing use of LAWS to affect that relationship. Equally interesting is the potential gap between intent and use, in terms of determining both user-based attribution (e.g., in terms of responsibility) and recipient-based remedies (e.g., for the likely harm caused). At a practical level, LAWS is likely to be stealthier, faster and harder to track, rendering it difficult to attribute a particular decision to a specific state. Similar 'problems of attribution' exist in the cyber domain, and there is real scope for this to be amplified in the physical domain once LAWS become more common.

---

[19]   See Human Rights Watch (2012), 'Losing Control: The Case Against Killer Robots' <https://www.hrw.org/report/2012/11/19/losing-humanity/case-against-killer-robots> accessed 1 March 2023; M Waxman, K Reisner and D Anderson, 'Adapting the Law of Armed Conflict to Autonomous Weapons Systems' (2014) 90 *International Law Studies*; and also J Kwik, 'A Practicable Operationalisation of Meaningful Human Control' (2022) 11(3) Laws.

CONCLUSION

As explored, the implications of LAWS on both the wide-ranging conceptual areas of IRT, as well as more specific applications relative to armed conflict, automation and autonomy, remain wide-ranging yet highly consequential in terms of clarifying understanding and insights of the potential impact of LAWS on relations between states.[20] Realist, liberal and constructivist churches all demonstrate a range of different capacities to theorise the potential impact of LAWS on armed conflict, by establishing the contours of power-based systemic structures or the permissive conditions that permit state-based cooperation. The chapter has on this basis sought to interrogate the overall use and consequences of LAWS against seminal IRT principles, while also reversing the equation and asking what technologically sophisticated weapons systems like LAWS reveal to us about the utility of IRT's axioms. Future scholarship and LAWS' technology are likely to develop in tandem, though not necessarily at the same rate. Overarching and uneasy questions have already emerged, the most salient of which is the propensity for automation in general and LAWS in particular to improve state behaviour or let it deteriorate, to act as a brake or an accelerator to the self-help credentials of anarchy – a buttress or a battering ram to collective cooperation.

Cynics may well argue that the emergence of weapons systems with AI-based components will only deepen the anarchical nature of international relations. Some IRT viewpoints are bleak indeed in conjecturing the full impact of LAWS on individual, hegemonic and collective state behaviour, arguing that automation contributes to political conflict by adding greater and greater degrees of unpredictability, prompting untrammelled escalation. Conversely, more encouraging perspectives, including those arising from core IR conflict theories, suggest that *escalation patterns* arise from human-to-human interaction and that a simple conversion to either human-to-machine and/or machine-to-machine interaction retains the indisputable human element, which itself is still broadly risk averse, a characteristic already embedded in the design, programming, choice and evaluation of the use of LAWS. Over time, however, this may well change, and IRT requires conceptual depth to deal with the practical consequences thereof. Generic escalation patterns may well come to reflect biases that humans themselves have programmed into a weapons system, whether risk averse or risk oriented. With such fast-paced and

---

[20] For an attempt to assess the impact of LAWS on armed conflict, see Leveringhaus (n 7).

unregulated developments, the scope for danger remains, particularly in scenarios where two separate weapons systems interact in unpredictable ways and trigger escalation. Would humans be able to establish control over these 'rogue' systems again? After all, the idea of LAWS, as outlined above, entails the ceding of control over the machine post-deployment. A final consideration is automation bias, which is a pivotal concept in cognitive engineering – and entails trust in the machine's ability. As a result, the escalation is perceived as real and elicits a fearful human response. It is not necessarily perceived for what it really is, namely two weapons interacting in unforeseen ways.

BIBLIOGRAPHY

Arkin R, 'The Case for Ethical Autonomy in Unmanned Systems' (2010) 9 Journal of Military Ethics.
Arkin R, *Governing Behaviour in Lethal Autonomous Robots* (Taylor & Francis 2009).
Boothby W, *Weapons and the Law of Armed Conflict*, 2nd edn (Oxford University Press 2016).
Forge J, *Designed to Kill: The Case against Weapons Research* (Springer 2013).
Gailliot J, MacIntosh D and Ohlin JD (eds), *Lethal Autonomous Weapons: Re-Examining the Law and Ethics of Robotic Warfare* (Oxford University Press 2021).
Human Rights Watch, 'Losing Humanity: The Case Against Killer Robots' (2012) <https://www.hrw.org/report/2012/11/19/losing-humanity/case-against-killer-robots>, accessed 1 March 2023.
International Institute of Strategic Studies (IISS), 'International competition over artificial intelligence' (2022) <https://www.iiss.org/publications/strategic-comments/2022/international-competition-over-artificial-intelligence> accessed 20 October 2022.
Kwik J, 'A Practicable Operationalisation of Meaningful Human Control' (2022) Laws 11 <https://www.mdpi.com/2075-471X/11/3/43> accessed 20 October 2022.
Leveringhaus A, 'Morally Repugnant Weaponry? Ethical Responses to the Prospect of Autonomous Weapons' in S Voeneky and others (eds), *The Cambridge Handbook of Responsible Artificial Intelligence* (Cambridge University Press 2022).
Leveringhaus A, 'Autonomous Weapons and the Future of Armed Conflict' in J Gailliot, D MacIntosh and JD Ohlin (eds), *Lethal Autonomous Weapons: Re-Examining the Law and Ethics of Robotic Warfare* (Oxford University Press 2021).
Leveringhaus A, *Ethics and Autonomous Weapons* (Palgrave 2016).
Maurer M and others (eds), *Autonomous Driving: Technical, Legal, and Social Aspects* (Springer Nature 2016).
New York Times, 'U.N. Expert Calls for Halt in Military Robot Development', <https://www.nytimes.com/2013/05/31/world/europe/united-nations-armed-robots.html> accessed 20 October 2022.

Sharkey N, 'Saying "No" to Lethal Autonomous Targeting' (2010) 9 Journal of Military Ethics.

Sharre P, *Army of None: Autonomous Weapons and the Future of War* (W. W. Norton 2019).

Sparrow R, 'Killer Robots' (2007) 24 Journal of Applied Philosophy.

Waxman M, Reisner D and Anderson K, 'Adapting the Law of Armed Conflict to Autonomous Weapons Systems' (2014) 90 International Law Studies.

Whitfield A, *Robotics: A Very Short Introduction* (Oxford University Press 2012).

7. Understanding emergent technology, instability and power in international political economy
Malcolm Campbell-Verduyn[1]

INTRODUCTION

At 14:42:44:075 on 6 May 2010 a 'tidal wave of data' of electronic orders overloaded the New York Stock Exchange and delayed its nearly real-time price calculation system. These short-lived delays sparked a rapid sell-off of stocks in what instigated a wider financial market panic. One trillion dollars of market value temporarily evaporated, only to return to near previous values within the span of just 20 minutes.[2] Widely dubbed as *the* flash crash and 'the most mysterious market crash in history',[3] the volatilities of May 6, 2010 were reported to be well in line with events occurring 'with alarming frequency'[4] as financial markets have progressively digitalized since the 1980s. Digital finance diminishes, though does not entirely eliminate, the roles of humans both in executing trades, as well as in programming instructions and parameters for increasingly artificial intelligence-driven algorithms that have become more and more able to 'learn from prior decisions, dynamically assess new information, and optimize their solutions to reflect new data'.[5] Yet the precise human and non-human contributions to rapid declines and recoveries of financial markets remain as disputed as the definition of 'flash crash'.[6] Going back

---

[1] The insightful feedback of the volume editors, as well as Marc Lenglet and Moritz Huetten, is gratefully acknowledged.

[2] Nanex, Nanex Flash Crash Summary Report (2010) <http://www.nanex.net/FlashCrashFinal/FlashCrashSummary.html> accessed 7 September 2022.

[3] Liam Vaughan, *Flash Crash: A Trading Savant, a Global Manhunt, and the Most Mysterious Market Crash in History* (Doubleday 2020).

[4] Graham Bowley, 'The Flash Crash, in Miniature' (*New York Times*, 8 November 2010).

[5] Gina-Gail Fletcher, 'Deterring Algorithmic Manipulation' (2021) 74 Vanderbilt Law Revue, 262.

[6] One effort to define the systemic impact of 'flash crashes' stresses the '4,4,6 rule' of 4% or larger swings in both the dollar–yen exchange rate or stock market index, as well as 6% or more swings in US 10-year Treasury yields; see Lananh

to 'Black Monday', when nearly a quarter of the value of the Dow Jones Industrial Average was erased within a few hours on 19 October 1987, officials and market participants have linked market crashes both to human herd behaviour and to the growth of computerized electronic trading.[7] To this day increasingly rapid crashes and recoveries in markets for novel, technology-enabled products such as 'crypto-assets' are blamed on combinations of technological glitches and the human propensity to bid up novel financial instruments.[8]

Flash crashes in markets for products ranging from inherently volatile cryptocurrencies to what are widely considered to be the safest financial assets remain poorly understood. Regulatory investigations of the 'dynamics that drove ... trading' in a 'broadly similar event' to the 2010 flash crash, the 15 October 2014 drop by 20% in the market for 10-year United States government bonds between 9:33 and 9:45, were inconclusive.[9] A similar lack of clarity surrounded flash crashes in financial instruments including forms of investment insurance,[10] as well as the following 'volatility events' identified by the International Organization of Securities Commissions:[11]

- 31 May 2016 – Chinese equity futures rapidly declined over 12.5% and returned to previous levels seconds later.

Nguyen, 'Citi: Maybe Flash Crashes Aren't So Bad, After All' *Bloomberg* (1 September 2015).

[7] Mark Carlson, *A Brief History of the 1987 Stock Market Crash with a Discussion of the Federal Reserve Response* (Finance and Economics Discussion Series Divisions of Research & Statistics and Monetary Affairs Federal Reserve Board, 2006) 4; Edemilson Paraná, *Digitalized Finance: Financial Capitalism and Informational Revolution* (Brill 2008) 84.

[8] Arjun Kharpal, 'Ethereum briefly crashed from $319 to 10 cents in seconds on one exchange after "multimillion dollar" trade' *CNBC* (22 June 2017); Bill Maurer, 'Re-risking in Realtime: On Possible Futures for Finance after the Blockchain' (2017) 9(2) Behemoth: A Journal on Civilisation.

[9] *Joint Staff Report of the Commodities Futures Trading Commission and Securities and Exchange Commission*, 'Findings Regarding the Market Events of May 6, 2010', <https://www.sec.gov/news/studies/2010/marketevents-report.pdf> accessed 7 September 2022; Donald MacKenzie, 'How Algorithms Interact: Goffman's 'Interaction Order' in Automated Trading' (2019) 36(2) Theory, Culture & Society.

[10] For example, West Texas Intermediate crude oil futures experienced nearly three dozen 'flash events' in the first half of 2015 alone.

[11] International Organization of Securities Commissions, 'Mechanisms Used by Trading Venues to Manage Extreme Volatility and Preserve Orderly Trading' (2018) <https://www.iosco.org/library/pubdocs/pdf/IOSCOPD607.pdf> accessed 7 September 2022.

- 6 October 2016 – The value of the British Pound dropped more than 6%, recovering to prior levels soon after.
- 16 February 2017 – French government bond (OAT) futures experienced a volatility event with yields falling 11bps within 85 seconds, in a period of significant illiquidity, before recovering most of the drop within 8 minutes.

If leading regulators have difficulties making sense of these 'mysterious' volatilities,[12] how can scholars and students of politics and governance understand the growing frequency and severity of flash crashes of markets increasingly driven by Big Data and artificial intelligence? How might the types of market instabilities accompanying these 'disruptive' digitizations of the global political economy productively be understood?

This chapter injects insight into the politics and governance of instability in an increasingly digitizing global economy by turning to perspectives provided in the field of International Political Economy (IPE). Bridging international economics and international politics, IPE is an interdiscipline offering of multiple and often contrasting approaches. While varying widely in their epistemological and ontological foundations, IPE perspectives can broadly be divided in two.[13] A first general group retains the central 'neoclassical' assumptions of economics holding that agent behaviour and expectations of others' agents in the global political economy conforms to instrumental rationality. In both financial markets and the global political economy more generally, agents whether they be consumers, firms, states and social classes are assumed to seek maximization of their interests and to expect others to do the same. This 'rational actors with rational expectations' (RARE) assumption, however, is set aside to varying degrees in a second group of IPE approaches. What can be generally assembled under the label of 'interpretivist' perspectives seeks to move 'beyond economism'[14] and integrate insights from cultural, feminist, media and social theory. The core assumptions of rational instrumentality are traded in favour of a stress on the intersubjective (re)construction of actor interests and expectations. This second group of perspectives also injects an emphasis on materiality by drawing insights from the field of Science and Technology Studies (STS), an interdiscipline that itself

---

[12]   Vaughan (n 3); Jethro Mullen, 'U.K. Pound Plunges More Than 6% in Mysterious Flash Crash' *CNN* (7 October 2016).
[13]   As will be noted, this is not a strict separation and in practice there are overlaps between these two broad groupings.
[14]   Marieke De Goede, 'Beyond Economism in International Political Economy' (2003) 29(1) Review of International Studies.

bridges insights from economic anthropology and economic sociology, amongst others.

This chapter proceeds to outline how the complementary strengths and weaknesses of two broad groups of IPE perspectives aid in making sense of the politics and governance of volatilities accompanying the digitization of financial markets. Two sections in turn review each of these broad sets of perspectives and the insights they provide into flash crashes. A third section then argues that the sum of the diverse perspectives IPE provides inject varying degrees of analytical complexity into understanding the broader contours of power in an increasingly complex and unstable global political economy. The chapter concludes by pointing to trading in so-called 'memestocks' as a key on-going yet poorly understood set of market volatilities that IPE is well positioned to make sense of.

INSTABILITY IN INSTRUMENTALIST IPE

A first, and traditionally most dominant, group of IPE perspectives bridging international politics and economics retains the central 'rational actors with rational expectations' (RARE) assumption of the 'dismal science'.[15] Although varying in their focus on levels of analysis – as this section will illustrate in the focus on the individual firm, state or social class level – liberal, mercantilist and critical perspectives, respectively, provide instrumental understandings of events such as flash crashes and other forms of 'disruption' accompanying the introduction of Big Data and artificial intelligence technologies into markets that span national borders. This section surveys how liberal individualism, mercantilist statism and critical structuralism each help to comprehend the *cui bono* question of who benefits from the 'disruptive' market instabilities accompanying digitization and the integration of emergent technologies in the global political economy. Focusing on the case of flash crashes in finance, the section concludes by pointing to some limits of these perspectives in tending towards overly deterministic analyses that struggle to deal with non-linear and unexpected events.

Liberal approaches in IPE foreground the rationality of individuals, whether experts and scientists developing technologies such as Big Data and AI or the entrepreneurs and firms deploying them, in attempting to achieve individual gains. With roots in idealism and other highly

---

[15]   Ivan Boldyrev and Ekaterina Svetlova, *Enacting Dismal Science: New Perspectives on the Performativity of Economics* (Palgrave Macmillan 2016).

optimistic perspectives, liberal perspectives tend to view market instabilities like flash crashes as aberrations. That is, abnormal events that are temporary deviations from longer-run tendencies towards general market equilibriums that, ultimately in the medium- to long run, benefit *all* agents. In the short term, however, liberal IPE perspectives recognize the existence of winners and losers from what are considered to be exceptional events like flash crashes. On the one hand, individual traders and firms can enjoy profit gains from periods of short but extreme market volatility when volumes of trades increase during moments of panic. While automating trading firms 'are only modestly profitable by the standards of other institutions in the financial sector',[16] in flash crashes they can become extremely profitable. Especially those agents best physically positioned vis-à-vis exchanges on which trading occurs can profit from being the fastest to buy and sell financial products in periods of turbulence. By 'co-locating' their servers in the same data centres housing those of the exchanges, certain market agents have for example been able to reduce time-lags between information flows and act in milliseconds faster than other market participants.[17] The material inequalities and 'advantageous network differentials [have] resulted in uneven spatial and temporal relations'[18] underpinning the ability of some firms to co-locate their servers with those of the exchanges they trade on is an important source of critique in other IPE perspectives. For the moment, what is important to stress is that in liberal IPE perspectives *individual* agency is emphasized above the structures in which market agents operate. The foregrounding of individual action and gains from 'disruption' is illustrated in journalistic accounts of the 'Flash Boys':[19] individual traders combatting large financial houses. These 'heroes' are emphasized alongside 'losers' in liberal accounts.

Case in point here is British trader Navinder Sarao, who became a multimillionaire in the aftermath of the 2010 flash crash only to find himself in jail just over a half decade later, when he was detained by British police after the American Department of Justice issued charges against him. These charges set off another half decade of media, policy and scholarly

---

[16]   Grahame F. Thompson, 'Time, Trading and Algorithms in Financial Sector Security' (2017) 22 New Political Economy.

[17]   James Angel and Douglas McCabe, 'Fairness in Financial Markets: The Case of High Frequency Trading' (2013) 112 Journal of Business Ethics.

[18]   Carolyn Hardin and Adam Rottinghaus, 'Introducing a Cultural Approach to Technology in Financial Markets' (2015) 8 Journal of Cultural Economy, 557.

[19]   Michael Lewis, *Flash Boys: A Wall Street Revolt* (W. W. Norton & Company 2014).

contemplation of whether an individual whose 2010 trades were conducted from his parents' basement could and should be the primary source responsible for a trillion dollars in market volatilities.[20] The central point of highlighting the widespread focus granted to the day trader Sarao in the aftermath of the 2010 flash crash is how it falls in line with the general stress of liberal IPE perspectives on individuals and their responsibility for both the benefits and harms of emergent technologies in the global political economy.

The Sarao case is illustrative, equally, of liberal stress on cooperative efforts to regulate general excesses and instabilities of markets in heralding improved collective outcomes in the global political economy. Cooperation between the United States and the United Kingdom was at the core of what became a 'global manhunt' for the alleged 2010 flash crash perpetrator. British authorities extradited Sarao to Chicago in 2016.[21] The charges Sarao faced emanated from cooperation between the infamously fractured and territorial American financial regulators, along with stock market operators, and the federal Department of Justice. In identifying Sarao as a 'trading savant'[22] whose activities contributed to the 2010 flash crash authorities drew on post-2010 reports into the flash crash produced by financial regulators known for jurisdictional turf battles. These reports were accompanied by a broader set of regulatory efforts following the 2010 flash crash to investigate and more formally govern the specific trading practices that Sarao and other traders had long utilized. In Chicago, Sarao pled guilty to charges of wire fraud and spoofing, the technique of flooding markets with fake orders 'to create an impression of false liquidity in the market and force asset prices to levels that benefit the investors behind this strategy.'[23] Spoofing, as part of a wider variety of practices aimed at fooling competitors and disguising what trades one is actually doing, was long informally tolerated and only infrequently 'subject to administrative action' and fines that could 'in effect be considered a business expense'.[24] Yet, a month after the 2010 flash crash, the US Congress adopted into law the Dodd–Frank Wall Street Reform and Consumer Protection Act, a sprawling reform measure whose section 747 'weakened

---

[20]   Christian Borch, 'High-Frequency Trading, Algorithmic Finance and the Flash Crash: Reflections on Eventalization' (2017) 45 Economy and Society; Andrew Keller, 'Robocops: Regulating High Frequency Trading after the Flash Crash of 2010' (2012) 73 Ohio State Law Journal.

[21]   Vaughan (n 3).

[22]   ibid.

[23]   Paraná (n 7) 89 n 40.

[24]   MacKenzie (n 9) 52.

the legal tests that have to be passed for a criminal prosecution for spoofing to succeed'.[25] Beyond the US, post-2010 financial market re-regulation in jurisdictions such as Germany enforced use of 'tags' on algorithms to detect individual market manipulation efforts.[26] Meanwhile, an update to the 'Markets in Financial Instruments Directive' of the European Union was implemented in 2018 with the aim of 'explicitly targeting the problems associated with new developments of algorithmic trading.'[27] Subsequently, under voluntary 'enhanced cooperation'[28] amongst member states a number of European countries implemented financial transactions taxes to 'slow down' the electronic trading at the heart of flash crashes.[29]

Despite its increased thrust and international coordination, global financial regulation immediately after the 2010 flash crash remained market-enabling. Liberal IPE perspectives emphasize how collective actions aimed at addressing instabilities in international financial markets – regulation – stresses market transparency in a way that leaves market players themselves to attend to problems such as flash crashes.[30] Understood as exceptions stemming from atypical individual activities and practices like spoofing, 'instability events' like the 2010 flash crash are regarded as 'immoral act[s] that regulators can attribute to one single individual.'[31] In following, the post-2010 attempts to tame instabilities are understood in liberal IPE perspectives as facilitating self-correcting market responses rather than imposing any major constraints on market activities beyond the types of fines that were issued by market self-regulatory organizations such as the Financial Industry Regulatory Authority (FINRA) in the US for firms undertaking spoofing-like practices in 2010.[32] The key insight here is that the persistence of pre-2010 structures of financial trading and

[25]   ibid.
[26]   Nathan Coombs, 'What is an Algorithm? Financial Regulation in the Era of High-Frequency Trading' (2016) 45 Economy and Society.
[27]   Marc Lenglet and J. Mol, 'Squaring the Speed of Light? Regulating Market Access in Algorithmic Finance' (2016) 45 Economy and Society, 45.
[28]   Niahm Hardiman and Saliha Metinsoy, 'Power, Ideas, and National Preferences: Ireland and the FTT' (2019) 26 Journal of European Public Policy.
[29]   Aukje Van Loon, 'European Financial Governance: FTT Reform, Controversies and Governments' Responsiveness' (2021) 9 Politics and Governance.
[30]   Robert Seyfert, 'Bugs, Predations or Manipulations? Incompatible Epistemic Regimes of High-Frequency Trading' (2016) 45 Economy and Society.
[31]   Christine Lange, 'High-Frequency Trading' in Christian Borch and Robert Wosnitzer (eds), *Routledge Handbook of Critical Finance Studies* (Routledge 2020), 255.
[32]   Frank Pasquale, 'Law's Acceleration of Finance: Redefining the Problem of High-Frequency Trading' (2014) 36 Cardozo Law Revue.

on-going 'instability events' are understood in liberal IPE perspectives as stemming from the rational pursuit of individual gains markets. It is 'bad apples' like Sarao and 'bad practices' like spoofing that can be purged in returning markets to equilibrium rather than undertaking more fundamental reforms, reconfigurations or restructuring of increasingly digitized markets themselves.

Mercantilist approaches in IPE, in turn, 'scale up' from the individual and firm-level analysis of liberals to also stress instrumental rationality in generating useful understanding the politics and governance of disruptions stemming from AI, Big Data and 'disruptive' technological change in financial markets and the global political economy more generally. The key individual agents here are the nation-states who set the structures for which all market agents operate in. Digital technologies like AI and Big Data are understood as providing countries the 'power to' achieve specific statist aims,[33] such as ensuring the prominence of American finance markets in areas of increased competition from Asian exchanges,[34] as well as efforts to ward off competitors who are themselves seeking to achieve 'data sovereignty' in Canada, Europe or Japan.[35] Leading US financial regulators like the Securities and Exchange Commission (SEC) have sought to maintain the prominence of American exchanges by undertaking post-2010 efforts such as inserting so-called 'circuit breakers' in order to curb trading in volatile periods, as well as mandating exchanges and their private sector regulator to develop centralized information archives on billions of financial trades. The launch of the Consolidated Audit Trail (CAT) in 2016 as a centralized trade repository exemplifies American national attempts to remain the dominant jurisdictions for financial trading. Not unlike liberal approaches, mercantilist approaches stress the rational instrumentalism of market regulating activities, yet more for the power and prestige of the state(s) enabling them rather than necessarily for the individual agents undertaking them – that is, the traders and leading market players. Indeed, American financial regulators like the SEC have long regulated the foundations of electronic communications

---

[33]   Guillaume Beaumier and others, 'Global Regulations for a Digital Economy: Between New and Old Challenges' (2020) 11 Global Policy.

[34]   Johannes Petry, 'Same Same, But Different: Varieties of Capital Markets, Chinese State Capitalism and the Global Financial Order' (2021) 25 Competition & Change.

[35]   Louise Amoore, 'Cloud Geographies: Computing, Data, Sovereignty' (2018) 42 Progress in Human Geography; Robert Herian, 'Regulating Disruption: Blockchain, GDPR, and Questions of Data Sovereignty' (2018) 22 Journal of Internet Law.

networks (ECNs) 'that facilitate the entry and execution of orders electronically by algorithms.'[36] For example, the SEC enforced standardized 'decimalization'[37] and the requirement for 'market participants automatically to route orders to the exchange offering the best price' through the creation of National Best Bid and Offer regulation.[38] The key insight from these statist perspectives, then, is efforts to govern markets are undertaken less in the service of markets themselves than in the wider interests of the nation-states hosting them. International power and prestige are regarded as flowing centrally through financial markets whose excesses, such as flash crashes, can be tamed to ensure national prominence.

Like mercantilist statism, *critical* IPE perspectives 'scale up' from the liberal focus on individuals to stress structural conflicts. Here, however, conflict is between social classes rather than states. Despite being more explicitly critical orientation towards 'neoclassical' economics, these approaches also tend to retain the RARE assumption. In understanding instabilities such as flash crashes, critical IPE perspectives emphasize the instrumental rationality of a class of market actors trading largely, if not solely, on quantified metrics. So-called 'quants' are finance professionals typically trained as mathematicians, physicists and computer engineers.[39] This class of professional actors design and operate the high frequency trading (HFT) algorithmic systems wherein automatically executing algorithms initiate buy and sell orders automatically at speeds of up to a millisecond, as well as in nanoseconds in the case of 'ultra-HFT'. These speeds far surpass the ability of existing classes of financial market actors, including the individual retail trader, to compete. Due to their technology-enabled ability to process increasingly large volumes and varieties of trade-relevant data, HFT firms and the quants they employ exercise varying forms of non-human 'artificial' intelligence. This variance is mainly in the extent to which algorithmic sets of instructions deployed to execute trading strategies are themselves 'able to "decide" when and how

---

[36]   Jerry Markham and Daniel Harty, 'For Whom the Bell Tolls: The Demise of Exchange Trading Floors and the Growth of ECNs' (2007) 33 Journal of Corporation Law.

[37]   Nathan Brown, 'The Rise of High Frequency Trading: The Role Algorithms, and the Lack of Regulations, Play in Today's Stock Market' (2011) 11 Appalachian Journal of Law, 212.

[38]   Ann-Christina Lange, Marc Lenglet and Robert Seyfert, 'Cultures of High-Frequency Trading: Mapping the Landscape of Algorithmic Developments in Contemporary Financial Markets' (2016) 45 Economy and Society, 153.

[39]   Malcolm Campbell-Verduyn, Marcel Goguen and Tony Porter, 'Big Data and Algorithmic Governance: The Case of Financial Practices' (2017) 22 New Political Economy.

to send orders without direct human intervention.'[40] In contrast to liberal emphasis on longer-term possibilities for mutual benefits, critical perspectives stress the profound, structural mismatches between social classes. In the case of financial trading, these tensions are between a new class of professional 'quants' and the HFT firms employing them on the one hand, and 'everyday' retail traders on the other hand. The mismatch in the instrumental power the two are able to exercise entails what has been characterized 'two-tiered markets – one for powerful insiders with access to the required technology, a second one for the retail investor whose orders are merely completed as an "afterthought" (Salkever, 2009).'[41] The 2010 flash crash and similar instabilities in increasingly volatile financial markets are understood as stemming from these structural inequalities between classes of traders with varying technology-enabled capacities to gain and act on, as well as profit from, data in more rapid and efficient manners.

Despite value in making sense of 'mysterious events' like flash crashes,[42] the trio of approaches making up this first group of IPE perspective suffers from a common flaw. Their central shortcoming lies in the inability to analytical deal with non-linear and unexpected events. The deterministic qualities of each set of instrumentalist perspectives are reflected generally in the 'one-size-fits-all' inevitability of which market, state, social classes seek to gain from 'instability events'.[43] Liberal accounts consider short-run disruptions from crashes but see market actors as enabling, eventually, long-run equilibrium for the benefit of all. Statist and critical accounts also take instabilities into account, but see events such as flash crashes inevitably as products of inter-state and inter-class conflicts. Even resistance efforts, for instance of moving to 'dark pools' where trading is slowed down by microseconds to permit degrees of equivalence between investors, are seen as inevitably doomed by class conflict between dark pool operators and state actors such as the SEC that have fined the likes of Barclays and Credit Suisse for allowing HFT trading to take place on their dark pools.

---

[40]   Marc Lenglet, 'Conflicting codes and codings: How algorithmic trading is reshaping financial regulation' (2011) 6 Theory, Culture & Society, 45.

[41]   Laureen Snider, 'Interrogating the Algorithm: Debt, Derivatives and the Social Reconstruction of Stock Market Trading' (2014) 40 Critical Sociology, 754, citing A Salkever, 'Wall Street Ripoff 2.0: High Speed Trading and Deep, Dark Pools' (2009), <http://www.dailyfinance.com/story/investing/wall-street-ripoff-2-0-high-speedtrading-anddeep-dark-pools/19116311>.

[42]   Vaughan (n 3).

[43]   Injoo Sohn, 'Toward Normative Fragmentation: An East Asian Financial Architecture in the Post-Global Crisis World' (2012) 19 Review of International Political Economy.

The determinism of this first set of IPE approaches also stems from their understanding of AI, Big Data and other technologies as neutral 'tools' of power rather than as affecting the exercise of power itself.[44] This instrumental view of technology echoes that of orthodox economics, which 'long treated technological phenomena as events transpiring inside a black box.'[45] The black box metaphor is particularly relevant to the case of flash crashes in which glitches, errors and errant events surrounding digital technologies are largely bracketed off in rationalist IPE accounts. That is, the inner workings of technologies matter only to the extent that they are *acted upon* in manipulations, frauds and nefarious activities. Such activities can always be considered to be at work particularly in a financial sector whose roots and contemporary practices involve illicit and illegitimate activities.[46] Yet, the purposeful and instrumental nature of market manipulation is often difficult even for leading financial regulators to locate, even if evidence of 'pump and dump' schemes arises frequently in markets for the likes of 'crypto-assets'.[47] A decade on from the 2010 flash crash, little evidence has been forthcoming of any purposeful 'setting off' of the 'tidal wave of data'[48] that overwhelmed the NYSE and resulted in delays that sparked the mass sell-off after 14:42:44:075pm on 6 May. What the linear rationalist expectations of profit-seeking individual and class behaviour and of inter-state competition struggle to consider then is what might be called the politics and governance of glitches, errors and errant behaviours. The complex systems designed and operated by market

---

[44]   Michael Talalay, Roger Tooze and Christopher Farrands, 'Technology, Culture, and Competitiveness: Change and the World Political Economy' in Christopher Farrands, Michael Talalay and Roger Tooze (eds), *Technology, Culture, and Competitiveness: Change and the World Political Economy* (Routledge 1997) 5; of importance to note here is that certain strands in critical IPE approaches, for instance those inspired by Gramscian theory, have long maintained how 'it is more realistic to see technology as being shaped by social forces at least as much as it shapes these forces' and that 'technology itself is a product of society and society's power relations': Robert Cox, *Production, Power, and World Order: Social Forces in the Making of History* (Columbia University Press 1987) 21.

[45]   Nathan Rosenberg, *Inside the Black Box: Technology and Economics* (Cambridge University Press 1982).

[46]   Rob Aitken, 'Capital at Its Fringes' (2006) 11 New Political Economy; Marieke De Goede, *Virtue, Fortune, and Faith: A Genealogy of Finance* (University of Minnesota Press 2001).

[47]   Josh Kamps and Bennett Kleinberg, 'To the Moon: Defining and Detecting Cryptocurrency Pump-and-Dumps' (2018) 7 Crime Science; Taro Tsuchiya, 'Profitability of Cryptocurrency Pump and Dump Schemes' (2019) 3 Digital Finance.

[48]   Nanex (n 2).

actors like the NYSE, or state regulators like the SEC, or as state-market hybrids like the CAT, have consistently remained vulnerable to technical glitches,[49] errant and unexpected events that less rationalist, instrumentalist and economistic IPE perspectives struggle to make sense of in an instrumental rationalist manner. As the next section elaborates, these unexpected malfunctions can be understood in less functionalist manners.

INSTABILITY IN INTERPRETIVIST IPE

A second set of IPE perspectives draws on a range of insights from cultural, feminist, media and social theory in drawing together politics and economics. The further cross-disciplinarity of what are generally labelled more interpretivist IPE approaches stems from on-going efforts to overcome the instrumentalism, rationalism and economism at the core of dominant IPE approaches surveyed in the previous section. The notion that power is instrumentally held by any actor or group of actors is jettisoned here in favour of more dispersed and capillary understandings of power theorized, amongst others, by the likes of French philosophers Deleuze and Foucault. The application of such insights for understanding digitizing markets, financial and otherwise, at times echo some of the insights generated in critical and mercantilist IPE perspectives stressing the augmentation of state and class power.[50]

The novelty of such accounts lies less on the inevitability of outcomes resulting from the instrumental, rational and linear exercise of power through technologies such as AI and Big Data. Instead, foregrounded here is the 'messiness, complexity and unintended consequences of technological change' in the less predictable and more fragile outcomes of continual

---

[49] Benjamin Bain, 'Audit Trail Could Boost Cybersecurity Threat, Exchanges Say' *Bloomberg*, 10 October 2017; Kate Fazzini and Liz Moyer, 'Hackers Broke into an SEC Database and Made Millions from Inside Information, says DOJ' *CNBC*, 15 January 2019.

[50] Rob Aitken, '"All data is credit data": Constituting the Unbanked' (2017) 21 Competition & Change; Alexander Barder, 'Neo-Materialist Ecologies and Global Systemic Crises' (2016) 13 Globalizations; Peter Dauvergne, *AI in the Wild: Sustainability in the Age of Artificial Intelligence* (MIT Press 2020); Julian Gruin, 'The Epistemic Evolution of Market Authority: Big Data, Blockchain and China's Neostatist Challenge to Neoliberalism' (2021) 25 Competition & Change; Ruben Kremers and James Brassett, 'Mobile Payments, Social Money: Everyday Politics of the Consumer Subject' (2017) 22 New Political Economy; Leanne Roderick, 'Discipline and Power in the Digital Age: The Case of the US consumer Data Broker Industry' (2017) 40 Critical Sociology.

evolving co-constitutions of power and technology.[51] Moving beyond ideational accounts solely stressing the social interpretation of events like crises, insights have been increasingly drawn from the interdiscipline of STS, which have been particularly influential in spurring growing attempts to 'open technological black boxes'[52] and draw out the often unexpected and unanticipated manners in which human activities in the 'international techno-political economy' are *co*produced with non-human matter.[53]

In particular, the fragilities of *relations* produced and reproduced between human practices and technical objectives are emphasized in STS-inspired notions of infrastructures. Not unlike the notion of 'assemblage' from Deleuze and Foucault, STS-inspired notions of infrastructure 'highlight the inseparability of ... financial activities from the materiality of the technical artefacts and local settings that enable them.'[54] In other words, infrastructures help to consider the fragile nature of relations between practices such as financial trading and the digital algorithms that both enable such activities and disable them through what are often unexpected and unacknowledged vulnerabilities. Specific examples include the increasing use of microwaves to enable the near real-time transmission of financial data, which have remained 'susceptible to atmospheric conditions' such as rains and heavy winds.[55] Similarly, the use of lasers for financial data transmission has remained highly vulnerable to fog.[56] The main insight here is that unexpected volatilities in activities undergoing

---

[51]   Malcolm Campbell-Verduyn, 'What Does Technology Do?' in Marijn Hoijtink and Matthias Leese (eds), *Technology and Agency in International Relations* (Routledge 2019) <https://academic.oup.com/edited-volume/35412> accessed 24 February 2023.

[52]   Donald MacKenzie, 'Opening the Black Boxes of Global Finance' (2005) 12 Review of International Political Economy.

[53]   Maximilian Mayer, Mariana Carpes and Ruth Knoblich, 'A Toolbox for Studying the Global Politics of Science and Technology' in Maximilian Mayer, Mariana Carpes and Ruth Knoblich (eds), *The Global Politics of Science and Technology: Vol. 2 Concepts from International Relations and Other Disciplines* (Springer 2014).

[54]   Malcolm Campbell-Verduyn, Marcel Goguen and Tony Porter, 'Finding Fault Lines in Long Chains of Financial Information' (2019) 26 Review of International Political Economy, 917.

[55]   Christian Borch, Kristian Bondo Hansen and Ann-Christina Lange, 'Markets, Bodies, and Rhythms: A Rhythmanalysis of Financial Markets from Open-Outcry Trading to High-Frequency Trading' (2015) 33 Environment and Planning D: Society and Space, 1092.

[56]   Donald MacKenzie, 'Be Grateful for Drizzle' (2014) 36 London Review of Books.

technological 'disruption', such as increasingly automated financial markets,[57] can be understood through human practices and non-human objects are integrally interrelated with one another in brittle manners.

One example of IPE insights drawing on STS scholarship is the extension of Bruno Latour's notion of 'long chains'[58] by Campbell-Verduyn, Goguen and Porter to conceive a four-phased pattern of the development and decoupling of informational infrastructures ('infostructures'). In a first phase – infostructure development – dispersed human actors and technical objects become integrated and form 'long chains' of financial information. Algorithms, fibre-optic cables and data centres for example are connected through electronic communications networks (ECNs) enabling flows of information that traders harness to conduct activities on financial exchanges.

In a second phase – infostructure expansion and risk accumulation – activities building on the establishment of relations between human practices and non-human objects grow rapidly and build up risks in ways that Campbell-Verduyn, Goguen and Porter liken to 'fault lines' underpinning earthquakes. In the lead-up to the 2010 flash crash electronic trading grew rapidly, if unevenly across markets for different financial products, drawing in a host of agents that are far less able to harness the material and cognitive advantages of firstcomers. The lead-up to the 2010 flash crash saw the introduction of a flurry of risks stemming from the 'arms race'[59] between HFT firms seeking to co-locate their computer servers directly at major exchanges, even though technical malfunction had led to numerous shutdowns and outages at major exchanges.[60] A similar set of risks stemmed from the herd-like behaviour of HFT firms, who programmed relatively similar automating trading strategies and began to draw on similar sources of data. Mini flash crashes that remain under-recognized beyond specialist communities occur here 'despite generally not becoming public knowledge'; these produce serious instabilities and risks for the markets.[61] The key point here is that, even when recognized

---

[57] Bo Hee Min and Christian Borch, 'Systemic Failures and Organizational Risk Management in Algorithmic Trading: Normal Accidents and High Reliability in Financial Markets' (2022) 52 Social Studies of Science.

[58] Bruno Latour, *Reassembling the Social: An Introduction to Actor-Network-Theory* (Oxford University Press 2005).

[59] Larry Harris, 'Stop the High-Frequency Trader Arms Race' *Financial Times* (27 December 2012).

[60] New York Times, 'A History of Stock Exchange Failures' <http://www.nytimes.com/interactive/2015/07/08/business/dealbook/history-of-stock-exchange-failures.html?_r=0> accessed 8 September 2022.

[61] Paraná (n 7) 81.

these risks remain largely unaddressed and develop 'fault lines' that can lead to have outsized impacts of what might otherwise be small 'shocks' or blockages in data flows.

In a third phase – infostructural decoupling – relatively minor break(s) in the long chain of financial data circulation can instigate wider market volatilities. Case in point is the 2010 flash crash in which short delays in the NYSE's Continuous Quotation System instigated a wider panic and sell-off as price data were not made readily available. Similarly, breaks can occur when false data appear, such as the erroneous story of an attack on then American president Obama that was tweeted and then nearly imme-diately retracted by Associated Press on 23 April 2013. Over the course of 5 minutes this tweet instigated a market crash and rapid recovery as pre-programmed automated trading algorithms responded to the false news and its subsequent correction. Dubbed the 'hash crash', this volatil-ity highlighted not only the roles of individual news and social media firms like Twitter and the Associated Press, but also how the pre-programming trading algorithms and machine-readable data feeds upon which HFT relies can have devastating consequences when they interpret the news incorrectly or simply impatiently.[62] A further instance of how a minor break in data flows can instigate wider panic occurred when a glitch in one of the algorithms operated by Knight Capital Partners (KCP) led to erratic trades on nearly 150 different stocks that this HFT firm had bought at a high price and then sold at a lower price. Over 30 minutes on 1 August 2012, KCP lost nearly a half-billion dollars. A private sector-led bailout of the firm had to be initiated.[63]

In a final phase – regulatory repair – efforts to attend to now well-recognized risks and 'fault lines' can lead to the introduction of a new informational infrastructure and, importantly, novel sets of risks. While not necessarily occurring, the development of new infostructure can be ushered in through regulatory responses to previous crises. In response to the flash crashes that occurred on 2 May 2010, the introduction of the CAT and repositories of trade data has instigated a host of new risks like cyber-attacks and hacking of these centralized informational archives. These risks, in turn, have in turn prompted the wider turn to integrate new material objects, such as distributed ledgers technologies (DLTs). The introduction of new technical objects in the form of DLTs such as

---

[62] Tero Karppi and Kate Crawford, 'Social Media, Financial Algorithms and the Hack Crash' (2016) 33 Theory, Culture & Society.

[63] Matthew Philips, 'Knight Shows How to Lose $440 Million in 30 Minutes' *Bloomberg* (2 August 2012).

blockchains to distribute data and render finance less vulnerable to hacks and cyber-attacks, has developed fragile relations with human practices of trade and production. In the initial years of blockchain-based 'decentralized finance' (DeFi) the re-introduction of intermediation and centralization of power was neither well recognized nor acted upon. Attempts at regulatory repair have been initiated only *after* small 'breaks' in data flows to the exchanges that have served in practice as centralized nodes in theoretically 'distributed networks'.[64] The production and trading of 'cryptocurrencies' like Bitcoin since its advent in 2009 through new types of 'mining' and exchanging these digital tokens has tended to mask the forms of centralization and intermediation underlying these activities that rapidly grew as new actors rushed into the initial and subsequent forms of 'decentralized finance' (DeFi). The fragilities in the relations between centralized human organization and technical objects in and across DeFi have broken in small events that have led to flash crashes. A wider systemic crash in traditional financial markets sparked by DeFi activities has not occurred, despite warnings by global financial regulators.[65] It also remains to be determined how precisely the fourth phase of 'regulatory repair' will develop and potentially spark new risks in turn. At the time of writing, hearings were being held in the US on cryptocurrencies and leading politicians were calling for echoing regulatory warnings of the risk of volatilities spreading from DeFi to traditional finance.[66] Meanwhile, the European Union introduced Markets in Crypto-Assets Regulation (MiCA) in 2020.[67]

In sum, the phased pattern Campbell-Verduyn, Goguen and Porter detailed here helps understand how otherwise small glitches can result in wider financial market crashes and recoveries. While highlighting a pattern, its phases are far from an inevitable or pre-destined 'cycle' or law. Identified in several periods of instability across decades, the phases

---

[64]   Kharpal, 'Ethereum Briefly Crashed from $319 to 10 Cents in Seconds on One Exchange after "Multimillion Dollar" Trade' *CNBC* (22 June 2017).

[65]   Financial Stability Board, 'Crypto-Asset Markets: Potential Channels for Future Financial Stability Implications' <https://www.fsb.org/2018/10/crypto-asset-markets-potential-channels-for-future-financial-stability-implications> accessed 8 September 2022).

[66]   United States Senate Committee on Banking, Housing and Urban Affairs, 'Cryptocurrencies: What Are They Good For?' <https://www.banking.senate.gov/hearings/cryptocurrencies-what-are-they-good-for> accessed 8 September 2022.

[67]   European Commission, 'Proposal for a Regulation of the European Parliament and of the Council on Markets in Crypto-assets, and amending Directive (EU) 2019/1937' <https://eur-lex.europa.eu/legal-content/EN/TXT/?uri=CELEX%3A52020PC0593> accessed 8 September 2022.

Table 7.1   Summary of phases in the development and decoupling of infostructures

Period	Phase One: Development	Phase Two: Expansion and Risk Accumulation	Phase Three: Break and Wider Instability	Phase Four: Regulatory Repair and New Risks
1980s–2010s	Computerized trading	Race for speed with (Ultra) High-Frequency Trading	Disrupted data flows leading to flash crashes	Centralization of information enhancing risks of hacking
2010s–present	Distributed ledger technology	Race for 'decentralization' introducing new intermediaries	Disruption of new intermediaries underpinning flash crashes	On-going and to be determined

Source: Adapted from Campbell-Verduyn, Goguen and Porter (2019).

summarized in Table 7.1 stress how 'instability events' can still be conceived in ways that move beyond the inevitabilities of the instrumental and linear emphasis of rationalist IPE perspectives. Attempts at regulatory repair *can* but do not necessary lead to subsequent crises. While injecting greater degrees of nuance into IPE by emphasizing how fragilities in the ways different actors and objects are brought together in enabling digital financial markets can lead to instabilities, the greater complexity of this and other interpretivist accounts can obscure where precisely power is exercised and lies in an increasingly digitizing global political economy. Embracing complexity has benefits in providing additional nuance and understanding of unexpected events. Yet, a drawback is the inability to pinpoint precisely where power is exercised in the same way that rationalist accounts illustrate the roles of specific states and market actors, as well as social classes.

As the concluding section argues, it is *together* that the two broad and diverging yet complementary sets of IPE approaches can provide insight into volatilities and other events related to the growing integration of emergent technologies like AI and Big Data in the global political economy.

CONCLUSION

This chapter has outlined and applied insights from two broad sets of IPE perspectives for understanding the origins and effects of volatility events in a rapidly digitizing global political economy. Complementary strengths of each were illustrated in making more nuanced sense of power and governance with varying degrees of analytical complexity in the case of flash crashes reoccurring in financial markets where the presence of Big Data and artificial intelligence has grown. While instrumental IPE perspectives foreground the power of state and market actors, as well as social classes, interpretivist approaches stress relations between human actors, practices and material objects. The central conclusion of this chapter's analysis is that, taken together, IPE's twin sets of perspectives inject complementary degrees of complexity in understanding the broader contours of power in increasingly complex and unstable global political economy generally, and financial markets in particular. This conclusion underlines the need for enhanced dialogue and engagement between the two broad strands of 'instrumentalist' and 'interpretivist' approaches to generate understanding of the wider politics and governance of instabilities surrounding flash crashes and other rapidly unfolding events in both finance and a wider global political economy being 'disrupted' by AI and Big Data.

Susan Strange[68] catalyzed the modern field of IPE in seeking to overcome what she identified as a 'dialogue of the deaf' between international economics and international politics. To bridge the growing of 'niches and networks'[69] within this interdiscipline, *internal* as well as *external* dialogues between IPE and other (inter-)disciplines are required to make more nuanced sense of instabilities evolving in an increasingly complex global political economy. This bridge-building is particularly required as 'massive market volatility' continues to occur in novel manners, with sudden spikes in the values of stocks that have become memes in online communities, a further set of poorly understood events attracting wider popular and regulatory attention at the time of writing.[70] A high-profile example of this volatility occurred in early 2021 with the one hundredfold increase in the stock of American consumer electronics firm GameStop

---

[68]   Susan Strange, 'International Economics and International Relations: A Case of Mutual Neglect' (1970) 46 International Affairs.
[69]   Leonard Seabrooke and Kevin Young, 'The Networks and Niches of International Political Economy' (2017) 24 Review of International Political Economy.
[70]   Sarah Min, 'A Washington Beating for Robinhood's CEO' *Chief Investment Officer* (19 February 2021).

allegedly stemming from retail investors using novel trading platforms such as Robinhood and coordinating their action in internet forums like Reddit's wallstreetbets. Hedge funds that had borrowed to take 'short' positions betting that GameStop stock would drop in price suffered heavy losses, with a nearly half-billion fund shutting down. Understanding these and other volatilities associated with so-called 'memestock' rallies will benefit from both instrumentalist and interpretivist IPE analysis. The former can help question initial accounts of this event as a 'counter-hegemonic'[71] power shift from elite professional wealth managers to retail investors. In particular, two emerging features of so-called 'Reddit rallies' challenge existing instrumentalist accounts of this novel set of volatilities:

1. their *origins* in trading strategies are devised and popularized by certi-fied financial analysts (CFAs) such as Keith Gill, whose YouTube videos were widely credited with initially spurring the 2021 rally in GameStop stock;
2. their *scaling* as hedge funds and other financial professionals cata-lyze market actions against competitors. US Congressional hearings prominently revealed how the main digital platform used to bid up GameStop stock, Robinhood, funded itself in part by selling customer order data to competing hedge funds.[72]

In short, existing understandings of 'memestock' rallies as one class of social actors (the 'unsophisticated dumb money' represented by small-time retail traders) challenging another (the 'sophisticated smart money' of large professional funds), can productively be complicated by more nuanced IPE *cui bono* analysis. This includes putting liberal, critical and mercantilist accounts in dialogue with more interpretivist accounts that, for instance, stress emotional drivers such as residual anger and desires for revenge for the 2007–2008 global financial crisis as gleaned from Reddit posts.[73] Going forward, memestock rallies and other instabilities under-stood as arising in what philosopher Luciano Floridi has dubbed the

---

[71]   Usman Chohan, 'Too Big to Fail, Too Small to Win: The Counter-Hegemony of WallStreetBets' <https://ssrn.com/abstract=3849770> accessed 8 September 2022.
[72]   Douglas MacMillan and Yeganeh Torbati, 'Robinhood and Citadel's rela-tionship comes into focus as Washington vows to examine stock-market moves' *Washington Post* (29 January 2021).
[73]   Tim Di Muzio, 'GameStop Capitalism: Wall Street vs. The Reddit Rally (Part I)' <https://www.econstor.eu/bitstream/10419/229951/1/20210200_di_muz io_gamestop_capitalism_part_1.pdf> accessed 8 September 2022.

'infosphere'[74] will benefit from engaging both broad sets of IPE perspectives to make more nuanced sense of whether and how 'disruptive' technological change alters or extends existing power relations in the global economy.

REFERENCES

Aitken R, '"All data is credit data": Constituting the Unbanked' (2017) 21 Competition & Change.

Aitken R, 'Capital at Its Fringes' (2006) 11 New Political Economy.

Amoore L, 'Cloud Geographies: Computing, Data, Sovereignty' (2018) 42 Progress in Human Geography.

Angel J and McCabe D, 'Fairness in Financial Markets: The Case of High Frequency Trading' (2013) 112 Journal of Business Ethics.

Bain B, 'Audit Trail Could Boost Cybersecurity Threat, Exchanges Say' *Bloomberg*, 10 October 2017.

Barder A, 'Neo-Materialist Ecologies and Global Systemic Crises' (2016) 13 Globalizations.

Beaumier G and others, 'Global Regulations for a Digital Economy: Between New and Old Challenges' (2020) 11 Global Policy.

Boldyrev I and Svetlova E, *Enacting Dismal Science: New Perspectives on the Performativity of Economics* (Palgrave Macmillan 2016).

Borch C, 'High-Frequency Trading, Algorithmic Finance and the Flash Crash: Reflections on Eventalization' (2017) 45 Economy and Society.

Borch C, Bondo Hansen K and Lange A-C, 'Markets, Bodies, and Rhythms: A Rhythmanalysis of Financial Markets from Open-Outcry Trading to High-Frequency Trading' (2015) 33 Environment and Planning D: Society and Space.

Bowley G, 'The Flash Crash, in Miniature' *New York Times* (8 November 2010).

Brown N, 'The Rise of High Frequency Trading: The Role Algorithms, and the Lack of Regulations, Play in Today's Stock Market' (2011) 11 Appalachian Journal of Law.

Campbell-Verduyn M, 'What Does Technology Do?' in Marijn Hoijtink and Matthias Leese (eds), *Technology and Agency in International Relations* (Routledge 2019).

Campbell-Verduyn M, Goguen M and Porter T, 'Big Data and Algorithmic Governance: The Case of Financial Practices' (2017) 22 New Political Economy.

Campbell-Verduyn M, Goguen M and Porter T, 'Finding Fault Lines in Long Chains of Financial Information' (2019) 26 Review of International Political Economy.

Carlson M, *A Brief History of the 1987 Stock Market Crash with a Discussion of the Federal Reserve Response* (Finance and Economics Discussion Series Divisions of Research & Statistics and Monetary Affairs Federal Reserve Board, 2006) 4.

---

[74] Luciano Floridi, *The Fourth Revolution: How the Infosphere Is Reshaping Human Reality* (Oxford University Press 2014).

Chohan U, 'Too Big to Fail, Too Small to Win: The Counter-Hegemony of WallStreetBets' <https://ssrn.com/abstract=3849770> accessed 8 September 2022.

Coombs N, 'What Is an Algorithm? Financial Regulation in the Era of High-Frequency Trading' (2016) 45 Economy and Society.

Cox R, *Production, Power, and World Order: Social Forces in the Making of History* (Columbia University Press 1987).

Dauvergne P, *AI in the Wild: Sustainability in the Age of Artificial Intelligence* (MIT Press 2020).

De Goede M, *Virtue, Fortune, and Faith: A Genealogy of Finance* (University of Minnesota Press 2001).

De Goede M, 'Beyond Economism in International Political Economy' (2003) 29 *Review of International Studies.*

Di Muzio T, 'GameStop Capitalism: Wall Street vs. The Reddit Rally (Part I)' <https://www.econstor.eu/bitstream/10419/229951/1/20210200_di_muzio_game stop_capitalism_part_1.pdf> accessed 8 September 2022.

European Commission, 'Proposal for a Regulation of the European Parliament and of the Council on Markets in Crypto-assets, and amending Directive (EU) 2019/1937' <https://eur-lex.europa.eu/legal-content/EN/TXT/?uri=CELEX%3A52020PC0593> accessed 8 September 2022.

Fazzini K and Moyer L, 'Hackers Broke into an SEC Database and Made Millions from Inside Information, Says DOJ' *CNBC*, 15 January 2019.

Financial Stability Board, 'Crypto-asset Markets: Potential Channels for Future Financial Stability Implications' <https://www.fsb.org/2018/10/crypto-asset-markets-potential-channels-for-future-financial-stability-implications/> acc essed 8 September 2022.

Fletcher G-G, 'Deterring Algorithmic Manipulation' (2021) 74 Vanderbilt Law Review.

Floridi L, *The Fourth Revolution: How the Infosphere Is Reshaping Human Reality* (Oxford University Press 2014).

Gruin J, 'The Epistemic Evolution of Market Authority: Big Data, Blockchain and China's Neostatist Challenge to Neoliberalism' (2021) 25 Competition & Change.

Hardiman N and Metinsoy S, 'Power, Ideas, and National Preferences: Ireland and the FTT' (2019) 26 Journal of European Public Policy.

Hardin C and Rottinghaus A, 'Introducing a Cultural Approach to Technology in Financial Markets' (2015) 8 Journal of Cultural Economy.

Harris L, 'Stop the High-Frequency Trader Arms Race' *Financial Times* (27 December 2012).

Herian R, 'Regulating Disruption: Blockchain, GDPR, and Questions of Data Sovereignty' (2018) 22 Journal of Internet Law.

International Organization of Securities Commissions, 'Mechanisms Used by Trading Venues to Manage Extreme Volatility and Preserve Orderly Trading' 2018 <https://www.iosco.org/library/pubdocs/pdf/IOSCOPD607.pdf> accessed 7 September 2022.

Joint Staff Report of the Commodities Futures Trading Commission and Securities and Exchange Commission, 'Findings Regarding the Market Events of May 6, 2010' <https://www.sec.gov/news/studies/2010/marketevents-report.pdf> accessed 20 February 2023.

Kamps J and Kleinberg B, 'To the Moon: Defining and Detecting Cryptocurrency Pump-and-Dumps' (2018) 7 Crime Science.

Karppi T and Crawford K, 'Social Media, Financial Algorithms and the Hack Crash' (2016) 33 Theory, Culture & Society.

Keller A, 'Robocops: Regulating High Frequency Trading after the Flash Crash of 2010' (2012) 73 Ohio State Law Journal.

Kharpal A, 'Ethereum Briefly Crashed from $319 to 10 Cents in Seconds on One Exchange after "Multimillion Dollar" Trade' *CNBC* (22 June 2017).

Kremers R and Brassett J, 'Mobile Payments, Social Money: Everyday Politics of the Consumer Subject' (2017) 22 New Political Economy.

Lange A-C, Lenglet M and Seyfert R, 'Cultures of High-Frequency Trading: Mapping the Landscape of Algorithmic Developments in Contemporary Financial Markets' (2016) 45 Economy and Society.

Lange C, 'High-Frequency Trading' in C Borch and R Wosnitzer (eds), *Routledge Handbook of Critical Finance Studies* (Routledge 2020).

Latour B, *Reassembling the Social: An Introduction to Actor-Network-Theory* (Oxford University Press 2005).

Lenglet M, 'Conflicting Codes and Codings: How Algorithmic Trading Is Reshaping Financial Regulation' (2011) 6 Theory, Culture & Society.

Lenglet M and Mol J, 'Squaring the Speed of Light? Regulating Market Access in Algorithmic Finance' (2016) 45 Economy and Society.

Lewis, M, *Flash Boys: A Wall Street Revolt* (W. W. Norton & Company 2014).

MacKenzie D, 'How Algorithms Interact: Goffman's "Interaction Order" in Automated Trading' (2019) 36(2) Theory, Culture & Society.

MacKenzie D, 'Be Grateful for Drizzle' (2014) 36 London Review of Books.

MacKenzie, D, 'Opening the Black Boxes of Global Finance' (2005) 12 Review of International Political Economy.

MacMillan D and Torbati Y, 'Robinhood and Citadel's Relationship Comes into Focus as Washington Vows to Examine Stock-Market Moves' *Washington Post* (29 January 2021).

Markham J and Harty D, 'For Whom the Bell Tolls: The Demise of Exchange Trading Floors and the Growth of ECNs' (2007) 33 Journal of Corporation Law.

Maurer B, 'Re-risking in Realtime: On Possible Futures for Finance after the Blockchain' (2017) 9(2) Behemoth: A Journal on Civilisation.

Mayer M, Carpes M and Knoblich R, 'A Toolbox for Studying the Global Politics of Science and Technology' in M Mayer, M Carpes and R Knoblich (eds), *The Global Politics of Science and Technology: Vol. 2 Concepts from International Relations and Other Disciplines* (Springer 2014).

Min BH and Borch C, 'Systemic Failures and Organizational Risk Management in Algorithmic Trading: Normal Accidents and High Reliability in Financial Markets' (2022) 52 Social Studies of Science.

Min S, 'A Washington Beating for Robinhood's CEO' *Chief Investment Officer* (19 February 2021).

Mullen J, 'U.K. Pound Plunges More Than 6% in Mysterious Flash Crash' *CNN* (7 October 2016).

Nanex, Nanex Flash Crash Summary Report (2010) <http://www.nanex.net/FlashCrashFinal/FlashCrashSummary.html> accessed 7 September 2022.

New York Times, 'A History of Stock Exchange Failures' <http://www.nytimes.com/interactive/2015/07/08/business/dealbook/history-of-stock-exchange-failures.html?_r=0> accessed 8 September 2022.

Nguyen L, 'Citi: Maybe Flash Crashes Aren't So Bad, After All' *Bloomberg* (1 September 2015).

Paraná E, *Digitalized Finance: Financial Capitalism and Informational Revolution* (Brill 2008).

Pasquale F, 'Law's Acceleration of Finance: Redefining the Problem of High-Frequency Trading' (2014) 36 Cardozo Law Review.

Petry J, 'Same Same, But Different: Varieties of Capital Markets, Chinese State Capitalism and the Global Financial Order' (2021) 25 Competition & Change.

Philips M, 'Knight Shows How to Lose $440 Million in 30 Minutes' *Bloomberg* (2 August 2012).

Roderick L, 'Discipline and Power in the Digital Age: The Case of the US Consumer Data Broker Industry' (2017) 40 Critical Sociology.

Rosenberg N, *Inside the Black Box: Technology and Economics* (Cambridge University Press 1982).

Seabrooke L and Young K, 'The Networks and Niches of International Political Economy' (2017) 24 Review of International Political Economy.

Seyfert R, 'Bugs, Predations or Manipulations? Incompatible Epistemic Regimes of High-Frequency Trading' (2016) 45 Economy and Society.

Snider L, 'Interrogating the Algorithm: Debt, Derivatives and the Social Reconstruction of Stock Market Trading' (2014) 40 Critical Sociology.

Sohn, I, 'Toward Normative Fragmentation: An East Asian Financial Architecture in the Post-Global Crisis World' (2012) 19 Review of International Political Economy.

Strange S, 'International Economics and International Relations: A Case of Mutual Neglect' (1970) 46 International Affairs.

Talalay M, Tooze R and Farrands C, 'Technology, Culture, and Competitiveness: Change and the World Political Economy' in C Farrands, M Talalay and R Tooze (eds), *Technology, Culture, and Competitiveness: Change and the World Political Economy* (Routledge 1997).

Thompson GF, 'Time, Trading and Algorithms in Financial Sector Security' (2017) 22 New Political Economy.

Tsuchiya T, 'Profitability of Cryptocurrency Pump and Dump Schemes' (2019) 3 Digital Finance.

United States Senate Committee on Banking, Housing and Urban Affairs, 'Cryptocurrencies: What Are They Good For?' <https://www.banking.senate.gov/hearings/cryptocurrencies-what-are-they-good-for> (accessed 8 September 2022).

Van Loon A, 'European Financial Governance: FTT Reform, Controversies and Governments' Responsiveness' (2021) 9 Politics and Governance.

Vaughan L, *Flash Crash: A Trading Savant, a Global Manhunt, and the Most Mysterious Market Crash in History* (Doubleday 2020).

8. Governance of AI and gender: building on International Human Rights Law and relevant regional frameworks
Elizabeth Coombs and Halefom H. Abraha

1. INTRODUCTION

Reports on AI,[1] of which there are many, generally start by stating that AI is fundamentally transforming societies; if not now, then in the near future. The global revenue for AI products and services is expected to increase from $US644 million in 2016 to $US36 billion in 2025.[2] Big Tech corporations are primarily responsible for driving the form and uses of AI-derived from their massive datasets.[3] These data have been supplied by individuals

---

[1] There are many definitions of AI. None fully captures the evolving nature of this technology. The 2018 definition of the European Commission is adopted for the purpose of this chapter: 'Artificial intelligence (AI) refers to systems designed by humans that, given a complex goal, act in the physical or digital world by perceiving their environment, interpreting the collected structured or unstructured data, reasoning on the knowledge derived from this data and deciding the best action(s) to take (according to pre-defined parameters) to achieve the given goal. AI systems can also be designed to learn to adapt their behaviour by analysing how the environment is affected by their previous actions. As a scientific discipline, AI includes several approaches and techniques, such as machine learning (of which deep learning and reinforcement learning are specific examples), machine reasoning (which includes planning, scheduling, knowledge representation and reasoning, search, and optimization), and robotics (which includes control, perception, sensors and actuators, as well as the integration of all other techniques into cyber-physical systems)' [internal quotations omitted]: The European Commission's High-Level Expert Group on Artificial Intelligence, 'Definition of AI: Main Capabilities and Scientific Disciplines', European Commission 2018, 7 <https://ec.europa.eu/futu rium/en/system/files/ged/ai_hleg_definition_of_ai_18_december_1.pdf> accessed 6 August 2021.
[2] Shoshana Zuboff, *The Age of Surveillance Capitalism: The Fight for a Human Future at the New Frontier of Power* (Profile Books 2019).
[3] While Big Tech dominates the field, small and medium-sized enterprises and the informal economy represent four out of five enterprises in the world, also warranting oversight. See 'Informal Economy' (*International Labour Organization*) <https://www.ilo.org/global/topics/employment-promotion/informal-economy/la ng--en/index.htm> accessed 6 August 2021.

through the many activities they undertake offline and online. States and governments are active also as data custodians and suppliers, markets, funders and developers.[4] While there is no doubt that AI systems can bring socio-economic benefits across industries and social activities, there are growing concerns that they also leave the door wide open for abuses. AI, for example, has been found to impact the right to equality/non-discrimination, the right to privacy and informational privacy, access to justice, the right to dignity, the right to social security and social assistance, the right to good administration, and the right to consumer protection.[5]

The impacts of AI on fundamental rights and freedom have recently gained significant policy and academic traction, given the fact that most AI systems are currently deployed in a regulatory vacuum.

Awareness of the potential impact of AI systems upon rights necessitates new responses to the reality that AI systems are neither neutral nor neutered.[6] 'Gender' stereotypes are part of AI's fabric.[7] 'Algorithmic bias'[8] is a recognised phenomenon, identified in areas as diverse as equal pay in the collaborative economy and platform work,[9] criminal justice systems,[10] loan

---

[4] 'The New Machinery of Government: Using Machine Technology in Administrative Decision-Making' NSW Ombudsman (2021) <https://www.parliament.nsw.gov.au/la/papers/Pages/tabled-paper-details.aspx?pk=81066&houseCode=LH> accessed 19 April 2022.

[5] FRA, 'Getting the Future Right: Artificial Intelligence and Fundamental Rights' (European Fundamental Rights Agency 2020).

[6] 'Dutch Scientific Council Knows: AI Is Neither Neutral Nor Always Rational – Racism and Technology Center' <https://racismandtechnology.center/2021/11/26/dutch-scientific-council-knows-ai-is-neither-neutral-nor-always-rational/> accessed 11 June 2022; Catherine Stinson, 'Algorithms Are Not Neutral: Bias in Collaborative Filtering' [2022] AI and Ethics.

[7] UNESCO, 'Artificial Intelligence and Gender Equality. Key Findings of UNESCO's Global Dialogue' (2020) <https://unesxcodoc.unesco.org/in/documentViewer.html?v=2.1.196&id+2020> accessed 15 June 2022.

[8] This expression is more inclusive than 'algorithmic discrimination', and is meant as placing privileged groups at a systemic advantage and unprivileged groups at a systemic disadvantage. See Janneke Gerards and Raphaële Xenidis, 'Algorithmic Discrimination in Europe: Challenges and Opportunities for EU Equality Law' (*European Futures*, 3 December 2020) 47 <https://www.europeanfutures.ed.ac.uk/algorithmic-discrimination-in-europe-challenges-and-opportunities-for-eu-equality-law/> accessed 5 August 2021.

[9] Gerards and Xenidis (n 8).

[10] Julia Angwin and others, 'Machine Bias' (*ProPublica*, May 2016) <https://www.propublica.org/article/machine-bias-risk-assessments-in-criminal-sentencing?token=PfkMUk0VOJFLCI7ofscfo7VgS3x9ll1i> accessed 5 August 2021.

and credit applications,[11] platform content moderation,[12] visa and migration approvals, recruitment and promotion,[13] airport screening systems,[14] through to (supposed) identification of sexual orientation.[15]

In addition to bias and discrimination, gendered technological harms also implicate autonomy, bodily integrity and personhood rights.[16] The risks of AI for women and gender-diverse individuals occur at various stages – from design, programming, building, training and testing to operating algorithms.[17] The harms that arise, although multifaceted, can be broadly classified into three forms: physical, institutional and psychological.[18] Physical harm denies bodily autonomy, for example, AI software that generates nude images from publicly available pictures; institutional harms arise from underperforming algorithms that deny access to services and support, particularly for marginalised groups, and anthropomorphised technology that reflects and entrenches harmful stereotypes producing humiliation and psychological damage.[19] Researchers have documented how inaccurate gender inference by social media

---

[11]   Gerards and Xenidis (n 8).

[12]   UN Special Rapporteur on the Right to Freedom of Opinion and Expression and Working Party Human Rights, Transnational Corporations and Other Business Enterprises, 'UN Special Rapporteur on the Right to Freedom of Opinion and Expression' (2020) OL OTH37/2020.

[13]   Jeffrey Dastin, 'Amazon Scraps Secret AI Recruiting Tool that Showed Bias against Women' *Reuters* (10 October 2018) <https://www.reuters.com/article/us-amazon-com-jobs-automation-insight-idUSKCN1MK08G> accessed 5 August 2021.

[14]   Sasha Costanza-Chock, 'Design Justice, A.I., and Escape from the Matrix of Domination DOI' <https://www.researchgate.net/publication/326618753_Design_Justice_AI_and_Escape_from_the_Matrix_of_Domination> accessed 15 June 2022.

[15]   Yilun Wang, 'Deep Neural Networks Are More Accurate than Humans at Detecting Sexual Orientation from Facial Images' (2018) 114 Journal of Personality and Social Psychology; for the flaws in this work see, for example Blaise Aguera y Arcas, 'Do Algorithms Reveal Sexual Orientation or Just Expose Our Stereotypes?' (*Medium*, 18 January 2018) <https://medium.com/@blaisea/do-algorithms-reveal-sexual-orientation-or-just-expose-our-stereotypes-d998fafd f477> accessed 6 August 2021.

[16]   The use of AI systems for the classification, detection and prediction of race and gender is particularly impactful. See Sarah Myers West, Meredith Whittaker and Kate Crawford, 'Discriminating Systems: Gender, Race and Power in AI' (AI Now Institute 2019).

[17]   Gerards and Xenidis (n 8).

[18]   Lena Wang, 'The Three Harms of Gendered Technology' (2020) 24 Australasian Journal of Information Systems: Selected Papers from 2019 AICE Conference.

[19]   ibid.

algorithms 'reinforces gender stereotypes, accentuates gender binarism, undermines privacy and autonomy, and may cause feelings of rejection, impacting people's self-esteem, confidence, and authenticity.'[20]

The following instances help illustrate the actual and potential harms of AI on gender:

- Amazon's infamous hiring algorithm, developed to select the best software engineers and later dropped for being discriminatory (if not outright sexist) against women applicants, illustrates how training AI systems with unrepresentative data can exacerbate systemic gender bias.[21]

- Algorithmic tools that underlie big social media platforms, such as Facebook and Google, could 'reinscribe gender, solidify the distinctions between male and female, and promote a dualistic realm via algorithms that depend on entrenched notions of what men and women want and need.'[22]

- A study commissioned by the European network of legal experts in gender equality and non-discrimination revealed, 'Gender-based algorithmic classification could ... lead to excluding gender non-conforming, trans and intersex individuals from access to certain goods, services and jobs or forcing them into categories with which they do not identify.'[23]

- AI systems can give rise to new gender-based bias and discrimination even if they are trained based on gender-neutral characteristics. Empirical studies have shown that, even if algorithmic gender-related harms do not exist at the design and implementation stage, they could also arise when these algorithms engage in 'proxy data', such as financial status and geolocation.[24] 'Proxy discrimination' occurs when an algorithm substitutes a facially neutral characteristic

---

[20]   Eduard Fosch-Villaronga and others, 'A Little Bird Told Me Your Gender: Gender Inferences in Social Media' (2021) 58 Information Processing and Management, 1.

[21]   Dastin (n 13).

[22]   Jonathan E Schroeder, 'Reinscribing Gender: Social Media, Algorithms, Bias' (2021) 37 Journal of Marketing Management, 376.

[23]   Gerards and Xenidis (n 8) 62.

[24]   Rebecca Kelly Slaughter, 'Algorithms and Economic Justice: A Taxonomy of Harms and a Path Forward for the Federal Trade Commission' (2021) 23 Yale Journal of Law & Technology; Sandra Wachter, 'Affinity Profiling and Discrimination by Association in Online Behavioural Advertising' (2020) 35 Berkeley Technology Law Journal.

for a protected class.[25] For instance, one empirical study revealed that job opportunities in Science, Technology, Engineering and Math are more likely to be shown to men than women even if these ads were explicitly intended to be gender-neutral.[26]

● An example of bias against gender-diverse individuals, is also provided by research showing 'intelligent' airport screening systems systematically signalling transsexual individuals for security searches.[27]

The choice and treatment of data points combined with the social, racial and cultural standpoints of *who* makes the assumptive determinations,[28] in AI systems shapes AI's gender expressions. Currently, the *who* tends to be white, educated males within western industrialised countries, whose values and norms are exported along with their technology[29] into new markets, trade agreements, global data flows and e-commerce. All of these shape the lives of individuals and communities.

AI systems, with 'black box' algorithms,[30] often produced at industrial scale, built into the backend of institutional decision-making, unseen and often unknown to those whose lives and opportunities they influence,[31] will present major challenges to gender equity. AI systems possess the ability to write a gendered future of automated and amplified prejudice

---

[25]   Audrey Adams, 'Algorithmic Decisions and Their Human Consequences | The Regulatory Review' (*The Regulatory Review*, 11 November 2021) <https://www.theregreview.org/2021/11/11/adams-algorithmic-decisions-human-consequences/> accessed 13 June 2022.

[26]   Anja Lambrecht and Catherine Tucker, 'Algorithmic Bias? An Empirical Study into Apparent Gender-Based Discrimination in the Display of STEM Career Ads' (2018) 65 Management Science.

[27]   Costanza-Chock (n 14).

[28]   Maggie Walter, 'Data Politics and Indigenous Representation in Australian Statistics' [2016] Researchgate <https://www.researchgate.net/publication/317656929_Data_politics_and_Indigenous_representation_in_Australian_statistics> accessed 6 August 2021.

[29]   West, Whittaker and Crawford (n 16); Lee Rainie and others, 'How Americans Think about Artificial Intelligence' (Pew Research Center 2022) <https://www.pewresearch.org/internet/2022/03/17/how-americans-think-about-artificial-intelligence/> accessed 18 April 2022.

[30]   That is, where it is not possible to discern the reason for certain decisions (European Commission's High-Level Expert Group on Artificial Intelligence, 'Definition of AI: Main Capabilities and Scientific Disciplines' (European Commission 2018) 7 <https://ec.europa.eu/futurium/en/system/files/ged/ai_hleg_definition_of_ai_18_december_1.pdf> accessed 6 August 2021.

[31]   West, Whittake and Crawford (n 16).

and harm,[32] inextricably associated with concepts of 'unfitness' or 'unworthiness' that rationalise these inequities.[33]

The risks and the resulting harms have been attributed, at least in part, to gender deficits in data used for training algorithms combined with the unrepresentative nature of the AI industry and existing structural inequality.[34] But AI gender issues will not be rectified solely by ensuring diverse representation in the AI sector, or by seeking to remove gender distortions in training datasets. While important, these actions are no match for the geopolitical, socio-economic dynamics underpinning AI rollouts and shaping regulatory formulation. When competitiveness depends upon existing structures that subordinate certain groups for social, economic and political purposes, the resulting marginalisation can be difficult to change.[35] Therefore, AI governance and regulation need to be fit for the purpose of recognising and addressing AI-induced gender harms – and this includes ensuring the adverse impacts of algorithms are not discretionary but of legal obligation.[36]

2.   THE NEED FOR REGULATORY RESPONSE

AI harms give rise to repeated calls for regulation.[37] These calls have not been the lone voice of activists and feminists. The general media since 2012 have seen growing calls for regulatory frameworks for AI technology,

---

[32]   Alex Antic, 'The I in Artificial Intelligence: A Reflection of Our Collective Conscience' <https://publicspectrum.co/the-i-in-artificial-intelligence-a-reflection-of-our-collective-conscience-2/> accessed 18 April 2022.

[33]   Walter (n 28) establishes the 'deficit data/problematic people' correlation in the context of data describing indigenous people and mechanisms for disenfranchising and dispossessing them.

[34]   West, Whittake and Crawford (n 16).

[35]   Gerald Midgley, 'Systemic Intervention' 2014 <https://www.researchgate.net/publication/315692826_Systemic_Intervention> accessed 14 June 2022.

[36]   Jessica Fjeld and others, 'Principled Artificial Intelligence: Mapping Consensus in Ethical and Rights-Based Approaches to Principles for AI' (Berkman Klein Center for Internet & Society, Harvard University 2020) <https://cyber.harvard.edu/publication/2020/principled-ai> accessed 15 June 2022.

[37]   For example, Kate Crawford, 'Time to Regulate AI that Interprets Human Emotions', Nature <https://www.nature.com/articles/d41586-021-00868-5> accessed 24 February 2023; Bruce Schneier, *Click Here to Kill Everybody Security and Survival in a Hyper-Connected World* (W. W. Norton & Company 2018); Toby Walsh, *2062: The World that AI Made* (La Trobe University Press and Black Inc 2018).

particularly in the USA and countries outside Europe.[38] Civil society, employees and community organisations are also stakeholders in AI,[39] and have advocated for more inclusive and equitable technology. Community-driven campaigns have sought legal restrictions on some uses of AI technologies, such as facial recognition by police.[40] Policy makers are grappling with how to regulate AI to maximise its benefits while addressing its actual and potential harms. The UN has called for a moratorium on the sale and use of artificial intelligence systems that pose a serious risk to human rights until adequate safeguards are put in place.[41] Further, Big Tech companies such as IBM and Microsoft, amongst others, have also looked for regulatory clarity.[42]

3. RELEVANT REGULATORY FRAMEWORKS

The governance of AI involves matters not only of normative values but also of global power and sovereignty as countries such as the United States, China, Russia, India and the European Union vie for global AI superpower.[43] In this environment, governments around the world increasingly are considering, proposing, passing or implementing AI governance. A recent example is China's regulation 'Provisions on the Management of

---

[38] Leila Ouchchy, Allen Coin and Veljko Dubljevic, 'AI in the Headlines: The Portrayal of the Ethical Issues of Artificial Intelligence in the Media' (2020) 35 AI & Society.

[39] Worker social responsibility initiatives, for example, have sought to shape and monitor AI products and services.

[40] West, Whittake and Crawford (n 16).

[41] 'Artificial Intelligence Risks to Privacy Demand Urgent Action – Bachelet' (*OHCHR*) <https://www.ohchr.org/EN/NewsEvents/Pages/DisplayNews.aspx?NewsID=27469&LangID=E> accessed 27 October 2021.

[42] For example, IBM Policy Lab, 'Precision Regulation for Artificial Intelligence' (*IBM THINKPolicy Blog*, 21 January 2020) <https://www.ibm.com/blogs/policy/ai-precision-regulation/> accessed 5 August 2021. See also Monica Nickelsburg, 'Microsoft President Brad Smith Calls for AI Regulation at Davos' *GeekWire* (21 January 2020) <https://www.geekwire.com/2020/microsoft-president-brad-smith-calls-ai-regulation-davos/> accessed 14 June 2022.

[43] Eric Schmidt, 'The AI Revolution and Strategic Competition with China | by Eric Schmidt' (*Project Syndicate*, 30 August 2021) <https://www.project-syndicate.org/commentary/ai-revolution-competition-with-china-democracy-vs-authoritarianism-by-eric-schmidt-2021-08> accessed 14 June 2022; Michael C Horowitz, 'Artificial Intelligence, International Competition, and the Balance of Power' (2018) 1 Texas National Security Review 36.

Algorithmic Recommendations in Internet Information Services', which became effective on 1 March 2022.[44]

In other parts of the world, AI regulation via specific national or regional legislation is still to be enacted. Where it does exist at the national level, some countries, such as the United Kingdom (UK), rely upon other related or overarching or sector-specific legislation, for example, in data protection, intellectual property, contract and tort, combined with sector-specific regulation, as in transport and healthcare.

Overarching legislation has deficiencies, as AI's effects generally and its specific gender effects do not fall neatly under data protection, anti-discrimination, anti-trust, consumer or equality law, and action to establish that harm has occurred can meet trade secrecy provisions that prevent outside scrutiny of algorithms.[45] For instance, equality and non-discrimination laws rely on an exhaustive list of protective grounds, which leave algorithmic proxy discrimination unaddressed.[46]

Data protection law's ability to meet the challenges of AI is limited by its singular purpose of protecting 'personal information', its focus upon individual interests (not collective interests), and its reliance upon concepts such as 'purpose specification and limitation' and 'consent'. Consent, for example, as a means for individual control over their personal data, is ineffective in situations where personal and non-personal data from sundry sources are mashed together. Further, most people's understanding of AI's capability would not meet the conditions for 'informed consent'.[47]

AI is not limited to 'personal information', and its ongoing dynamic evolution eludes traditional data protection principles. Machine learning, for example, is about exploring the unknown, of using all manner of datasets to infer patterns that can lead to decisions applied to individuals and categories of individuals. Inferential analyses have targeted sensitive

---

44   Ed Sander, 'Is China Showing Us the Way in Regulating Algorithms?' (ChinaTalk, 7 January 2022) <https://www.chinatalk.nl/is-china-showing-us-the-way-in-regulating-algorithms/> accessed 18 April 2022.

45   West, Whittaker and Crawford (n 16).

46   For detailed analysis of how EU equality and non-discrimination law falls short in addressing algorithmic discrimination, see European Commission, Directorate General for Justice and Consumers and European network of legal experts in gender equality and non-discrimination, *Algorithmic Discrimination in Europe: Challenges and Opportunities for Gender Equality and Non-Discrimination Law* (Publications Office 2021) 44 <https://data.europa.eu/doi/10.2838/544956> accessed 14 January 2022.

47   Neil M Richards and Woodrow Hartzog, 'The Pathology of Digital Consent' (2019) 96 Washington University Law Review.

characteristics such as gender.[48] Such analyses challenge data protection law. Even the current world's most comprehensive data protection model, the General Data Protection Regulation's (GDPR) provisions concerning the rights to know (art. 13–15), to rectify (art. 16), to delete (art. 17), to object (art. 21), or to data portability (art. 20) are significantly curtailed for inferences.[49]

The GDPR, an influential regional instrument, also provides insufficient protection for sensitive inferences (art. 9) or remedies for important decisions based on them (art. 22(3)), and hence for those concerning gender. The GDPR only prohibits the 'processing of personal data revealing a natural person's sex life or sexual orientation',[50] not 'sex' or 'gender' as in EU gender equality and non-discrimination law.[51] The GDPR is not an isolated case. This gap tends to be the case around the world within data protection law that is, 'gender' is absent from categories of 'sensitive personal data'. Further, discussion of gender is also largely absent from most data protection authorities' guidance on AI.[52]

Some general GDPR provisions might protect against gender-based incursions of informational privacy, such as the right not to be subject to automated individual decision-making (art. 22), the right to erasure (art. 17), the right to data portability (art. 20), the right to explanation (art. 21), and data protection impact assessments (DPIAs, art. 35), as well as the mandatory consultation with the supervisory authority when risks cannot be mitigated. But while there is the right not to be subject to a decision based solely on automated processing, the form of the human supervision and its purpose are unspecified (Recital 71 GDPR), and the DPIA is limited to 'high-risk' personal data, excluding other rights.[53] Calls for further guidance have been made to the European Data Protection Board and the European Data Protection Supervisor for more effective implementation of GDPR provisions directly applying to AI.[54]

---

[48] Sandra Wachter and Brent Mittelstadt, 'A Right to Reasonable Inferences: Re-Thinking Data Protection Law in the Age of Big Data and AI' [2019] Colombia Business Law Review 494.

[49] ibid.

[50] Article 9(1), Recital 51 GDPR.

[51] Sexual orientation is a component of gender not its totality; see Gerards and Xenidis (n 8).

[52] For example, Information Commissioner's Office, 'Big Data, Artificial Intelligence, Machine Learning and Data Protection' (2017) <https://ico.org.uk/media/for-organisations/documents/2013559/big-data-ai-ml-and-data-protection.pdf> accessed 14 June 2022.

[53] FRA (n 5) FRA Opinion 5.

[54] ibid.

European gender equality and non-discrimination law also have limited ability to address algorithmic discrimination due to their scope;[55] hidden uses of AI; difficulties in detecting, identifying and establishing algorithmic discrimination; jurisdictional issues; and challenges in determining responsibility for the design and use of algorithms that discriminate.[56] Anti-discrimination laws around the world also face the same challenge of establishing algorithmic discrimination. Even the decision logic of *disclosed* algorithms is likely to be difficult to concretely verify in practice – let alone when the algorithm is hidden or unavailable.

AI regulatory initiatives emanating from the European Union and the Council of Europe have attracted considerable attention.

In April 2021 the European Union proposed a Regulation on Artificial Intelligence (the AI Act), which has been described as 'a pivotal moment in the global regulation of artificial intelligence.'[57] The proposed Act 'specifically aims at strengthening Europe's competitiveness and industrial basis in AI',[58] while seeking to protect fundamental rights contained in the EU Charter of Fundamental Rights including the right to human dignity (art. 1), respect for private life and protection of personal data (arts 7 and 8), non-discrimination (art. 21), and equality between women and men (art. 23).[59]

That said, the Act is 'patchy' in its coverage of these rights. It classifies AI systems according to whether they are prohibited, high risk, low risk with obligations, or low risk with no obligations. The systems prohibited are those deploying subliminal techniques or exploiting vulnerabilities due to age or disability, real-time remote biometric identification systems, and social scoring. The risk-based appraisals for determining in which

---

[55]   A narrower form of 'algorithmic bias' relating to grounds protected under Art. 19 TFEU.

[56]   Gerards and Xenidis (n 8).

[57]   Graham Greenleaf, 'The "Brussels Effect" of the EU's "AI Act" on Data Privacy Outside Europe' (2021) 171(1) Privacy Laws & Business International Report, 3–7 UNSW Law Research, 2.

[58]   Proposal for a Regulation of the European Parliament and of the Council Laying Down Harmonised Rules on Artificial Intelligence (Artificial Intelligence Act) and Amending Certain Union Legislative Acts {SEC(2021) 167 final} – {SWD(2021) 84 final} – {SWD(2021) 85 final}, para 3.4.

[59]   Additional rights addressed include freedom of expression (art. 11), freedom of assembly (art. 12), the right to an effective remedy and to a fair trial, the rights of defence and the presumption of innocence (arts 47 and 48), workers' rights to fair and just working conditions (art. 31), a high level of consumer protection (art. 28), the rights of the child (art. 24) and the integration of persons with disabilities (art. 26), the right to a high level of environmental protection and the improvement of the quality of the environment (art. 37). ibid, para 3.5.

category the AI system belongs, are undertaken by providers, presumably the AI industry. Most AI systems will fall within the category of 'lower risk systems with no obligations.'[60] Clearly, it will be against business interests to find their systems are high risk.

Many, including those advocating for greater attention to gender in AI regulation, find the proposal disappointing. From a gender governance perspective, it is difficult to discern adequate recognition of 'gender' or direct prevention and protection against infringement of the rights of individuals based on their gender. The AI Act is criticised also for the absence of a requirement for a fundamental rights impact assessment before deployment,[61] which would help avoid placing a disproportionately high burden upon individuals to establish the impact of AI on their rights. The Council of Europe's Modernised Convention No. 108 art. 10(2) by placing the onus upon controllers and processors (where applicable), is more attuned to the difficulties faced by individuals in vulnerable situations.[62]

The draft provisions only partially alleviate specific concerns arising from gender and AI findings – for example, while there is a ban upon the use of real-time biometric identification systems by law enforcement, its use by other entities is not prohibited. Similarly, the ban on social scoring by public authorities does not extend to the private sector.

Notably, the European Data Protection Board and the European Data Protection Supervisor have recommended the proposal, amongst other things:[63]

a) assess and mitigate societal risks for groups of individuals,
b) generally ban any use of AI for automated recognition of human features in publicly accessible spaces in any context, and
c) ban AI systems using biometrics to categorise individuals into clusters using grounds prohibited under Article 21 of the European Charter of Fundamental Rights – that is, 'sex' and race, colour, ethnic or social origin, genetic features, language, religion or belief, political or any

---

[60] Greenleaf (n 57) 3.

[61] See for instance, Lilian Edwards, 'Expert Opinion: Regulating AI in Europe' (Ada Lovelace Institute 2022) <https://www.adalovelaceinstitute.org/report/regulating-ai-in-europe/> accessed 19 April 2022.

[62] Convention 108 + 'Convention for the protection of individuals with regard to the processing of personal data 108', 2018 <https://www.coe.int/en/web/data-protection/convention108-and-protocol> accessed 15 June 2022.

[63] EDPS–EDPB Joint Opinion on the proposal for a Regulation of the European Parliament and of the Council laying down harmonised rules on artificial intelligence (Artificial Intelligence Act), 18 June 2021 <https://edps.europa.eu/node/7140_en> accessed 18 June 2021.

other opinion, membership of a national minority, property, birth, disability, age, or sexual orientation.

However, given the many forms of AI able to generate harm, application beyond biometrics would be appropriate, and grounding protections in Article 21 needs to include 'gender'.

The AI Act, which is expected to be negotiated in 2023, will follow other EU regulations in the digital sphere such as the Digital Services Act and the Digital Markets Act.[64] Once passed, its expansive extraterritorial scope will potentially affect jurisdictions beyond the European Union, in the same way the GDPR has via the 'Brussels Effect'.[65] The AI Act would apply to providers located or established in third countries if the providers place on the market or put into service AI systems in the Union.[66]

Also from Europe but with potential international effect, the Council of Europe's Ad hoc Committee on Artificial Intelligence (CAHAI) in December 2021 recommended the development of a legally binding transversal instrument based on Council of Europe standards, and which could facilitate accession by States outside of the regions that share those standards.

The framework proposed by the CAHAI is based on risk management where the potential risks of unequal access or treatment, various forms of bias and discrimination, and gender inequality were identified for assessment. It was recommended that the legally binding transversal instrument contain provisions to uphold gender equality and rights related to vulnerable groups and people in vulnerable situations, throughout the lifecycle of artificial intelligence systems.

The successor to the CAHAI, the Committee on Artificial Intelligence, is to deliver by mid-November 2023 an 'Appropriate legal instrument on the development, design, and application of artificial intelligence systems based on the Council of Europe's standards on human rights, democracy

---

[64]   Goda Naujokaitytė, 'Parliament Gives EU a Push to Move Faster on Artificial Intelligence' (*Science|Business*) <https://sciencebusiness.net/news/parlia ment-gives-eu-push-move-faster-artificial-intelligence> accessed 14 June 2022.

[65]   Alex Engler, 'The EU AI Act Will Have Global Impact, but a Limited Brussels Effect' (*Brookings*, 8 June 2022) <https://www.brookings.edu/research/ the-eu-ai-act-will-have-global-impact-but-a-limited-brussels-effect/> accessed 14 June 2022; Greenleaf (n 57); see also Anu Bradford, *The Brussels Effect: How the European Union Rules the World* (Oxford University Press 2022).

[66]   Art. 2, Proposal for a Regulation of the European Parliament and of the Council Laying Down Harmonised Rules on Artificial Intelligence (Artificial Intelligence Act) and Amending Certain Union Legislative Acts COM/2021/206 final 206 <https://eur-lex.europa.eu/legal-content/EN/TXT/?uri= CELEX%3A52021PC0206> accessed 15 June 2022.

and the rule of law, and conducive to innovation.'[67] The potential of an international legally binding transversal treaty is highly attractive. There are several precedents of Council of Europe treaties applied beyond the European region, notably the Budapest Convention (Cybercrime) and the Convention for the Protection of Individuals with regard to Automatic Processing of Personal Data (CETS No. 108). These two instruments currently have 66 and 55 parties respectively, many of which are not Member States of the Council of Europe.[68] In this regard, the Council of Europe's proposal for an international legally binding transversal treaty is cause for cautious optimism.[69]

China, in contrast, has already adopted a relatively comprehensive regulation of algorithmic systems, such as those used in making recommendations.[70] Based on some reports, it is possible that the regulatory framework enables not only governance of AI content recommendation systems, but also 'governance of gender' via morality and societal well-being provisions that require companies to 'uphold mainstream value orientations', 'vigorously disseminate positive energy' and 'prevent or reduce controversies or disputes.'[71] As the framework was introduced in March 2022, it is too early to be definitive on this issue.

There have been three different Chinese approaches to the system of AI governance, each led by a different branch of the Chinese bureaucracy, with each at a different level of maturity as evidenced by available documents.[72] The rules for online algorithms published by the Cyberspace Administration of China, exist alongside the China Academy

---

[67]   Council of Europe, <https://rm.coe.int/terms-of-reference-of-the-committee-on-artificial-intelligence-for-202/1680a4ee36> accessed 15 June 2022.

[68]   Council of Europe, Ad Hoc Committee on Artificial Intelligence, 'Possible elements of a legal framework on artificial intelligence, based on the Council of Europe's standards on human rights, democracy and the rule of law', Strasbourg, 3 December 2021, CAHAI(2021)09rev. <https://rm.coe.int/cahai-2021-09rev-elements/1680a6d90d> accessed 15 June 2022.

[69]   'Council of Europe and Artificial Intelligence' (*Council of Europe*) <https://www.coe.int/en/web/artificial-intelligence/home> accessed 14 June 2022.

[70]   Although several countries have introduced regulatory frameworks, most of these laws are sector-specific, focusing on certain AI systems such as face recognition.

[71]   Jennifer Conrad and Will Knight, 'China Is About to Regulate AI—and the World Is Watching' Wired <https://www.wired.com/story/china-regulate-ai-world-watching/> accessed 19 April 2022.

[72]   Matt Sheehan, 'China's New AI Governance Initiatives Shouldn't Be Ignored' (Carnegie Endowment for International Peace) <https://carnegieendowment.org/2022/01/04/china-s-new-ai-governance-initiatives-shouldn-t-be-ignored-pub-86127> accessed 19 April 2022.

of Information and Communications Technology's tools for testing and certifying 'trustworthy AI' systems, and the Ministry of Science and Technology's AI ethics principles and tech ethics review boards within companies and research institutions. As a combined package of AI regulation, China's initiatives may have global implications.[73]

In Latin America, in September 2021, Brazil's Congress in an emergency proceeding, passed a Bill to create a legal framework for artificial intelligence. Most of the principles included in the 'Legal Framework for Artificial Intelligence' (*Marco Legal da Inteligência Artificial*, PL 21/2020) are supportive of protecting gender:

- beneficial purpose: the pursuit of beneficial outcomes for humanity;
- human-centric AI: respect for human dignity, privacy, personal data protection and fundamental rights;
- non-discrimination: AI systems must not be used for discriminatory, unlawful or abusive purposes;
- neutrality: AI systems must be structured, developed, implemented and used in a way that reduces the possibility of unlawful bias;
- transparency: the right of individuals to be informed in a clear, accessible and accurate manner about the use of AI solutions – unless they are subject to trade and industry secrecy;
- security and prevention: the management and mitigation of security risks arising from AI systems' operations throughout their entire life cycle and continued operation;
- responsible innovation: agents involved in AI systems' development and operations must document their internal management processes and would be held liable for any issues involving such systems;
- data availability: non-infringement of copyright arising from the use of data, databases and texts protected by it for training purposes of AI models.[74]

The Bill was criticised on the grounds it may help perpetuate algorithmic discrimination through provisions hindering the accountability for AI-induced errors, and restricting the scope of rights established in Brazil's General Data Protection Legislation and its Constitution. Of particular concern are the provisions that could weaken remedy mechanisms

---

[73]   ibid (n 72).
[74]   'The upcoming Brazilian Artificial Intelligence Act: what businesses need to know' *Mattos Filho*, 18 April 2022) <https://www.mattosfilho.com.br/en/unico/brazilian-artificial-intelligence/> accessed 14 June 2022.

providing adequate compensation (contained in Brazil's tort liability regime) and reduce the application scope of the non-discrimination principle in the Brazilian Data Protection Legislation. This prohibits personal data processing for illicit or abusive discriminatory purposes. Without an obligation for guaranteeing fair, non-discriminative AI systems, accountability for AI discriminatory biases may be harder to achieve.[75]

In early 2022, Brazil's Senate appointed a commission of jurists chaired by a member of the Superior Court of Justice, to draft a proposal to regulate AI, based on the already-approved PLs 21/2020, 5.051/2019 and 872/2021. Reports indicate the commission will consult with the private sector, civil society, as well as intergovernmental and multilateral organisations to address the social–economic contexts and benefits of AI; sustainable development and well-being; innovation; AI research and development (funding resources and public–private partnerships); public security; agriculture; industry; digital services; information technology; and healthcare robots. The commission will address the use of personal and non-personal data; data mining issues; 'unacceptable risks' linked to the application of AI; the use of the 'precautionary principle'; and industrial and trade secrets.[76]

In the US, while the US Federal Trade Commission has expressed its intent to play a greater regulatory role in AI,[77] progress on national legislation has been slow. In October 2022, the White House Office of Science and Technology Policy released a 'Blueprint for an AI Bill of Rights: Making Automated Systems Work for the American People'.[78] This framework was released after public engagement. The Blueprint is non-binding and does not constitute government policy but is 'intended to support the development of policies and practices that protect civil

---

[75] Thiago Guimarães Moraes and José Renato Laranjeira de Pereira, 'Promoting Irresponsible AI: Lessons from a Brazilian Bill | Heinrich Böll Stiftung | Brussels Office – European Union' (*Heinrich-Böll-Stiftung*) <https://eu.boell.org/en/2022/02/14/promoting-irresponsible-ai-lessons-brazilian-bill> accessed 14 June 2022.

[76] Brasil Senate News Agency, 'Brasil poderá ter marco regulatório para a inteligência artificial', Da Agência Senado, 30 March 2022 <https://www12.senado.leg.br/noticias/materias/2022/03/30/brasil-podera-ter-marco-regulatorio-para-a-inteligencia-artificial (translated with DeepL Translating, accessed 6 October 2022).

[77] Elisa Jillson, 'Aiming for Truth, Fairness, and Equity in Your Company's Use of AI' (Federal Trade Commission, 19 April 2021) <https://www.ftc.gov/news-events/blogs/business-blog/2021/04/aiming-truth-fairness-equity-your-companys-use-ai> accessed 6 August 2021.

[78] The White House Office of Science and Technology Policy, 'Blueprint for an AI Bill of Rights Making Automated Systems Work for the American People', October 2022 <https://www.whitehouse.gov/ostp/ai-bill-of-rights/#applying> accessed 5 October 2022.

rights'.[79] However, gender is mentioned once, not as an integral component but as a possible form of algorithmic discrimination.

Below the Federal government, American State legislatures have been active. During 2021, at least seventeen States introduced general artificial intelligence bills or resolutions, with Alabama, Colorado (two pieces), Illinois and Mississippi enacting legislation.[80] The introduced laws in Alabama and Colorado specifically address gender, with Colorado including protections against gender discrimination in insurance practices.[81] The still-pending Californian Automated Decision Systems Accountability Act aims to ensure government algorithms making 'high-risk' decisions are fair, free from bias and work as advertised by encouraging developers and agencies to complete an impact assessment before purchasing and deploying a high-risk automated decision system. It also requires the creation of an inventory of existing high-risk automated decision systems in use by State agencies.[82]

The UK government, when announcing the Brexit Freedoms Bill, stated that the Bill aims to facilitate the UK's 'moving in a faster, more agile way to regulate new digital markets and AI and creating a more proportionate and less burdensome data rights regime compared to the EU's GDPR.'[83] The distancing from the European omnibus regulatory approach of adopting rules applying to AI generally, is explicit in the July 2022 Department for Digital, Culture, Media and Sport paper 'Establishing a pro-innovation approach to regulating AI. An overview of the UK's emerging approach'.[84] The EU form of AI regulation is seen as

---

[79]   ibid 2.

[80]   'Legislation Related to Artificial Intelligence' (National Conference of State Legislatures)   <https://www.ncsl.org/research/telecommunications-and-informati on-technology/2020-legislation-related-to-artificial-intelligence.aspx> accessed 19 April 2022.

[81]   See for instance, Senate Bill 21-169 concerning protecting consumers from unfair discrimination in insurance practices 2022.

[82]   Greenlining, 'The Automated Decisions Systems Accountability Act (AB 13) Explained', <https://greenlining.org/blog-category/2021/automated-decisions-accountability-act-ab-13/> accessed 14 June 2022.

[83]   Laura Linkomies, 'UK: Data Protection Shake-up Looks Certain' (2022) 120 Privacy Laws & Business <https://www.privacylaws.com/reports-gateway/ articles/uk120/uk120uk/> accessed 14 June 2022.

[84]   UK Department for Digital, Culture, Media and Sport (DCMS), 'Establishing a Pro-Innovation Approach to Regulating AI: An Overview of the UK's Emerging Approach', 18 July 2022, <https://assets.publishing.service. gov.uk/government/uploads/system/uploads/attachment_data/file/1092630/_CP_7 28__-_Establishing_a_pro-innovation_approach_to_regulating_AI.pdf> accessed 14 June 2022.

a threat to innovation within the UK. The paper's focus is upon general cross-sectoral principles issued as general non-statutory guidance to be interpreted and applied by sector-specific regulators within their existing remit. Regulatory intervention is envisaged as 'light touch' and enforcement as secondary to innovation. Described as 'pretty much mom and apple pie for AI regulation',[85] the UK's direction does not depart from existing norms and embedded blindness to both gender and the differential harms of AI according to gender.

4. CURRENT DEBATES ON AI GOVERNANCE

The work of the Council of Europe's AI Committees and the EU's proposed AI Act have brought direct reference to fundamental human rights. Globally, the current debate on AI regulation has tended towards approaching AI regulation via ethics. The ethical approach has been expressed in terms such as 'Trustworthy AI', 'AI for Good' and 'Ethical AI' contained in at least 173 ethic frameworks/guidelines produced internationally, regionally, nationally.[86] Examples have been produced by the EU and countries such as Australia, Canada, Singapore, Dubai and Malta. Professional associations and standard setting agencies have also produced such guidelines, as have some state governments within federated countries.[87]

---

[85]   Lilian Edwards, Professor of Law, Innovation and Society, Newcastle University, UK quoted in #RISK 2022, 'Will the UK's "Light Touch" AI Regulation Plans Increase AI Risks?' Robert Bateman, 1 August 2022, <https://www.grcworldforums.com/risk-2022/will-the-uks-light-touch-ai-regulation-plans-increase-ai-risks/6281> 5 September 2022.

[86]   Algorithm Watch, 'AI Ethics Guidelines Global Inventory' <https://algorithmwatch.org/en/ai-ethics-guidelines-global-inventory> accessed 6 August 2021.

[87]   'Dubai AI Principles & Ethics' <https://www.smartdubai.ae/initiatives/ai-principles-ethics> accessed 6 August 2021; 'White Paper on Artificial Intelligence – A European Approach to Excellence and Trust' (European Commission, COM(2020) 65 final 2019) <https://rm.coe.int/cahai-2021-09rev-elements/1680a6d90d> accessed 6 August 2021; METI, 'Japan Contract Guidelines on Utilization of AI and Data Released' <https://www.meti.go.jp/english/press/2019/0404_001.html> accessed 6 August 2021; Parliamentary secretariat for financial services, digital economy and innovation, 'Malta towards Trustworthy AI' (Parliamentary secretariat for financial services, digital economy and innovation 2019) <https://malta.ai/wp-content/uploads/2019/08/Malta_Towards_Ethical_and_Trustworthy_AI.pdf> accessed 9 June 2022; SG:D, Infocomm Media Development Authority and Personal data Protection Commission 2020, 'Singapore Model Artificial Intelligence Governance Framework' <https://www.pdpc.gov.sg/-/media/Files/PDPC/PDF-Files/Resource-for-Organisation/AI/SGModelAIGovFramework2.

Ethical guidance espouses broad, abstract principles that meta studies have categorised under clusters of 'AI ethic principles' sharing a common underlying value. The groupings complied in these meta studies are set out in Table 8.1, providing insights into areas where guidance has been identified as necessary – and where it has not.

Across these meta studies, there is a reasonable concurrence upon broad principle classifications. The common clusters of principles are 'accountability/responsibility'; 'explainability/transparency'; 'safety/non-maleficence'; 'privacy'; and 'equality and non-discrimination'. Few ethical guidelines indicate oversight or enforcement mechanisms, or guidance on operationalising them.[88] In addition, while research on their effectiveness as governance tools appears limited, some work suggests the ability of ethics to influence decision-making is doubtful.[89]

Principles generally, and these specifically, are open to wide interpretation. AI ethics' high-level principles relate to broad notions and values, for example, 'promotion of human values' and 'fairness'. AI gender issues appear to be reflected in the ethical guidelines by principles clustered around 'equality/non-discrimination/fairness' but not in a specific or substantive manner.[90] These principles, 'equality/non-discrimination/fairness', poorly

---

pdf> accessed 15 June 2022; IEEE, 'IEEE Global A/IS Ethics Initiative Newsletter' <https://ieeeforms.wufoo.com/forms/r54n5um1cu3h0f/> accessed 6 August 2021; ISO, 'ISO/IEC JTC 1/SC 42 – Artificial Intelligence' <https://www.iso.org/cms/render/live/en/sites/isoorg/contents/data/committee/67/94/6794475.html> accessed 6 August 2021.

88   AccessNow, 'Can We Move beyond the AI Hype to Defend Human Rights?' (AccessNow 2020) <https://www.accessnow.org/can-we-move-beyond-the-ai-hype-to-defend-human-rights/> accessed 14 June 2022; Algorithm Watch (n 82); Thilo Hagendorff, 'The Ethics of AI Ethics: An Evaluation of Guidelines' (2020) 30 Minds and Machines; Anna Jobin, Marcello Ienca and Effy Vayena, 'The Global Landscape of AI Ethics Guidelines' (2019) 1 Nature Machine Intelligence; Brent Mittelstadt, 'Principles Alone Cannot Guarantee Ethical AI' [2019] Nature Machine Intelligence; Ben Wagner, 'Ethics as an Escape from Regulation: From Ethics-Washing to Ethics-Shopping' in Emre Bayamlioğlu and others (eds), *Being Profiled: Cogitas Ergo Sum: 10 Years of Profiling the European Citizen* (Amsterdam University Press 2019).

89   For example, Andrew McNamara, Justin Smith and Emerson Murphy-Hill, 'Does ACM's Code of Ethics Change Ethical Decision Making in Software Development?', *ESEC/FSE '18, November 4–9, 2018*, found no evidence that ethical guidelines of the Association for Computing Machinery (ACM) affected the decision-making of software developers (63 software engineering students and 105 professional software developers).

90   Hagendorff (n 88); Mislav Jurić, Agneza Šandić and Mario Brcic, 'AI Safety: State of the Field through Quantitative Lens', 43rd International Convention on Information and Communication Technology, Electronics and Microelectronics

Table 8.1   Principle clusters in ethical guidelines, meta studies 2019–2021

Clusters/Generic principles	Study
Accountability Equality/non-discrimination Safety and transparency	Algorithm Watch, 2021: studied 173 guidelines provided by contributors (n 86).
Accountability Explainability/transparency Fairness/non-discrimination Human control of technology Privacy Professional responsibility Promotion of human values Safety/security	Fjeld and others, 2020: examined 36 prominent AI principles documents, using a purposive sampling method to provide a manageable dataset representing a diversity of viewpoints, for example stakeholders, content, geography, date, and more (n 36).
Accountability Explainability Privacy	Hagendorff, 2020: undertook meta-analysis of main ethical guidelines published in last five years (n 88).
Justice Non-maleficence Privacy Responsibility Transparency	Jobin and others, 2019: examined 84 documents from all countries responsible for existing AI ethical guidelines (see n 88).
Justice Non-maleficence Privacy Responsibility Transparency	CAHAI (Ienca and Vayena), 2020: reviewed 116 documents published by governmental agencies, non-governmental organisations, academic institutions and private companies (n 96).

address the wider range of gender harms arising from AI that go beyond bias. For example, a quantitative bibliographic survey of AI safety research and its foci, found only two of the twenty-two most relevant ethical guidelines published in the last five years, mentioned the lack of diversity in the AI industry.[91]

Each abstract principle cluster provides broad direction and appears relevant and easily understood. While subsequently appealing, principles are abstract concepts, where abstraction hides elements constituting human experiences of socio-political situations. Feminist scholars stress the

---

(MIPRO), URL = <https://Arxiv.Org/Ftp/Arxiv/Papers/2002/2002.05671.Pdf> accessed 12 June 2022.

[91]   Hagendorff (n 88).

importance of environmental materialities, concrete contexts and practice to the actual experiencing of gender.[92] Abstraction not only removes the realities of human experience; it also removes responsibility for them, as revealed by the minimal attention to the need for remedy amongst these ethic principles clusters. The gap is especially problematic in the AI context given its opacity. This blindness to gender and remedy within AI ethical guidelines, brings to mind Zuboff's concepts of 'radical indifference', 'observation without witness' and 'equivalence without equality'.[93]

Like AI products themselves, AI ethical guidelines reflect the core values of the culture and society developing them,[94] while securing and maintaining existing power structures. They are 'blind' to historical inequalities affecting past and current data collections or the root causes of biases and social inequalities pertaining to race and gender.[95] It is noteworthy that more than half of the globe was excluded from the debate about which ethical principles and regulatory strategies should guide the AI contained in the services and products being exported to them.[96] Similarly, only 37.1% of AI ethics guidelines were found to have female authors.[97]

These issues make it clear we cannot only address the treatment of gender by AI systems; we must also consider the treatment of gender within governance frameworks and regulation applied to AI. Examining data protection law and AI ethics guidance with a view to what is included and what is not, reveals existing governance frameworks and regulations are ill suited to address gender harms embedded in AI.[98] AI requires not only regulation, but regulation incorporating gender as a mainstreamed element.

---

[92]   For example, the discussion in Sharlene Ngy Hesse-Biber (ed.), *Handbook of Feminist Research: Theory and Praxis* (SAGE Publications 2014) <https://methods.sagepub.com/base/download/BookChapter/handbook-of-feminist-research/n1.xml> accessed 14 June 2022.

[93]   Zuboff (n 2).

[94]   MIT, 'The Global AI Agenda: Latin America' (2020) <https://mittrinsights.s3.amazonaws.com/AIagenda2020/LatAmAIagenda.pdf> accessed 14 June 2022.

[95]   Catherine D'Ignazio and Lauren F. Klein, *Data Feminism* (MIT Press 2020) <https://data-feminism.mitpress.mit.edu/> accessed 6 August 2021.

[96]   Eugenio V Garcia, 'The Militarization of Artificial Intelligence: A Wake-Up Call for the Global South' (SSRN Electronic Journal, doi: 102139/ssrn3452323, 2019); Marcello Ienca and Effy Vayena, 'AI Ethics Guidelines: European and Global Perspectives' (Ad Hoc Committee on Artificial Intelligence (CAHAI) 2020) <https://rm.coe.int/cahai-2020-07-fin-en-report-ienca-vayena/16809eccac> accessed 13 June 2022; Jobin, Ienca and Vayena (n 88); Hagendorff (n 88).

[97]   Hagendorff (n 88).

[98]   Ada Lovelace Institute 2019, 'Beyond Face Value: Public Attitudes to Facial Recognition Technology', <https://perma.cc/M4EG-N5MY> accessed 6 August 2021.

Regulation blind to the differential and biased effect of AI technologies upon women and gender-diverse individuals is not 'fit for purpose' – in the same way technology causing or exacerbating gender harms is not 'fit for purpose'. Those managing AI production, including legislators with influence on technological development, have a responsibility to prevent harms, particularly harms to groups with increased vulnerability due to their gender and resulting social marginalisation.[99] An integral part of responding appropriately is to incorporate gender governance.

In other areas, some States have recognised that more harm can fall to certain groups because of their gender and are adopting 'gender' as a key concept in laws and policies protecting, for example, women and LGBT individuals against violence and discrimination.[100] These initiatives provide exemplars for the explicit incorporation of gender into the regulation of AI.

Changing how States and corporations address gender issues within AI technologies requires legislative specification to make regulation of modern digital technologies a systemic intervention – that is, purposeful action designed to create change in the setting of inclusive boundaries for marginalised populations.[101] Such regulation could even accelerate gender equality by better visualising, measuring, detecting and correcting biases.[102]

5.   MOVING BEYOND ETHICAL PRINCIPLES

AI ethics may be a means to bridge the gap between current law and the pace of AI development; however, many AI ethic narratives side-line the regulatory role of the State to emphasise the private technological sector.[103] While the involvement of the industry is necessary for effective AI governance, the power to regulate and to enforce breaches against the

---

[99]   Wang (n 18).

[100]   The law of inclusion: Report of the Independent Expert on protection against violence and discrimination based on sexual orientation and gender identity, Victor Madrigal-Borloz (2 June 2021), A/HRC/47/27.

[101]   Gerald Midgley, 'The Systemic Intervention Approach' [2021] Researchgate <https://www.researchgate.net/publication/349054424_The_Systemic_Intervention_Approach> accessed 14 June 2022.

[102]   It is possible to correct (some) gender biases, e.g. while gender stereotypes can be amplified through machine learning techniques, 'de-biasing' methodologies for removing gender stereotypes from word embedding do exist. See Tolga Bolukbasi and others, 'Man Is to Computer Programmer as Woman Is to Home-Maker? Debiasing Word Embeddings' (2016) <https://arxiv.org/abs/1607.06520> accessed 6 August 2021; UNESCO (n 6).

[103]   Wagner (n 88).

law, are powers of the State. As the Council of Europe Commissioner for Human Rights aptly notes, 'Since states bear the responsibility of respecting, protecting and fulfilling every person's human rights, it is their duty to ensure that private companies which design, develop or use AI systems do not violate human rights standards.'[104]

Industry cannot be both gamekeeper and poacher, particularly when AI ethical guidelines are invariably voluntary commitments. Self-regulation of voluntary commitments are beset by conflicts of interests presented by:

a) the scale as well as the proprietary and economic interests of the AI industry,
b) the significant socio-political and material impacts of AI,[105]
c) the requirements of, and returns generated by Big Tech business models,[106] and
d) the power of virtual monopolies such as Google, Apple, Facebook, Amazon and Microsoft, providing services akin to 'utilities'.[107]

The interests of individuals pale against such forces. Such significant market power asymmetries are traditionally regarded as constituting market failure, requiring legally enforceable restrictions in the public interest.[108] In the burgeoning and aggressive data economy supporting AI, self-regulation is neither an effective nor an appropriate form of governance. There is a need to re-focus the debate on AI regulation to move it beyond voluntary guidelines of abstract ethical principles to comprehensive, enforceable regulatory frameworks that recognise the pervasive nature of AI impacts including those upon human autonomy and dignity.[109]

---

[104] 'Human Rights in the Era of Artificial Intelligence in Europe as a Setter of International Standards in the Field of Artificial Intelligence' *Council of Europe* (20 January 2021) <https://www.coe.int/ru/web/commissioner/view/-/asset_publisher/ugj3i6qSEkhZ/content/high-level-conference-human-rights-in-the-era-of-artificial-intelligence> accessed 14 June 2022.

[105] D'Ignazio and Klein (n 95); Nicholas Kluge Corrêa and Nythamar de Oliveria, 'Good AI for the Present of Humanity Democratizing AI Governance' (2021) 2 AI Ethics Journal; Mittelstadt (n 88).

[106] Zuboff (n 2).

[107] Pieter Nooren and others, 'Should We Regulate Digital Platforms? A New Framework for Evaluating Policy Options, Policy and Internet' (2018) 10 Policy & Internet.

[108] ibid; Jobin, Ienca and Vayena (n 88); Wagner (n 88); Jillson (n 77).

[109] Ienca and Vayena (n 92); The Toronto Declaration, 'The Toronto Declaration' <https://www.torontodeclaration.org/declaration-text/english/> accessed 6 August 2021.

Human dignity is a concept firmly grounded in human rights. Governance framework based on AI ethic principles enables circumvention of human rights frameworks, or those parts inconvenient to governments and the AI sector.[110] While a number of AI ethic guidelines claim to be based on human rights, these position fundamental rights not as innate or existing rights, but as *potential* rights stripped of enforcement options or commitment to their implementation.[111] Investigating the applicability of human rights and international human rights law to AI is necessary in view of the global nature of AI, the digital economy, competing national interests and potential adverse effects of AI.

6. HUMAN RIGHTS AND INTERNATIONAL HUMAN RIGHTS INSTRUMENTS

The major international human rights overarching conventions are the International Convention of Civil and Political Rights (ICCPR) and the International Convention of Economic, Social and Cultural Rights (ICESCR). Drawing from the UN Universal Declaration of Human Rights (UNDHR), the ICCPR and ICESCR provide each individual with equal and inalienable rights, and require the creation of conditions for these to be enjoyed. These two conventions are already globally recognised by 173 and 171 State Parties respectively with established structures and status a newly emergent framework would struggle to match.[112]

Currently, no international legal instrument comprehensively and specifically applies to AI systems and human rights.[113] Moreover, none applies to AI systems, human rights *and* gender. However, the UN Guiding Principles (UNGPs) on Business and Human Rights, accompanied by the Gender Dimensions of the Guiding Principles on Business and Human Rights,[114] provide a sound and existing regime for the regulation

---

[110] Rodrigo Ochigame, 'The Invention of "Ethical AI": How Big Tech Manipulates Academia to Avoid Regulation' *The Intercept* (20 December 2019) <https://theintercept.com/2019/12/20/mit-ethical-ai-artificial-intelligence/> accessed 6 August 2021; Jobin, Ienca and Vayena (n 88).

[111] Wagner (n 88).

[112] Working Party Human Rights, Transnational Corporations and Other Business Enterprises (2021).

[113] Ienca and Vayena (n 96).

[114] UNDP and the United Nations Working Group on Business and Human Rights, 'Gender Dimensions of the Guiding Principles on Business and Human Rights' https://www.ohchr.org/Documents/Issues/Business/BookletGenderDimensionsGuidingPrinciples.pdf> accessed 15 June 2022.

of AI,[115] and one which incorporates gender as a specific recognised need. The UNGPs were unanimously endorsed by the Human Rights Council in June 2011.[116]

Under the UNGPs, States have an obligation to protect the human rights of all people within their jurisdiction from violations, caused either by their own policies or practices, or by the acts of third parties, such as businesses. Protecting human rights against business-related abuse is, in most cases, a legal obligation upon States through their ratification of legally binding international human rights treaties containing provisions to this effect. The State duty to protect is derived from these obligations.

Notably, the UNGPs position business responses as accountability rather than corporate philanthropy.[117] Companies are required through regular human rights impact assessments of their products, operations and policies, to implement proactive due diligence processes to prevent or mitigate actual or potential adverse impacts on human rights.[118] This strengthens the probability of detecting inbuilt gender issues, while providing greater legal certainty and other benefits.[119]

Sensitivity to gender impacts is also enhanced by the requirement to give special attention to unique experiences and structural discrimination or barriers – a requirement placed on both States and business enterprises.[120] The supplementary UNGP 'Gender Dimensions' enables the avoidance of the downsides of abstraction by illustrating implementation in specific situations; this ensures the UNGPs are properly interpreted from a gender perspective.

The UNGPs' alignment with 'gender governance' also derives from its lateral mechanisms, a capability similar to 'multilevel governance',[121]

---

[115]   Fjeld and others (n 36).

[116]   Report of the Special Representative of the Secretary-General on the issue of human rights and transnational corporations and other business enterprises, John Ruggie, Guiding Principles on Business and Human Rights: Implementing the United Nations 'Protect, Respect and Remedy' Framework A/HRC/RES/17/31 <https://www.ohchr.org/sites/default/files/Documents/Issues/Business/A-HRC-17-31_AEV.pdf> accessed 10 June 2022.

[117]   Fjeld and others (n 36).

[118]   Corporate responsibility to respect human rights is recognised also in the OECD Guidelines for Multinational Enterprises and the UN Global Compact.

[119]   'Report of Working Group on Human Rights and Transnational Corporations and Other Business Enterprises' (Working Group on human rights and transnational corporations and other business enterprises 2021).

[120]   Commentary to Principle 3 (States) and Commentary to Principle 20 (business enterprises) concerning 'issues of gender, vulnerability and/or marginalization'.

[121]   Katherine A. Daniell and Adrian Kay, 'Multi-Level Governance: An Introduction' in Katherine A. Daniell and Adrian Kay (eds), *Multi-level*

enabling involvement of various stakeholders including individuals and representative associations, and dispersion of authority across levels of government as well as across spheres and sectors, including States, markets and civil society. This approach to governance with its holistic and intersectional capacity is better attuned to the variety of manifestations of gender impacts possible from AI systems.

The use of the UNGPs specifically for AI technologies, was recommended by the Council of Europe's Human Rights Commissioner.[122] Their applicability was further reinforced in July 2021 by the Human Rights Council resolution to develop the UNGPs further for application to new technologies.[123] This is in addition to the UNGPs' existing international standing arising from being cited in English, American and Canadian courts, and providing the basis for the Council of Europe's 'Implement Human Rights and Business – Recommendation CM/Rec (2016) of the Committee of Ministers to Member States (2016)', including gender-related risks[124] and the European Commission's proposed 'Directive on corporate sustainability due diligence'.[125] Further, the ISO 26000 standard on social responsibility incorporates the UNGPs' corporate human rights due diligence process,[126] and the International Labour Organization's revised 2017 'Tripartite Declaration of Principles Concerning Multinational Enterprises and Social Policy' also draws upon the UNGPs.

Governance: Conceptual Challenges and Case Studies from Australia (ANU Press 2017). The term, with 'adaptive governance', 'polycentric governance' and 'collaborative governance', is found also in environmental and natural resource management literature.

[122] Council of Europe, 'Unboxing Artificial Intelligence: 10 Steps to Protect Human Rights' (Council of Europe Commissioner for Human Rights 2019) <https://rm.coe.int/unboxing-artificial-intelligence-10-steps-to-protect-human-rights-reco/1680946e64> accessed 6 August 2021.

[123] Resolution adopted by the Human Rights Council on 13 July 2021 47/23, 'New and emerging digital technologies and human rights', A/HRC/RES/47/23, <https://documents-dds-ny.un.org/doc/UNDOC/GEN/G21/192/18/PDF/G2119218.pdf?OpenElement> accessed 14 June 2022.

[124] Council of Europe, 'Implement Human Rights and business – Recommendation CM/Rec(2016) of the Committee of Ministers to Member States (2016)' <https://edoc.coe.int/en/fundamental-freedoms/7302-human-rights-and-business-recommendation-cmrec20163-of-the-committee-of-ministers-to-member-states.html> accessed 18 April 2022.

[125] Stefano Spinaci, 'Corporate Sustainability Due Diligence: Could Value Chains Integrate Human Rights and Environmental Concerns?' (BRIEFING: EU Legislation in Progress Members' Research Service, PE 729.424, May 2022).

[126] ISO, 'ISO 26000: Social Responsibility' <https://www.iso.org/iso-26000-social-responsibility.html> accessed 6 August 2021.

Guidance for the implementation of AI within an international human rights framework can be found also in other documents, for example, the Toronto Declaration,[127] but most specifically within the UN Special Rapporteur on the right to privacy (UNSRP)'s 'Recommendations on privacy protection for the development and operation of artificial intelligence solutions'.[128] The additional elements in the latter provide structural rigour while being supportive of governance cognisant of gender issues.

The UNSRP has proposed a common international human rights baseline for AI solutions, especially those implemented at the domestic level. It makes explicit reference to the UNGPs (para 15) and is based on the Universal Declaration of Human Rights, particularly articles 7 (non-discrimination) and 12 (right to privacy), which are obligations upon States that have ratified the ICCPR. Mandatory considerations for the planning, development and implementation of AI solutions are outlined, such as holistic human rights assessments alongside data protection assessments of all AI solutions *before* deployment, 'red lines' for the use of AI solutions, inclusion of cross-sectoral, cross-industry, civil society and user communities into the development, testing and monitoring of AI solutions, and a transnational regulatory framework.[129] Necessary extra- and intra-organisational arrangements, such as independent competent regulators, judicial and non-judicial remedies for violations, and risk mitigation based on international standards, for example, those published jointly by the International Organization for Standardization and the International Electrotechnical Commission in the ISO/IEC 27000 series (information security management systems), are set out.

7.   CONCLUSION

AI systems include social not just technical and industrial infrastructures.[130] As a global phenomenon, AI is affecting all humanity.[131] If the current

---

[127]   The Toronto Declaration was published on 16 May 2018 by Amnesty International and Access Now, and launched at RightsCon 2018 in Toronto, Canada.

[128]   UN Special Rapporteur on the Right to Privacy (2021) 'UN Special Rapporteur on the Right to Privacy on Artificial intelligence and privacy, and children's privacy' Human Rights Council 46th Session, A/HRC/46/37, pps 2–10. https://documents-dds-ny.un.org/doc/UNDOC/GEN/G21/015/65/PDF/G2101565.pdf?OpenElement, accessed 15 June 2021.

[129]   In the absence of a transnational framework, options are outlined.

[130]   Crawford (n 37).

[131]   'Declaration on Ethics and Data Protection in Artificial Intelligence', *40th International Conference of Data Protection and Privacy Commissioners* (European

regulatory vacuum persists, allowing AI systems to carry forward encoded gender inequality and marginalisation, the future of women and gender-diverse individuals and communities, will be determined by AI's algorithms.

While not all business models relying on AI systems, undermine human rights or gender equality, this examination found existing governance and regulatory data protection, anti-discrimination, and ethics frameworks incompletely or poorly address AI systems' gender harms, and to inadequately reflect the nature of 'gender' or address the gender effects of AI.

Companies profiting from AI solutions in asymmetrical marketplaces, need clear operating and sanction parameters on these issues. Ethical guidelines as an effective AI governance mechanism lack substance due to their voluntary nature and reliance upon principles separated from social context, rights, or politics – matters so closely intertwined with gender experiences.[132] Greater capacity exists in international human rights law to protect individuals vulnerable to the effects of AI because of their gender. Explicit AI regulation based on international human rights instruments incorporating gender, such as the UNGPs, is required.

While the human rights framework is not infallible, human rights are more representative, legitimate and concerned with protecting the vulnerable than 'the ethical compasses of Silicon Valley.'[133] The international framework of human rights matches the global nature of AI systems; the number of countries that have formally adopted these instruments, and the functionality of the existing well-established standards, procedures for determining human rights violations, and mechanisms for remedy and redress.

Accordingly, the challenge of countering AI's harmful effects requires the implementation of human rights by legislative specification to regulate these digital technologies. Society has given the powers of passing and enforcing laws to governments. And society is concerned about AI and wants governments to ensure positive outcomes for humanity. Governments' policy development and legislative powers enable the setting of governance requirements that respect human rights as an integral part

---

Date Protection Supervisor 2018) <https://edps.europa.eu/data-protection/our-work/publications/international-conferences/resolutions-and-declaration-2018_en> accessed 19 April 2022.

[132]   Anaïs Rességuier and Rowena Rodrigues, 'AI Ethics Should Not Remain Toothless? A Call to Bring Back the Teeth of Ethics' (2020) July–Dec Big Data & Society.

[133]   Hannah Hilligoss, Filippo A. Raso and Vivek Krishnamurthy, 'It's Not Enough for AI to Be "Ethical"; It Must Also Be "Rights Respecting"' (2018) <https://medium.com/berkman-klein-center/its-not-enough-for-ai-to-be-ethical-it-must-also-be-rights-respecting-b87f7e215b97> accessed 6 August 2021.

of doing business.[134] The evolving technological context and speed of AI evolution requires matching commitment from States to ensure AI does not render equality a human value under threat of extinction.[135]

ACKNOWLEDGEMENTS

Special thanks to the reviewers and Colette Mahieu for invaluable feedback. The usual disclaimers apply.

REFERENCES

AccessNow, 'Can We Move beyond the AI Hype to Defend Human Rights?' (2020) <https://www.accessnow.org/can-we-move-beyond-the-ai-hype-to-defend-human-rights/> accessed 14 June 2022.

Ada Lovelace Institute, 'Beyond Face Value: Public Attitudes to Facial Recognition Technology' (2019) <https://perma.cc/M4EG-N5MY> accessed 6 August 2021.

Adams A, 'Algorithmic Decisions and Their Human Consequences | The Regulatory Review' (*The Regulatory Review*, 11 November 2021) <https://www.theregreview.org/2021/11/11/adams-algorithmic-decisions-human-consequences/>, accessed 13 June 2022.

Aguera y Arcas B, 'Do Algorithms Reveal Sexual Orientation or Just Expose Our Stereotypes?' (*Medium*, 18 January 2018) <https://medium.com/@blaisea/do-algorithms-reveal-sexual-orientation-or-just-expose-our-stereotypes-d998fafdf477> accessed 6 August 2021.

Algorithm Watch, 'AI Ethics Guidelines Global Inventory' <https://algorithmwatch.org/en/ai-ethics-guidelines-global-inventory> accessed 6 August 2021.

Angwin J and others, 'Machine Bias' (*ProPublica*, May 2016) <https://www.propublica.org/article/machine-bias-risk-assessments-in-criminal-sentencing?token=PfkMUk0VOJFLCI7ofscfo7VgS3x9ll1i>, accessed 5 August 2021.

Antic A, 'The I in Artificial Intelligence: A Reflection of Our Collective Conscience' <https://publicspectrum.co/the-i-in-artificial-intelligence-a-reflection-of-our-collective-conscience-2/> accessed 18 April 2022.

'Artificial Intelligence Risks to Privacy Demand Urgent Action – Bachelet' (*OHCHR*) <https://www.ohchr.org/EN/NewsEvents/Pages/DisplayNews.aspx?NewsID=27469&LangID=E> accessed 27 October 2021.

Bolukbasi T and others, 'Man Is to Computer Programmer as Woman Is to Home-Maker? Debiasing Word Embeddings' (2016) <https://arxiv.org/abs/1607.06520> accessed 6 August 2021.

Bradford A, *The Brussels Effect: How the European Union Rules the World* (Oxford University Press 2022).

Brasil Senate News Agency, 'Brasil poderá ter marco regulatório para a inteligência

---

[134]　Special Representative of the Secretary-General on the issue of human rights and transnational corporations and other business enterprises, John Ruggie, 'Protect, Respect and Remedy: A Framework for Business and Human Rights' (2008) A/HRC/8/5.

[135]　Walsh (n 37).

artificial', Da Agência Senado, 30 March 2022 <https://www12.senado.leg.br/noticias/materias/2022/03/30/brasil-podera-ter-marco-regulatorio-para-a-inteligencia-artificial (translated with DeepL Translating, accessed 6 October 2022).

Conrad J and Knight W, 'China Is About to Regulate AI—and the World Is Watching' Wired <https://www.wired.com/story/china-regulate-ai-world-watching/> accessed 19 April 2022.

Convention 108 + 'Convention for the protection of individuals with regard to the processing of personal data 108', 2018 <https://www.coe.int/en/web/data-protection/convention108-and-protocol> accessed 15 June 2022.

Corrêa NK and de Oliveria N, 'Good AI for the Present of Humanity Democratizing AI Governance' (2021) 2 AI Ethics Journal.

Costanza-Chock S, 'Design Justice, A.I., and Escape from the Matrix of Domination DOI' <https://www.researchgate.net/publication/326618753_Design_Justice_AI_and_Escape_from_the_Matrix_of_Domination> accessed 15 June 2022.

Council of Europe, Ad Hoc Committee on Artificial Intelligence, 'Possible elements of a legal framework on artificial intelligence, based on the Council of Europe's standards on human rights, democracy and the rule of law', Strasbourg, 3 December 2021, CAHAI(2021)09rev.

Council of Europe, 'Implement Human Rights and business – Recommendation CM/Rec(2016) of the Committee of Ministers to Member States (2016)' <https://edoc.coe.int/en/fundamental-freedoms/7302-human-rights-and-business-recommendation-cmrec20163-of-the-committee-of-ministers-to-member-states.html> accessed 18 April 2022.

Council of Europe, 'Unboxing Artificial Intelligence: 10 Steps to Protect Human Rights' (Council of Europe Commissioner for Human Rights 2019) <https://rm.coe.int/unboxing-artificial-intelligence-10-steps-to-protect-human-rights-reco/1680946e64> accessed 6 August 2021.

'Council of Europe and Artificial Intelligence' (Council of Europe) <https://www.coe.int/en/web/artificial-intelligence/home> accessed 14 June 2022.

Crawford K, 'Time to Regulate AI that Interprets Human Emotions' Nature <https://www-nature-com.ejounrals.um.edu.mt/articles/d411586-021-00868-5> accessed 14 June 2022.

D'Ignazio C and Klein LF, *Data Feminism* (MIT Press 2020) <https://data-feminism.mitpress.mit.edu/> accessed 6 August 2021.

Daniell KA and Kay A, 'Multi-Level Governance: An Introduction' in KA Daniell and A Kay (eds), *Multi-level Governance: Conceptual Challenges and Case Studies from Australia* (ANU Press 2017).

Dastin J, 'Amazon Scraps Secret AI Recruiting Tool that Showed Bias against Women' *Reuters* (10 October 2018) <https://www.reuters.com/article/us-amazon-com-jobs-automation-insight-idUSKCN1MK08G> accessed 5 August 2021.

'Declaration on Ethics and Data Protection in Artificial Intelligence', *40th International Conference of Data Protection and Privacy Commissioners* (European Date Protection Supervisor 2018) <https://edps.europa.eu/data-protection/our-work/publications/international-conferences/resolutions-and-declaration-2018_en> accessed 19 April 2022.

'Dubai AI Principles & Ethics' <https://www.smartdubai.ae/initiatives/ai-principles-ethics> accessed 6 August 2021; 'White Paper on Artificial Intelligence – A European Approach to Excellence and Trust' (European Commission, COM(2020) 65 final 2019) <https://rm.coe.int/cahai-2021-09rev-elements/1680a6d90d> accessed 6 August 2021.

'Dutch Scientific Council Knows AI Is Neither Neutral nor Always Rational' Racism and Technology Center <https://racismandtechnology.center/2021/11/26/dutch-scientific-council-knows-ai-is-neither-neutral-nor-always-rational/> accessed 11 June 2022.

EDPS–EDPB Joint Opinion on the proposal for a Regulation of the European Parliament and of the Council laying down harmonised rules on artificial intelligence (Artificial Intelligence Act), 18 June 2021 <https://edps.europa.eu/node/7140_en> accessed 18 June 2021.

Edwards L, 'Expert Opinion: Regulating AI in Europe' (Ada Lovelace Institute 2022) <https://www.adalovelaceinstitute.org/report/regulating-ai-in-europe/> accessed 19 April 2022.

Engler A, 'The EU AI Act Will Have Global Impact, but a Limited Brussels Effect' (*Brookings*, 8 June 2022) <https://www.brookings.edu/research/the-eu-ai-act-will-have-global-impact-but-a-limited-brussels-effect/> accessed 14 June 2022.

European Commission, Directorate General for Justice and Consumers and European network of legal experts in gender equality and non-discrimination, *Algorithmic Discrimination in Europe: Challenges and Opportunities for Gender Equality and Non-Discrimination Law* (Publications Office 2021) 44 <https://data.europa.eu/doi/10.2838/544956> accessed 14 January 2022.

Fjeld J and others, 'Principled Artificial Intelligence: Mapping Consensus in Ethical and Rights-Based Approaches to Principles for AI' (Berkman Klein Center for Internet & Society, Harvard University 2020) <https://cyber.harvard.edu/publication/2020/principled-ai> accessed 15 June 2022.

Fosch-Villaronga E and others, 'A Little Bird Told Me Your Gender: Gender Inferences in Social Media' (2021) 58 Information Processing and Management.

FRA, 'Getting the Future Right: Artificial Intelligence and Fundamental Rights' (European Fundamental Rights Agency 2020).

Garcia EV, 'The Militarization of Artificial Intelligence: A Wake-Up Call for the Global South' (SSRN Electronic Journal, doi: 102139/ssrn3452323, 2019).

Gerards J and Xenidis R, 'Algorithmic Discrimination in Europe: Challenges and Opportunities for EU Equality Law' (*European Futures*, 3 December 2020) 47 <https://www.europeanfutures.ed.ac.uk/algorithmic-discrimination-in-europe-challenges-and-opportunities-for-eu-equality-law/> accessed 5 August 2021.

Greenleaf G, 'The "Brussels Effect" of the EU's "AI Act" on Data Privacy Outside Europe' (2021) 171(1) Privacy Laws & Business International Report.

Hagendorff T, 'The Ethics of AI Ethics: An Evaluation of Guidelines' (2020) 30 Minds and Machines.

Hilligoss H, Raso FA and Krishnamurthy V, 'It's Not Enough for AI to Be "Ethical"; It Must Also Be "Rights Respecting' (2018) <https://medium.com/berkman-klein-center/its-not-enough-for-ai-to-be-ethical-it-must-also-be-rights-respecting-b87f7e215b97> accessed 6 August 2022.

Horowitz MC, 'Artificial Intelligence, International Competition, and the Balance of Power' (2018) 1 Texas National Security Review.

'Human Rights in the Era of Artificial Intelligence in Europe as a Setter of International Standards in the Field of Artificial Intelligence' *Council of Europe* (20 January 2021) <https://www.coe.int/ru/web/commissioner/view/-/asset_publisher/ugj3i6qSEkhZ/content/high-level-conference-human-rights-in-the-era-of-artificial-intelligence> accessed 11 June 2022.

IBM Policy Lab, 'Precision Regulation for Artificial Intelligence' (*IBM THINKPolicy Blog*, 21 January 2020) <https://www.ibm.com/blogs/policy/ai-precision-regulation/> accessed 5 August 2021.

Ienca M and Vayena E, 'AI Ethics Guidelines: European and Global Perspectives' (Ad Hoc Committee on Artificial Intelligence (CAHAI) 2020) <https://rm.coe.int/cahai-2020-07-fin-en-report-ienca-vayena/16809eccac> accessed 13 June 2022.

'Informal Economy' *International Labour Organization* <https://www.ilo.org/global/topics/employment-promotion/informal-economy/lang--en/index.htm> accessed 6 August 2021.

ISO, 'ISO 26000: Social Responsibility' <https://www.iso.org/iso-26000-social-responsibility.html> accessed 6 August 2021.

ISO, 'ISO/IEC JTC 1/SC 42 – Artificial Intelligence' <https://www.iso.org/cms/render/live/en/sites/isoorg/contents/data/committee/67/94/6794475.html> accessed 6 August 2021.

Jillson E, 'Aiming for Truth, Fairness, and Equity in Your Company's Use of AI' (Federal Trade Commission, 19 April 2021) <https://www.ftc.gov/news-events/blogs/

business-blog/2021/04/aiming-truth-fairness-equity-your-companys-use-ai> accessed 6 August 2021.

Jobin A, Ienca I and Vayena E, 'The Global Landscape of AI Ethics Guidelines' (2019) 1 Nature Machine Intelligence.

Jurić M, Šandić A and Brcic M, 'AI Safety: State of the Field through Quantitative Lens, 43rd International Convention on Information and Communication Technology, Electronics and Microelectronics (MIPRO2020) <https://Arxiv.Org/Ftp/Arxiv/Papers/2002/2002.05671.Pdf> accessed 12 June 2022.

Lambrecht A and Tucker C, 'Algorithmic Bias? An Empirical Study into Apparent Gender-Based Discrimination in the Display of STEM Career Ads' (2018) 65 Management Science.

'Legislation Related to Artificial Intelligence' National Conference of State Legislatures <https://www.ncsl.org/research/telecommunications-and-information-technology/2020-legislation-related-to-artificial-intelligence.aspx> accessed 19 April 2022.

Linkomies L, 'UK: Data Protection Shake-up Looks Certain' (Privacy Laws & Business, issue 120 2022) <https://www.privacylaws.com/reports-gateway/articles/uk120/uk120 uk/> accessed 14 June 2022.

McNamara A, Smith J and Murphy-Hill E, 'Does ACM's Code of Ethics Change Ethical Decision Making in Software Development?' *ESEC/FSE* '18, 4–9 November 2018.

METI, 'Japan Contract Guidelines on Utilization of AI and Data Released' <https://www.meti.go.jp/english/press/2019/0404_001.html> accessed 6 August 2022.

Midgley G, 'Systemic Intervention' 2014 <https://www.researchgate.net/publication/31569 2826_Systemic_Intervention> accessed 14 June 2022.

MIT, 'The Global AI Agenda: Latin America' (2020) <https://mittrinsights.s3.amazonaws.com/AIagenda2020/LatAmAIagenda.pdf> accessed 14 June 2022.

Mittelstadt B, 'Principles Alone Cannot Guarantee Ethical AI' [2019] Nature Machine Intelligence.

Moraes TG and de Pereira JRL, 'Promoting Irresponsible AI: Lessons from a Brazilian Bill' (*Heinrich-Böll-Stiftung*) <https://eu.boell.org/en/2022/02/14/promoting-irresponsi ble-ai-lessons-brazilian-bill> accessed 14 June 2022.

Naujokaitytė G, 'Parliament Gives EU a Push to Move Faster on Artificial Intelligence' *Science|Business* <https://sciencebusiness.net/news/parliament-gives-eu-push-move-fast er-artificial-intelligence> accessed 14 June 2022.

Ngy Hesse-Biber S, (ed.), *Handbook of Feminist Research: Theory and Praxis* (SAGE Publications 2014) <https://methods.sagepub.com/base/download/BookChapter/hand book-of-feminist-research/n1.xml> accessed 14 June 2022.

Nickelsburg M, 'Microsoft President Brad Smith Calls for AI Regulation at Davos' (*GeekWire*, 21 January 2020) <https://www.geekwire.com/2020/microsoft-president-brad-smith-calls-ai-regulation-davos/>, accessed 14 June 2022.

Nooren P and others, 'Should We Regulate Digital Platforms? A New Framework for Evaluating Policy Options, Policy and Internet' (2018) 10 Policy & Internet.

Ochigame R, 'The Invention of "Ethical AI": How Big Tech Manipulates Academia to Avoid Regulation' *The Intercept* (20 December 2019) <https://theintercept.com/2019/12/20/mit-ethical-ai-artificial-intelligence/> accessed 6 August 2021.

Ouchchy L, Coin A and Dubljevic V, 'AI in the Headlines: The Portrayal of the Ethical Issues of Artificial Intelligence in the Media' (2020) 35 AI & Society.

Parliamentary secretariat for financial services, digital economy and innovation, 'Malta towards Trustworthy AI' (Parliamentary secretariat for financial services, digital economy and innovation 2019) <https://malta.ai/wp-content/uploads/2019/08/Malta_ Towards_Ethical_and_Trustworthy_AI.pdf> accessed 9 June 2022.

Proposal for a Regulation of the European Parliament and of the Council Laying Down Harmonised Rules on Artificial Intelligence (Artificial Intelligence Act) and Amending Certain Union Legislative Acts COM/2021/206 final 206 <https://eur-lex.europa.eu/legal-content/EN/TXT/?uri=CELEX%3A52021PC0206> accessed 15 June 2022.

Rainie L and others, 'How Americans Think about Artificial Intelligence' (Pew Research

Center 2022) <https://www.pewresearch.org/internet/2022/03/17/how-americans-think-about-artificial-intelligence/> accessed 18 April 2022.

Report of the Special Representative of the Secretary-General on the issue of human rights and transnational corporations and other business enterprises, John Ruggie, Guiding Principles on Business and Human Rights: Implementing the United Nations 'Protect, Respect and Remedy' Framework A/HRC/ RES/17/31 <https://www.ohchr. org/sites/default/files/Documents/Issues/Business/A-HRC-17-31_AEV.pdf> accessed 10 June 2022.

'Report of Working Group on Human Rights and Transnational Corporations and Other Business Enterprises' (Working Group on human rights and transnational corporations and other business enterprises 2021).

Rességuier A and Rodrigues R, 'AI Ethics Should Not Remain Toothless? A Call to Bring Back the Teeth of Ethics' (2020) July–Dec Big Data & Society 1.

Richards NM and Hartzog W, 'The Pathology of Digital Consent' (2019) 96 Washington University Law Review.

Ruggie J, Guiding Principles on Business and Human Rights: Implementing the United Nations 'Protect, Respect and Remedy' Framework A/HRC/RES/17/31, <https://www.ohchr.org/sites/default/files/Documents/Issues/Business/A-HRC-17-31_AEV.pdf> accessed 15 June 2022.

Ruggie J, 'Protect, Respect and Remedy: A Framework for Business and Human Rights' (2008) A/HRC/8/5, Special Representative of the Secretary-General on the issue of human rights and transnational corporations and other business enterprises, 2008 A/HRC/8/5.

Sander E, 'Is China Showing Us the Way in Regulating Algorithms?' (ChinaTalk, 7 January 2022) <https://www.chinatalk.nl/is-china-showing-us-the-way-in-regulating-algorithms/> accessed 18 April 2022.

Schmidt E, 'The AI Revolution and Strategic Competition with China | by Eric Schmidt' (*Project Syndicate*, 30 August 2021) <https://www.project-syndicate.org/commentary/ai-revolution-competition-with-china-democracy-vs-authoritarianism-by-eric-schmidt-2021-08>, accessed 14 June 2022.

Schneier B, *Click Here to Kill Everybody Security and Survival in a Hyper-Connected World* (W. W. Norton & Company 2018).

Schroeder JE, 'Reinscribing Gender: Social Media, Algorithms, Bias' (2021) 37 Journal of Marketing Management 376.

Senate Bill 21-169 concerning protecting consumers from unfair discrimination in insurance practices 2022.

SG:D, Infocomm Media Development Authority and Personal data Protection Commission, 'Singapore Model Artificial Intelligence Governance Framework' <https://www.pdpc.gov.sg/-/media/Files/PDPC/PDF-Files/Resource-for-Organisation/AI/SGModelAIGovFramework2.pdf> accessed 15 June 2022.

Sheehan M, 'China's New AI Governance Initiatives Shouldn't Be Ignored' (Carnegie Endowment for International Peace) <https://carnegieendowment.org/2022/01/04/china-s-new-ai-governance-initiatives-shouldn-t-be-ignored-pub-86127> accessed 19 April 2022.

Slaughter RK, 'Algorithms and Economic Justice: A Taxonomy of Harms and a Path Forward for the Federal Trade Commission' (2021) 23 Yale Journal of Law & Technology.

Special Representative of the Secretary-General on the issue of human rights and transnational corporations and other business enterprises, John Ruggie, 'Protect, Respect and Remedy: A Framework for Business and Human Rights' (2008) A/HRC/8/5.

Spinaci S, 'Corporate Sustainability Due Diligence: Could Value Chains Integrate Human Rights and Environmental Concerns?' (BRIEFING: EU Legislation in Progress Members' Research Service, PE 729.424, May 2022).

Stinson C, 'Algorithms Are Not Neutral: Bias in Collaborative Filtering' [2022] AI and Ethics.

'The New Machinery of Government: Using Machine Technology in Administrative Decision-Making' NSW Ombudsman (2021) <https://www.parliament.nsw.gov.au/la/papers/Pages/tabled-paper-details.aspx?pk=81066&houseCode=LH> accessed 19 April 2022.

The Toronto Declaration, 'The Toronto Declaration' <https://www.torontodeclaration.org/declaration-text/english/> accessed 6 August 2021.

'The upcoming Brazilian Artificial Intelligence Act: what businesses need to know' *Mattos Filho*, 18 April 2022) <https://www.mattosfilho.com.br/en/unico/ brazilian-artificial-intelligence/> accessed 14 June 2022.

The White House Office of Science and Technology Policy, 'Blueprint for an AI Bill of Rights Making Automated Systems Work for the American People', October 2022 <https://www.whitehouse.gov/ostp/ai-bill-of-rights/#applying> accessed 5 October 2022.

UNDP and the United Nations Working Group on Business and Human Rights, 'Gender Dimensions of the Guiding Principles on Business and Human Rights' https://www.ohchr.org/Documents/Issues/Business/BookletGenderDimensionsGuidingPrinciples.pdf> accessed 15 June 2022.

UK Department for Digital, Culture, Media and Sport (DCMS), 'Establishing a Pro-Innovation Approach to Regulating AI: An Overview of the UK's Emerging Approach', 18 July 2022 <https://assets.publishing.service.gov.uk/government/uploads/system/uploads/attachment_data/file/1092630/_CP_728__-_Establishing_a_pro-innovation_approach_to_regulating_AI.pdf> accessed 14 June 2022.

UN Special Rapporteur on the Right to Freedom of Opinion and Expression and Working Party Human Rights, Transnational Corporations and Other Business Enterprises, 'UN Special Rapporteur on the Right to Freedom of Opinion and Expression' (2020) OL OTH37/2020.

UNESCO, 'Artificial Intelligence and Gender Equality: Key Findings of UNESCO's Global Dialogue' (2020) <https://unesxcodoc.unesco.org/in/documentViewer.html?v=2.1.196&id+2020> accessed 15 June 2022.

Wachter S, 'Affinity Profiling and Discrimination by Association in Online Behavioural Advertising' (2020) 35 Berkeley Technology Law Journal.

Wachter S and Mittelstadt B, 'A Right to Reasonable Inferences: Re-Thinking Data Protection Law in the Age of Big Data and AI' [2019] Colombia Business Law Review.

Wagner B, 'Ethics as an Escape from Regulation: From Ethics-Washing to Ethics-Shopping' in Emre Bayamlioğlu and others (eds), *Being Profiled: Cogitas Ergo Sum: 10 Years of Profiling the European Citizen* (Amsterdam University Press 2019).

Walsh C, *2062: The World That AI Made* (La Trobe University Press and Black Inc 2018).

Walter M, 'Data Politics and Indigenous Representation in Australian Statistics' [2016] <https://www.researchgate.net/publication/317656929_Data_politics_and_Indigenous_representation_in_Australian_statistics> accessed 6 August 2021.

Wang L, 'The Three Harms of Gendered Technology' (2020) 24 Australasian Journal of Information Systems: Selected papers from 2019 AICE Conference.

Wang Y, 'Deep Neural Networks Are More Accurate than Humans at Detecting Sexual Orientation from Facial Images' (2018) 114 Journal of Personality and Social Psychology.

West SM, Whittaker M and Crawford K, 'Discriminating Systems: Gender, Race and Power in AI' (AI Now Institute 2019).

'White Paper on Artificial Intelligence – A European Approach to Excellence and Trust' (European Commission, COM(2020) 65 final 2019) <https://rm.coe.int/cahai-2021-09rev-elements/1680a6d90d> accessed 6 August 2021.

Zuboff S, *The Age of Surveillance Capitalism: The Fight for a Human Future at the New Frontier of Power* (Profile Books 2019).

PART IV

SECTORAL APPROACHES TO THE GOVERNANCE OF BIG DATA AND AI

9. Better technological security solutions through human-centred design and development

Andrew B. Wootton, Caroline L. Davey, Dagmar Heinrich and Maximilian Querbach

1. INTRODUCTION

The Design Against Crime Solution Centre at the University of Salford has spent the last two decades undertaking action research around design-led crime prevention. The authors have focused on the role of design – of products, communications, processes, systems and environments – in reducing harm and improving safety and security. This has included research into the analysis and mapping of police-recorded crime incident data to better target preventative action by law enforcement and partner agencies. As proponents of human-centred design, the authors have been critical of overly *technology-driven* approaches that tend not to fully consider contextual requirements, roles, values and responsibilities of the human stakeholders within a design system. The rise of big data analytics might be considered a prime example of a *solution* emerging from a technological development – a capability searching for a well-defined problem.

Much has been written about the application of big data analytics to law enforcement, often in what has been termed *predictive policing*.[1] Predictive policing is traditionally defined as,

> a multidisciplinary, law enforcement-based strategy that brings together advanced technologies, criminological theory, predictive analysis, and tactical

---

[1] Dennis Broeders and others, 'Big Data and Security Policies: Towards a Framework for Regulating the Phases of Analytics and Use of Big Data' (2017) 33 Computer Law and Security Law Review; Andrew Guthrie Ferguson, *The Rise of Big Data Policing* (New York University Press 2017); Pietro Costanzo, Francesca D'Onofrio and Julia Friedl, 'Big Data and the Italian Legal Framework: Opportunities for Police Forces' in B Akhgar and others (eds), *Application of Big Data for National Security* (Oxford 2015).

operations that ultimately lead to results and outcomes – crime reduction, management efficiency, and safer communities.[2]

In 2019 Meijer and Wessels further, and arguably more practically, defined predictive policing as,

> the collection and analysis of data about previous crimes for identification and statistical prediction of individuals or geospatial areas with an increased probability of criminal activity to help in developing policing intervention and prevention strategies and tactics.[3]

While the focus was initially on the potential for predictive policing to modernise and improve policing, later studies highlighted the ethical, legal and social impacts of the approach.[4]

This chapter draws on research carried out as part of the EU-funded *Cutting Crime Impact* (CCI) project. The overall aim of the CCI project was to prevent high-impact crime and reduce its negative effect on citizens through the use of a human-centred design approach.[5] The focus of CCI was directed by six partner law enforcement agencies (LEAs), with the aim to develop tools that met their needs and requirements. Consequently, CCI addressed four LEA-defined 'focus areas' related to the prevention of crime and insecurity. The focus area chosen by the Landeskriminalamt (LKA) in Lower Saxony, Germany, was predictive policing. The LKA was supported in adopting a human-centred design approach to address issues around predictive policing in Lower Saxony.[6]

This chapter details CCI research in Lower Saxony into the application and use of predictive policing, undertaken using a human-centred design approach. Research conducted in Lower Saxony revealed that the new system was not actually transforming police operations in the way it was planned. Using a human-centred design approach, the LKA was able to better understand and reframe the problem, as well as develop a solution tailored to the needs of end-users.

---

[2]   Craig D Uchida, 'Predictive Policing' in Gerban Bruinsma and David Weisburd (eds), *Encyclopedia of Criminology and Criminal Justice* (Springer 2014) 3871.

[3]   Albert Meijer and Martijn Wessels, 'Predictive Policing: Review of Benefits and Drawbacks' (2019) 42 International Journal of Public Administration, 1033.

[4]   Oskar J Gstrein, Anno Bunnik and Andrei Zwitter, 'Ethical, Legal and Social Challenges of Predictive Policing' (2019) 3 Católica Law Review 77.

[5]   CCI, 'Introduction to CCI' (cuttingcrimeimpact.eu, 2021) <https://www.cuttingcrimeimpact.eu/about/introduction-to-cci/> accessed 7 July 2022.

[6]   ibid.

2.   THE DESIGN APPROACH TO RESEARCH

The *Design Against Crime Solution Centre* undertakes design research within the broad domain of safety and security. As a means of creating tools, processes and systems that support the security goals of end-users, adopting a design approach offers several benefits.

For designers, the needs of the human user are central to understanding problems, evaluating options and resolving issues – an approach often described as *human centred*:

> human-centred design focuses on the roles, requirements, abilities and perceptions of all the humans in the problem domain being examined.[7]

The CCI project adopted a human-centred design approach to the delivery of tools for its partner LEAs, focusing on the human participants within the various design systems being studied – in this case, LEAs and their stakeholder organisations.[8] From a human-centred perspective, the application of predictive policing must respect the requirements and values of the humans in the design system. In order to do so, designers must gain insight into end-users' needs, limitations and contexts.

2.1   Human-centred Design

As in other disciplines, design is characterised by a specialised vocabulary that illuminates certain aspects of the lived experience and constructs a particular worldview. This design discourse resides in the work of communities of academic and professional practice.[9] The design literature identifies at least four key features that in combination might be considered distinctive of design and which the authors suggest are fundamental to design research.

1.   Design explores possible futures while producing tangible results
      Designers have the ability to imagine and convincingly communicate possible futures, explore different means of pursuing such futures,

---

[7]   Caroline L Davey and Andrew B Wootton, *Design Against Crime: A Human-Centred Approach to Designing for Safety and Security* (Routledge 2017) 30.

[8]   CCI, 'Project Design' (cuttingcrimeimpact.eu, 2021) <https://www.cuttingcrimeimpact.eu/about/project-design/> accessed 4 August 2022.

[9]   Klaus Krippendorff, 'Design Discourse: A Way to Redesign Design' [1998] Keynote Address to the Society for Science of Design Studies 6 December 1998 01–5 <https://repository.upenn.edu/asc_papers/227> accessed 29 June 2022.

and work towards achieving those that are chosen. In the process, a stockpile of meaningful artefacts is amassed, such as sketches, drawings, models and specifications.[10] The role of design in addressing societal challenges and helping create improved and more sustainable solutions is emphasised within a range of design approaches, including socially responsible design and transformation design.[11]

2. Design challenges assumptions to provoke new perspectives and ideas

Designers pursue possibilities for change, overcoming barriers and opening doors that appear closed. In pursuing change, designers challenge what others take for granted, creating space for new ideas and for improvement.[12] Indeed, the process of challenging assumptions is often a form of *provocation* aimed at exposing alternative perspectives and new ideas, rather than being a solution itself.

3. Design is human-centred, embracing the depth and diversity of human experience

For designers, the needs of the human user are central to understanding problems, evaluating options and resolving issues – the essence of being *human-centred*.[13] Design research seeks to embrace the diversity of practical, psychological and emotional understandings that humans bring to artefacts and situations. This draws on empathetic observation, visual and physical prototyping, and creative analysis to gain rich understanding and insight.

Human-centred design moves beyond ergonomics or human factors approaches, which traditionally focus on efficiency of use, perceptual biases and mistakes. Designers appreciate the social and psychological impact of their work; how the creation of new artefacts alters how we live together. As Krippendorf identifies, 'We do not react to the physical properties of things but act on what they mean to us.'[14]

Unlike other change-oriented disciplines, such as engineering, design is primarily concerned with the creation of artefacts that are

---

[10]   ibid.
[11]   Caroline L Davey and Andrew B Wootton, 'Transformation Design – Creating security & wellbeing' in Wolfgang Jonas, Kristof Von Anshelm and Sarah Zerwas (eds), *Transformation Design* (BIRD 2016).
[12]   Krippendorff (n 9).
[13]   Davey and Wootton (n 7) 11.
[14]   Krippendorff (n 9) 8.

perceived as meaningful by others.[15] Thus, empathy and emotional intelligence are important design research skills.

4.   Design involves prototyping and progressive refinement
    Design research involves controlled revelation of research outputs to the world to test if and how they function, and then progressively refining them.[16] Product designers refer to prototyping – which may suggest a physical product, test rig or *demo*. However, there are numerous forms of 'prototyping' in design research – from narrative descriptions, through drawings and conceptual models, to three-dimensional models and data analyses. These may all be used to test, validate and refine outputs of design research.

2.2   Human Centred vs Technology Driven

The results of human-centred design contrast with technology-driven solutions, which, as identified by the Technology Hype Cycle,[17] often fail to meet early expectations. Predictive policing is perhaps a prime example of a technology-driven solution,[18] with a number of police forces reducing or ending their use of predictive policing technologies.[19] For instance, Kent Police – the first UK police force to try predictive policing – ended its £100,000 per year contract in March 2018, after five years. While PredPol – the system deployed – was considered to have a good record in predicting the location of crime, there was no evidence that this information was being used to actually reduce crime.[20]

---

[15]   Richard Buchanan, 'Declaration by Design: Rhetoric, Argument, and Demonstration in Design Practice' in Victor Margolin (ed.), *Design Discourse: History, Theory, Criticism* (The University of Chicago Press 1989).

[16]   Allan Collins, Diana Joseph and Katerine Bielaczyc, 'Design Research: Theoretical and Methodological Issues' (2004) 13(1) The Journal of the Learning Sciences.

[17]   Ozgur Dedehayir and Martin Steinert, 'The Hype Cycle Model: A Review and Future Directions' (2016) 108 Technological Forecasting and Social Change.

[18]   Guy Adams 'LAPD's sci-fi solution to real crime' *Independent* (London, 11 January 2012) 32.

[19]   Johana Bhuiyan, 'LAPD Ended Predictive Policing Programs amid Public Outcry: A New Effort Shares Many of Their Flaws' *The Guardian* (8 November 2021) <https://www.theguardian.com/us-news/2021/nov/07/lapd-predictive-policing-surveillance-reform> accessed 2 August 2022; Annie Gilbertson, 'Data-Informed Predictive Policing Was Heralded As Less Biased. Is It?' *The Markup* (NY, 20 August 2020) <https://themarkup.org/the-breakdown/2020/08/20/does-predictive-police-technology-contribute-to-bias> accessed 2 August 2022.

[20]   Patricia Nilsson, 'First UK Police Force to Try Predictive Policing Ends Contract' *Financial Times* (London, 26 November 2018).

From a human-centred perspective, the application of predictive polic-ing needs to respect the needs, requirements and values of the humans in the design system. Design outputs, such as tools, must be designed to support the roles and actions of those humans within a system who are responsible for its successful implementation and/or delivery. Consequently, human-centred objectives rather than technology should drive the design process, these being:

1. To enhance human abilities
    – *Human abilities should be identified, understood and cultivated*
2. To overcome human limitations
    – *Identify these and devise compensatory mechanisms/processes*
3. To foster human acceptance
    – *Understand and address preferences, concerns and values.*[21]

To do this, requires deep insight into end-users' needs, requirements and contexts. LEA partners in the CCI project were supported to undertake design research to gain such insight about the design systems upon which their problem areas focused. As outlined above, the focus of design research is not merely data, but insight gained from research into stake-holder needs and contexts.[22] Such insight can act as the catalyst for new ways of thinking about problems or issues, from which successful solution ideas can be developed.[23] This search for insight requires not just the social science skills of the ethnographer, but also empathy, introspection and emotional intelligence.

3.   GREAT EXPECTATIONS: PREDICTIVE POLICING AND BIG DATA

In recent years, considerable attention has been given to big data, and claims for its potential value to business,[24] science and medicine.[25]

---

[21]   William B Rouse, *Design for Success: A Human-Centered Approach to Designing Successful Products and Systems* (Wiley 1991).

[22]   Davey and Wootton (n 11) 62.

[23]   ibid.

[24]   Andrew McAfee and Erik Brynjolfsson, 'Big Data: The Management Revolution' (Harvard Business Review, October 2012) <https://hbr.org/2012/10/big-data-the-management-revolution> accessed 6 April 2022.

[25]   Mary Mallappallil and others, 'A Review of Big Data and Medical Research' (2020) 8 SAGE open Med 1.

Big data analytics is the use of advanced analytic techniques to analyse large and diverse data sets coming from different sources. Such data may be structured, semi-structured or unstructured, and range in size from terabytes to zettabytes.[26] Big data is characterised by high data volume, data velocity and data variety – the so-called '3V definition'.[27] Such big data sets must be managed by computer networks geared towards the processing of high volumes of data messages with minimal delay.[28] Sources are more complex than traditional sources of data, being often the output of artificial intelligence (AI), mobile devices, social media and the Internet of Things (IoT).[29]

3.1 The Original Promise of Predictive Policing

Big data analytics is a technology that promises to fuel better and faster decision-making, modelling and predicting future outcomes, and providing enhanced business intelligence.[30] Recognising its potential to support decision-making in the field of law enforcement, products using big data analytics were developed for police forces and marketed under the term *Predictive Policing*.

While large companies like IBM also make predictive policing tools, one of the most widely deployed products in the US comes from a small company in Santa Cruz.[31] The sales literature identifies a range of uses for predictive policing – a list of technological *could do*s. However, in essence, predictive policing is quite simple. Core to predictive policing is a product, or more specifically a software application, designed to analyse past crime data, in terms of the type of crime, when it happened and where. Based on

---

[26]   IBM, 'Big Data Analytics' (IBM.com, ND) <https://www.ibm.com/analyt ics/big-data-analytics> accessed 6 April 2022.

[27]   Doug Laney, '3D Data Management: Controlling Data Volume, Velocity and Variety' Gartner (2 February 2001) <https://studylib.net/doc/8647594/3d-data-management--controlling-data-volume--velocity--an...> accessed 14 July 2022; Rosamunde van Brakel, 'Pre-Emptive Big Data Surveillance and its (Dis) Empowering Consequences: The Case of Predictive Policing' in Bart van der Sloot and others (eds), *Exploring the Boundaries of Big Data* (Amsterdam University Press 2016).

[28]   Salvador García and others, 'Big Data Preprocessing: Methods and Prospects' (2016) 1(9) Big Data Analytics.

[29]   IBM (n 26).

[30]   ibid.

[31]   Alexis C. Madrigal, 'The Future of Crime-Fighting or the Future of Racial Profiling? Inside the Effects of Predictive Policing' (HuffPost.com, 28 March 2016) <https://www.huffpost.com/entry/predictive-policing-video_n_56f898c9e4b 0a372181a42ef> accessed 5 April 2022.

an analysis of this data, predictive policing systems generate more or less accurate predictions about where and when future crimes are more likely to occur.[32] Systems may be used to predict individuals at risk of offending (or reoffending) or to identify locations where crime is likely to occur[33] – the latter being the focus for this chapter.

In relation to some products, such as PredPol (used in the US and UK),[34] the system represents predictions in terms of 150 metre square red boxes overlaid onto a Google map. These red boxes are the areas at risk of crime that police officers should patrol, when they are not actively responding to a call. By focusing their attention on areas where there is a higher likelihood of crimes being committed, it is argued, patrolling efforts will be more effective and the number of crime incidents in that location will be reduced.

The new technology and its application of predictive policing to law enforcement was heralded as ground-breaking. Indeed, in 2011 *TIME* magazine named predictive policing – and its application in the city of Santa Cruz – as one of the 50 best inventions of that year.[35] Santa Cruz's Police Chief Kevin Vogel said of the accolade,

> We are honored to be recognized by Time magazine for our predictive policing program[.] Innovation is the key to modern policing, and we're proud to be leveraging technology in a way that keeps our community safer.[36]

The new technology was credited with making police operations more effective, without requiring additional resources. According to Zach Friends, a spokesman and crime analyst for the police department, 'since the program was implemented, the department has seen a large reduction in crimes.'[37]

---

[32]   ibid.

[33]   van Brakel (n 27).

[34]   PredPol 'Predictive policing: The Predictive Policing Company' (2015) <www.predpol.com> accessed 18 July 2022; Kentonline, 'Predpol Software which Targets Crime Down to Small Zones Has Slashed North Kent Crime by 6%' (Kent, 2013) <www.kentonline.co.uk/kent/news/crime-innorth-kent-slashed-4672> accessed 18 July 2022.

[35]   Jessica M. Pasko, 'Time Magazine Names Santa Cruz Police Program to Predict Crime One of the Year's Top Inventions' *The Mercury News* (Santa Cruz, 23 November 2011) <https://www.mercurynews.com/2011/11/23/time-magazine-names-santa-cruz-police-program-to-predict-crime-one-of-the-years-top-inventions/> accessed 6 April 2022.

[36]   ibid.

[37]   ibid.

Most senior police officers would probably like to be able to demonstrate that their force has become more effective, while spending less.[38] More likely than not, senior police officers are also under pressure to modernise and address specific issues – often identified by those outside the force, responsible for local or national policies. Like other organisations, police senior managers are influenced by current trends in organisational management and change, as well as the hype that often seems to surround a new technology.[39] Under the circumstances, it is perhaps not surprising that police forces in the US were willing to risk experimenting with the new technology.

Predictive policing was first piloted by the Los Angeles Police Department (LAPD) in 2010,[40] with the city of Minneapolis an early adopter of the approach.[41] Other cities in the US soon followed, with New York City Police Commissioner William Bratton calling predictive policing 'the wave of the future'.[42] Police forces across the world rushed to adopt the use of data analysis methods to inform deployment of police resources, often reduced due to public spending cuts after the 2008 financial crisis. Deemed innovative and forward looking, predictive policing was heralded as the beginning of a new era in 21st-century policing by politicians and police leaders alike.[43] According to a report funded by the US Department of Justice, by 2017 28% of large US police agencies were using predictive analytics software, with a further 22% planning to implement it by 2019.[44] Predictive policing was also considered *promising* for LEAs

---

[38] HV Jagadish, 'The Promise and Perils of Predictive Policing Based on Big Data' (TheConversation.com, 16 November 2016) <https://theconversation.com/the-promise-and-perils-of-predictive-policing-based-on-big-data-48366> accessed 6 April 2022.

[39] ibid.

[40] Gstrein and others (n 4).

[41] Jeff Egge, 'Experimenting with Future-Oriented Analysis at Crime Hot Spots in Minneapolis' (2011) 2(4) Geography & Public Safety <https://www.ojp.gov/ncjrs/virtual-library/abstracts/experimenting-future-oriented-analysis-crime-hot-spots-minneapolis> accessed 7 April 2022.

[42] Ali Winston, 'Predictive Policing is "Wave of the Future," NY Commissioner Says' (revealnews.org, 31 July 2015) <https://revealnews.org/article/predictive-policing-is-wave-of-the-future-ny-commissioner-says/> accessed 7 April 2022.

[43] Beth Pearsall, 'Predictive Policing: The Future of Law Enforcement?' (2010) 266 National Institute of Justice Journal <https://www.ojp.gov/pdffiles1/nij/230414.pdf> accessed 3 August 2022; Pasko (n 35).

[44] Kevin Strom, 'Research on the Impact of Technology on Policing Strategy in the 21st Century, Final Report' (Office of Justice Programs' National Criminal Justice Reference Service, May 2016) <https://www.ojp.gov/pdffiles1/nij/grants/251140.pdf> accessed 7 April 2022.

across Europe.[45] However, it was not long before criticisms and shortcomings emerged – especially in relation to the experience of applying predictive policing in the US – and police forces began to abandon the approach.[46]

4.   PARADISE LOST?

The term predictive policing suggests that the police can anticipate a crime and be there to stop it before it happens and/or apprehend the culprits right away. Prior to the development of predictive policing, police forces mapped the geographical location of different crime types to identify neighbourhoods with higher crime rates. Since the 1980s, criminological research has provided insight into how burglars operate – and such knowledge has helped police forces identify when and where future burglaries might occur.[47]

Predictive policing algorithms may be good at analysing a combination of factors to determine where crimes are more likely to happen and who is more likely to commit them. However, as data analysts are aware, predictions come nowhere near close to certainty, even with advanced technology. The accuracy of predictions depends upon the quality of the data input to the system. However, the data inputted to predictive policing systems is often inaccurate and prone to errors.[48]

In a previous project, *City Centre Crime*, which investigated crime hotspots in Greater Manchester (UK), the location for incidents of crime had to be corrected by the researcher in around 50% of cases. This is a time-consuming process that involves checking location data against other, more qualitative information about the incident.[49]

---

[45]   Bart Custers and Bas Vergouw, 'Promising Policing Technologies: Experiences, Obstacles and Police Needs regarding Law Enforcement Technologies' (2015) 31(4) Computer Law & Security Review.

[46]   Martin Degeling and Bettina Berendt, 'What is Wrong about Robocops as Consultants? A Technology-Centric Critique of Predictive Policing' (2018) 33 AI & Society.

[47]   Portland State University, Criminology and Criminal Justice Senior Capstone, 'Prevention of Residential Burglary: A Review of the Literature' (2010) Criminology and Criminal Justice Senior Capstone Project 3 <https://pdxscholar.library.pdx.edu/ccj_capstone/3> accessed 14 July 2022.

[48]   HV Jagadish, 'Big Data Analyses Depend on Starting with Clean Data Points' (TheConversation.com, 4 August 2015) <https://theconversation.com/big-data-analyses-depend-on-starting-with-clean-data-points-43687> accessed 7 April 2022.

[49]   Andrew B Wootton, Melissa Marselle and Caroline L Davey, 'City Centre Crime: Design thinking for safer city centres', Proceedings from the 8th European Academy of Design Conference 2009 – 1, 2 and 3 April 2009, The Robert Gordon University, Aberdeen, Scotland.

Even if the data were cleaned prior to input to reduce such errors, the algorithms are only determining correlations. All that the best algorithm can do is to say it is likely, but not certain, that a burglary will be committed in a particular location. Many intervening variables can prevent a burglary from taking place. Predictive policing tools simply provide police forces with probabilities based on statistical modelling, rather than certainty. A police department may add up these probabilities across all houses in a neighbourhood to estimate how likely it is that there will be a burglary. They can then place more officers in neighbourhoods with higher probabilities for crime on the basis that police presence may deter incidents. There does seem to be some evidence that targeted use of police resources does indeed reduce crime rates.[50] But are the data provided by predictive policing systems significantly better than the knowledge held by officers with many years of experience patrolling an area, or that gained from existing GIS-based incident recording systems? Either of these can allow police resources to be targeted to areas where one or more incidents (e.g., burglaries) have already taken place. However, this in itself is not always straightforward.

The placing of police officers in a particular location can have social and ethical consequences. The presence of police officers can result in more offences being detected – from traffic violations, through incivilities to illegal drug possession and dealing. Consequently, this may more strongly associate the neighbourhood and communities that live there with crime, which has the potential to result in more intense policing leading to particular communities being overly targeted.[51] In the US, the targeting of particular individuals and groups by the police has raised serious concerns about civil liberties.[52] Police in the US have a poor record in terms of

---

[50]   Stuart Wolpert, 'Predictive Policing Test Substantially Reduces Crime' (universityofcalifornia.edu, 7 October 2015). <https://www.universityofcalifornia.edu/news/predictive-policing-test-substantially-reduces-crime> accessed 7 April 2022.

[51]   Media Freedom & Information Access Clinic, 'Algorithmic Accountability: The Need for a New Approach to Transparency and Accountability When Government Functions Are Performed by Algorithms' [2022] Abrams Institute for Freedom of Expression, Yale Law School <https://law.yale.edu/sites/default/files/area/center/mfia/document/algorithmic_accountability_report.pdf> accessed 7 July 2022.

[52]   Lindsey Barret, 'Reasonably Suspicious Algorithms: Predictive Policing at the United States Border' (2018) 41 N.Y.U. Review of Law & Social Change 3.   <https://socialchangenyu.com/review/reasonably-suspicious-algorithms-predictive-policing-at-the-united-states-border/> accessed 7 July 2022.

compliance with human rights,[53] and this has been exacerbated through the use of predictive policing to identify individuals likely to offend, rather than locations of risk.[54]

In Germany, where predictive policing has also been adopted, ethical and social issues were considered and addressed during their particular implementation of the approach.

5.   EXPLORATION OF PREDICTIVE POLICING ADOPTION IN GERMANY

Germany comprises 16 federal states, each with its own governing body and state police service. There are also three federal law enforcement agencies, one of which is the Federal Police.[55] Desk research, a survey and interviews were conducted as part of CCI to investigate use of predictive policing across Germany. Between 2014 and 2018, LEAs in six German states were working with predictive policing, having purchased a system from an external company or developed their own system in house. These were: Berlin, Bavaria, Baden-Württemberg, Hessen, Lower Saxony and North Rhine-Westphalia.[56] In addition, LEAs in a number of other German states were planning to introduce predictive policing over the next couple of years.[57]

German use of predictive policing focused initially on the identification of areas at higher risk of burglary. The main driver for this was the rising rate of domestic burglary in Germany as a whole and the low clearance

---

[53]   Rashida Richardson, Jason Schultz and Kate Crawford, 'Dirty Data, Bad Predictions: How Civil Rights Violations Impact Police Data, Predictive Policing Systems, and Justice' (2019) 94 NYU Law Review Online <https://papers.ssrn.com/sol3/papers.cfm?abstract_id=3333423> accessed 20 July 2022.

[54]   ibid.

[55]   Federal Ministry of the Interior and Community, 'The Federal Police' (bmi.bund.de, ND) <https://www.bmi.bund.de/EN/topics/security/federal-police/federal-police-node.html> accessed 5 April 2022.

[56]   Kai Seidensticker, Felix Bode and Florian Stoffel, 'Predictive Policing in Germany' [2018] 2 <http://nbn-resolving.de/urn:nbn:de:bsz:352-2-14sbvox1ik0z06> accessed 7 August 2022.

[57]   Maximillian Querbach, Marian Krom and Armando Jongejan, 'Review of State of the Art: Predictive Policing' (Cutting Crime Impact (CCI) Deliverable 2.3, Salford, UK, August 2020) <https://www.cuttingcrimeimpact.eu/resources/public-results/predictive-policing-/titulo/> accessed 6 April 2022; Alexander Gluba and Alexander Pett, 'Predictive Policing – ein (un)bekannter Ansatz – Definition, Ursprung und Rahmenbedingungen' in Martin HW Möllers and Robert C van Ooyen (eds), *Jahrbuch Öffentliche Sicherheit 2016/2017* (Nomos 2017).

rates for burglaries in the affected federal states.[58] It was recognised that domestic burglaries impact negatively on society, and result in financial and psychological harm to victims.[59] Due to intensive media attention, politicians and senior police officers were under significant public pressure to address the problem and allocate resources to burglary prevention.[60]

While other European countries, such as the UK and the Netherlands, were keeping burglary rates down through better design and security of residential areas, such approaches were less well established in Germany. In addition, burglaries were largely attributed to 'professional burglars' – career criminals that were entering Germany via the Netherlands.[61]

In October 2016, the interior ministers of the Netherlands, Belgium, Germany and the federal states of North Rhine-Westphalia, Rhineland-Palatinate and Lower Saxony signed the *Aachen Declaration*. This document recorded their agreement to strengthen cross-border cooperation in combating property crime. A variety of steps were taken to prevent burglary, one of which was the implementation of predictive policing.[62]

The use of algorithms to identify potential risk areas was perceived as an innovative approach to addressing public concerns about burglary and improving traditional policing methods.[63] With Germany somewhat

---

[58]   Bundesministerium des Innern, 'Polizeiliche Kriminalstatistik 2015' (May 2016) 3 <https://www.bmi.bund.de/SharedDocs/downloads/DE/publikationen/themen/sicherheit/pks-2015.html> accessed 20 July 2022.

[59]   Gina Rosa Wollinger and others, 'Wohnungseinbruch – Tat und Folgen – Ergebnisse einer Betroffenenbefragung in fünf Großstädten' (KFN-Forschungsberichte 124 Hannover 2014).

[60]   Querbach and others (n 57).

[61]   Gina Rosa Wollinger and Nadine Jukschat, 'Reisende und zugereiste Täter des Wohnungseinbruchs. Ergebnisse einer qualitativen Interviewstudie mit verurteilten Tätern' (Kriminologisches Forschungsinstitut Niedersachsen e.V. 2017) <https://kfn.de/wp-content/uploads/Forschungsberichte/FB_133.pdf> accessed 26 February 2023; Gina Rosa Wollinger and Nadine Jukschat, 'Foreign Burglars: Primary Results of an Interview Study with Arrested Offenders in Germany' (2017) 6 International Journal of Criminology and Sociology; Gina Rosa Wollinger and others, 'Offender Organization and Criminal Investigations with regard to Organised Residential Burglary Law Enforcement: Results of an International Expert Survey' (Kriminologisches Forschungsinstitut Niedersachsen e.V. (KFN) 2018) <https://kfn.de/wp-content/uploads/Forschungsberichte/FB_147%20en.pdf> accessed 3 August 2022.

[62]   Landesregierung Nordrhein-Westfalen, 'Aachener Erklärung zur besseren Bekämpfung der grenzüberschreitenden Eigentumskriminalität' (31 October 2016) <https://www.land.nrw/pressemitteilung/aachener-erklaerung-zur-besseren-bekaempfung-der-grenzueberschreitenden> accessed 7 August 2022; Querbach and others (n 57).

[63]   Querbach and others (n 57) 13.

lagging behind other European countries in terms of digitalisation, predictive policing may also have been seen as a welcome opportunity for the country to modernise.

Since 2014 and 2015 respectively, the states of Bavaria and Baden-Württemberg have been using a predictive policing system called *Precobs*. This system predicts domestic burglaries based on the near-repeat approach. The near-repeat phenomenon suggests that when a crime occurs in a specific location, the area surrounding that location may experience an increased risk of a similar crime occurring for a distinct period of time.[64] The system was developed by the institute for pattern-based forecasting technology in Oberhausen, Germany.[65] Precobs was tested in several cities and areas in Bavaria, before being adopted by the police.[66] The implementation of Precobs in Baden-Württemberg was evaluated by the Max Planck Institute for Foreign and International Criminal Law. However, the results proved inconsistent due to the problem of being able to attribute causal effects solely to the use of predictive policing – a common problem in evaluating policing practice.[67] In December 2018, the state of Saxony started a pilot project with the Precobs system.[68]

In 2015, the federal state of North Rhine-Westphalia developed a predictive policing tool, called SKALA, that brings together near-repeat and socio-economic theories about crime.[69] The in-house system predicts locations and times not only for domestic burglary, but also for commercial

---

64   Tasha J Youstin and others, 'Assessing the Generalizability of the Near Repeat Phenomenon' (2011) 38(10) Criminal Justice and Behavior; Jerry H Ratcliffe and George F Rengert, 'Near Repeat Patterns in Philadelphia Shootings' (2008) 21(1–2) Security Journal.

65   Tobias Knobloch, 'Vor die Lage kommen – Predictive Policing in Deutschland – Chancen und Gefahren datenanalytischer Prognosetechnik und Empfehlungen für den Einsatz in der Polizeiarbeit' (Gütersloh 2018) <https://www.bertelsmann-stiftung.de/fileadmin/files/BSt/Publikationen/GrauePublikationen/predictive.policing.pdf> accessed 26 February 2023.

66   Bayerisches Staatsministerium des Inneren, für Bau und Verkehr, 'Kooperationsvereinbarung Bayern – Baden-Württemberg zur Bekämpfung Wohnungseinbruchskriminalität' (2015) <https://www.stmi.bayern.de/med/pressemitteilungen/pressear-chiv/2015/248b/index.php> accessed 7 August 2022.

67   Dominik Gerstner, 'Predictive Policing in the Context of Residential Burglary: An Empirical Illustration on the basis of a Pilot Project in Baden-Württemberg, Germany' (2018) 3(2) European Journal for Security Research.

68   Querbach and others (n 57).

69   Simon Egbert, 'Predictive Policing in Deutschland: Grundlagen, Risiken, (mögliche) Zukunft' in Strafverteidigervereinigungen (ed.), *Räume der Unfreiheit: Texte und Ergebnisse des 42. Strafverteidigertages Münster* (Organisationsbüro der Strafverteidigervereinigungen 2018).

burglary and automobile-related offences (car theft and theft from cars). In its pilot phase, SKALA was tested in six cities in North Rhine-Westphalia, with the probable risk of the offences predicted for each district.[70] After being scientifically evaluated, SKALA was rolled out in 16 police departments within North Rhine-Westphalia.[71]

The State of Hessen developed a system in house, called KLB-operativ, which brings together crime-related data from police sources and socio-economic census-data.[72] Information about burglaries was initially provided via a web app, but was subsequently also made available via mobile phones. Information about burglaries over the previous ten days is displayed on an interactive map. The data are updated daily to enable police forces to deploy officers in a more targeted manner. KLB-operativ was piloted in the winter of 2015, when burglaries rates were particularly high.[73]

Police in the city-state of Berlin developed a system called KrimPro, which predicts crimes in 400×400m areas based on police data and freely accessible infrastructure and demographic data.[74] Working together with Microsoft, KrimPro was piloted in two districts in 2016, before being rolled out throughout the city of Berlin.[75]

---

[70] Landeskriminalamt NRW, 'Abschlussbericht Projekt SKALA – Kurzfassung' (Düsseldorf 2018a) <https://lka.polizei.nrw/sites/default/files/2018-06/180208_Abschlussbericht_SKALA.pdf> accessed 26 February 2023; Landeskriminalamt NRW, 'Kooperative Evaluation des Projektes SKALA. Abschlussbericht der Zentralstelle Evaluation beim LKA NRW (ZEVA) und der Gesellschaft für innovative Sozialforschung und Sozialplanung e.V. Bremen (GISS)' (Düsseldorf 2018b) <https://lka.polizei.nrw/sites/default/files/2018-06/160131_Evaluationsbericht_SKALA_Kurzfassung.pdf> accessed 26 February 2023.

[71] ibid; Seidensticker and others (n 56) 5; Querbach and others (n 57).

[72] D Anbau, 'KLB-operativ – ein neues Instrument zur Bekämpfung des Wohnungseinbruchdiebstahls' in Bund Deutscher Kriminalbeamter (eds), *Hessen-Extra, Sonderausgabe zum Landesdelegiertentag* (2016); Egbert (n 69).

[73] Querbach and others (n 57).

[74] Alexander Dinger, 'Vorhersage-Software: So genau ist das Programm der Polizei' *Berliner Morgenpost* (Berlin 2019) <https://www.morgenpost.de/berlin/article216410297/Vorhersage-Software-So-genau-ist-das-Programm-der-Polizei.html> accessed 20 July 2022; Egbert (n 69); Michael Graupner, 'Kommissar Glaskugel: Polizei-Software sagt jetzt Einbrüche voraus' *BZ* (19 October 2017) <https://www.bz-berlin.de/archiv-artikel/polizei-software-sagt-jetzt-einbrueche-voraus> accessed 7 August 2022.

[75] Seidensticker and others (n 56) 3.

5.1   Palantir

Hessen, North Rhine-Westphalia and Bavaria are currently using software from Palantir, a US-based big data analytics company. Other federal states (including Baden-Württemberg and Bremen) are also considering following suit. The software from Palantir should make police work easier, but its use is considered controversial.[76]

Since 2014, police in the federal state of Lower Saxony in Germany have tested, developed and deployed a predictive policing model.

5.2   Predictive Policing in Lower Saxony

The Landeskriminalamt (LKA) in Lower Saxony – a partner on *Cutting Crime Impact* – was one of the first in Germany to experiment with predictive policing.

In-house approach
Predictive software was initially jointly developed by the LKA in Lower Saxony with the IBM corporation and Karlsruhe Institute for Technology (KIT).[77] However, the LKA decided to complete development of the technology in house due to a number of issues, including:

- concerns about sharing with an external commercial partner confidential crime incident data and potentially sensitive crime predictions produced by the system, and
- a concern that, if developed by an external third party, the resulting system would essentially be a 'black box' to the LKA, in

---

[76]   JA Allen, 'Controversial software from Palantir also on the rise in Germany. the police arc in the lead "Gotham" a' (*then24*, 5 June 2022) <https://then24.com/2022/06/05/controversial-software-from-palantir-also-on-the-rise-in-germany-the-police-are-in-the-lead-gotham-a/> accessed 3 August 2022; Jannis Brühl, 'German Police Deploy Controversial Silicon Valley Surveillance Tool' (*WORLDCRUNCH*, 20 November 2018) <https://worldcrunch.com/tech-science/german-police-deploy-controversial-silicon-valley-surveillance-tool> accessed 3 August 2022.
[77]   Alexander Gluba, 'Predictive Policing – eine Bestandsaufnahme' (2014) 6 Kriminalistik; Alexander Gluba, Stefan Heitmann and Nina Hermes, 'Reviktimisierungen bei Wohnungseinbrüchen – Eine empirische Untersuchung zur Bedeutung des Phänomens der (Near) Repeat Victimisation im Landkreis Harburg' (2015) 6 Kriminalistik; Alexander Gluba, 'Mehr offene Fragen als Antworten – Was vor einer Bewertung des Nutzens von Predictive Policing noch zu klären ist' (2016) 2 Die Polizei; Gluba and Pett (n 57) 436.

that they would not fully understand how the system generated predictions.[78]

Understanding and controlling the selection of data and information used to create crime predictions was prioritised by the LKA in Lower Saxony. By developing the system in house, the LKA has a comprehensive understanding of both the data being inputted into the system to generate predictions, and how results generated by the system are interpreted. Consequently, rather than purchasing an off-the-shelf predictive policing product, the LKA developed its own software system – PreMAP (Predictive Mobile Analytics for Police).

Mapping the risk of burglary
The LKA's PreMAP system uses geospatial data to identify locations that have a high probability of burglary. In addition, the system generates a map – sometimes called a 'crime radar' map – showing all relevant, police-recorded criminal offences from the previous four weeks.[79]

Using the near-repeat approach, PreMAP calculates a score that represents the probability of another burglary occurring within the next 72 hours in a radius of 400m of a previously recorded burglary incident. If the score exceeds a pre-set threshold, the system draws a 'risk area' (i.e., a red-lined area) on an interactive map. Specially trained officers have the ability to refine the prediction based on local intelligence by manually deactivating – or indeed activating – a risk area. The additional 'crime radar' map provides an overview of the last four weeks of police-recorded crime. Together with PreMAP's predictions, this is used to assess current crime trends.[80]

To feed the PreMAP system, the police in Lower Saxony collect detailed data about burglaries. All relevant prediction parameters are recorded by the police officers using the LKA's case management system, NIVADIS. This includes: incident location; type of property targeted; date and time of offence; offender *modus operandi*; and details of any stolen items. If no information is available regarding the specific time, the burglary is omitted from the prediction modelling. As is standard practice in Germany, when making the analysis, no personal data on the victim or perpetrator are

---

[78] Cutting Crime Impact Practice sheet, 'Predictive Policing Tool: Can Algorithmic Prediction of Crime Really Facilitate the Work of the Police?' (CCI University of Salford, 2021) <https://www.cuttingcrimeimpact.eu/resources/prac tice-sheets/the-lka-predictive-policing-tool/?lang=en> accessed 8 April 2022.
[79] ibid.
[80] Querbach and others (n 57).

used.[81] The fact that the system was being used to forecast locations at risk of crime – not individual risk of offending – reduced some of the ethical issues associated with predictive policing. The idea is that PreMAP results inform the choice of areas patrolled by the police, with officers prioritising areas designated by the system as being at risk of burglary.[82] It is proposed that increased police presence in the area will both deter offenders and increase the likelihood of their apprehension.

PreMAP testing and implementation

PreMAP was tested initially in 2016 in six police departments in Lower Saxony: Salzgitter, Peine, Wolfenbüttel and the city of Wolfsburg, and subsequently Hanover and Osnabrück.[83] The pilot phase identified areas for improvement in communicating risk areas to police officers and ensuring deployment of officers. Nevertheless, it was generally felt that PreMAP would be accepted by police officers due to its simple design:

> The communication and implementation of PreMAP within the departments was satisfactory. The simple design of the program and its predicting approach ensured a high level of communicability and thus a high level of acceptance of the tool among police officers.[84]

Feedback from the piloting of PreMAP suggested that it generated additional benefits, including improving the supply of police-relevant data.

From an ethical perspective, the implementation of predictive policing using German in-house systems like PreMAP avoids several thorny issues relating to data protection and human rights. Knobloch sums this up as follows: 'Experience shows that ... predictive policing, as currently practised in Germany, does not constitute an encroachment on civil rights.'[85] This is because the various systems in use in Germany, such as PreMAP, mainly process location-based information, not personal data.[86]

---

[81]   Seidensticker and others (n 56).

[82]   Querbach and others (n 57).

[83]   Landeskriminalamt, 'PreMAP – Predictive Policing (Vorausschauende Polizeiarbeit) in Niedersachsen' (lka.polizei-nds.de, ND) <https://www.lka.polizei-nds.de/startseite/kriminalitaet/forschung/premap/predictive-policing-in-niedersachsen-das-projekt-premap-114083.html> accessed 8 April 2022.

[84]   Querbach and others (n 57) 15.

[85]   Knobloch (n 65) 5 (translated from German).

[86]   Vanessa K Bauer, 'Predictive Policing in Germany: Opportunities and Challenges of Data-Analytical Forecasting Technology in order to Prevent Crime' (2019) Management Center Innsbruck <https://www.researchgate.net/publication/338411808_Predictive_Policing_in_Germany_Opportunities_and_chal

Within the CCI project, the LKA in Lower Saxony originally aimed to improve the technical use and effectiveness of PreMAP and predictive policing. In the event, the human-centred design approach adopted by CCI revealed different priorities.

6.   CASE EXAMPLE: DEVELOPMENT OF THE CCI PREDICTIVE POLICING TOOL

6.1   Human-Centred Design within the CCI project

Led by the *Design Against Crime Solution Centre*, the CCI project adopted a human-centred design approach to the research and delivery of tools for partner law enforcement agencies (LEAs).[87] To this end, CCI focused on researching the human participants within the various design systems – in this case, LEAs and their stakeholder organisations.[88] For the CCI partners, this design research resulted in assumptions being challenged, initial problems being reframed and the tools eventually developed addressing fundamental issues that, in a number of cases, were previously hidden.

The CCI project delivery was characterised by three principles:

1) the inclusion of end-users (e.g., frontline practitioners) and a focus on the humans that would use the design solutions to be developed,
2) the collaboration and exchange of knowledge and experience between stakeholders and across different professional disciplines to enable problem framing and solution ideation (e.g., in *DesignLab* workshops), and
3) the early development of solution prototypes, and prototype testing with end-users to support solution validation, feasibility testing and design decision-making.[89]

The development and testing of design solutions is an iterative process – one in which solutions can be amended and improved in response to feedback from those who will ultimately use and benefit from them. For CCI,

---

lenges_of_data-analytical_forecasting_technology_in_order_to_prevent_crime> accessed 21 July 2022; Querbach and others (n 57).

[87]   Cutting Crime Impact Practice Sheet (n 78).

[88]   CCI, 'Toolkits' (cuttingcrimeimpact.eu, 2021) <https://www.cuttingcrim eimpact.eu/cci-toolkits/> accessed 4 August 2022.

[89]   CCI (n 8).

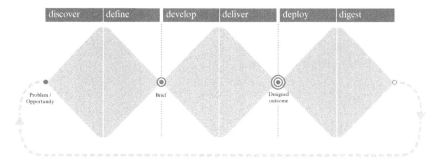

Figure 9.1   Triple Diamond model of the design process[90]

end-users were LEA practitioners and their delivery partners, while the design solutions were the tools developed during the project.[91]

In researching the predictive policing problem domain, LKA researchers worked closely with the different police officers that used PreMAP. This allowed them to gain insight into the problems end-users faced, the context in which they operated and the requirements the CCI tool needed to fulfil. In line with CCI's human-centred design approach, research, development and delivery of the tool followed the Triple Diamond model of design development.

6.2   The Triple Diamond Design Process Model

The Triple Diamond model, developed by Wootton and Davey in 2011, represents the design process as sequential phases of divergent and convergent thinking named *Discover*, *Define*, *Develop*, *Deliver*, *Deploy* and *Digest*, respectively (see Figure 9.1).[92]

During the *Discover* phase, divergent design research methods are used to support discovery and reframing of problems and deep understanding of the problem context.[93] This is followed by the *Define* phase, in which analysis methods and convergent thinking are used to generate insight and define the Design Brief. This leads to the *Develop* phase, in which ideation, concept generation and divergent thinking methods are employed to

---

[90]   Design Council, 'Designing Out Crime: A Designer's Guide' (Design Council: London 2011) <https://www.designcouncil.org.uk/sites/default/files/asset/document/designersGuide_digital_0_0.pdf> accessed 21 July 2022.

[91]   CCI (n 8).

[92]   Design Council (n 90).

[93]   ibid.

develop, prototype, test and resolve design options that meet the brief.[94] In the *Deliver* phase, the validated design option is refined, finalised and produced (i.e., made real) and preparations made for launch of the designed outcome. In the *Deploy* phase, the finished, delivered design is launched and deployed into its use context. This then kicks off the *Digest* phase, in which the designed outcome begins its life of being used, operated and maintained. Over time, potential problems and opportunities may be revealed, which themselves might feed into and be the catalyst for the Discover phase of a new design development process.[95]

6.3   Requirements Capture Research in the Discover Phase

The problem that the LKA in Lower Saxony ended up addressing emerged at the outset of the CCI research, in the *Discover* phase. In order to understand how the PreMAP system was being used in an operational policing context, LKA researchers identified a number of key end-user groups, including police officers, shift managers and data analysts. Observational research provided insights into the everyday activities of end-users, without interrupting or influencing their flow.[96] These insights also informed the ensuing interviews, allowing researchers to refine and target the questions they posed to stakeholders. During six months of requirements capture, the LKA undertook ethnographic (shadowing and observation), interview and focus group research.

Observational research conducted by the LKA revealed significant issues regarding the implementation of PreMAP.[97] The headline finding was that PreMAP was not in fact being used by frontline police officers at all. Predictive results were not being used by police officers to guide their patrol activities, and computer tablets provided for this purpose were not even being charged. Flat screen displays installed in police stations to present data resulting from PreMAP analysis were not being used for their intended purpose.[98] In short, investment in predictive policing

---

[94]   ibid.
[95]   ibid.
[96]   CCI, 'PIM Toolkit 1: LKA Tool' (cuttingcrimeimpact.eu, 2021) <https://www.cuttingcrimeimpact.eu/resources/public-results/predictive-policing-/pim-toolkit-1-lka-tool-/> accessed 7 August 2022.
[97]   Cutting Crime Impact Practice Sheet, 'Predictive Policing Tool: Can algorithmic prediction of crime really facilitate the work of police?' (www.cuttingcrimeimpact.eu, ND) <https://www.cuttingcrimeimpact.eu/resources/practice-sheets/the-lka-predictive-policing-tool/?lang=en> accessed 21 July 2022.
[98]   ibid.

systems and equipment was having little if any influence on frontline policing. Interviews and focus groups revealed police officers to be generally sceptical of the value of the data provided by PreMAP. In addition, reported technical issues regarding the speed and usability of the system were significant barriers to adoption by already busy police officers. For example, logging in to the tablet devices was perceived as overly slow and complicated.[99]

6.4   Problem Exploration and Reframing in the Define Phase

The problems identified in the Discover phase were presented by the LKA and creatively explored by the whole consortium during the *DesignLab* session held at the beginning of the *Define* phase of CCI tool development.[100] The DesignLab is a facilitated, collaborative ideation event, during which requirements capture findings are presented, research insights discussed, problems reframed and initial solution concepts developed.

Multiple stakeholders participated in the DesignLab, representing a diverse array of disciplinary backgrounds and professional experiences, and enabling creative thinking. Divided into four teams, the DesignLab concluded with each team presenting short 'pitches' for their two favourite concept solutions. Thus, the DesignLab generated eight more developed tool concepts, along with all the other ideas developed by the team on their journey to these 'favourites'. Finally, all the DesignLab participants were asked to vote on the different tool concepts presented.[101]

Following the DesignLab, the Design Against Crime Solution Centre analysed the resulting concepts and ideas produced by the participating teams. While not fully resolved tools, this material provided a pool of evidence-based, creative thinking demonstrating innovative interpretations of requirements directly linked to specific issues identified by the research. From this material, a number of potential '*solution directions*' for tool development were identified. These were discussed with the LKA and the design concept that led to the final tool was selected.[102]

---

[99]   ibid.

[100]   CCI, 'Report on Results of DesignLab 1' (cuttingcrimeimpact.eu, 2021) <https://www.cuttingcrimeimpact.eu/resources/public-results/predictive-policing-/report-on-results-of-designlab-1-/> accessed 7 August 2022.

[101]   ibid.

[102]   CCI, 'PATROL' (cuttingcrimeimpact.eu, 2021) <https://www.cuttingcrimeimpact.eu/toolkits/patrol/lka/> accessed 8 April 2022.

6.5   Solution Design and Prototyping in the Develop Phase

The design concept was developed, prototyped, tested and refined during the third (*Develop*) phase and finalised and produced during the fourth (*Deliver*) phase of CCI. Research with end-users during the *Develop* phase revealed that PreMAP data comprised only one of a number of types of information that should be provided more systematically in daily patrol briefings.

Consequently, a tool was designed to provide a standardised process for the internal communication, dissemination and use of both predictive data and general police data. The design aimed to also support the sharing of expertise by individual officers on a shift. Such a tool would ensure shift managers provided officers with essential information about risk areas and current crime trends, as well as important information from earlier shifts – which research showed was not always communicated between shift managers. In discussion with end-users, the LKA sought to optimise how information was shared with police officers, as this was found to vary widely, and often depended on the individual preferences of shift managers and analysts.[103]

6.6   The PATROL Tool

The final LKA tool was named PATROL, deriving its name from the German acronym *Polizeiliches Analysetool zur Recherche und Organisation von Lageinformationen im Einsatz- und Streifendienst.*

The PATROL tool provides a new process specifically designed to meet the needs of police officers and enable an intelligence-enhanced approach to patrolling. Using PATROL, valuable data, information and experience is communicated to police officers of the operations and patrol service quickly, and when needed.[104]

The tool comprises four main components:

1) The Analyst Manual: a guide for analysts processing current crime and situation-related information. This supports the creation of daily situation reports that contain all the information relevant to colleagues in the operation and patrol service.
2) A standardised briefing process: a new process of daily briefings for shift managers to more effectively communicate information on

---

[103]   ibid.
[104]   ibid.

current events and relevant developments in the area to the different shifts of police officers undertaking patrol duties.

3) The Briefing Manual: a guide for shift managers on the preparation and delivery of PATROL briefings to different shifts, including briefing templates for the various types of incidents and issues that are communicated.

4) Online information-sharing: PATROL enables exchange of information between patrolling officers through the Niedersachsen Messenger or NiMes-Channel – an existing secure online communication platform available to all police officers via their smartphones.[105]

The PATROL tool is being rolled out across Lower Saxony, and has been disseminated to police forces in Germany and across Europe. Options for evaluation of the impact of the PATROL tool – as well as all other tools developed by the CCI project – are currently being explored.

7.   DISCUSSION AND CONCLUSION

7.1   The Practical Politics of Predictive Policing

The LKA in Lower Saxony is far from alone in wanting to operationalise the analysis of crime incident data to forecast and prevent future offences.[106] From a human-centred design perspective, the problem is that technology-driven solutions, especially at the concept stage, are often promoted using what we term *could dos*. Potential use options are described in the form, 'With this technology, you could do X. You could do Y. You could do Z.' The problem arises in translating a technological *could do* into practical reality and developing a means of influencing the decisions of officers about where they choose to patrol between dealing with specific incidents.

Ambitious *could dos* easily transform into *hype*, especially when concerning new or as-yet-unimplemented technology. The hype surrounding predictive analytics has unsurprisingly attracted political interest and influenced decision-making around policing strategy. Nevertheless, the promise of applying predictive analytics to accurately forecast crime

---

[105]   ibid.

[106]   Simon Egbert and Matthias Leese, *Criminal Futures – Predictive Policing and Everyday Police Work*, 1st edn (Routledge 2021); Seidensticker and others (n 56).

remains tantalisingly out of reach.[107] Despite this, the technological *could do* of predictive policing remains a siren call to policymakers and technologists alike, with frontline police officers seldom involved in any meaningful way.

7.2 The Value of a Human-centred Approach

The human-centred design approach adopted by CCI revealed practical problems on the frontline of predictive policing.[108] In many ways, these reflected a lack of understanding of policing by technologists and software system developers. The inability to sell the practical benefits of predictive policing to frontline officers results in such systems being distrusted and at best ignored. It is problematic for busy frontline officers to be expected to plan their movements around areas they know well using data that have questionable accuracy.

Police officers have significant autonomy in how they discharge their duties and deliver their role. Predictive policing can be seen as an attempt to place an analytics system in charge of policing delivery in an area, with implementation reduced to a problem of *acceptance* by police officers. Technologists seem insensitive to the degree to which this undermines the self-perception and roles of individuals to whom their job is often a vocation. Rather than seeking to support and amplify the work of such intrinsically motivated individuals, predictive policing often appears to be aimed at controlling or even replacing it.

Human-centred design recognises that the promise of technology can only be realised through understanding, supporting and *delighting* the humans in a design system. As Steve Jobs famously remarked of Apple's ethos in this regard, 'It is technology married with the humanities that yields us the results that make our hearts sing.'[109] Successful solutions are not solely technology driven, but need to be tempered with an appreciation and understanding of the human context.

The main issues impacting practical implementation of predictive policing by the LKA in Lower Saxony were not technical. Problems were not related to analysis software or algorithms, but rather to the poor integration of the technological system (and its results) with the practical job of police patrolling, and the needs and preferences of those in this role.

---

[107] Jagadish (n 38).
[108] Querbach and others (n 57).
[109] Steve Jobs, iPad 2 launch, 2 March 2011.

Adopting a human-centred design approach allowed the LKA to reframe the problem from:

'How can we improve the predictive policing system and get police patrol officers to accept and follow its predictions?'

to:

'How might we better support the information needs of the police officers responsible for patrolling?'

This refocusing led to the insight that the systematic inclusion of many different types of relevant information was lacking from police officers' daily briefings. Information, intelligence and insights from fellow officers were not being shared across different teams and between shifts. This included – but importantly was not limited to – predictions generated by PreMAP, which was now viewed as one component of a more integrated, intelligence-informed model of police patrolling.

In developing their tool, the LKA shifted from a technology-centred focus on the PreMAP predictive policing system, to a human-centred focus on police patrolling and improving the quality, clarity and flow of information to the police officers responsible for this. End-user research during the *fuzzy front end* of the CCI tool development process enabled this problem reframing. Indeed, the results of this research with end-users would have been difficult to ignore.

At the outset of the CCI project, LKA researchers held a number of assumptions about the nature of the tool they would develop. Observational research was fundamental to confronting the LKA with the stark reality of end-users' operational context, challenging their assumptions and necessitating a reframing of the original problem. Researchers' observations supported development of more pertinent and fruitful questions for qualitative research with end-users. By understanding and clearly articulating end-user requirements and constraints, the CCI project was able to support the LKA through a human-centred design development process that resulted in a practical solution suited to the problem context.

As mentioned in section 2.1 above, design explores possible futures while producing tangible results. Importantly, such design futures are not limited to consideration of a technical capability – i.e., technology centred – but consider implications for the wider human experience of different stakeholders. This human-centred approach thereby allows consideration of the impact of proposed *solutions* on individual and social systems – and allows the optimisation of solutions for real-world contexts. Too often, proposals resulting from technology-driven design reflect only technical requirements, with fundamental non-technical aspects (relating, for example, to human, social and political outcomes) minimised as of secondary importance. These are often only considered during implementation, after the design process is complete, in terms of narrowly conceptualised issues such as end-user *acceptance*. Unfortunately, it is often these more complex, poorly understood phenomena that are revealed as a *fatal flaw*, hindering successful implementation of such solutions and resulting in performance shortfall – especially in relation to early inflated expectations. However, it would seem that there is always another technology bus coming along to attract the attention of managers and decision-makers.

7.3 Innovation is about Good Design, not just New Technology

Public- and private-sector organisations alike are urged to embrace innovation in order to save time, reduce costs, solve problems or achieve competitive advantage over other (less innovative) organisations. According to the Collins English dictionary, innovation is 'the introduction of new ideas, methods, or things. An innovation is a new thing or a new method of doing something'.[110]

Too often, however, innovation is simply equated with technology – generally information technologies – in what David Rotman refers to as 'techno-optimism'.[111] This perspective on technology 'raged in the late 1990s and early 2000s and then dried up and turned to pessimism during the last decade – [but] is once again bubbling up.'[112]

Despite some pessimism about, for example, the real-world impact of social media, the unbounded hope – a kind of faith – that new technologies will solve all our problems remains strong. Until recently, this was certainly the case with big data and its application to predictive policing.

Of course, innovation should not solely be equated with technological development, but also understood as taking a variety of forms: new products, services, processes, systems of working or communication methods. Technology can be an enabler of any of these, but is not required for something to be considered innovative. In the case of the PATROL tool, the innovation was not technological, but rather involved:

---

[110] Collins English Dictionary <https://www.collinsdictionary.com/dictionary/english/innovation> accessed 7 August 2022.

[111] David Rotman, 'An Uber-Optimistic View of the Future' (*MIT Technology Review*, 27 October 2021) <https://www.technologyreview.com/2021/10/27/1037169/book-review-azeem-azhar/> accessed 8 April 2022.

[112] ibid 1.

- A *new service* within the police provided to brief and inform police officers of priority issues and ongoing tasking during their shift.
- *New processes* for (i) managing the flow and organisation of information from PreMAP analysts, and (ii) managing the briefing of police officers.
- *New* use of the NiMes *system* for, (i) the provision of briefing information (including from crime analysts) to police officers during their shifts, and (ii) the updating and exchange of information between police officers themselves.

The development and application of PATROL by the LKA in Lower Saxony was therefore a significant innovation with many practical benefits for officers and the communities they serve. In addition, the PATROL tool and principles underpinning it have the potential to be exploited by LEAs in other federal states in Germany, and potentially across other European countries.

Finally, if and when predictive policing technology improves in the accuracy and usefulness of its predictive outputs, the human-centred design underpinnings of PATROL ensures that there is an effective process in place to more effectively operationalise these while meeting end-user needs.

ACKNOWLEDGEMENTS

The CCI project received funding from the European Union's Horizon 2020 Research and Innovation programme under grant agreement no. 787100. However, this chapter reflects the views only of the authors, and the European Commission cannot be held responsible for any use which may be made of the information contained therein.

NOTE

BIBLIOGRAPHY

Adams G, 'LAPD's Sci-Fi Solution to Real Crime' *Independent* (London, 11 January 2012) 32.

Allen JA, 'Controversial Software from Palantir also on the Rise in Germany: The Police Are in the Lead "Gotham"' A' (*then24*, 5 June 2022) <https://then24.com/2022/06/05/controversial-software-from-palantir-also-on-the-rise-in-germany-the-police-are-in-the-lead-gotham-a/> accessed 3 August 2022.

Anbau D, 'KLB-operativ – ein neues Instrument zur Bekämpfung des Wohnungseinbruchdiebstahls' in Bund Deutscher Kriminalbeamter (eds), *Hessen-Extra, Sonderausgabe zum Landesdelegiertentag* (2016).

Barret L, 'Reasonably Suspicious Algorithms: Predictive Policing at the United States Border' (2018) 41, 3 N.Y.U. Review of Law & Social Change <https://socialchangenyu.com/review/reasonably-suspicious-algorithms-predictive-policing-at-the-united-states-border/> accessed 7 July 2022.

Bauer VK, 'Predictive Policing in Germany: Opportunities and Challenges of Data-Analytical Forecasting Technology in order to Prevent Crime' (2019) Management Center Innsbruck <https://www.researchgate.net/publication/338411808_Predictive_Policing_in_Germany_Opportunities_and_challenges_of_data-analytical_forecasting_technology_in_order_to_prevent_crime> accessed 21 July 2022.

Bayerisches Staatsministerium des Inneren, für Bau und Verkehr, 'Kooperationsvereinbarung Bayern – Baden-Württemberg zur Bekämpfung Wohnungseinbruchskriminalität' (2015) <https://www.stmi.bayern.de/med/pressemitteilungen/pressear-chiv/2015/248b/index.php> accessed 7 August 2022.

Bhuiyan J, 'LAPD Ended Predictive Policing Programs amid Public Outcry: A New Effort Shares Many of Their Flaws' *The Guardian* (8 November 2021) <https://www.theguardian.com/us-news/2021/nov/07/lapd-predictive-policing-surveillance-reform> accessed 2 August 2022.

Broeders D and others, 'Big Data and Security Policies: Towards a Framework for Regulating the Phases of Analytics and Use of Big Data' (2017) 33 Computer Law and Security Law Review.

Brühl J, 'German Police Deploy Controversial Silicon Valley Surveillance Tool' (*WORLDCRUNCH*, 20 November 2018) <https://worldcrunch.com/tech-science/german-police-deploy-controversial-silicon-valley-surveillance-tool> accessed 3 August 2022.

Buchanan R, 'Declaration by Design: Rhetoric, Argument, and Demonstration in Design Practice' in V Margolin (eds), *Design Discourse: History, Theory, Criticism* (The University of Chicago Press 1989).

Bundesministerium des Innern, 'Polizeiliche Kriminalstatistik 2015' (May 2016) <https://www.bmi.bund.de/SharedDocs/downloads/DE/publikationen/themen/sicherheit/pks-2015.html> accessed 20 July 2022.

CCI, 'Introduction to CCI' (cuttingcrimeimpact.eu, 2021) <https://www.cuttingcrimeimpact.eu/about/introduction-to-cci/> accessed 7 July 2022.

CCI, 'PATROL' (cuttingcrimeimpact.eu, 2021) <https://www.cuttingcrimeimpact.eu/toolkits/patrol/lka/> accessed 8 April 2022.

CCI, 'PIM Toolkit 1: LKA Tool' (cuttingcrimeimpact.eu, 2021) <https://www.cuttingcrimeimpact.eu/resources/public-results/predictive-policing-/pim-toolkit-1-lka-tool-/> accessed 7 August 2022.

CCI, 'Project Design' (cuttingcrimeimpact.eu, 2021) <https://www.cuttingcrimeim pact.eu/about/project-design/> accessed 4 August 2022.

CCI, 'Report on Results of DesignLab 1' (cuttingcrimeimpact.eu, 2021) <https:// www.cuttingcrimeimpact.eu/resources/public-results/predictive-policing-/ report-on-results-of-designlab-1-/> accessed 7 August 2022.

CCI, 'Toolkits' (cuttingcrimeimpact.eu, 2021) <https://www.cuttingcrimeimpact. eu/cci-toolkits/> accessed 4 August 2022.

Collins English Dictionary <https://www.collinsdictionary.com/dictionary/ english/innovation> accessed 7 August 2022.

Collins A, Joseph D and Bielaczyc K, 'Design Research: Theoretical and Methodological Issues' (2004) 13(1) The Journal of the Learning Sciences.

Costanzo P, D'Onofrio F. and Friedl J, 'Big Data and the Italian Legal Framework: Opportunities for Police Forces' in B Akhgar and others (eds), *Application of Big Data for National Security* (Oxford 2015).

Custers B and Vergouw B, 'Promising Policing Technologies: Experiences, Obstacles and Police Needs Regarding Law Enforcement Technologies' (2015) 31(4) Computer Law & Security Review.

Cutting Crime Impact Practice Sheet, 'Predictive Policing Tool: Can Algorithmic Prediction of Crime Really Facilitate the Work of Police?' (www.cuttingcrimeim pact.eu, 2021) <https://www.cuttingcrimeimpact.eu/resources/practice-sheets/ the-lka-predictive-policing-tool/?lang=en> accessed 21 July 2022.

Davey CL and Wootton AB, *Design against Crime: A Human-Centred Approach to Designing for Safety and Security* (Routledge 2017).

Davey CL and Wootton AB, 'Transformation Design – Creating Security & Wellbeing' in W Jonas, K Von Anshelm and S Zerwas (eds), *Transformation Design* (BIRD 2016).

Dedehayir O and Steinert M, 'The Hype Cycle Model: A Review and Future Directions' (2016) 108 Technological Forecasting and Social Change.

Degeling M. and Berendt B, 'What is Wrong about Robocops as Consultants? A Technology-Centric Critique of Predictive Policing' (2018) 33 AI & Society.

Design Council, 'Designing Out Crime: A Designer's Guide' (Design Council: London 2011) <https://www.designcouncil.org.uk/sites/default/files/asset/docu ment/designersGuide_digital_0_0.pdf> accessed 21 July 2022.

Dinger A, 'Vorhersage-Software: So genau ist das Programm der Polizei' Berliner Morgenpost (Berlin, 2019) <https://www.morgenpost.de/berlin/article2164102 97/Vorhersage-Software-So-genau-ist-das-Programm-der-Polizei.html> accessed 20 July 2022.

Egbert S and Leese M, *Criminal Futures: Predictive Policing and Everyday Police Work*, 1st edn (Routledge 2021).

Egbert S, 'Predictive Policing in Deutschland. Grundlagen, Risiken, (mögliche) Zukunft' in Strafverteidigervereinigungen (ed.), Räume der Unfreiheit. Texte und Ergebnisse des 42. Strafverteidigertages Münster (Organisationsbüro der Strafverteidigervereinigungen 2018).

Egge J, 'Experimenting with Future-Oriented Analysis at Crime Hot Spots in Minneapolis' (2011) 2(4) Geography & Public Safety <https://www.ojp.gov/ ncjrs/virtual-library/abstracts/experimenting-future-oriented-analysis-crime-hot- spots-minneapolis> accessed 7 April 2022.

Federal Ministry of the Interior and Community, 'The Federal Police' (bmi.bund. de, ND) <https://www.bmi.bund.de/EN/topics/security/federal-police/federal- police-node.html> accessed 5 April 2022.

Ferguson AG, *The Rise of Big Data Policing* (New York University Press 2017).

García S, Ramírez-Gallego S, Luengo J, Benítez JM and Herrera F, 'Big Data Preprocessing: Methods and Prospects' (2016) 1(9) Big Data Analytics.

Gerstner G, 'Predictive Policing in the Context of Residential Burglary: An Empirical Illustration on the basis of a Pilot Project in Baden-Württemberg, Germany' (2018) 3(2) European Journal for Security Research 2.

Gilbertson A, 'Data-Informed Predictive Policing Was Heralded As Less Biased. Is It?' *The Markup* (NY, 20 August 2020) <https://themarkup.org/the-break down/2020/08/20/does-predictive-police-technology-contribute-to-bias> accessed 2 August 2022.

Gluba A, 'Predictive Policing – eine Bestandsaufnahme' (2014) 6 Kriminalistik.

Gluba A, Heitmann S and Hermes N, 'Reviktimisierungen bei Wohnungseinbrüchen – Eine empirische Untersuchung zur Bedeutung des Phänomens der (Near) Repeat Victimisation im Landkreis Harburg' (2015) 6 Kriminalistik.

Gluba A, 'Mehr offene Fragen als Antworten – Was vor einer Bewertung des Nutzens von Predictive Policing noch zu klären ist' (2016) 2 Die Polizei.

Gluba A and Pett A, 'Predictive Policing – ein (un)bekannter Ansatz – Definition, Ursprung und Rahmenbedingungen' in MHW Möllers and RC van Ooyen (eds), *Jahrbuch Öffentliche Sicherheit 2016/2017* (Nomos 2017).

Graupner M, 'Kommissar Glaskugel. Polizei-Software sagt jetzt Einbrüche voraus' *BZ* (Berlin, 19 October 2017) <https://www.bz-berlin.de/archiv-artikel/ polizei-software-sagt-jetzt-einbrueche-voraus> accessed 7 August 2022.

Gstrein OJ, Bunnik A and Zwitter A, 'Ethical, Legal and Social Challenges of Predictive Policing' (2019) 3 Católica Law Review.

IBM, 'Big Data Analytics' (IBM.com, ND) <https://www.ibm.com/analytics/ big-data-analytics> accessed 6 April 2022.

Jagadish HV, 'Big Data Analyses Depend on Starting with Clean Data Points' (TheConversation.com, 4 August 2015) <https://theconversation.com/big-data-analyses-depend-on-starting-with-clean-data-points-43687> accessed 7 April 2022.

Jagadish HV, 'The Promise and Perils of Predictive Policing based on Big Data' (TheConversation.com, 16 November 2016) <https://theconversation.com/the-promise-and-perils-of-predictive-policing-based-on-big-data-48366> accessed 6 April 2022.

Kentonline, 'Predpol Software which Targets Crime Down to Small Zones Has Slashed North Kent Crime by 6%' (Kent, 2013) <www.kentonline.co.uk/kent/ news/crime-innorth-kent-slashed-4672> accessed 18 July 2022.

Knobloch T, 'Vor die Lage kommen – Predictive Policing in Deutschland – Chancen und Gefahren datenanalytischer Prognosetechnik und Empfehlungen für den Einsatz in der Polizeiarbeit' (Gütersloh 2018) <https://www.bertels mann-stiftung.de/fileadmin/files/BSt/Publikationen/GrauePublikationen/predic tive.policing.pdf> accessed 26 February 2023.

Krippendorff K, Design Discourse: A Way to Redesign Design. Keynote Address to the Society for Science of Design Studies, 6 December 1998. Available from Scholarly Commons, University of Pennsylvania.

Landeskriminalamt, 'PreMAP – Predictive Policing (Vorausschauende Polizeiarbeit) in Niedersachsen' (lka.polizei-nds.de, ND) <https:// www.lka.polizei-nds.de/startseite/kriminalitaet/forschung/premap/

predictive-policing-in-niedersachsen-das-projekt-premap-114083.html>
accessed 8 April 2022.
Landeskriminalamt NRW, 'Abschlussbericht Projekt SKALA – Kurzfassung'
(Düsseldorf 2018a) <https://lka.polizei.nrw/sites/default/files/2018-06/180208_
Abschlussbericht_SKALA.pdf> accessed 26 February 2023.
Landeskriminalamt NRW, 'Kooperative Evaluation des Projektes SKALA.
Abschlussbericht der Zentralstelle Evaluation beim LKA NRW (ZEVA)
und der Gesellschaft für innovative Sozialforschung und Sozialplanung e.V.
Bremen (GISS)' (Düsseldorf 2018b) <https://lka.polizei.nrw/sites/default/
files/2018-06/160131_Evaluationsbericht_SKALA_Kurzfassung.pdf> accessed
26 February 2023.
Landesregierung Nordrhein-Westfalen, 'Aachener Erklärung zur besseren
Bekämpfung der grenzüberschreitenden Eigentumskriminalität' (31 October
2016) <https://www.land.nrw/pressemitteilung/aachener-erklaerung-zur-besse
ren-bekaempfung-der-grenzueberschreitenden> accessed 7 August 2022.
Laney D, '3D Data Management: Controlling Data Volume, Velocity and
Variety' Gartner, 2 February 2001 <https://studylib.net/doc/8647594/3d-da
ta-management--controlling-data-volume--velocity--an...> accessed 14 July
2022.
Madrigal AC, 'The Future of Crime-Fighting or the Future of Racial Profiling?
Inside the Effects of Predictive Policing' (HuffPost.com, 28 March 2016) <https://
www.huffpost.com/entry/predictive-policing-video_n_56f898c9e4b0a372181a4
2ef> accessed 5 April 2022.
Mallappallil M, Sabu J, Gruessner A and Salifu M, 'A Review of Big Data and
Medical Research' (2020) 8 SAGE open Med 1.
McAfee A and Brynjolfsson E, 'Big Data: The Management Revolution' (Harvard
Business Review, October 2012) <https://hbr.org/2012/10/big-data-the-manage
ment-revolution> accessed 6 April 2022.
Media Freedom & Information Access Clinic, 'Algorithmic Accountability:
The Need for a New Approach to Transparency and Accountability When
Government Functions Are Performed by Algorithms' (2022) Abrams Institute
for Freedom of Expression, Yale Law School <https://law.yale.edu/sites/
default/files/area/center/mfia/document/algorithmic_accountability_report.pdf>
accessed 7 July 2022.
Meijer A and Wessels M, 'Predictive Policing: Review of Benefits and Drawbacks'
(2019) 42 International Journal of Public Administration.
Nilsson P, 'First UK Police Force to Try Predictive Policing Ends Contract'
Financial Times (London, 26 November 2018).
Pasko JM, 'Time Magazine Names Santa Cruz Police Program to Predict
Crime One of the Year's Top Inventions' *The Mercury News* (Santa Cruz, 23
November 2011) <https://www.mercurynews.com/2011/11/23/time-magazine-
names-santa-cruz-police-program-to-predict-crime-one-of-the-years-top-inven
tions/> accessed 6 April 2022.
Pearsall B, 'Predictive Policing: The Future of Law Enforcement?' (2010) 266 NIJ
Journal 16 <https://www.ojp.gov/pdffiles1/nij/230414.pdf> accessed 3 August
2022.
Portland State University, Criminology and Criminal Justice Senior Capstone,
'Prevention of Residential Burglary: A Review of the Literature' (2010)
Criminology and Criminal Justice Senior Capstone Project 3 <https://pdxsch
olar.library.pdx.edu/ccj_capstone/3> accessed 14 July 2022.

PredPol, 'Predictive Policing: The Predictive Policing Company' (2015) <www. predpol.com> accessed 18 July 2022.

Querbach M, Krom M and Jongejan A, 'Review of State of the Art: Predictive Policing' (Cutting Crime Impact (CCI) Deliverable 2.3, Salford, UK, August 2020) <https://www.cuttingcrimeimpact.eu/resources/public-results/predictive-policing-/titulo/> accessed 6 April 2022.

Ratcliffe JH and Rengert GF, 'Near Repeat Patterns in Philadelphia Shootings' (2008) 21(1–2) Security Journal.

Richardson R, Schultz J and Crawford K, 'Dirty Data, Bad Predictions: How Civil Rights Violations Impact Police Data, Predictive Policing Systems, and Justice' (2019) 94 NYU Law Review Online <https://papers.ssrn.com/sol3/papers.cfm?abstract_id=3333423> accessed 20 July 2022.

Rotman D, 'An Uber-Optimistic View of the Future' (*MIT Technology Review*, 27 October 2021) <https://www.technologyreview.com/2021/10/27/1037169/book-review-azeem-azhar/> accessed 8 April 2022.

Rouse WB, *Design for Success: A Human-Centered Approach to Designing Successful Products and Systems* (Wiley 1991).

Seidensticker K, Bode F and Stoffel F, 'Predictive Policing in Germany' [2018] 2 <http://nbn-resolving.de/urn:nbn:de:bsz:352-2-14sbvox1ik0z06> accessed 7 August 2022.

Strom K, 'Research on the Impact of Technology on Policing Strategy in the 21st Century, Final Report' (Office of Justice Programs' National Criminal Justice Reference Service, May 2016) <https://www.ojp.gov/pdffiles1/nij/grants/251140.pdf> accessed 7 April 2022.

Uchida CD, 'Predictive Policing' in Gerban Bruinsma and David Weisburd (eds), *Encyclopedia of Criminology and Criminal Justice* (Springer 2014).

van Brakel R, 'Pre-Emptive Big Data Surveillance and Its (Dis)Empowering Consequences: The Case of Predictive Policing' in Bart van der Sloot and others (eds), *Exploring the Boundaries of Big Data* (Amsterdam University Press 2016).

Winston A, 'Predictive Policing Is "Wave of the Future," NY commissioner says' (revealnews.org, 31 July 2015) <https://revealnews.org/article/predictive-polic ing-is-wave-of-the-future-ny-commissioner-says/> accessed 7 April 2022.

Wollinger GR and others, 'Wohnungseinbruch – Tat und Folgen – Ergebnisse einer Betroffenenbefragung in fünf Großstädten' (KFN-Forschungsberichte 124 Hannover 2014).

Wollinger GR and Jukschat N, 'Reisende und zugereiste Täter des Wohnungseinbruchs. Ergebnisse einer qualitativen Interviewstudie mit verur-teilten Tätern' (Kriminologisches Forschungsinstitut Niedersachsen e.V. 2017) <https://kfn.de/wp-content/uploads/Forschungsberichte/FB_133.pdf> accessed 26 February 2023.

Wollinger GR and Jukschat N, 'Foreign Burglars: Primary Results of an Interview Study with Arrested Offenders in Germany' (2017) 6 International Journal of Criminology and Sociology.

Wollinger GR and others, 'Offender Organization and Criminal Investigations with regard to Organised Residential Burglary Law Enforcement: Results of an International Expert Survey' (Kriminologisches Forschungsinstitut Niedersachsen e.V. 2018) <https://kfn.de/wp-content/uploads/Forschungsber ichte/FB_147%20en.pdf> accessed 3 August 2022.

Wolpert S, 'Predictive policing test substantially reduces crime' (universityof california.edu, 7 October 2015) <https://www.universityofcalifornia.edu/news/predictive-policing-test-substantially-reduces-crime> accessed 7 April 2022.

Wootton AB, Marselle M and Davey CL, 'City Centre Crime: Design thinking for safer city centres', Proceedings from the 8th European Academy of Design Conference 2009 – 1, 2 and 3 April 2009, The Robert Gordon University, Aberdeen, Scotland.

Youstin TJ and others, 'Assessing the Generalizability of the Near Repeat Phenomenon' (2011) 38(10) Criminal Justice and Behavior.

10. On the governance of privacy-preserving systems for the web: should Privacy Sandbox be governed?

Lukasz Olejnik

1. INTRODUCTION

User tracking on the web was a developing and rising issue in the decades of the 2000s and 2010s.[1] The developing web economy ecosystems coupled with the new advertising technologies lead to the proliferation and uncontrolled spread of ubiquitous tracking on the web.[2] Such tracking had various forms, for example:

- tracking pixels or scripts 'monitored' user interactions across the browsed websites to enable the construction of user profiles,
- third-party cookies, making such tracking rather simple,[3]
- the various forms of fingerprinting (such as browser-configuration types or Canvas[4]) making the technical possibility of tracking even stronger,
- various types of 'web plugins' (e.g., the Facebook Like button) or libraries that were functionally deploying the tracking capabilities,
- the increasing issue of behavioural monitoring, including the tracking of keystrokes or mouse movements.

[1]   Jonathan R Mayer and John C Mitchell, 'Third-party Web Tracking: Policy and Technology' (2012) <https://jonathanmayer.org/publications/tracking survey12.pdf> accessed 1 July 2022.

[2]   Mayer and Mitchell (n 1); Balachander Krishnamurthy and Craig Wills, 'Privacy Diffusion on the Web: A Longitudinal Perspective' (2009) Proceedings of the 18th International Conference on World Wide Web; José Estrada-Jiménez and others, 'Online Advertising: Analysis of Privacy Threats and Protection Approaches' (2017) 100 Computer Communications 32.

[3]   Franziska Roesner, Tadayoshi Kohno and David Wetherall, 'Detecting and Defending against Third-Party Tracking on the Web' (2012) Presented as part of the 9th USENIX Symposium on Networked Systems Design and Implementation (NSDI 12).

[4]   Pierre Laperdrix and others, 'Browser Fingerprinting: A Survey' (2020) 14(2) ACM Transactions on the Web (TWEB).

This growing problem likely culminated around the years of 2014–2016.[5] While tracking-protection technologies, such as web browser plugins, were always present, the landscape is evolving since web browser vendors entered the game. Approaches of web browser vendors such as Mozilla, Apple or Microsoft vary, but it is widely accepted that Apple is the vendor that first seriously considered the risk of web privacy.[6] Since then, the web is on a trajectory to 'civilise' the associated technologies, curbing unsanctioned tracking.

Privacy is constantly at the centre of today's shifts in web technologies, such as web browsers, as evidenced with the regular changes in the privacy user interface and new technical features deployed in web browsers, both implementing Internet Engineering Task Force (IETF) and World Wide Web Consortium (W3C) standards, and going beyond. Significant changes continue to be introduced. Web browser vendors have decided to take action to address growing user concerns due to the rising privacy problem of web tracking. The previous decade witnessed the growing trend of content filtering and blocking. Anti-tracking measures built in by the major web browser vendors are changing how the web ecosystem works. There is currently an abrupt backlash from the third-party cookies mechanism, the primary vehicle of user tracking. This is evidenced with the growing popularity of privacy-focused web extensions, and the changing default treatment of third-party cookies in major web browsers such as Mozilla Firefox, Apple's Safari and Google Chrome's vow to disable third-party cookies.

Apple's Safari does not support the mechanism of third-party cookies, and deploys a specialised Intelligent Tracking Prevention.[7] Mozilla Firefox ships Enhanced Tracking Prevention, and likewise scrutinises third-party cookies and interactions.[8] Finally, Chrome announced the intention to

---

[5]   Author's own independent and humble assessment, based on many years of observations, and including due to the fact that it was around these years when some web browser vendors started to build countermeasures.

[6]   Apple was certainly the first big technology firm strictly underlining the privacy guarantees built in with technology. Such a serious take on privacy was famously stressed for the first time in the company's 2015 annual keynote speech while releasing new products; see also Natasha Lomas, 'Apple stresses user privacy at WWDC' <https://techcrunch.com/2015/06/08/apple-stresses-user-privacy-at-wwdc/> (accessed 1 July 2022). Such communications have been consistently maintained since 2015.

[7]   John Wilander, Intelligent Tracking Prevention (2017) <https://webkit.org/blog/7675/ intelligent-tracking-prevention/> accessed 1 July 2022.

[8]   Mozilla Firefox, Enhanced Tracking Protection in Firefox for desktop (2019) <https:// support.mozilla.org/en-US/kb/enhanced-tracking-protection-firefox-desktop> accessed 1 July 2022.

remove third-party cookies in 2022,[9] conditioned on '*satisfactory changes*' to the web platform, a timeline already delayed to 2023.[10] Such modifications are called *Privacy Sandbox*, and they aim to tighten the control over privacy, at the same time allowing ads to be displayed in a '*privacy-preserving manner*'. In other words, the third-party cookie,[11] today's primary tracking vehicle, is going away.

Privacy Sandbox foresees several web browser features that might be deployed by web browser vendors to (1) guarantee future user privacy protection by limiting the potential of abuses, and (2) uphold the web economy model based on web advertisements. The so-called Privacy Sandbox proposals were introduced in 2019,[12] and the co-design and co-development happen in the open within the discussion venues of the W3C standardisation body, primarily in the Improving Web Advertising Business Group (WAB), and in the later-formed Private Advertising Technology Community Group (PATCG). Some parts of designs appear to be consistent with past well-researched proposals in privacy-preserving digital advertising systems.[13] Early evidence demonstrates openness to proposals submitted during the design discussions within the W3C venue.[14] Approaching conclusions on how such interactions would look like in the future, in general, is premature. Nothing compels the technology controller (i.e., Google, owner of Chrome;

---

[9]   Justin Schuh, Building a More Private Web: A Path towards Making Third Party Cookies Obsolete (2020) <https://blog.chromium.org/2020/01/building-more-private-web-path-towards.html> accessed 1 July 2022.

[10]   Vinay Goel, An Updated Timeline for Privacy Sandbox Milestones (2021) <https://blog.google/products/chrome/updated-timeline-privacy-sandbox-mile stones/> accessed 1 July 2022.

[11]   Roesner, Kohno and Wetherall (n 3).

[12]   Justin Schuh, 'Building a More Private Web' (2019) <https://www.blog.google/products/chrome/building-a-more-private-web> accessed 1 July 2022.

[13]   Vincent Toubiana and others, 'Adnostic: Privacy Preserving Targeted Advertising' (2010) Proceedings of the 2010 Network and Distributed System Security Symposium; Saikat Guha, Bin Cheng and Paul Francis, 'Privad: Practical Privacy in Online Advertising' (2011) USENIX Conference on Networked Systems Design and Implementation; Michael Backes and others, 'Obliviad: Provably Secure and Practical Online Behavioral Advertising' (2012) IEEE Symposium on Security and Privacy <https://ieeexplore.ieee.org/document/6234417> accessed 1 July 2022; Minh-Dung Tran, Gergely Acs and Claude Castelluccia, 'Retargeting without Tracking' [2014] arXiv preprint arXiv:1404.4533; Lukasz Olejnik, 'Are We Reaching Privacy Preserving Digital Advertising? Historical View' (2020) <https://blog.lukaszolejnik.com/are-we-reaching-privacy-preserving-digital-advertising-hi storical-view/> accessed 1 July 2022.

[14]   Justin Schuh and Marshall Vale, 'Progress Update on the Privacy Sandbox Initiative (2021) <https://developer.chrome.com/blog/privacy-sandbox-update-2021-jan/> accessed 1 July 2022.

or other web browser vendors, such as Mozilla, should they be involved[15]) to guarantee the future aspects of Privacy Sandbox.[16]

1.1   Privacy, Competition, Governance

Signs of an increased convergence between *privacy* and *competition* protection are beginning to appear. However, such links between these two spheres are in line with previous predictions of the European Data Protection Supervisor (since 2014)[17] or the U.S. Federal Trade Commission (since 2017).[18]

Google's web browser Chrome has an estimated 69% of the global user-base, and many businesses depend on the web browser as a gateway technology. Recent changes made to web browsers (particularly, Google's plans) appear to have gathered significant interest from competitors,[19] regulators[20] and civil society.[21] Such privacy and competition concerns ought to illuminate the public debate.

---

[15]   Martin Thomson, 'Privacy Preserving Attribution for Advertising' (2022) <https://blog.mozilla.org/en/mozilla/privacy-preserving-attribution-for-advertising/> accessed 1 July 2022.

[16]   'Killed by Google' <https://killedbygoogle.com/> accessed 1 July 2022.

[17]   Christian D'Cunha, 'Best of Frenemies? Reflections on Privacy and Competition Four Years after the EDPS Preliminary Opinion' (2018) 8(3) International Data Privacy Law; P Hustinx, 'Privacy and Competitiveness in the Age of Big Data: Preliminary Opinion of the European Data Protection Supervisor' [2014]   <https://edps.europa.eu/data-protection/our-work/publications/opinions/privacy-and-competitiveness-age-big-data_en> accessed 1 July 2022.

[18]   Julie Brill, 'The Intersection of Consumer Protection and Competition in the New World of Privacy' (2011) 7(1) Competition Policy International.

[19]   Natasha Lomas, 'Digital Marketing Firms File UK Competition Complaint against Google's Privacy Sandbox' (2020) <https://techcrunch.com/2020/11/23/digital-marketing-firms-file-uk-competition-complaint-against-googles-privacy-sandbox/> accessed 1 July 2022.

[20]   UK Competition and Markets Authority, 'Investigation into Google's "Privacy Sandbox" Browser Changes' (2021) <https://www.gov.uk/cma-cases/investigation-into-googles-privacy-sandbox-browser-changes> accessed 1 July 2022; Australian Competition and Consumer Commission, 'Digital Advertising Services Inquiry' (2021) <https://www.accc.gov.au/focus-areas/inquiries-ongoing/digital-advertising-services-inquiry/interim-report> accessed 1 July 2022; European Commission, 'Antitrust: Commission Opens Investigation into Possible Anticompetitive Conduct by Google in the Online Advertising Technology Sector (2021) <https://ec.europa.eu/commission/presscorner/detail/en/ip_21_3143> accessed 1 July 2022.

[21]   Bennet Cyphers, 'Don't Play in Google's Privacy Sandbox' (2019) <https://www.eff.org/deeplinks/2019/08/dont-play-googles-privacy-sandbox-1> accessed 1 July 2022.

However, in this context it is worth noting that the following are unclear at the time of writing: (1) how the privacy input would or should be considered, and by whom; (2) how the existing competition controversies will be reconciled in the future; (3) if in the future the Privacy Sandbox proposals would be maintained, developed or even kept as part of the web browsers.[22]

Technically speaking, these questions touch the issue of governance, a political science term describing a collective process of effective and legitimate decision-making.[23] Governance is also a process well known in the technology landscape.

In this chapter, the focus is positioned on the related issues of governance of potential privacy-preserving digital advertising systems.

1.2 Alternatives to Privacy Sandbox?

Privacy Sandbox is presented as a realisation of a privacy-preserving online ad system. As such there is currently no substantial competition, but it is pertinent to mention the potential alternatives.

One rigid approach could be the complete removal, or the minimisation, of all the technologies with tracking potential, including third-party cookies, fingerprinting, etc. – without any other intervention. In the case of privacy, that would limit the risks and issues of concern. However, it would likely have a significant impact on some market players in online e-commerce, including publishers and advertisers that rely on cookies (e.g., to monitor user behaviour, or to facilitate the 'shopping cart' functionality with cookies – not third-party cookies when performed on the example web store site) or web advertising (e.g., to track conversions, whether the seen ad was linked with a particular user action such as purchase). Hence, anti-competition complaints are being made, and investigations are being conducted. It seems that in the market economy this may not be so simple. In fact, the matter is the subject of anti-competition proceedings,[24] specifically

---

[22] 'Killed by Google' (n 16).
[23] Vasudha Chhotray and Gerry Stoker, *Governance Theory and Practice: A Cross-Disciplinary Approach* (Palgrave Macmillan 2008).
[24] UK Competition and Markets Authority (n 20); Lomas (n 19); District Court, EDTexas, 'Anti-Competition Complaints against Google's Plan to Replace Third-Party Cookies with Privacy Sandbox'; UK Competition and Markets Authority, 'Notice of Intention to Accept Commitments Offered by Google in relation to its Privacy Sandbox Proposals', case number 50972 (2021) <https://assets.publishing.service.gov.uk/media/60c21e54d3bf7f4bcc0652cd/Notice_of_intention_to_accept_binding_commitments_offered_by_Google_publication.pdf> accessed 1 July 2022; European Commission (n 20).

with the focus on the dominant web browser, Chrome. It turns out that having a dominating market position opens a player to a potential anti-competition proceeding. And in fact, the United Kingdom's Competition and Markets Authority (CMA) and Google worked towards an agreement, where the final say over the removal of third-party cookies and the acceptance of '*alternative technologies*' will (!) actually be with the UK's CMA.[25] In June 2021 CMA had an intention to accept Google's commitments, de facto becoming a key regulator with respect to the competitive practices of this technology.[26] The commitments were formally accepted in February 2022.[27] The European Commission is following a similar path, initiating an independent investigation.[28]

Still, the final structure of the Privacy Sandbox is not finalised yet. There are many proposals aspiring to be picked up and considered seriously (e.g., some by Mozilla,[29] but also those of many other proponents). These intra-competitions may be viewed as 'alternatives' too.

2.   TECHNOLOGY GOVERNANCE

From the high-level and generic challenges such as internet governance,[30] through the deliberations about AI governance,[31] to the many practical setups in standardisation, the problem of technology governance is in general a challenge. But the topics of internet and AI are complex and compounded, and they involve many actors. Issues of technology

---

[25]   UK Competition and Markets Authority, 'Notice of Intention' (n 24); District Court, EDTexas (n 24).

[26]   UK Competition and Markets Authority, 'CMA to Have Key Oversight Role over Google's Planned Removal of Third-Party Cookies' (2021) <https:// www.gov.uk/government/news/cma-to-have-key-oversight-role-over-google-s-pla nned-removal-of-third-party-cookies> accessed 1 July 2022.

[27]   UK Competition and Markets Authority, 'CMA to Keep "Close Eye" on Google as It Secures Final Privacy Sandbox Commitments' (2022) <https://www. gov.uk/government/news/cma-to-keep-close-eye-on-google-as-it-secures-final-pri vacy-sandbox-commitments> accessed 1 July 2022.

[28]   European Commission (n 20).

[29]   Thomson (n 15).

[30]   Laura DeNardis, 'The Emerging Field of Internet Governance' [2010] Yale Information Society Project Working Paper Series; John E Savage and Bruce W McConnell, 'Exploring Multi-Stakeholder Internet Governance' (2015) <https:// www.eastwest.ngo/sites/default/files/Exploring%20Multi-Stakeholder%20Internet %20Governance_0.pdf> accessed 1 July 2022.

[31]   Allan Dafoe, 'AI Governance: A Research Agenda' (2018) Governance of AI Program, Future of Humanity Institute, University of Oxford, Oxford, UK.

governance arise also in other dimensions of modern technologies in the broader deployment phase.[32]

For example, when many actors are involved, and the stability of the product for its users is an asset, governance issues arise when multiple and various factors play a role. In general, designing a governance model may need to account for known or predictable challenges, for example reaching an agreement among diversified numbers of actors. Standardisation bodies such as W3C, with its Advisory Board (AB) and Technical Architecture Group (TAG), or the IETF, with the Internet Architecture Board (IAB), form good model examples. These bodies strive to reconcile the policy and technical design issues with their specially designated advisory bodies. The processes at work have been present for many decades now. They have withstood the test of time and proved themselves to be working models offering advantages when the goal is stable and mature technical standards. In these respects, the standardisation processes at the IETF or W3C are a de facto standard in themselves.

Governance-like structures exist in the case of other technologies as well. These include the Accelerated Mobile Pages (AMP),[33] which 'delegates the technical leadership of the AMP project to the AMP Technical Steering Committee', the JS Foundation's Technical Advisory Committee (and its technical leadership structure),[34] the OpenJS Foundation's Cross Project Council,[35] that is, 'the technical governing body of the OpenJS Foundation', or even the Facebook's Oversight Board,[36] which is tasked with advisory help concerning content moderation. Other significant standardisation bodies, such as the Institute of Electrical and Electronics Engineers Standards Association (IEEE-SA), the European Telecommunications Standards Institute (ETSI) or the International Organization for Standardization (ISO), are not considered. While these are versatile standards developments organisations, the focus of this work is on information technologies, the internet, and

---

[32]   Paul Timmers, 'There Will Be No Global 6G unless We Resolve Sovereignty Concerns in 5G Governance' (2020) 3(1) Nature Electronics.

[33]   AMP, AMP Governance Structures (2020) <https://amp.dev/community/governance/> accessed 1 July 2022.

[34]   JS Foundation, 'Technical Advisory Committee (TAC) Charter v1.0' (2016)   <https://github.com/JSFoundation/TAC/blob/master/TAC-Charter.md> accessed 1 July 2022.

[35]   The OpenJS Foundation, 'The OpenJS Foundation Cross Project Council' (2020) <https://github.com/openjs-foundation/cross-project-council/> accessed 1 July 2022.

[36]   Facebook AB, 'Facebook's Oversight Board's Charter' (2020) <https://oversightboard.com/governance/> accessed 1 July 2022.

most particularly, the specialised aspects concerning the web or the platforms functioning on the web.

The overarching theme based on such governance structures strongly suggests that for successful technology governance to happen, some prerequisites must be met. A technology must either exist or be emerging. Involvement of several stakeholders is necessary. Mechanisms of decision-making that impact technology control, development or management, must exist. To achieve these tasks transparently and predictably from the point of view of all the stakeholders, technical consortiums typically give rise to forms of advisory bodies.

The core intention of the work in this chapter is to offer a potential future vision of technology governance of the 'Privacy Sandbox' and its associated deliverables. To propose a governance framework, the sincere commitments of the involved proponents and actors in the development of Privacy Sandbox must be assumed. Therefore, it is assumed that Privacy Sandbox and the related web browser features would be eventually deployed and in use (there is limited rationale for designing a governance structure for something that is not of practical relevance). This will introduce several future challenges, for example the need to design a transparent future mechanism of steering the development and deployment of Privacy Sandbox, including the advisory aspects.

At stake is the future of web privacy, while considering the impact of technologies on competition might also be relevant.[37] Therefore it might be constructive to offer a governance and advisory structure that would guarantee future privacy protections, considering also the competition factor.

Today, no technology governance structure comes to mind that concerns itself with matters of technology and privacy, considering the aspects of competition. It is therefore pertinent to consider these issues as of importance to proposals such as 'Privacy Sandbox'. This observation stems from the existing evidence of interest from data protection and competition protection authorities.[38] Technology or standards assessments are often concerned with the consideration of security, privacy, ethics, or perhaps human rights aspects. Less focus is typically placed on the technical conceptions of competition. The proposal analysed in this chapter is

---

[37]   UK Competition and Markets Authority, 'Investigation' (n 20); Australian Competition and Consumer Commission (n 20); D'Cunha (n 17); European Commission, 'Antitrust' (n 20).

[38]   UK Competition and Markets Authority, 'Investigation' (n 20); Australian Competition and Consumer Commission (n 20); European Commission, 'Antitrust' (n 20).

based on the author's experience in web standardisation and privacy, as well as the awareness of the ongoing policy and regulatory processes.

The chapter is grounded on certain premises: that users expect privacy when browsing the web; that this aspect is clearly within the scope of data protection regulators' interest; that competition authorities are increasingly focusing on the actions of technology vendors; and that technology standardisation, 'albeit voluntary in nature, can impose de facto rules for a particular sector and hence become coercive.'[39]

Governance structures should guarantee the decisional equality of the Members who form a representation of the concerned communities and industries. While some Members may be inclined to favour their own industries or even individual firms, a well-designed governance structure should be about individual motivations, leading to the creation of broadly acceptable recommendations and standards. Evidence suggests that competitors tend to be involved in the same standardisation initiatives,[40] and such natural competition improves the end product. This is opposed by self-standardisation ('de facto') when standards are simply built and implemented by a single vendor, not involving any external actors. Collaborative standardisation tends to be the favoured approach by the modern developer circles, including open source developers. For example, within W3C, it is standard procedure to involve the wider community, including in the process of horizontal reviews, such as the assessment of accessibility, or security and privacy.

Good governance design must guarantee satisfactory composition of the governance or advisory structure, such as the appropriate Member representation and the Member expertise, or the practical issues of legitimacy based on the decision process whether consensus based or voting.[41] Ultimately the decisions or advice must be adopted and accepted by all stakeholders, which in practice would mean that the controllers of the technology in question must implement the specified changes in the technology (i.e., the web browser, in this case), and the users of the technology must agree to use the functionality.

---

[39]   Olia Kanevskaia, 'Governance within Standards Development Organizations: WHO Owns the Game?' (2017) ITU Kaleidoscope: Challenges for a Data-Driven Society, IEEE, 3.

[40]   Justus Baron and Tim Pohlmann, 'Who Cooperates in Standards Consortia—Rivals or Complementors?' (2013) 9(4) Journal of Competition Law and Economics.

[41]   Justus Baron and others, 'Making the Rules: The Governance of Standard Development Organizations and Their Policies on Intellectual Property Rights' (2019) 29655 JRC Science for Policy Report, EUR.

The primary source of legitimacy would be the respect of such voluntary standards. Another factor may be the reasons for considering regulations. While a governance body may be devised as a structure upholding self-regulation, it may be possible to go beyond this by linking such a governance structure with vehicles offered by existing lawful mechanisms of regulatory oversight or those offered by regulations. For example, European law considers the issues of standardisation explicitly,[42] and technology standards are used to fulfil the needs of various regulations.

As will be shown in the case of the European Union, legal texts to consider could include GDPR,[43] but also the DSA.[44] Both these frameworks foresee the use of codes of conduct. For the GDPR, Europe's leadership in data protection standards is accepted – as is evidenced in the world's data protection frameworks modelled over the GDPR.[45] Likewise, linking an existing governance structure to European law could be broadly accepted as a model guarantee. The added advantage would be guaranteeing that the governance structure is to some degree based on existing laws, effectively constituting an additional source of legitimacy, and perhaps even enforcement.

2.1   Alternatives to Privacy Sandbox

Privacy Sandbox is a stack of proposals that intend to (1) improve the privacy footprints of certain web-browsing experiences, and (2) introduce a potential form of privacy-preserving advertisement systems. As such, no viable alternatives to the Sandbox exist. That said, there are many various competing proposals introduced in the scope of individual proposals.

---

[42]   'Regulation 1025/2012 of 25 October 2012 on European standardisation (2012), Official Journal of the European Union L 316/12' (2012-10-25) L 316/12 OJ.

[43]   General Data Protection Regulation, 'Regulation EU 2016/679 of the European Parliament and of the Council of 27 April 2016' [2016] Official Journal of the European Union <https://eur-lex.europa.eu/eli/reg/2016/679/oj> accessed 1 July 2022.

[44]   European Commission, 'Proposal for a Regulation of the European Parliament and of the Council on a Single Market for Digital Services (Digital Services Act) and amending Directive 2000/31/EC COM/2020/825 final' [2020] <https://eur-lex.europa.eu/legal-content/en/TXT/?uri=COM:2020:825:FIN> accessed 1 July 2022.

[45]   Graham Greenleaf, 'Global Data Privacy Laws 2019: 132 National Laws & Many Bills' (2019) 157 Privacy Laws & Business International Report <https://ssrn.com/abstract=3381593> accessed 1 July 2022.

For example, in the case of the Turtledove proposal,[46] many variations or even competing solutions were put forward for consideration. Some of such input has been picked up by Google, and at the time of writing it is due to be tested during the trials of Turtledove (called 'FLEDGE'[47]) conducted in 2022 and 2023. Furthermore, the final name of this quite complex proposal is now Protected Audience API.[48]

Privacy Sandbox is introduced as a possible avenue for amending the web architecture. It is advocated as the minimum change that would lead to the option of phasing out the current standard web-tracking mechanism, third-party cookies, from the most popular Chrome web browser. Still, it is necessary to point out that other web-browser vendors (in particular, Apple's Safari or Mozilla Firefox) already restrict tracking by default. This chapter does not seek to elaborate further on such already-existing deployments. Rather, the focus is on the potential ways of governing the Privacy Sandbox stack of proposals.

3. EXISTING TECHNOLOGY GOVERNANCE FRAMEWORK SPECIAL TO INTERNET AND WEB

In this section, the governance configuration relating to existing technologies and associated problems is analysed. The focus is on web technologies, so the governance and standardisation consideration should be as close as possible to existing frameworks of that kind. Here it must be noted that the inclusion of Facebook's Oversight Board in the considerations is motivated by the fact that this structure is devised to 'regulate' what happens on a technology platform (that uses the web).

Therefore, the assessment and the proposals are based on analysis of the rules of W3C's Technical Architecture Group, the IETF's Internet Architecture Board, the AMP,[49] the JS Foundation's Technical Advisory Committee,[50] the OpenJS Foundation's Cross Project Council,[51] and the

---

[46] TURTLEDOVE (2022) <https://github.com/WICG/turtledove> accessed 1 July 2022.

[47] Michael Kleber, 'First Experiment (FLEDGE)' (2021) <https://github.com/WICG/turtledove/blob/main/FLEDGE.md> accessed 1 July 2022.

[48] Paul Jensen, 'Protected Audience API' (2023) Draft community report <https://wicg.github.io/turtledove/> accessed 31 April 2023.

[49] AMP Governance Structures (n 33).

[50] Technical Advisory Committee (TAC) Charter v1.0 (n 34).

[51] The OpenJS Foundation Cross Project Council (n 35).

admittedly differing in topical interest – Facebook's Oversight Board.[52] The analysis will help to distil a proposal for a governance framework for privacy-preserving ad systems;[53] in practice, considering such a system based on Google Chrome's Privacy Sandbox proposals. This choice is made for the reasons that Google's Chrome is the most popular web browser, that Google kick-started this particular debate, and that the initiative has garnered interest from many other vendors or companies.

3.1   W3C's Technical Architecture Group and Advisory Board

The W3C Process explicitly states that web development is a consensus-based activity.[54] Crucially, the Process defines two specialised groups: the Advisory Board (AB, 'to help resolve Consortium-wide non-technical issues') and the Technical Architecture Group (TAG, 'to help resolve Consortium-wide technical issues'). The W3C Advisory Committee (AC) is a body composed of the representatives of the current W3C Members. It reviews the W3C works, and 'elects' Members to the AB and to the TAG. In this sense, the AC forms a source of legitimacy as it expresses the views of W3C Members. Specifically, 'the Advisory Board provides ongoing guidance to the Team on issues of strategy, management, legal matters, process, and conflict resolution', while 'the mission of the TAG is steward-ship of the Web architecture.' In practice, this work is done by the follow-ing actions: 'to document and build consensus around principles of Web architecture and to interpret and clarify these principles when necessary; to resolve issues involving general Web architecture brought to the TAG; to help coordinate cross-technology architecture developments inside and outside W3C.' The detailed description is in the TAG Charter.[55]

This structure of W3C advisory bodies makes for a strict organisation-policy and technical division. The TAG was first bootstrapped by the W3C director Tim Berners-Lee, who appointed the initial Members,[56] and some seats are still filled by the Director. But the current general process of election of AB and TAG Members is defined in detail. Election of a TAG Member for a two-year term requires the current W3C Member to nominate

---

[52]   Facebook's Oversight Board's Charter (n 36).

[53]   Toubiana and others (n 13).

[54]   Elika Etemad and Floian Rivoal, 'W3C Process Document' (2020) <https://www.w3.org/2020/Process-20200915/> accessed 1 July 2022.

[55]   Ian Jacobs, 'Technical Architecture Group (TAG) Charter' (2004) <https://www.w3.org/2004/10/27-tag-charter.html> accessed 1 July 2022.

[56]   Jean-François Abramatic and others, 'Technical Architecture Group (TAG) Charter' (2001) <https://www.w3.org/2001/07/19-tag> accessed 1 July 2022.

an individual; the Members vote for individuals; and the seats are assigned according to a vote process that happens each year. The TAG Members' terms are staggered; each year there are elections for some freed seats.

Crucially, the Members of the AB and the TAG are representing themselves, not their companies or organisations. Members themselves may be employed by W3C Member organisations, but they may also be external Invited Experts, unaffiliated with any formal Member. The process contains numerous precautions, for example to ensure there are not two participants with the same primary affiliation occupying seats at the same time, a measure likely meant to avoid the risk of unbalanced composition. Moreover, the formally defined election process[57] considers the need to compose a nominating statement explaining the motivations and aims of the candidate. Candidates should have the following traits: 'Technical competence in one's role; [t]he ability to act fairly; [s]ocial competence in one's role.'[58]

At W3C, including the groups such as the AB or the TAG, decisions are made by *consensus*. This requires the need to include and consider the views, objections and opinions of legitimate parties. Signalled problems should be addressed in ways such that all the parties are satisfied to a degree that there may even be unanimity. The Process document defines consensus as, 'substantial number of individuals in the set supporting the decision and nobody in the set registering a Formal Objection.' But in practice, after a lengthy process is executed, the final decision may be resolved by voting or even by the W3C Director (CEO, or COO) decision, in matters of special controversy. When holding the voting, no quorum is formally defined; a quorum may be defined in the case of individual groups.

While no quorums might be defined, the required votes may amount to a supermajority (exceeding the 50% mark). While voting may be a last resort, the Process documents stipulate that groups should 'favor proposals that create the weakest objections.'

W3C favours 'rapid progress'. This is ensured by favouring a small size of Working Groups, typically composed of fewer than 15 Members. The existing and formal TAG review process may benefit from the many existing Working Groups, especially on the level of horizontal review of a considered proposal for a standard. In practice, the TAG may request an opinion (for a review) from an external group or even from an individual, for example in the case of security and privacy reviews, or to assess the impact of a feature on accessibility. What matters is

---

[57] W3C, 'How to Organize an Advisory Board or TAG Election' (2002) <https://www.w3.org/2002/10/election-howto> accessed 1 July 2022.

[58] Etemad and Rivoal (n 54).

for proposals to undergo a *wide review* – including consideration of the views of the wider community. This *wide review* means that other W3C groups may be involved, but it may also involve external actors such as civil society, or independent individuals. Today, the evidence of a wider review would typically constitute a collection of links to statements or analyses, for example, posted on a GitHub discussion board, and/or to the mailing list.

Finally, it is necessary to understand that W3C is involved in the development of technical specifications. It is not to be involved in the competitive practices of W3C's Members 'nor in any way restrict competition.' The legal obligations of participants are at their sole discretion, and W3C is not the venue to reconcile such issues.[59]

How is this relevant to the Privacy Sandbox? Web standards governance happens within the W3C, but in the case of individual projects, the activity is limited to standards development. That said, it is clear the works within the W3C venue are directly relevant to the Privacy Sandbox, if just because of the fact that the W3C Improving Web Advertising Business (WAB) (or the Private Advertising Technology Community Group, PATCG) is the venue of choice when deciding on feature designs.

While the Privacy Sandbox concerns web technology, no clear path for linking it with the W3C process appears to exist, at least based on the W3C Process document.[60] In this case, the works concerning the design of Privacy Sandbox are discussed in the devoted WAB and PATCG groups. But there seems to be no clear governance path, the work being limited to standards development, and only concerned with the delivery of technical standards.

It is not possible, for example, to task the W3C Technical Architecture Group with a direct oversight mandate. The TAG is an advisory body of the wider W3C, and its works concern the web platform's architecture. As such, the TAG is reviewing the works delivered by individual Working Groups. The TAG considers matters of web architecture, and it can even link to privacy or competition aspects.[61] But it is less clear to what extent the TAG could impact the enforcement or impact on the final decisions made by the feature authored or the vendors (the TAG has no formal powers).

Important discussions and deliberations may still happen in the specialised WAB group, and any potential Privacy Sandbox governance

---

[59]   Wendy Seltzer, 'Antitrust and Competition Guidance' (2017) <https://www.w3.org/Consortium/Legal/2017/antitrust-guidance> accessed 1 July 2022.

[60]   Etemad and Rivoal (n 54).

[61]   Amy Guy, 'Early Design Review for the FLoC API #601' (2021) <https://github.com/w3ctag/design-reviews/issues/601%5C#issuecomment-783780556> accessed 1 July 2022.

structure must consider this open and transparent nature of the process, as well as the collaboration venue of choice (the W3C WAB or PATCG).

3.2 The IETF's Internet Architecture Board

According to the IETF's Internet Architecture Board (IAB) Charter,[62] the IAB is composed of a fixed number of 13 Members who come from the IETF community. As in the case of the W3C TAG, IAB Members represent themselves, not the organisations with which they may be affiliated. According to the Charter, 'The IAB acts as a source of advice and guidance to the Board of Trustees and Officers of the Internet Society concerning technical, architectural, procedural, and (where appropriate) policy matters pertaining to the Internet and its enabling technologies. If necessary the IAB may convene panels of knowledgeable people, hold hearings, and otherwise pursue the investigation.' In this sense, the IAB directs both technical and policy advice, and it may ask for external input, including from the wider community. IAB is tasked with a long-term oversight of internet protocols, and 'is expected to pay attention to important long-term issues in the Internet, and to make sure that these issues are brought to the attention of the group(s) that are in a position to address them.'

The decision process in IAB strives to be *unanimous*. If reaching unanimity is not possible in practice, a consensus is sought. Voting is possible: 'the chair may conduct informal polls to determine consensus.' Such a governance mechanism, as in the case of W3C groups, is meant to reduce the risks of group lockup (paralysis), ensuring that decisions are being made. As in the case of W3C, following each meeting or decision made, proceedings are made available to the public, to ensure transparency.

Candidate nomination and the election process are formalised and defined in detail.[63] The term of elected persons is two years. In the context of the election process, the IETF IAB also has a dispute resolution mechanism, where the party concerned sends their input to the Internet Society's President. Subsequently, a then-established independent arbiter is tasked with making an investigation, striving to understand all sides of the dispute. The voting requires the majority of 3/4.

---

[62]   B Carpenter, 'Charter of the Internet Architecture Board' (2000) <https://www.iab.org/about/charter/> accessed 1 July 2022.

[63]   M Kucherawy, R Hinden and J Livingood, 'IAB, IESG, IETF Trust and IETF LLC Selection, Confirmation, and Recall Process: Operation of the IETF Nominating and Recall Committees' (2020) <https://tools.ietf.org/html/bcp10> accessed 1 July 2022.

The day-to-day work of the IETF concerns the standardisation process, described in Best Current Practice 9.[64] Among the goals are 'technical excellence; prior implementation and testing; clear, concise, and easily understood documentation; openness and fairness; and timeliness.' Work procedures are construed to guarantee such desirable properties, and they describe each phase of a standard. All the crucial deliberations and decisions are communicated openly, in a transparent fashion. Clarity of the process and decision transparency make it possible to reason as to how and why particular decisions were reached. It is, for example, stressed that the IAB group 'have an existence as leaders in the community. As leaders in the Internet technical community, these entities should have an outlet to propose ideas to stimulate work in a particular area, to raise the community's sensitivity to a certain issue, to make a statement of architectural principle, or to communicate their thoughts on other matters.' This makes it clear that the IAB is tasked with resolving disputes and finding consensus. It is accepted that the IAB's decisions are final.

3.3   AMP Advisory and Technical Steering Group

The Accelerated Mobile Pages (AMP) governance body is closely related to the publisher (i.e., website) side. As such, its charter may be understood as the principles facilitating the technical work closely linked to the functioning of websites. The Advisory Committee (AC) is representative in the sense that it includes Members from 'major AMP constituencies (Collaborators, Contributors, Users and End-Users).' The number of AMP AC Members is not fixed, but a situation of having between 6 and 12 persons is favoured, possibly to balance the need for representation and allow a smooth and practical approach to working. Once initially established, the AMP AC self-assigns future Members via consensus. Compared with W3C's and the IETF's strict limits on representation, AMP allows multiple individuals from single employers ('no more than 1/3 of the Advisory Committee should be from one employer').

In the case of AMP, the technical leadership is realised at the Technical Steering Committee (TSC). Crucially, the TSC may 'designate entities to perform security and privacy reviews of AMP code/features', and also direct legal questions to upstream to the OpenJS Foundation. The ability to request legal support is not the norm at governance bodies.

---

[64]   S Bradner, 'The Internet Standards Process – Revision 3' (1996) <https://tools.ietf.org/ html/bcp9> accessed 1 July 2022.

The TSC 'shall be composed of members with significant experience contributing to AMP on a technical and product level.' This limits the participation to Members contributing on a technical or product layer and potentially reduces the involvement of bodies such as civil society or academia. But the nature of the AMP deliverables are quite specific, and such a broad oversight might not be needed on the level of the TSC.

Like the AMP AC, the TSC is composed of an arbitrary number of Members (aiming at 6–12 Members), with not more than 1/3 Members from a single organisation. Some seats may be pre-filled with individuals from organisations contributing funds to the AMP project: 'Entities (such as a company) may be granted seats on the TSC. In these cases certain conditions may be placed on the seat (such as maintaining committed resources to the project).' In this sense, paying Members would be viewed as those holding stakes in the committee and AMP, and would expect to have an influence on the works.

The TSC defines mandates of each Working Group working on particular features. In this sense, the TSC is the source of legitimacy of the Working Groups, while the source of legitimacy of the TSC are the Members. It is important to note that the Members of the first AC and TSC were initially assigned 'upfront' and directly, as is made clear by the Google-affiliated post.[65] Decisions at the AC, TSC and the Working Groups are reached via consensus, with a possibility of voting.

AMP 'enables the creation of websites and ads. Publishers and advertisers can decide how to present their content that emphasizes a user-first experience.' Processes related to AMP may be seen as relevant to the Privacy Sandbox in the sense that both projects focus on fixed areas of web technologies. The differences lie in the topical focus. For example, AMP concerns only the presentation layer), and Privacy Sandbox would need to be specially assessed to measure its privacy aspects.

3.4   The JS Foundation Technical Advisory Committee

Since the rules are roughly comparable to the previous bodies, this section concerning the JS Foundation TAC has been simplified.

The TAC's responsibilities are 'ensuring collaboration is the driving principle within a Project, between JS Foundation Projects, and between JS Foundation Projects and the broader community.' Its tasks include

---

[65]   Malte Ubl, 'An Open Governance Model for the AMP Project' (2018) <https://blog.amp.dev/2018/09/18/governance/> accessed 1 July 2022.

conflict resolution among the projects (in the JS Foundation, projects are self-governing), and providing guidelines.

The Members of the TAC are elected for 1 year.[66] The body is set at a fixed size of 25 seats, with Members consisting of people from the JS Foundation's Platinum Member organisation (1 seat), the Node.js Foundation (1 seat) and the broader community. It is the existing TAC and the Board that hold the election. Such an obligation required the bootstrapping of the first TAC, setting it up in some way.

As in the previous cases, there is a strict limit on the number of Members from the same employer (no more than a quarter), a clause that is the norm.

3.5   Facebook's Oversight Board

Facebook's Oversight Board is an advisory body admittedly different from the ones described previously. This governance structure is of interest because it relates to a closed platform maintained entirely by Facebook. The Charter defines the operation of the Oversight Board.[67] The need for the Board in the closed platform of Facebook is motivated directly: 'Free expression is paramount, but there are times when speech can be at odds with authenticity, safety, privacy, and dignity. Some expression can endanger other people's ability to express themselves freely. Therefore, it must be balanced against these considerations.' The standards set are not standards in a technical sense (i.e., as in the context of the bodies previously described that worked on actual technology standards), but relate to the content placed on the platform by its users: 'internet services have a responsibility to set standards for what is and is not acceptable to share on their platforms.' The practical work of the Board is transparency, with decisions communicated to the public.

The Board counts at least 11 diversified Members, with Members having broad expertise, assumed to be able to arrive at 'neutral, independent judgment'. The members must have advanced competencies, being 'skilled at making and explaining decisions based on a set of policies or standards; and have familiarity with matters relating to digital content and governance, including free expression, civic discourse, safety, privacy and technology.' Such framing deliberately mixes policy and technology competencies. The composition of the first Oversight Board was

---

[66]   JS Foundation (n 34).
[67]   Facebook AB (n 36).

bootstrapped directly by Facebook. Members serve for a three-year term and a maximum of three terms. The terms are staggered – each year new members are accepted. The decision-making process at the Board is consensus, when this is not possible, a majority vote can be held.

The board also pays attention to human rights – 'When reviewing decisions, the board will pay particular attention to the impact of removing content in light of human rights norms protecting free expression' – even though the concrete human rights in question are not listed. The Board's work revolves around the interpretation of Facebook's Community Standards and applying them to Facebook's decisions with the option of overturning or upholding them. According to the Charter, the Board's decisions are binding: Facebook must adopt them. In this sense, Facebook is taking a unilateral vow to respect the Board's decision, a form of self-governance.

Members are compensated for their work. Furthermore, the Oversight Board has the support of employed staff who handle administrative tasks. The work process is open to external input: 'including through subject matter experts, research requests or translation services.' Funding comes from an independent trust: 'both the board and its administration are funded by an independent trust and supported by an independent company that is separate from Facebook' (funded by Facebook).

3.6 Summary

The previous sections described various approaches to technology governance, revolving around standardisation, advice or even decision enforcement. Each body can be analysed in the context of the specific features and overarching rules.

- *The aims.* The scope of the governance structure typically revolves around facilitating the development work, providing advice about current and future work and challenges, as well as oversight. The aims usually include the oversight of the production of satisfactory deliverables and well-balanced opinions that are fair and acceptable to the Members.
- *The composition.* A governance structure is composed of interested individuals. This may be employees of member organisations or external individuals. Typically there are bounds on the numbers of individuals having the same employer. Additionally, Facebook's Oversight Board pays attention to geographic representation. Geographical or gender considerations may be an important aspect to guarantee the representativeness.

- *The nature of representation.* In the analysed cases concerning web technology standardisation, members of governance structures represent themselves, not their employers. While this differs in the case of other bodies, such as ISO (organisation representation) or ITU (country representation), such governance structures are outside the scope of this analysis.
- *The rules.* The rules of operating a governance structure are always formalised in some form (i.e., a charter). The length and complexity of the charter rules vary from the simpler (as in the case of AMP) to the long and precise (as in the case of the W3C TAG or the IETF IAB).
- *Decision-making.* While unanimity may be an asset, the decisions are often made via consensus, which strives to obtain a result that is acceptable to all the involved parties. In practice, if consensus is difficult to obtain, voting can be held, with various majority needs (1/2, 2/3, 3/4, etc.), and with an option of filing a dissenting opinion or even a formal objection. Unanimity is favoured at the IETF IAB, but it is accepted that voting might be needed (fallback to consensus if unanimity not possible). Voting may be performed to gauge the 'feeling' of the members for a particular decision, for example at the IETF.
- *Legitimacy.* The composition of the high-level governing structures varies but the source of legitimacy is typically other higher-level governing structures, the Members and/or participants from the broader community. In this place, a special status existing in the W3C is important, where unaffiliated individuals may participate as Invited Experts, making the process open to the wider community.
- *Bootstrapping.* The members of the governing structures are typically elected. But initially, there is a need to establish the starting composition. This might be a choice made by an influential member organisation or respected individual. For example, it was Google in the case of the initial AMP governing body, it was Facebook in the case of the Oversight Board, and it was the W3C Director in the case of the W3C TAG.
- *Mode of work.* Governance bodies usually perform work on a needs basis, holding regular meetings, and often pro-active activities, for example the issuing opinions or assessments, or preparations of guidelines.
- *Transparency.* Typically, all the important work details are made public in an accessible place, such as a GitHub repository. Discussion may also happen within a designated Working Group, such as in the case of W3C. Sometimes, face-to-face meetings may be held, but the proceedings of such meetings are also published.

- *Translation to practice.* Certain bodies (i.e., the W3C TAG), while influential, do not exercise any formal powers (web browser vendors independently decide what to implement and how). Others (i.e., Facebook's Oversight Board) have a different role and their decisions should in principle be binding (in this case, voluntarily accepted by Facebook). Translating deliberations, opinions or decisions into practice is a challenge. For example, W3C is a venue for developing voluntary standards, meaning that implementors themselves decide what to implement and how.
- *Compensation.* This is a more practical matter of work. It varies greatly, and some bodies support the governance structures financially (such as AMP or Facebook's Oversight Board), while others do not.
- *Interactions with laws and regulations.* While some of the governance structures are tasked with making business or policy advice, the work conducted by the analysed governance structures typically does not directly intersect with regulations and policies. While of course there is an impact and overlap in this sphere (e.g., the Web Content Accessibility Guidelines 2.1 were codified on the level of a directive of the European Union,[68] standardisation bodies typically do not directly interact with the legal frameworks within various jurisdictions. There are caveats of a different nature. For example, the W3C expects its members to guarantee a patent-free policy (so that the deliverables remain unencumbered) and, equally, places responsibility in the case of anti-trust and competition with the members. That said, the new laws such as the GDPR exert an influence on the works performed within the body.

4. GOVERNANCE OF PRIVACY-PRESERVING ADS TECHNOLOGY: 'PRIVACY SANDBOX' GOVERNANCE

4.1 Understanding of the Technical Meaning of Privacy and Competition

In many respects, it may be more useful to construe privacy not as a focus on secrecy, right to control or even the mere processing of data, but as

---

[68] Directive (EU) 2016/2102 of the European Parliament and of the Council of 26 October 2016 on the accessibility of the websites and mobile applications of public sector bodies' (2016-10-26) L 327 OJ.

the right to appropriate flows of personal information, something that may be summarised as *norms of information flow*.[69] Although compliance with data protection regimes is a separate, if serious, issue, this concise definition is sufficient in terms of considering the privacy footprint of the Privacy Sandbox. That said, the reader should understand that other notions of privacy may differ, and the specific focus of data protection laws may have plenty of complex principles that must also be taken into account. Here it is important to note that respect for privacy is the core tenet for fulfilling the data protection requirements, as introduced by existing regulations, such as the General Data Protection Regulation, or the ePrivacy Directive (or the upcoming Regulation, still in works in 2022). This definition, though, slightly differs from the notion of GDPR, which is focused on data protection and where the term 'privacy' is not used (instead, *'data protection'* is in use). Subsequently, it is explained how the Code of Conduct vehicle of the GDPR may be used to offer certain guarantees of the governance structure discussed in this work. In the end, the potential tensions between competition and data protection need more attention.

In the case of a specialised integrated[70] product such as the Privacy Sandbox concept, additional aspects may need to be considered: specifically, privacy.[71] To some degree, the role of competition aspects play a role as well.[72] This is also the case with the contents of the W3C TAG review of the Federated Learning of Cohorts proposal,[73] where the issue has been highlighted. The issue of competition is additionally stressed in light of the formal investigations.[74] To ensure acceptable deliverables, it is likely that the assessment of both aspects (privacy, competition) may need to be built into any 'governance' structure.

It is perhaps a paradox that, while many resources (including research) were devoted to the development of security and privacy assessment methods, a similar focus was never put on competition. Although the links between privacy and competition were investigated,[75] the impacts

---

[69]   Helen Nissenbaum, *Privacy in Context* (Stanford University Press 2020) and 'Privacy as Contextual Integrity' (2004) 79 Washington Law Review.

[70]   When the full deliverable only works if all its parts function.

[71]   As judged by the name, *Privacy* Sandbox.

[72]   Frank Pasquale, 'Privacy, Antitrust, and Power' (2012) 20 George Mason Law Review; D'Cunha (n 17).

[73]   Guy (n 61).

[74]   UK Competition and Markets Authority, 'Investigation' (n 20); Australian Competition and Consumer Commission (n 20); European Commission, 'Antitrust' (n 20).

[75]   D'Cunha (n 17); Pasquale (n 72).

of technologies on competition are today the prime subject of regulatory scrutiny,[76] creating the motivation to consider the competition aspects in the design of potentially significant technologies. Competition is recently also becoming a topic of regulatory interventions.[77] Competition considerations are for example recognised by W3C,[78] although limited in this case to a policy and a legal framing, with less focus on the technical meaning. The W3C competition clause is very short and it states, 'W3C does not play any role in the competitive decisions of W3C participants.' It also mentions, 'Participants must ensure that their conduct does not violate antitrust and competition laws and regulations. For example, participants should not discuss product pricing, methods or channels of product distribution, division of markets, allocation of customers, or any other topic that should not be discussed among competitors.' In other words, the long-term design consequences on entire ecosystems are not exactly foreseen directly, but in any case the responsibility is put on W3C Members, such as the companies participating in standards development process. Indeed, while many security and privacy technical assessments exist (and are created), no similar assessment frameworks appear to exist in the case of competition. Perhaps this is the case because it is a less structured horizontal issue, generally less defined technically. It may seem that the sole reason and motivation to consider the competitive aspects of technology developments is the interest of regulators, due to the actions of big market players. For the purposes of this chapter, the technical meaning of competition is defined as *all the technical processes and changes that may have impacts on market conditions and competitive behaviour of existing market participants.*[79] This definition should include the possible impacts of technology changes on the ability or inability to function by market participants, and to deliver services. It should also include the ability to compete on special grounds, such as the level of privacy.

In the case of standardisation, such a definition should also consider the priority of constituencies at the standards bodies. For example, W3C and the IETF understandably prioritise the well-being of users – not the servers or companies. While in this chapter user privacy is prioritised, it is likewise preferable to refrain from engaging in philosophical discussions

---

[76] UK Competition and Markets Authority, 'Investigation' (n 20); Australian Competition and Consumer Commission (n 20); European Commission, 'Antitrust' (n 20).

[77] European Commission, 'Proposal' (n 44).

[78] Seltzer (n 59).

[79] Author-proposed broad definition.

considering the tangible or intangible 'inherent' value of market competition. It is also not the intention of this chapter to discuss any 'trade-offs between privacy and competition'. The priority of constituencies as defined by the IETF and W3C, specifically the user, must be respected.

4.2   The Need for Mediating and Receiving Input concerning the Design Layer

During the design of a system intending to work on a broad scale, voices of many sides and parties must be taken into consideration. For example, in February 2021 the W3C Technical Architecture Group review of a Privacy Sandbox component (the Federated Learning of Cohorts, FLoC, now a discontinued proposal, following significant criticism of this proposed solution[80]), indicated the need for having a way of designating the privacy parameters of the systems. For example, such configuration aspects concern which websites are considered 'sensitive' by the system.[81] Apart from the technical aims, it is necessary to understand who would be making such decisions, and how. In principle, they could be made by Google Chrome's engineers. But crucially, the TAG review suggests reaching some particular decisions 'by a diverse set of stakeholders, so that the definition of "sensitive" is not biased by the backgrounds of implementors alone.' This means that there should be some input and analysis phase during the discussions and before the decisions are made.

Other relevant ideas from the early W3C TAG review directly motivating the needs for governance are, 'a persistent and authoritative means of documenting what they are that is not tied to a single implementor or company', 'how such documentation can be updated and maintained in the long run', and 'what the spec[ification] can do to ensure implementers actually abide by restrictions around sensitive categories.' In other words, these comments concern the long-term decision-making process and stability of the decisions, as well as the legitimisation of the decision process. Some of the concerns relate to the protection of individuals (and their privacy), while others in these comments actually seem to be motivated in thinking about aspects of competition.

---

[80]   It is difficult not to think of FLoC as a type of 'lightning arrester', as FLoC absorbed strong criticism from academia, NGOs, the media, and so on, which did not reach other Sandbox proposals. After so much initial focus on FLoC, it appears that the community has lost impetus and lesser criticism was directed at other proposals.

[81]   Guy (n 61).

4.2.1   Can governance of Privacy Sandbox happen in the W3C?

Ultimately, the TAG review comments highlight the need to gauge the opinions of users and of other involved actors. The next step after a W3C TAG review typically is the consideration of its contents and an appropriate reply. The review's contents are directed at the specification authors, in this particular case meaning Google. Assuming that the 'process of design governance' of Privacy Sandbox is entirely focused on W3C, this could work as follows. Discussions happening in the W3C WAB/PATCG (or others) group should be open to external opinions. In principle, voices should be taken into consideration by feature developers. Nearing the end of this process, a TAG review is requested and implementation is created, possibly later taking into account the external input and the TAG review. In this case, the decisions happen entirely at the discretion of the implementor.

Assuming goodwill of collaborators in the standardisation venue, as well as the goodwill of the implementers (web browser vendors, i.e. Google Chrome) such a process could function, if in principle at least. But it is important to understand that nothing compels or binds recipients of the W3C TAG review, nor any other review. This means that the perception and the later changes are solely within the control of the feature developers and implementers. In the next sections, the possibilities of going forward, or beyond, are explored.

4.2.2   Dedicated governance structure?

It is imaginable that the current consensus-based process within the W3C work venue would function, and work would be continued. However, in practice there is no guarantee as to what this process would look like in the future. What is certain is the apparent interest of data protection and competition regulators in the changes introduced to the web ecosystem (particularly, online ads capabilities). In such an atmosphere, to avoid risks to the development and implementation of such a platform as the Privacy Sandbox within the web architecture, a specialised governance structure could be envisioned. This would be a structure offering clear assumptions as to transparency, legitimisation and decision-making. The structure in question could function as an additional advisory board, including in matters of assessing privacy and technical aspects of the technical proposals. It is of course assumed that Privacy Sandbox, as any other web technology, will undergo future changes and development. An additional governing structure, independent of a single actor, could help to alleviate concerns and reconcile the potential conflicts during such evolution and development.

Such a structure would not be an entirely new thing (i.e., not a precedent). As explained in the previous section, many web, internet and platform technology governance bodies exist. These preceding examples could function as a model for the creation of an additional legitimate (i.e., independent and impartial) governing or advisory body. The design of such a governance structure could even go beyond the traditional governance means. Such an outcome could be achieved by closely aligning the works with some existing or emerging self-regulatory and regulatory levers.

From now on, such a structure will be referred to as the 'Privacy Sandbox Governance'.

4.3   Potential Privacy Sandbox Governance Structure

To design a governance structure, several prerequisites must be considered. These points are extracted and summarised from the analysis of other practical venues of the kind, explained in the previous section. Specifically important aspects to consider are the aims, the composition, the nature of representation, the rules, legitimacy, bootstrapping, mode of work, transparency, translation into practice.

Whether there would be a dedicated Trust, a Consortium or a Body that unites collaborators and supports the work in the field of privacy-preserving ads ('Privacy Sandbox') is a separate 'operational' problem, external to the considerations of this work. In this section, another voluntary 'assurance' aspect should be mentioned: the linking of the governance structure with existing regulatory frameworks to guarantee decision enforcement and trust.

4.3.1   Aims

The aims and scope of such a governance structure should be simple: oversight of the design and the delivery of privacy-preserving ads technologies that would constitute an ecosystem. The focus on privacy should be obligatory. The aim should not be the finding of 'rotten compromises'. Rather, the aims should include the provision of advice and guidance around the development of privacy-preserving digital online ad capabilities. The opinions should be well balanced, and acceptable to all the relevant actors.

4.3.2   Composition

Such a governance structure should be composed of individuals representing themselves, not their organisations, exactly as in the case of similar governance bodies. The number of individuals with the same affiliation should be binding (perhaps no more than 1 or 2 such individuals). Such a structure could have between 7 and 15 Members (and an odd number).

4.3.3 Nature of representation

The participants represent themselves, but they should come from various (including demographic) backgrounds and organisations. These should include important stakeholders such as the major web-browser vendors (representative, so with substantial market participation), others with stakes in such a system (perhaps the members of the W3C WAB/PATCG group) as the ads technology active in privacy-preserving advertising (i.e., representatives from demand-side platforms or supply-side platforms), publishers, civil society, independent researchers and experts. Relevant candidates for membership should be competent in the problems of privacy, technology, web, standardisation and ads systems, having demonstrated a suitable track record.

Mentioning the initial proponent of Privacy Sandbox, Google, a company with a dominant position and the most popular web browser, Chrome, is unavoidable. Google-affiliated members should abide by the limits of participants, but it has to be assumed that opinions of any participant from the implementers' side (like Google Chrome) would carry weight.

4.3.4 Rules

As in the case of all governance bodies, rules should be formalised in a public charter. Additional documents providing topical precision should be created and published by the governance body itself. The rules should be flexible enough to offer smooth work, while not leaving too much room for interpretation.

4.3.5 Legitimacy

Legitimacy is challenging in such a structure because online ads concern every web user, and many websites or firms. The source of legitimisation should be the potential Members of the body where the collaborators contribute (i.e., W3C/WAB), the contributors, the relevant and competent experts, or members of the relevant civil society. However, such a governance structure would be tasked with oversight of a precise piece of technology.

Prior to the election, candidates should publish statements describing their candidacy. Legitimacy is undermined if the decisions put forward by the governance body are not translated into practice. A specific process should be defined.

4.3.6 Bootstrapping

Bootstrapping also impacts legitimisation. How should the members of the initial governance structure be chosen? Procedures varied historically, but it is accepted that individuals with adequate expertise were initially assigned authoritatively. For example, it was Google that chose and assigned the initial Members in the case of the governing body of AMP, it was the W3C Director who assigned the initial people to the Technical Architecture Group, and it was Facebook who unilaterally and independently filled seats of their content moderation advisory body, the Oversight Board. After the initial process of bootstrapping, elections should be held to fill the available seats in the governance group on a rolling basis.

4.4 Decision-making Process

The core process of decision-making should be identical to that of W3C, namely, seeking consensus. Decisions and consensus must be justified with source material (evidence). If consensus is impossible to reach, voting should be allowed, with a pre-defined majority type, such as 2/3 majority of votes, and perhaps 3/4 in the case of certain crucial decisions. Unanimity might be inadequate for practical reasons, as this form of decision-making may risk paralysis of the works by a single participant.

Task groups working on specific deliverables could be created. After a proposal receives adequate scrutiny, and is reviewed and accepted by the governance structure (possibly with the involvement of external structures such as the W3C TAG, since Privacy Sandbox concerns the web platform), the governance body should arrive at a decision, issuing a public communication. Subsequently, it would be expected that, following a decision, such as approval of a design document or other feature in question, this is then translated into practice: a document is published and must be considered in the future, or a design feature is ready to be implemented, shipped by the web browser and used by publishes or users.

All actors must accept the decisions made using a formal process. Otherwise, the legitimisation of the governing body would be undermined, as would trust in such a privacy-preserving ads technology component.

4.4.1 Mode of work
Regular meetings should be held. Input from the wider community should be considered. Such a governing structure should accept input from external actors in matters of technology, policy and regulations. The governance body should provide opinions, advice, reviews, and so on.

4.4.2 Transparency
All the proceedings or documents from the work of such a governing body should be made public, including the transcripts of the meetings and the

adopted decisions. It should be the Chair's responsibility to make sure that the work proceedings are made public.

In principle, the work could be performed in the open over GitHub, such as happens in the current dedicated W3C WAB and PATCG groups. Currently, deliberations concerning the design and other issues take place on the W3C WAB and PATCG groups, Early evidence suggests that changes to the design and implementation are made in response to such discussions.[82]

4.4.3 Translation into practice

Implementers should accept the opinions, guidance and proposals of the governing body, and implement them when they are mature. In practice, such a decision would always be voluntary on the side of implementers. A good example is W3C. Nothing can compel a vendor to implement a particular feature if the will is not present. There are features that are not being implemented, or features that are were removed (e.g., due to privacy concerns).

Actually enforcing decisions could be imaginable if the governance structure's body is linked to some existing regulatory or enforcement vehicle, such as the data protection authorities, the competition authorities or even the respective regulations. The potential of linking with regulatory levers is covered in the section below.

4.4.4 Compensation

In general, governing bodies do not offer compensation (with the exception of Facebook's Oversight Board). While it is accepted that not being compensated for one's work perhaps may be seen as an idealistic goal of guaranteeing independence,[83] financing issues should be addressed either by a specifically designed Trust or by the Members of such a project.

The financing source should cover costs such as the operation of the governance structure, face-to-face meetings, and perhaps the work of the governing structure Members.

4.4.5 Summary

An alternative process could include the establishment of a typical W3C Working Group, with a dedicated charter, an option to join by Members,

---

[82] First Experiment (FLEDGE) (n 47); Progress update on the Privacy Sandbox initiative (n 14).

[83] Even if at the same time typically being employed, so compensated, by stakeholder organisations, which is not always the case.

and the linkage to the typical W3C work process. Concerning the ideas laid out in the previous points, a typical W3C Working Group structure would simplify the rules around the development of voluntary technical standards. But such a work process would not take into consideration advanced matters of privacy (though this sphere of interest has a dedicated point within W3C) or even competition, a point expressly outside W3C consideration.[84] It would also potentially be challenging to persuade some parties such as the civil society groups or publishers (specific websites) to join W3C solely to participate in the fraction of works of such a Working Group, although their views should always be incorporated on the time of work and review of prepared deliverables.

4.5   Regulatory Levers

Law is a type of a regulatory system.[85] Vendors desiring to demonstrate extra sensitivity or to extend extra guarantees could benefit from regulatory vehicles that would allow linking the technical and business decisions with a form of oversight or limitations.

4.5.1   General Data Protection Regulation

In the European regulatory regime, the General Data Protection Regulation[86] offers a way of designating and accepting a Code of Conduct by which controllers may abide to demonstrate guarantees of respecting data protection laws. These frameworks are used in this chapter as potential world standards.[87] Theoretically, a code of conduct of this kind could be prepared to guarantee the privacy level of privacy-preserving ads systems, including the acceptance of the decisions made by the governance structure. Subsequently, any vendor decision that would violate the advice of the governance structure could be seen as a violation of the code of conduct in question, and an evidence of a worse stance when it comes to data protection guarantees. Article 40(9) of the GDPR[88] stipulates that a code of conduct may be accepted and adopted by the European

---

[84]   Seltzer (n 59).

[85]   Ugo Pagallo, Pompeu Casanovas and Robert Madelin, 'The Middle-Out Approach: Assessing Models of Legal Governance in Data Protection, Artificial Intelligence, and the Web of Data' (2019) 7(1) The Theory and Practice of Legislation <https://doi.org/10.1080/20508840.2019.1664543> accessed 1 July 2022.

[86]   General Data Protection Regulation (n 43).

[87]   Greenleaf (n 45).

[88]   General Data Protection Regulation (n 43).

Commission through the issuing of a formal implementing act (and thus be binding in the whole European Union), even though until now this article has never been used. In principle, adherence to the code of conduct is stipulated in the GDPR's Article 24 ('responsibility of the controller'): 'to demonstrate compliance with the obligations of the controller.' While the GDPR is a legal framework developed in line of European values,[89] it is conceivable that considering its emergence as a world standard,[90] grounding a privacy-preserving technical system on a regulatory footing, would give it additional credence.

4.5.2 Digital Services Act

Perhaps a superior voluntary regulatory lever is contained in the proposal for a Digital Services Act in the EU,[91] specifically Article 36 ('Codes of conduct for online advertising'). This article is encouraging the creation of voluntary codes of conduct in the area of online advertising. The article also concerns *data protection and competition aspects at the same time*: 'competitive, transparent and fair environment in online advertising, in accordance with Union and national law, in particular on competition and the protection of personal data.' This is made even more precise by Recital 70: 'Codes of conducts should support and complement the transparency obligations relating to advertisement for online platforms and very large online platforms set out in this Regulation in order to provide for flexible and effective mechanisms to facilitate and enhance the compliance with those obligations, notably as concerns the modalities of the transmission of the relevant information. The involvement of a wide range of stakeholders should ensure that those codes of conduct are widely supported, technically sound, effective and offer the highest levels of user- friendliness to ensure that the transparency obligations achieve their objectives.' Such a code of conduct could then voluntarily stipulate that decisions of a structure governing the design of a privacy-preserving advertising system (i.e., Privacy Sandbox) are binding, should be translated into a practical operation (or implementation or deployment), and should respect user's privacy. Enforcement is a separate issue. While non-acceptance of decisions may undermine the legitimisation of the governing body, and generally result in a public relations crisis or even backlash from the solution, is it possible to voluntarily

---

[89]   Amelia Andersdotter and Lukasz Olejnik, 'Policy Strategies for Value-Based Technology Standards' (2021) 10(3) Internet Policy Review.

[90]   Greenleaf (n 45).

[91]   European Commission, 'Proposal' (n 44).

go beyond? The Digital Services Act foresees fines for non-compliance: 'the Commission may impose on the very large online platform concerned fines not exceeding 6% of its total turnover in the preceding financial year' in the case of infringement of 'relevant provisions of this Regulation' (Article 59(1)(a)). While it is unclear whether such fines relate to non-compliance with a voluntary code of conduct (i.e., Article 36), the regulation project is as of now not yet finalised. It is expected that this particular issue will be clarified in the future.

In summary, if a very large company would seriously intend to respect the privacy and competition guarantees of a Privacy Sandbox-like mechanism, self-regulatory opportunities such as the adoption and acceptance of a code of conduct are potentially an option. Such measures might be acceptable and reassuring to regulators, for example to the European Commission, to the market participants, and perhaps to the users. It could also constitute an additional form of legitimisation of the work of the governance structure.

5. CONCLUSION

In this chapter, the landscape of standardisation of web technologies with a special focus on the various existing governing structures was investigated. The analysis included the common governance frameworks such as the legitimisation, the mode of work or the practical aspects such as how decision-making is made. Such an analysis allowed us to consider a possible governance structure of the future privacy-preserving advertising ecosystem, a flexible proposal that would foresee the acceptance of input from multiple stakeholders, offering advice, and issuing biding decisions about the operation, maintenance and development of privacy-preserving ads systems components. The practical realisation of such a technical system might be Google Chrome's proposal of Privacy Sandbox. The practical associated governance structure should be an independent entity, with works done in the public. The primary objective of such a structure should be user privacy on the web and technical soundness.

In this work, the intersections of privacy and competition is also considered. Historically, this area is often considered by legal scholars or data protection regulators. However, it must be noted that the technical understanding of the meaning of 'competition' is not mature or well understood, unlike in the case of other horizontal aspects such as security and privacy. While when designing application programming interfaces (APIs) privacy aspects may well be considered, it is perhaps not so simple to include into the considerations a possibly even more high-level issue such as 'competition'. At the same time, some design choices may clearly be regarded as anti-competitive – the implications are simply not immediately clear.

While the growing interest of market competition authorities in web technologies (and the actions of certain players) is perhaps a testament to current times, the potential ability to connect technical and standardisation work with regulatory frameworks may conceivably be seen as surprising. This is likely a consequence of the growing importance of technology policy. Notably, the proposal for a Digital Services Act offers flexible options of self-governing frameworks relating to data protection and competition.

REFERENCES

Abramatic J-F and others, 'Technical Architecture Group (TAG) Charter (2001)' <https://www. w3.org/2001/07/19-tag> accessed 1 July 2022.

AMP, 'AMP Governance Structures' (2020) <https://amp.dev/community/gov ernance/> accessed 1 July 2022.

Andersdotter A and Olejnik L, 'Policy Strategies for Value-Based Technology Standards' (2021) 10(3) Internet Policy Review.

Australian Competition and Consumer Commission, 'Digital Advertising Services Inquiry' (2021) <https://www.accc.gov.au/focus-areas/inquiries-ongoing/digi tal-advertising-services-inquiry/interim-report> accessed 1 July 2022.

Backes M and others, 'Obliviad: Provably Secure and Practical Online Behavioral Advertising' (2012) IEEE Symposium on Security and Privacy <https://ieeex plore.ieee.org/document/6234417> accessed 1 July 2022.

Baron J and Pohlmann T, 'Who Cooperates in Standards Consortia— Rivals or Complementors?' (2013) 9(4) Journal of Competition Law and Economics.

Baron J and others, 'Making the Rules: The Governance of Standard Development Organizations and Their Policies on Intellectual Property Rights' (2019) 29655 JRC Science for Policy Report, EUR.

Bennet Cyphers, 'Don't Play in Google's Privacy Sandbox' (2019) <https://www. eff.org/deeplinks/2019/08/dont-play-googles-privacy-sandbox-1> accessed 1 July 2022.

Bradner S, 'The Internet Standards Process – Revision 3' (1996) <https://tools.ietf. org/html/bcp9> accessed 1 July 2022.

Brill J, 'The Intersection of Consumer Protection and Competition in the New World of Privacy' (2011) 7(1) Competition Policy International.

Carpenter B, 'Charter of the Internet Architecture Board' (2000) <https:// www. iab.org/about/charter/> accessed 1 July 2022.

Chhotray V and Stoker G, *Governance Theory and Practice: A Cross-Disciplinary Approach* (Palgrave Macmillan 2008).

D'Cunha C, 'Best of Frenemies? Reflections on Privacy and Competition Four Years after the EDPS Preliminary Opinion' (2018) 8(3) International Data Privacy Law.

Dafoe A, 'AI Governance: A Research Agenda' [2018] Governance of AI Program, Future of Humanity Institute, University of Oxford, Oxford, UK.

DeNardis L, 'The Emerging Field of Internet Governance' [2010] Yale Information Society Project Working Paper Series.

'Directive (EU) 2016/2102 of the European Parliament and of the Council of 26 October 2016 on the accessibility of the websites and mobile applications of public sector bodies' (2016-10-26) L 327 OJ.

District Court, EDTexas, 'Anti-Competition Complaints against Google's Plan to Replace Third-Party Cookies with Privacy Sandbox'.

Estrada-Jiménez J and others, 'Online Advertising: Analysis of Privacy Threats and Protection Approaches' (2017) 100 Computer Communications.

Etemad E and Rivoal F, 'W3C Process Document' (2020) <https://www.w3.org/2020/Process-20200915/> accessed 1 July 2022.

European Commission, 'Proposal for a Regulation of the European Parliament and of the Council on a Single Market For Digital Services (Digital Services Act) and Amending Directive 2000/31/EC COM/2020/825 final' [2020] <https://eur-lex.europa.eu/legal-content/en/TXT/?uri=COM:2020:825:FIN> accessed 1 July 2022.

European Commission, 'Antitrust: Commission opens Investigation into Possible Anticompetitive Conduct by Google in the Online Advertising Technology Sector' (2021) <https://ec.europa.cu/commission/presscorner/detail/en/ip_21_3143> accessed 1 July 2022.

Facebook AB, 'Facebook's Oversight Board's Charter' (2020) <https://oversight board. com/governance/> accessed 1 July 2022.

Goel V, 'An Updated Timeline for Privacy Sandbox Milestones' (2021) <https://blog.google/products/chrome/updated-timeline-privacy-sandbox-milestones/> accessed 1 July 2022.

Greenleaf G, 'Global Data Privacy Laws 2019: 132 National Laws & Many Bills' (2019) 157 Privacy Laws & Business International Report <https://ssrn.com/abstract=3381593> accessed 1 July 2022.

Guha S, Cheng B and Francis P, 'Privad: Practical Privacy in Online Advertising' (2011) USENIX Conference on Networked Systems Design and Implementation.

Guy A, 'Early Design Review for the FLoC API #601' (2021) <https://github.com/w3ctag/design-reviews/issues/601%5C#issuecomment-783780556> accessed 1 July 2022.

Hustinx P, 'Privacy and Competitiveness in the Age of Big Data: Preliminary Opinion of the European Data Protection Supervisor' [2014] <https://edps.europa.eu/data-protection/our-work/publications/opinions/privacy-and-compe titiveness-age-big-data_en> accessed 1 July 2022.

Jacobs I, 'Technical Architecture Group (TAG) Charter (2004)' <https://www.w3.org/2004/10/27-tag-charter.html> accessed 1 July 2022.

JS Foundation, 'Technical Advisory Committee (TAC) Charter v1.0' (2016) <https://github.com/JSFoundation/TAC/blob/master/TAC-Charter.md> accessed 1 July 2022.

Kanevskaia O, 'Governance within Standards Development Organizations: WHO Owns the Game?' (2017) ITU Kaleidoscope: Challenges for a Data-Driven Society, IEEE.

'Killed by Google' <https://killedbygoogle.com/> accessed 1 July 2022.

Kleber M, 'First Experiment (FLEDGE)' (2021) <https://github.com/WICG/tur tledove/blob/main/FLEDGE.md> accessed 1 July 2022.

Krishnamurthy B and Wills C, 'Privacy Diffusion on the Web: A Longitudinal Perspective' (2009) Proceedings of the 18th International Conference on World Wide Web.

Kucherawy M, Hinden R and Livingood J, 'IAB, IESG, IETF Trust, and IETF LLC Selection, Confirmation, and Recall Process: Operation of the IETF Nominating and Recall Committees' (2020) <https://tools.ietf.org/html/bcp10> accessed 1 July 2022.

Laperdrix P and others, 'Browser Fingerprinting: A Survey' (2020) 14(2) ACM Transactions on the Web (TWEB).

Lomas N, 'Digital Marketing Firms File UK Competition Complaint against Google's Privacy Sandbox' (2020) <https://techcrunch.com/2020/11/23/digital-marketing-firms-file-uk-competition-complaint-against-googles-privacy-sandbox/> accessed 1 July 2022.

Mayer JR and Mitchell JC, 'Third-Party Web Tracking: Policy and Technology' (2012) <https://jonathanmayer.org/publications/trackingsurvey12.pdf> accessed 1 July 2022.

Mozilla Firefox, 'Enhanced Tracking Protection in Firefox for Desktop' (2019) <https://support.mozilla.org/en-US/kb/enhanced-tracking-protection-firefox-desktop> accessed 1 July 2022.

Nissenbaum H, 'Privacy as Contextual Integrity' (2004) 79 Washington Law Review.

Nissenbaum H, *Privacy in Context* (Stanford University Press 2020).

Olejnik L, 'Are We Reaching Privacy Preserving Digital Advertising? Historical View' (2020) <https://blog.lukaszolejnik.com/are-we-reaching-privacy-preserving-digital-advertising-historical-view/> accessed 1 July 2022.

Pagallo U, Casanovas P and Madelin R, 'The Middle-Out Approach: Assessing Models of Legal Governance in Data Protection, Artificial Intelligence, and the Web of Data' (2019) 7(1) The Theory and Practice of Legislation <https://doi.org/10.1080/20508840.2019.1664543> accessed 1 July 2022.

Pasquale F, 'Privacy, Antitrust, and Power' (2012) 20 George Mason Law Review.

'Regulation 1025/2012 of 25 October 2012 on European standardisation (2012), Official Journal of the European Union L 316/12' (2012-10-25) L 316/12 OJ.

Regulation GDP, 'Regulation EU 2016/679 of the European Parliament and of the Council of 27 April 2016' [2016] Official Journal of the European Union <https://eur-lex.europa.eu/eli/reg/2016/679/oj> accessed 1 July 2022.

Roesner F, Kohno T and Wetherall D, 'Detecting and Defending against Third-Party Tracking on the Web' (2012) Presented as part of the 9th USENIX Symposium on Networked Systems Design and Implementation (NSDI 12).

Savage JE and McConnell BW, 'Exploring Multi-Stakeholder Internet Governance' (2015) <https://www.eastwest.ngo/sites/default/files/Exploring%20Multi-Stakeholder%20Internet%20Governance_0.pdf> accessed 1 July 2022.

Schuh J, 'Building a More Private Web' (2019) <https://www.blog.google/products/chrome/building-a-more-private-web> accessed 1 July 2022.

Schuh J and Vale M, 'Progress Update on the Privacy Sandbox Initiative' (2021) <https://developer.chrome.com/blog/privacy-sandbox-update-2021-jan/> accessed 1 July 2022.

Seltzer W, 'Antitrust and Competition Guidance' (2017) <https://www.w3.org/Consortium/Legal/2017/antitrust-guidance> accessed 1 July 2022.

The OpenJS Foundation, 'The OpenJS Foundation Cross Project Council' (2020) <https://github.com/openjs-foundation/cross-project-council/> accessed 1 July 2022.

Thomson M, 'Privacy Preserving Attribution for Advertising' (2022) <https://blog.mozilla.org/en/mozilla/privacy-preserving-attribution-for-advertising/> accessed 1 July 2022.

Timmers P, 'There Will Be No Global 6G unless We Resolve Sovereignty Concerns in 5G Governance' (2020) 3(1) Nature Electronics.

Toubiana V and others, 'Adnostic: Privacy Preserving Targeted Advertising' (2010) Proceedings of the 2010 Network and Distributed System Security Symposium.

Tran M-D, Acs G and Castelluccia C, 'Retargeting without Tracking' [2014] arXiv preprint arXiv:1404.4533.

TURTLEDOVE (2022) <https://github.com/WICG/turtledove>.

Ubl M, 'An Open Governance Model for the AMP Project' (2018) <https://blog. amp.dev/2018/09/18/governance/> accessed 1 July 2022.

UK Competition and Markets Authority, 'CMA to Have Key Oversight Role over Google's Planned Removal of Third-Party Cookies (2021) <https://www.gov. uk/government/news/cma-to-have-key-oversight-role-over-google-s-planned-re moval-of-third-party-cookies> accessed 1 July 2022.

UK Competition and Markets Authority, 'Investigation into Google's "Privacy Sandbox" Browser Changes (2021) <https://www.gov.uk/cma-cases/investiga tion-into-googles-privacy-sandbox-browser-changes> accessed 1 July 2022.

UK Competition and Markets Authority, 'Notice of Intention to Accept Commitments Offered by Google in relation to its Privacy Sandbox Proposals', case number 50972 (2021) <https://assets.publishing.service.gov. uk/media/60c21e54d3bf7f4bcc0652cd/Notice_of_intention_to_accept_binding_ commitments_offered_by_Google_publication.pdf> accessed 1 July 2022.

UK Competition and Markets Authority, 'CMA to Keep "Close Eye" on Google as it Secures Final Privacy Sandbox Commitments' (2022) <https://www.gov. uk/government/news/cma-to-keep-close-eye-on-google-as-it-secures-final-priva cy-sandbox-commitments> accessed 1 July 2022.

W3C, 'How to Organize an Advisory Board or TAG Election' (2002) <https:// www.w3.org/2002/10/election-howto> accessed 1 July 2022.

Wilander J, 'Intelligent Tracking Prevention (2017)' <https://webkit.org/blog/7675/ intelligent-tracking-prevention/> accessed 1 July 2022.

11. Experiments with facial recognition technologies in public spaces: in search of an EU governance framework[*]
Catherine Jasserand

1. INTRODUCTION

The use of facial recognition technologies (FRTs) to monitor individuals in public spaces has become an issue of concern in many countries worldwide, including in democratic countries.[1] The widespread use of these technologies to monitor publicly accessible areas (including sports stadiums, event areas, shopping centres and train stations) can significantly affect the freedoms and rights of individuals (including their right to privacy, freedom of expression, freedom of opinion and freedom of assembly).[2] In 2020, EDRi (European Digital Rights), a civil rights organisation, conducted a survey that revealed at least 15 European countries had already used or experimented with FRTs in public spaces without much public debate.[3] Yet, these technologies capture the distinctive facial characteristics of individuals to identify them at a distance and without their cooperation or knowledge.

This chapter builds on the experiments carried out by public authorities (mainly police authorities and municipalities) in France and in the United Kingdom (UK). These two countries constitute prime examples

[*] This project has received funding from the European Union's Horizon 2020 research and innovation programme under the Marie Skłodowska-Curie grant agreement No. 895978 (DATAFACE).
[1] Iman Ghosh, 'Mapped: The State of Facial Recognition Around the World' (Visual Capitalist, 22 May 2020) <https://www.visualcapitalist.com/facial-recogni tion-world-map/> accessed 1 July 2022.
[2] E.g. Surveillance Camera Commissioner, 'Facing the Camera, Good Practice and Guidance for the Police Use of Overt Surveillance Camera Systems Incorporating Facial Recognition Technology to Locate Persons on a Watchlist, in Public Places in England and Wales' (2020) 29–30.
[3] European Digital Rights (EDRi), 'Ban Biometric Mass Surveillance: A Set of Fundamental Rights Demands for the European Commission and EU Member States' (13 May 2020) <https://edri.org/wp-content/uploads/2020/05/Paper-Ban-Biometric-Mass-Surveillance.pdf> accessed 1 July 2022.

due to the high number of trials carried out by the police (UK) and the active role of the data protection authorities on these topics (France and UK). Although the UK is not part of the EU anymore, the experiments were conducted under the EU data protection rules and led to a landmark case on the legality of the use of FRTs by police forces (in South Wales). Besides, the Information Commissioner's Office (ICO) has published influential guidance on facial recognition, which is still relevant for interpreting the EU data protection rules. Finally, the chapter draws some comparisons with experiments conducted in the Netherlands in the context of 'living labs', which are dedicated environments involving the public and private sectors. Experimentations with facial recognition technologies were envisaged in the living lab around the Johan Cruijff ArenA, a large-scale facility used for football games and public events.[4] The chapter discusses the experiments in this specific environment.

Although the analysis in this chapter focuses on these three countries, insights from other jurisdictions are brought in as appropriate. The existence (or inexistence) of an adequate legal framework for testing and deploying facial recognition technologies in public spaces is a crucial issue. The EU data protection frameworks (the General Data Protection Regulation (GDPR) and the Law Enforcement Directive (LED)) regulate the processing of biometric data. Yet, whether these rules are sufficient to regulate experiments with biometric technologies, including pilot testing combining policing operations, is uncertain. In addition to the data protection frameworks, this chapter also mentions the proposal of the European Commission to regulate the development, use and placing on the internal market of Artificial Intelligence systems (Draft AI Act). A part of the proposal focuses on biometric systems. These include 'remote biometric identification systems', for which the European Commission proposed to prohibit law enforcement authorities from using these technologies in real-time and publicly accessible spaces.[5] Broad exceptions to this interdiction are also proposed.[6] Although the term 'facial recognition system' is not mentioned in the proposal, these systems are the ones that

---

[4]   'Digitale Perimeter' <https://www.amsterdam.nl/innovatie/digitalisering-tec hnologie/digitale-perimeter/> accessed 1 July 2022.

[5]   European Commission, 'Proposal for a Regulation of the European Parliament and of the Council Laying Down Harmonised Rules on Artificial Intelligence (Artificial Intelligence Act) and Amending Certain Union Legislative Acts' COM (2021) 206 final [Draft AI Act].

[6]   Art 5.1 (d)(i)–(iii) of the Draft AI Act.

the Commission initially wanted to regulate.[7] By choosing a more generic term, the Commission does not limit the application of the rules to FRTs. At the time of writing, the negotiations of the proposal are ongoing. Therefore, it remains to be seen what the rules will be once the EU institutions have agreed on the final text of the regulation.

Finally, the chapter focuses on *public* spaces, understood as areas 'publicly owned or of public use, accessible and enjoyable by all for free.'[8] For the purpose of this chapter, the term also includes *publicly accessible areas*, which might be privately owned but are accessible to everyone for social interactions or having a public interest (e.g., sports and concert arenas, shopping centres, public transport).[9] However, strictly speaking, the two notions are different.[10]

After this introduction, the remainder of the chapter is structured as follows. Section 2 explains the functioning and use of facial recognition technologies. Section 3 describes the experiments conducted by public authorities in the three countries that are featured most prominently in this chapter. Building on these examples, section 4 discusses the findings of the experiments and the regulatory frameworks under which the experiments were carried out. Finally, section 5 discusses whether a specific framework to experiment with biometric technologies such as facial recognition in public spaces is needed. Without replacing the public debate on

---

[7]   See European Commission, leaked draft White Paper entitled 'Structure for the White Paper on Artificial Intelligence – a European Approach', 14–15, Euractiv <https://www.euractiv.com/wp-content/uploads/sites/2/2020/01/AI-white-paper-E URACTIV.pdf> accessed 1 July 2022; and European Commission, 'White Paper – on Artificial Intelligence – A European Approach to Excellence and Trust', 19 February 2020, COM(2020) 65 final, 21–22.

[8]   As defined in UN Habitat, 'Global Public Space Toolkit: From Global Principles to Local Policies and Practice' (*United Nations*, 2015) 127.

[9]   The Draft AI Act defines 'publicly accessible space' as 'any physical place accessible to the public, regardless of whether certain conditions for access may apply' (Art. 3(39) Draft AI Act).

[10]   See literature on the definition(s) of public space, e.g. Daniel Moeckli, *Exclusion from Public Space: A Comparative Constitutional Analysis* (Cambridge University Press 2016); Jeremy Németh and Stephan Schmid, 'Publicly Accessible Space and Quality of Life: A Tool for Measuring the Openness of Urban Spaces' in Megha Budruk and Ronda Philipps (eds), *Quality-of-Life Community Indicators for Parks, Recreation and Tourism Management* (Springer 2011); and the distinction made between 'public space' and 'public place' in Bert-Jaap Koops and Maša Galič, 'Conceptualising Space and Place: Lessons from Geography for the Debate on Privacy in Public' in Tjerk Timan, Bryce Newell and Bert-Jaap Koops (eds), *Privacy in Public Space: Conceptual and Regulatory Challenges* (Edward Elgar Publishing 2017).

whether FRTs should be trialled in public spaces (including for policing and public security purposes), this last section presents some arguments and tools to reflect on an experimental approach to test the technologies. These tools include risk-assessment mechanisms such as Data Protection Impact Assessments (DPIAs), experimental legislation and regulatory sandboxes (introduced in the proposal for the Artificial Intelligence Act).

2.   BACKGROUND

Traditional CCTV (Closed-Circuit Television) cameras have been monitoring public and private spaces for a long time. CCTV is part of daily life in the UK, with more than 5 million surveillance cameras deployed to monitor public areas and business and domestic properties.[11] The history of CCTV in the UK dates back to the 1950s, when the police used the first surveillance cameras during the Queen's coronation.[12] By 1961, the first permanent CCTV system was installed at the London Train Station.[13] In 2018, the UK was considered the country with 'the most CCTV cameras per head per country in the world',[14] a figure since surpassed in China.[15] While the use of CCTVs in Asia and other regions of the world has gained increasing attention,[16] the UK is far from being the only European country to monitor public spaces with CCTVs.

---

[11]   As reported in November 2020, CCTV.co.uk, 'Number of CCTV Cameras in the UK reaches 5.2 million' (November 2020) <https://www.cctv.co.uk/number-of-cctv-cameras-in-the-uk-reaches-5-2-million/> accessed 1 July 2022.

[12]   E.g. Pete Fussey, 'Beyond Liberty, Beyond Security: The Politics of Public Surveillance' (2008) 3(1) British Politics.

[13]   BBC, 'How We Are Being Watched' (3 November 2006); Kristie Ball and others, 'A Report on the Surveillance Society: For the Information Commissioner by the Surveillance Studies Network' (2006) 19 <https://www.personuvernd.is/media/frettir/surveillance_society_full_report_final.pdf> accessed 1 July 2022; referring as well to Chris Williams, 'Police Surveillance and the Emergence of CCTV in the 1960s' (2003) 5(3) Crime Prevention and Community Safety.

[14]   Jess Young, 'A History of CCTV Surveillance in Britain' (*QSwns*, 22 January 2018) <https://stories.swns.com/news/history-cctv-surveillance-britain-93449/> accessed 1 July 2022; Peter Fussey and Daragh Murray, 'Policing Uses of Live Facial Recognition in the United Kingdom' in Amba Kak (ed.), *Regulating Biometrics: Global Approaches and Urgent Questions*, AI Now Institute, September 2020.

[15]   Paul Bischoff, 'Surveillance Camera Statistics: Which Cities Have the Most CCTV Cameras?' (*Comparitech*, 17 May 2021) <https://www.comparitech.com/vpn-privacy/the-worlds-most-surveilled-cities/> accessed 1 July 2022.

[16]   Ghosh (n 1).

The use of CCTVs in public spaces affects a broad range of fundamental rights and freedoms, including the right to privacy.[17] The way these technologies are used begs the question of how they are regulated by international organisations, such as the European Union (EU). In several EU Member States, the use and deployment of surveillance cameras by public authorities are regulated.[18] But, while surveillance cameras film people in a given area and record images, cameras equipped with facial recognition technology allow the identification of individuals thanks to advanced video analytics systems. The systems capture faces to transform them into biometric data for comparison purposes. If these operations are performed in real-time and on a mass scale,[19] they can lead to mass surveillance.[20]

According to the UK's former Biometrics Commissioner, the real-time identification of individuals is made possible thanks to the combination of 'three technologies – biometric matching, artificial intelligence and big data analytics [that] are reinforcing each other and producing technical improvements very rapidly.'[21] Diverse applications of facial recognition exist, but they do not impact fundamental rights in the same way.[22] For instance, unlocking a device or controlling access to premises with facial

---

[17]   E.g. EDPB, 'Guidelines 3/2019 on Processing of Personal Data through Video Devices' Version 2.0 (adopted on 29 January 2020); European Court of Human Rights' case law on video surveillance, Press Unit, Fact Sheet on New Technologies <https://www.echr.coe.int/Documents/FS_New_technologies_ENG.pdf> accessed 1 July 2022.

[18]   Through specific legislation, such as Article L.251-2 of the French Code of Domestic Security (Code de la Sécurité Intérieure) setting up the conditions under which public authorities can transfer and record images in public areas or Codes of Practice, such as the UK Home Office's Surveillance Camera Code of Practice.

[19]   E.g. Facing the Camera (n 2) 15; CNIL, 'Facial Recognition: For a Debate Living Up to the Challenges' (2019) 3 <https://www.cnil.fr/sites/default/files/atoms/files/facial-recognition.pdf> accessed 1 July 2022; EDPB's Response to Sophie in't Veld, MEP, regarding the use of Automatic Image Recognition Systems on migrants in Italy (10 August 2021) 2 <https://edpb.europa.eu/system/files/2021-08/edpb_letter_out_2021_00130_mepveld_facialrecognition_publica tion.pdf> accessed 1 July 2022.

[20]   As denounced by several civil rights organisations, see the civil society initiative 'Reclaim Your Face' <https://reclaimyourface.eu> accessed 1 July 2022.

[21]   Biometrics Commissioner, 'Automated Facial Recognition: Biometrics Commissioner Response to Court Judgment on South Wales Police's Use of Automated Facial Recognition Technology' (10 September 2019) <https://www.gov.uk/government/news/automated-facial-recognition> accessed 1 July 2022.

[22]   ICO, 'Blog: Information Commissioner's Opinion Addresses Privacy Concerns on the Use of Live Facial Recognition Technology in Public Places' (*ICO*, 18 June 2021) <https://ico.org.uk/about-the-ico/media-centre/information-com

recognition tools has a lesser impact than monitoring public spaces with the same technology. As observed by the UK Information Commissioner, 'when the technology and its algorithms are used to scan people's faces in real-time and in more public contexts, the risks to people's privacy increase.'[23] This chapter focuses on this specific use of facial recognition, which is affecting the fundamental rights of individuals to a greater degree.

A facial recognition system measures the similarity between two faces to determine the probability that they belong to the same individual. To compare the data, the technology captures a facial image and enhances the distinctive biometric characteristics that will be used for recognition purposes. The system captures, for instance, the geometry of a face (i.e., the distance between the different salient points: between the eyes, the chin and the mouth). It then transforms these facial features into a mathematical representation to compare them with other captured data.[24] This comparison produces a statistical score of a match between the extracted features of a given face and other data presented to the system. The different technical stages run against various technical challenges: from the image format (2D, 3D, live video feeds or still images) to methods used to detect a face, extract and convert the characteristics into machine-understandable data.[25] Besides, researchers have recently discovered that facial recognition systems were prone to gender and ethnicity biases due to their imbalanced training datasets,[26] leading to a high risk of misidentification for groups of people and discrimination.[27]

Finally, no identification is possible without an existing database (such as a criminal watchlist) to compare the facial features. A live facial recognition system needs, therefore, to be coupled with one or several databases.

---

missioner-s-opinion-addresses-privacy-concerns-on-the-use-of-live-facial-recogn ition-technology-in-public-places/> accessed 1 July 2022.

[23]　ibid.

[24]　Alex Martinez, 'Face Recognition, Overview' in *Encyclopedia of Biometrics* (Springer 2009).

[25]　For further details on facial recognition systems, see Anil K Jain and others, *Introduction to Biometrics* (Springer 2011) 109–111.

[26]　These can also replicate societal biases.

[27]　Joy Buolamwini and Timnit Gebru, 'Gender Shades: Intersectional Accuracy Disparities in Commercial Gender Classification' (2018) 81 Proceedings of Machine Learning Research.

3.   EXPERIMENTS

3.1   United Kingdom

In September 2019, the Home Office acknowledged the existence of the trials carried out by the London Metropolitan Police (the MET) and South Wales Police (SWP).[28] However, according to Big Brother Watch, a civil rights organisation, no fewer than ten police forces have tested the technologies in public spaces or publicly accessible areas.[29] The Leicestershire police were the first to trial the technology at a rock festival in 2015, where they checked the participants against a European criminal database.[30] The MET and SWP are the police authorities that most trialled live FRTs in public spaces.[31] For this reason, the section focuses on these two police forces. Besides, the legality of SWP's trials was challenged before the domestic Courts, resulting in a landmark case for police use of facial recognition in public spaces.[32]

3.1.1   London Metropolitan Police
Between 2016 and 2019, the MET deployed FRTs on ten occasions.[33] The first trial happened during the Notting Hill Carnival, where the police used

---

[28]   Home Office, 'Fact Sheet on Live Facial Recognition Used by Police' (2019) <https://homeofficemedia.blog.gov.uk/2019/09/04/fact-sheet-on-live-facial-recogn ition-used-by-police/> accessed 1 July 2022.

[29]   The London Metropolitan Police, the South Wales Police, the South Yorkshire Police, the police of Manchester, Leicestershire, Birmingham, Liverpool, Waltham Forest, Bradford, and Brighton; See Big Brother Watch, 'Map: UK Facial Recognition in Detail' <https://bigbrotherwatch.org.uk/campaigns/stop-facial-recognition/#facial-recognition-uk> accessed 1 July 2022.

[30]   Alexander Martin, 'Cops Turn Download Festival into an Orwellian Spy Paradise' (*The Register*, 11 June 2015) <https://www.theregister.com/2015/06/11/download_festival_big_brother_playground_leicestershire_police?page=1> accessed 1 July 2022.

[31]   Most of the literature, opinions, reports, policy documents relate to their trials.

[32]   R(Bridges) v the Chief Constable of South Wales Police [2019] EWHC 2341 (Admin) [High Court's decision]; and R(on the application of Edward Bridges) v the Chief Constable of South Wales Police, Appeal [2020] EWCA Civ 1058 [Court of Appeal's decision].

[33]   See Big Brother Watch, Map (n 29); number confirmed by the MET in their report, National Physical Laboratory and Metropolitan Police, 'Metropolitan Police Service Live Facial Recognition Trials' (February 2020) 3.

the technology in 2016 and 2017.[34] According to Big Brother Watch,[35] the system was highly inaccurate.[36] As revealed by the MET much after their first trials,[37] they had constituted ad-hoc watchlists of 'wanted' persons for each trial. Each time an individual passed by the cameras, their image was compared with photos stored in the watchlist. However, who was a 'wanted' individual was not clear or consistent across the trials.[38] For instance, for the deployment during Remembrance Day, the watchlist included individuals who had some mental issues but were neither prohibited from attending the event nor 'wanted' by the police.[39] Once the trials were over, the police decided to roll out live FRTs in public spaces,[40] which raised much concern to civil rights organisations.[41]

3.1.2 South Wales Police

Funded by the Home Office,[42] SWP trialled seventy times FRTs at public events (including sports, concerts, entertainment events) and on public

---

[34] Vikram Dodd, 'Met Police to Use Facial Recognition Software at Notting Hill Carnival' (*The Guardian*, 5 August 2017) <https://www.theguardian.com/uk-news/2017/aug/05/met-police-facial-recognition-software-notting-hill-carnival> accessed 1 July 2022.

[35] Big Brother Watch, 'Face Off: The Lawless Growth of Facial Recognition in UK Policing' (*Big Brother Watch*, May 2018).

[36] Vikram Dodd, 'UK Police Use of Facial Recognition Technology a Failure, Says Report' (*The Guardian*, 15 May 2018) <https://www.theguardian.com/uk-news/2018/may/15/uk-police-use-of-facial-recognition-technology-failure> accessed 1 July 2022.

[37] See Report (n.33) 22 et seqs.

[38] See Fussey's and Murray's analysis on the criterion of being 'wanted' in Pete Fussey and Daragh Murray, 'Independent Report on the London Metropolitan Police Service's Trial of Live Facial Recognition Technology' (2019) 10 <https://repository.essex.ac.uk/24946/1/London-Met-Police-Trial-of-Facial-Recognition-Tech-Report-2.pdf> accessed 1 July 2022.

[39] Mark Townsend, 'Police to Use Facial Recognition Cameras at Cenotaph Service' (*The Guardian*, 12 November 2017) <https://www.theguardian.com/technology/2017/nov/12/metropolitan-police-to-use-facial-recognition-technology-remembrance-sunday-cenotaph> accessed 1 July 2022.

[40] Danyal Hussain, 'Met Police Make First Arrest Using Facial Recognition Technology as They Hold Woman, 35, Over Alleged Serious Assault on Emergency Service Worker' (*Daily Mail Online*, 28 February 2020) <https://www.dailymail.co.uk/news/article-8055001/Met-Police-make-arrest-using-facial-recognition-technology.html> accessed 1 July 2022.

[41] Jessie Mathewson, 'MET Facial Recognition to Face Legal Challenge' (*City Matters*, 30 January 2020) <https://www.citymatters.london/met-facial-recognition-face-legal-challenge/> accessed 1 July 2022.

[42] SWP received more than £1.9m as reported by Bethan Davies and others, *An Evaluation of South Wales Police's Use of Automated Facial Recognition* (Universities' Police Science Institute 2018) 9.

streets.[43] The technology was used for the first time, in May 2017, in an uncontrolled environment during the Final Week of the UEFA Champions League football event in Cardiff. According to Big Brother Watch, thousands of people were wrongly identified.[44] The system used, called 'AFR Locate', scanned faces of the public in real-time to find matches against a pre-determined watchlist.[45] Watchlists were constituted for each deployment. Like the watchlists established by the MET, the ones used by SWP raised concerns over the criteria for inclusion. For instance, the lists contained faces of individuals of 'possible interest to the police' and 'individuals whose presence at a particular event causes particular concern.'[46] According to Davies et al., who assessed the FRT deployments between May 2017 and March 2018, SWP used the technology as an '*assisting*' rather than an automated tool.[47] The system flagged matching suggestions, which were reviewed by a human operator. Arguably, the fact that a human operator was involved in the decision-making process did not lift the fundamental rights issues resulting from the use of live FRTs in the first place.[48] According to the SWP's website,[49] the police forces interrupted their trials with live FRTs in January 2020 but resumed them in March 2022 after the College of Policing published its guidance on the use of FRTs by the police.[50]

---

[43]　At <https://afr.south-wales.police.uk/wp-content/uploads/2021/04/All-Dep loyments.pdf> accessed 1 July 2022.

[44]　Big Brother Watch (n 29); Press Association, 'Welsh Police Wrongly Identify Thousands as Potential Criminals' (*The Guardian*, 5 May 2018) <https://www.theguardian.com/uk-news/2018/may/05/welsh-police-wrongly-identify-thou sands-as-potential-criminals> accessed 1 July 2022; contested by Davies and others (n 42) 39–41.

[45]　Another functionality of the system, which compares images of unknown individuals to police custody images (AFR Identify) was not used; see Davies and others (n 42) 6.

[46]　R(Bridges) (2020) (n 32) [13].

[47]　Davies and others (n 42); see also Pete Fussey and others, '"Assisted" Facial Recognition and the Reinvention of Suspicion and Discretion in Digital Policing' (2021) 61(2) The British Journal of Criminology.

[48]　Equality and Human Rights Commission, 'Facial Recognition Technology and Predictive Policing Algorithms Out-Pacing the Law' (12 March 2020) <https://www.equalityhumanrights.com/en/our-work/news/facial-recognition-technology-and-predictive-policing-algorithms-out-pacing-law> accessed 1 July 2022; Robert Booth, 'Halt Public Use of Facial Recognition Tech, says Equality Watchdog' (*The Guardian*, 12 March 2020) <https://www.theguardian.com/uk-news/2020/mar/12/halt-public-use-of-facial-recognition-tech-says-equality-watchdog> accessed 1 July 2022.

[49]　See n 43.

[50]　SWP, 'Live Facial Recognition Technology Results' (2022) <https://www.south-wales.police.uk/news/south-wales/news/2022/maw-mar/results-of-live-fa

The civil rights organisations have played an essential role in disclosing the police forces' trials of live FRTs in public spaces.[51] Even if the police forces advertised the FRT deployments on social media and placed signs on location, it was not sufficient for the public to become aware of the operations and the processing of their biometric data when they passed in front of the FRT cameras.[52]

3.2   France

In France, only one official experiment was conducted by the local police and the municipality of Nice during the Nice Carnival in 2019. In the report written after the experiment, the municipality justified the use of FRTs through the necessity to secure public spaces, describing the technologies as one of the emerging tools to prevent offences against persons or property and terrorist attacks.[53] With these objectives in mind, the municipality tested FRTs on volunteers in a dedicated area of the Carnival for three days. Six CCTV cameras equipped with facial recognition technology were used at one of the entrance areas of the event. An ad-hoc watchlist had been constituted for the event, composed of pictures provided by the volunteers before the event or taken on-site. Several pre-determined scenarios were tested on 50 participants, who had consented to the experiment. Faces of passers-by were also scanned to be discarded. More than seven hundred passers-by agreed to have their faces processed by the cameras. They indicated their consent by wearing a bracelet of colour. They also received information about the experiment.[54] As explained in the next section, the experiment did not have to be formally authorised by the data protection authority, which was only informed a few weeks before it started. The experiment was also limited to volunteer participation, as there is currently no specific legal framework in France that would allow the use and deployment of FRTs in public spaces. The legal conditions under which the experiment was conducted are further detailed in the next sections of this chapter.

---

cial-recognition-technology-on-190322/> accessed 1 July 2022; BBC News, 'Facial Recognition Plan "Hammer Blow to Privacy" Claim' (22 March 2022) <https://www.bbc.com/news/uk-wales-60831816> accessed 1 July 2022.

[51]   E.g. Big Brother Watch, Liberty, whose concerns were further echoed by media reporting.

[52]   R(Bridges) (2019) (n 32) [39]–[40], and R(Bridges) (2020) (n 32) [19]–[20].

[53]   Ville de Nice, 'Rapport: Expérimentation Reconnaissance Faciale' (20 June 2019) 11 <https://data.technopolice.fr/api/files/1568560839337an2i6yk04kp.pdf> accessed 1 July 2022.

[54]   ibid.

Besides this official experiment, Nice and other municipalities tried to test other biometric technologies, but the French data protection authority halted the experiments.[55] For instance, during the first lockdown related to the COVID-19 pandemic, the municipality of Cannes used face-mask recognition software to check whether individuals were wearing mouth caps. The Paris Metro started a similar experiment until the CNIL stopped it.[56] In Saint-Etienne also, the municipality planned to deploy sound sensors coupled with CCTV cameras to detect abnormal noises. The CNIL warned against the project, which was abandoned.[57] Although they relied on biometric technologies, the experiments did not intend to process biometric data for biometric recognition purposes. The experiments were meant to check the compliance with the coronavirus measures[58] or the safety of the streets by monitoring street noises.[59] Finally, it is worth mentioning that the regional public authorities in the South of France authorised two high schools to trial FRTs on their premises for access control and security purposes.[60] Before the pilots were deployed, the Administrative Court of Marseille stopped them by invalidating the authorisation given by the regional authorities.[61]

---

[55] Violaine III, 'Un logiciel pour décoder les émotions des usagers du tramway de Nice' (*FranceBleu.fr*, 4 January 2019) <https://www.francebleu.fr/infos/societe/un-logiciel-pour-decoder-les-emotions-des-usagers-du-tramway-de-nice-1546621455> accessed 1 July 2022.

[56] But, in March 2021, the Government adopted a decree allowing it, see Décret 2021–269 [Decree no. 2021–269 of 10 March 2021 concerning the use of smart surveillance cameras to measure the mouth cap use in transports] <https://www.legifrance.gouv.fr/jorf/id/JORFTEXT000043235679> accessed 1 July 2022.

[57] France Bleu Saint-Etienne, 'Capteurs sonores à Saint-Etienne: la mise en garde de la CNIL' (France Bleu, 29 October 2019) <https://www.francebleu.fr/infos/societe/capteurs-sonores-a-saint-etienne-la-mise-en-garde-de-la-cnil-1572343225> accessed 1 July 2022; extracts of the letter sent by the CNIL to the Municipality can be found on Télérama <https://www.telerama.fr/medias/la-cnil-tire-les-oreilles-intelligentes-de-saint-etienne,n6492439.php> accessed 1 July 2022.

[58] CNIL, 'La CNIL publie son avis sur le décret relatif à l'utilisation de la vidéo intelligente pour mesurer le port du masque dans les transports' (12 March 2021) <https://www.cnil.fr/fr/avis-sur-le-decret-video-intelligente-port-du-masque> accessed 1 July 2022.

[59] ibid.

[60] Provence-Alpes-Côte d'Azur Région, Decision 18–893 of 14 December 2018, <https://www.laquadrature.net/wp-content/uploads/sites/8/2019/02/4.-D%C3%A9lib%C3%A9ration-attaqu%C3%A9e.pdf> accessed 1 July 2022.

[61] TA Marseille (Administrative Court in Marseille), 27 February 2020, no. 1901249 <http://marseille.tribunal-administratif.fr/content/download/178764/1756210/version/1/file/1901249.pdf> accessed 1 July 2022.

3.3　The Netherlands

In the Netherlands, numerous experiments with emerging technologies are conducted in the context of 'living labs' – that is, under real-life settings with real users.[62] These laboratories are presented as experimental co-initiatives involving users and citizens in the process. But the citizens are rarely placed at the centre of these experiments, which involve public and private partnerships (including the police).[63] In Eindhoven, Amsterdam or Rotterdam, several of these initiatives have emerged.[64]

One of these living labs, the *Digitale Perimeter*, was set up in 2019 around the Amsterdam football stadium. It results from a collaboration between the municipality of Amsterdam, the football stadium Johan Cruijff ArenA, the national police and TNO, an independent research institute specialised in applied sciences.[65] One of its objectives is to 'collaborate with partners to develop and implement the solutions' to 'increase both fan experience and safety and security within an assigned perimeter.'[66] At the start of the project, the partners had planned several types of experiments, including with facial recognition [*gezichtsherkenning*].[67] The initial description of the experiments is no longer available on the website of the municipality. Still, it can be found in the report written by the Dutch civil rights organisation, Bits of Freedom.[68] TNO also published a report in January 2021 in which it explored the possible use cases of FRTs in the context of the *Digitale Perimeter*.[69] The current description of the project and experiments

---

[62]　Elke den Ouden, Rianne Valkenburg and Steef Blok, 'Exploring the Future of Living Labs' (2016) Research Report <https://www.tue-lighthouse.nl/Images/Livinglabs/20160210%20Exploring%20the%20future%20or%20Living%20Labs%20-%20LR%20ebook.pdf> accessed 1 July 2022.

[63]　E.g. Maša Galič, 'Surveillance and Privacy in Smart Cities and Living Labs: Conceptualising Privacy for Public Space' (PhD thesis, Tilburg University 2019) 48–51.

[64]　E.g. <https://living-lab.nl> accessed 1 July 2022.

[65]　'Digitale Perimeter' (n 4).

[66]　ibid.

[67]　Bits of Freedom, 'Op Waarden Geschat, Living Lab Digitale Perimeter' (30 April 2021) <https://www.bitsoffreedom.nl/wp-content/uploads/2021/05/2021-rapport-digitale-perimeter-bof.pdf> accessed 1 July 2022. The initial description of the experiments is no longer available on the website of the project but can be found in the Bits of Freedom's Report; see as well description in English referring to facial recognition <https://amsterdamsmartcity.com/updates/project/digital-perimeter> accessed 1 July 2022.

[68]　ibid.

[69]　TNO's report 'Privacy bescherming bij niet-coöperatieve gezichtsherkenning', Appendix E describing the possible use cases with FRT, 21 January

refers to research on *gelaatsvergelijking*, which could be roughly translated as face comparison, instead of experiments with *gezichtsherkenning*, which means facial recognition in Dutch. The terminology used to describe the experiments does not seem to be meaningless. Instead, it seems to echo the communication made by the Dutch police in the media. The police claimed having never used or tested facial recognition but only facial comparison – that is, they did not link the images with any identity.[70] The nuance of terminology is subtle, but according to technical experts, there is not much difference between facial recognition and face comparison.[71] Face comparison is, in any event, a technical stage of the facial recognition process. The change of wording to describe the experiments also seems to be linked to the investigation made by Bits of Freedom on the experiments conducted in the *Digitale Perimeter*.[72] Besides the terminology used to describe the experiments – which changed over time – what comes out from this investigation is the lack of transparency. Yet the municipality of Amsterdam has set up and pledged to respect a new policy for the use of data, known as the TADA manifest.[73] The manifest comprises six principles: inclusive, control (of individuals over their data), tailored to people, legitimate and monitored, open and transparent (including which data are collected for what purposes), and from and for everyone.[74] As challenged by Bits of Freedom, the municipality of Amsterdam seems to have failed to comply

---

2021 <https://www.tno.nl/nl/newsroom/2021/02/nieuwe-mijlpaal-waarborgen-pri vacy/> accessed 1 July 2022.

[70] In particular, in the context of the criminal database CATCH. See Paula Hooyman, 'Het ware gezicht van gezichtsherkennings-technologie' (*Bits of Freedom*, 30 October 2019) <https://www.bitsoffreedom.nl/wp-content/uploads/2019/11/ het-ware-gezicht-van-gezichtsherkenningstechnologie.pdf> accessed 1 July 2022; Lianne Tijhaar, 'Vroeg of laat moet de politie gezichtsherkenning gaan gebruiken' (*Kennislink*, 6 January 2021) <https://www.nemokennislink.nl/publicaties/vroeg-of-laat-moet-de-politie-gezichtsherkenning-gaan-gebruiken/> accessed 1 July 2022.

[71] Niels Waarlo and Laurens Verhagen, 'De stand van gezichtsherkenning in Nederland' (*De Volkskrant*, 27 March 2020) <https://www.volkskrant.nl/ kijkverder/v/2020/de-stand-van-gezichtsherkenning-in-nederland~v91028/> accessed 1 July 2022.

[72] Bits of Freedom's Report (n 67), see also Rosa Oosterhoff, 'Amsterdam Is Watching You, naar hoe zorgvuldig gebeurt dat?' (*AT5*, 18 February 2021) <https://www.at5.nl/artikelen/207283/amsterdam-is-watching-you-maar-hoe-zor gvuldig-gebeurt-dat> accessed 1 July 2022.

[73] At <https://waag.org/en/article/amsterdam-lays-foundation-new-digital-policy> accessed 1 July 2022.

[74] TADA <https://tada.city/en/home-en/> accessed 1 July 2022.

with these principles with regard to the experiments in the context of the *Digitale Perimeter*.[75] After the publication of the Bits of Freedom's report, the Green Party (GroenLinks) asked the municipality to clarify whether facial recognition had been tested in the *Digitale Perimeter* and to be transparent about the experiments.[76] In the context of the *Digitale Perimeter*, the partners had expressed the wish to test facial recognition at the beginning of the project and ahead of the UEFA EURO 2020. But despite the investigation made, there is no evidence that the technologies were ever tested in that context.

In the Netherlands, facial recognition technologies have, however, been used in a different context, and in particular by a supermarket, for security purposes. In 2019, the media revealed that a supermarket experimented with the technology to scan the faces of its customers so as to compare them with the faces of individuals who were banned from entering the supermarket.[77] After the Dutch Data Protection Authority (DPA) had requested information about the experiment, the supermarket disabled the technology with the wish to reactivate it. In December 2020, the Dutch DPA issued a formal warning against the supermarket specifying that the technology could only be used if people had given their explicit consent (as entering the supermarket does not equal explicit consent) or in case of substantial public interest (which was absent here).[78]

The next section discusses the findings of the experiments, focusing on the scope of the trials, the applicable rules and the oversight of the experiments.

---

[75]   Bits of Freedom, 'Washed in Blue: Living Lab Digital Perimeter in Amsterdam', 19 May 2021 <https://edri.org/our-work/washed-in-blue-living-lab-digital-perimeter-in-amsterdam/> accessed 1 July 2022.

[76]   Gemeente Amsterdam, written question, <https://amsterdam.raadsinformatie.nl/document/10131215/1/180%20sv%20IJmker%20onderzoek%20Digitaleo%20Perimeter> accessed 1 July 2022; at the time of writing, the answer provided by the municipality was not publicly known.

[77]   RTLnieuws, 'Tientallen camera's houden klanten van filiaal Jumbo in de gaten: willen we dit?' (RTLnieuws, 3 December 2019) <https://www.rtlnieuws.nl/nieuws/nederland/artikel/4941596/gezichtsherkenning-biometrie-alphen-jumbo-privacy> accessed 1 July 2022.

[78]   De Autoriteit Persoonsgegevens, 'Formele waarschuwing AP aan supermarkt om gezichtsherkenning' (15 December 2020) <https://autoriteitpersoonsgegevens.nl/nl/nieuws/formele-waarschuwing-ap-aan-supermarkt-om-gezichtsherkenning> accessed 1 July 2022; see also Rules established by the Authority for the use of FRTs in supermarkets (1 May 2020) <https://autoriteitpersoonsgegevens.nl/sites/default/files/atoms/files/brief_regels_voor_gezichtsherkenning_in_supermarkten.pdf> accessed 1 July 2022.

4. EXPERIMENTS' FINDINGS

The experiments conducted in the UK and in France are different. In France, FRT was tested in a controlled environment, i.e. on volunteers whose faces were compared with an ad-hoc watchlist containing their pictures. By contrast, in the UK, the technologies were deployed on the public, and the captured faces matched in real-time against 'criminal' watchlists composed of photographs of 'wanted' individuals. The findings concerning the situation in the Netherlands are limited as there is no established evidence that FRT trials occurred in the context of the living lab around the event arena, even though they were initially envisaged by the partners.

4.1 No Definition of Trials and No Protocol

As stressed in various reports and in the testimony of the UK Biometrics Commissioner,[79] the police forces did not define the trials, explain the purpose of the operations, or communicate on a specific methodology until the trials drew the attention of the regulators and civil rights organisations. For instance, the Biometrics Commissioner challenged the term 'trial' to describe the operations. In his view, 'the conclusion of a trial is a process when you take the decision on a basis of evidence you gathered on whether it is appropriate to go forward.' [80] The police forces had indeed combined technology trials with policing operations.[81] The ICO also expressed concerns about the ambiguous nature of the trials and launched an investigation in 2018.[82] As observed by Fussey and Murray, the police trials were mainly approached from a technical perspective as the focus of the police was on 'the performance of the technology in live settings.'[83]

---

[79] House of Commons Science and Technology Committee, Oral Evidence, 'The Work of the Biometrics Commissioner and the Forensic Science Regulator' HC 1970 (19 March 2019) Q 53 <http://data.parliament.uk/writtenevidence/com mitteeevidence.svc/evidencedocument/science-and-technology-committee/the-wo rk-of-the-biometrics-commissioner-and-the-forensic-science-regulator/oral/98556. html> accessed 1 July 2022; Fussey and Murray (n 38) 7–8.

[80] Oral Evidence (ibid).

[81] Fussey and Murray (n 38) 7.

[82] ICO, 'ICO Investigation into How the Police Use Facial Recognition Technology in Public Places' (31 October 2019) <https://ico.org.uk/media/about-the-ico/documents/2616185/live-frt-law-enforcement-report-20191031.pdf> accessed 1 July 2022.

[83] Fussey and Murray (n 38) 7.

The 'non-technical objectives' (such as the impact of the trials on the public) were not assessed.[84]

In France, the objective of the experiment conducted by the municipality of Nice was limited to testing the technical system, as noted by the CNIL.[85] Based on the information published by the municipality, it seems that the experiment did not follow a strict design-and-evaluation methodology.[86] Yet, the purpose of the experiment was to test the system from a technical perspective. As reported by *Le Monde*,[87] the report clearly lacked the technical details to enable the French data protection authority to properly assess the experiment, the performance of the facial recognition software used during the experiment, and the usefulness of the experiment. The end report only mentioned whether the software could recognise individuals in different settings; it did not provide any performance metrics, such as the percentage of false positives, false negatives or the average time to compare the faces.

4.2   Lack of Specific Legal Frameworks

None of the three countries under review has adopted a specific legal framework for testing or using (live) facial recognition by the public or private sector.[88] The authorities relied on existing data protection rules. As the deployment of FRTs in public spaces, whether on an experimental or operational basis, affects the fundamental rights to privacy and data protection,[89] the chapter now focuses on these rights.

---

[84]   ibid.

[85]   AFP, 'Test de reconnaissance faciale à Nice: Précisions de la CNIL' (*Public Sénat*, 19 February 2019) <https://www.publicsenat.fr/article/politique/test-de-reconnaissance-faciale-a-nice-precisions-de-la-cnil-138122> accessed 1 July 2022.

[86]   Municipality Report (n 53).

[87]   Martin Untersinger, 'Reconnaissance faciale: la CNIL toque sur le bilan de l'expérience niçoise' (*Le Monde*, 29 August 2019) <https://www.lemonde.fr/pixels/article/2019/08/28/reconnaissance-faciale-la-cnil-tique-sur-le-bilan-de-l-exp erience-nicoise_5503769_4408996.html> accessed 1 July 2022.

[88]   But some European countries (e.g., France) have adopted specific rules allowing the police to use post-event facial recognition, Article R.40–26 of the Code of Criminal Procedure allows post-event use of facial recognition to identify individuals already registered in a criminal record police file called TAJ.

[89]   And other fundamental rights and freedoms (non-discrimination, freedom of expression, assembly, opinion, association, and human dignity), as acknowledged in 'Facing the Camera' (n 2) 20, and FRA, 'Facial Recognition Technology: Fundamental Rights Considerations in the Context of Law Enforcement' (2019) 18–32.

4.2.1 Rights to privacy and data protection

Facial recognition technologies deployed in public spaces are highly intrusive,[90] ubiquitous and potentially lead to mass surveillance.[91] Capturing the public's faces affects both the rights to privacy and data protection, as enshrined in the European Convention on Human Rights (Article 8)[92] and the Charter of Fundamental Rights (Articles 7 and 8).[93] Limitations to these rights are possible if they pursue specific (public) interests and are provided by law, besides being necessary and proportionate.[94] Each condition (legality, proportionality, necessity) has been reflected in a test shaped through the case law of the European Courts. Concerning facial recognition, neither the European Court of Human Rights (ECtHR) nor the European Court of Justice (ECJ) had to answer the question of whether experiments with FRTs in public spaces by the police infringe the right to privacy (and data protection) and if so, whether it is justified.

However, the High Court and Court of Appeal in the UK examined these questions in more detail. In a landmark case opposing a civil liberties

---

[90] E.g. EDPB and EDPS, 'Joint Opinion 5/2021 on the proposal for a Regulation of the European Parliament and of the Council laying down harmonised rules on artificial intelligence (Artificial Intelligence Act)' 11.

[91] EDRi (n 3); Big Brother Watch (n 35).

[92] Article 8 ECHR ('the right to respect for private and family life' known as right to privacy) reads as follows: '1. Everyone has the right to respect for his private and family life, his home and his correspondence. 2. There shall be no interference by a public authority with the exercise of this right except such as is in accordance with the law and is necessary in a democratic society in the interests of national security, public safety or the economic well-being of the country, for the prevention of disorder or crime, for the protection of health or morals, or for the protection of the rights and freedoms of others.'

[93] Article 7 of the Charter, mirroring Article 8 ECHR, reads as follows: 'Everyone has the right to respect for his or her private and family life, home and communications' (right to privacy); whereas Article 8 of the Charter holds, '1. Everyone has the right to the protection of personal data concerning him or her. 2. Such data must be processed fairly for specified purposes and on the basis of the consent of the person concerned or some other legitimate basis laid down by law. Everyone has the right of access to data which has been collected concerning him or her, and the right to have it rectified. 3. Compliance with these rules shall be subject to control by an independent authority' (Right to the protection of personal data).

[94] Art 8(2) ECHR (n 92); and Art 52(1) Charter, which provides: 'Any limitation on the exercise of the rights and freedoms recognised by this Charter must be provided for by law and respect the essence of those rights and freedoms. Subject to the principle of proportionality, limitations may be made only if they are necessary and genuinely meet objectives of general interest recognised by the Union or the need to protect the rights and freedoms of others.'

campaigner, Mr Bridges, to the South Wales Police, the Courts reviewed the legality of the SWP's trials using live facial recognition in public spaces.[95] Both courts ruled that the police deployments had interfered with the fundamental right to privacy, but they disagreed on whether the interference was justified. The High Court identified the legal framework applicable to the trials composed of the right to privacy (i.e., Article 8 ECHR producing effect in national law through the Human Rights Act 1998), Part 3 of the Data Protection Act 2018 (implementing the LED), the Surveillance Camera Code of Practice and the relevant policies of SWP.[96] The High Court was of the opinion that the legal framework was clear and sufficient. The Court of Appeal had a different appreciation. The appeal judges declared the interference with the right to privacy unjustified because the legal framework left too much discretion to the police for the constitution of the watchlists and the deployment locations.[97]

In France, the only Court decision taken in the context of facial recognition is linked to planned trials of FRTs in two public high schools. These trials were authorised by regional public authorities but stopped before being deployed. In December 2018, the public authorities of the South of France (Provence–Alpes–Côte d'Azur) adopted a resolution to allow two high schools, in Marseille and Nice, to experiment with FRTs for access control and security purposes.[98] In February 2019, several civil rights organisations appealed the decision of the regional authorities to the Administrative Court in Marseille. In the meantime, the regional authorities had started discussions with the French data protection authority to obtain its advice on the trials. In October 2019, the CNIL delivered negative advice for carrying out the experiments as it found the measures disproportionate and unnecessary. There were less intrusive means to reach the same goal, such as the use of badges.[99] On 27 February 2020, the Administrative Court invalidated the decision of the regional authorities and ended the experiments based on arguments similar to those of the CNIL. The Court also specified that the consent of the students or their

---

[95]   R(Bridges) [2019] (High Court's decision) (n 32); R(Bridges) [2020] (Court of Appeal's decision) (n 32).

[96]   R(Bridges) [2019] (n 32) [85]–[97].

[97]   R(Bridges) [2020] (n 32) [121]–[130]; besides the Court found that the DPIA conducted by the police before the deployments was insufficient in [152]–[154], and that the police had also failed with their duty of equality in [199]–[201].

[98]   Decision 18–893 of 14 December 2018 (n 60).

[99]   CNIL, 'Expérimentation de la reconnaissance faciale dans deux lycées: la CNIL précise sa position' (29 October 2019) <https://www.cnil.fr/fr/experimen tation-de-la-reconnaissance-faciale-dans-deux-lycees-la-cnil-precise-sa-position> accessed 1 July 2022.

parents (on their behalf) was not an appropriate legal basis as the students were in a relationship of authority with the schools, depriving them of giving free consent.[100]

After the experiment conducted during the Nice Carnival, the CNIL called for a public debate on facial recognition and drew red lines concerning experimentations. The supervisory authority identified areas and groups of individuals that should be excluded from them (such as minors or vulnerable people).[101] The CNIL also reminded key requirements for future experiments with the technologies (such as transparency, necessity, proportionality, legitimacy and public acceptability).[102]

4.2.2   Data protection legislation

The fundamental right to data protection is further detailed in EU secondary legislation, namely the GDPR (general instrument) and the LED (specific instrument for law enforcement) as implemented at the national level.[103] In both instruments, biometric data processed to 'uniquely identify' an individual are considered sensitive data. This type of data benefits from a higher level of protection, but the GDPR and the LED follow a different approach concerning the conditions for processing sensitive data. In the GDPR, the processing of sensitive data is prohibited unless an exception allows it, as listed in Article 9(2) GDPR. For instance, the processing of sensitive data can be based on individuals' explicit consent (Article 9(2)(a) GDPR), a substantial public interest based on law (Article 9(2)(g) GDPR), the protection of vital interests (Article 9(2)(c) GDPR) or the necessity to process the data for scientific research purposes (also based on law) (Article 9(2)(j) GDPR).[104] Following the LED, the processing of sensitive data is not prohibited but authorised under the conditions of legality and strict necessity. The legality covers three scenarios: the processing is expressly authorised by law, is performed to protect vital interests, or it relates to data manifestly made public by the data subject themselves (Article 10 LED).[105] Due to their nature and

---

[100]   TA Marseille (n 61) para. 12.

[101]   CNIL (n 19) 9.

[102]   ibid.

[103]   As well as other legal instruments not relevant for the purpose of this chapter.

[104]   Art 9(2) GDPR provides a list of ten exceptions. But the CNIL considers that only the individual's explicit consent, the protection of their vital interests or a substantial public interest can serve as a legal basis for biometric processing, see CNIL's Report (n 19) 6.

[105]   Following Art 10 LED, the processing of sensitive data 'shall be allowed only where strictly necessary, subject to appropriate safeguards for the rights and

objectives, the trials conducted in the UK and in Nice were not based on the same legal instrument.

In the UK, the trials did not involve volunteers and led to some arrests.[106] As analysed by the Biometrics Commissioner and legal scholars, they were not merely experiments but a mix of trials with operational policing deployments.[107] In the Bridges case, the UK Courts acknowledged this nature as the data protection rules applicable to the 'trials' were those applicable to police operations, i.e. Part 3 of the DPA 2018 implementing the LED rather than the GDPR rules.[108] Unfortunately, the Court of Appeal did not assess whether the domestic legislation and, in particular, Section 35 DPA 2018 (on sensitive processing in law enforcement context) were adequate for the use of FRTs by police forces. The judges considered that such an assessment, requested by the ICO as an intervening party, went beyond the request made by the defendant. His request was indeed limited to the interpretation of the right to privacy.[109] In its intervention, the ICO had asked the Court to recognise the inadequacy of the domestic legislation for lacking clarity, precision and foreseeability. Following the ICO's assessment, Section 35 DPA 2018 did not meet the criteria of legality.[110]

After the Court's decision was published, the ICO called for the Government to provide 'a clearer and more specific legal framework to govern the use of LFR [Live Facial Recognition] by the police.'[111] In its Nineteenth Report, the Parliamentary Science and Technology Committee also asked the Government to suspend the police use and trials of live FRTs until the adoption of a specific legislative framework and the issuance of guidance on trial protocols.[112] In May 2021, the College of Policing issued a consultation paper to establish new policy guidance

---

freedoms of the data subject, and only: (a) where authorized by Union or Member State law [legality]; (b) to protect the vital interests of the data subject or of another natural person; or (c) where such processing relates to data which are manifestly made public by the data subject.'

[106] E.g. Fussey and Murray (n 38) 11.

[107] House of Commons Science and Technology Committee (n 79).

[108] R(Bridges) [2019] (n 32).

[109] R(Bridges) (2020) (n 32) [107]–[108].

[110] ibid.

[111] ICO, 'Information Commissioner's Opinion: The Use of Live Facial Recognition Technology in Public Places' (18 June 2021) 10.

[112] House of Commons Science and Technology Committee, 'The Work of the Biometrics Commissioner and the Forensic Science Regulator, Nineteenth Report of Session 2017–19' (*Parliament*, 17 July 2019) 4 <https://publications.parliament.uk/pa/cm201719/cmselect/cmsctech/1970/1970.pdf> accessed 1 July 2022.

on the use of live FRTs by the police in public spaces based on the existing rules.[113] By March 2022, the College of Policing had published its new Authorised Professional Practice on Live Facial Recognition, on which SWP relied to resume their trials.[114] Soon after the publication, the Biometrics and Surveillance Commissioner expressed concerns about the scope of the Authorised Professional Practice, the testing methodologies and the specific use of live FRTs in counter-terrorism.[115] In June 2022, the Ada Lovelace Institute published the report that it had commissioned to a group of experts on the governance of biometric data. Known as the Ryder Review, the study concluded the need for a new statutory framework and legislation for the use of biometric technologies.[116] And until the adoption of the rules, the experts called for the suspension of live FRTs.[117] However, despite the conclusions of the report and the ICO's request, the UK Government has not announced any specific legal framework to govern the police use of live FRTs.

In France, the experiment conducted during the Nice Carnival was based on the explicit consent of the participants, in line with Article 9(2) GDPR. In its position paper on facial recognition, the CNIL considered that only three of the ten exceptions are suitable in the context of facial recognition: the individuals' explicit consent, the necessity to protect their vital interest (based on law) and the existence of substantial public interest (also based on law). In the absence of explicit consent, the processing

---

[113]   Government Response to the Committee's Nineteenth Report of Session 2017–19 (*Parliament*, 19 March 2021) para 22 <https://publications.parliament.uk/pa/cm5801/cmselect/cmsctech/1319/131902.htm> accessed 1 July 2022; College of Policing, 'Authorised Professional Practice Live Facial Recognition, Consultation: Guidance for the Overt Deployment of Live Facial Recognition Technology to Locate Persons on a Watchlist' <https://paas-s3-broker-prod-lon-6453d964-1d1a-432a-9260-5e0ba7d2fc51.s3.eu-west-2.amazonaws.com/s3fs-public/2021-05/live-facial-recognition-app.pdf> accessed 1 July 2022.

[114]   College of Policing, 'Authorised Professional Practice' <https://www.college.police.uk/app/live-facial-recognition> accessed 1 July 2022; see also n 50.

[115]   The UK Government, News, 'The Biometrics and Surveillance Camera Commissioner's Response to the College of Policing APP on Live Facial Recognition' (Gov.uk, 6 April 2022) <https://www.gov.uk/government/news/the-biometrics-and-surveillance-camera-commissioners-response-to-the-college-of-policing-app-on-live-facial-recognition> accessed 1 July 2022.

[116]   The Ryder Review (June 2022), <https://www.adalovelaceinstitute.org/wp-content/uploads/2022/06/The-Ryder-Review-Independent-legal-review-of-the-governance-of-biometric-data-in-England-and-Wales-Ada-Lovelace-Institute-June-2022.pdf> accessed 1 July 2022.

[117]   ibid, Recommendation 5.

of biometric data needs first to be authorised by law.[118] Concerning the experiment in Nice, the purpose of the trial did not relate to security but to scientific testing of the software.[119] In the absence of a specific law allowing the processing of biometric data, the explicit consent of individuals whose facial images were captured was the only possible legal basis.[120] The consent had to be obtained from the volunteers and the passers-by using the Carnival's entrance monitored by facial recognition cameras. As further analysed by the CNIL, any operational deployment of FRTs by the police for security purposes, crime prevention or criminal investigation falls under the national rules implementing the LED.[121] As a result, a specific law (or at minima a decree adopted by the Council of State) is necessary to authorise the police to deploy live FRTs in public spaces and process the public's biometric data.[122] No such law or decree exists, even if there have been several attempts by Members of the French Parliament and the Government to create regulatory frameworks to experiment with and use FRTs. For instance, in 2019, the Government communicated in the media about its plan to launch a national experiment with FRTs without providing much detail about the purpose and legal basis for the experiment.[123] In May 2021, several MPs introduced a legislative proposal (*proposition de loi*) to adopt an experimental law that would set a framework for the scientific analysis and the citizens' consultation to use AI-enabled facial recognition systems.[124] But as explained in the next section, the proposal has never been scheduled for discussion by the National Assembly. As a result of the current French legislative framework, French police forces are not authorised to deploy FRTs in public spaces for law enforcement purposes.

---

[118]   CNIL (n 19) 6.

[119]   AFP (n 85).

[120]   CNIL (n 19) 6.

[121]   AFP (n 85).

[122]   CNIL's tweets, 7 <https://twitter.com/CNIL/status/1097789738176708608> accessed 1 July 2022. This results from the implementation of Article 10 LED.

[123]   Martin Untersinger, 'Cédric O: «Expérimenter la reconnaissance faciale est nécessaire pour que nos industriels progressent»' (*Le Monde*, 14 October 2019) <https://www.lemonde.fr/economie/article/2019/10/14/cedric-o-experimenter-la-reconnaissance-faciale-est-necessaire-pour-que-nos-industriels-progressent_6015395_3234.html> accessed 1 July 2022.

[124]   See Didier Baichère and others, 'Proposition de loi d'expérimentation créant un cadre d'analyse scientifique et une consultation citoyenne sur les dispositifs de reconnaissance faciale par l'intelligence artificielle' (Proposal for an experimental law, no 4127, 4 May 2021).

Besides data protection rules, the police use of FRTs in public spaces is subject to other rules. Those include criminal procedural rules, policy rules and rules applicable to the use of CCTVs in public spaces. These rules set forth the conditions under which public authorities can process images from the surveillance cameras, where they can deploy these cameras, for how long they can retain the images, and for which purposes they can use them.[125] In France, for instance, these rules are part of the French Code of Domestic Security. The provisions that allow the use of CCTVs in public spaces for crime prevention or detection, criminal investigation or prosecution, implement the LED. The other purposes, such as traffic management or prevention of natural risks, are based on the GDPR. The French data protection authority is in charge of controlling compliance with the rules.[126]

4.3   Fragmented Oversight

In the UK, there is no clear answer about who has oversight over these trials. The UK regulatory landscape in that field is complex.[127] Three regulators are at least involved, but none has a leading role in overseeing the police's use of FRTs and only the data protection authority has an enforcement role. These regulators are the Information Commissioner's Office or ICO (data protection), the former Biometrics Commissioner (police use and retention of biometric materials), the former Surveillance Camera Commissioner (monitoring the Surveillance Camera Code of Practice) and the Forensic Science Regulator (standards for biometrics).[128] They got involved during the trials but were not informed before they had started.[129] This observation contrasts with the

---

[125]   E.g. Guiding principles in the Surveillance Camera Code of Practice (n 2) as updated in November 2021 <https://assets.publishing.service.gov.uk/governm ent/uploads/system/uploads/attachment_data/file/1035067/Surveillance_Camera_ CoP_Accessible_PDF.pdf> accessed 1 July 2022; also Art 251-2 French Code of Domestic Security (n 18).

[126]   CNIL, 'Vidéoprotection: Quelles sont les dispositions applicables?' 13 December 2019 <https://www.cnil.fr/fr/videoprotection-quelles-sont-les-disposit ions-applicables> accessed 1 July 2022.

[127]   Christopher James Lawless, 'The Evolution, Devolution and Distribution of UK Biometric Imaginaries' (2022) 17 BioSocieties.

[128]   Home Office, 'Biometrics Strategy: Better Public Services Maintaining Public Trust' (June 2018) 16–17 <https://assets.publishing.service.gov.uk/gover nment/uploads/system/uploads/attachment_data/file/720850/Home_Office_Biom etrics_Strategy_-_2018-06-28.pdf> accessed 1 July 2022.

[129]   ICO started an investigation on the trials once informed, and the Biometrics Commissioner and Surveillance Camera Commissioner could observe some of the trials.

views of the Home Office. The Government considered that there were enough regulators, although it did not explain their respective roles. In 2019, the Science and Technology Committee of the House of Commons asked the Government to establish regulatory oversight of the police trials.[130] In its answer to the report, the Government considered that it had already taken steps to simplify the oversight structure by merging the functions of the Biometrics Commissioner and the Surveillance Camera Commissioner.[131] However, the UK government has not designated a leading supervisory authority with an enforcement role for the trials and deployments of FRTs.[132]

In France, the CNIL was informed about the experiment in Nice briefly before it started.[133] The supervisory authority provided some recommendations to the municipality, but it did not formally authorise the experiment.[134] Since the adoption of the GDPR, the procedure of authorisation (and prior notification) has been replaced by record-keeping and Data Protection Impact Assessment obligations. Besides, the CNIL only enforces compliance with data protection rules. Other rules impacted by the deployment of FRT fall outside its role and authority.

In the Netherlands, scholars and civil society have expressed concerns about the rapid development of experimental labs and their impact on fundamental rights in public spaces.[135] These labs harvest a considerable amount of data, including personal data, without needing the cooperation of the data subjects.[136] Besides, once informed that they are entering an experimental area, individuals and groups might change their behaviour because they feel monitored. The legal basis of these experiments also

---

[130] Science and Technology Committee (n 112) 4.
[131] Replaced by the 'Biometrics and Surveillance Camera Commissioner', see Government Response (2021) (n 112) para 22.
[132] Although the ICO seems the most suitable one to oversee the police's trials.
[133] CNIL's tweets (n 122) 1.
[134] AFP (n 85).
[135] EDRi, 'Washed in Blue: Living Lab Digital Perimeter in Amsterdam' (19 May 2021) <https://edri.org/our-work/washed-in-blue-living-lab-digital-perimeter-in-amsterdam/> accessed 1 July 2022; Bart van der Sloot and Marjolein Lanzing, 'The Continued Transformation of the Public Sphere: On the Road to Smart Cities, Living Labs and a New Understanding of Society' in Michael Nagenborg and others (eds), *Technology and the City: Towards a Philosophy of Urban Technologies* (Springer 2021).
[136] Saskia Naafs, '*Living Laboratories*: The Dutch Cities Amassing Data on Oblivious Residents' (*The Guardian*, 1 March 2018) <https://www.theguardian.com/cities/2018/mar/01/smart-cities-data-privacy-eindhoven-utrecht> accessed 1 July 2022; Galič (n 63).

remains uncertain. As analysed by van der Sloot and Lanzing, experiments conducted by municipalities in the context of living labs do not seem to be grounded on a specific legal basis.[137] Galič and Gellert also observed the difficulty of relying on data protection rules due to the design of the experiments and the purposes of the experiments involving both private parties and law enforcement authorities.[138] Concerning *the Digitale Perimeter*, civil rights organisations have investigated whether the police and municipality of Amsterdam trialled FRTs without finding evidence of such experiments,[139] whereas discussions on the regulation of facial recognition technologies are still ongoing in the Netherlands.[140]

In a nutshell, (operational) experiments in the UK and the technology-testing experiment in France followed existing, albeit not specific, data protection rules. However, it is questionable whether these rules would be sufficient to generalise experiments with facial recognition in public spaces (under the GDPR rules) and to operationally roll out the technologies for security, crime prevention and criminal investigation purposes (under the rules established by the LED).

The next section provides some elements for a reflection on an experimental approach based on existing and emerging regulatory tools, without prejudging the outcomes of a public debate on whether it is acceptable, in a democratic society, to experiment with these technologies in public spaces.

5. ELEMENTS FOR AN EXPERIMENTAL APPROACH

Without replacing the public debate on the topic, this section provides some arguments and tools for a reflection on an experimental regulatory approach to test FRTs. It does not address the trial design, protocol and evaluation methodology, which should, however, be an inherent part of

---

[137]   van der Sloot and Lanzing (n 135).

[138]   Maša Galič and Raphael Gellert, 'Data Protection Law beyond Identifiability? Atmospheric Profiles, Nudging and the Stratumseind Living Lab' (2021) 40 Computer Law & Security Review.

[139]   On the investigation conducted by Bits of Freedom, see <https://www.bitsoffreedom.nl/dossiers/gezichtsherkenning/> accessed 1 July 2022.

[140]   Esther Keymolen, 'Dutch Experiment with Facial Recognition: Privacy Risks Require Legislative Choices' <https://www.tilburguniversity.edu/current/press-releases/privacy-risks-facial-recognition-technology> accessed 1 July 2022.

the experiments should such experiments occur.[141] This section weighs several options. Some tools are already in place, such as Data Protection Impact Assessments (DPIAs). Others only exist at national levels (normative experimental legislation). Finally, some are prospective mechanisms in the context of the future EU AI regulation (regulatory sandboxes), currently discussed by the European institutions.

5.1   DPIA, a Necessary but Insufficient Tool

The GDPR and LED have introduced DPIA mechanisms to assess the risks that processing operations might pose to the fundamental rights and freedoms of individuals (including, but not limited to, the rights to privacy and data protection). Following Article 35 GDPR and Article 27 LED, data controllers must conduct a DPIA when the processing operations envisaged are 'likely to result in a high risk' to individuals' rights and freedoms. In its Guidelines on DPIAs, the Article 29 Data Protection Working Party, replaced by the European Data Protection Board (EDPB), suggested nine factors to assess 'high-risk' processing operations. The obligation to conduct a DPIA is triggered by the combination of two of these factors.[142] Article 29 identified the use of new technologies, the systematic monitoring of public spaces and the processing of sensitive data on a large scale among the factors.[143] Experiments with FRTs in public spaces combine three of them at least. Therefore, there is no doubt that public authorities planning to trial these technologies in public spaces must first conduct a DPIA. This document will describe the processing operations (purpose and legality of the processing), assess the necessity of the processing and proportionality of the operations, identify the risks (i.e., the effects of the processing operations on an individual's fundamental rights and freedoms) and find mitigating solutions (to overcome the risks). Several data protection authorities have designed models of DPIAs to help data controllers to carry them: see, for instance, the models developed by the CNIL (France), the Agencia española de protección de datos (AEPD)

---

[141]   Several institutions and regulators have called for the development of trial designs (definition, hypothesis tested) and evaluation methodology; also echoed by Castellucia and Le Métayer, who proposed a methodology in Claude Castellucia and Daniel le Métayer, 'Impact Analysis of Facial Recognition' (2020) HAL, 24 <https://hal.inria.fr/hal-02480647/document> accessed 1 July 2022.

[142]   Art 29 WP 'Guidelines on Data Protection Impact Assessment (DPIA)' (2017) WP248 rev.01.

[143]   Art 35 (3) GDPR and criteria established by Art 29 WP in its Guidelines on DPIA (n 142).

(Spain),[144] the ICO (UK)[145] or the German data protection authorities.[146] These models are steps to be followed and criteria to assess the severity of harms and the likelihood of risks (low, medium and high). As noted by Friedewald et al., these models are based on existing methodologies (CNIL), ISO/IEC standards (ICO) or doctrine (Germany).[147]

A distinction between true and hybrid experiments should be made to determine which legal instrument is applicable. Purely experimental trials will be subject to the GDPR. In France, for instance, in the absence of specific law allowing the processing of biometric data for facial recognition purposes in public spaces,[148] the individual's explicit consent should be identified, in the DPIA, as the applicable legal basis to trial FRTs in public spaces. Besides, data controllers will have to demonstrate the necessity (i.e., demonstrating that other less intrusive means are inadequate) and proportionality (i.e., balancing the processing objectives with the impact on individuals' rights and freedoms) of the processing operations.[149] The validity of a DPIA to experiment with FRTs in public spaces might also depend on the number and status of individuals (whether they are volunteers or passers-by), the area covered, the duration of the experiment and the number of cameras. The assessment will be made case by case.

By contrast, hybrid experiments, i.e. combining the testing of technologies with a policing operation, are subject to the implementing rules of the LED. The UK Courts expressly acknowledged it in the Bridges case (reviewing the legality of SWP's trials) and the French data protection authority took the same position in its analysis of the experimentation conducted in Nice. In application of the LED rules, the processing of biometric data can only be allowed if based on law and if strictly necessary

---

[144]   AEPD (2021) <https://www.aepd.es/sites/default/files/2019-09/guia-evaluaciones-de-impacto-rgpd.pdf> accessed 1 July 2022.

[145]   ICO, Data Protection Impact Assessments <https://ico.org.uk/for-organisations/guide-to-data-protection/guide-to-the-general-data-protection-regulation-gdpr/accountability-and-governance/data-protection-impact-assessments/?msclkid=3b86403fb58611ec9ce9f3a413668fd9> accessed 1 July 2022.

[146]   Conference of the Independent Data Protection Supervisory Authorities of the Federation and the Länder (2020) <https://www.datenschutzzentrum.de/uploads/sdm/SDM-Methodology_V2.0b.pdf> accessed 1 July 2022.

[147]   Michael Friedewald and others, 'Data Protection Impact Assessments in Practice' (2022) Lecture Notes in Computer Science, Conference Paper (13106).

[148]   As analysed by the CNIL.

[149]   As suggested by the CNIL (n 19) 9.

and proportionate.[150] If hybrid experimentations are not permitted by law in France, the UK domestic legislation allows the police to use FRTs only 'when it is strictly necessary for reasons of substantial public interest.'[151] This strict necessity is assessed, considering the number of people involved, the seriousness of the offence, the location, the definition of the purpose, and the justification to trial FRTs in real-life settings and on the public.[152] So whether police forces might be able to deploy hybrid experiments depends on the applicable national law. Some changes will, most likely, be introduced once the EU Commission's proposal for AI Regulation is adopted.[153] However, this new piece of legislation will not apply in the UK, which is no longer part of the EU.

A DPIA seems like a necessary tool but is not sufficient in itself. First, the scope of a DPIA relates to the impact of processing operations. Yet, not all the issues linked to the experiment with FRTs are connected to the processing of individuals' facial images. For instance, the chilling effect of FRTs on the freedom of assembly is not linked to the processing of the images of people but to the presence of cameras in public spaces. Second, data controllers (i.e., the police and public authorities) are not obliged to publish DPIAs. Thus, the public is not aware of the risks data controllers have identified and the proposed solutions. Likewise, data controllers are not obliged to submit their DPIA to the data protection authorities before starting the processing unless they cannot mitigate the risks.[154] Last, experiments with FRTs in public spaces cannot be generalised based on DPIA mechanisms, which should be assessed on a case-by-case basis.

For a more holistic approach, DPIAs could be complemented by Human Rights Impact Assessment (HRIA) Tools.[155] There is no single

---

[150] The other legal grounds, data manifestly made available by the data subjects themselves and data processed in the vital interests, are not suitable; see Art 10 LED.

[151] ICO, 'Investigation' (2019) (n 82) 10; s35(5) DPA 2018 (relating to conditions for sensitive data processing for law enforcement purposes).

[152] ICO, 'Information Commissioner's Opinion: The Use of Live Facial Recognition Technology by Law Enforcement in Public Places' (October 2019) 14–15 <https://ico.org.uk/media/about-the-ico/documents/2616184/live-frt-law-enforcement-opinion-20191031.pdf> accessed 1 July 2022.

[153] Proposal (n 5).

[154] Art 36 GDPR and Art 28 LED.

[155] On the concept and use for AI systems, e.g. Heleen L Janssen, 'An Approach for a Fundamental Rights Impact Assessment to Automated Decision-Making' (2020) 10 (1) International Data Privacy Law; also Alessandro Mantelero, 'AI and Big Data: A Blueprint for a Human Rights, Social and Ethical Impact Assessment' (2018) 34(4) Computer Law & Security Review.

approach to HRIA, but the Council of Europe's Commissioner for Human Rights has recommended Member States to 'establish a legal framework to impose on public authorities to carry out human rights impact assessments (HRIAs) on AI systems acquired, developed and/or deployed by those authorities.'[156] In his recommendation, facial recognition systems are identified as systems that should be subject to HRIAs.[157] The Recommendation identifies the key areas, principles and obligations that should be considered in the HRIA of AI systems. Besides the impact on data protection and privacy, public authorities should assess the discrimination risks that AI systems might pose to (groups of) individuals and other human or fundamental rights that could be affected.[158] Those include the freedom of expression, assembly, association and the right to work.[159] HRIAs are meant to assess the impacts that activities from the public and private sectors have on people (not as data subjects, but as consumers, citizens, workers, patients, etc.). HRIAs go beyond privacy and data protection issues and do not result from a legal obligation (yet) but could be very helpful in assessing the impact that the experimentation and the deployment of FRTs in public areas and publicly accessible spaces could have on individuals and society. Some methodologies exist but have been mainly developed until now for business activities (such as by the Danish Institute for Human Rights)[160] or in specific areas (e.g. health).[161]

5.2   Normative Exceptions for Experimentation Purposes

Another option could be the adoption of experimental legislation, which would derogate from existing rules (including data protection rules). According to Philipsen et al., 'one way to enable experiments is by creating a statutory basis for the experiment. Such a basis offers the

---

[156]   Council of Europe, Recommendation, 'Unboxing Artificial Intelligence: 10 Steps to Protect Human Rights', May 2019, 7, <https://rm.coe.int/unboxing-artificial-intelligence-10-steps-to-protect-human-rights-reco/1680946e64> accessed 1 July 2022.

[157]   ibid 13.

[158]   ibid 11.

[159]   ibid 12.

[160]   Handbook on Human Rights Impact Assessment (2019) <https://www.humanrights.dk/sites/humanrights.dk/files/media/dokumenter/business/hria_toolbox/hria_guidance_and_toolbox_final_feb2016.pdf> accessed 1 July 2022.

[161]   Gillian MacNaughton, 'Human Rights Impact Assessment: A Method for Healthy Policymaking' (2015) 17(1) Health and Human Rights.

executive a competence to deviate from existing norms by toying around with a new idea.'[162]

In France, the Constitution has allowed regulatory experiments by public authorities since its revision in 2003. Articles 37-1 and 72 (para 4) permit the adoption of derogatory measures on an experimental basis for a limited time at the national and regional levels. In a report published in 2019 on experimentations at national and local levels, the Council of State identified that more than 250 experimentations have been conducted since 2003.[163] But the normative experimental framework presents two critical limits. First, some fields should be excluded from the experimentation's scope because of their impact on fundamental rights or specific groups of individuals (such as vulnerable people).[164] Second, the framework is not suitable for sectors harmonised at EU level.[165] Therefore, it is difficult to argue that experiments with FRTs in public spaces could benefit from national derogatory legislation as they would occur in an area harmonised at EU level (through data protection rules and the future rules applicable to AI systems) and would have a significant impact on fundamental rights.

Despite the limits identified by the French Council of State, the Government announced in October 2019 a plan to launch a national experiment with FRTs. But the Government did not provide any details to determine whether the experiment would be based on an experimental law and when it would be launched.[166] This announcement followed the Senate Committee on Sciences and Technology's Report, which had called in July 2019 for a legislative framework to allow experiments with FRTs under

---

[162]   Stefan Philipsen and others, 'Legal Enclaves as a Test Environment for Innovative Products: Toward Legally Resilient Experimentation Policies' (2021) 15 Regulation and Governance; and for a detailed account of the concept of experimental legislation, see Sofia Ranchordás, 'The Whys and Woes of Experimental Legislation' (2013) 1 (3) Theory and Practice of Legislation.

[163]   Conseil d'Etat, 'Les Expérimentations: Comment innover dans la conduite des politiques publiques' [Experimentations: How to Innovate in the Conduct of Public Policies] (3 October 2019) <https://www.vie-publique.fr/catalogue/270979-les-experimentations-comment-innover-dans-la-conduite-des-politiques-publiques> accessed 1 July 2022.

[164]   ibid, 'internal constraints', 33.

[165]   ibid, 'external constraints', 33.

[166]   Untersinger (n 123); Caroline Piquet, 'Reconnaissance faciale: Cédric O n'est "pas certain" qu'Alicem soit un jour déployée' (*Le Parisien*, 24 December 2019) <https://www.leparisien.fr/high-tech/reconnaissance-faciale-cedric-o-n-est-pas-certain-qu-alicem-soit-un-jour-deployee-24-12-2019-8223705.php> accessed 1 July 2022.

real-life conditions.[167] The idea of experimenting with FRTs seemed to be gaining ground in France. In November 2020, the French Ministry of Interiors published a White Paper on Internal Security, including several proposals for facial recognition use by public authorities.[168] One of these proposals related to experimentation with FRTs in public spaces.[169] The report suggested testing the technologies in three phases: stage 1, experiments on volunteers; stage 2, experiments under real conditions with notification to the public; and stage 3, limited experiments (geographically and temporarily) without prior notification to the public. The experiment in Nice only reached the first stage. In May 2021, several Members of Parliament introduced a legislative proposal to create an experimental legal framework to test FRTs in public spaces and consult citizens.[170] The proposal was never tabled by the National Assembly (the lower house of the French Parliament) and thus never examined. In September 2021, though, the Prime Minister received a parliamentary report on the use of new technologies in the field of security, also suggesting similar experiments.[171] In anticipation of the Olympic Games in 2024 and the Rugby World Cup in 2023, the report suggested that the Government proposes a national experimental law to test facial recognition systems for verification purposes (identity checks) and considers experimenting with FRTs under real conditions (i.e., not based on individuals' consent) in public spaces.[172] This proposal looks very similar to the hybrid experiments conducted by the UK police forces. It also echoes the request by the Mayor of Nice after the Carnival experiment. He lamented the absence of a derogatory legal framework to test the technologies in real conditions and large-scale settings. But these proposals do not seem to be in line with the CNIL's position, which considers that experimentations with facial

---

[167] French Senate [Sénat], Science and Technology Briefings, Parliamentary Office for Scientific and Technological Assessment, Briefing 14, 'Facial Recognition' (July 2019) 3 <https://www2.assemblee-nationale.fr/content/down load/179314/1794787/version/2/file/Note%20Reconnaissance%20Faciale%20-%20 EN.pdf> accessed 1 July 2022.
[168] Ministère de l'Intérieur, 'Livre Blanc de la Sécurité Intérieure' (2020) <https://www.interieur.gouv.fr/sites/minint/files/medias/documents/2021-06//livr e-blanc-de-la-securite-interieure.pdf> accessed 1 July 2022.
[169] ibid 263–265.
[170] Proposal for an experimental law (n 124).
[171] Jean-Michel Mis, 'Pour un usage responsable et acceptable par la société des technologies de sécurité' (Report to the Prime Minister for a Responsible and Acceptable Use of Technologies for Security Purposes), vols 1 and 2, September 2021.
[172] ibid.

recognition should follow a strict methodology and comply with data protection rules (instead of derogating from them).[173] In May 2022, the French Senate Commission of Law published a report on facial recognition in which it proposed thirty recommendations to regulate facial recognition (including its use in public spaces).[174] Among them, the report calls for the adoption of an experimental law for a period of three years to set the conditions and purposes of experiments with biometric technologies (i.e., facial recognition) by public actors and possibly in public spaces.[175] This recommendation looks like a regulatory sandbox mechanism, as it would involve a committee of scientists and experts in ethics to assess the experiments. The role played by the CNIL in the context of these experiments is, however, not clarified.

At EU level, the European Data Protection Supervisor and European Data Protection Board have called for a general ban on facial recognition technologies in publicly accessible areas in the EU Commission's proposal for AI Regulation.[176] It is, thus, hard to imagine that these two authorities would support (temporary) derogation from data protection rules to experiment with facial recognition technologies in public spaces due to the fundamental rights issues that their use raises.

5.3 Regulatory Sandboxes, a Policy Tool within an Existing Framework

Regulatory sandboxes have become extremely popular as experimental tools for innovation purposes. The term originates from the financial sector, where it was first applied.[177] However, there is no single definition or type,[178] but as described by Philipsen et al., a regulatory sandbox 'is

---

[173] CNIL's Report (n 19).
[174] French Senate, Commission of Law, Information Report on Facial Recognition and the Risks Posed to the Protection of Civil Liberties [Rapport d'information fait au nom de la commission des lois constitutionnelles, de législation, du suffrage universel, du Règlement et d'administration générale sur la reconnaissance faciale et ses risques au regard de la protection des libertés individuelles], no 627, 10 May 2022 <https://www.senat.fr/rap/r21-627/r21-6271.pdf> accessed 1 July 2022.
[175] ibid, recommendation no 7.
[176] EDPB–EDPS Joint Opinion 5/2021 (n 90).
[177] Term coined by the British Financial Conduct Authority that launched the first regulatory sandbox in 2016; see Hilary Allen, 'Sandbox Boundaries' (2020) 22(2) Vanderbilt Journal of Entertainment and Technology Law.
[178] E.g. Hilary Allen, 'Regulatory Sandboxes' (2019) 87 The George Washington Law Review.

not a form of regulation but a policy regarding the enforcement of the existing legal framework.'[179] Regulatory sandboxes allow the testing of innovative technologies in a controlled environment (i.e., under regulatory supervision). Their use in the data protection area is very recent. The British DPA was the first data protection authority to launch an initiative of regulatory sandboxes to accompany projects from September 2020.[180] The ICO identified projects involving biometric technologies as potentially eligible for sandbox pilots.[181] As conceived by the ICO, regulatory sandboxes do not replace DPIAs nor exempt its participants from conducting a DPIA. A DPIA with the ICO's prior consultation is an inherent part of the mechanism in the UK.[182] The Norwegian data protection authority, Datatilsynet, and the CNIL have also launched their own programmes.[183]

The European Commission has also introduced a mechanism to set up regulatory sandboxes in the Draft AI Act. The AI regulatory sandboxes will allow the development and testing of AI systems in a controlled environment and under a supervisory authority's monitoring.[184] In principle, AI regulatory sandboxes should not derogate from data protection rules. However, the EDPS and EDPB asked in their joint opinion to clarify that the objective of a regulatory sandbox would be limited to the testing and could not fall under the LED.[185] As a consequence, hybrid experiments, such as the ones conducted in the UK, should be excluded from the scope of regulatory sandboxes. But the current wording of Article 54(1) of the proposal allows the development and testing of AI systems for substantial public interest using personal data lawfully collected for other purposes. Among those purposes are personal data collected in police and criminal

---

[179]   Philipsen and others (n 162) 5.
[180]   ICO, 'Sandbox Beta Phase, Discussion Paper' (30 January 2019) <https://ico.org.uk/media/about-the-ico/documents/2614219/sandbox-discussion-paper-20190130.pdf> accessed 1 July 2022.
[181]   ibid 1.
[182]   ICO, 'The Guide to the Sandbox' <https://ico.org.uk/for-organisations/regulatory-sandbox/the-guide-to-the-sandbox/> accessed 1 July 2022; CNIL, Bac à sable (15 February 2021) <https://www.cnil.fr/fr/bac-a-sable-2021> accessed 1 July 2022.
[183]   Datatilsynet, 'Framework for the Regulatory Sandbox' (13 January 2021) <https://www.datatilsynet.no/en/regulations-and-tools/sandbox-for-artificial-intelligence/framework-for-the-regulatory-sandbox/> accessed 1 July 2022; CNIL, Bac à sable (n 182).
[184]   Arts 53 and 54 Draft AI Act (n 5).
[185]   EDPB–EDPS Joint Opinion 5/2021 (n 90).

justice contexts.[186] According to Article 54(1)(a)(i), such processing should be expressly allowed by law. If adopted, one may wonder if this provision will not allow police authorities to experiment with real-time FRTs in public spaces.[187]

6.   CONCLUSION

Lequesne Roth and her colleagues observed that the public debate on facial recognition is happening in many countries, but several fundamental issues still need to be addressed.[188] To paraphrase these scholars, it remains to determine which uses are appropriate (efficiency), which uses are legal (legality principle) and which uses are acceptable (legitimacy principle).[189] If this chapter did not answer all the questions – which should result from a democratic debate – it provided some food for thought. First, it revealed the disparities between the UK and France concerning the experiments held with FRTs in public spaces. While the experiment in France was limited to technology testing, the trials in the UK were policing operations (under the umbrella of 'pilot projects'). Second, it identified some gaps (the lack of trial methodology, specific legal frameworks and oversight). Third, it investigated whether DPIA mechanisms, experimental legislation and the regulatory sandbox tools could play a role in defining an experimental approach to test real-time FRTs in public spaces. But it also calls for caution as any experimental framework will have to be weighed against the impact on fundamental rights and delimited by red lines resulting from a public debate on the trials and use of these technologies.

---

[186]   Article 54(1)(a)(i) Draft AI Act.
[187]   See the discussions following the publication of the proposal for AI Regulation as reported in Theodore Christakis, 'Facial Recognition in the Draft European AI Regulation: Final Report on the High-Level Workshop Held on 26 April 2021' <https://ai-regulation.com/facial-recognition-in-the-draft-european-ai-regulation-final-report-on-the-high-level-workshop-held-on-april-26-2021/> accessed 1 July 2022.
[188]   Caroline Lequesne Roth and others, 'La reconnaissance faciale dans l'espace public: Une cartographie juridique européenne', Fablex DL4T Report (April 2020) <https://droit.univ-cotedazur.fr/dl4t/la-reconnaissance-faciale-dans-lespace---une-cartographie-juridique-europeenne> accessed 1 July 2022.
[189]   ibid 12.

REFERENCES

AEPD (2021) <https://www.aepd.es/sites/default/files/2019-09/guia-evaluaciones-de-impacto-rgpd.pdf?msclkid=cb207782b58611ec8fc0d575e8250a57> accessed 1 July 2022.

AFP, 'Test de reconnaissance faciale à Nice: Précisions de la CNIL' (*Public Sénat*, 19 February 2019) <https://www.publicsenat.fr/article/politique/test-de-recon naissance-faciale-a-nice-precisions-de-la-cnil-138122> accessed 1 July 2022.

Allen H, 'Regulatory Sandboxes' (2019) 87 The George Washington Law Review.

Allen H, 'Sandbox Boundaries' (2020) 22(2) Vanderbilt Journal of Entertainment and Technology Law.

Art 29 WP 'Guidelines on Data Protection Impact Assessment (DPIA)' (2017) WP248 rev.01.

Baichère D and others, 'Proposition de loi d'expérimentation créant un cadre d'analyse scientifique et une consultation citoyenne sur les dispositifs de reconnaissance faciale par l'intelligence artificielle' (no. 4127) <https://www.assemblee-nationale.fr/dyn/15/textes/l15b4127_proposition-loi> accessed 1 July 2022.

Ball K and others, 'A Report on the Surveillance Society: For the Information Commissioner by the Surveillance Studies Network' (September 2006) <https://www.personuvernd.is/media/frettir/surveillance_society_full_report_final.pdf> accessed 1 July 2022.

BBC, 'How We are Being Watched' (3 November 2006) <http://news.bbc.co.uk/2/hi/uk_news/6110866.stm> accessed 1 July 2022.

BBC News, 'Facial Recognition Plan "Hammer Blow to Privacy" Claim' (22 March 2022) <https://www.bbc.com/news/uk-wales-60831816> accessed 1 July 2022.

Big Brother Watch, 'Face Off: The Lawless Growth of Facial Recognition in UK Policing' (May 2018).

Big Brother Watch, 'Map: UK Facial Recognition in Detail' <https://bigbr otherwatch.org.uk/campaigns/stop-facial-recognition/#facial-recognition-uk> accessed 1 July 2022.

Biometrics and Surveillance Camera Commissioner, 'Amended Surveillance Camera Code of Practice' <https://assets.publishing.service.gov.uk/governme nt/uploads/system/uploads/attachment_data/file/1035067/Surveillance_Came ra_CoP_Accessible_PDF.pdf> accessed 1 July 2022.

Biometrics Commissioner, 'Automated Facial Recognition: Biometrics Commissioner Response to Court Judgment on South Wales Police's Use of Automated Facial Recognition Technology' (10 September 2019) <https://www.gov.uk/government/news/automated-facial-recognition> accessed 1 July 2022.

Bischoff P, 'Surveillance Camera Statistics: Which Cities Have the Most CCTV Cameras?' (*Comparitech*, 17 May 2021) <https://www.comparitech.com/vpn-privacy/the-worlds-most-surveilled-cities/> accessed 1 July 2022.

Bits of Freedom, 'Op Waarden Geschat, Living Lab Digitale Perimeter' (30 April 2021) <https://www.bitsoffreedom.nl/wp-content/uploads/2021/05/2021-rapport-digitale-perimeter-bof.pdf> accessed 1 July 2022.

Bits of Freedom, 'Washed in Blue: Living Lab Digital Perimeter in Amsterdam' (19 May 2021) <https://edri.org/our-work/washed-in-blue-living-lab-digital-perimeter-in-amsterdam/> accessed 1 July 2022.

Booth R, 'Halt Public Use of Facial Recognition Tech, says Equality Watchdog' (*The Guardian*, 12 March 2020) <https://www.theguardian.com/uk-news/2020/mar/12/halt-public-use-of-facial-recognition-tech-says-equality-watchdog>.

Buolamwini J and Gebru T, 'Gender Shades: Intersectional Accuracy Disparities in Commercial Gender Classification' (2018) 81 Proceedings of Machine Learning Research.

Castellucia C and le Métayer D, 'Impact Analysis of Facial Recognition' (HAL 2020) <https://hal.inria.fr/hal-02480647/document> accessed 1 July 2022.

CCTV.co.uk, 'Number of CCTV Cameras in the UK Reaches 5.2 Million' (November 2020) <https://www.cctv.co.uk/number-of-cctv-cameras-in-the-uk-reaches-5-2-million/> accessed 1 July 2022.

Christakis T, 'Facial Recognition in the Draft European AI Regulation: Final Report on the High-Level Workshop Held on 26 April 2021' <https://ai-regulation.com/facial-recognition-in-the-draft-european-ai-regulation-final-report-on-the-high-level-workshop-held-on-april-26-2021/> accessed 1 July 2022.

CNIL, 'Expérimentation de la reconnaissance faciale dans deux lycées: la CNIL précise sa position' (29 October 2019) <https://www.cnil.fr/fr/experimentation-dc-la-reconnaissance-faciale-dans-deux-lycees-la-cnil-precise-sa-position> accessed 1 July 2022.

CNIL, 'Facial Recognition: For a Debate Living Up to the Challenges' (2019) <https://www.cnil.fr/sites/default/files/atoms/files/facial-recognition.pdf> accessed 1 July 2022.

CNIL, 'Vidéoprotection: Quelles sont les dispositions applicables?' (December 2019) <https://www.cnil.fr/fr/videoprotection-quelles-sont-les-dispositions-applicables> accessed 1 July 2022.

CNIL, Bac à sable (February 2021) <https://www.cnil.fr/fr/bac-a-sable-2021> accessed 1 July 2022.

CNIL, 'La CNIL publie son Avis sur le décret vidéo-intelligente port du masque' (March 2021) <https://www.cnil.fr/fr/avis-sur-le-decret-video-intelligente-port-du-masque> accessed 1 July 2022.

Code de la Sécurité Intérieure <https://www.legifrance.gouv.fr/codes/id/LEGITEXT000025503132/> accessed 1 July 2022.

College of Policing, 'Authorised Professional Practice Live Facial Recognition, Consultation: Guidance for the Overt Deployment of Live Facial Recognition Technology to Locate Persons on a Watchlist' <https://paas-s3-broker-prod-lon-6453d964-1d1a-432a-9260-5e0ba7d2fc51.s3.eu-west-2.amazonaws.com/s3fs-public/2021-05/live-facial-recognition-app.pdf> accessed 1 July 2022.

College of Policing, 'Authorised Professional Practice' <https://www.college.police.uk/app/live-facial-recognition> accessed 1 July 2022.

Conference of the Independent Data Protection Supervisory Authorities of the Federation and the Länder (April 2020) <https://www.datenschutzzentrum.de/uploads/sdm/SDM-Methodology_V2.0b.pdf> accessed 1 July 2022.

Conseil d'Etat, 'Les Expérimentations: Comment innover dans la conduite des politiques publiques' (October 2019) <https://www.vie-publique.fr/catalogue/270979-les-experimentations-comment-innover-dans-la-conduite-des-politiques-publiques> accessed 1 July 2022.

Council of Europe, Recommendation, 'Unboxing Artificial Intelligence: 10 Steps to Protect Human Rights' (May 2019) <https://rm.coe.int/unboxing-artificial-intelligence-10-steps-to-protect-human-rights-reco/1680946e64> accessed 1 July 2022.

Datatilsynet, 'Framework for the Regulatory Sandbox' (January 2021) <https://www.datatilsynet.no/en/regulations-and-tools/sandbox-for-artificial-intelligence/framework-for-the-regulatory-sandbox/> accessed 1 July 2022.

Davies B and others, 'An Evaluation of South Wales Police's Use of Automated Facial Recognition' (2018) <https://static1.squarespace.com/static/51b06364e4b02de2f57fd72e/t/5bfd4fbc21c67c2cdd692fa8/1543327693640/AFR+Report+%5BDigital%5D.pdf> accessed 1 July 2022.

De Autoriteit Persoonsgegevens, 'Formele waarschuwing AP aan supermarkt om gezichtskerkenning' (15 December 2020) <https://autoriteitpersoonsgegevens.nl/nl/nieuws/formele-waarschuwing-ap-aan-supermarkt-om-gezichtsherkenning> accessed 1 July 2022.

De Autoriteit Persoonsgegevens, 'Voorlichting – regels voor gezichtsherkenning in supermarkten (1 May 2020) <https://autoriteitpersoonsgegevens.nl/sites/default/files/atoms/files/brief_regels_voor_gezichtsherkenning_in_supermarkten.pdf> accessed 1 July 2022.

Décret n. 2021-269 du 10 mars 2021 relatif au recours à la vidéo intelligente pour mesurer le taux de port du masque dans les transports <https://www.legifrance.gouv.fr/jorf/id/JORFTEXT000043235679> accessed 1 July 2022.

den Ouden E and others, 'Exploring the Future of Living Labs' (2016) Research Report <https://www.tue-lighthouse.nl/Images/Livinglabs/20160210%20Exploring%20the%20future%20or%20Living%20Labs%20-%20LR%20ebook.pdf> accessed 1 July 2022.

Digitale Perimeter <https://www.amsterdam.nl/innovatie/digitalisering-technologie/digitale-perimeter/> accessed 1 July 2022.

Dodd V, 'Met Police to Use Facial Recognition Software at Notting Hill Carnival' (*The Guardian*, 5 August 2017) <https://www.theguardian.com/uk-news/2017/aug/05/met-police-facial-recognition-software-notting-hill-carnival> accessed 1 July 2022.

Dodd V, 'UK Police Use of Facial Recognition Technology a Failure, Says Report' (*The Guardian*, 15 May 2018) <https://www.theguardian.com/uk-news/2018/may/15/uk-police-use-of-facial-recognition-technology-failure> accessed 1 July 2022.

EDPB, 'Guidelines 3/2019 on Processing of Personal Data through Video Devices' Version 2.0 (adopted on 29 January 2020).

EDPB, Response to Sophie in't Veld, MEP, regarding the use of Automatic Image Recognition Systems on migrants in Italy, 10 August 2021 <https://edpb.europa.eu/system/files/2021-08/edpb_letter_out_2021_00130_mepveld_facialrecognition_publication.pdf> accessed 1 July 2022.

EDPB and EDPS, 'Joint Opinion 5/2021 on the Proposal for a Regulation of the European Parliament and of the Council Laying Down Harmonised Rules on Artificial Intelligence (Artificial Intelligence Act)'.

Equality and Human Rights Commission, 'Facial Recognition Technology and Predictive Policing Algorithms Out-Pacing the Law' (March 2020) <https://www.equalityhumanrights.com/en/our-work/news/facial-recognition-technology-and-predictive-policing-algorithms-out-pacing-law> accessed 1 July 2022.

Euractiv, European Commission, leaked draft paper entitled 'Structure for the White Paper on Artificial Intelligence – a European Approach' (*Euractiv*, 2 February 2021) <https://www.euractiv.com/wp-content/uploads/sites/2/2020/01/AI-white-paper-EURACTIV.pdf> accessed 1 July 2022.

European Commission, 'Proposal for a Regulation of the European Parliament and of the Council Laying Down Harmonised Rules on Artificial Intelligence (Artificial Intelligence Act) and Amending Certain Union Legislative Acts' COM (2021) 206 final.

European Commission, 'White Paper – on Artificial Intelligence – A European Approach to Excellence and Trust', 19 February 2020, COM (2020) 65 final.

European Court of Human Rights, Press Unit, Factsheet 'New Technologies' <https://www.echr.coe.int/Documents/FS_New_technologies_ENG.pdf> accessed 1 July 2022.

European Digital Rights (EDRi), 'Ban Biometric Mass Surveillance: A Set of Fundamental Rights Demands for the European Commission and EU Member States' (*EDRi*, 13 May 2020) <https://edri.org/wp-content/uploads/2020/05/Paper-Ban-Biometric-Mass-Surveillance.pdf> accessed 1 July 2022.

EDRi, 'Washed in Blue: Living Lab Digital Perimeter in Amsterdam' (19 May 2021) <https://edri.org/our-work/washed-in-blue-living-lab-digital-perimeter-in-amsterdam/> accessed 1 July 2022.

France Bleu Saint-Etienne, 'Capteurs sonores à Saint-Etienne: la mise en garde de la CNIL' (29 October 2019) <https://www.francebleu.fr/infos/societe/capteurs-sonores-a-saint-etienne-la-mise-en-garde-de-la-cnil-1572343225> accessed 1 July 2022.

Friedewald M and others, 'Data Protection Impact Assessments in Practice' (2022) Lecture Notes in Computer Science, Conference Paper (13106).

Fussey P, 'Beyond Liberty, Beyond Security: The Politics of Public Surveillance' (2008) 3(1) British Politics.

Fussey P and Murray D, 'Independent Report on the London Metropolitan Police Service's Trial of Live Facial Recognition Technology' (2019) 10 <https://repository.essex.ac.uk/24946/1/London-Met-Police-Trial-of-Facial-Recognition-Tech-Report-2.pdf> accessed 1 July 2022.

Fussey P and Murray D, 'Policing Uses of Live Facial Recognition in the United Kingdom' in A Kak (ed.), *Regulating Biometrics: Global Approaches and Urgent Questions*, AI Now Institute (September 2020) <https://ainowinstitute.org/regulatingbiometrics.pdf> accessed 1 July 2022.

Fussey P and others, '"Assisted" Facial Recognition and the Reinvention of Suspicion and Discretion in Digital Policing' (2021) 61(2) The British Journal of Criminology.

Galič M, 'Surveillance and Privacy in Smart Cities and Living Labs: Conceptualising Privacy for Public Space' (PhD thesis, Tilburg University 2019).

Galič M and Gellert R, 'Data Protection Law beyond Identifiability? Atmospheric Profiles, Nudging and the Stratumseind Living Lab' (2021) 40 Computer Law & Security Review.

Gemeente Amsterdam, written question, <https://amsterdam.raadsinformatie.nl/document/10131215/1/180%20sv%20IJmker%20onderzoek%20Digitaleo%20Perimeter> accessed 1 July 2022.

Ghosh I, 'Mapped: The State of Facial Recognition Around the World', 22 May 2020, Visual Capitalist <https://www.visualcapitalist.com/facial-recognition-world-map/> accessed 1 July 2022.

Handbook on Human Rights Impact Assessment (2019) <https://www.humanrights.dk/sites/humanrights.dk/files/media/dokumenter/business/hria/hria_toolbox/hria_guidance_and_toolbox_final_feb2016.pdf> accessed 1 July 2022.

Home Office, 'Biometrics Strategy: Better Public Services Maintaining Public Trust' (June 2018) <https://assets.publishing.service.gov.uk/government/uploads/syst em/uploads/attachment_data/file/720850/Home_Office_Biometrics_Strategy_-_ 2018-06-28.pdf> accessed 1 July 2022.

Home Office, 'Fact Sheet on Live Facial Recognition Used by Police' (September 2019) <https://homeofficemedia.blog.gov.uk/2019/09/04/fact-sheet-on-live-fac ial-recognition-used-by-police/> accessed 1 July 2022.

Hooyman P, 'Het ware gezicht van gezichtsherkennings-technologie' (*Bits of Freedom*, 30 October 2019) <https://www.bitsoffreedom.nl/wp-content/uploa ds/2019/11/het-ware-gezicht-van-gezichtsherkenningstechnologie.pdf> accessed 1 July 2022.

House of Commons Science and Technology Committee, Oral Evidence, 'The Work of the Biometrics Commissioner and the Forensic Science Regulator' HC 1970 (*Parliament*, 19 March 2019) <http://data.parliament.uk/writtenevidence/ committeeevidence.svc/evidencedocument/science-and-technology-committee/ the-work-of-the-biometrics-commissioner-and-the-forensic-science-regulator/o ral/98556.html> accessed 1 July 2022.

House of Commons Science and Technology Committee, 'The Work of the Biometrics Commissioner and the Forensic Science Regulator, Nineteenth Report of Session 2017-19' (*Parliament*, 17 July 2019) <https://publications. parliament.uk/pa/cm201719/cmselect/cmsctech/1970/1970.pdf>.

Hussain D, 'Met Police Make First Arrest Using Facial Recognition Technology as They Hold Woman, 35, Over Alleged Serious Assault on Emergency Service Worker' (*Daily Mail Online*, 28 February 2020) <https://www.dailymail.co.uk/ news/article-8055001/Met-Police-make-arrest-using-facial-recognition-technolo gy.html> accessed 1 July 2022.

ICO, 'Sandbox Beta Phase, Discussion Paper' (January 2019) <https://ico.org.uk/ media/about-the-ico/documents/2614219/sandbox-discussion-paper-20190130. pdf> accessed 1 July 2022.

ICO, 'The Guide to the Sandbox' <https://ico.org.uk/for-organisations/regula tory-sandbox/the-guide-to-the-sandbox/> accessed 1 July 2022.

ICO, 'Information Commissioner's Opinion: The Use of Live Facial Recognition Technology by Law Enforcement in Public Places' (October 2019) <https://ico. org.uk/media/about-the-ico/documents/2616184/live-frt-law-enforcement-opini on-20191031.pdf> accessed 1 July 2022.

ICO, 'Blog: Information Commissioner's Opinion Addresses Privacy Concerns on the Use of Live Facial Recognition Technology in Public Places' (18 June 2021) <https://ico.org.uk/about-the-ico/media-centre/information-commissioner-s-op inion-addresses-privacy-concerns-on-the-use-of-live-facial-recognition-technol ogy-in-public-places/> accessed 1 July 2022.

ICO, 'Information Commissioner's Opinion: The Use of Live Facial Recognition Technology in Public Places' (June 2021) <https://ico.org.uk/media/about-the- ico/documents/2619985/ico-opinion-the-use-of-lfr-in-public-places-20210618. pdf> accessed 1 July 2022.

ICO, 'ICO Investigation into how the Police Use Facial Recognition Technology in Public Places' (31 October 2019) <https://ico.org.uk/media/about-the-ico/ documents/2616185/live-frt-law-enforcement-report-20191031.pdf> accessed 1 July 2022.

ICO, 'Data Protection Impact Assessment' <https://ico.org.uk/for-organisations/ guide-to-data-protection/guide-to-the-general-data-protection-regulation-gdpr/

accountability-and-governance/data-protection-impact-assessments/?msclkid=
3b86403fb58611ec9ce9f3a413668fd9> accessed 1 July 2022.
Jain AK and others, *Introduction to Biometrics* (Springer 2011).
Janssen HL, 'An Approach for a Fundamental Rights Impact Assessment to
Automated Decision-Making' (2020) 10 International Data Privacy Law 1.
Keymolen E, 'Dutch Experiment with Facial Recognition: Privacy Risks Require
Legislative Choices' <https://www.tilburguniversity.edu/current/press-releases/
privacy-risks-facial-recognition-technology> accessed 1 July 2022.
Koops BJ and Galič M, 'Conceptualising Space and Place: Lessons from
Geography for the Debate on Privacy in Public' in T Timan and others (eds),
Privacy in Public Space: Conceptual and Regulatory Challenges (Edward Elgar
Publishing 2017).
Lawless CJ, 'The Evolution, Devolution and Distribution of UK Biometric
Imaginaries' (2022) 17 BioSocieties.
Lequesne Roth C and others, 'La reconnaissance faciale dans l'espace public: Une
cartographie juridique européenne', Fablex DL4T Report (April 2020) <https://
droit.univ-cotedazur.fr/dl4t/la-reconnaissance-faciale-dans-lespace---une-carto
graphie-juridique-europeenne> accessed 1 July 2022.
MacNaughton G, 'Human Rights Impact Assessment: A Method for Healthy
Policymaking' (2015) 17(1) Health and Human Rights.
Mantelero A, 'AI and Big Data: A Blueprint for a Human Rights, Social and
Ethical Impact Assessment' (2018) 34(3) Computer Law & Security Review.
Martin A, 'Cops Turn Download Festival into an Orwellian Spy Paradise' (*The
Register*, 11 June 2015) <https://www.theregister.com/2015/06/11/download_
festival_big_brother_playground_leicestershire_police?page=1> accessed 1 July
2022.
Martinez A, 'Face Recognition, Overview' in SZ Li and A Jain (eds), *Encyclopedia
of Biometrics* (Springer 2009).
Mathewson J, 'MET Facial Recognition to Face Legal Challenge' (*City Matters*,
30 January 2020) <https://www.citymatters.london/met-facial-recognition-face-
legal-challenge/> accessed 1 July 2022.
Ministère de l'Intérieur, 'Livre Blanc de la Sécurité Intérieure' (2020) <https://
www.interieur.gouv.fr/sites/minint/files/medias/documents/2021-06//livre-bla
nc-de-la-securite-interieure.pdf> accessed 1 July 2022.
Mis JM, 'Pour un usage responsable et acceptable par la société des technologies de sécurité' vols 1 and 2 (September 2021) <https://www.vie-publique.fr/
rapport/281424-pour-un-usage-responsable-et-acceptable-par-la-societe-des-tec
hnologies> accessed 1 July 2022.
Moeckli D, *Exclusion from Public Space: A Comparative Constitutional Analysis*
(Cambridge University Press 2016).
Naafs S, '*Living Laboratories*: The Dutch Cities Amassing Data on Oblivious
Residents' (*The Guardian*, 1 March 2018) <https://www.theguardian.com/
cities/2018/mar/01/smart-cities-data-privacy-eindhoven-utrecht> accessed 1
July 2022.
National Physical Laboratory and Metropolitan Police, 'Metropolitan Police
Service Live Facial Recognition Trials' (February 2020).
Németh J and Schmid S, 'Publicly Accessible Space and Quality of Life: A Tool for
Measuring the Openness of Urban Spaces' in M Budruk and R Philipps, *Quality-
of-Life Community Indicators for Parks, Recreation and Tourism Management*
(Springer 2011).

Oosterhoff R, 'Amsterdam Is Watching You, naar hoe zorgvuldig gebeurt dat?' (*AT5*, 18 February 2021) <https://www.at5.nl/artikelen/207283/amsterdam-is-watching-you-maar-hoe-zorgvuldig-gebeurt-dat> accessed 1 July 2022.

Philipsen S and others, 'Legal Enclaves as a Test Environment for Innovative Products: Toward Legally Resilient Experimentation Policies' (2021) 15 Regulation and Governance.

Piquet C, 'Reconnaissance faciale: Cédric O n'est "pas certain" qu'Alicem soit un jour déployée' (*Le Parisien*, 24 December 2019) <https://www.leparisien.fr/high-tech/reconnaissance-faciale-cedric-o-n-est-pas-certain-qu-alicem-soit-un-jour-deployee-24-12-2019-8223705.php> accessed 1 July 2022.

Press Association, 'Welsh Police Wrongly Identify Thousands as Potential Criminals' (*The Guardian*, 5 May 2018) <https://www.theguardian.com/uk-news/2018/may/05/welsh-police-wrongly-identify-thousands-as-potential-criminals> accessed 1 July 2022.

Provence-Alpes-Côte d'Azur Région, Décision 18-893 (14 December 2018) <https://www.laquadrature.net/wp-content/uploads/sites/8/2019/02/4.-D%C3%A9lib%C3%A9ration-attaqu%C3%A9e.pdf> accessed 1 July 2022.

R(Bridges) v the Chief Constable of South Wales Police, [2019] EWHC 2341 (Admin).

R(on the application of Edward Bridges) v the Chief Constable of South Wales Police, Appeal [2020] EWCA Civ 1058.

Ranchordás S, 'The Whys and Woes of Experimental Legislation' (2013) 1(3) Theory and Practice of Legislation.

'Reclaim Your Face' <https://reclaimyourface.eu> accessed 1 July 2022.

RTLnieuws, 'Tientallen camera's houden klanten van filiaal Jumbo in de gaten: willen we dit?' (*RTLnieuws*, 3 December 2019) <https://www.rtlnieuws.nl/nieuws/nederland/artikel/4941596/gezichtsherkenning-biometrie-alphen-jumbo-privacy> accessed 1 July 2022.

Sénat, Science and Technology Briefings, Parliamentary Office for Scientific and Technological Assessment, Briefing 14, 'Facial Recognition' (July 2019) <https://www2.assemblee-nationale.fr/content/download/179314/1794787/version/2/file/Note%20Reconnaissance%20Faciale%20-%20EN.pdf> accessed 1 July 2022.

Sénat, Rapport d'information fait au nom de la commission des lois constitutionnelles, de législation, du suffrage universel, du Règlement et d'administration générale sur la reconnaissance faciale et ses risques au regard de la protection des libertés individuelles, no 627, 10 May 2022 <https://www.senat.fr/rap/r21-627/r21-6271.pdf> accessed 1 July 2022.

South Wales Police, 'Smarter Recognition, Safer Community, Deployments' <https://afr.south-wales.police.uk/wp-content/uploads/2021/04/All-Deployments.pdf> accessed 1 July 2022.

South Wales Police, 'Live Facial Recognition Technology Results' <https://www.south-wales.police.uk/news/south-wales/news/2022/maw-mar/results-of-live-facial-recognition-technology-on-190322/> accessed 1 July 2022.

Surveillance Camera Commissioner, 'Facing the Camera, Good Practice and Guidance for the Police Use of Overt Surveillance Camera Systems Incorporating Facial Recognition Technology to Locate Persons on a Watchlist, in Public Places in England and Wales' (November 2020) <https://assets.publishing.service.gov.uk/government/uploads/system/uploads/attachment_data/file/940386/6.7024_SCC_Facial_recognition_report_v3_WEB.pdf> accessed 1 July 2022.

TA Marseille (Administrative Court in Marseille), 27 February 2020, no. 1901249 <http://marseille.tribunal-administratif.fr/content/download/178764/1756210/version/1/file/1901249.pdf> accessed 1 July 2022.

TADA <https://tada.city/en/home-en/> accessed 1 July 2022.

Tesquet O, 'Des micros dans la rue: la CNIL tire les oreilles (intelligentes) de Saint-Etienne (*Télérama*, 29 October 2019) <https://www.telerama.fr/medias/la-cnil-tire-les-oreilles-intelligentes-de-saint-etienne,n6492439.php> accessed 1 July 2022.

The Ryder Review (June 2022) <https://www.adalovelaceinstitute.org/wp-content/uploads/2022/06/The-Ryder-Review-Independent-legal-review-of-the-governa nce-of-biometric-data-in-England-and-Wales-Ada-Lovelace-Institute-June-20 22.pdf> accessed 1 July 2022.

Tijhaar L, 'Vroeg of laat moet de politie gezichtsherkenning gaan gebruiken' (*Kennislink*, 6 January 2021) <https://www.nemokennislink.nl/publicaties/vroeg-of-laat-moet-de-politie-gezichtsherkenning-gaan-gebruiken/> accessed 1 July 2022.

TNO's report 'Privacy bescherming bij niet-coöperatieve gezichtsherkenning', Appendix E describing the possible use cases with FRT (21 January 2021) <https://www.tno.nl/nl/newsroom/2021/02/nieuwe-mijlpaal-waarborgen-priva cy/> accessed 1 July 2022.

Townsend M, 'Police to Use Facial Recognition Cameras at Cenotaph Service' (*The Guardian*, 12 November 2017) <https://www.theguardian.com/tec hnology/2017/nov/12/metropolitan-police-to-use-facial-recognition-technology-remembrance-sunday-cenotaph> accessed 1 July 2022.

Tribunal Administratif (TA) Marseille, no. 1901249 (27 February 2020) <http://marseille.tribunal-administratif.fr/content/download/178764/1756210/version/1/file/1901249.pdf> accessed 1 July 2022.

UK Government, Response to the Committee's Nineteenth Report of Session 2017–19 (*Parliament*, 19 March 2021) <https://publications.parliament.uk/pa/cm5801/cmselect/cmsctech/1319/131902.htm> accessed 1 July 2022.

UK Government, News, 'The Biometrics and Surveillance Camera Commissioner's Response to the College of Policing APP on Live Facial Recognition' (Gov.uk, 6 April 2022) <https://www.gov.uk/government/news/the-biometrics-and-sur veillance-camera-commissioners-response-to-the-college-of-policing-app-on-liv e-facial-recognition> accessed 1 July 2022.

UN Habitat, 'Global Public Space Toolkit: From Global Principles to Local Policies and Practice' (*United Nations*, 2015).

Untersinger M, 'Reconnaissance faciale : la CNIL toque sur le bilan de l'expérience niçoise' (*Le Monde*, 29 August 2019) <https://www.lemonde.fr/pixels/article/2019/08/28/reconnaissance-faciale-la-cnil-tique-sur-le-bilan-de-l-experience-nicoise_5503769_4408996.html> accessed 1 July 2022.

Untersinger M, 'Cédric O: "Expérimenter la reconnaissance faciale est nécessaire pour que nos industriels progressent"' (*Le Monde*, 14 October 2019) <https ://www.lemonde.fr/economie/article/2019/10/14/cedric-o-experimenter-la-reconna issance-faciale-est-necessaire-pour-que-nos-industriels-progressent_6015395_32 34.html> accessed 1 July 2022.

van der Sloot B and Lanzing M, 'The Continued Transformation of the Public Sphere: On the Road to Smart Cities, Living Labs and a New Understanding of Society' in M Nagenborg and others (eds), *Technology and the City: Towards a Philosophy of Urban Technologies* (Springer 2021).

Ville de Nice, 'Rapport: Expérimentation Reconnaissance Faciale' (20 June 2019) <https://data.technopolice.fr/api/files/1568560839337an2i6yk04kp.pdf> accessed 1 July 2022.

Violaine III, 'Un logiciel pour décoder les émotions des usagers du tramway de Nice' (*FranceBleu.fr*, 4 January 2019) <https://www.francebleu.fr/infos/societe/un-logiciel-pour-decoder-les-emotions-des-usagers-du-tramway-de-nice-154662 1455> accessed 1 July 2022.

Waarlo N and Verhagen L, 'De stand van gezichtsherkenning in Nederland' (*De Volkskrant*, 27 March 2020) <https://www.volkskrant.nl/kijkverder/v/2020/de-stand-van-gezichtsherkenning-in-nederland~v91028/> accessed 1 July 2022.

Williams C, 'Police Surveillance and the Emergence of CCTV in the 1960s' (2003) 5(3) Crime Prevention and Community Safety.

Young J, 'A History of CCTV Surveillance in Britain' (*QSwns*, 22 January 2018) <https://stories.swns.com/news/history-cctv-surveillance-britain-93449/> accessed 1 July 2022.

12. Big Data, AI and health data: between national, European, and international legal frameworks

Nikolaus Forgó, Emily Johnson, Iana Kazeeva and Elisabeth Steindl[1]

INTRODUCTION

The purpose of this chapter is to examine how health data is treated in the EU from a data protection point of view and whether this treatment has an impact on the development of Big Data and AI-driven medical treatment and research, as well as on patients' rights. EU data protection norms, in particular the General Data Protection Regulation 216/679 (hereinafter referred to as 'GDPR'),[2] have become, as many say, a global point of reference for regulatory ambitions in order to ensure the protection of (sensitive) personal data. By choosing a wide territorial scope,[3] addressing the transfer of data outside the EU and the EEA,[4] and by externalising its data protection requirements outside its borders through market power and market mechanisms, European data protection law has become an essential factor to consider not only within the Union but also far beyond. However, GDPR can and needs to be put into context as its standards and its values are not the only ones found in Europe. On a second level, this chapter is therefore using the example of the legal situations on the same topic in other jurisdictions, particularly the UK and

---

[1]   Department of Innovation and Digitalisation in Law, University of Vienna.

[2]   EU General Data Protection Regulation (GDPR), Regulation (EU) 2016/679 of the European Parliament and of the Council of 27 April 2016 on the protection of natural persons with regard to the processing of personal data and on the free movement of such data, and repealing Directive 95/46/EC (General Data Protection Regulation), OJ 2016 L 119/1.

[3]   Art 3(1) GDPR provides that the regulation applies to the processing of a controller or a processor in the Union, regardless of whether the processing takes place in the Union or not, and to the processing of personal data of data subjects within the Union by a processor or controller not established in the Union provided it is related to the offering of goods or services within the Union (Art 3(2) (b) GDPR), or to the monitoring of their behaviour therein (Art 3(2)(a) GDPR).

[4]   See Chapter 5 of the GDPR.

Russia for reasons of comparison. The UK and Russia are chosen due to their regulatory approaches, different from EU procedures, and serve as points of reference for further EU assessments.

In examining legislative shifts with regard to emerging technologies, this chapter is well aware of the substantial benefits of using Big Data and AI for the sector of health and care. In all knowledge-based fields this kind of data processing leads to informational insights. For the field of medical research and treatment, new technologies arguably have the potential to result in an exponential leap in personalised and precise medicine as well as in significant advancements in the collective fight against life-threatening individual diseases as well as against pandemics.[5] However, these insights and advancements must not be achieved with no sensitivity for the fundamental rights-related implications they might come with.

Looking beyond EU legislative responses and initiatives to address the challenges provoked by emerging technologies allows for a wider horizon and legal reflections against the background of a global health market. The developments in the UK in the area of health-related data and AI are of specific interest, particularly due to the work of a number of private research companies that are considered frontrunners in AI and health data, as well as government-driven initiatives. The UK's National Data Strategy, launched in 2020,[6] provides insight regarding the dynamics post-Brexit, allowing for consideration of what the European values on privacy mean and how they can be upheld when facing the needs of new technologies. As part of the National Data Strategy, the UK has proposed a reform of its data protection laws with the aim of securing 'pro-growth and [a] trusted data regime.'[7] This legal reform proposes a divergence from

---

[5]   See e.g. EPRS (STOA) (2022), 'Artificial Intelligence in Healthcare: Applications, Risks, and Ethical and Societal Impacts' <https://www.europarl. europa.eu/RegData/etudes/STUD/2022/729512/EPRS_STU(2022)729512_EN.pdf> accessed 7 July 2022; Apple/Google, Exposure Notification Privacy-preserving Analytics (ENPA) White Paper <https://covid19-static.cdn-apple.com/ap plications/covid19/current/static/contact-tracing/pdf/ENPA_White_Paper.pdf> accessed 25 February 2023; see Ryan Browne, 'Why Coronavirus Contact-Tracing Apps Aren't Yet the "Game Changer" Authorities Hoped They'd Be' <https:// www.cnbc.com/2020/07/03/why-coronavirus-contact-tracing-apps-havent-been-a-game-changer.html> accessed 25 February 2023.

[6]   GOV.UK, 'National Data Strategy' (9 December 2020) <https://www.gov. uk/government/publications/uk-national-data-strategy/national-data-strategy> accessed 6 July 2022.

[7]   GOV.UK, 'Data: A New Direction – Government Response to Consultation' (updated 23 June 2022) <https://www.gov.uk/government/consultations/data-a-new-direction/outcome/data-a-new-direction-government-response-to-consultat ion> accessed 6 July 2022.

the EU's approach to data protection, which it considers impeding and 'overcautious'.[8]

The specific interest in the legal situation in Russia is triggered by the recent regulatory attempts to further AI and Big-Data data processing, also in health-related areas, under a 'sandbox' privilege. The Russian example provides a perspective, different from that of the EU and UK, wherein the right to data protection is *de facto* being neglected for the sake of expedited and unconstrained development of AI technologies. Furthermore, using a sandbox regime for development of AI systems is of relevance, particularly in light of the EU's first pilot sandbox initiative on AI, launched by the Government of Spain in October 2022.[9] This initiative aims to support the implementation of the proposed AI Act by working with competent authorities and private actors to develop best practices in line with the proposed Act.

Part I of this chapter discusses the data protection and security issues with regard to health-related data in the context of the GDPR. Special emphasis is put on the challenges created by the use of Big Data and AI in the area of healthcare and the Commission's most recent attempt to introduce regulatory sandboxes in the draft Artificial Intelligence Act, proposed in April 2021. Part II focuses on the analysis of the plans of the UK government with regard to the processing of health-related data in the context of Brexit and provides an overview of the work of private research organisations, such as DeepMind. Part III of the chapter describes the approach taken by the Russian Government to data protection and the use of health-related data for the purposes of AI experimental regimes, focusing on the example of the AI regulatory 'sandbox' introduced in Moscow in July 2020.

PART I: THE EUROPEAN UNION

Data-fuelled technologies have remarkable potential for the governance of health and care. Data and new data-intense technologies are the key elements in endeavours to make this transformation. Digitalisation could help European healthcare systems in overcoming structural and

---

[8]   ibid.

[9]   Ministerio de Asuntos Económicos y Transformación Digital. El Gobierno de España presenta, en colaboración con la Comisión Europea, el primer piloto del sandbox de regulación de Inteligencia Artificial en la UE <https://portal.mineco.gob.es/en-us/comunicacion/Pages/20220627-PR_AI_Sandbox.aspx> accessed 4 July 2022.

financial challenges, such as an ageing population, chronic diseases, unequal access, quality of service and shortage of health professionals.[10] Accordingly, the digital transformation of health and care in the Digital Single Market has been on the agenda of the European Commission for many years. Improved health data management and secured access to data to foster research, as well as better treatment and building a healthier society, are considered crucial in this transformation.[11] The Commission has highlighted three priorities for the digital future for health and care in a communication released in 2018: (i) citizens' secure access to their health data, including across borders; (ii) better data to advance research, disease prevention, and personalised health and care; and (iii) digital tools for citizen empowerment and person-centred care. Furthermore, the Commission acknowledged that success depended on the quality and the quantity of the data available together with the appropriate regulatory frameworks.[12]

The Covid-19 pandemic has accelerated the demand for supra-regional digital solutions, such as for contact tracing, the digital green certificate, and vaccine development and manufacturing. Simultaneously, it has made the prevailing poor level of access to health data for public health purposes, as well as the need to share data for research purposes within EU borders, beyond apparent.[13] Member States showed a multitude of national (legal) approaches in how to manage the fight against the virus

---

[10] See e.g. European Commission, 'Shaping Europe's Digital Future: eHealth' <https://digital-strategy.ec.europa.eu/en/policies/ehealth> accessed 24 January 2022 and European Commission, 'Digital Health and Care' (2018) <https://ec.eu ropa.eu/health/sites/default/files/ehealth/docs/2018_ehealth_infographic_en.pdf> accessed 23 November 2021.

[11] European Commission, 'Shaping Europe's Digital Future: Managing Health Data' <https://digital-strategy.ec.europa.eu/en/policies/health-data> accessed 24 January 2022.

[12] European Commission, 'Communication from the Commission to the European Parliament, the Council, the European Economic and Social Committee and the Committee of the Regions on enabling the Digital Transformation of Health and Care in the Digital Single Market', COM (2018) 233 final.

[13] For reflections on a common data strategy with regard to health data see: EPRS, 'EU Health Data Centre and a Common Data Strategy for Public Health', Study Panel for the Future of Science and Technology. Scientific Foresight Unit (STOA) (2021).For the regulatory challenges of collecting health data in the European research context see e.g. Jos Dumortier and Mahault Piéchaud Boura, 'European-wide Big Health Data Analytics under the GDPR' in Maria Tzanou (ed.), *Health Data Privacy under the GDPR: Big Data Challenges and Regulatory Responses* (Routledge 2020).

and share relevant data, which made data sharing all the more difficult.[14] Stakeholders noticed that next to a lack of comparability of data and data sets, which are scattered over multiple providers, the use of different legal bases caused difficulties to share health data for public health purposes; in addition, they recognised a high demand for more pseudonymised data for public health purposes and for data altruism, which eventually could open the gate to more adventurous and effective research approaches in the future.[15]

Alongside the impact on people's physical health, the Covid-19 crisis has also exposed and exacerbated the ongoing silent epidemic in the mental health ecosystem. Given the associated risks for the data subjects, developments in digital mental health and protection of mental health data should be given the utmost attention by regulators. Here, it will serve as an exemplary case to discuss some of the legal concerns of data protection and privacy raised by new technologies.

The focal point of reference for data protection of personal health data in Europe is the above-mentioned General Data Protection Regulation 216/679 ('GDPR').[16] The GDPR builds the common framework on EU secondary law level governing all processing of personal data (data relating to an identified or identifiable natural person). The rules under the GDPR for processing of health-related data have to be applied in the national legal context of the Member States and with regard to the national health system and the national provision of healthcare. The GDPR itself allows Member States to adjust the application of the regulation in certain aspects to their national situation. In particular, one such opening clause specifically concerns the processing of health data. According to Article 9(4) GDPR, Member States are allowed to maintain or introduce their own conditions, including limitations with regard to the processing of genetic, biometric or health data. Article 89(2) GDPR states that Member States' law may provide for derogations from data subject's rights if the processing is undertaken for scientific purposes.

Consequently, in the area of health, neither does the GDPR set all necessary rules by itself nor is the GDPR applied in the same manner in each

---

[14]   European Commission, 'Assessment of the EU Member States' Rules on Health Data in the Light of the GDPR' (2021).

[15]   ibid 53f.

[16]   EU General Data Protection Regulation (GDPR): Regulation (EU) 2016/679 of the European Parliament and of the Council of 27 April 2016 on the protection of natural persons with regard to the processing of personal data and on the free movement of such data, and repealing Directive 95/46/EC (General Data Protection Regulation), OJ 2016 L 119/1.

Member State or within one Member State supposing that regional legislation applies; this has contributed to the difficulties in a common European attempt to fight the pandemic, as mentioned above.

The legal definition for health data encompasses all 'personal data related to the physical or mental health of a natural person, including the provision of healthcare services, which reveal information about his or her health status' (Article 4(15) GDPR). As clear as it seems at first sight, this definition leaves room for interpretation since the terms 'health' or 'physical health' and 'mental health' are not explained anywhere in the GDPR.[17] Recital 35 specifies that health data includes all relevant information relating to the past, current or future health status and covers registration as well as provision of healthcare services as referred to in Directive 2011/24/EU.[18] Comprehensively interpreted, health data comprises genetic data and biometric data as well as data collected by patients through mhealth (mobile health) tools, wearables, apps and self-reported information, as is the case in numerous AI applications for mental and physical health.[19] Anonymised health data does not fall within the scope of the GDPR, whereas pseudonymised health data continues to be personally (re-) identifiable and therefore has to comply with all provisions of the GDPR (Recital 26 GDPR).

According to Article 9(1) GDPR, (inter alia) data concerning health is considered a special category of data. This type of data is, in the eyes of the European legislator, by its nature particularly sensitive and requires specific protection reflecting the risks that processing might cause to the fundamental rights and freedoms of a natural person (Recital 51 GDPR). Processing of special category data is generally prohibited. Article 9(2) GDPR lists ten possible exceptions to the general prohibition; seven of these derogations are applicable to the processing of health data and build a possible legal basis.[20] Noteworthy here, is that if consent is the legal basis

---

[17]   For the definitional uncertainties of health data see: Maria Tzanou, 'The GDPR and (Big) Health Data: Assessing the EU Legislator's Choices' in Maria Tzanou (ed.), *Health Data Privacy under the GDPR: Big Data Challenges and Regulatory Responses* (Routledge 2020), here 6.

[18]   Directive 2011/24/EU of the European Parliament and of the Council of 9 March 2011 on the application of patients' rights in cross-border healthcare. OJ 2011 L 88/45.

[19]   See Boris P Paal and Daniel A Pauly (eds), *Datenschutz-Grundverordnung Bundesdatenschutzgesetz: DS-GVO BDSG*, 3rd edn (Beck 2021), Article 4, Margin number 106–110.

[20]   Article 9(2), (a) explicit consent to the processing for one or more specified purposes; (b) obligations and exercising rights in the field of employment and social security and social protection law; (c) vital interests of the data subject where

of choice, the processing of health data requires explicit consent as the strongest form of agreement as opposed to (only) regular consent (Article 6(1)(a) GDPR) required for the processing of non-sensitive data.[21]

The distinction of sensitive and non-sensitive data by the GDPR that results in different regimes of protection is in itself a challenge with regard to Big Data, new forms of data collection and data analytics. Merging big sets of traditionally non-health data with additional information and applying algorithms and data analytics can turn almost any data into health or other forms of sensitive data and reveal details about the mental or physical health of data subjects. Other than what the (static) binary categorisation of data in the GDPR is suggesting, Big Data combined with AI makes data dynamic.[22] Data that at some point did not contain any sensitive information can at another point and combined with other details or data sets become health data. Hence, such data can 'inadvertently shift from one category to another, every one of which requires the application of a different set of legal rules.'[23]

The terms 'AI', 'Big Data', or related concepts are not mentioned in the GDPR. This is on the one hand due to the fact that the GDPR is (at least in technological terms) rather outdated already. The Commission's proposal was presented more than 10 years ago, in January 2012, and many of the conceptual decisions were taken years before, some of them going back to the 1970s.[24] However, the GDPR explicitly tries to follow a

---

the data subject is physically or legally incapable of giving consent; (g) substantial public interest; (h) for the purposes of preventive or occupational medicine, for the assessment of the working capacity of the employee, medical diagnosis, the provision of health or social care or treatment or the management of health or social care systems and services; (i) public interest in the area of public health, such as protecting against serious cross-border threats to health or ensuring standards of quality and safety of healthcare and of medicinal products or medical devices; and (j) archiving purposes in the public interest, scientific or historical research purposes or statistical purposes in accordance with Article 89(1) GDPR.

[21]   For the question of consent requirement according to GDPR in the context of health research see e.g. Mary Donnelly and Maeve McDonagh, 'Health Research, Consent and the GDPR Exemption' (2019) 26 European Journal of Health Law. DOI: 10.1163/15718093-12262427.

[22]   On the problematic binary distinction of data in sensitive health data versus non-sensitive non-health data by the GDPR and the consequences resulting from it, see e.g. Tzanou (n 17).

[23]   Tal Z Zarsky, 'Incompatible: The GDPR in the Age of Big Data' (2017) 47 Seton Hall Law Review, 1013.

[24]   See, for example, the very first Data Protection Law in Hessen, Germany, from 1970, already introducing a Data Protection Officer <https://starweb.hessen.de/cache/GVBL/1970/00041.pdf> accessed 25 February 2023.

technology-neutral approach covering all possible fields of data processing in the same way, no matter how they might further develop, so that technology-specific rules are not incorporated. GDPR also follows a 'one-size-fits-all' approach, different from, for example, the US (HIIPA[25]), so that specificities of particular sectors are to be generally regulated.

Nonetheless, many if not most AI applications in health and care involve the processing of great quantities of personal data and can include the targeting and personalised treatment of individuals on the basis of such data. A large number of the provisions of the GDPR therefore are relevant to the use of AI and Big Data in health; some are indeed challenged by them as, in particular, most of the principles enumerated in Article 5 GDPR. Many of these principles are much older than the GDPR and have their roots in the 1970s and 1980s, when computers looked and operated very differently from today.

According to these principles, processing must be lawful, fair and transparent (Article 5(1)(a) GDPR). Fairness and transparency as understood by the GDPR provide that the collection and further processing of data is done in alignment with the (reasonable) expectations of the data subject and undertaken in a clear and open manner. Both, however, clash with the nature and possibilities of new technologies for exploiting their full potential and most likely will involve methods and patterns leading to results that neither the controller nor the data subject could have imagined at the time of collection.[26] In particular, transparency is an issue in AI as it can be impossible to say why the AI system reacts in a specific way. 'Explainable AI' is only a sub-discipline within the larger field of computer science-related research on AI, so that it is not the exception but more the rule that the machine acts like a 'blackbox'.[27] Lawfulness and fairness are also at stake whenever big amounts of data are processed in a way that is (mostly) unforeseeable for humans.

Purpose limitation is yet another principle challenged by the needs and possibilities of AI and Big Data. Article 5(1)(b) GDPR provides that only processing for specified, explicit and legitimate purposes is in conformity with data protection law; personal data shall not be further processed in a manner that is incompatible with the purposes for which the data

---

[25]   Health Insurance Portability and Accountability Act of 1996, HIPAA, is a US federal law protecting sensitive patient health information. See <https://www.hhs.gov/hipaa/for-professionals/compliance-enforcement/index.html> accessed 25 February 2023 for further information.

[26]   Tzanou (n 17) 111.

[27]   See e.g. Frank A Pasquale, 'The Black Box Society. The Secret Algorithms that Control Money and Information' (2015) 96 Book Gallery.

was collected. Recital 50 GDPR stresses that the data subject should be informed on those other purposes and on his or her rights including the right to object. According to Article 29 Working Party,[28] the gap between the new and the original purpose is decisive for determining compatibility; the new purpose has to be in alignment with the expectations of the data subject, the nature of the data and their impact on the data subjects' interests, and the safeguards adopted. This again seems to go against the very idea of Big Data, which is to collect as much data as possible and to exploit it repeatedly from different angles, to combine it with new information and to thus retrieve results that were unforeseen at the time of collection.[29] Mental health serves as an exquisite example of the difficulties of GDPR-compliant processing of health data when deploying new technologies. The multiple ways to infer information for mental health diagnosis and prediction from originally non-sensitive data (e.g., by inference inter alia from GPS data, amount of social contact, typing or scrolling patterns, linguistic patterns in social media entries, etc.) call into question whether inferences of that kind are indeed within the scope of intention when the data was collected and are in alignment with reasonable expectations of the data subject.

Related to the principle of purpose limitation are the principles of data minimisation in Article 5(1)(c) GDPR, according to which personal data should be 'adequate, relevant and limited to what is necessary in relation to the purposes for which they are processed', and storage limitation (Article 5(1)(e)). Both again can stand in contrast with the very nature of Big Data, which combines AI and statistical methods to find out about unexpected and so far unknown correlations in big data sets. The requirement of keeping the data set as little as possible and deleting it as soon as possible thus could undermine the potential success and utility of Big Data.[30]

The principle of accuracy (Article 5(1)(d)) is equally discussed in relation to GDPR compliance, as training sets with biases, such as biases concerning gender or race, reduce drastically the accuracy of health predictions and medical research for groups that are not reflected adequately in the training set.

---

28   Article 29 Data Protection Working Party, 'Opinion 03/2013 on Purpose Limitation' (adopted 2 April 2013).

29   See e.g. Bart van der Sloot and Sascha van Schendel, 'Ten Questions for Future Regulation of Big Data: A Comparative and Empirical Legal Study' (2016) 7 Journal of Intellectual Property, Information Technology and Electronic Commerce Law.

30   See Zarsky (n 23) 1013.

Among the great strengths of data-intense technologies is their exceptional potential for automation in addition to evaluative and/or predictive aspects. AI and Big Data combined allow for automated decision-making and profiling in fields that demand complex choices with a multitude of factors while relying on criteria that are not always entirely predefined and with results that not only save costs but also are more precise and impartial than human decision-making.[31] Health and care certainly belong to these domains.

Article 22 GDPR provides a general prohibition of solely automated decision-making, including profiling, followed by a number of exemptions. Data subjects have a right not to be subject to automated processing, including profiling, without meaningful human involvement if this causes legal effects or similarly affects the data subject. For special category data, such as health data, Article 22(4) GDPR specifies that only explicit consent (Article 9(2)(a) GDPR) and substantial public interest (Article 9(2)(g) GDPR) are a lawful basis for solely automated decision-making. In case sensitive and non-sensitive data are merged, which as shown above is one of the special features of new technologies, to the point that separation of the data becomes impossible, Article 22(4) GDPR is understood to apply to the complete data set.[32]

With the increased use of Big Data and the creation of new health data infrastructures for a better discoverability and usability of different (big) data sets, cybersecurity, too, is gaining even more relevance than before. As demonstrated by the reported attack on the European Medicines Agency (EMA) related to Covid-19 medicine and vaccines,[33] as well as by two recent possible cyberattacks to the Irish health system[34] and a hospital in New Zealand,[35] the risk for attacks on critical health infrastructures is growing. A cyberattack in October 2020 on a Finnish mental health

---

[31] EPRS, 'The Impact of the General Data Protection Regulation (GDPR) on Artificial Intelligence' (2020) <https://www.europarl.europa.eu/RegData/etudes/STUD/2020/641530/EPRS_STU(2020)641530_EN.pdf> accessed 23 November 2021.

[32] Paal and Pauly (n 19), Article 22, Margin number 41a.

[33] EMA, 'Cyberattack on EMA' <https://www.ema.europa.eu/en/news/cyberattack-ema-update-5> accessed 23 November 2021.

[34] BBC, 'Cyber Attack "Most Significant on Irish State"' (14 May 2021) <https://www.bbc.com/news/world-europe-57111615> accessed 23 November 2021.

[35] Sara Barker, 'IT Systems Down at Waikato Hospital & DHB, "Cybersecurity Incident" Confirmed' (Security Brief, 19 May 2021) <https://securitybrief.co.nz/story/breaking-it-systems-down-at-waikato-hospital-dhb-cybersecurity-incident-confirmed> accessed 23 November 2021.

start-up illustrates the seriousness of a similar attack or data breach, and possible implications: patients' notes revealing details about adulterous relationships, suicide attempts, paedophilic thoughts, alcoholism and abuse have supposedly been hacked; patients have been blackmailed individually to pay ransom money; the list of patients affected included politicians and public figures, according to reports in the media.[36]

The drastic consequences of violations of data protection law and privacy, as described in some examples in this chapter, make clear, once again, why caution should be exercised with the processing of sensitive data such as health data, and why data protection rules in the GDPR are as strict as they are.

At the same time and as shown above, the deployment of data-driven technologies to the best of their potential and for the benefit of the patients runs against numerous points of friction with the GDPR. Critics admonish that, due to the current legal framework, Europe is lagging behind in the international digital development while patients are not sufficiently protected either. As pointed out above, the European legislation for health data processing, in particular the GDPR as the most relevant piece of data protection legislation, is seen by many as technologically outdated and thus obstructing the usage and development of new technologies to the detriment of individual and public health.[37]

In recent years, many of the regulatory attempts within the European legal framework that aimed to foster the development of AI and Big Data followed a soft law approach of a somewhat general nature, such as the Ethics Guidelines for Trustworthy Artificial Intelligence,[38] the Report on liability for Artificial Intelligence and other emerging Technologies,[39] the

---

[36]   William Ralston, 'They Told Their Therapists Everything: Hackers Leaked It All' (Wired, 05 April 2021) <https://www.wired.com/story/vastaamo-psycho therapy-patients-hack-data-breach/> accessed 23 November 2021.

[37]   See, as a recent (Austrian) example, statements made in the Austrian Parliament during debates on the Covid-19 pandemic such as <https://www. parliament.gv.at/PAKT/VHG/XXVII/NRSITZ/NRSITZ_00129/B_-_11_38_45_ 00255837.html> accessed 25 February 2023 ('one can see that data protection leads to health problems in Austria').

[38]   European Commission, Directorate-General for Communications Networks, Content and Technology, 'Ethics Guidelines for Trustworthy AI', Publications Office (2019) <https://data.europa.eu/doi/10.2759/177365> accessed 25 February 2023.

[39]   European Commission, Directorate-General for Justice and Consumers, 'Liability for Artificial Intelligence and Other Emerging Digital Technologies', Publications Office (2019) <https://data.europa.eu/doi/10.2838/25362> accessed 25 February 2023.

White Paper on AI[40] or Ursula von der Leyen's agenda for Europe.[41] The past months, however, could become the starting point for a complete overhaul of the prevailing legal framework with regard to new technologies. The goal of the Commission's regulatory efforts is to ensure data protection rights on the one hand and to support technological development on the other hand. In alignment with the EU's aspiration towards becoming a global power and role model for digital regulation, the Commission has been zealous to propose new pieces of legislation such as the Artificial Intelligence Act (hereinafter referred to as 'the AI Act').[42] Sector-specific legislation is on the horizon as well, in particular by the creation of a European Health Data Space,[43] allowing for health data (electronic health records, genomics data, data from patient registries, etc.) to be collected, used, re-used and exchanged across borders in a secure environment.

Among other provisions, the AI Act introduces regulatory sandboxes, which could serve as one of the possible escape mechanisms to the above-outlined problems. The purpose of such a sandbox is to 'foster AI innovation by establishing a controlled experimentation and testing environment in the development and pre-marketing phase with a view to ensuring compliance of the innovative AI systems with this Regulation and other relevant Union and Member States legislation.'[44] The sandbox does not exempt from existing regulatory limitations so that GDPR rules continue to be fully applicable.

Article 53(1) of the proposed AI Act explains that the purpose of a sandbox is to develop 'a controlled environment that facilitates the development, testing and validation of innovative AI systems for a limited time before their placement on the market or putting into service pursuant to a specific plan.' Data protection authorities are not expected to give developers of innovative AI solutions a 'carte blanche', but to closely collaborate, monitor and guide them in order to help them to stay within legal boundaries (Article 53(2)).

---

[40]   European Commission, 'White Paper on Artificial Intelligence: A European Approach to Excellence and Trust', COM(2020) 65 final.

[41]   Ursula von der Leyen, 'A Union That Strives For More, My Agenda for Europe: Political Guidelines for the Next European Commission 2019–2024' <https://op.europa.eu/en/publication-detail/-/publication/43a17056-ebf1-11e9-9c4 e-01aa75ed71a1> accessed 25 February 2023.

[42]   Proposal for a Regulation of the European Parliament and of the Council Laying Down Harmonised Rules on Artificial Intelligence (Artificial Intelligence Act) and Amending Certain Union Legislative Acts, COM/2021/206 final.

[43]   For further details see: European Commission, 'European Health Data Space' <https://ec.europa.eu/health/ehealth/dataspace_en> accessed 23 November 2021.

[44]   ibid., Recital 72.

Health risks of AI solutions that are within a regulatory sandbox are explicitly highlighted: 'Any significant risks to health and safety and fundamental rights identified during the development and testing of such systems shall result in immediate mitigation and, failing that, in the suspension of the development and testing process until such mitigation takes place' (Article 53(3)). Data controllers participating in a sandbox remain liable for any harm inflicted on third parties as a result from the experimentation taking place in the sandbox (Article 53(4)). This means in particular that European and national rules on torts, such as product liability and liability for negligence, are not superseded.

Interestingly, the proposed AI regulation has a specific clause on data protection-related issues of regulatory sandboxes – Article 54. Data that were lawfully collected for one purpose (such as medical treatment) may be processed for another purpose – the developing and testing of innovative AI systems in the sandbox – (inter alia) for 'public health, including disease prevention, control and treatment' (Article 54(1)(a)(ii)). In such a case additional safeguards apply, such as effective monitoring and functional separation (Article 54 1(b)–(j)). The ethical and legal impact of these conditions could be long and problematic, as one can see quite clearly when assessing how, for example, data on (individual) Covid-19 vaccinations might now be used for purposes of enforcing obligatory vaccination mandates prescribed in a (later) law. Austria is a quite stunning example for this problem, as the Austrian Vaccination Act – introducing an obligation to get vaccinated against Covid-19 – foresees the usage of (mainly) treatment related data for this purpose.[45]

Article 54(2), however, states that all the reliefs in the regulatory sandbox are 'without prejudice to Union or Member States legislation excluding processing for other purposes than those explicitly mentioned in that legislation.' This means that all controller's issues coming with the processing of personal data for other purposes (e.g., research purposes), as well as all problems with Article 89(5)(2) and 6(4) GDPR, are not resolved. This means, in particular, that the issue as to whether data that was originally collected for a purpose such as medical treatment may be processed – and if so, under which conditions – for purposes of medical research without explicit consent, remains unsolved.

In addition, the processing of personal data in the context of the sandbox must not lead to 'measures or decisions affecting the data

---

[45]   § 6 Vaccination Code ('Impfpflichtgesetz') <https://www.ris.bka.gv.at/GeltendeFassung.wxe?Abfrage=Bundesnormen&Gesetzesnummer=20011811&FassungVom=2022-03-17> accessed 25 February 2023.

subjects'; this can be problematic in cases in which the AI system discovers an instrument (treatment, therapy, drug, etc.) that would help a patient who provided their data. If the mentioned rule has to be applied verbatim, it would be impossible to let this patient profit from the (incidental) finding although this would be technically feasible.

The factual outcome of the regulatory sandbox will therefore most likely only be some kind of 'privileged access' to Data Protection Authorities for developers in the form of a 'direct communication line' to use for regulatory questions and issues, but no deviation from the dense (and complex) protective shield for personal health data in research environments.

However, should the processing of health data for AI and Big Data purposes remain to be governed by such legal complexity as outlined, the question arises whether transferring the data beyond European borders could be a viable and more practical option for industry and research. Outsourcing the data and their processing into countries outside the EU might be an attractive line of thinking. Each decision to outsource data for reasons of a less strict regime, though, can come with a price paid, for example in less protection for data, serious ethical concerns or higher costs due to implications by an unknown foreign legal regime. The following sections will therefore explore noteworthy developments in two countries, firstly the UK with seemingly similar data protection law, and then the Russian Federation, by way of providing an example of a jurisdiction not guided by EU data protection law.

PART II: THE UNITED KINGDOM

Brexit and the GDPR

From the previous discussion, it is clear that the necessity for data sharing within the context of Big Data, AI and health goes beyond the EU. Exacerbated by the Covid-19 pandemic, research and commercial development in medicine has expanded beyond political or economic borders. Yet, as discussed in the previous section, the legal complexities associated with Big Data processing using AI are numerous. This section discusses the current state of EU–UK data sharing from a legal perspective after Brexit. It outlines the UK GDPR, as well as ongoing concerns between the UK and EU in the area of health and Big Data. An analysis of the ongoing plans of the UK government concerning the large-scale processing of health data for research purposes under the NHS Digital initiative will be carried out. Similarly, the work of the private UK-based organisation, DeepMind, will also be explored in relation to legal concerns and the compatibility of current activities with EU data protection law.

The date 31 December 2020 marked the end of the Brexit transition period, after which the UK officially left the EU. However, the conclusion of the transition period did not result in an immediate end to the free movement of personal data between the UK and the EU. Instead, from 1 January 2021, the EU–UK Trade and Cooperation Agreement (TCA) regulates any transfers of personal data.[46] Under the TCA, an interim period for data transfers was extended to 1 May 2021 and to 1 July 2021, if necessary while an adequacy decision is being determined. During this bridging phase, the UK was not to be considered as a third party with regard to data transfers between the EU and the UK, 'provided that the data protection legislation of the United Kingdom on 31 December 2020, as it is saved and incorporated into United Kingdom law', applies.[47]

From 19 February 2021, the European Commission commenced the adequacy decision procedures for both the GDPR, and Directive 2016/680.[48] The European Data Protection Board (EDPB), which was advising on the process, expressed, 'there is a need for further clarification and assessment of bulk interceptions', in particular whether 'the access to personal data meets the threshold set by the CJEU',[49] which is aimed at safeguarding fundamental rights. Furthermore, MEPs debated the potential UK–EU adequacy decision in light of the *Schrems II* of the Court of Justice.[50] The overall concern was that, while the UK's data protection regime is very similar to that of the EU, UK law permits large-scale and indiscriminate access and retention of data, methods that go against the GDPR and CJEU rulings.[51]

---

[46]   Trade and Cooperation Agreement between the European Union and the European Atomic Energy Community, of the One Part, and the United Kingdom of Great Britain and Northern Ireland, of the Other Part (31 December 2020).

[47]   ibid, Article FINPROV.10A.

[48]   European Commission, 'Brexit' <https://ec.europa.eu/info/law/law-topic/data-protection/international-dimension-data-protection/brexit_en> accessed 14 June 2021.

[49]   EDPB, 'Opinion 14/2021 regarding the European Commission Draft Implementing Decision Pursuant to Regulation (EU) 2016/679 on the Adequate Protection of Personal Data in the United Kingdom' (EDPB, 13 April 2021) 9.

[50]   Case C-311/18, *Data Protection Commissioner v Facebook Ireland, Maximilian Schrems and others* [2020] ECLI:EU:C:2020:559.

[51]   European Commission (n 48).

While the UK was a part of the EU, the Data Protection Act 2018,[52] which received royal assent on 23 May 2018, applied the legislative standards set out in the GDPR. However, post-Brexit, UK legislators introduced new legislation titled 'the UK GDPR', which came into effect from 1 January 2021. This system relies upon the requirements of the GDPR as already enacted in UK domestic law. As such, this permitted the EU Exit Regulations 2019 to amend the Data Protection Act 2018 thereby creating the UK GDPR,[53] a 'UK specific data protection regime that works in a UK context after Brexit as part of the DPA 2018.'[54] The UK GDPR ensures consistency between UK and EU data protection legislation. For example, all of the data protection principles, the legal bases for processing, data subject rights, and the obligations for controllers and processors remain harmonious between the EU GDPR and the UK GDPR. However, there are some differences between the two pieces of legislation. For example, the UK GDPR lowers the age of consent to processing to 13 years old. Additionally, the UK GDPR employs a more limited definition of 'personal data' than that used in the EU GDPR.

As a result of efforts by the UK to retain EU data protection standards, despite reservations, the UK was granted an adequacy decision by the European Commission on 28 June 2021. As highlighted by the EDPB, the UK is under the jurisdiction of international human rights law, including the European Convention on Human Rights as well as Convention 108, and it has signed Convention 108+,[55] which is currently being ratified.[56] The integration of EU data protection law within the UK's legal system as well as international legal obligations contributed to the granting of the adequacy decision of the GDPR. Věra Jourová, the Vice-President for Values and Transparency, stated that, although the UK has left the

---

[52] Data Protection Act (2018), c.12 <https://www.legislation.gov.uk/ukpga/2018/12/contents/enacted> accessed 15 June 2021.
[53] The Data Protection, Privacy and Electronic Communications (Amendments etc.) (EU Exit) Regulations 2019, No. 419 <https://www.legislation.gov.uk/uksi/2019/419/introduction/made> accessed 15 June 2021.
[54] Itgovernance, 'Data Protection and Brexit' <https://www.itgovernance.co.uk/eu-gdpr-uk-dpa-2018-uk-gdpr> accessed 15 June 2021.
[55] Protocol Amending the Convention for the Protection of Individuals with regard to Automatic Processing of Personal Data ('Convention 108+'), 18 May 2018.
[56] EDPB, 'Opinion 15/2021 Regarding the European Commission Draft Implementing Decision Pursuant to Directive (EU) 2016/680 on the Adequate Protection of Personal Data in the United Kingdom' (adopted on 13 April 2021) 8.

EU, 'today its legal regime of protection personal data is as it was.'[57] Consequently, in line with Article 45 GDPR, any transfers of personal data from the EU to the UK do not require specific authorisation or additional safeguards.

While the UK has received an adequacy decision, as mentioned above, the UK government has launched a consultation 'Data: A New Direction'[58] to reform data protection law with the aim of establishing 'the UK as the most attractive global data market place.' This reform includes the simplification of legal requirements to benefit scientific research, the removal of 'the right to human review of automated decisions', and the removal of Data Protection Impact Assessments and Data Protection Officers. These legislative shifts away from EU data protection law requirements raise questions about whether the adequacy decision will be impacted and how data flows between the UK and the EU will be affected. Indeed, this point was raised in the Consultation with the UK Government, the latter responding that it is both 'possible and reasonable to expect the UK maintain EU adequacy as it designs a future regime.'[59] While it is true that an adequacy decision does not rely on the third country mirroring the GDPR, the UK's proposed legislative changes nevertheless raise questions about whether it can maintain an adequate level of data protection and privacy protection for data subjects.

Regarding the use of AI, the Consultation focuses heavily on fairness in AI systems.[60] The Consultation acknowledged that there is a lack of clarity regarding how fairness in data protection law interacts with the concept of fairness in non-discrimination law. Nevertheless, the consultation identified agreement on the necessity for the concept of fairness to be included in data protection as part of 'a holistic approach to AI governance'. It is not yet clear how this will be implemented in practice.[61] Moreover, the need for trustworthy AI and bias mitigation in the use of AI were highlighted, with respondents noting that legislative clarity is needed. The Consultation

---

[57]   European Commission, 'Data Protection: Commission Adopts Adequacy Decisions for the UK' (28 June 2021) <https://ec.europa.eu/commission/press corner/detail/en/ip_21_3183> accessed 17 November 2021.

[58]   GOV.UK, 'Consultation Outcome: Data: A New Direction' (last updated 23 June 2022) <https://www.gov.uk/government/consultations/data-a-new-direc tion> accessed 6 July 2022.

[59]   GOV.UK, 'Data: A New Direction – Government Response to Consultation' (updated 23 June 2022) <https://www.gov.uk/government/consultations/data-a-new-direction/outcome/data-a-new-direction-government-response-to-consultati on> accessed 6 July 2022.

[60]   ibid.

[61]   ibid.

had proposed the removal of the requirement for human oversight in automated decision-making and profiling from the UK GDPR; however, a substantial majority opposed this. This opposition is unsurprising given that human oversight aims to provide a safeguard mechanism to providing fair and trustworthy AI.

While the Consultation demonstrates engagement with the public and private sector on proposed legislative developments, thereby providing transparency for the public, there is a clear intention to stray from EU data protection law. It is unclear whether or how this will affect the UK adequacy decision and the future of EU–UK data flows.

Health Data

The benefits of the adequacy decision echo beyond the UK as they are also of value to the EU. In the UK, the NHS has a huge wealth of health data, making the mass of data increasingly appealing for research initiatives. One leading researcher stated, '[t]he UK has a phenomenal resource in its raw data, and its people.'[62] Further, the Covid-19 pandemic has demonstrated the significance of health data and research, showing the world the importance of high-quality science and access to the necessary resources to aid public health, assisting in care and treatment. The collective value of health data, whether concerning nations, smaller populations or particular groups, can aid in obtaining knowledge and also providing better medical treatment and even prevention. However, the value of these data does not supersede the autonomy, rights, interests and freedoms of the patients it concerns.

Under the NHS General Practice Data for Planning and Research (NHS GPDPR), the NHS aims to amalgamate patient medical records held by general practitioners across England. The aim of this mass data collection is, according to NHS Digital, to 'support health and care planning and research in England' and to help 'to find better treatments and improve patient outcomes for everyone.'[63] Despite these intentions, this mass data grab was met with contention, leading to the NHS deferring

---

[62]   Department of Health and Social Care, 'Press Release: New Review into Use of Health Data for Research and Analysis' (Gov.uk, 9 February 2021) <https://www.gov.uk/government/news/new-review-into-use-of-health-data-for-research-and-analysis> accessed 15 June 2021.

[63]   NHS Digital, 'General Practice Data for Planning and Research (GPDPR)' <https://digital.nhs.uk/data-and-information/data-collections-and-data-sets/data-collections/general-practice-data-for-planning-and-research> accessed 16 June 2021.

their data collection from the initially planned date of 1 July 2021 to 1 September 2021. However, the deferred date of 1 September 2021 was then postponed indefinitely 'to provide more time to speak with patients, doctors, health charities and others', according to the NHS.[64]

The NHS has said that NHS Digital will not collect the names or addresses of patients, nor will it collect 'any other data that could directly identify patients (such as NHS Number, date of birth, full postcode).'[65] Instead, personal data will be pseudonymised before the data are shared with NHS Digital. This method of pseudonymisation adds an additional security layer to the data processing in line with Article 32 GDPR, and aims to ensure that those using NHS Digital cannot identify patients using direct identifiers. However, one of the foremost concerns is that additional special categories of personal data are collected, and the security techniques applied to these data sets are omitted from NHS Digital public information. For example, data are collected 'about diagnoses, symptoms, observations, test results, medications, allergies, immunisations, referrals, recalls and appointments, including information about physical, mental and sexual health' as well as 'data on sex, ethnicity and sexual orientation'. Several of these data categories fall into the Article 9(1) GDPR definition of a 'special category of personal data', meaning that additional safeguards are required to process such data. Yet, despite the sensitivity of these data sets from both a legal and an ethical perspective, very little information is provided regarding the security measures protecting these data.

Moreover, this mass data collection was based on an opt-out scheme, which raises concerns about both the autonomy and the awareness of the patient. Further questions arise regarding the legal basis of the collection of these data, and particularly of the special categories of personal data. An opt-out scheme cannot be considered a basis for consent to data processing and especially not explicit consent. The GDPR requires that consent be an 'unambiguous indication of the data subject's wishes by which he or she, by a statement or by a clear affirmative action signifies agreement to the processing of personal data relating to him or her.'[66]

NHS Digital has the possibility to collect data on 61 million patients, provided they do not opt out of the scheme. This large-scale collection of several categories of sensitive data without significant consultation has led not only to the perpetual postponement of the data grab but also to vocalised conflict. The legal activist group Foxglove raised concerns with regard

---

[64]   ibid.
[65]   ibid.
[66]   GDPR, Article 4(11).

to the failure to inform patients sufficiently about data collection and the possibility of identifying patients in relation to highly personal information.[67] The Royal College of General Practitioners expressed similar concern regarding the poor communication of NHS Digital to share their plans with members of the public and offer them an adequate timeframe to opt out of the data collection.[68]

Additionally, the ability for NHS Digital to share this data with third parties raises concerns over the security of the data and patient autonomy. NHS Digital states that it only shares health and care data in line with security practices and rules relating to privacy and confidentiality, as well as in line with data protection rules. However, there remain questions regarding with whom this patient data may be shared. NHS Digital provides a non-exhaustive list of a broad assortment of organisations ranging from government organisations, NHS authorities, care networks, local authorities and 'research organisations, including universities, charities, clinical research organisations that run clinical trials and pharmaceutical companies.'[69] This wide-ranging list of third parties who could have access to sensitive personal data raises serious concerns about patient autonomy. How can data subjects access their rights and have autonomy over their own personal data when they are not sufficiently informed about the processing, or the processors? This question becomes even more significant in the context of Big Data and AI as the transparency of the processing and the exercise of data subject rights can become more difficult depending on the type and transparency of AI system being employed.

Given that NHS Digital makes no mention of data subject rights, including the right to be informed in their 'Transparency notice', it is unsurprising that an extension has been placed on the implementation of this mass health data seizure. There is also no information on how NHS Digital will assess the security measures or ongoing legal obligations of the third parties with whom they will share health and care data.

---

[67] Foxglove, 'Stop the NHS GP Data Grab' (4 June 2021) <https://www.fox glove.org.uk/news/stop-the-nhs-gp-data-grab> accessed 18 June 2021.

[68] Sarah Marsh, 'GPs Warn over Plans to Share Patient Data with Third Parties in England' (*The Guardian*, 30 May 2021) <https://www.theguardian.com/ society/2021/may/30/gps-warn-plans-share-patient-data-third-parties-england> accessed 15 June 2021.

[69] NHS Digital, 'General Practice Data for Planning and Research: NHS Digital Transparency' <https://digital.nhs.uk/data-and-information/data-collec tions-and-data-sets/data-collections/general-practice-data-for-planning-and-rese arch/transparency-notice#who-we-share-patient-data-with> accessed 18 June 2021.

These security and confidentiality concerns are well founded. In 2016, DeepMind, the AI research organisation, now owned by Google, implemented a five-year-long data sharing agreement with the NHS Foundation Trust as the Royal Free Hospital in London.[70] However, the Information Commissioner's Office (ICO) determined that, in entering into this agreement, which permitted the sharing of the personal data of 1.6 million patients, the London Royal Free hospital was in breach of the Data Protection Act.[71] The aim of this data transfer was to create an app for the diagnosis, detection and alert of acute kidney injury.[72] However, after the transfer of patient data, this app continued to undergo testing. The ICO found, 'patients were not adequately informed that their data would be used as part of the test' and nor would they 'have reasonably expected their information to have been used in this way', noting that the NHS Foundation Trust should have provided patients with more transparency about the data processing.[73] Based on an independent review of DeepMind Health being used by the NHS, concerns were highlighted regarding data sharing with private companies, privacy and confidentiality, and the lack of transparency of the data processing, particularly in relation to sharing agreements.[74] The ICO's Elizabeth Denham expressed the value in the use of clinical data in research and patient care but noted, 'the price of innovation does not need to be the erosion of fundamental privacy rights.'[75] Furthermore, the ICO also expressed concern about the

---

[70]   NHS Royal Free London, 'Our Work with Google Health UK' <https://www.royalfree.nhs.uk/patients-visitors/how-we-use-patient-information/our-work-with-deepmind/> accessed 18 November 2021.

[71]   Alex Hern, 'Royal Free Breached UK Data Law in 1.6m Patient Deal with Google's DeepMind' (*The Guardian*, 3 July 2017) <https://www.theguardian.com/technology/2017/jul/03/google-deepmind-16m-patient-royal-free-deal-data-protection-act> accessed 18 June 2021.

[72]   DeepMind, 'Working with the NHS to Build Lifesaving Technology' (22 November 2016) <https://deepmind.com/blog/announcements/working-nhs-build-lifesaving-technology> accessed 18 June 2021.

[73]   ICO, 'Royal Free – Google DeepMind Trial Failed to Comply with Data Protection Law' (3 July 2017) <https://ico.org.uk/about-the-ico/news-and-events/news-and-blogs/2017/07/royal-free-google-deepmind-trial-failed-to-comply-with-data-protection-law/> accessed 18 June 2021.

[74]   Mike Bracken and others, 'DeepMind Health Independent Review Panel Annual Report' (DeepMind Health, July 2017) <https://kstatic.googleuserconte nt.com/files/7e0b35e4cb6ccb750cba03fb160a69cc4f24456358042b8313b88943c49 dfbce46037e9c89fad32fae986bd08a84e90c792656e0208d1276f1db895dcb42386b> accessed 27 January 2022.

[75]   Laura Stevens, 'Royal Free and Google DeepMind Trial Did Not Comply with DPA' (DigitalHealth, 3 July 2017) <https://www.digitalhealth.

'processing of such a large volume of records containing sensitive health data [as it] was not subject to a full privacy impact assessment ahead of the project's commencement.'[76] This case demonstrates not only the value in patient data in assisting clinicians and benefitting patients, but also more fervently the requirement for concrete and transparent data protection compliance schemes prior to the data processing. This way, the rights and autonomy of patients can be adequately evaluated and protected in line with data protection laws.

To comply with national data protection law and human rights obligations, this approach must be taken in the NHS GPDPR Big Data acquisition and future Big-Data processing. Patients were not adequately informed about the initial data collection and it is unclear how this large-scale set of sensitive data will be used and secured, and precisely with whom it will be shared. It is easy to overlook the individual in Big-Data processing, and instead favour the value of information for the collective. However, EU data protection law places the data subject at the centre of the legislative structure. Thus, to gain insights into health and clinical data legitimately, organisations must first establish a foundation in data protection and privacy law that adequately respects the rights and interests of the patient. This means that all data processing must be in accordance with UK, EU and international legal obligations whether in national, secondary or primary law. For the UK, legal compliance in Big-Data processing in line with the GDPR and as outlined earlier in this text, particularly in the area of health and medical research, is paramount for retaining the EU adequacy decision. Lawful data processing not only aids political relations between the UK and the EU, but more significantly, it would bolster research and innovation to the benefit of everyone. From this perspective, there are a vast number of other countries, many lacking an adequacy decision, with whom the EU could share data to the benefit of the research community and innovation in general. The following section will look at the example of Russia as a non-EU country without such an adequacy decision in place, but with the aspiration to bolster the use of health data using AI technologies.

---

net/2017/07/royal-free-and-deepmind-did-not-comply-with-dpa-ico/> accessed 27 January 2022.

[76] ICO, 'Letter: Investigation on the Provision of Patient Data to DeepMind' (3 July 2017) <https://ico.org.uk/media/action-weve-taken/undertakings/2014353/undertaking-cover-letter-revised-04072017-to-first-person.pdf> accessed 27 January 2022.

PART III: RUSSIAN FEDERATION

In recent years, the development of AI technologies has become one of the priorities for the Russian Federation. Following the adoption of the National Strategy for the Development of AI until 2030 in October 2019,[77] a number of political and legislative initiatives have been undertaken by the Russian Government. Such initiatives include the approval of the first state standards in the area of AI in 2019,[78] the launch of a federal project on 'Artificial Intelligence' in August 2020,[79] as well as the adoption of a regulation to provide a Framework for AI and robot technologies.[80]

One of the most notable recent projects involving the processing of personal health-related data is the launch of an experimental legal regime (regulatory 'sandbox') to develop AI in Moscow. The relevant Federal Law governing the experiment (the 'AI Law') became effective on 1 July 2020 and has the objective of providing favourable conditions for the development and implementation of AI technologies in Russia.[81]

---

[77]   Presidential Decree, 'On Development of AI in the Russian Federation' (10 October 2019) <https://www.garant.ru/products/ipo/prime/doc/72738946/> accessed 17 May 2021.

[78]   Namely, State Standard GOST R 58776-2019, 'Means of Monitoring Behaviour and Predicting People's Intentions. Terms and Definitions' and State Standard GOST R 5877-2019, 'Air Transport. Airports. Technical Means of Inspection. Methodology for Determining the Quality Indicators for the Recognition of Illegal Contents by Shadow X-Ray Images'; see Federal Agency on Technical Regulating and Metrology, News, 'The First Standards in the Area of AI Have Been Approved' (25 December 2019) <https://www.rst.gov.ru/portal/gost/home/presscenter/news?portal:componentId=88beae40-0e16-414c-b176-d0ab5de82e16&navigationalstate=JBPNS_rO0ABXczAAZhY3Rpb24AAAABAA5zaW5nbGVOZXdzVmlldwACaWQAAAABAAQ2NTY2AAdfX0VPRl9f> accessed 17 May 2021.

[79]   Ministry of Economic Development of the Russian Federation. Federal Project, 'Artificial Intelligence' <https://www.economy.gov.ru/material/directions/tehnologicheskoe_razvitie/federalnyy_proekt_iskusstvennyy_intellekt/> accessed 17 May 2021.

[80]   Order of the Government of the Russian Federation No. 2129-p dated 19 August 2020, 'On Approval of the Framework for Development of Artificial Intelligence and Robot Technologies Regulation until 2024' <https://www.economy.gov.ru/material/file/57ff642339b16c479b12030fb5f1b6e3/19082020_2129-p.pdf> accessed 17 May 2021.

[81]   Federal Law No. 123-FZ, 'On the Experiment on Establishing a Special Regulatory Regime for Creation of Necessary Conditions for Development and Implementation of Artificial Intelligence Technologies in Moscow, A Constituent Entity of the Russian Federation and a City of Federal Importance, and on Amending Articles 6 and 10 of the Federal Law "On Personal Data"' (24 April 2020), Corpus of Legislative Acts of the Russian Federation, 2020, No. 17, Article 2701.

Under the new law, legal entities and entrepreneurs registered in Moscow that are engaged in the creation, development, implementation or sale of AI technologies can become participants. They must apply for registration in a dedicated 'register' (database) (Articles 2 and 5 of the AI Law). Their activities could relate to the fields of computer vision, natural language processing, speech recognition and synthesis, as well as other emerging AI methods. According to Article 1 of the law, the experiment is planned to last for five years. It will be monitored by a special coordination council, chaired by the Mayor of Moscow, who will submit legislative proposals to the Government of Russia after the end of the experiment.[82]

The experimental AI regime is generally viewed as an ambitious and innovative project.[83] With the special legal framework, created specifically to encourage the development of AI, such a 'sandbox' regime can make available new products and technologies at lower regulatory costs and less time expense as (informed) consent is not needed as a legal basis for the processing. The new technologies can broadly be applied, also in the field of healthcare. This could foster AI-driven medical treatment and research in Russia. However, one of the most controversial issues of the regulatory 'sandbox' regime in Moscow is the treatment of personal data, particularly health-related data, which the participants of the 'sandbox' and public authorities make use of in the course of the experiment.

Such controversy, causing major concern among data protection specialists, is based on the amendments that the AI legal framework has introduced into the Federal Law 'On Personal Data'[84] (the 'Law on Personal Data'), which is the main legal instrument regulating processing and protection of personal data in Russia. The provisions of the Law on personal data are in compliance with the Convention for the Protection of Individuals with Regard to Automatic Processing of Personal Data, signed and ratified by Russia.[85] The law defines personal data as 'any

---

[82]   See 'Statute of the Coordination Council for the Experimental Legal Regime, Approved by the Resolution of the Moscow Government No. 2135-ПП' (3 December 2020) <https://docs.cntd.ru/document/573103470> accessed 17 May 2021.

[83]   Alexander Gusev and others, 'Development of Artificial Intelligence in Healthcare in Russia' in Chee-Peng Lim and others (eds), *Handbook of Artificial Intelligence in Healthcare. Vol 2: Practicalities and Prospects* (Springer Nature 2022).

[84]   Federal Law No. 152-FZ, 'On Personal Data' (27 July 2006), Corpus of Legislative Acts of the Russian Federation, 2006, No. 31 (Part I), Article 3451.

[85]   However, the amending Protocol No. 223 signed by Russia in October 2018 still lacks ratification. See Council of Europe, 'Treaty List for the Russian Federation' <https://www.coe.int/en/web/conventions/full-list?module=treaties-ful l-list-signature&CodePays=RUS> accessed 16 March 2023. It is unclear whether

information which, directly or indirectly, is related to any identified or identifiable person' (Article 3) and sets the basic principles related to processing of personal data, such as lawfulness and fairness of processing, purpose limitation, data minimisation and accuracy, storage limitation, and confidentiality (Article 5). The bases for lawful processing of personal data are listed in Article 6 and look similar to what is known from GDPR. In particular, they include consent (which should be 'specific, informed, and wilful'), processing necessary for the performance of a task carried out in the exercise of official authority, and other bases that are generally in line with the lawful bases for processing of personal data under Article 6 of the GDPR. Article 10 regulates the processing of special categories of personal data, which include personal data revealing racial or ethnic origin, political opinions, religious or philosophical beliefs, state of health, and sex life. Processing of such data is generally prohibited, except for a limited number of cases, such as based on a written consent of the data subject, processing necessary for the purposes of preventive or occupational medicine, and so on.

The AI Law has amended the Law on personal data by broadening the list of bases for lawful processing of 'regular' (Article 6) and special categories (Article 10) of personal data. Specifically, processing of personal data (including special categories thereof), 'obtained as the result of depersonalisation of personal data', is now allowed 'for the purposes of maximising effectiveness of state and municipal administration, as well as for other purposes specified in the [AI Law]' (Article 7 of the AI Law). Thus, the participants of the 'sandbox' regime, as well as public authorities, can process 'depersonalised personal data', including health-related data, for the purposes of the experiment and without the consents of the data subjects. The concept of depersonalisation of personal data is understood as one or more actions that make it impossible, without the use of additional information, to attribute personal data to a specific data subject (Article 3 of the Law on personal data).[86] Thus, the term 'depersonalisation' under Russian law is similar to 'pseudonymisation' under the GDPR.[87] As with

---

and when the Protocol will be ratified by Russia, in view of Russia's exclusion from the Council of Europe following the invasion of Ukraine in February 2022. See Council of Europe, 1428ter meeting, 16 March 2022 <https://search.coe.int/cm/pages/result_details.aspx?objectid=0900001680a5d7d9> accessed 16 March 2022.

[86]   'Depersonalisation of personal data' is our own translation of the Russian term 'обезличивание персональных данных' used in the Law on personal data.

[87]   'Pseudonymisation' means the processing of personal data in such a manner that the personal data can no longer be attributed to a specific data subject without the use of additional information, provided that such additional information is

pseudonymised data, the process of depersonalisation can be reversed, putting at risk the security of personal data.

Although the amendment to the Law on personal data is the central part of the 'sandbox' legal framework, it provides little legal certainty and raises numerous legal questions as to its precise scope of application, data protection and privacy guarantees, and responsibility of participants in the experiment and public authorities. First, the new basis for lawful processing is worded very broadly. In particular, the purpose of maximising effectiveness of state and municipal administration, as well as other purposes listed in the AI Law, such as improving the quality of life or enhancing the effectiveness of implementation of AI technologies, could cover any processing of personal data.[88] Second, it is unclear how exactly the data will be used and in which ways the legal entities and entrepreneurs participating in the experiment will ensure confidentiality and security of such data. Third, there are major legal uncertainties and serious preoccupation as to the reliability of depersonalisation of personal data.

Under the experimental regime, depersonalisation is performed by the operator of personal data,[89] which is in most cases the participant of the experiment itself. Processing of depersonalised data is based on a special agreement, which must be concluded between a participant of the experiment and the Moscow City IT Department ('processing agreement'). Depersonalised data can be transferred from the participants of the experiment to the IT Department of the city of Moscow, or to other public authorities in case the participants are operators of personal data,[90] or owners of photo and video surveillance systems and services where they

---

kept separately and is subject to technical and organisational measures to ensure that the personal data is not attributed to an identified or identifiable natural person (Article 4 GDPR).

[88] Besides, it is unclear from the wording of Article 7 of the AI Law whether the purpose of 'maximising effectiveness of state and municipal administration' should be considered as a separate basis for lawful processing of personal data. Also, the words 'in accordance with the provisions of the AI Law' would be more precise as opposed to the wording 'for the purposes specified in the AI Law'.

[89] Unlike the GDPR, which distinguishes between the roles of controller and processor, the Russian Law on personal data uses only the term 'operator', which is defined as a state or municipal authority, or natural or legal person, which processes personal data and determines the purposes and means for such processing (Article 3 of the Law on personal data).

[90] See Sections 2, 3–5 and 9 of the Rules for processing of de-personalised personal data by participants of the experimental regime for creation of the necessary conditions for development and implementation of artificial intelligence technologies in Moscow, as well as for further possible application of the results of the use of artificial intelligence, approved by the Resolution of the Moscow

can potentially be used, inter alia, for purposes of political persecution.[91] Besides, the Moscow City IT Department can transfer depersonalised data to participants of the experiment based on their applications for such transfer.

There are a number of legal requirements to the processing agreements, which are intended to guarantee privacy and data protection. Specifically, according to the Rules for processing of depersonalised personal data by participants of the experimental regime approved by the Resolution of the Moscow Government, processing agreements should include provisions ensuring confidentiality, security of transfer and processing, as well as the purposes of processing of depersonalised data, which have to correspond to the results that the participant is planning to achieve through its participation in the experimental regime.[92] Besides, depersonalised data must not be transferred to non-participants of the experiment and are not allowed to be stored outside of Moscow, which is a stricter prohibition than the general legal requirement of personal data localisation solely in Russia[93] (Article 4 of the AI Law).

However, the general and vaguely worded provisions of the few publicly available regulations provide very little information on how exactly the processing of depersonalised data will be performed by the different subjects involved. In fact, they raise more questions than they provide answers and clarity. In which cases will depersonalised data (including health-related data or data received via photo and video surveillance systems) be transferred to the Moscow City IT Department and other public authorities? How and for which purposes will these data

---

Government No. 2138-ПП dated 3 December 2020 <https://docs.cntd.ru/document/573103472> accessed 17 May 2021.

[91]   See Section 1 of the Rules for transfer of images and granting access to photo and video surveillance systems and services by owners of such systems and services for the purposes of creating necessary conditions for development and implementation of artificial intelligence technologies in Moscow, approved by the Resolution of the Moscow Government No. 2136-ПП dated 3 December 2020 <https://docs.cntd.ru/document/573103471> accessed 17 May 2021.

[92]   See Annex to the Rules for processing of depersonalised personal data by participants of the experimental regime for creation of the necessary conditions for development and implementation of artificial intelligence technologies in Moscow, as well as for further possible application of the results of the use of artificial intelligence, approved by the Resolution of the Moscow Government No. 2138-ПП dated 3 December 2020 <https://docs.cntd.ru/document/573103472> accessed 17 May 2021.

[93]   The personal data localisation requirement was introduced in the Federal Law No. 149-FZ, 'On Information, Information Technologies, and Protection of Information' (2014) and became effective on 1 September 2015.

be processed? Which legal remedies will be available for data subjects whose personal data have leaked or have been unlawfully disclosed? A number of important legal issues, such as the purposes of processing of depersonalised data or the rules for granting access to photo and video surveillance systems, are to be addressed in the processing agreements, which, however, are not publicly available. The Russian Federal Service for Supervision of Communications, Information Technology and Mass Media ('Roskomnadzor'),[94] which is responsible for enforcement of data protection laws, has commented neither on the experimental AI regime, nor on the amendments to the Law on personal data. At the same time, the courts are often unwilling to take the side of the data subject, which was demonstrated in the 2020 case decided by the Moscow City Court brought by a political activist Alena Popova against the Moscow City IT Department and Main Directorate of Internal Affairs of the City of Moscow claiming that the use of facial recognition technologies in the streets of Moscow violated Russian data protection and privacy laws.[95]

Thus, the innovative 'sandbox' AI regime in Moscow, although being designed to foster technological development, also in the field of healthcare, in fact provides Moscow residents with very little to no control over their personal, including health-related, data. Broad and imprecise bases for processing, little reliability of depersonalisation process, lack of transparency, and unclear legal remedies available for data subjects – all these factors expose personal data to a substantial risk and raise questions of compatibility of the 'sandbox' legal framework with the data protection and privacy laws, including the constitutional provisions,[96] as well as Article 8 of the European Convention on Human Rights. As human rights lawyers have commented, with the AI Law, the Moscow authorities not

---

[94]   Roskomnadzor, established in 2008, is responsible for control and supervision in the areas of mass media and communications (including limiting access to information resources), television and radio broadcasting, information technologies, and data protection. Unlike the European Data Protection Supervisor in the EU, Roskomnadzor is not an independent authority and is subordinate to the Russian Ministry of Communications <http://eng.pd.rkn.gov.ru/> accessed 26 January 2022.

[95]   Official Portal of the General Jurisdiction Courts of the City of Moscow, Moscow City Court, Information on case no. 33a-0707/2020 <https://mos-gorsud.ru/mgs/services/cases/appeal-admin/details/6c9dfe4c-ecc7-4626-90f4-dea208d54b5 f?participants=%D0%BF%D0%BE%D0%BF%D0%BE%D0%B2%D0%B0+%D 0%B0.%D0%B2> accessed 26 January 2022.

[96]   The Constitution of the Russian Federation guarantees inviolability of private life, personal and family secrets (Article 23) and prohibits collection, storage, use, and distribution of information about a person's private life without his or her consent (Article 24).

only neglect the national legislation on personal data, but also disregard international standards.[97]

Data protection concerns surrounding the experimental regime have been raised by a group of members of the State Duma, the lower house of the Russian parliament. In a draft law, they suggested postponing the amendments to the Law on personal data until 1 July 2025 (i.e., for the whole term of the experiment), arguing that the usage and implementation of AI technologies, including surveillance and facial recognition systems, raise serious concerns among Russian citizens. Given that currently there are no mechanisms ensuring protection from data leakage or unlawful use of personal data, as well as no regulations covering responsibility of public authorities for unlawful use of AI technologies, the proposed postponement would allow the time to address these legislative gaps. However, neither the State Duma nor the Russian Government upheld the proposed amendments, stating that processing of depersonalised data is crucial for the 'sandbox' AI regime, and postponing the amendments to the Law on personal data would undermine the experiment.[98]

As seen with the experimental AI regime in Moscow, the development of AI-driven technologies is a clear strategic preference for Russia, even though such 'sandboxes' put the security of personal data at risk. This approach to the 'sandbox' AI regime in Moscow stands in contrast to the approach taken by the Commission in the proposed AI Act, as described in Part I of this chapter. As mentioned above, the GDPR should remain fully applicable to the regulatory 'sandboxes' envisioned by the AI Act, and significant risks to health, safety or fundamental rights could lead to suspension of the experimentation. However, the public authorities in Russia attribute utmost importance to the experimental AI regime,[99]

---

[97]   Human Rights Watch, Russia: Broad Facial Recognition Use Undermines Rights (15 September 2021) <https://www.hrw.org/news/2021/09/15/russia-broad-facial-recognition-use-undermines-rights> accessed 26 January 2022.

[98]   See Draft Law No. 950900-7, 'On Amending Article 8 of the Federal Law "On the experiment on establishing a special regulatory regime for creation of necessary conditions for Development and Implementation of Artificial Intelligence Technologies in Moscow, a Constituent Entity of the Russian Federation and a City of Federal Importance", and on Amending Articles 6 and 10 of the Federal Law "On Personal Data" proposed on 30 April 2020' <https://sozd.duma.gov.ru/bill/950900-7> accessed 17 May 2021.

[99]   The President of Russia, Artificial Intelligence Journey, 2020 Conference <http://www.kremlin.ru/events/president/transcripts/64545> accessed 26 January 2022. In particular, President Putin has instructed the Government to 'promptly prepare draft laws on the introduction of experimental legal regimes for the use of artificial intelligence technologies in the economic and social spheres.'

insomuch as to amend the Law on personal data by adding a special basis for lawful processing of personal data exclusively for the purposes of the experiment and as to deny parliamentarians' remarks on risks to data protection and privacy rights.

Notably, the experimental regulatory 'sandbox' regime in Moscow is to some extent similar to the DeepMind case in the UK described in Part II of this chapter. In both cases private organisations are entering into data-sharing agreements with the objective of fostering the development of AI technologies. The prospective political and strategic advantages from quick development of AI systems prompt Russia to move quickly in this area overlooking data protection standards and privacy rights of data subjects. This is even more problematic as independent oversight structures seem inefficient. While the UK ICO disagrees with such a technology-focused approach by stating, 'the price of innovation does not need to be the erosion of fundamental privacy rights',[100] the Russian Government seems to be willing to pay this price.

Nevertheless, it is doubtful whether such a regulatory 'sandbox' turns out to be a competitive advantage that will allow the fostering of technological innovation. Effective data-protection mechanisms, political stability and transparency in public administration are central components to enable sustainable economic development, especially for economies willing to create a favourable and stable climate for investment. At the same time, technologies based on the processing of sensitive categories of data, including health-related data, also require effective security and oversight mechanisms. The 'sandbox' regime as introduced in Moscow guarantees little to no protection of personal data and does not seem to be a viable option for the responsible development and implementation of AI-driven technologies that could be used in the medical sector.

CONCLUSION

This chapter has examined how health data is regulated throughout the EU, delving into the legislative impact on the use of Big Data in relation to the technological advancements in AI within the context of health and medical research. It began by looking at the legislative sphere in the EU, discussing the benefits of health and medical research, which is increasingly highlighted as a result of the Covid-19 pandemic. It then outlined the legislative considerations under the GDPR for the regulation of the

---

[100]   See n 75.

processing of personal data and the specific legal concerns associated with the processing of data concerning health. After that, the text examined the intersection of AI technologies with data processing and regulation in this area.

Part I of the chapter provided an overview of the relevant data protection law in the areas of health and medical research, while simultaneously acknowledging the concerns associated with the use of AI to process these data on a large scale. The text then looked at two extra-territorial examples of health data processing, AI, Big Data and the associated data protection legislation. First focusing on the UK, Part II set out the development of EU–UK data protection legislation post Brexit. A number of the AI and health research initiatives taking place in the UK in both the public and private settings were examined in relation to data protection legislation. From here, common problems associated with data subject awareness and rights in the areas of medical research, particularly when processing large datasets, were highlighted. After looking at legislative developments in the EU in the first part, including new legal instruments such as regulatory sandboxes, Part III of this chapter looked at the Russian Federation as an example of a non-EU country without an adequacy decision. This section outlined the legislative attempts by Russia to develop a legal framework that fosters technological developments in AI and Big Data processing and the ways in which this compares with the initiatives in the EU. By comparing these non-EU countries with the situation in the bloc, not only do we see how the different legal and political spheres influence legislation, but we can also get a glimpse of medical research taking place beyond the EU and the value in this research as well as the legislative limits.

At first sight, the strict legal regime for the processing of health data in Europe can appear too tight or even outdated and hindering development and innovation. However, the EU legislators have put it in place for good reason and out of concern about possible detrimental effects for the data subjects. Lifting or mitigating the high standard of data protection in a critical sector such as health and care can only happen in full alignment with the very core values and principles of European primary legislation and its guarantees for the fundamental rights of the individual. A technophilic 'anything goes' is just as unfeasible as a technophobic 'no progress allowed' approach. We will see how far the EU legislator's attempts to outbalance sufficient guarantees for the data subjects on the one hand and sufficient flexibility for developers on the other hand, via an instrument such as the regulatory sandboxes, will further develop.

This chapter, however, has shown that at the time of writing neither the UK nor the Russian example is a fully convincing alternative model that provides the appropriate equilibrium between data protection as well as privacy for the data subject on the one hand, and freedom for innovative technological as well as medical advancement on the other hand. Instead of simply imitating or following one or both of these examples, the European legislator should therefore rather continue to create and elaborate an autonomous legislative way. This is a process that has already started by proposing the discussed draft regulations. It will then be particularly interesting to see how the position of the European Parliament and the European Council will shape the final form of these regulatory frameworks.

BIBLIOGRAPHY

Annex to the Rules for processing of depersonalised personal data by participants of the experimental regime for creation of the necessary conditions for development and implementation of artificial intelligence technologies in Moscow, as well as for further possible application of the results of the use of artificial intelligence, approved by the Resolution of the Moscow Government No. 2138-ПП dated 3 December 2020 <https://docs.cntd.ru/document/573103472> accessed 17 May 2021.

Apple/Google, Exposure Notification Privacy-preserving Analytics (ENPA) White Paper, <https://covid19-static.cdn-apple.com/applications/covid19/current/static/contact-tracing/pdf/ENPA_White_Paper.pdf> accessed 25 February 2023.

Article 29 Data Protection Working Party, 'Opinion 03/2013 on Purpose Limitation' (adopted 2 April 2013).

Barker S, 'IT Systems Down at Waikato Hospital & DHB, "Cybersecurity Incident" Confirmed' (Security Brief, 19 May 2021) <https://securitybrief.co.nz/story/breaking-it-systems-down-at-waikato-hospital-dhb-cybersecurity-incident-confirmed> accessed 23 November 2021.

BBC, 'Cyber Attack "Most Significant on Irish State" (14 May 2021) <https://www.bbc.com/news/world-europe-57111615> accessed 23 November 2021.

Bracken M and others, 'DeepMind Health Independent Review Panel Annual Report' (DeepMind Health, July 2017) <https://kstatic.googleusercontent.com/files/7e0b35e4cb6ccb750cba03fb160a69cc4f24456358042b8313b88943c49dfbce46037e9c89fad32fae986bd08a84e90c792656e0208d1276f1db895dcb42386b> accessed 27 January 2022.

Browne R, 'Why Coronavirus Contact-Tracing Apps Aren't Yet the "Game Changer" Authorities Hoped They'd Be' <https://www.cnbc.com/2020/07/03/why-coronavirus-contact-tracing-apps-havent-been-a-game-changer.html> accessed 25 February 2023.

Case C-311/18, *Data Protection Commissioner v Facebook Ireland, Maximilian Schrems and others* [2020] ECLI:EU:C:2020:559.

Data Protection Act 2018, c.12 <https://www.legislation.gov.uk/ukpga/2018/12/contents/enacted> (accessed 15 June 2021).

DeepMind, 'Working with the NHS to Build Lifesaving Technology' (22 November 2016) <https://deepmind.com/blog/announcements/working-nhs-build-lifesaving-technology> accessed 18 June 2021.

Department of Health and Social Care, 'Press Release: New Review into Use of Health Data for Research and Analysis' (Gov.uk, 9 February 2021) <https://www.gov.uk/government/news/new-review-into-use-of-health-data-for-research-and-analysis> accessed 15 June 2021.

Directive 2011/24/EU of the European Parliament and of the Council of 9 March 2011 on the Application of Patients' Rights in Cross-Border Healthcare, OJ 2011 L 88/45.

Donnelly M and McDonagh M, 'Health Research, Consent and the GDPR Exemption' [2019] 26 European Journal of Health Law. DOI: 10.1163/15718093-12262427.

Draft Law No. 950900-7, 'On amending Article 8 of the Federal Law "On the Experiment on Establishing a Special Regulatory Regime for Creation of Necessary Conditions for Development and Implementation of Artificial Intelligence Technologies in Moscow, a Constituent Entity of the Russian Federation and a City of Federal Importance, and on Amending Articles 6 and 10 of the Federal Law "On Personal Data" Proposed on 30 April 2020' <https://sozd.duma.gov.ru/bill/950900-7> accessed 17 May 2021.

Dumortier J and Boura MP, 'European-wide Big Health Data Analytics under the GDPR' in Maria Tzanou (ed.), *Health Data Privacy under the GDPR: Big Data Challenges and Regulatory Responses* (Routledge 2020).

EDPB, 'Opinion 14/2021 Regarding the European Commission Draft Implementing Decision Pursuant to Regulation (EU) 2016/679 on the Adequate Protection of Personal Data in the United Kingdom' (13 April 2021).

EDPB, 'Opinion 15/2021 Regarding the European Commission Draft Implementing Decision Pursuant to Directive (EU) 2016/680 on the Adequate Protection of Personal Data in the United Kingdom' (adopted on 13 April 2021).

EMA, 'Cyberattack on EMA' <https://www.ema.europa.eu/en/news/cyberattack-ema-update-5> accessed 23 November 2021.

EPRS, 'EU Health Data Centre and a Common Data Strategy for Public Health', Study Panel for the Future of Science and Technology, Scientific Foresight Unit (STOA) (2021).

EPRS, 'The Impact of the General Data Protection Regulation (GDPR) on Artificial Intelligence' (2020) <https://www.europarl.europa.eu/RegData/etudes/STUD/2020/641530/EPRS_STU(2020)641530_EN.pdf> accessed 23 November 2021.

EPRS (STOA) (2022), 'Artificial Intelligence in Healthcare: Applications, Risks, and Ethical and Societal Impacts' <https://www.europarl.europa.eu/RegData/etudes/STUD/2022/729512/EPRS_STU(2022)729512_EN.pdf> accessed 7 July 2022.

EU General Data Protection Regulation (GDPR), Regulation (EU) 2016/679 of the European Parliament and of the Council of 27 April 2016 on the protection of natural persons with regard to the processing of personal data and on the free movement of such data, and repealing Directive 95/46/EC (General Data Protection Regulation), OJ 2016 L 119/1.

European Commission, 'Assessment of the EU Member States' Rules on Health Data in the Light of the GDPR' (2021).

European Commission, 'Brexit' <https://ec.europa.eu/info/law/law-topic/data-protection/international-dimension-data-protection/brexit_en> accessed 14 June 2021.

European Commission, 'Communication from the Commission to the European Parliament, the Council, the European Economic and Social Committee and the Committee of the Regions on enabling the Digital Transformation of Health and Care in the Digital Single Market', COM (2018) 233 final.

European Commission, 'Assessment of the EU Member States' Rules on Health Data in the Light of the GDPR' (2021).

European Commission, 'Data Protection: Commission Adopts Adequacy Decisions for the UK' (European Commission, 28 June 2021) <https://ec.europa.eu/commission/presscorner/detail/en/ip_21_3183> accessed 17 November 2021.

European Commission, 'Digital Health and Care' (2018) <https://ec.europa.eu/health/sites/default/files/ehealth/docs/2018_ehealth_infographic_en.pdf> accessed 23 November 2021.

European Commission, 'European Health Data Space' <https://ec.europa.eu/health/ehealth/dataspace_en> accessed 23 November 2021.

European Commission, 'Shaping Europe's digital future. eHealth' <https://digital-strategy.ec.europa.eu/en/policies/ehealth> accessed 24 January 2022.

European Commission, 'White Paper on Artificial Intelligence: A European Approach to Excellence And Trust', COM(2020) 65 final.

European Commission, Directorate-General for Communications Networks, Content and Technology, 'Ethics Guidelines for Trustworthy AI', Publications Office (2019) <https://data.europa.eu/doi/10.2759/177365> accessed 25 February 2023.

European Commission, Directorate-General for Justice and Consumers, 'Liability for Artificial Intelligence and Other Emerging Digital Technologies', Publications Office (2019), <https://data.europa.eu/doi/10.2838/25362> accessed 25 February 2023.

Federal Agency on Technical Regulating and Metrology, News, 'The First Standards in the Area of AI Have Been Approved' (25 December 2019) <https://www.rst.gov.ru/portal/gost/home/presscenter/news?portal:componentId=88bea e40-0e16-414c-b176-d0ab5de82e16&navigationalstate=JBPNS_rO0ABXczAA ZhY3Rpb24AAAABAA5zaW5nbGVOZXdzVmlldwACaWQAAAABAAQ2 NTY2AAdfX0VPRl9f> accessed 17 May 2021.

Federal Law No. 123-FZ, 'On the Experiment on Establishing a Special Regulatory Regime for Creation of Necessary Conditions for Development and Implementation of Artificial Intelligence Technologies in Moscow, a Constituent Entity of the Russian Federation and a City of Federal Importance, and on Amending Articles 6 and 10 of the Federal Law "On Personal Data"' (24 April 2020), Corpus of Legislative Acts of the Russian Federation, 2020, No. 17, Article 2701.

Federal Law No. 152-FZ, 'On Personal Data' (27 July 2006), Corpus of Legislative Acts of the Russian Federation, 2006, No. 31 (Part I), Article 3451.

Foxglove, 'Stop the NHS GP Data Grab' (4 June 2021) <https://www.foxglove.org.uk/news/stop-the-nhs-gp-data-grab> accessed 18 June 2021.

GOV.UK, 'Consultation Outcome: Data: A New Direction' (last updated 23 June 2022) <https://www.gov.uk/government/consultations/data-a-new-direction> accessed 6 July 2022.

GOV.UK, 'Data: A New Direction – Government Response to Consultation' (updated 23 June 2022) <https://www.gov.uk/government/consultations/data-a-new-direction/outcome/data-a-new-direction-government-response-to-consul tation> accessed 6 July 2022.

GOV.UK, 'National Data Strategy' (9 December 2020) <https://www.gov.uk/government/publications/uk-national-data-strategy/national-data-strategy> accessed 6 July 2022.

Gusev A and others, 'Development of Artificial Intelligence in Healthcare in Russia' in C-P Lim and others (eds), *Handbook of Artificial Intelligence in Healthcare. Vol 2: Practicalities and Prospects* (Springer Nature 2022).

Hern A, 'Royal Free Breached UK Data Law in 1.6m Patient Deal with Google's DeepMind' (*The Guardian*, 3 July 2017) <https://www.theguardian.com/technology/2017/jul/03/google-deepmind-16m-patient-royal-free-deal-data-protection-act> accessed 18 June 2021.

Human Rights Watch, 'Russia: Broad Facial Recognition Use Undermines Rights' (15 September 2021) <https://www.hrw.org/news/2021/09/15/russia-broad-facial-recognition-use-undermines-rights> accessed 26 January 2022.

ICO, 'Letter: Investigation on the Provision of Patient Data to DeepMind' (3 July 2017) <https://ico.org.uk/media/action-weve-taken/undertakings/2014353/undertaking-cover-letter-revised-04072017-to-first-person.pdf> accessed 27 January 2022.

ICO, 'Royal Free – Google DeepMind Trial Failed to Comply with Data Protection Law' (3 July 2017) <https://ico.org.uk/about-the-ico/news-and-events/news-and-blogs/2017/07/royal-free-google-deepmind-trial-failed-to-comply-with-data-protection-law/> accessed 18 June 2021.

Itgovernance, 'Data Protection and Brexit' <https://www.itgovernance.co.uk/eu-gdpr-uk-dpa-2018-uk-gdpr> accessed 15 June 2021.

Marsh S, 'GPs Warn over Plans to Share Patient Data with Third Parties in England' (*The Guardian*, 30 May 2021) <https://www.theguardian.com/society/2021/may/30/gps-warn-plans-share-patient-data-third-parties-england> accessed 15 June 2021.

Ministerio de Asuntos Económicos y Transformación Digital, 'El Gobierno de España presenta, en colaboración con la Comisión Europea, el primer piloto del sandbox de regulación de Inteligencia Artificial en la UE' <https://portal.mineco.gob.es/en-us/comunicacion/Pages/20220627-PR_AI_Sandbox.aspx> accessed 4 July 2022.

Ministry of Economic Development of the Russian Federation, Federal Project, 'Artificial Intelligence' <https://www.economy.gov.ru/material/directions/tehnologicheskoe_razvitie/federalnyy_proekt_iskusstvennyy_intellekt/> accessed 17 May 2021.

NHS Digital, 'General Practice Data for Planning and Research (GPDPR)' <https://digital.nhs.uk/data-and-information/data-collections-and-data-sets/data-collections/general-practice-data-for-planning-and-research> accessed 16 June 2021.

NHS Royal Free London, 'Our Work with Google Health UK' <https://www.royalfree.nhs.uk/patients-visitors/how-we-use-patient-information/our-work-with-deepmind/> accessed 18 November 2021.

Official Portal of the General Jurisdiction Courts of the City of Moscow, Moscow City Court, Information on case no. 33a-0707/2020 <https://mos-gorsud.ru/mgs/services/cases/appeal-admin/details/6c9dfe4c-ecc7-4626-90f4-dea208d54b5f?participants=%D0%BF%D0%BE%D0%BF%D0%BE%D0%B2%D0%B0+%D0%B0.%D0%B2> accessed 26 January 2022.

Order of the Government of the Russian Federation No. 2129-p dated 19 August 2020, 'On Approval of the Framework for Development of Artificial Intelligence and Robot Technologies Regulation until 2024' <https://www.economy.gov.ru/material/file/57ff642339b16c479b12030fb5f1b6e3/19082020_2129-p.pdf> accessed 17 May 2021.

Paal BP and Pauly DA (eds), *Datenschutz-Grundverordnung Bundesdatenschutzgesetz: DS-GVO BDSG*, 3rd edn (Beck 2021).

Pasquale FA, 'The Black Box Society: The Secret Algorithms that Control Money and Information' (2015) 96 Book Gallery.

Presidential Decree, 'On Development of AI in the Russian Federation' (10 October 2019) <https://www.garant.ru/products/ipo/prime/doc/72738946/> accessed 17 May 2021.

Proposal for a Regulation of the European Parliament and of the Council laying down Harmonised Rules on Artificial Intelligence (Artificial Intelligence Act) and amending certain Union Legislative Acts, COM/2021/206 final.

Protocol Amending the Convention for the Protection of Individuals with regard to Automatic Processing of Personal Data ('Convention 108+'), 18 May 2018.

Ralston W, 'They Told Their Therapists Everything: Hackers Leaked It All' (Wired, 5 April 2021) <https://www.wired.com/story/vastaamo-psychotherapy-patients-hack-data-breach/> accessed 23 November 2021.

Rules for processing of de-personalised personal data by participants of the experimental regime for creation of the necessary conditions for development and implementation of artificial intelligence technologies in Moscow, as well as for further possible application of the results of the use of artificial intelligence, approved by the Resolution of the Moscow Government No. 2138-ПП dated 3 December 2020 <https://docs.cntd.ru/document/573103472> accessed 17 May 2021.

Rules for transfer of images and granting access to photo and video surveillance systems and services by owners of such systems and services for the purposes of creating necessary conditions for development and implementation of artificial intelligence technologies in Moscow, approved by the Resolution of the Moscow Government No. 2136-ПП dated 3 December 2020 <https://docs.cntd.ru/document/573103471> accessed 17 May 2021.

State Standard GOST R 58776-2019, 'Means of Monitoring Behaviour and Predicting People's Intentions. Terms and Definitions'.

State Standard GOST R 5877-2019, 'Air Transport. Airports. Technical Means of Inspection. Methodology for Determining the Quality Indicators for the Recognition of Illegal Contents by Shadow X-Ray Images'.

'Statute of the Coordination Council for the Experimental Legal Regime, Approved by the Resolution of the Moscow Government No. 2135-ПП' (3 December 2020) <https://docs.cntd.ru/document/573103470> accessed 17 May 2021.

Stevens L, 'Royal Free and Google DeepMind Trial Did Not Comply with DPA' (DigitalHealth, 3 July 2017) <https://www.digitalhealth.net/2017/07/royal-free-and-deepmind-did-not-comply-with-dpa-ico/> accessed 27 January 2022.

The Data Protection, Privacy and Electronic Communications (Amendments etc.) (EU Exit) Regulations 2019, No. 419 <https://www.legislation.gov.uk/uksi/2019/419/introduction/made> accessed 15 June 2021.

The President of Russia, Artificial Intelligence Journey 2020 Conference <http://www.kremlin.ru/events/president/transcripts/64545> accessed 26 January 2022.

Trade and Cooperation Agreement between the European Union and the European Atomic Energy Community, of the One Part, and the United Kingdom of Great Britain and Northern Ireland, of the Other Part (31 December 2020).

Tzanou M, 'Addressing Big Data and AI Challenges: A Taxonomy and Why the GDPR Cannot Provide a One-Size-Fits-All Solution' in Maria Tzanou (ed.), *Health Data Privacy under the GDPR: Big Data Challenges and Regulatory Responses* (Routledge 2020).

Tzanou M, 'The GDPR and (Big) Health Data: Assessing the EU Legislator's Choices' in Maria Tzanou (ed.), *Health Data Privacy under the GDPR: Big Data Challenges and Regulatory Responses* (Routledge 2020).

Van der Sloot B and Van Schendel S, 'Ten Questions for Future Regulation of Big Data: A Comparative and Empirical Legal Study' (2016) 7 Journal of Intellectual Property, Information Technology and Electronic Commerce Law.

Von der Leyen U, 'A Union that Strives for More, My Agenda for Europe: Political Guidelines for the Next European Commission 2019–2024', <https:// op.europa.eu/en/publication-detail/-/publication/43a17056-ebf1-11e9-9c4e-01a a75ed71a1> accessed 25 February 2023.

Zarsky TZ, 'Incompatible: The GDPR in the Age of Big Data' (2017) 47 Seton Hall Law Review.

13. Governing the 'datafied' school: bridging the divergence between universal education and student autonomy
Theresa Henne and Oskar J. Gstrein

1. INTRODUCTION

The COVID-19 pandemic affected many sectors of society in unforeseen and profound ways. Among them is the educational sector, which experienced an amplification of trends that remained on the backburner for some time. Certainly, enhanced data collection and connectivity in the context of personalised learning and school management, the use of Big Data infrastructure to train 'smart algorithms' and 'artificial intelligence' (AI), as well as the implementation of emerging technologies, such as mixed/virtual/augmented reality in educational concepts, have been discussed for decades now.[1] However, the pandemic has drastically and rapidly increased demand for such services and applications – typically referred to as 'edtech' or 'edutech'. They are now used in ever-growing numbers by school and university students, parents and teachers all across the world.[2] The sudden urgency to provide education at scale over distance, combined with the difficulty for most (public) schools to do so instantly and effectively, can be seen as the result of the inability (or unwillingness?) of educational institutions to address seemingly unavoidable trends.[3] At the same time, the economic interest from the private sector in edtech

---

[1] To highlight just two examples see Vaughan Prain and others, 'Personalised Learning: Lessons to Be Learnt' [2012] 39(4) British Educational Research Journal; L Rosenblum, 'Virtual and Augmented Reality 2020' (2000) 20 IEEE Computer Graphics and Applications; Francois St-Hilaire and others, 'A New Era: Intelligent Tutoring Systems Will Transform Online Learning for Millions' <https://arxiv.org/abs/2203.03724> accessed 25 March 2022.

[2] Samual Amponsah, Micheal M van Wyk and Michael Kojo Kolugu, 'Academic Experiences of "Zoom-Fatigue" as a Virtual Streaming Phenomenon during the COVID-19 Pandemic' (2022) 17(1) International Journal of Web-Based Learning and Teaching Technologies.

[3] Yasmeen Shamsi Rizvi and Asma Nabi, 'Transformation of Learning from Real to Virtual: An Exploratory-Descriptive Analysis of Issues and Challenges' (2021) 14(1) Journal of Research in Innovative Teaching & Learning.

grows, with one report valuing the market at around USD 85 billion in 2021 with an expectation to grow up to USD 218 billion by 2027.[4]

In this chapter we consider how the datafication of schools is being shaped through emerging Big Data and AI infrastructures and investigate the situation of students in Germany during the year 2021. We focus on how this transformation affects the personal development of students as they develop from kids into teenagers and young adults. We analyse and discuss the datafication of schools in relation to privacy, data protection, as well as personal development, which we approach through the lens of 'informational self-determination'.

Whereas privacy and data protection are widely established in legal frameworks, it is particular to Germany that informational self-determination also has a formal status as a legally binding fundamental right. It is because of this unique legal framework and the high socio-economic status that we chose Germany as the field of study.[5]

In the context of this chapter, we consider how aforementioned individual rights, governance principles and legal guarantees apply to minors in primary and secondary education. As more and more data on the learning processes and administrative practices in schools are generated, one would expect legal frameworks such as privacy and data protection laws or associated constitutional rights to safeguard the autonomous space of children and their families. Through such protection they would allow and encourage students to become critical and independent citizens, capable of making meaningful decisions for democratic societies.

However, as we argue based on the analysis below, the existing governance approach in a seemingly advanced democratic country such as Germany lacks effective safeguards and remedies for minors. Especially the current generation of students is going through an educational process that is more data-dependent than ever before, and the effects on the future personal development of students might be particularly severe with the process of datafication starting at such a young age. The diverse landscape

---

4   Infinium Global Research, 'EdTech Market: Global Industry Analysis, Trends, Market Size, and Forecasts up to 2027' (2021) <https://www.researc handmarkets.com/reports/5401915/edtech-market-global-industry-analysis-tren ds?utm_source=BW&utm_medium=PressRelease&utm_code=3tc325&utm_cam paign=1620048+-+Global+EdTech+Market+Report+2021%3a+Industry+An alysis%2c+Trends%2c+Market+Size%2c+and+Forecasts+2019-2027&utm_exe c=chdo54prd> accessed 21 March 2022.
5   United Nations Development Programme, *Human Development Report 2020: The Next Frontier – Human Development and the Anthropocene* (United Nations 2020) 389 <https://www.un-ilibrary.org/content/books/9789210055161> accessed 29 March 2022.

of educational institutions is increasingly populated by private, semi-private and international schools, which to a smaller degree are subject to state regulation.[6] Furthermore, many of the concerns raised in this chapter will likewise be applicable to data processing in higher education, which, however, differs insofar as most data subjects are no longer minors. The focus of this chapter, however, lies solely on public schools in primary and secondary education.

2. WHAT IS POTENTIALLY LOST WITH DATAFICATION OF SCHOOLS?

The COVID-19 pandemic forced schools all over the world and in Germany to shift to remote home schooling or hybrid classroom formats.[7] This need for rapid adaptation once more exposed the existing global inequalities in public education.[8] Where possible, the inadequacies were sought to be levelled out by investments in hard- and software, that alongside facilitating teaching and learning gathered data on students and the entire school community. Whereas some authors frame the pandemic as a long-overdue momentum to catch up with digital forerunners, such as Singapore, Denmark or and Sweden,[9] others fear the consequences of ad-hoc digitalisation and the increasing influence of private players in public education.[10] Already before the pandemic educators and academics raised concerns about the effects

---

[6] Marcel Helbig, Rita Nikolai and Michael Wrase, 'Privatschulen und die soziale Frage Wirkung rechtlicher Vorgaben zum Sonderungsverbot in den Bundesländern' (2017) 45 Leviathan.

[7] OECD, 'The State of School Education: One Year into the COVID Pandemic' (2021) <https://www.oecd-ilibrary.org/education/the-state-of-school-education_201dde84-en> accessed 25 February 2022.

[8] ibid; Velislava Hillman, João Pedro Martins and Emmanuel C Ogu, 'Debates about EdTech in a Time of Pandemics Should Include Youth's Voices' (2021) 3 Postdigital Science and Education; Karla Zavala Barreda, 'Fuar de Alcance: Educación a Distancia En Zonas Rurales Peruanas Durante La Pandemia' in Stefania Milan, Emiliano Treré and Silvia Masiero (eds), *COVID-19 from the Margins* (Institute of Network Cultures 2021); Raquel Tarullo, 'COVID-19 in Argentina: When the Micro-Practices of Activism Fit in a WhatsApp Message' in Stefania Milan, Emiliano Treré and Silvia Masiero (eds), *COVID-19 from the Margins* (Institute of Network Cultures 2021).

[9] OECD, 'Were Schools Equipped to Teach – and Were Students Ready to Learn – Remotely?' (2020) 108 PISA in Focus.

[10] Linda Castañeda and Ben Williamson, 'Assembling New Toolboxes of Methods and Theories for Innovative Critical Research on Educational

of datafication on the privacy and autonomy of students, as well as the educational system as a whole.[11]

Besides real-time monitoring of the cognitive activities of students, an abundance of other data types, such as demographics, physiological and emotion metrics, and social media activities, are explored for assessing the knowledge of students, their skills and learning patterns, as well as for improving their health and wellbeing.[12] These trends are likely to increase with the introduction of augmented, mixed- and virtual reality devices in classrooms, which can offer even more behavioural data.

The generated data can be modelled into 'data doubles' or 'digital twins' of students, which might act as a basis for categorising their abilities and individual character.[13] This makes predictions on their future behaviour and potentials possible, which might result in recommending certain pathways in education or employment while discouraging others.[14] If such categorisations and predictions are based on immature and hardly tested technology, incomplete or biased data sets, or are applied uncritically, they severely limit the potential for personal development of the students concerned.[15] The models, which underpin the response of institutions and which define what is considered a 'successful'

Technology' (2021) 10 Journal of New Approaches in Educational Research; Hillman, Martins and Ogu (n 8).

[11]   Audrey Watters, *Teaching Machines: The History of Personalized Learning* (The MIT Press 2021) <https://direct.mit.edu/books/book/5138/Teaching-MachinesThe-History-of-Personalized> accessed 26 February 2022; Ben Williamson, 'Calculating Children in the Dataveillance School: Personal and Learning Analytics' in Emmeline Taylor and Tonya Rooney (eds), *Surveillance Futures: Social and Ethical Implications of New Technologies for Children and Young People* (Routledge, Taylor & Francis Group 2017).

[12]   Xiaoming Zhai, 'Practices and Theories: How Can Machine Learning Assist in Innovative Assessment Practices in Science Education' (2021) 30 Journal of Science Education and Technology; Billy Tak-ming Wong and Kam Cheong Li, 'A Review of Learning Analytics Intervention in Higher Education (2011–2018)' (2020) 7 Journal of Computers in Education; Deborah Lupton and Ben Williamson, 'The Datafied Child: The Dataveillance of Children and Implications for Their Rights' (2017) 19 New Media & Society.

[13]   Kyle ML Jones and Chase McCoy, 'Reconsidering Data in Learning Analytics: Opportunities for Critical Research Using a Documentation Studies Framework' (2019) 44 Learning, Media and Technology.

[14]   Christine Broughan and Paul Prinsloo, '(Re)Centring Students in Learning Analytics: In Conversation with Paulo Freire' (2020) 45 Assessment & Evaluation in Higher Education; Kyle ML Jones, 'Advising the Whole Student: EAdvising Analytics and the Contextual Suppression of Advisor Values' (2019) 24 Education and Information Technologies.

[15]   Jones and McCoy (n 13); Williamson (n 11).

student, are regularly untransparent and opaque.[16] Often student data is masked as an objective truth ignoring its political, inherently incomplete and often erroneous nature.[17] Jones argues, '[e]ven with noble and good ends in mind—namely improving learning (however defined)',[18] the surveillance and intervention in the life of students undermine their agency and voice, whereas it should be the purpose of public education to nurture it.

Next to the invasion of the privacy of minors that comes with the exploitation of individuals as data sources,[19] critics also point to the effects of datafication of students on public education and democracy. The logics of datafication, personalisation and commodification, which already govern large parts of society as Van Dijck illustrates, also threaten to permeate a public education that 'has long been one of the most precious common goods and the backbone of Western democracies.'[20] With private companies entering the educational spheres, the privilege of the state to govern what and how students learn may be challenged by commercial interests.[21] Public education or '*Bildung*' (loosely, formation) builds on the pedagogic

---

[16]   Broughan and Prinsloo (n 14).

[17]   Jones and McCoy (n 13); Sharon Slade and Paul Prinsloo, 'Learning Analytics: Ethical Issues and Dilemmas' (2013) 57 American Behavioral Scientist.

[18]   Kyle ML Jones, 'Learning Analytics and Higher Education: A Proposed Model for Establishing Informed Consent Mechanisms to Promote Student Privacy and Autonomy' (2019) 16(1) International Journal of Educational Technology in Higher Education <https://doi.org/10.1186/s41239-019-0155-0>.

[19]   Ingrida Milkaite and others, 'Children's Reflections on Privacy and the Protection of Their Personal Data: A Child-Centric Approach to Data Protection Information Formats' (2021) 129 Children and Youth Services Review; Sonja Livingstone, Mariya Stoilova and Rishita Nandagiri, 'Children's Data and Privacy Online Growing up in a Digital Age – An Evidence Review' (2018) <https://www.lse.ac.uk/media-and-communications/assets/documents/research/projects/childrens-privacy-online/Evidence-review-final.pdf> accessed 27 June 2002; Leah Plunkett and Urs Gasser, 'Student Privacy and Ed Tech (K-12) Research Briefing' <https://cyber.harvard.edu/publications/2016/StudentPrivacyBriefing>; JC Buitelaar, 'Child's Best Interest and Informational Self-Determination: What the GDPR Can Learn from Children's Rights' (2018) 8 International Data Privacy Law.

[20]   José van Dijck, Thomas Poell and Martijn de Waal, *The Platform Society*, vol 1 (Oxford University Press 2018) 117 <https://oxford.universitypressscholarship.com/view/10.1093/oso/9780190889760.001.0001/oso-9780190889760> accessed 20 January 2022.

[21]   David Lundie, Andrej Janko Zwitter and Dipayan Ghosh, 'Corporatized Education and State Sovereignty' (*Brookings*, 31 January 2022) <https://www.brookings.edu/blog/techtank/2022/01/31/corporatized-education-and-state-sovereignty/> accessed 17 June 2022.

qualities and autonomy of the teacher, the social momentum of learning, and the discovery that making mistakes is part of self-development.[22] Certainly, the personal development of the individual has also been guided in traditional settings of education by the teachers and the learning environment. It is the task of educational institutions to expose students to thoughts, objects and practices that they would not encounter through their families, friends or algorithmic predictions and inspire them to pick up professions and hobbies.[23] Still, ultimately it is the mind of the student that combines and assesses all of these influences and decides which interests to pursue.

Through the lens of enlightenment, the purpose of education is to transform students into autonomous citizens on their way in life and society – along the notion of Immanuel Kant's famous quote 'sapere aude' or 'Have courage to use your own reason.' These values are considered at threat with the introduction of technology that transforms people and their practices into data and monitors them permanently while constantly extrapolating potential paths of thinking and action.[24] This also coincides with a style of teaching that cuts education into (micro-)learning units, that aims at optimising the skills of a future workforce ('human capital'), rather than treating students as future citizens with curious minds and maturing characters. If 'individualised' learning comes down to using the personal data insights for means of nudging a student into what is considered an optimising behaviour, the individual right to personal development and the opportunity to have a free and informed opinion are lost in public education.

When investigating the realities of German schools as elaborated in section 4, images such as Williamson's 'dataveillance school',[25] in which children are reduced to a calculable actor and judged upon their data doubles, seem not to fit the perception of local actors. Also, the notion of public schools as spaces of surveillance and social control is certainly not a new idea. Foucault, Deleuze and others have highlighted and discussed this function long before the emergence of Big Data and AI.[26] Yet, only a look at documented cases in countries such as the United

---

[22]   Lupton and Williamson (n 12).

[23]   Watters (n 11).

[24]   Anne Beaulieu and Sabina Leonelli, *Data and Society: A Critical Introduction* (SAGE Publications Ltd 2022); Jones and McCoy (n 13).

[25]   (n 11).

[26]   Maša Galič, Tjerk Timan and Bert-Jaap Koops, 'Bentham, Deleuze and Beyond: An Overview of Surveillance Theories from the Panopticon to Participation' (2017) 30(1) Philosophy & Technology.

Kingdom, France, Sweden and Bulgaria is required to understand that invasive technologies such as facial recognition are already deployed at scale in schools.[27] Corporations such as Intel are increasingly exploring this space, promising to be able to detect student emotions remotely using machine learning.[28] Without meaning to reproduce the alarmist tone that commonly accompanies most discussions in Germany involving 'Big Data', 'artificial intelligence' and 'education',[29] we find evidence that raises questions about the direction that public education is heading when it comes to nurturing personal development, free thought and critical thinking. Yet there are indications that Germany's educational landscape might differ from other countries, which already rely much more on Big Tech solutions and do not know the notion of informational self-determination. Hence, Germany might provide an exceptional space for developing 'edtech' and governance mechanisms that promote democratic values and counter exploitative data logics.

3.   FRAMING THE DATAFIED SCHOOL THROUGH DATA PROTECTION LAW AND INFORMATIONAL SELF-DETERMINATION

In this section, we examine the existing legal privacy and data protection framework applicable to the data collection in German schools on a national level.[30] Based on this legal analysis, we argue that the consideration of novel concepts is required to address the challenges of growing up

---

[27]   Mark Andrejevic and Neil Selwyn, 'Facial Recognition Technology in Schools: Critical Questions and Concerns' (2020) 45 Learning, Media and Technology 115; Sebastião Barros Vale and Gabriela Zanfir-Fortuna, 'Automated Decision-Making under the GDPR: Practical Cases from Courts and Data Protection Authorities' (Future of Privacy Forum 2022) 42 <https://fpf.org/wp-content/uploads/2022/05/FPF-ADM-Report-R2-singles.pdf> accessed 19 May 2022.

[28]   Kate Kaye, 'Intel Thinks Its AI Knows What Students Think and Feel in Class' (*Protocol*, 17 April 2022) <https://www.protocol.com/enterprise/emotion-ai-school-intel-edutech> accessed 22 April 2022.

[29]   Christian Füller, 'Schülerdaten – Das gläserne Klassenzimmer' (*Deutschlandfunk Kultur*, 10 November 2020) <https://www.deutschlandfunkkultur.de/schuelerdaten-das-glaeserne-klassenzimmer-100.html> accessed 11 April 2022.

[30]   This includes the caveat that we exclude the sixteen federal school laws of German states since they would exceed the scope of this chapter and seem irrelevant for drawing the main conclusions.

in the digital age. To build on the status quo, we explore the potential of a conceptual reframing of the right to informational self-determination as a means of resistance to the harmful effects of datafication.

3.1   Specific Protection of Minors in the General Data Protection Regulation (GDPR)

A central piece of legislation within the German and European data governance framework is the 2016 GDPR, which is generally perceived as setting high standards for the protection of personal data worldwide.[31] The universal scope of the regulation is likewise applicable to educational institutions and any third parties. The legal framework for public educational institutions and private entities, such as edtech companies, nevertheless differs regarding the purposes they commonly pursue. Data processing that is performed for a public interest, such as providing universal education, justifies greater interferences with individual rights. However, according to the GDPR, an additional EU or national law is required to define the public interest. Commercial interests can be pursued by relying, for instance, on the legitimate interest provisions under Art. 6 (1) lit f, yet must be carefully balanced with the rights and freedoms of the data subject. Regularly, however, the different interests mix – for instance, when a private company is tasked by a school to process the data of students to provide (digital) services to them. Commonly the responsibility for the data processing remains with the educational institutions in such instances, which is considered the data controller, whereas the third party processes such data within the bounds of the terms and conditions defined by the school. Although the GDPR adopts a principle-based and technology-neutral approach that includes a set of measures to restrict the scope of collection and use of personal data – e.g., necessity of valid legal basis before using data, transparency, purpose limitation or data minimisation – the regulation is also subject to criticism. For instance, Purtova admonishes that comprehensive data protection law in a datafied society will make it 'the law of everything',[32] with practically no real-life situation imaginable where the regulation is not applicable.

---

[31]   Oskar Josef Gstrein, 'Right to Be Forgotten: European Data Imperialism, National Privilege, or Universal Human Right?' [2020] Review of European Administrative Law (REALaw).

[32]   Nadezhda Purtova, 'The Law of Everything: Broad Concept of Personal Data and Future of EU Data Protection Law' (2018) 10 Law, Innovation and Technology.

Whereas the 1995 EU Data Protection Directive 95/46 EC that preceded the GDPR did not entail a single notion indicating the necessity of special treatment of the personal data of minors, the GDPR contains some improvements. Recital 38 serves as a starting point for this investigation since it provides insights into the reasoning why minors should be treated differently than adults. It is argued that their personal data should be subject to specific protection measures because children 'may be less aware of the risks, consequences and safeguards concerned and their rights in relation to the processing of personal data.'

Hence, the GDPR fails to recognise that children require specific protection not only because their capacity to exercise reason is immature but more so because child- and teenagerhood together is a sensitive and formative phase. Data harms occurring at a young age might be particular severe and might interfere in the personal development of the child more profoundly than in adulthood. Justifying specific data protection measures based only on the cognitive immaturity of minors misses addressing the more significant objective, namely to establish extended safeguards against the invasions of privacy and autonomy and for the protection of personal development.

Building on a lacking analysis of why children need special protection, the proposed measures of the GDPR are far from satisfactory. We begin by outlining the GDPR's primary response to the identified vulnerability of children, namely to limit the legal bases on which the data of minors can be processed, followed by a discussion on the relevance of the right to erasure ('right to be forgotten'), child-friendly transparency requirements and automated decision-making.

3.1.1 Legal basis for processing personal data

Personal data processing under the GDPR must be based on one of six legal bases listed in Art. 6 (1), of which four remain indifferent to the age of the data subject. If personal data is processed for the implementation of a contract, compliance with a legal obligation, protection of the vital interest of the data subject or the performance of a task in public interest, data controllers do not need to adhere to any further restrictions in cases where the data of minors is involved.[33]

---

[33] Sonja Kress and Daniel Nagel, 'The GDPR and Its Magic Spells Protecting Little Princes and Princesses: Special Regulations for the Protection of Children within the GDPR' (2017) 18 Computer Law Review International <https://www.degruyter.com/document/doi/10.9785/cri-2017-0103/html> accessed 28 February 2022.

In order to justify, in accordance with Art. 6 (1) lite, the processing necessary for the performance of a task carried out in the public interest, the respective tasks must be laid down by a EU or national law, as Art. 6 (3) states. The respective federal German state laws on data processing in educational institutions – despite a few exemptions – do not explicitly cover data collection beyond the name, address and grades of students. The federal state of Berlin, however, reformed its educational law in 2021, so it incorporates data processing by the school for the purpose of using digital teaching and learning tools insofar as this is necessary for the fulfilment of their educational mandate.[34] In most other federal states, legal uncertainty remains regarding which legal basis schools refer to when cooperating with edtech companies.

Another potential legal basis that edtech companies can rely on when processing student data is the legitimate interest provision in Art. 6 (1) lit f. However, data processing based on the legitimate interest of the data controller (or another third party) can be overridden by the interests, fundamental rights and freedoms of the data subject, 'in particular where the data subject is a child'. Hence, the proportionality of the interference must be carefully weighed against the rights of the children that result from potential data harms.[35] Still, it remains unclear under which conditions an edtech provider can rely on the legitimate interest provision for processing data. Given that students will hardly expect that data collected in the classroom are used for purposes outside of the educational context, it is highly questionable whether the legitimate interest of a private company to develop its technology or market its products outweighs the rights of the child.

Furthermore, referring to the most prominently applied legal basis for data processing[36] – the consent of the data subject – is limited in cases where the data subject is a child. Art. 8 (1) of the GDPR states that, where 'information society services' are offered to a child directly,[37] the

---

[34]   Berliner Beauftragte für Datenschutz und Informationsfreiheit, 'Berliner Schulgesetz: Reform Stärkt Den Datenschutz im Bildungsbereich' <https://www.dat enschutz-berlin.de/fileadmin/user_upload/pdf/pressemitteilungen/2021/20210917-PM_Schulgesetz.pdf> accessed 17 June 2022.

[35]   Kress and Nagel (n 33) 9.

[36]   L Jasmontaite and P De Hert, 'The EU, Children under 13 Years, and Parental Consent: A Human Rights Analysis of a New, Age-Based Bright-Line for the Protection of Children on the Internet' (2014) 5(1) International Data Privacy Law.

[37]   According to Kess and Nagel, under the leading doctrine not only services that do not exclusively target children fall under Art 8 (1); so too do so-called 'dual-use' services such as WhatsApp or Instagram that are likewise used by adults and children.

data subject must reach the age of 16 years for being able to agree to the processing based on Art. 6 (1) lit a. Children below the age of 16 rely on their parents to provide consent on their behalf. National member states, however, may with national law lower the age for consent to 13 years. In practice, this leads to a scattered GDPR landscape when it comes to the age required to provide legitimate consent. At the end of 2019 nine (of the then twenty-eight) EU member states required a minimum age of 13 for consent, six an age of 14, three an age of 15 and ten the age of 16.[38] In the context of datafied education, the age limitation for consent will regularly exclude students from making related decisions, who instead rely on their parents to agree or disagree with processing of their data.

Furthermore, the immense informational burden coming with the scale and complexity of the data economy makes it impossible for the individual to assess the risks and consequences of the data processing to which they agree.[39] Hence, the condition of lacking cognitive capacity, which Recital 38 attributes to children and based on which it justifies the limitation of their right to consent, can likewise be diagnosed among adults. Consequently, transferring the responsibility for assessing the risk of data processing to the legal guardians of a child will often not lead to adequate protection of the child. Rather, it might worsen the situation since parents who already struggle with managing their own data flows will likely react with practical indifference due to informational overload – and agree to terms without considering potential data harms.[40]

Corresponding to the criticism outlined above, Buitelaar points to the lack of empirical evidence that people over the age of 16 are more capable of overseeing the risks relating to their personal data.[41] It is therefore questionable why 16-year-olds should be expected to make good decisions from this age onwards, in particular since the vast majority of EU

---

[38] Ingrida Milkaite and Eva Lievens, 'Status Quo Regarding the Child's Article 8 GDPR Age of Consent for Data Processing across the EU' (*BIK Portal*, 20 December 2019) <https://www.betterinternetforkids.eu/practice/awareness/article> accessed 24 March 2022.

[39] Daniel J Solove, 'Privacy Self-Management and the Consent Dilemma' <https://papers.ssrn.com/abstract=2171018> accessed 13 February 2022.

[40] I van Ooijen and Helena U Vrabec, 'Does the GDPR Enhance Consumers' Control over Personal Data? An Analysis from a Behavioural Perspective' (2019) 42 Journal of Consumer Policy; F J Zuiderveen Borgesius and others, 'Tracking Walls, Take-It-Or-Leave-It Choices, the GDPR, and the EPrivacy Regulation' (2017) 3 European Data Protection Law Review.

[41] Buitelaar (n 19).

member states only grants full legal capacity at the age of 18 years.[42] Buitelaar further criticises the GDPR age limitation regime as an 'on–off approach' that does not sufficiently consider 'the evolving capacities of the child'. The latter is introduced as a legal concept in the Convention on the Rights of the Child (CRC) and encourages parents to involve children in (co-)determining their life with respect to their development.[43]

3.1.2   The Right to Be Forgotten as a remedy for minors

Article 17 GDPR stipulates an individual right to demand erasure of personal data. The provision is also commonly referred to as the 'right to be forgotten', although this is not entirely accurate and requires more nuance.[44] Article 17 GDPR contains several conditions to erase personal data, of which one specifically refers to children.[45] According to Art 17 (1) lit f GDPR in combination with Art 8 (1) GDPR, a data subject may withdraw consent that has initially been given by their parents. Unfortunately, this provision is rather vague. It is not further clarified whether the child itself must reach the age for legally providing consent for making use of it. However, given that otherwise Art. 17 (1) lit f GDPR would be conflicting with the authority granted to legal guardians in Art. 8 (1) GDPR, the same age limitation must be assumed for demanding erasure. Therefore, this facet of the right seems drafted as a remedy for minors who disagree with past decisions of legal guardians such as parents. Recital 65 of the regulation further clarifies that the right to erasure is also relevant in cases where a minor was legally allowed to give consent – sometimes as early as at the age of 13 – but was not fully aware of the potential harms involved when agreeing to the data collection and processing. Hence, Recital 65 recognises that, despite the age limitation, children might still be put into the position of making unsafe choices.

However, whether retrospective deletion of personal data can be considered a satisfactory remedy for the diverse harms potentially stemming from data collection and processing is questionable. Frequently, it will be neither apparent to minors (or their legal guardians) how data trails might result

---

[42]   European Union Agency for Fundamental Rights, 'Age of Majority' (12 November 2017) <https://fra.europa.eu/en/publication/2017/mapping-minimum-age-requirements/age-majority> accessed 28 February 2022; Buitelaar (n 19).

[43]   (n 19).

[44]   Gstrein (n 31) 125–127.

[45]   Jef Ausloos, *The Right to Erasure in EU Data Protection Law*, 1st edn (Oxford University Press 2020) <https://oxford.universitypressscholarship.com/view/10.1093/oso/9780198847977.001.0001/oso-9780198847977> accessed 8 November 2020.

in harm over a longer period.[46] Furthermore, these types of harms are not easily revisable or reparable once they occur. To make this more concrete just with two examples, one can only speculate how the data trails of minors impact future choices of educational institutions, or potential employers who increasingly use AI tools to create personality profiles of their applicants?[47] Finally, the debate about material compensation for infringements of GDPR data protection rights is active, but still in its infancy.[48]

3.1.3   Review of child-friendly transparency and automated (faulty) decisions

The principle of transparency, which is enshrined in Art. 5 GDPR and fundamental for several rights of data subjects, is another GDPR mechanism that acknowledges child-specific needs. According to Art. 12, GDPR information on data processing must be provided 'in a concise, transparent, intelligible, and easily accessible form, using clear and plain language.' This applies according to Art. 12 to any information addressed to a child in particular. In practice, child-friendly transparency, however, is rarely provided.[49] Based on the investigation of the privacy policies of Instagram, Snapchat and TikTok, Milkaike concludes that such policies are still largely text-based and complex. More effort needs to be taken to develop child-specific communication formats.[50] In the empirical analysis in section 4, we conclude that the stakeholders of public schools likewise struggle to provide students with sufficient transparency. Again, the discussion of child-specific measures mirrors a broader debate on the dilemma between not overwhelming the audience with information while at the same time not over-simplifying the terms and conditions of the data-processing agreements.[51]

---

[46]   Aisling McMahon, Alena Buyx and Barbara Prainsack, 'Big Data Governance Needs More Collective Responsibility: The Role of Harm Mitigation in the Governance of Data Use in Medicine and Beyond' [2019] Medical Law Review <https://academic.oup.com/medlaw/advance-article/doi/10.1093/medlaw/fwz016/5543530> accessed 12 May 2022.

[47]   Hilke Schellmann and others, 'Podcast: Beating the AI Hiring Machines' (*MIT Technology Review*, 4 August 2021) <https://www.technologyreview.com/2021/08/04/1030513/podcast-beating-the-ai-hiring-machines/> accessed 29 March 2022.

[48]   Tobias Jacquemain, *Der deliktische Schadensersatz im europäischen Datenschutzprivatrecht: unter besonderer Berücksichtigung der Schadensbemessung* (1. Auflage, Nomos 2017).

[49]   Milkaite and others (n 19).

[50]   ibid.

[51]   Solove (n 39).

Closely related with the notion of transparency is the right not to be subject to a decision based solely on automated processing of personal data that produces legal or similarly significant affects in Art 22 GDPR. Sometimes this is also being referred to as a right to human review or explanation of automated decisions 'made by algorithms'.[52] However, the academic discussion of the precise scope, meaning and practical feasibility of this provision is still lively and ongoing. The language of the regulation has been criticised as being overly vague.[53] It is not entirely clear who needs to explain what to whom, in what detail, when and how. More questions can be raised around multi-staged decision-making processes, where different groups of humans closely interact with complex data models at different stages of a problem analysis and strategy development.[54] Given, however, that the decisions made by automated systems in the educational context – e.g., for grading, providing feedback or recommending learning pathways – might have significant effects on the future pathway of an individual, it is of utmost importance to enable young people to understand, evaluate and challenge the output of such systems.

To summarise, the constructional flaws of informed consent, the resulting inadequacy of transferring consent rights to the legal guardian, the insufficiency of the right to erasure/be 'forgotten' to act as a remedy for data exposure, the lacking implementation of child-friendly transparency standards, as well as the unclear notion of what it means to review/explain automated decisions, broadly undermine the attempts of the GDPR to provide specific protection to children. This is not to say that the GDPR leaves minors without protection, since most of the requirements and safeguards of the regulation are applicable to the processing of personal data regardless of the age of the data subject. However, the GDPR fails to provide *child-specific* protection, despite the good intentions mentioned in Recital 38.

Whereas currently the primary response of the regulation to the vulnerability of children is to limit the legal bases on which their data can be processed,[55] general requirements or limitations for processing the data of minors may be equally or more effective. For instance, during the

---

[52]   Barros Vale and Zanfir-Fortuna (n 27).

[53]   Sandra Wachter, Brent Mittelstadt and Luciano Floridi, 'Why a Right to Explanation of Automated Decision-Making Does Not Exist in the General Data Protection Regulation' (2017) 7 International Data Privacy Law.

[54]   Reuben Binns and Michael Veale, 'Is That Your Final Decision? Multi-Stage Profiling, Selective Effects, and Article 22 of the GDPR' (2021) 11 International Data Privacy Law.

[55]   Kress and Nagel (n 33) 7.

discussions for the adoption of a the Digital Service Act (DSA) the European Parliament adopted an amendment that prohibits online platforms from using personal data 'for commercial purposes related to direct marketing, profiling and behaviourally targeted advertising of minors.'[56] At the same time, discussions in the EU are ongoing on the adoption of an Artificial Intelligence Act (AIA),[57] where many applications relating to decisions being made in education (e.g., exam assessment) are labelled as high risk and might therefore become subject to strict standardisation.[58] How all of these policy initiatives affect datafication in schools over the longer term will be seen as the regulatory frameworks materialise.

3.2 Informational Self-determination as Additional Concept to Address Datafication

Since the existing European governance framework faces substantial deficits in addressing the needs of minors, it is necessary to investigate the potential of other concepts. In the following, we introduce and examine the right to informational self-determination and its ability to address the risks of minors. In particular, it seems promising to us since the right proposes a distinct rationale for why data flows must be restricted, namely the protection of the development of the personality.[59]

To elaborate on the background of the right, the German Federal Constitutional Court established the right to informational self-determination in a famous ruling of 15 December 1983 on the Census Act ('*Volkszählungsurteil*').[60] At the time, the government of West

---

[56] European Parliament, 'Amendments Adopted by the European Parliament on 20 January 2022 on the Proposal for a Regulation of the European Parliament and of the Council on a Single Market for Digital Services (Digital Services Act) and Amending Directive 2000/31/EC (COM(2020)0825 – C9-0418/2020 – 2020/0361(COD))(1)' (20 January 2022) s Amendments 57 and 498 Proposal for a regulation Recital 52 <https://www.europarl.europa.eu/doceo/document/TA-9-2022-0014_EN.html> accessed 28 February 2022.

[57] European Commission, Proposal for a Regulation of the European Parliament and of the Council Laying Down Harmonised Rules on Artificial Intelligence (Artificial Intelligence Act) and Amending Certain Union Legislative Acts 2021.

[58] Inês de Matos Pinto, 'The Draft AI Act: A Success Story of Strengthening Parliament's Right of Legislative Initiative?' (2021) 22 ERA Forum 619, 630–639.

[59] René Mahieu, 'The Right of Access to Personal Data: A Genealogy' [2021] Technology and Regulation.

[60] Oskar J Gstrein and Anne Beaulieu, 'How to Protect Privacy in a Datafied Society? A Presentation of Multiple Legal and Conceptual Approaches' (2022) 35 Philosophy & Technology; *Urteil vom 15 Dezember 1983, 1 BvR 209/83* (Bundesverfassungsgericht).

Germany announced a large-scale census program to collect personal and household data. The formal objective was to inform planning decisions and policymaking, but the plan sparked concerns about the power relationship between citizens and their government. Considering the technological capabilities of the time from the perspective of today, the judgment of the court seems prophetic in outlining the threats to individual freedoms stemming from unlimited collection, storage, use and disclosure of personal data. For addressing the risks, the right to informational self-determination grants the individual, in principle, the authority of the disclosure and use of their data as well as general measures aiming at 'keeping data flows limited, transparent, and geared towards what is necessary for a free and democratic society.'[61]

Conceptually, informational self-determination has many parallels to data protection, yet remains different with an objective that goes beyond the formal protection of personal data. It has a two-pronged origin, combining two constitutional guarantees enshrined in the first two articles of the German Basic Law ('*Grundgesetz*') that came into effect in 1949. First, 'every person shall have the right to free development of his [*sic*] personality', as enshrined in Art 2 (1) of the Basic Law. Secondly, 'human dignity shall be inviolable', as stated in Art 1 (1) of the Basic Law. In the census judgment from 1983, the court decided that such space of personal discretion must also exist in the informational sphere and is therefore not limited to the physical domain.[62] The evolution of the traditional notion of privacy is a challenge for many jurisdictions as they try to apply and interpret them in the digital age.[63]

Another interesting consideration is whether and how this right applies to minors and their personal development. The original judgment from 1983 is not directly engaging with this question, but it can be argued that the right to informational self-determination applies to minors since the law on data collection during the 1983 census also required collection of data relating to their living circumstances (e.g., are they keeping a household, how many of them live in a household).[64]

The right to informational self-determination has seen some development over the past decades. More recently, in two decisions from

---

[61]   Mahieu (n 59) 69.
[62]   *Volkszählungsurteil* (n 60) 1.
[63]   Gstrein and Beaulieu (n 60) 10; 17–20.
[64]   *Volkszählungsurteil* (n 60) 8.

2019 in relation to the right to be forgotten,[65] the judges reinterpreted informational self-determination to include commercial exploitation of data along the lines of Zuboff's surveillance capitalism.[66] This could be a new development in the history of informational self-determination, that expands it beyond the focus on state interference to establish a duty of the state to create an environment where also private parties among themselves guarantee the right. This could be particularly relevant where power asymmetries come into play, such as in relation to consumers and Big Tech firms, or students who must attend public or private schools that are increasingly datafied.

While such developments seem promising for those who lament the shortcomings of traditional data protection and privacy law in the context of datafied education, the question remains as to how informational self-determination can make a difference in practice. Critics such as Veil highlight that the concept has a metaphysical character that is almost impossible to grasp and translate into concrete practices.[67] Also, it is a very national concept, which raises the question of how relevant it could be beyond the territorial borders of Germany. Potentially, one could argue that it might also be transferrable to the entire EU, as Article 1 of the Charter of Fundamental Rights of the EU includes a legally binding commitment to human dignity – modelled after the German constitution.[68] Yet it is uncertain what the future of the right looks like, certainly internationally and beyond Europe.

4. DATAFICATION OF PUBLIC EDUCATION IN GERMANY

The data collection of schools may have been a rather mundane and redundant affair for decades. It turned the magical process of 'Bildung' into a bureaucratic deed and allowed for a pre-selection of students for

---

[65] Gstrein (n 31) 136–139.

[66] Shoshana Zuboff, 'Surveillance Capitalism and the Challenge of Collective Action' (2019) 28(1) New Labor Forum.

[67] Winfried Veil, 'The GDPR: The Emperor's New Clothes – On the Structural Shortcomings of Both the Old and the New Data Protection Law' [2018] Neue Zeitschrift für Verwaltungsrecht 686, 687–688.

[68] Steve Peers and others (eds), *The EU Charter of Fundamental Rights: A Commentary* (Hart Publishing 2021) <http://www.bloomsburycollections.com/book/the-eu-charter-of-fundamental-rights-a-commentary-1> accessed 30 March 2022.

the labour market. The 'datafication' of public education, however, refers to processes that are not much older than 20 years and seem to redefine the profane everyday politics of student data. This process is closely intertwined with the introduction of digital devices and services in the classroom and in the homes of students. In this section, we have a closer look at Germany's educational landscape, compare its state of digitalisation to international standards and outline the peculiarities of the federated system. The meta-observations are complemented by empirical investigation of two use cases, in which we explore the current data practices of two German schools and reflect upon the implication of the status quo on students' privacy, autonomy and personal development.

4.1   Meta-Observations: In 2021, German Schools Are Still Without Wi-Fi

The digitalisation of education in Germany was pushed forward in recent years by numerous public and private entities.[69] Despite these efforts, Germany is generally regarded as a latecomer in terms of digital education. In a study that explored the readiness of OECD countries for remote education, Germany ranked generally low despite its socio-economic status.[70] Little more than 30% of the German headmasters surveyed in 2018 indicated that their school had an effective online learning support platform. In contrast, in top-ranking countries such as Singapore or Denmark, above 90% of schools were equipped to provide remote learning effectively. Concerning the question of whether effective professional resources were available for teachers to learn how to use digital devices, Germany ranked third from the bottom, indicating that such resources were only provided at 40% of the German schools.

Furthermore, also within the German education system, great disparities exist when it comes to the ability to provide digital education.[71]

---

[69]   Annina Förschler, 'Der wachsende politische Einfluss privater (EdTech-) Akteure im Kontext digitaler Bildungsbeobachtung und -steuerung' (2021) 67 Zeitschrift für Pädagogik.
[70]   OECD (n 9).
[71]   Martin Riethmüller and others, 'Digitalisierung im Schulsystem – 2021 Arbeitszeit, Arbeitsbedingungen, Rahmenbedingungen und Perspektiven von Lehrkräften in Deutschland' (2021) <https://www.gew.de/fileadmin/media/son stige_downloads/hv/Service/Presse/2021/2021-09-29-STUDIE-Digitalisierung-im-Schulsystem-2021-Gesamtbericht-web.pdf> accessed 19 November 2021.

Those schools that are considered digital pioneers possess a high-performance infrastructure and digital strategy, whereas even the most fundamental resources are lacking in others. Despite the catalysing force of the pandemic, in 2021 not even half of German schools provided Wi-Fi to their students, and still more than 40% of them did not incorporate a learning management system into their infrastructure.

One explanation of this fragmented digital education landscape lies in the federal structure of Germany, which confers the educational sovereignty to the Länder (federal states). In a survey across the sixteen German states concerning which learning platforms are used,[72] the vast majority indicated that no unified learning management system was implemented across all schools. Rather, a variety of solutions was offered on a voluntary basis. For example, Bavaria provided the learning platform 'mebis' to schools. However, only 12.5% of the Bavarian students used it. At the beginning of the pandemic, some schools also used more mainstream solutions such as Microsoft Teams. However, due to heavy criticism from federal data protection authorities, such as Hessen and Baden-Württemberg, the licences were terminated.[73] Still to date, the use of tools provided by US-based companies is discouraged, which is a consequence of the judgments of the Court of Justice of the EU in the Schrems cases.[74] These fragmented governance approaches, the lack of basic internet infrastructure, as well as high data protection standards hamper the access to the German edtech market.[75] In order to promote digitalisation, Förschler observes that since 2012, but in particular since 2016, a growing number of networks and initiatives have been formed that lobby for a transfer of educational competencies to the national level and facilitate the introduction of a common national (data) infrastructure.

To summarise, the federal states are relying on a mix of corporate and public solutions. There is a lack of evidence concerning which solutions

---

[72] Sven Rieken, 'Corona-Krise: Welches Land setzt auf welche Lernplattform?' (15 January 2021) <https://www.zdf.de/uri/8a56b6da-7ded-4c51-b576-fad70 23cc5d1> accessed 25 February 2022.

[73] Corinna Budras, 'Datenschutz: "Microsoft ist zu riskant für die Schule"' *FAZ.NET* <https://www.faz.net/aktuell/wirtschaft/digitec/microsoft-produkte-in-schulen-datenschutz-bedenken-17339890.html> accessed 12 April 2022.

[74] Oskar Josef Gstrein and Andrej Janko Zwitter, 'Extraterritorial Application of the GDPR: Promoting European Values or Power?' (2021) 10 Internet Policy Review <https://policyreview.info/articles/analysis/extraterritorial-applica tion-gdpr-promoting-european-values-or-power> accessed 26 January 2022.

[75] Förschler (n 69).

are implemented on school level, since no unified standards and requirements are defined on the national or federal level. To get a better understanding of the 'situation on the ground', we investigate the practices of two German schools in the next subsection.

4.2   On the Ground: Investigating the Data Practices of Two German Schools

The research that informs this part of the chapter was conducted in spring 2021. It aimed at gaining an insight into the data practices at German schools and the related perceptions of stakeholders to explore the potentials and risks of datafied public education. Therefore, four workshops were organised, of which the first two, which aimed at mapping the data ecosystem of two use cases, are discussed below. The findings from two Multi-Stakeholder Workshops inviting a wider set of participants to reflect upon the status quo of 'student data' and (desirable) future trajectories are presented in Section 4.3.

The two schools investigated as use cases, namely the Universitätsschule (US) Dresden (grades 1–6) and the John Lennon Gymnasium (JLG) Berlin (grades 7–12), are considered as forerunners in terms of digitalisation. Both schools were awarded by the industry association Bitkom, which honours so-called 'Smart Schools' based on criteria such as digital infrastructure, digital teaching, training of educators, and the school's strategy and vision for a digital future.[76] Correspondingly, the schools had incorporated learning management systems (LMSs) and other software systems into their pedagogical concept already before the pandemic hit in March 2020. At the JLG Berlin, the Norwegian LMS provider 'itslearning' facilitated the collection of the learning data of students. The US Dresden has the privilege of cooperating with the Technical University Dresden and a Czech company in developing a custom-made LMS that fits the needs of the school. Given the digital divide inside of Germany's educational sector,[77] the data infrastructure of many other German schools is far less developed than the one described here. Hence, these two use cases should not be understood as representing the average German school. Rather, they represent stakeholders that are driving present developments and whose experiences are key to manifesting best practices for the entire German school system.

---

[76]   'Was ist eine Smart School? | Smart Schools' <https://www.smart-school.de/de/Smart-School> accessed 8 March 2022.

[77]   Riethmüller and others (n 71).

In the two use cases investigated, next to the LMS the schools also employed software systems that served mainly administrative and organisational purposes – such as generating timetables, checking the attendance of students or providing information. In both use cases, learning data is generated when students interact with the LMS by accessing materials, completing tasks online or submitting assignments. In the future, the US Dresden might consider applying AI-based techniques for analysing student data: 'The data is great for use with AI, something to think about in five, six or seven years.'[78]

In general, the data practices of the two investigated schools entail basic monitoring, aggregation and visualisation of the learning process. The degree of automatisation and personalisation of education in the use cases is limited. Rather than framing the current state as a missed opportunity or deficit, the empirical data indicates that in the two cases it was a deliberate decision of the stakeholders to employ certain technical elements and to refrain from using others. Clearly, teachers at the US Dresden had more possibilities for shaping the technical infrastructure to their needs and pedagogical concept given that they are co-designers of their LMS. Also, the LMS itslearning provides the teachers at the JLG Berlin with a vast variety of choices for designing and supporting the learning process. Although the JLG has several years of experience with itslearning, it is pointed out that teachers only 'use about 20 to 30 percent of the possibilities.'[79] Furthermore, it was mentioned that, although the teachers of the JLG wished to provide students with 'their own space, [which they could use] to develop their media competence', the school decided against using existing services such as 'Google suites' for this end, one of the prime reasons being data protection concerns.

However, it has also become clear from the workshops that both schools already invest substantial resources in managing and developing their digital infrastructure, and that their visions often conflict with the realities of school life, in which time and finances are chronically short. Considering the digital divide in the educational system, many German schools will not have the privilege of fitting their data ecosystem to their needs and visions. Instead, teachers, students, and all other stakeholders of the school community will either work with a minimum of digitalisation, in which exercises are sent via mail or WhatsApp and printed out

---

[78]   'Man hat auch wunderbare Daten bezogen auf KI, darüber hat man in 5,6,7 Jahren nachzudenken.'

[79]   'Wir nutzen wahrscheinlich irgendwas zwischen 20 bis 30 Prozent der Möglichkeiten.'

by the students, or will accept whatever digital tools are provided to them irrespective of whether they enable a form of learning that they consider relevant. The space for shaping digitalisation will be scarce at many schools. Hence, it is even more important that the lessons learned from those schools who have such capacities are conveyed to benefit the entire school system.

4.3   Critical Reflection: Balancing Privacy and Autonomy with Feasibility and Efficiency

A fundamental question concerning the politics of student data is what data types shall be collected to serve whose interests. The literature typically assumes a depiction of a data ecosystem that is mainly built around commercial and institutional interests and exploits students as passive data providers, resulting in calls for 'student-centred approaches', which allow individuals to take control of their data.[80] These narratives suggest that schools are either a place of modern surveillance, or a site of empowerment and rights for students. However, neither of the two scenarios seems to fit the fuzzy realities of the daily school life, in which many more stakeholders than edtech companies and students meet.

This subsection continues by discussing the risk and potentials for student data building on the empirical insights of two Multi-Stakeholder Workshops that were conducted in spring 2021. The workshops invited a wide group of stakeholders in public education: representatives of students from Berlin and Dresden, members of civil society, providers of edtech and learning platforms, as well as teachers, parents and researchers from the TU Dresden. A summary of the findings can be found in the Appendix.

Although the participants shared many of the concerns already raised in the datafication literature (see section 2 above), this did not result in the demand for providing more control to students or a demonisation of edtech. Rather, the accounts of the participants display the complexities that data flows in public education produce, and which serve the functioning of the educational apparatus. The following section highlights the risks to the privacy, autonomy and agency of students discussed in the Multi-Stakeholder Workshops. Furthermore, the accounts of participants are depicted, displaying the impediments to realising a data infrastructure in public education that respects the rights of minors and balances interests.

---

[80]   Broughan and Prinsloo (n 14); Jones and McCoy (n 13); Slade and Prinsloo (n 17).

The data derived from schools are a valuable resource for a diverse set of objectives. The participants in the two workshops agreed that the data of school students are very sensitive. Therefore, they are facing a dilemma resulting from the tension that student data are insightful and useful for supporting the learning process, while posing great risks to the autonomy and privacy of the minors. For example, comprehensive tracking of the learning activities over longer periods can enable a deeper understanding of the learning patterns of minors and allows for 'more meaningful' formative assessment methods. At the same time, this activity can also provide sensitive insights into the private and family life of the monitored persons. A participating student representative recalls a case of a learning platform from Schleswig-Holstein, which enabled teachers to see at what times a student had accessed a data file. The participant said students are afraid of becoming overly transparent to the teacher, who observes not only the result of an assignment, but also the process of the development, which the conditions of remote schooling made more difficult than usually.

Another participant, who is a teacher at the US Dresden, notes that safe spaces are required to support the development of students holistically. Students should not be afraid of being monitored, but encouraged to experiment, act and speak freely. For this aim, the teacher argues, 'anonymity or at least an exclusive digital space, to which parents, peers and learning facilitators have only limited access, can be important to support the development of the student.'[81]

The empirical accounts display that the use of student data, also for means beneficial to the minors, must be balanced with their developing autonomy, agency and privacy. A pre-condition for weighing risks and potentials is a comprehensive understanding of which data types serve which objective and are relevant to whom within the data ecosystem of a school. This is an issue that still requires the attention of researchers, argues a participant who himself conducts research at the USD. In effect, student data might not be collected systematically or with a clear purpose, despite the sensitive nature of the data. Instead of first determining which data types are valuable for the student or for researchers, a participant from civil society states, simply the data that are most easily accessible are collected: 'Currently the cart is put before the horse. At first, it is considered which data [are] available or could be collected and what can possibly

---

[81] 'Da kann Anonymität, oder zumindest ein begrenzter, digitaler Raum wichtig sein, der nur begrenzt von Eltern, Lernbegleitern, Mitschülern zugänglich ist, um die Entwicklung des Schülers zu unterstützen'.

be done with [these] data at some point in the future, although one should first be thinking about the objectives.'[82]

A great concern to the participant was the sharing of student data with external entities outside the school. A primary fear was that data are exploited for commercial interests and are assigned with a price. A student representative argues, 'it is already hard to be accompanied in life by the final mark of the Abitur [end exam grade]. Such data, however, which is so comprehensive and outlines in detail how a person functions, must not be sold, especially not to employers.'[83] In both workshops, the groups highlighted the importance of the 'right to be forgotten',[84] which in their understanding must ensure that students are free to decide which data points sustain over time. Past data must not lead to path dependencies and thereby limit the prospects of a student. Therefore, when data are shared with third parties, it must be safeguarded that personal data does not affect students negatively in their futures.

A participant who himself develops edtech products, points out that currently the biggest concern of the German educational ministries is that student data is employed for personalised advertisement. Learning platforms that are employed in school could use the data to their advantage and target minors and their parents to offer personalised learning tools outside the classroom: 'Many learning providers have an additional, fee-based after-school offer. The fear is that information generated within the school setting will then be used to sell something to the parents. In the sense of 'if you want your child to graduate from high school, then you have to make use of these after-school programs.'[85] Therefore, the edtech developer proposed that student data should only be shared with private third parties if they adhere to a number of principles, such as the prohibitions of using the data for advertisement or of matching the data with other data sets.

---

[82] 'Momentan wird das Pferd von hinten aufgezäumt. Es wird erst geschaut welche Daten man hat, bzw. man sammeln könnte und was man irgendwann mit diesen Daten machen kann. [...] Dabei sollte man vom Ziel her denken.'

[83] 'Es ist schon schwer, dass einen sein Leben lang die Abiturnote begleitet. Aber solche Daten, die so umfangreich sind und so gut skizzieren, wie dieser Mensch funktioniert, dürfen nicht verkauft werden, insbesondere nicht an Arbeitgeber.'

[84] Gstrein (n 31) 125.

[85] 'Viele Lernanbieter haben ein zusätzliches, kostenpflichtiges Nachmittagsangebot. Die Befürchtung ist, dass Erkenntnisse aus dem schulischen Bereich generiert werden, die dann genutzt werden, um den Eltern etwas zu verkaufen. Im Sinne von "sie wollen doch das das ihr Kind Abi macht, dann müssen sie aber auch diese Nachmittagsangebot nutzen."'

A strong consensus existed among the participants that public and private players must provide more transparency concerning the student data they collect. As showcased by the example from Schleswig-Holstein, knowing which data are collected and accessed by whom is a pre-condition for an inclusive discussion concerning data practices within schools. Yet, despite the willingness to provide more transparency to students, participants working at the US Dresden indicated that they simply did not see the available capacity to perform such a task among the current members of the school community (e.g., teachers or IT managers). 'Although transparency is a right of the GDPR,' the former data privacy officer of a private learning platform adds to the discussion, 'schools and data processor are struggling with providing it.'[86]

Another issue raised by the participants, which shows that current legal requirements clash with common practices, is the requirement that parents and students must sign a consent form in order to allow the processing of student data by private parties. The participants made clear that the concept of informed and explicit consent, which assumes that the individual has free choice to agree or disagree, is not properly applicable in the school context. Since there are no equal 'analogue' alternatives to digital education, in practice students and parents would suffer from great disadvantages if they decided not to consent to the data processing. In particular, under the situation of pandemic-related restrictions 'a group pressure is created' to accept the suggested digital tools.[87] Even though the current conduct of informed consent is likely not to be upheld in front of courts, it is still used as schools are lacking an adequate alternative legal basis. Such an alternative could be the 'public interest' provision of Art. 6 (1) lit e GDPR, which outlines that processing is lawful if 'necessary for the performance of a task carried out in the public interest.' However, to rely on this legal basis a specific law is required that outlines the purpose and conditions of the data processing for the respective public interest, and potentially includes individual remedies and safeguards against data abuse. Establishing such a new provision within the Education Acts of German states would be the best solution under the GDPR, argues one participant.

Nevertheless, establishing a novel legal framework without considering the necessity that educational institutions must be trusted and competent to protect students' data falls short of solving the issue. Once enacted, such a legal basis would potentially undermine the ability of minors and parents

---

[86] 'Transparenz ist ein Recht nach der DSGVO, aber die Schulen und Datenverarbeiter tun sich schwer diese herzustellen.'

[87] 'Es besteht ein Gruppendruck.'

to opt out of data processing that takes place with tools of private players. On the one hand, a student representative considered the possibility to opt out on an individual basis necessary, while pointing to 'unsafe' data infrastructure choices made by schools in the haste of the pandemic. On the other hand, if students and parents would be provided with better options for restricting the data collection according to their preferences, this would conflict with the public mandate of schools to provide education to all children and the smooth functioning of the school life. A participant argues that even though he considers 'informational self-determination as very important, in some cases it clearly misses the mark. We have compulsory education. [...] At the same time, however, we now have an excessive right to object to pedagogical [data] uses. This very quickly creates an absolute divergence.'[88]

To summarise, the main conflicts surrounding the collection and use of student data are balancing the privacy and autonomy of minors with the benefits of monitoring and analysing the learning process, providing meaningful transparency despite limited resources, and finding an adequate legal framework for data processing.

5.   CONCLUSION

In this chapter we investigated how the datafication of schools with increasing dependence on data-intense infrastructure affects the privacy and autonomy of students. We argued that the situation of students in Germany is of particular relevance, as we analysed and discussed the datafication of schools in relation to privacy, data protection, as well as personal development. Despite the numerous requirements and safeguards envisioned by the European framework around the protection of personal data, it delivers no satisfactory results. As we showed in section 3, formal guarantees such as the transparency principle, necessity to provide consent, a right to be forgotten, a right to not being solely dependent on automated decisions and many others seem well intended. However, ultimately they do not seem to readjust the forces within the data economy and have little effect on the day-to-day data practices of schools. Additionally, we have looked at the concept of informational self-determination, which aims at

---

[88]   'Die informationelle Selbstbestimmung ist enorm wichtig, aber teilweise schießt man mit diesem Rechtsanspruch deutlich über das Ziel hinaus. Wir haben eine Schulpflicht. [...] Gleichzeitig haben wir aber jetzt ein überbordendes Einspruchsrecht der pädagogischen Nutzung. Da entsteht sehr schnell eine absolute Divergenz.'

protecting the personal space for development – an objective relevant in the context of datafied education. On the one hand, this right seems fascinating with its clear political mission, fostering democratic ideals and autonomy. On the other hand, much more consistent work and practice seem required to make it a reality and translate it into a governance framework and practice.

As we demonstrated based on a literature review and two case studies in pioneering schools (section 4), many of the stakeholders are aware of the dilemmas and trade-offs the practice of the datafied school faces. It is also clear that the peculiarities of the German federated education system so far have hindered the development and implementation of an overarching vision. Yet, they also enabled the thriving of promising local initiatives. The learnings from these examples, however, illustrate that engaging actively in shaping the digital infrastructure binds substantial resources that most German schools likely are lacking. Regularly, consideration of the purpose and effect of datafication will hence remain only an afterthought.

At the end of this chapter, we must admit that more questions remain open than were answered, which is in itself a finding that should be considered. The engagement of all stakeholders in education will be necessary to develop a (more) common and inclusive vision of the datafied school that opposes invasive data logics commonly connected with Big Tech. It will be a key challenge for educational institutions to prove that they can be trusted with such sensitive data as produced over years in the learning context. Therefore, novel concepts such as 'data trusts' or 'data stewards' (*Datentreuhand*), which are envisioned as independent intermediaries overseeing the data flows and ensuring the rights of the individuals, might be promising in the domain of public education and help to relieve schools from the burden of securing data protection.[89] Finally, this chapter has also made clear that the traditional Western ideals of education – such as free thought and expression – are under pressure. This has serious repercussions for democracies and free societies, which are dependent on humans who can develop and excel in unexpected ways.

---

[89]   The potential of a data trust for student data has been discussed in detail by Theresa Henne in earlier research. Please contact the author for more information.

LITERATURE

Amponsah S, van Wyk MM and Kolugu MK, 'Academic Experiences of "Zoom-Fatigue" as a Virtual Streaming Phenomenon during the COVID-19 Pandemic' (2022) 17(1) International Journal of Web-Based Learning and Teaching Technologies.

Andrejevic M and Selwyn N, 'Facial Recognition Technology in Schools: Critical Questions and Concerns' (2020) 45 Learning, Media and Technology.

Ausloos J, *The Right to Erasure in EU Data Protection Law*, 1st edn (Oxford University Press 2020) <https://oxford.universitypressscholarship.com/view/10.1093/oso/9780198847977.001.0001/oso-9780198847977> accessed 8 November 2020.

Barros Vale S and Zanfir-Fortuna G, 'Automated Decision-Making under the GDPR: Practical Cases from Courts and Data Protection Authorities' (Future of Privacy Forum 2022) <https://fpf.org/wp-content/uploads/2022/05/FPF-ADM-Report-R2-singles.pdf> accessed 19 May 2022.

Beaulieu A and Leonelli S, *Data and Society: A Critical Introduction* (SAGE Publications Ltd 2022).

Berliner Beauftragte für Datenschutz und Informationsfreiheit, 'Berliner Schulgesetz: Reform Stärkt Den Datenschutz im Bildungsbereich' <https://www.datens chutz-berlin.de/fileadmin/user_upload/pdf/pressemitteilungen/2021/20210917-P M_Schulgesetz.pdf> accessed 17 June 2022.

Binns R and Veale M, 'Is That Your Final Decision? Multi-Stage Profiling, Selective Effects, and Article 22 of the GDPR' (2021) 11 International Data Privacy Law.

Broughan C and Prinsloo P, '(Re)Centring Students in Learning Analytics: In Conversation with Paulo Freire' (2020) 45 Assessment & Evaluation in Higher Education.

Budras C, 'Datenschutz: Microsoft ist zu riskant für die Schule"' faz.net <https://www.faz.net/aktuell/wirtschaft/digitec/microsoft-produkte-in-schulen-datensch utz-bedenken-17339890.html> accessed 12 April 2022.

Buitelaar JC, 'Child's Best Interest and Informational Self-Determination: What the GDPR Can Learn from Children's Rights' (2018) 8 International Data Privacy Law.

Castañeda L and Williamson B, 'Assembling New Toolboxes of Methods and Theories for Innovative Critical Research on Educational Technology' (2021) 10(1) Journal of New Approaches in Educational Research.

de Matos Pinto I, 'The Draft AI Act: A Success Story of Strengthening Parliament's Right of Legislative Initiative?' (2021) 22 ERA Forum.

European Parliament, 'Amendments Adopted by the European Parliament on 20 January 2022 on the Proposal for a Regulation of the European Parliament and of the Council on a Single Market For Digital Services (Digital Services Act) and Amending Directive 2000/31/EC (COM(2020)0825 – C9-0418/2020 – 2020/0361(COD))(1)' (20 January 2022) <https://www.europarl.europa.eu/doceo/document/TA-9-2022-0014_EN.html> accessed 28 February 2022.

European Union Agency for Fundamental Rights, 'Age of Majority' (12 November 2017) <https://fra.europa.eu/en/publication/2017/mapping-minimum-age-requ irements/age-majority> accessed 28 February 2022.

Förschler A, 'Der wachsende politische Einfluss privater (EdTech-)Akteure im Kontext digitaler Bildungsbeobachtung und -steuerung' (2021) 67 Zeitschrift für Pädagogik.

Füller C, 'Schülerdaten – Das gläserne Klassenzimmer' (*Deutschlandfunk Kultur*, 10 November 2020) <https://www.deutschlandfunkkultur.de/schuelerdaten-das-glaeserne-klassenzimmer-100.html> accessed 11 April 2022.

Galič M, Timan T and Koops B-J, 'Bentham, Deleuze and Beyond: An Overview of Surveillance Theories from the Panopticon to Participation' (2017) 30(1) Philosophy & Technology 9.

Gstrein OJ, 'Right to Be Forgotten: European Data Imperialism, National Privilege, or Universal Human Right?' [2020] Review of European Administrative Law (REALaw).

Gstrein OJ and Beaulieu A, 'How to Protect Privacy in a Datafied Society? A Presentation of Multiple Legal and Conceptual Approaches' (2022) 35 Philosophy & Technology.

Gstrein OJ and Zwitter AJ, 'Extraterritorial Application of the GDPR: Promoting European Values or Power?' (2021) 10 Internet Policy Review <https://policyreview.info/articles/analysis/extraterritorial-application-gdpr-promoting-european-values-or-power> accessed 26 January 2022.

Helbig M, Nikolai R and Wrase M, 'Privatschulen und die soziale Frage Wirkung rechtlicher Vorgaben zum Sonderungsverbot in den Bundesländern' (2017) 45 Leviathan.

Hillman V, Martins JP and Ogu EC, 'Debates about EdTech in a Time of Pandemics Should Include Youth's Voices' (2021) 3 Postdigital Science and Education.

Infinium Global Research, 'EdTech Market: Global Industry Analysis, Trends, Market Size, and Forecasts up to 2027' (2021) <https://www.researchandmarkets.com/reports/5401915/edtech-market-global-industry-analysis-trends?utm_source=BW&utm_medium=PressRelease&utm_code=3tc325&utm_campaign=1620048+-+Global+EdTech+Market+Report+2021%3a+Industry+Analysis%2c+Trends%2c+Market+Size%2c+and+Forecasts+2019-2027&utm_exec=chdo54prd> accessed 21 March 2022.

Jacquemain T, *Der deliktische Schadensersatz im europäischen Datenschutzprivatrecht: unter besonderer Berücksichtigung der Schadensbemessung*, 1st edn (Nomos 2017).

Jasmontaite L and De Hert P, 'The EU, Children under 13 Years, and Parental Consent: A Human Rights Analysis of a New, Age-Based Bright-Line for the Protection of Children on the Internet' (2014) 5(1) International Data Privacy Law.

Jones KML, 'Advising the Whole Student: EAdvising Analytics and the Contextual Suppression of Advisor Values' (2019) 24 Education and Information Technologies.

Jones KML and McCoy C, 'Reconsidering Data in Learning Analytics: Opportunities for Critical Research Using a Documentation Studies Framework' (2019) 44(1) Learning, Media and Technology.

Jones KML, Rubel A and LeClere E, 'A Matter of Trust: Higher Education Institutions as Information Fiduciaries in an Age of Educational Data Mining and Learning Analytics' (2020) 71 Journal of the Association for Information Science and Technology.

Kaye K, 'Intel Thinks Its AI Knows What Students Think and Feel in Class' (*Protocol*, 17 April 2022) <https://www.protocol.com/enterprise/emotion-ai-school-intel-edutech> accessed 22 April 2022.

Kress S and Nagel D, 'The GDPR and Its Magic Spells Protecting Little Princes and Princesses: Special Regulations for the Protection of Children within the

GDPR' (2017) 18 Computer Law Review International <https://www.degruyter.com/document/doi/10.9785/cri-2017-0103/html> accessed 28 February 2022.

Livingstone S, Stoilova M and Nandagiri R, 'Children's Data and Privacy Online Growing Up in a Digital Age – An Evidence Review' (2018) <https://www.lse.ac.uk/media-and-communications/assets/documents/research/projects/childrens-privacy-online/Evidence-review-final.pdf> accessed 27 June 2022.

Livingstone S, Stoilova M and Nandagiri R, 'Data and Privacy Literacy: The Role of the School in Educating Children in a Datafied Society' in Ingrid Stapf and others (eds), *Aufwachsen in überwachten Umgebungen* (Nomos Verlagsgesellschaft mbH & Co KG 2021) <https://www.nomos-elibrary.de/index.php?doi=10.5771/9783748921639-219> accessed 20 January 2022.

Lundie D, Zwitter AJ and Ghosh D, 'Corporatized Education and State Sovereignty' (*Brookings*, 31 January 2022) <https://www.brookings.edu/blog/techtank/2022/01/31/corporatized-education-and-state-sovereignty/> accessed 17 June 2022.

Lupton D and Williamson B, 'The Datafied Child: The Dataveillance of Children and Implications for Their Rights' (2017) 19 New Media & Society.

Mahieu R, 'The Right of Access to Personal Data: A Genealogy' [2021] Technology and Regulation.

McMahon A, Buyx A and Prainsack B, 'Big Data Governance Needs More Collective Responsibility: The Role of Harm Mitigation in the Governance of Data Use in Medicine and Beyond' [2019] Medical Law Review <https://academic.oup.com/medlaw/advance-article/doi/10.1093/medlaw/fwz016/5543530> accessed 12 May 2022.

Milkaite I and Lievens E, 'Status Quo Regarding the Child's Article 8 GDPR Age of Consent for Data Processing across the EU' (*BIK Portal*, 20 December 2019) <https://www.betterinternetforkids.eu/practice/awareness/article> accessed 24 March 2022.

Milkaite I and others, 'Children's Reflections on Privacy and the Protection of Their Personal Data: A Child-Centric Approach to Data Protection Information Formats' (2021) 129 Children and Youth Services Review.

OECD, 'Were Schools Equipped to Teach – and Were Students Ready to Learn – Remotely?' (2020) PISA in Focus 108.

OECD, 'The State of School Education: One Year into the COVID Pandemic' (2021) <https://www.oecd-ilibrary.org/education/the-state-of-school-education_201dde84-en> accessed 25 February 2022.

Peers S and others (eds), *The EU Charter of Fundamental Rights: A Commentary* (Hart Publishing 2021) <http://www.bloomsburycollections.com/book/the-eu-charter-of-fundamental-rights-a-commentary-1> accessed 30 March 2022.

Plunkett L and Gasser U, 'Student Privacy and Ed Tech (K-12) Research Briefing' <https://cyber.harvard.edu/publications/2016/StudentPrivacyBriefing>.

Prain V and others, 'Personalised Learning: Lessons to Be Learnt' (2012) 39(4) British Educational Research Journal.

Purtova N, 'The Law of Everything: Broad Concept of Personal Data and Future of EU Data Protection Law' (2018) 10(1) Law, Innovation and Technology.

Rieken S, 'Corona-Krise: Welches Land setzt auf welche Lernplattform?' (15 January 2021) <https://www.zdf.de/uri/8a56b6da-7ded-4c51-b576-fad7023cc5d1> accessed 25 February 2022.

Riethmüller M and others, 'Digitalisierung im Schulsystem – 2021 Arbeitszeit, Arbeitsbedingungen, Rahmenbedingungen und Perspektiven von Lehrkräften in Deutschland' (2021) <https://www.gew.de/fileadmin/media/sonstige_down loads/hv/Service/Presse/2021/2021-09-29-STUDIE-Digitalisierung-im-Schulsys tem-2021-Gesamtbericht-web.pdf> accessed 19 November 2021.

Rizvi YS and Nabi A, 'Transformation of Learning from Real to Virtual: An Exploratory-Descriptive Analysis of Issues and Challenges' (2021) 14(1) Journal of Research in Innovative Teaching & Learning.

Rosenblum L, 'Virtual and Augmented Reality 2020' (2000) 20 IEEE Computer Graphics and Applications.

Schellmann H and others, 'Podcast: Beating the AI Hiring Machines' (*MIT Technology Review*, 4 August 2021) <https://www.technologyreview. com/2021/08/04/1030513/podcast-beating-the-ai-hiring-machines/> accessed 29 March 2022.

Slade S and Prinsloo P, 'Learning Analytics: Ethical Issues and Dilemmas' (2013) 57 American Behavioral Scientist.

Solove DJ, 'Privacy Self-Management and the Consent Dilemma' <https://papers. ssrn.com/abstract=2171018> accessed 13 February 2022.

St-Hilaire F and others, 'A New Era: Intelligent Tutoring Systems Will Transform Online Learning for Millions' <https://arxiv.org/abs/2203.03724> accessed 25 March 2022.

Tarullo R, 'COVID-19 in Argentina: When the Micro-Practices of Activism Fit in a WhatsApp Message' in S Milan, E Treré and S Masiero (eds), *COVID-19 from the Margins* (Institute of Network Cultures 2021).

United Nations Development Programme, *Human Development Report 2020: The Next Frontier – Human Development and the Anthropocene* (United Nations 2020) <https://www.un-ilibrary.org/content/books/9789210055161> accessed 29 March 2022.

Urteil vom 15 Dezember 1983, 1 BvR 209/83 (Bundesverfassungsgericht) European Commission, Proposal for a Regulation of the European Parliament and of the Council Laying Down Harmonised Rules on Artificial Intelligence (Artificial Intelligence Act) and Amending Certain Union Legislative Acts 2021.

van Dijck J, Poell T and de Waal M, *The Platform Society*, vol. 1 (Oxford University Press 2018) <https://oxford.universitypressscholarship.com/ view/10.1093/oso/9780190889760.001.0001/oso-9780190889760> accessed 20 January 2022.

van Ooijen I and Vrabec HU, 'Does the GDPR Enhance Consumers' Control over Personal Data? An Analysis from a Behavioural Perspective' (2019) 42 Journal of Consumer Policy.

Veil W, 'The GDPR: The Emperor's New Clothes – On the Structural Shortcomings of both the Old and the New Data Protection Law' [2018] Neue Zeitschrift für Verwaltungsrecht.

Wachter S, Mittelstadt B and Floridi L, 'Why a Right to Explanation of Automated Decision-Making Does Not Exist in the General Data Protection Regulation' (2017) 7 International Data Privacy Law.

'Was ist eine Smart School? | Smart Schools' <https://www.smart-school.de/de/ Smart-School> accessed 8 March 2022.

Watters A, *Teaching Machines: The History of Personalized Learning* (The MIT Press 2021) <https://direct.mit.edu/books/book/5138/Teaching-MachinesThe-History-of-Personalized> accessed 26 February 2022.

Williamson B, 'Calculating Children in the Dataveillance School: Personal and Learning Analytics' in E Taylor and T Rooney (eds), *Surveillance Futures: Social and Ethical Implications of New Technologies For Children and Young People* (Routledge, Taylor & Francis Group 2017).

Wong BT and Li KC, 'A Review of Learning Analytics Intervention in Higher Education (2011–2018)' (2020) 7 Journal of Computers in Education.

Zavala Barreda K, 'Fuar de Alcance: Educación a Distancia en Zonas Rurales Peruanas Durante la Pandemia' in S Milan, E Treré and S Masiero (eds), *COVID-19 from the Margins* (Institute of Network Cultures 2021).

Zhai X, 'Practices and Theories: How Can Machine Learning Assist in Innovative Assessment Practices in Science Education' (2021) 30 Journal of Science Education and Technology.

Zuboff S, 'Surveillance Capitalism and the Challenge of Collective Action' (2019) 28(1) New Labor Forum.

Zuiderveen Borgesius F and others, 'Tracking Walls, Take-It-Or-Leave-It Choices, the GDPR, and the EPrivacy Regulation' (2017) 3 European Data Protection Law Review 353.

APPENDIX

Table 13.A1 displays risks and potentials perceived by the participants of two Multi-Stakeholder Workshops and differentiates between internal data flows within the school and external data uses by third parties, such as edtech companies, public authorities and researchers.

Table 13.A1 Summary of findings, 'Risks and potential of collection and use of student data'

Potentials & Uses	Risks & Challenges
Internal data use	Internal data use
Better organisation and communication of daily school processes	Usability vs complexity of the IT system
	Sustainable data management
Support of teacher in capturing the student's knowledge and skill level, which enables early detection of problems and better support	Data 'overflow', audience-targeted communication
	Development of role-specific access rights
Better, more meaningful assessment formats	Despite monitoring, schools must remain a safe space to support students' development holistically
Better understanding of students learning process and long-term development	Efficiency gains are used to reduce cost and personnel instead of improving quality of the education
Individualised learning	Student data enables sensitive insights in students' private life
External data uses	Both internal and external data use
Research on the effectiveness of pedagogical concepts and the development of didactic models	Lack of transparency on the collection, use and sharing of student data for students and parents
Meta-monitoring and evidence-based education policymaking	Students are discriminated against based on student data, student data creates stereotypes
Improvement and innovation of learning platforms and tools	Past data influences students' future pathway, possibly creating path dependencies
	Data disclosure because of cyber-attacks, vulnerability of IT systems and human mistake
	Lack of understanding what data types are relevant to purposes of stakeholders

Table 13.A1   (continued)

Potentials & Uses	Risks & Challenges
	External data use
	Illegitimate access by third parties
	Students' data becomes object of commercial interests
	Student data is used to target parents and students with personalised advertisement
	No systematic data collection across schools and regions
	Consistent procedure for data anonymisation and pseudonymisation
	General lack of transparency concerning data collection and use of private players
	Deanonymisation

PART V

AUTONOMOUS SYSTEMS, RIGHTS AND DUTIES

14. Artificial Intelligence and international human rights law: implications for humans and technology in the 21st century and beyond

Joshua C. Gellers and David J. Gunkel

INTRODUCTION

Legal systems often struggle to adapt to technological changes. Although there is evidence that the dilemmas posed by such innovations 'rarely persist indefinitely',[1] emerging technologies such as artificial intelligence (AI), virtual reality (VR), Internet of Things (IoT) and others have exposed critical weaknesses in extant legal paradigms.[2] The goals of maintaining an orderly society and providing justice, especially for society's most vulnerable, hinge on the ability of the law to adjust to these stressors. At the same time, technology companies are rightly criticized for testing the limits of the law in the name of innovation or profit-seeking.[3] Why should industry be permitted to develop, market and sell products that pose a threat to existing laws and regulations, leaving policymakers scrambling to make necessary adjustments to regulatory systems? Further, what is the appropriate scale of change to governing structures urged by technological advancements? Is it enough to tweak extant laws, policies and institutions, or must these developments be met with systemic disruptions to the status quo? Do current rules need updating, or perhaps might we find better ways to enforce existing rules?

---

[1] Lyria Bennett Moses, 'Agents of Change: How the Law "Copes" with Technological Change' (2011) 20 Griffith Law Review, 763.

[2] W Keith Robinson and Joshua T Smith, 'Emerging Technologies Challenging Current Legal Paradigms' (2018) 19 Minnesota Journal of Law, Science and Technology.

[3] See, e.g., Dirk Helbing and others, 'Will Democracy Survive Big Data and Artificial Intelligence?' [2017] Scientific American <https://www.scientificameri can.com/article/will-democracy-survive-big-data-and-artificial-intelligence/> accessed 22 July 2022; Paul Nemitz, 'Constitutional Democracy and Technology in the Age of Artificial Intelligence' (2018) 376 Philosophical Transactions of the Royal Society A: Mathematical, Physical and Engineering Sciences.

A prime example of an area where these concerns abound involves the challenges that AI poses to existing human rights.

In general, the scope and magnitude of impacts that technological developments hold for human rights remain uncertain. Meanwhile, news reports regularly publicize dramatic affronts to human rights tied to the (mis)use of novel technologies. On a more abstract level, emerging technologies destabilize taken-for-granted concepts in the law and invite intellectually demanding conversations about controversial issues, such as what it means to be human and who or what occupies a place within our moral and legal universes. These discussions occur against a background of global movements actively seeking to promote the rights of animals and nature, natural non-human entities whose evolving status might hold direct implications for the rights of artefactual non-human forms such as AI. Although early efforts to take stock of these impacts and address relevant existential questions have provided some clarity, much work remains to be done. In particular, the variety of human rights impacts needs to be expanded and the notion of rights for technological entities needs to be situated within the context of contemporaneous initiatives regarding the rights of other non-humans. Can the existing corpus of international human rights law (IHRL) accommodate the inclusion of technological entities or must existing paradigms be replaced?

This chapter critically examines the extent to which current IHRL is hospitable (or not) to AI. First, we review the philosophical foundations of rights. Second, we present methodological and critical insights regarding the extant literature before using a two-step framework to highlight less obvious ways in which emerging technologies like AI intersect with IHRL. Third, we explore the opportunities and challenges of extending rights to technological beings such as robots. We conclude with a call to enlarge the ontological scope of rights on theoretical and practical levels, and offer recommendations designed to assist in the governance of AI with an eye toward protecting the rights of human and non-human entities alike.

BACKGROUND ON THE PHILOSOPHY OF RIGHTS

Like 'time' in *The Confessions of St. Augustine*,[4] 'rights' is one of those words that we are all fairly certain of knowing what it means up to the

---

[4]   Saint Augustine, *The Confessions of St. Augustine*, trans. Edward B Pusey (PF Collier & Son 1909) 54.

point when someone asks us to define it. Then we run into difficulties and confusions. This is neither unexpected nor uncommon. One hundred years ago, an American jurist, Wesley Hohfeld, observed that even experienced legal professionals tend to misunderstand the term, often using contradictory or insufficient formulations during a decision or even in a single sentence.[5]

In response to this problem, Hohfeld developed a typology that categorizes rights into four components or what he called 'incidents': claims, powers, privileges and immunities. His point was simple and direct: a right, like the right one has over a piece of property, can be defined and operationalized by one or more of these incidents. It can, for instance, be formulated as a claim that an owner has over and against another individual. Or it could be formulated as an exclusive privilege for use and possession that is granted to the owner of the object. Or it could be a combination of these.

Hohfeld also recognized that rights are fundamentally social and relational. The four types of rights or incidents only make sense to the extent that each one necessitates a correlative duty that is imposed on at least one other individual. 'The "currency" of rights', as Johannes Marx and Christine Tiefensee explain, 'would not be of much value if rights did not impose any constraints on the actions of others. Rather, for rights to be effective they must be linked with correlated duties.'[6] Hohfeld, therefore, presents and describes the four incidents in terms of rights/duties pairs:

- If A has a Privilege, then someone (B) has a No-claim.
- If A has a Claim, then someone (B) has a Duty.
- If A has a Power, then someone (B) has a Liability.
- If A has an Immunity, then someone (B) has a Disability.

This means that a right—like a claim to property ownership—means little or nothing if there is not, at the same time, some other individual who is obligated to respect this claim. Or as Jacob Turner explains, mobilizing an example that finds expression in both European literature and philosophical thought experiments, 'It would not make sense for a person marooned alone on a desert island to claim that she has a right to life, because there

---

5   Wesley Hohfeld, *Fundamental Legal Conceptions as Applied in Judicial Reasoning* (Yale University Press 1920).
6   Johannes Marx and Christine Tiefensee. 'Of Animals, Robots and Men' (2015) 40 Historical Social Research (Köln) <https://doi.org/10.12759/hsr.40.2015.4.70-91> accessed 27 July 2021.

is no one else against which she can claim that right.'[7] On Hohfeld's account, then, rights are a social phenomenon.[8] A solitary human being living alone without any contact with another person (something that is arguably a fiction) would have no need for rights. Furthermore, and as a direct consequence of this, rights can be perceived and formulated either from the side of the possessor of the right (e.g., the power, privilege, claim or immunity that one has or is endowed with), which is a 'patient-oriented' way of looking at a moral, legal or political situation, or from the side of the agent (e.g., what obligations are imposed on another who stands in relationship to this individual), which considers the responsibilities of the producer of a moral, legal or social/political action. These incidents provide the foundation for modern human rights.

INTERNATIONAL HUMAN RIGHTS LAW AND AI

Over four decades have passed since Karel Vašák first characterized IHRL in terms of three distinct 'generations'.[9] These generations correspond to the major international treaties comprising what is commonly referred to as the International Bill of Human Rights—the Universal Declaration of Human Rights (UDHR), International Covenant on Civil and Political Rights (ICCPR), and International Covenant on Economic, Social and Cultural Rights (ICESCR). In addition to these treaties, IHRL derives from customary practices and general principles of law found among states and within regional systems.[10]

The first generation consists mostly of negative rights (that is, prohibitions against government interference in the enjoyment of certain liberties) related to civil and political freedoms held by individuals. Examples include the freedom of movement (Art. 12), the right to be presumed innocent until proven guilty (Art. 14), and the freedom of thought,

---

[7] Jacob Turner, *Robot Rules: Regulating Artificial Intelligence* (Palgrave Macmillan 2019) 135.

[8] Although this insight is widely shared by many contemporary philosophers and legal theorists, it is not universally accepted as the only possible formulation. Idealists and natural rights advocates, for instance, argue that the rights of human beings are grounded not in social institutions and recognitions but in 'human nature' itself.

[9] Karel Vašák, 'A 30-Year Struggle: The Sustained Efforts to Give Force of Law to the Universal Declaration of Human Rights' [1977] The UNESCO Courier, 29.

[10] Dinah L Shelton, *Advanced Introduction to International Human Rights Law* (Edward Elgar Publishing 2014) ch 4.

conscience and religion (Art. 18).[11] The second generation involves mostly positive rights (that is, guarantees that the state will take action to realize certain entitlements) related to economic, social and cultural affordances. Examples include the right to work (Art. 6), the right of everyone to the enjoyment of the highest attainable standard of physical and mental health (Art. 12), and the right to education (Art. 13).[12] It should also be noted that some second-generation rights, such as the right to take part in cultural life (Art. 15),[13] qualify as 'collective rights' because they focus on the protection and preservation of groups that share common cultural traits.[14] The third generation, so-called 'solidarity' rights, entails broad goals that can only be achieved through the widespread participation of actors at all levels of society, from individuals to governments and including both public and private institutions.[15] Examples include the right to development, the right to a healthy environment and the right to peace.[16] Unlike the preceding two generations, this third one finds expression in international and domestic law, but not in a separate global treaty. More recently, scholars have increasingly identified a fourth generation of rights defined by the need to safeguard human life in the face of technological innovations.[17] This category of rights tends to focus on the individual, strive for the protection of human dignity and interface with existing human rights in novel ways that necessitate the articulation of new entitlements. Examples include the right to change sex,[18] freedom from genetic harm,[19] and the right to social media.[20] As mentioned above, much of the

---

[11]   International Covenant on Civil and Political Rights (adopted 16 December 1966, entered into force 23 March 1976) 999 UNTS 171 (ICCPR).

[12]   International Covenant on Economic, Social and Cultural Rights (adopted 19 December 1966, entered into force 3 January 1976) 993 UNTS 3 (ICESCR).

[13]   ibid.

[14]   Douglas Sanders, 'Collective Rights' (1991) 13 Human Rights Quarterly 368, 369.

[15]   Vašák (n 9).

[16]   Carl Wellman, 'Solidarity, the Individual and Human Rights' (2000) 22 Human Rights Quarterly.

[17]   Mathias Risse, 'The Fourth Generation of Human Rights: Epistemic Rights in Digital Lifeworlds' [2021] 5 Moral Philosophy and Politics <https://www.degruyter.com/document/doi/10.1515/mopp-2020-0039/html> accessed 24 July 2021.

[18]   Olena Ivanii, Andrii Kuchuk and Olena Orlova, 'Biotechnology as Factor for the Fourth Generation of Human Rights Formation' (2020) 9 Journal of History Culture and Art Research.

[19]   Erick Valdés, 'Bioderecho, Daño Genético y Derechos Humanos de Cuarta Generación' (2015) 144 Boletín Mexicano de Derecho Comparado.

[20]   Brian Christopher Jones, 'Is Social Media a Human Right? Exploring the Scope of Internet Rights' (*International Journal of Constitutional Law Blog*,

literature on human rights and emerging technologies has understandably focused on impacts related to the first generation in IHRL. The present work seeks to contribute additional insights by examining the implications such technologies hold for subsequent generations, which have been neglected in the literature.

The concept of dignity looms large in discussions about the extent to which technology impacts human rights. Yet, its meaning has shifted over time and its role remains highly contested. Daly distinguishes between ancient (circa the Byzantine Empire) and modern (post-World War II) understandings of dignity, where the former indicates a vaunted status conferred on the privileged few and the latter refers to the respect and honor to which all humans are entitled 'just by virtue of having been born human.'[21] The contemporary variant can be observed in instruments of IHRL such as the UDHR, which begins by stating, 'recognition of the inherent dignity and of the equal and inalienable rights of all members of the human family is the foundation of freedom, justice and peace in the world.'[22] While some have gone as far as to claim that dignity is a concept devoid of meaning,[23] in the context of technology others have argued it represents a fundamental basis for human rights like the right to privacy.[24] Following Krämer, a productive way of resolving this tension might be to avoid use of the term dignity altogether and instead focus on precisely articulating the nature of an alleged harm (e.g., lack of respect for one's moral or legal status).[25]

Several academic studies and government reports published over the past few years have sought to unpack the relationship between AI and IHRL.[26] In general, these works have looked to the International Bill

---

5 December 2014) <http://www.iconnectblog.com/2014/11/is-social-media-a-> accessed 24 July 2021.

[21]   Erin Daly, *Dignity Rights: Courts, Constitutions, and the Worth of the Human Person* (University of Pennsylvania Press 2012) 14.

[22]   Universal Declaration of Human Rights (adopted 10 December 1948) UNGA Res 217 A(III) (UDHR) pmbl.

[23]   Justin Bates, 'Human Dignity – An Empty Phrase in Search of Meaning?' (2005) 10 Judicial Review.

[24]   Luciano Floridi, 'On Human Dignity as a Foundation for the Right to Privacy' (2016) 29 Philosophy & Technology.

[25]   Carmen Krämer, 'Can Robots Have Dignity?' in Benedikt Paul Göcke and Astrid Rosenthal-von der Pütten (eds), *Artificial Intelligence: Reflections in Philosophy, Theology, and the Social Sciences* (Brill 2020).

[26]   HLEGAI, 'High-Level Expert Group on Artificial Intelligence, EU – Ethics Guidelines for Trustworthy AI' (2019) <https://ec.europa.eu/digital-single-market/en/news/ethics-guidelines-trustworthy-ai> accessed 23 July 2021; Proposal for a Regulation of the European Parliament and the Council: Laying

of Human Rights, UN Guiding Principles on Business and Human Rights, European agreements (e.g., EU Charter, European Convention on Human Rights, etc.), and a few select international conventions for guidance. They often organize their analyses along sectoral lines, identify a non-exhaustive list of relevant (almost exclusively first- and second-generation) rights, and exemplify human rights impacts by exploring well-known use cases. The most robust of these efforts admits the complexity inherent in the analytical exercise conducted, offers a tentative qualitative assessment of the directionality of impact (e.g., positive or negative), and explains the human rights implications evident at various stages in the design and deployment of emerging technologies.[27]

The present chapter endeavors to build upon these recent works and move the discussion of AI and human rights in productive directions while acknowledging some key limitations up front. First, we do not attempt to provide an exhaustive list of all human rights impacts that might result from the creation or use of emerging technologies. Second, we do not

---

Down Harmonised Rules on Artificial Intelligence (Artificial Intelligence Act) and Amending Certain Union Legislative Acts 2021; Helmut Philipp Aust, 'Undermining Human Agency and Democratic Infrastructures? The Algorithmic Challenge to the Universal Declaration of Human Rights' (2018) 112 American Journal of International Law; Mark Latonero, 'Governing Artificial Intelligence: Upholding Human Rights and Dignity' (Data & Society 2018) <https://data society.net/wp-content/uploads/2018/10/DataSociety_Governing_Artificial_ Intelligence_Upholding_Human_Rights.pdf>; Alessandro Mantelero, 'AI and Big Data: A Blueprint for a Human Rights, Social and Ethical Impact Assessment' (2018) 34 Computer Law & Security Review; Filippo Raso and others, 'Artificial Intelligence and Human Rights: Opportunities and Risks' (Berkman Klein Center for Internet & Society, Harvard University 2018) <https://cyber.harvard.edu/publication/2018/artificial-intelligence-human-rig hts> accessed 27 July 2021; Eileen Donahoe and Megan MacDuffee Metzger, 'Artificial Intelligence and Human Rights' (2019) 30 Journal of Democracy; Janneke Gerards, 'The Fundamental Rights Challenges of Algorithms' (2019) 37 Netherlands Quarterly of Human Rights; Lorna McGregor, Daragh Murray and Vivian Ng, 'International Human Rights Law as a Framework for Algorithmic Accountability' (2019) 68 International & Comparative Law Quarterly; Mathias Risse, 'Human Rights and Artificial Intelligence: An Urgently Needed Agenda' (2019) 41(1) Human Rights Quarterly; Evgeni Aizenberg and Jeroen van den Hoven, 'Designing for Human Rights in AI' (2020) 7 Big Data & Society; Nathalie A Smuha, 'Beyond a Human Rights-Based Approach to AI Governance: Promise, Pitfalls, Plea' [2020] Philosophy & Technology; Karen Yeung, Andrew Howes and Ganna Pogrebna, 'AI Governance by Human Rights-Centered Design, Deliberation, and Oversight: An End to Ethics Washing' in Markus D Dubber, Frank Pasquale and Sunit Das (eds), *The Oxford Handbook of Ethics of AI* (Oxford University Press 2020).

27   Raso and others (n 26).

present a rigorous accounting (qualitative or quantitative) of either the direction or magnitude of human rights impacts related to a select number of technologies or sectors in which they are deployed. This is a task better suited for showcasing the utility of a comprehensive assessment tool such as the Human Rights, Ethical and Social Impact Assessment (HRESIA),[28] or the Trustworthy AI Assessment List.[29] Instead, our more circumspect goals include describing a framework useful for assessing human rights impacts, delivering a critical perspective on extant scholarship's reliance on IHRL as the foundation for AI ethics (which may not reflect how the conversation is proceeding in policy circles) and expanding the purview of how we should think about the scope of potential impacts on the less often acknowledged generations of human rights.

To begin, determining the human rights consequences associated with AI may be assisted using a simple, two-part framework. While previous work has roughly estimated the positive, negative or indeterminate effects of AI on a set of 30 human rights (stratified by the sector in which the technology is used),[30] missing from this approach is a way of accounting for less immediate impacts that nevertheless may hold serious human rights implications. One way to capture these knock-on effects is to follow the approach taken by Sætra,[31] who evaluates the relationship between AI and the Sustainable Development Goals (SDGs) by probing the level of analysis and discriminating among direct/indirect effects and impacts at varying levels of intensity. To accomplish this, he first proposes a nested model in which impacts are reviewed at the micro (individual or within-state), meso (state) and macro (international) levels of analysis simultaneously. Next, he arranges a kind of three-dimensional matrix that separates direct from indirect effects and then further subdivides impacts according to their intensity (high, medium or minor) and the extent to which ripple effects can be observed (major or minor). For present purposes, only direct/indirect effects and high/medium/minor impacts will be used since it is beyond the scope of this chapter to decipher the ripple effects of technology. We contend that an analytical tool capable of capturing both spatial interactions and the interrelationships between effects and impacts provides a richer, more complex scheme for assessing the human rights

---

[28]   Alessandro Mantelero, *Beyond Data: Human Rights, Ethical and Social Impact Assessment in AI* (Springer 2022).

[29]   HLEGAI (n 27).

[30]   Raso and others (n 26).

[31]   Henrik Skaug Sætra, 'AI in Context and the Sustainable Development Goals: Factoring in the Unsustainability of the Sociotechnical System' (2021) 13 Sustainability.

impacts of emerging technologies than others found in the literature. Such a framework may be better positioned to reflect the messy reality that '[a] single AI application can impact a panoply of civil, political, economic, social, and cultural rights, with simultaneous positive and negative impacts on the same right for different people.'[32]

Next, several scholars claim that IHRL represents the strongest possible foundation for translating AI ethics into practice.[33] There is good reason to put stock in this assertion. After all, IHRL enjoys near-universal acceptance across most cultures,[34] comes equipped with procedures and enforcement mechanisms available at multiple levels of governance,[35] and is grounded in specific, international norms (unlike AI ethics codes featuring principles 'effectively plucked out of the air'[36]).

However, there are also plenty of reasons why IHRL might not be the ideal benchmark for AI governance. First, IHRL suffers from jurisdictional issues that frustrate the governance of AI.[37] For one, the regulatory regime surrounding emerging technologies is driven primarily by non-state actors, not nation-states that are party to human rights treaties. In addition, these technologies operate without regard for national boundaries, making the application of law under the traditional notion of jurisdiction complicated. Second, much of IHRL places a premium on individual rights,[38] neglecting the unique features of AI that create cause for concern with respect to new kinds of groups and attendant legal constructs designed to protect them. For instance, companies engaging in online 'affinity profiling' use algorithms to 'group people according to their assumed interests rather than solely their personal traits',[39] which can

---

[32]   Raso and others (n 26) 58.

[33]   ibid; McGregor, Murray and Ng (n 27); Michael Pizzi, Mila Romanoff and Tim Engelhardt, 'AI for Humanitarian Action: Human Rights and Ethics' (2020) 102 International Review of the Red Cross 145; Yeung, Howes and Pogrebna (n 26).

[34]   Linda Camp Keith, 'Constitutional Provisions for Individual Human Rights (1977–1996): Are They More than Mere "Window Dressing?"' (2002) 55 Political Research Quarterly.

[35]   Douglass Cassel, 'Does International Human Rights Law Make a Difference?' (2001) 2 Chicago Journal of International Law.

[36]   Yeung, Howes and Pogrebna (n 27) 4.

[37]   Jason Pielemeier, 'The Advantages and Limitations of Applying the International Human Rights Framework to Artificial Intelligence' (*Data & Society: Points*, 2019) <https://points.datasociety.net/the-advantages-and-limitations-of-applying-the-international-human-rights-framework-to-artificial-291a2dfe1d8a> accessed 27 July 2021.

[38]   Smuha (n 27).

[39]   Sandra Wachter, 'Affinity Profiling and Discrimination by Association in Online Behavioral Advertising' (2020) 35 Berkeley Technology Law Journal, 367.

result in discrimination experienced by people who do not even know they are members of such collectives.[40] Third, IHRL's claim of universality is undercut by its Eurocentric colonial roots that continuously seek to bring non-Western societies into compliance with Western ideals while failing to account for historic injustices.[41] For example, the uncritical manner with which some Western scholars advocate for the application of IHRL to AI ethics ignores persistent global inequities, such as the degree to which the development of new technologies is likely to exacerbate existing economic disparities between the Global North and South.[42] All of this is to say that the promotion of IHRL as a framework for AI governance needs to confront these challenges with sincerity, humility and intentionality so as to avoid the pitfalls of ineffectiveness, under-inclusiveness and neo-colonialism.

Considering the preceding two sections, how might we assess the human rights impacts of AI in a manner that better reflects the complex relationship between emerging technologies and rights, especially those overlooked in the literature? Here we demonstrate how this might be accomplished by applying the two-step framework described above to use cases that intersect with second-, third- and fourth-generation rights.

The right to housing, a second-generation right, falls under the UDHR (Art. 25) and ICESCR (Art. 11), specifically as a corollary to the right to an adequate standard of living. It can also be found in several international treaties and soft law documents.[43] The Committee on Economic, Social and Cultural Rights elaborated on the contents of this right in General Comment No. 4, which further specified that the right entails legal security of tenure; availability of services, materials, facilities and infrastructure; affordability; habitability; accessibility; location; and cultural adequacy.[44]

---

[40] Mantelero (n 27) 764.

[41] Makau Mutua, 'Savages, Victims, and Saviors: The Metaphor of Human Rights' (2001) 42 Harvard International Law Journal.

[42] Jacques Bughin and others, 'Modeling the Global Economic Impact of AI' (*McKinsey Global Institute*, 4 September 2018) <https://www.mckinsey.com/featured-insights/artificial-intelligence/notes-from-the-AI-frontier-modeling-the-impact-of-ai-on-the-world-economy> accessed 27 July 2021; Cristian Alonso, Siddharth Kothari and Sidra Rehman, 'How Artificial Intelligence Could Widen the Gap Between Rich and Poor Nations' (*IMF Blog*, 2 December 2020) <https://blogs.imf.org/2020/12/02/how-artificial-intelligence-could-widen-the-gap-between-rich-and-poor-nations/> accessed 27 July 2021.

[43] Joshua C Gellers, 'The Great Indoors: Linking Human Rights and the Built Environment' (2016) 7 Journal of Human Rights and the Environment 243, 249.

[44] UN Committee on Economic, Social and Cultural Rights (CESCR), 'General Comment No. 4: The Right to Adequate Housing (Art. 11(1) of

AI relying on Big Data, such as machine-learning algorithms, poses a threat to the fulfillment of this right where it produces biased recommendations for public housing tenant selection that disproportionately reject applications from communities of color.[45] Applying the two-step framework helps to illustrate the breadth and magnitude of human rights impacts generated by this particular application of AI. In terms of levels of analysis, racially biased automated decisions regarding tenant applications diminish an individual's or family's housing accessibility (micro level) while also having spillover effects for others within their personal networks, who might be unfairly characterized as poor candidates for government-subsidized accommodations due to a kind of automated 'guilt[] by association'[46] (meso level). This discriminatory practice could amplify domestic economic inequality and frustrate upward economic mobility, thus negatively affecting a country's status in the global economy (macro level). The effects of discriminatory algorithmic housing allocation might be direct and high impact for the immediately affected individuals or families denied access to public housing, but indirect and high impact for affected members of their network, and indirect and medium impact for the country overall.

The right to the environment, a third-generation right, stems not from binding international treaties, but rather from state custom and soft law. While scholars often trace its inception back to the 1972 Stockholm Declaration,[47] this substantive guarantee is most often found in national constitutions and phrased in terms of a positive right individuals possess to enjoy a certain level of environmental quality.[48] In fact, some have argued that this right has attained the status of customary international law (and thus IHRL) by virtue of its widespread proliferation at the state level.[49]

---

the Covenant)' <https://www.refworld.org/pdfid/47a7079a1.pdf> accessed 31 July 2021.

[45]   Valerie Schneider, 'Locked out by Big Data: How Big Data Algorithms and Machine Learning May Undermine Housing Justice' (2020) 52 Columbia Human Rights Law Review.

[46]   Danah Boyd, Karen Levy and Alice Marwick, 'The Networked Nature of Algorithmic Discrimination' (Open Technology Institute 2014) <http://www.danah.org/papers/2014/DataDiscrimination.pdf> accessed 31 July 2021.

[47]   Declaration of the United Nations Conference on the Human Environment, Stockholm Conference, UN Doc.A/CONF.48/14/Rev.1 (adopted 16 June 1972).

[48]   James R May and Erin Daly, *Global Environmental Constitutionalism* (Cambridge University Press 2015).

[49]   Rebecca M Bratspies, 'Reasoning Up: Environmental Rights as Customary International Law' in John H Knox and Ramin Pejan (eds), *The Human Right*

Essentially, IBM's Green Horizons smart city initiative, which relies on Big Data, cognitive computing and IoT, can assist in the realization of environmental rights by forecasting pollution with great accuracy. This technology allows officials to better monitor ambient air quality, alert citizens to poor environmental conditions, optimize renewable energy generation and take actions to temporarily reduce greenhouse gases.[50] But the rise of smart technologies used for environmentally beneficial applications does not come without drawbacks. For instance, Green Horizons makes use of 'thousands of sensors across physical and man-made environments,'[51] which require batteries or other energy sources.[52] They eventually produce electronic waste that often winds up in developing countries.[53] Using the two-step framework, the deployment of smart sensors to monitor and predict local pollution levels might help safeguard the environmental rights of individual city dwellers (micro level) while reducing the emissions of the entire country (meso level) and yet producing down-stream harms to people employed in the metals recovery industry abroad (macro level). The benefits conferred upon those living in the city might be direct and medium impact and for those elsewhere in the country the impacts might be indirect and minor, whereas those residing in the Global South who make a living by combing through discarded electronics for valuable raw materials might endure indirect but high negative impacts (violating their right to health).

As mentioned earlier, fourth-generation rights represent the latest entrant into the IHRL lineage and as such they are not yet pervasive across the world. But despite their nascent status, given that they explicitly relate to emerging technologies it stands to reason that their impacts should at least be tentatively explored here. One example of a fourth-generation

---

to a Healthy Environment (Cambridge University Press 2018) <https://www.cambridge.org/core/books/human-right-to-a-healthy-environment/reasoning-up/52A3CFD53D62ECBCEF7D4EE5B80207C0> (accessed 27 July 2021).

[50] Peter Dauvergne, *AI in the Wild: Sustainability in the Age of Artificial Intelligence* (MIT Press 2020).

[51] IBM, 'Green Horizons: Harnesses Power of Cognitive Computing & IoT to Fight Climate Change' (*IBM Research*) <https://www.research.ibm.com/green-horizons/www.research.ibm.com/green-horizons> accessed 31 July 2021.

[52] SC Mukhopadhyay and NK Suryadevara, 'Internet of Things: Challenges and Opportunities' in Subhas Chandra Mukhopadhyay (ed.), *Internet of Things: Challenges and Opportunities* (Springer 2014) 13 <https://doi.org/10.1007/978-3-319-04223-7_1> accessed 31 July 2021.

[53] Michelle Heacock and others, 'E-Waste and Harm to Vulnerable Populations: A Growing Global Problem' (2016) 124 Environmental Health Perspectives.

right is the 'right to social media', which involves freedoms of association, expression and information on online platforms owned by private companies.[54]

This indicative, albeit cursory, survey of the ways in which AI interacts with human rights suggests three main takeaways. First, the framework shows that human rights impacts may not be uniformly positive or negative across different scales. Any analysis of emerging technologies and human rights should, at the very least, examine potential direct and indirect impacts at varying levels of abstraction, from the end-user or data subject to other countries. Second, the use of AI often holds implications for several human rights concurrently. This means that the decision to adopt a new technology will likely involve significant trade-offs among and within the generations of human rights that must be considered and articulated to all potentially affected parties. Finally, the way AI is deployed may lead to both novel challenges for existing human rights and new fourth-generation entitlements. Policymakers, scholars and the public alike will need to contribute to discussions surrounding changes or additions to IHRL and collaboratively decide how they can best be managed in the presence of diverse contexts, cultures and experiences.

RIGHTS FOR AI

Ensuring the integrity of human rights protections in the face of new technological challenges is only one side of the coin. The other side concerns uncertainty regarding the moral and legal status of novel technologies such as AI. In fact, the question of rights or moral consideration for AI is the site of a robust and rather polarizing conflict, one that has been documented in a 2021 literature review conducted by Jamie Harris and Jacy Reese Anthis.[55] In their analysis, the authors identify just under 300 publications on the subject and classify each one on a five-point scale extending from 'argues forcefully against' the idea of AI moral status to argues forcefully for AI being a moral subject.[56] As their research demonstrates, the debate is polarizing, with the one side opposing what the other promotes. One side, for instance, argues that rights for robots

---

[54]   Jones (n 21).
[55]   Jamie Harris and Jacy Reese Anthis, 'The Moral Consideration of Artificial Entities: A Literature Review' (2021) 27 Science and Engineering Ethics.
[56]   ibid.

opens the opportunity for thinking about the limitations of existing moral and legal systems. Thereby, this side follows and contributes to similar efforts supporting animal rights and the rights of nature. In contrast, the other side argues that focusing attention on what are human-designed and -manufactured artifacts distracts us from the more important and pressing moral, legal and social matters that confront us, thereby risking further harm to already vulnerable populations. One side suggests that, as robots and AI get increasingly capable, sentient and maybe even conscious, we will need to consider their interests and well-being in a manner that is no different from the way we perceive other persons, like human beings or even non-human animals. The other side argues that, because robots with consciousness or sentience would need the protections of rights, it would be prudent to avoid ever making things that we would feel obligated to safeguard. One side proposes that resolving questions regarding the rights of robots and the legal standing of AI will help us resolve problems of liability and responsibility in a world where artifacts make (or at least seem to make) independent decisions. The other side asserts that doing so will only exacerbate existing problems with responsibility gaps, shell companies and liability shields.

Despite their differences, one thing both sides in the debate already agree on is that rights are valuable and important. Both sides argue for the protection of rights and respect the concept. The problem—and often the point of conflict—derives from misunderstandings about attribution, specifically who or what has a claim to rights. An all-too-common error—one that has been perpetrated by both sides—results from the mistaken assumption that 'rights' must mean and can only mean *human* rights as formulated in IHRL. Evidence of this can be seen all over the popular press with eye-catching headlines such as, 'Do humanlike machines deserve human rights?', 'When will robots deserve human rights?', 'Do robots deserve human rights?' and 'Should sentient robots have the same rights as humans?'[57] It is also operative in the scientific and academic literature on

---

[57]   Daniel Roh, 'Do Humanlike Machines Deserve Human Rights?' *Wired* (2009) <https://www.wired.com/2009/01/st-essay-16> accessed 27 July 2021; Georg Dvorsky, 'When Will Robots Deserve Human Rights?' *Gizmodo* (2 June 2017) <https://gizmodo.com/when-will-robots-deserve-human-rights-1794599063> accessed 27 July 2021; Lauren Sigfusson, 'Do Robots Deserve Human Rights?' *Discover* (5 December 2017) <https://www.discov ermagazine.com/technology/do-robots-deserve-human-rights> accessed 27 July 2021; Hugh McLachlan, 'Ethics of AI: Should Sentient Robots Have the Same Rights as Humans?' *Independent* (26 June 2019) <https://www.independ ent.co.uk/news/science/ai-robots-human-rights-tech-science-ethics-a8965441. html> accessed 27 July 2021.

the subject,[58] with journal articles and book chapters bearing titles such as, 'Granting Automata Human Rights', 'We Hold These Truths to Be Self-Evident, That All Robots Are Created Equal', 'The Constitutional Rights of Advanced Robots (and of Human Beings)' and 'Can Robots Have Dignity?'[59] Complicating the picture is the fact that, even in cases where the word 'rights' appears in a seemingly generic and unspecified sense, the way it is operationalized often denotes 'human' rights.

Conflating rights with human rights is something that is both understandable and expedient. It is understandable to the extent that so much of the interest in and attention circulating around the subject of rights typically is presented and discussed in terms of human rights and human rights abuses, which are all too prevalent in our daily dose of world news. Even though experts in the field have been careful to distinguish and explain that human rights are 'a special, narrow category of rights',[60] there is a tendency to immediately assume that any talk of rights must mean or at least involve the interests and protections stipulated in IHRL. It is expedient because proceeding from this assumption has turned out to be an effective way to win arguments, capture attention and sell content. Pitching the contest in terms of 'human rights' helps generate a kind of self-righteous indignation and moral outrage, with different configurations of this 'outrage' serving to advance the interests and objectives of both sides in the debate.

For many on the 'argues forcefully for' side of the dispute, this can be (and has been) mobilized as a kind of clarion call that is implicitly justified by nominal associations with previous liberation efforts focused on the human experience. As Peter Asaro has characterized it, 'robots might simply demand their rights. Perhaps because morally intelligent robots might achieve some form of moral self-recognition, [they might] question

---

[58]   John-Stewart Gordon and Ausrine Pasvenskiene provide a much-needed critical review of this literature in the essay 'Human Rights for Robots? A Literature Review' (2021) AI & Society <https://doi.org/10.1007/s43681-021-00050-7> accessed 27 July 2021.

[59]   Lantz Fleming Miller, 'Granting Automata Human Rights: Challenge to a Basis of Full-Rights Privilege' (2015) 16 Human Rights Review <https://doi.org/10.1007/s12142-015-0387-x> accessed 27 July 2021; Amanda Wurah, 'We Hold These Truths to be Self-Evident, that All Robots are Created Equal' (2017) 22 Journal of Futures Studies <https://doi.org/10.6531/JFS.2017.22(2).A61> accessed 27 July 2021; R George Wright, 'The Constitutional Rights of Advanced Robots (and of Human Beings)' (2019) 71 Arkansas Law Review 613 <https://scholarworks.uark.edu/alr/vol71/iss3/2> accessed 27 July 2021; Krämer (n 23).

[60]   Andrew Clapham, *Human Rights: A Very Short Introduction* (Oxford University Press 2007) 4.

why they should be treated differently from other moral agents .... This would follow the path of many subjugated groups of humans who fought to establish respect for their rights against powerful sociopolitical groups who have suppressed, argued and fought against granting them equal rights.'[61]

This is undeniably persuasive and even dramatic. Connecting the dots between the history of previous liberation movements and proposals for considering something similar for other kinds of entities like robots or AI sounds appealing if not intuitively right. 'Human history', as Sohail Inayatullah and Phil McNally point out in what is one of the earliest publications on the subject, 'is the history of exclusion and power. Humans have defined numerous groups as less than human: slaves, woman, the "other races," children and foreigners. These are the wretched who have been defined as stateless, personless, as suspect, as rightless. This is the present realm of robotic rights.'[62] Amedeo Santosuosso not only follows this line of reasoning but makes a direct connection to IHRL: 'Assuming that even an artificial entity may have a certain degree of consciousness would mean that, despite its artificiality, such entity shares with humans something that, according to the legal tradition intertwined into the Universal Declaration of Human Rights, is considered an exclusively human quality. That is a matter of human rights or, better, of extended human rights to machines.'[63]

The problem with this formulation is that it can be and has been criticized for fostering and facilitating what are questionable associations between previously 'subjugated' groups of humans who have endured centuries of oppression at the hands of those in power, and robots or AI that are often developed by and serve the interests of those same powerful sociopolitical groups doing the oppressing. The associations might be rhetorically expedient, tapping into and making connections to the history of previous liberations efforts (e.g., social movements that are celebrated as important progressive innovations), but they also risk being insensitive

---

[61]   Peter Asaro, 'What Should We Want from a Robot Ethic?' (2006) 6(12) International Review of Information Ethics <http://www.i-r-i-e.net/inhalt/006/006_full.pdf> accessed 27 July 2021.
[62]   Sohail Inayatullah and Phil McNally, 'The Rights of Robots: Technology, Culture and Law in the 21st Century' (1988) 20 Futures.
[63]   Amedeo Santosuosso, 'The Human Rights of Nonhuman Artificial Entities: An Oxymoron?' (2016) 19 Jahrbuch für Wissenschaft und Ethik <https://doi.org/10.1515/jwiet-2015-0114> accessed 27 July 2021. Though not directly mentioned by Santosuosso, this formulation also has potential connections to various modern and postmodern forms of pantheism, including the work of Baruch Spinoza and recent innovations in New Materialism.

and tone deaf to the very real social conditions and material circumstances that have contributed to actual oppression and human suffering. Critics on the 'argue forcefully against' side of the debate have been quick and entirely correct to focus on this issue and point it out, calling the entire escapade of robot rights a 'first-world problem' that might be fun to contemplate as a kind of mental gymnastics but is actually something 'detestable to consider as a pressing ethical issue in light of real threats and harms imposed on society's most vulnerable.'[64]

For those on this side, the moral outrage proceeds and is derived from this very problem. If the term 'rights' is immediately and unqualifiedly assumed to be co-extensive with 'human' rights and the stipulations provided in IHRL, then any proposal or inquiry regarding rights for artifacts can be summarily dismissed and disarmed as being woefully insensitive to the plight of real human individuals and communities. Contemplating the very notion of rights for AI or robots is criticized for being at best a distracting exercise for ivory tower navel gazers and at worst a degrading insult to those human individuals and communities who unfortunately suffer the indignity of oppression, subjugation, exploitation and human rights abuses.

Consider, for example, a famous (or perhaps notorious) event involving the Hanson Robotics humanoid robot Sophia. In October 2017, Sophia was bestowed with 'honorary citizenship' by the Kingdom of Saudi Arabia during the Future Investment Initiative conference that was held in Riyadh.[65] Many experts in the field of AI and robotics, like Joanna Bryson and Yann LeCun, who was at that time director of Facebook AI Research, immediately criticized the spectacle as 'bullshit' and dismissed the entire affair as little more than a PR stunt.[66] Others, such as Robert David Hart, found it demoralizing and degrading: 'In a country where the laws allowing women to drive were only passed last year and where a multitude of oppressive rules are still actively enforced (such as women still requiring a male guardian to make financial and legal decisions), it's simply insulting.

---

[64]   Abeba Birhane and Jelle van Dijk, 'A Misdirected Application of AI Ethics' (*Noema*, 18 June 2020) <https://www.noemamag.com/a-misdirected-application-of-ai-ethics/> accessed 27 July 2021.

[65]   In the case of Sophia, the entire debate is caused by similar confusion/conflation—the assumption that 'honorary citizenship' must be (and can only be) the same as 'citizenship'. But this is not the case. Sophia is not a legal citizen of the Kingdom of Saudi Arabia; the robot does not hold a Saudi passport and is not required to procure entry visas for traveling across national borders.

[66]   Daniel Estrada, 'Sophia and Her Critics' (*Medium*, 17 June 2018) <https://medium.com/@eripsa/sophia-and-her-critics-5bd22d859b9c> accessed 27 July 2021.

Sophia seems to have more rights than half of the humans living in Saudi Arabia.'[67] Statements such as 'Saudi Arabia's robot citizen is eroding human rights'[68] (which was the title of Hart's story) are designed to trigger moral outrage and pack an undeniably powerful rhetorical punch. Formulated in this fashion, anyone who truly values and supports human rights cannot help but find the very idea of AI or robot rights detestable, demoralizing and even dangerous.

However, all of this—the entire conflict and dispute—proceeds from an initial error or miscalculation. In both cases, the moral outrage and righteous indignation are the result of an often-unacknowledged category mistake. The question concerning rights is immediately assumed to entail or involve 'human' rights (so much so that the word 'human' is often not even present but inferred from the mere use of the term 'rights'), not recognizing that the set of possible rights (as broken down and formulated in terms of specific Hohfeldian incidents) belonging to one category of entity, such as an animal or an artifact, is not necessarily equivalent to nor the same as that enjoyed by another category of entity, like a human being. 'Rights' does not automatically mean 'human' rights. A good illustration of how and why this difference makes a difference can be found with actual efforts involving the rights of non-human animals.

Since 2018, the organization Nonhuman Rights Project has been working to secure a writ of *habeas corpus* for an elephant named Happy. Granting this one narrowly tailored protection to this specific animal does not mean nor does it necessitate that the full set of human rights be extended to this one particular elephant, all elephants or all animals. Following this precedent, it is clear that, whatever rights come to be recognized for or attributed to an AI, robot or other non-human artifact, they will not be nor must they entail the full set of existing human rights as specified in IHRL.

Developments in the rapidly expanding rights of nature movement similarly demonstrate that the kinds of rights to which non-human natural entities might be entitled would not correspond directly to the generations of international human rights covered earlier. With philosophical roots in Indigenous cultures and ancient religions that have long recognized the fundamental interconnectedness among humans and the environment,[69]

---

[67] Robert David Hart, 'Saudi Arabia's Robot Citizen Is Eroding Human Rights' (*Quartz*, 14 February 2017) <https://qz.com/1205017/saudi-arabias-robot-citizen-is-eroding-human-rights/> accessed 27 July 2021.

[68] ibid.

[69] David R Boyd, *The Rights of Nature: A Legal Revolution that could Save the World* (ECW 2017) xxix.

the rights of nature have found concrete instantiation in constitutions, court decisions and citizen referenda over the past fifteen years. In terms of specific rights that have been recognized, the decision in the Ecuadorian case of *Wheeler c. Director de la Procuraduria General Del Estado de Loja*,[70] cited authoritatively the right of ecosystems 'to exist and follow their own vital processes.'[71] This specific phrasing does not appear anywhere in the International Bill of Human Rights.

In terms of rights for AI, one could, for example, advance the proposal—introduced by the French legal team of Alain and Jérémy Bensoussan—that domestic social robots have a right to privacy (or what they call 'digital dignity') for the purposes of protecting the user's personal private information.[72] But considering this one rights claim does not and should not mean that we also need to give such robots the right to vote. Additionally, recognizing this one claim or immunity for this one type of social-interactive technology not only does not take anything away from human beings, but it also might serve to protect the rights and interests of the human users of the device.

The problem with both sides in the existing arguments is that they often fail to appreciate how robot rights (whatever bundle of claims, powers, privileges or immunities that might entail) would be significantly different from human rights. Their arguments and conclusions, which typically have the effect of generating forms of moral outrage that are dramatic and rhetorically expedient, proceed from an erroneous starting point, namely that any and all rights are and can only be equivalent to 'the entire suite of legal rights expressed in major international human rights documents.'[73] But whatever rights might be attributable to a non-human artifact, like forms of AI, they can be and will most certainly be different from the set of incidents we currently recognize under existing IHRL. Simply put, AI is different from humans. Only human beings have a claim to what is formulated and defined as 'human rights'. AI and robots, by contrast (if they can or even should have some access to rights in existing legal systems), would have 'robot rights'. There is a difference, and that difference makes a difference.

---

[70]   *Wheeler c. Director de la Procuraduria General Del Estado de Loja*, Juicio No. 111212011-0010 (2011) <https://elaw.org/system/files/ec.wheeler.loja_.pdf> accessed 27 July 2021.

[71]   ibid 3–4.

[72]   Alain Bensoussan and Jérémy Bensoussan, *Droit des Robots* (Éditions Larcier 2015).

[73]   Joshua C. Gellers, *Rights for Robots: Artificial Intelligence, Animal and Environmental Law* (Routledge 2020) 16–17.

CONCLUSION: GOVERNANCE AND RIGHTS FOR ALL?

While the modern corpus of IHRL has been around for over half a century, recent social, legal and technological developments suggest it might be time to critically reimagine the enterprise of rights. Not only have emerging technologies, Big Data applications, and increasingly unclear boundaries between humans and artifacts spurred a vibrant discourse around fourth-generation rights, but non-human rights movements have provided philosophical and legal grounds for extending apex protections to even non-natural, technological entities. Given the explicit emphasis that IHRL places on humans, perhaps it is time to think of rights at the international level as consisting of two registers—established and unfolding entitlements granted to humans and as-yet-unresolved sets of guarantees reserved for certain types of non-humans. This expansive reframing entails articulating two sides (e.g., human and non-human) of the same coin (e.g., rights). We need not erase the previous generations of human rights, focused as they are exclusively on humans, however. Rather, we might incorporate the ongoing expansion of rights-holders into a complementary dimension that captures this diverse group of morally and legally significant entities.

How might we translate the foregoing insights about IHRL and rights for AI into practical recommendations designed to address the unique governance challenges of the digital age? On the human side of the rights coin, governments and businesses should apply the two-step framework articulated above when considering whether to adopt emerging technologies at all stages of policy or product lifecycles. The objective here is to identify the scope and magnitude of potential threats to the human rights of various stakeholders prior to implementation so that they might be proactively mitigated. In addition, states should consider proposing a new international human rights treaty specifically focused on protecting human dignity in the context of AI and/or requesting additional guidance on interpreting existing IHRL with respect to AI from the various UN human rights treaty bodies.[74] One model worth examining toward this end is the UN Framework Convention on Climate Change. That is, states could agree to a common framework that provides the structure

---

[74] See, e.g., UN Committee on Rights of the Child (CRC), 'General Comment No. 25 (2021) on Children's Rights in Relation to the Digital Environment' <https://tbinternet.ohchr.org/_layouts/15/treatybodyexternal/Download.aspx?symbolno=CRC/C/GC/25&Lang=en> accessed 11 August 2021.

for adopting future protocols that deal with specific issues such as data privacy, biotechnology, VR or AR crimes, and so on. This approach would avoid the hazard inherent in trying to legalize solutions in a single omnibus treaty, which might require constant revision considering the pace of technological advancement. Finally, regional institutions and national governments should enact, where appropriate, policies on AI that harmonize IHRL with geographically and culturally particularized priorities.

On the non-human side of the rights coin, jurisdictionally specific legal innovations may need to be advanced to resolve conflicts that emerge as new technological entities become integrated into human societies. Importantly, these alterations to legal landscapes should strive to be logically and doctrinally compatible with the treatment of other non-humans, including animals and nature. Examples of legal innovations worthy of consideration include classifying certain AI as 'non-personal subjects of law',[75] or using a contingent, context-dependent and relational framework for determining an entity's eligibility for legal personhood and thus legal rights.[76] The point here is that the extension of legal status, personhood or rights to AI, robots or other technologies should be employed on pragmatic and culturally appropriate grounds when legal disputes arise. At the same time, many of the often-unquestioned assumptions underlying international 'human' rights law (e.g., dignity, individualism, Eurocentrism) might also require a more fundamental recalibration as humanity increasingly interfaces with natural and artefactual non-humans in situations that present serious moral or ethical dilemmas not currently reconcilable under the current IHRL paradigm.

This chapter was not intended to provide an exhaustive or dispositive list of strategies for overcoming the many existential, legal and ontological disruptions caused by emerging technologies. Our more modest goals have been to propose a two-step framework and two-dimension reformulation of rights that decision makers might find useful when seeking to proactively identify or resolve novel and technology-driven issues emerging in the 21st century. In doing so, our objective has been to provide guidance for getting rights 'right' so that we—individually, collectively and globally—may respond to the challenges of governance in an era of rapid technological change and increasingly uncertain biophysical boundaries.

---

[75]   Tomasz Pietrzykowski, *Personhood Beyond Humanism: Animals, Chimeras, Autonomous Agents and the Law* (Springer 2018) 97.

[76]   Gellers (n 74) 151–155.

REFERENCES

Aizenberg E and van den Hoven J, 'Designing for Human Rights in AI' (2020) 7 Big Data & Society.

Alonso C, Kothari S and Rehman S, 'How Artificial Intelligence Could Widen the Gap Between Rich and Poor Nations' (*IMF Blog*, 2 December 2020) <https://blogs.imf.org/2020/12/02/how-artificial-intelligence-could-widen-the-gap-between-rich-and-poor-nations/> accessed 27 July 2021.

Asaro P, 'What Should We Want from a Robot Ethic?' (2006) 6(12) International Review of Information Ethics <http://www.i-r-i-e.net/inhalt/006/006_full.pdf> accessed 27 July 2021.

Augustine S, *The Confessions of St. Augustine*, trans. EB Pusey (PF Collier & Son 1909).

Aust HP, 'Undermining Human Agency and Democratic Infrastructures? The Algorithmic Challenge to The Universal Declaration of Human Rights' (2018) 112 American Journal of International Law.

Bates J, 'Human Dignity – An Empty Phrase in Search of Meaning?' (2005) 10 Judicial Review.

Bensoussan A and Bensoussan J, *Droit des Robots* (Éditions Larcier 2015).

Birhane A and van Dijk J, 'A Misdirected Application of AI Ethics' (*Noema*, 18 June 2020) <https://www.noemamag.com/a-misdirected-application-of-ai-ethics/> accessed 27 July 2021.

Boyd D, Levy K and Marwick A, 'The Networked Nature of Algorithmic Discrimination' (Open Technology Institute 2014) <http://www.danah.org/papers/2014/DataDiscrimination.pdf> accessed 31 July 2021.

Boyd DR, *The Rights of Nature: A Legal Revolution That Could Save the World* (ECW 2017).

Bratspies RM, 'Reasoning Up: Environmental Rights as Customary International Law' in JH Knox and R Pejan (eds), *The Human Right to a Healthy Environment* (Cambridge University Press 2018) <https://www.cambridge.org/core/books/human-right-to-a-healthy-environment/reasoning-up/52A3CFD53D62ECBCEF7D4EE5B80207C0> (accessed 27 July 2021).

Bughin J and others, 'Modeling the Global Economic Impact of AI' (*McKinsey Global Institute*, 4 September 2018) <https://www.mckinsey.com/featured-insights/artificial-intelligence/notes-from-the-AI-frontier-modeling-the-impact-of-ai-on-the-world-economy> accessed 27 July 2021.

Camp KL, 'Constitutional Provisions for Individual Human Rights (1977–1996): Are They More than Mere "Window Dressing?"' (2002) 55 Political Research Quarterly.

Cassel D, 'Does International Human Rights Law Make a Difference?' (2001) 2 Chicago Journal of International Law.

Clapham A, *Human Rights: A Very Short Introduction* (Oxford University Press 2007).

Daly E, *Dignity Rights: Courts, Constitutions, and the Worth of the Human Person* (University of Pennsylvania Press 2012).

Dauvergne P, *AI in the Wild: Sustainability in the Age of Artificial Intelligence* (MIT Press 2020).

Declaration of the United Nations Conference on the Human Environment, Stockholm Conference, UN Doc.A/CONF.48/14/Rev.1 (adopted 16 June 1972).

Donahoe E and Metzger MM, 'Artificial Intelligence and Human Rights' (2019) 30 Journal of Democracy.

Dvorsky G, 'When Will Robots Deserve Human Rights?' (*Gizmodo*, 2 June 2017) <https://gizmodo.com/when-will-robots-deserve-human-rights-1794599063> accessed 27 July 2021.

Estrada D, 'Sophia and Her Critics' (*Medium*, 17 June 2018) <https://medium.com/@eripsa/sophia-and-her-critics-5bd22d859b9c> accessed 27 July 2021.

Floridi L, 'On Human Dignity as a Foundation for the Right to Privacy' (2016) 29 Philosophy & Technology.

Gerards J, 'The Fundamental Rights Challenges of Algorithms' (2019) 37 Netherlands Quarterly of Human Rights.

Gellers JC, 'The Great Indoors: Linking Human Rights and the Built Environment' (2016) 7 Journal of Human Rights and the Environment.

Gellers JC, *Rights for Robots: Artificial Intelligence, Animal and Environmental Law* (Routledge 2020).

Gordon J-S and Pasvenskiene A, 'Human Rights for Robots? A Literature Review' (2021) 1 AI and Ethics <https://doi.org/10.1007/s43681-021-00050-7> accessed 27 July 2021.

Harris J and Anthis JR, 'The Moral Consideration of Artificial Entities: A Literature Review' (2021) 27 Science and Engineering Ethics.

Hart RD, 'Saudi Arabia's Robot Citizen is Eroding Human Rights' (*Quartz*, 14 February 2017) <https://qz.com/1205017/saudi-arabias-robot-citizen-is-eroding-human-rights/> accessed 27 July 2021.

Heacock M and others, 'E-Waste and Harm to Vulnerable Populations: A Growing Global Problem' (2016) 124 Environmental Health Perspectives.

Helbing D and others, 'Will Democracy Survive Big Data and Artificial Intelligence?' [2017] *Scientific American* <https://www.scientificamerican.com/article/will-democracy-survive-big-data-and-artificial-intelligence/> accessed 22 July 2022.

HLEGAI, 'High-Level Expert Group on Artificial Intelligence, EU – Ethics Guidelines for Trustworthy AI' (2019) <https://ec.europa.eu/digital-single-market/en/news/ethics-guidelines-trustworthy-ai> accessed 23 July 2021.

Hohfeld W, *Fundamental Legal Conceptions as Applied in Judicial Reasoning* (Yale University Press 1920).

IBM, 'Green Horizons: Harnesses Power of Cognitive Computing & IoT to Fight Climate Change' (*IBM Research*) <https://www.research.ibm.com/green-horizons/www.research.ibm.com/green-horizons> accessed 31 July 2021.

Inayatullah S and McNally P, 'The Rights of Robots: Technology, Culture and Law in the 21st Century' (1988) 20 Futures.

International Covenant on Civil and Political Rights (adopted 16 December 1966, entered into force 23 March 1976) 999 UNTS 171 (ICCPR).

International Covenant on Economic, Social and Cultural Rights (adopted 19 December 1966, entered into force 3 January 1976) 993 UNTS 3 (ICESCR).

Ivanii O, Kuchuk A and Orlova O, 'Biotechnology as Factor for the Fourth Generation of Human Rights Formation' (2020) 9 Journal of History Culture and Art Research.

Jones BC, 'Is Social Media a Human Right? Exploring the Scope of Internet Rights' (*International Journal of Constitutional Law Blog*, 5 December 2014) <http://www.iconnectblog.com/2014/11/is-social-media-a-> accessed 24 July 2021.

Krämer C, 'Can Robots Have Dignity?' in Benedikt Paul Göcke and Astrid Rosenthal-von der Pütten (eds), *Artificial Intelligence: Reflections in Philosophy, Theology, and the Social Sciences* (Brill 2020).

Latonero M, 'Governing Artificial Intelligence: Upholding Human Rights and Dignity' (Data & Society 2018) <https://datasociety.net/wp-content/uploads/2018/10/DataSociety_Governing_Artificial_Intelligence_Upholding_Human_Rights.pdf> accessed 27 July 2021.

Mantelero A, 'AI and Big Data: A Blueprint for a Human Rights, Social and Ethical Impact Assessment' (2018) 34 Computer Law & Security Review.

Mantelero A, *Beyond Data: Human Rights, Ethical and Social Impact Assessment in AI* (Springer 2022).

Marx J and Tiefensee C, 'Of Animals, Robots and Men' (2015) 40 Historical Social Research (Köln) <https://doi.org/10.12759/hsr.40.2015.4.70-91> accessed 27 July 2021.

May JR and Daly E, *Global Environmental Constitutionalism* (Cambridge University Press 2015).

McGregor L, Murray D and Ng V, 'International Human Rights Law as a Framework for Algorithmic Accountability' (2019) 68 International & Comparative Law Quarterly.

McLachlan H, 'Ethics of AI: Should Sentient Robots Have the Same Rights as Humans?' *Independent* (26 June 2019) <https://www.independent.co.uk/news/science/ai-robots-human-rights-tech-science-ethics-a8965441.html> accessed 27 July 2021.

Miller LF, 'Granting Automata Human Rights: Challenge to a Basis of Full-Rights Privilege' (2015) 16 Human Rights Review <https://doi.org/10.1007/s12142-015-0387-x> accessed 27 July 2021.

Moses LB, 'Agents of Change: How the Law "Copes" with Technological Change' (2011) 20 Griffith Law Review, 763.

Mukhopadhyay SC and Suryadevara NK, 'Internet of Things: Challenges and Opportunities' in SC Mukhopadhyay (ed.), *Internet of Things: Challenges and Opportunities* (Springer 2014) <https://doi.org/10.1007/978-3-319-04223-7_1> accessed 31 July 2021.

Mutua M, 'Savages, Victims, and Saviors: The Metaphor of Human Rights' (2001) 42 Harvard International Law Journal.

Nemitz P, 'Constitutional Democracy and Technology in the Age of Artificial Intelligence' (2018) 376 Philosophical Transactions of the Royal Society A: Mathematical, Physical and Engineering Sciences.

Pielemeier J, 'The Advantages and Limitations of Applying the International Human Rights Framework to Artificial Intelligence' (*Data & Society: Points*, 2019) <https://points.datasociety.net/the-advantages-and-limitations-of-applying-the-international-human-rights-framework-to-artificial-291a2dfe1d8a> accessed 27 July 2021.

Pietrzykowski T, *Personhood beyond Humanism: Animals, Chimeras, Autonomous Agents and the Law* (Springer 2018).

Pizzi M, Romanoff M and Engelhardt T, 'AI for Humanitarian Action: Human Rights and Ethics' (2020) 102 International Review of the Red Cross.

Proposal for a Regulation of the European Parliament and the Council: Laying Down Harmonised Rules on Artificial Intelligence (Artificial Intelligence Act) and Amending Certain Union Legislative Acts 2021.

Raso F and others, 'Artificial Intelligence and Human Rights: Opportunities and Risks' (Berkman Klein Center for Internet & Society, Harvard University 2018) <https://cyber.harvard.edu/publication/2018/artificial-intelligence-human-rights> accessed 27 July 2021.

Risse M, 'Human Rights and Artificial Intelligence: An Urgently Needed Agenda' (2019) 41(1) Human Rights Quarterly.

Risse M, 'The Fourth Generation of Human Rights: Epistemic Rights in Digital Lifeworlds' [2021] 5 Moral Philosophy and Politics <https://www.degruyter.com/document/doi/10.1515/mopp-2020-0039/html> accessed 24 July 2021.

Robinson WK and Smith JT, 'Emerging Technologies Challenging Current Legal Paradigms' (2018) 19 Minnesota Journal of Law, Science and Technology.

Roh D, 'Do Humanlike Machines Deserve Human Rights?' (*Wired*, 2009) <https://www.wired.com/2009/01/st-essay-16> accessed 27 July 2021.

Sætra HS, 'AI in Context and the Sustainable Development Goals: Factoring in the Unsustainability of the Sociotechnical System' (2021) 13 Sustainability.

Sanders D, 'Collective Rights' (1991) 13 Human Rights Quarterly.

Santosuosso A, 'The Human Rights of Nonhuman Artificial Entities: An Oxymoron?' (2016) 19 Jahrbuch für Wissenschaft und Ethik 204 <https://doi.org/10.1515/jwiet-2015-0114> accessed 27 July 2021.

Schneider V, 'Locked out by Big Data: How Big Data Algorithms and Machine Learning May Undermine Housing Justice' (2020) 52 Columbia Human Rights Law Review.

Shelton DL, *Advanced Introduction to International Human Rights Law* (Edward Elgar Publishing 2014).

Sigfusson L, 'Do Robots Deserve Human Rights?' (*Discover*, 5 December 2017) <https://www.discovermagazine.com/technology/do-robots-deserve-human-rights> accessed 27 July 2021.

Smuha NA, 'Beyond a Human Rights-Based Approach to AI Governance: Promise, Pitfalls, Plea' [2020] Philosophy & Technology.

Turner J, *Robot Rules: Regulating Artificial Intelligence* (Palgrave Macmillan 2019).

UN Committee on Economic, Social and Cultural Rights (CESCR), 'General Comment No. 4: The Right to Adequate Housing (Art. 11(1) of the Covenant)' <https://www.refworld.org/pdfid/47a7079a1.pdf> accessed 31 July 2021.

UN Committee on Rights of the Child (CRC), 'General Comment No. 25 (2021) on Children's Rights in Relation to the Digital Environment' <https://tbinternet.ohchr.org/_layouts/15/treatybodyexternal/Download.aspx?symbolno=CRC/C/GC/25&Lang=cn> accessed 11 August 2021.

Universal Declaration of Human Rights (adopted 10 December 1948) UNGA Res 217 A(III) (UDHR) pmbl.

Valdés E, 'Bioderecho, Daño Genético y Derechos Humanos de Cuarta Generación' (2015) 144 Boletín Mexicano de Derecho Comparado.

Vašák K, 'A 30-Year Struggle: The Sustained Efforts to Give Force of Law to the Universal Declaration of Human Rights' [1977] The UNESCO Courier.

Wachter S, 'Affinity Profiling and Discrimination by Association in Online Behavioral Advertising' (2020) 35 Berkeley Technology Law Journal.

Wellman C, 'Solidarity, the Individual and Human Rights' (2000) 22 Human Rights Quarterly.

Wheeler c. Director de la Procuraduria General del Estado de Loja, Juicio No. 111212011-0010 (2011) <https://elaw.org/system/files/ec.wheeler.loja_.pdf> accessed 27 July 2021.

Wright RG, 'The Constitutional Rights of Advanced Robots (and of Human Beings)' (2019) 71 Arkansas Law Review <https://scholarworks.uark.edu/alr/vol71/iss3/2> accessed 27 July 2021.

Wurah A, 'We Hold These Truths to be Self-Evident, that All Robots are Created Equal' (2017) 22 Journal of Futures Studies <https://doi.org/ 10.6531/ JFS.2017.22(2).A61> accessed 27 July 2021.

Yeung K, Howes A and Pogrebna G, 'AI Governance by Human Rights-Centered Design, Deliberation, and Oversights: An End to Ethics Washing' in Markus D Dubber, Frank Pasquale and Sunit Das (eds), *The Oxford Handbook of Ethics of AI* (Oxford University Press 2020).

15. Challenges posed by autonomous systems to liability regimes: finding a balance

Nynke E. Vellinga

INTRODUCTION

Autonomous systems are becoming more prevalent in our everyday lives, from health care to the mobility sector. These systems are able to gather information, analyse it and perform one or multiple actions to achieve a goal. In doing so, human error is eliminated from the specific action performed. Autonomous systems are thereby expected to enhance safety and efficiency.

However, autonomous systems will not be infallible: poor design can make them incapable of living up to their tasks, sensors can get damaged, a software glitch can lead to the incorrect analysis of data provided and cybersecurity vulnerabilities can be exploited to cause harm. This can lead to significant damage of persons and property. Therefore, questions of liability arise.

In recent years there have already been instances where autonomous systems caused such damage: in October 2018 and March 2019 the so-called Maneuvering Characteristics Augmentation System or MCAS of the Boeing 737 MAX 8 airplane caused two airplanes to crash, resulting in the death of 350 people. The MCAS was incapable of addressing design flaws of the airplane, which eventually lead to a nosedive based on input from a malfunctioning sensor.[1] In another case from March 2018, an Uber self-driving vehicle performing test drives on public roads in Arizona (US) caused a fatal accident with a pedestrian, as the system of the vehicle was unable to classify the pedestrian correctly.[2] Recently, the US

---

[1] Dominic Gates, 'Q&A: What led to Boeing's 737 MAX crisis' (*The Seattle Times*, 22 November 2020) <https://www.seattletimes.com/business/boeing-aerospace/what-led-to-boeings-737-max-crisis-a-qa/> accessed 14 July 2021.

[2] National Transport Safety Board, 'Collision Between Vehicle Controlled by Developmental Automated Driving System and Pedestrian Tempe, Arizona, March 18, 2018' (Accident Report NTSB/HAR-19/03 PB2019-101402, NTSB 2019).

National Transport Highway Safety Administration has started investigation into accidents between vehicles from Tesla with 'Autopilot' engaged and emergency vehicles.[3] This highlights the importance of addressing questions on liability concerning damage caused by autonomous systems.

The development of autonomous systems puts the existing liability regimes under pressure as these autonomous systems have the capability of causing damage without any human interference. Existing liability regimes have traditionally been designed around human conduct leading to damage. Damage can consist of personal injury, financial loss, but, depending on the jurisdiction, also other non-pecuniary loss (e.g., pain, grief). A causal link between the human conduct and the damage will be required for establishing liability. Van Dam describes this causation as 'an elastic feature which can be stretched and shrunk according to the magnitude of the other requirements' such as negligence and damage.[4] There is, therefore, not one single way to establish a causal link between human conduct and damage.

Given the importance of human conduct in existing liability regimes, the question appears as to whether autonomous systems causing damage unrelated to any human conduct should fall within the scope of these existing liability regimes. Therefore, there is a need to identify and address any shortcomings existing liability regimes may have in the light of the development of autonomous systems. The development of autonomous systems could thereby prove to be a driving force for the transformation of current liability regimes. Moreover, liability regimes as well as insurance and compensation funds can influence the acceptance of autonomous systems and can potentially influence the development of innovations.

This chapter focuses on these challenges posed to existing liability regimes. This requires, first, addressing what constitutes an *autonomous system* for the purpose of this chapter. Secondly, the main features of existing liability regimes are outlined, providing a clear picture of two types of liability: strict liability and negligence. In addition, the functions of tort law are discussed. In light of tort law, it is particularly important to address the question of whether an autonomous system has legal personhood and to explore whether the functions of tort law are also fulfilled if a system can be held liable for damage caused. In other words, can an autonomous system as such be liable for 'its own actions'? Moreover, the

---

[3]   National Highway Traffic Safety Administration, 'ODI Resume: Investigation PE21-020' (US Department of Transportation, 13 August 2021) <https://static. nhtsa.gov/odi/inv/2021/INOA-PE21020-1893.PDF> accessed 1 December 2021.

[4]   Cees van Dam, *European Tort Law*, 2nd edn (Oxford University Press 2013) 1101.

liability of other involved parties will be analysed. These parties influence the functioning of the autonomous system by developing the system (the manufacturer), by using the system (the user) or by having control over the risks involved in the use of these systems (the owner). Such parties can all play an important role in the compensation of damage caused by an autonomous system. This will bring a potential negative effect of liability law, the so-called chilling effect of liability, to the surface. In response to this chilling effect, insurance and compensation funds are discussed as both instruments can play an important role in the indemnification of damage suffered in connection with liability.

This chapter hereby aims to provide clarity on the current legal framework, addressing liability for damage caused by an autonomous system, as well as providing a way forward to ensure a balanced approach in both compensating the injured party for damage caused by an autonomous system and providing incentives to prevent damage in the first place.

DEFINING AUTONOMOUS SYSTEMS

Before discussing who might be liable for damage caused by an autonomous system, it is necessary to discuss what autonomous systems are. They are defined and described in various ways, often in relation to a specific context such as autonomous weapons or autonomous vehicles.[5] For the purpose of this chapter, the following definition by the United States' National Aeronautics and Space Administration (NASA) will be adhered to. NASA has described *autonomy* as 'the ability of a system to achieve goals while operating independently of external control [...]. Autonomy is not the same as artificial intelligence (AI), but may make use of AI methods.'[6]

This requires elements of situational awareness and self-awareness, a decision-making process based on the information gathered and the

---

[5]   For instance: Michael C Horowitz, 'Why Words Matter: the Real World Consequences of Defining Autonomous Weapon Systems' (2016) 30 Temple International & Comparative Law Journal; SAE International, 'Taxonomy and Definitions for Terms Related to Driving Automation Systems for On-Road Motor Vehicles, Standard J3016' (*SAE International*, April 2021) para 7.1.1; Christoph Hubig, 'Benefits and Limits of Autonomous Systems in Public Security' (2020) 5 European Journal for Security Research.

[6]   Terrence W Fong and others, 'Autonomous Systems Taxonomy' (NASA Technical Reports Server 2018) <https://ntrs.nasa.gov/citations/20180003082> accessed 12 July 2021.

subsequent acting to achieve a (pre-defined) goal.[7] An autonomous system, therefore, can make decisions independently and self-sufficiently.[8] It does not require any human input. This does not preclude human monitoring. However, if a system depends on cooperation or communication with outside entities, it is not qualified as autonomous but as cooperative.[9]

A *system* is described by NASA as the combination of hardware, software and other relevant elements necessary to achieve this autonomy.[10] An autonomous system could therefore be a combination of hardware and software that analyses several test results to determine and administer the right dose of treatment to a patient, or a system in an airplane that decides on its position based on the input from sensors to achieve the goal of remaining at the correct altitude, like the previously mentioned MCAS. Autonomous weapons also fit this definition of autonomous systems but will be discussed in another chapter of this handbook. Hence, the focus of this chapter will be autonomous systems used by and for consumers, such as autonomous systems used in health care, autonomous vehicles and robots used to assist in the household.

LIABILITY FOR DAMAGE CAUSED BY AN AUTONOMOUS SYSTEM

Terminology

In this chapter both the terms 'tort' and 'liability' will be used. Tort is a term originating from common law systems. Although it does not have a true equivalent in European continental law systems, it is commonly used in European comparative law to indicate extra-contractual liability excluding agency without authority and unjust enrichment.[11] In the context of this chapter, 'liability' also excludes extra-contractual liability excluding agency without authority and unjust enrichment. In addition, it should be noted that this chapter covers liability and insurance in general terms. The exact elaboration and details of these subjects depend (largely) on national law. In addition, the party suffering damage is referred to as the injured party. Moreover, the party that faces the liability claim is referred to as the defendant.

---

[7]   ibid.
[8]   SAE International (n 5).
[9]   ibid.
[10]   Fong and others (n 6).
[11]   van Dam (n 4) 101–102.

The Functions of Tort Law

Compensation and *prevention* are generally acknowledged as the main functions of tort law.[12] Starting with *compensation*, tort law aims to bring the injured party in the same economic position as before the harm was inflicted.[13] Tort law sets the boundaries as to which harm, under what circumstances, needs to be compensated.[14] Under Dutch liability rules, for instance, damage suffered because of an 'ongelukkige samenloop van omstandigheden' (an unfortunate turn of events or unfortunate coincidence) is not a ground for compensation.[15] Important to note is that the function of compensation is not one of a punitive character; it is merely a restorative function as it compensates for the harm caused. In other words, it aims to restore the situation to the situation before the harm was caused. However, in some jurisdictions tort law does also have a punitive character in the form of punitive damages.[16] For example, punitive damages are an established part of US tort law.[17]

The prospect of having to compensate damage and the inherent costs of the compensation can encourage a defendant to abstain from the harm-inflicting conduct. It might also lead to a more careful consideration of the potential risk of activities. This is the *prevention* function of tort law.[18] Through this function, the desirable behaviour is being stimulated, whereas undesirable behaviour, the harm-inflicting behaviour, is being discouraged.[19]

Tort in General: The Protection of Rights and Interests

The functions of tort law are served by its substantive requirements. Generally, liability consists of several elements: there is an interest that

---

[12]   See for instance Fokko T Oldenhuis, 'GS Onrechtmatige daad: Afdeling 2 Boek 6 BW' (Wolters Kluwer 2021) section A, sub-s 4.3.

[13]   Christian Förster, 'BGB § 823 Schadensersatzpflicht' (*BeckOK BGB Hau/ Poseck*, 58th edn, Beck online 2021) Rn 7–8.

[14]   Gerhard Wagner, 'Vorbemerkung (Vor § 823)' (*Münchener Kommentar zum BGB*, 8th edn, Beck online 2021) Rn 43–44.

[15]   For example: Hoge Raad 19 October 1990, ECLI:NL:HR:1990:AD1456, *NJ* 1992/621 (Tennisbal).

[16]   See also Förster (n 13) Rn 12–14; Wagner (n 14) Rn 49–52.

[17]   See on the functions of punitive damages: Guido Calabresi, 'The Complexity of Torts – The Case of Punitive Damages' in M Stuart Madden (ed.), *Exploring Tort Law* (Cambridge University Press 2005).

[18]   Also referred to as the *deterrence* function of tort law.

[19]   Förster (n 13) Rn 9.

is protected, this interest is harmed and there is a remedy for the harm or damage caused.[20] Tort, therefore, serves an important purpose in protecting the rights and interests of individuals. Various rights and interests can be protected by tort law, such as life and physical integrity, privacy and property rights.[21] If one or more of these rights are harmed and damage is done, the injured party can seek compensation from the party who inflicted the harm.[22] Damage can, for instance, consist of personal injury, damage to property, financial loss. The defendant is not necessarily liable simply because he has caused damage to the other; if the defendant has been careless (fault liability) or if he bears the risk that has materialized (strict liability), he could be held liable for the damage caused.

The defendant can be a human and, depending on the jurisdiction, a legal person such as a company or foundation. Given the definition of autonomous system and the lack of human input, the question arises as to whether it would also be possible for an autonomous system to be assigned legal personhood and to become a defendant in a liability case.

The Autonomous System as Defendant?

The question of whether legal personhood can be assigned to non-human actors has been discussed for many, many years. Solum points to the Temples in Rome and church buildings in the Middle Ages that were the subject of legal rights.[23] The Te Awa Tupua or Whanganui River in New Zealand is the first river to have been assigned legal personhood, as it states in the Te Awa Tupua (Whanganui River Claims Settlement) Act 2017: 'Te Awa Tupua is a legal person and has all the rights, powers, duties, and liabilities of a legal person.'[24] Recently, hippos were deemed to be 'interested persons' in court proceedings by court order of the United States District Court for Southern District of Ohio.[25] For several years

---

[20] Peter Cane, *The Anatomy of Tort Law* (Hart Publishing 1997).

[21] van Dam (n 4) 701.

[22] The focus in this chapter is on the monetary compensation of damage suffered. See for other forms of reparation: van Dam (n 4) 1202–1203.

[23] Lawrence B Solum, 'Legal Personhood for Artificial Intelligences' (1992) 70 North Carolina Review.

[24] See on the legal status of rivers: Cristy Clark and others, 'Can You Hear the Rivers Sing? Legal Personhood, Ontology, and the Nitty-Gritty of Governance' (2018) 45 Ecology Law Quarterly, 787.

[25] Associated Press, 'Pablo Escobar's "Cocaine Hippos" Are People Too, US Court Rules' (*The Guardian*, 25 October 2021) <https://www.theguardian.com/world/2021/oct/25/pablo-escobar-colombian-hippos-granted-rights-interested-persons-us-court> accessed 1 December 2021.

now, the question of whether an autonomous system or robot has legal personhood has also been discussed by scholars and policymakers alike.[26]

Generally, those subject to legal rights and duties are considered to have legal personhood.[27] Natural persons, but also companies and other legal constructs such as foundations can have legal personhood, depending on domestic legislation. These are all legal entities that, as described by Van der Hoven van Genderen, 'have to have the power and legal status to perform economic acts with legal consequences and have to have legal credibility.'[28]

In its resolution on Civil Law Rules on Robotics (2017), the European Parliament recommended the European Commission to consider 'a specific legal status for robots.'[29] In an open letter to the European Commission, robotics experts, ethics and legal experts, together with industry leaders, expressed their concerns on creating legal personhood for robots.[30] This highlights the legal, but also moral and ethical perspectives in the discussion on legal personhood for autonomous systems. It goes beyond the scope of this chapter to discuss all perspectives and arguments. Therefore, only the consequences of legal personhood in the tort law framework will be briefly addressed.

One could argue that autonomous systems too must have power and legal status to perform economic acts with legal consequences. Human-like robot Sophia by Hanson Robotics, for instance, was granted citizenship by the Kingdom of Saudi Arabia, which could indicate some form of legal personhood.[31]

If autonomous systems were to have legal personhood status, they can be held liable for their conduct and would thereby shield the manufacturer

---

[26] Among others: Solum (n 23); Ugo Pagallo, 'Vital, Sophia, and Co.—The Quest for the Legal Personhood of Robots' (2018) 9 Information; John-Stewart Gordon, 'Artificial Moral and Legal Personhood' (2020) 36 AI & Society; Simon Chesterman, 'Artificial Intelligence and the Limits of Legal Personality' (2020) 69 International & Comparative Law Quarterly.

[27] Bryant Smith, 'Legal personality' (1928) 37 Yale Law Journal; Solum (n 23). See also the discussion in this handbook by Gellers and Gunkel (Ch. 14).

[28] Robert van den Hoven van Genderen, 'Do We Need New Legal Personhood in the Age of Robots and AI?' in Marcelo Corrales, Mark Fenwick and Nikolaus Forgó (eds), *Robotics, AI and the Future of Law* (Springer 2018) 21.

[29] Resolution of the European Parliament 2015/2103(INL) of 16 February 2017 with recommendations to the Commission on Civil Law Rules on Robotics [2015] OJ C 252/239 (Resolution on Robotics 2015/2103(INL)), para 59(f).

[30] 'Open Letter to the European Commission on Artificial Intelligence and Robotics' (robotics-openletter.eu) <www.robotics-openletter.eu/> accessed 14 July 2021.

[31] Pagallo (n 26).

or another party from liability.[32] This should encourage, not hinder, innovation. It would avoid lengthy procedures on the question as to which of the stakeholders (manufacturer, software designer, original equipment manufacturer, owner, user, etc.) involved might be liable for the damage caused, as the injured party would directly claim damages from the autonomous system itself. In other words, it offers one entry point for litigation.[33] Questions on whether it was the software that failed, whether the design of the system was flawed, whether the system was misused, etc. are all replaced by one question: can the autonomous system be held liable for the damage caused?

Granting legal personhood to autonomous systems would lead to autonomous systems taking part in litigation procedures as defendant. Moreover, it can be argued that these systems are subject to certain rights.[34] Solum discusses the possibility of AI having the right to freedom of speech.[35] He raises three objections: AI systems are not humans, they lack critical elements of personhood (feelings, consciousness, free will, etc.) and AI can never be more than human property.[36] Pagallo advises to, 'in the mid-term, skip any hypothesis of granting AI robots full legal personhood.'[37] Wagner avoids the objections raised by Solum, by exploring a limited legal personhood for autonomous systems, specifically in the context of liability: 'they [autonomous systems, NEV] are recognized as persons for the sole purpose of serving as a defendant in tort suits.'[38] Wagner explains that these systems do not have the full range of rights that 'full' legal persons (humans, companies, etc.) enjoy; they are only concerned legal persons in the context of tort law.[39]

This approach is interesting, but nevertheless it poses a problem in relation to the functions of tort law. As the autonomous system has no assets, it cannot pay the damages. The compensation function of tort law would thereby erode. Legal personhood for autonomous systems as described here offers thus a substantial disadvantage compared with the existing legal framework in which the compensation function is secured.

---

[32]   Gerhard Wagner, 'Robot, Inc.: Personhood for Autonomous Systems?' (2019) 88 Fordham Law Review; Pagallo (n 26).

[33]   Andrea Bertolini, 'Artificial Intelligence and Civil Liability' (study requested by the JURY Committee of the European Parliament 2020).

[34]   Solum (n 23).

[35]   ibid.

[36]   ibid. See also Pagallo (n 26).

[37]   Pagallo (n 26).

[38]   Wagner, 'Robot, Inc.: Personhood for Autonomous Systems?' (n 32).

[39]   ibid.

To solve this problem, stakeholders involved in the development could set up a fund for the autonomous to which they all contribute.[40] The autonomous system with limited legal personhood can subsequently pay the damages from that fund. Another option is to put a mandatory insurance in place.[41] However, this risks dulling the incentive for the stakeholders to produce as safe a system as possible as the fund can serve as a 'liability shield'.[42] This puts the tort law function of prevention under pressure. Therefore, assigning (limited) legal personhood to an autonomous system does not sufficiently safeguard the functions of tort law and is thus not desirable.

At the moment, the discussion on legal personhood for autonomous systems is still ongoing. Generally, autonomous systems do not have legal personhood. This being the case, an autonomous system has no legal rights and duties. As a result, an autonomous system cannot be held liable for damage the system itself inflicted on the injured party. Therefore, the question arises as to which parties could be held liable for damage caused by the autonomous system.

Fault Liability and the Wrongdoing of an Autonomous System

As an autonomous system lacks legal personhood and thus cannot be held liable for its own actions, the focus lies on other actors who could be held liable for the damage caused by an autonomous system. In principle, the owner of an autonomous system, the user or the manufacturer could all be liable for damage caused by the system.

In general, two main liability approaches can be distinguished: fault liability and strict liability. In between these two types of liability, liability for damage caused by violating a statutory rule is situated.[43] Especially statutory safety rules will be of importance in the context of autonomous systems, or as Van Dam puts it: 'Whereas statutory safety rules are the warning signs and barriers at the top of the cliff, tort law can be considered to be the ambulance waiting at the bottom.'[44] Here, liability differs more strongly per jurisdiction.[45] The breach of a statutory rule can, for instance, contribute to negligence. However, complying with a statutory rule does not necessarily mean that liability can be avoided.

---

[40]   Resolution on Robotics 2015/2103(INL) (n 29).
[41]   2015/2103(INL) (n 40); Solum (n 23); Wagner, 'Robot, Inc.: Personhood for Autonomous Systems?' (n 32).
[42]   Pagallo (n 26).
[43]   van Dam (n 4) 901.
[44]   van Dam (n 4) 901.
[45]   More extensively: ibid 901ff.

Strict liability is discussed separately in the next section. It should, however, be noted that in practice, fault liability and strict liability are not clearly separated. Strict liability can have elements similar to fault liability, such as the availability of certain defences or justifications to the defendant.[46]

Fault liability is centred on the conduct of the defendant. This becomes very clear from the general liability clause from the French Civil Code, which states that any act of man which causes damage to another, obliges the person by whose fault it was done to repair it.[47] This example shows how the defendant's conduct is the pivotal point in fault liability. Generally, if the defendant intentionally or negligently causes damage, he can be held liable for this damage.[48] For the purpose of this chapter, the focus will be on negligent conduct, as this is where the most questions arise regarding autonomous systems.

Negligence can require the breach of a duty of care.[49] In order to establish if such a duty exists and whether it has been breached, the defendant's conduct is generally compared with the conduct of the figures of, what is generally referred to, a 'reasonable man' or a 'good family father'.[50] This reasonable man is not someone who knows everything, has the best skill set and never makes a mistake. Rather, the average person who is careful but nevertheless sometimes makes mistakes, does not have skills to resolve every problem and does not have infinite knowledge, serves as point of reference to assess negligence. Van Dam explains, 'people may expect other people to behave in an objectively careful way and if this standard is not met, there is good reason to vindicate their infringed rights and to compensate the harm caused.'[51] Moreover, the rights and interests that have been violated put weight into the scale: highly valued rights generally require a high level of care.[52] So, if a doctor uses an autonomous system on a patient during surgery, a higher level of care is required from the doctor (e.g. frequently checking whether the autonomous system is functioning

---

[46] See for instance with regard to Germany: Förster (n 13) Rn 26–36.
[47] Art 1382 C Civ: 'Tout fait quelconque de l'homme, qui cause à autrui un dommage, oblige celui par la faute duquel il est arrivé à le réparer.'
[48] van Dam (n 4) 801.
[49] ibid, 804. In relation to liability based on the general lability clause of Article 1401 of the Dutch Burgerlijk Wetboek (now: Art 6:162 BW) see for example Hoge Raad 31 januari 1919, ECLI:NL:HR:1919:AG1776, *NJ* 1919/161 (Lindenbaum/Cohen) on the 'algemene zorgvuldigheidsplicht' (general duty of care).
[50] van Dam (n 4) 802, 811–812. As Van Dam rightfully points out, there is no reference made to the 'reasonable woman' or 'good family mother'.
[51] ibid.
[52] ibid 801.

the way it should) then when an autonomous system is used to clean an empty operating theatre.

Negligence can consist of an act and of an omission. The question whether the defendant not acted, whereas the 'reasonable man' would have acted or whether the defendant did act whereas the 'reasonable man' would not have acted, is therefore pivotal to establishing negligence. The violation of a codified rule can indicate negligence and unlawfulness. The latter is required under, for example, German *Deliktsrecht* ('Rechtswidrigkeit').[53]

Besides negligence or intent, elements such as damage, a causal link between the negligent or intentional conduct and attributability can all play a role in establishing fault liability. Moreover, the defendant might have certain defences to his disposal or justifications for his conduct.

Negligence in relation to autonomous systems could exist, for instance, in using the autonomous system in a situation for which it was not designed. If the autonomous system subsequently causes damage, the user of that system could face liability claims based on negligence; it can be argued he did not exercise proper care when using the autonomous system. Take, for example, an autonomous vehicle: if the vehicle is designed for use only on a highway, but is used for driving in a crowded city centre and subsequently causes damage, the user of the vehicle has likely behaved negligently. In addition, not providing regular maintenance to the autonomous system could constitute negligence of the owner of the system, depending on the exact circumstances. Moreover, the manufacturer of the software might act negligently if he does not provide a software update for a known vulnerability in the system. Factors such as time after initial release of the software, how well known the vulnerability was, and so on, can all be taken into account when assessing negligence. If the manufacturer has provided a software update, but the owner of the system has decided not to install the update, this could constitute negligence of the owner.

The updating of software of autonomous systems will become increasingly more important given the increasing cybersecurity risks.[54] In case of a cybersecurity breach, a hacker will be liable for any damage caused, but he might be untraceable. However, given the duties of care resting with the

---

[53]   § 823 Abs 1 Bürgerliches Gesetzbuch (BGB): 'Wer vorsätzlich oder fahrlässig das Leben, den Körper, die Gesundheit, die Freiheit, das Eigentum oder ein sonstiges Recht eines anderen widerrechtlich verletzt, ist dem anderen zum Ersatz des daraus entstehenden Schadens verpflichtet.'

[54]   Jean-Paul A Yaacoub and others, 'Robotics Cyber Security: Vulnerabilities, Attacks, Countermeasures, and Recommendations' (2021) 21 International Journal of Information Security, 121.

owner and manufacturer of the autonomous system, they might be liable for damage caused by a hacked autonomous system. This could be the case if the manufacturer has failed to provide a software update that could have prevented the hack or the damage caused, or if the owner has failed to install such an update. If, however, these parties exercise the necessary care or if these parties do not have a duty of care to provide or install software updates, fault liability will not provide a route to compensation. For instance, when the hacked autonomous system has been designed to conform to the 'state of the art', equipped with the best fail safe systems and with the best measures in place to prevent hacking, the manufacturer might not have acted negligently as he has taken all reasonable precautions. Here, strict liability could offer a solution.

Strict Liability: Accountability for Risks Created

Other than for fault liability, strict liability does not require that the defendant was at fault.[55] Strict liability revolves around a risk that has been created by the defendant, expressed by the German term 'Gefährdungshaftung' and the Dutch term 'risicoaansprakelijkheid'. If this risk subsequently materializes and damage is caused to another party, the defendant can be held strictly liable.

Strict liability regimes are often in place for activities or objects that are inherently dangerous, such as the development of a new product (product liability) and driving or owning a vehicle.[56] Due to this inherent risk, a strict liability regime is often deemed more suitable than a fault-based liability regime to address the compensation of the party suffering damage caused by an autonomous system.[57] A strict liability regime provides the injured party with a more accessible route to compensation as there is no need to proof the other party's fault or negligent behaviour. The party suffering damage will, generally, only proof its damage, that the inherently dangerous activity or object caused this damage (causation) and, in case of a product liability matter, the defect of the product. Therefore, one could argue that a strict liability regime caters to the needs of the victim as it is more efficient in settling claims.[58]

---

[55]   van Dam (n 4) 1001.
[56]   Such as, in relation to motor vehicles, in particular Article 2 of the French Loi Badinter, see Loi n° 85–677 du 5 juillet 1985 tendant à l'amélioration de la situation des victimes d'accidents de la circulation et à l'accélération des procédures d'indemnisation, art 2.
[57]   van Dam (n 4) 1002.
[58]   ibid.

If strict liability is deemed too 'strict', legislators could offer the defendant defences to invoke to not be deemed liable. The defendant can, for instance, be excused by *force majeure*,[59] which typically means an unforeseen event beyond the control of either of the parties. The defendant can also invoke a defence known such as the *development risk defence*, as seen in the EU Product Liability Directive.[60] For the manufacturer of a product to be liable under the EU Product Liability Directive, the injured party will have to prove his damage, the defect of the product, and the causal link between the damage and the defect.[61] Under the development risk defence, the manufacturer of a defective product is not liable for the damage caused by his defective product if he proves that 'the state of scientific and technical knowledge at the time when he put the product into circulation was not such as to enable the existence of the defect to be discovered.'[62] Hereby, elements of fault liability find their way into strict liability regimes: proper conduct can lead to a defendant avoiding liability for damage caused by a risk he created.

Strict liability can be in place for some autonomous systems. For instance, as autonomous road vehicles also qualify as motor vehicles, strict liability rules on damage caused by motor vehicles will also apply to autonomous vehicles. Autonomous systems might also qualify as products, meaning they would fall within the scope of current product liability regimes. Consequently, the owner of an autonomous vehicle and the manufacturer of an autonomous system can be held liable for damage caused by the vehicle or system without being at fault. So even when the owner and the manufacturer have taken all precautions to avoid damage, have been more careful than the 'reasonable man', they could still be liable for the damage caused. This protects the injured party: he will not have to proof any negligence on the side of the owner or manufacturer, thereby making it less challenging to successfully claim damage from these parties.

---

[59]   For example, Article 185 of the Dutch Road Traffic Act (Wegenverkeerswet 1994) states: 'Indien een motorrijtuig waarmee op de weg wordt gereden, betrokken is bij een verkeersongeval waardoor schade wordt toegebracht aan, niet door dat motorrijtuig vervoerde, personen of zaken, is de eigenaar van het motorrijtuig of […] verplicht om die schade te vergoeden, tenzij aannemelijk is dat het ongeval is te wijten aan overmacht', see Art 185 Wegenverkeerswet 1994, Stb 1994, 475 (WVW).

[60]   Council Directive 85/374/EEC of 25 July 1985 on the approximation of the laws, regulations and administrative provisions of the Member States concerning liability for defective products [1985] OJ L210/29 (Product Liability Directive), art 7(e).

[61]   ibid, art 4.

[62]   ibid, art 7(e).

Consequently, strict liability provides a strong incentive to provide for excellent maintenance of a vehicle or to only bring the safest of products to the market.

THE CHILLING EFFECT OF LIABILITY

Liability – or the threat of liability – can lead to the adjustment of the conduct of the defendant. On the one hand, this can lead to the socially desired conduct and prevent any future damage. On the other hand, the defendant might become too careful, fearing high compensation claims for damage the defendant might have little control over. When the regime for the liability for damage caused by products has this effect, defendants abstain from the development of new products because of the possibility of being confronted with liability claims. This 'chilling effect' thereby hinders innovation.[63] How serious this risk of a chilling effect is, is unclear. It can be argued that products posing a liability risk for the manufacturer should be banned from the market anyway as they apparently pose too great of a safety risk. However, it would not be beneficial for society as a whole when new innovative products with clear societal benefits but also unknown safety risks are kept from the market out of fear for liability for these unknown risks. The unknown safety risks thereby play a key role in the chilling effect discussion. Who should bear these unknown risks?

Defences such as the development risk defence can reallocate risks and thereby dampen such a chilling effect of tort law. Moreover, insurance as well as compensation funds can play a role in keeping the chilling effect of liability at bay while ensuring the compensation of the injured party.[64]

INSURANCE

The Role of Insurance

Insurance and liability together form a complex system. The importance of an insurance is twofold: it ensures that the damage suffered can be compensated, and it ensures that the risks the liable party must bear remain manageable from an economic perspective. An insurance can be

---

[63]   Maurice Schellekens, 'Self-driving cars and the chilling effect of liability law' (2015) 31 Computer Law & Security Review.

[64]   See also, ibid.

mandatory, which ensures indemnification of the injured party. A mandatory insurance is common, for example, in relation to motor vehicle liability. Especially in relation to strict liability, insurance can keep risks at bay for a defendant, thereby limiting the chilling effect of liability law.

Third-party Insurance vs First-party Insurance

The two main types of insurance are the first-party insurance and the third-party insurance. To start with the latter, a third-party insurance is generally an insurance that covers the *liability* of party A by compensating the damage party A has inflicted on party B. In other words, it compensates for the damage suffered by a third party (B), damage for which the insured (A) is liable. Therefore, one will have to be able to identify the liable party. This type of insurance is common in the automotive context.[65]

A first-party insurance is an insurance that is not connected to the liability question. Party A takes out an insurance to cover the *damage* he suffers, regardless of whether someone is liable for that damage. So, if party A suffers damage, A's insurer will cover this damage. The insurer could decide to seek redress to whomever might be liable for the damage suffered by party A, but this is not a matter with which the insured party is confronted. In contrast to the third-part insurance, the first-party insurance evolves around damage, not liability. An example of a common first-party insurance is a general accident insurance, where an insurer compensates the damage suffered by the insured, injured party.

Compensation Fund

In addition to insurance, compensation funds can also play their part. A compensation fund can compensate damage caused by someone who was uninsured. Such a fund is a mandatory feature of the EU Motor Insurance Directive, which requires Member States to have a compensation fund in place to compensate the damage inflicted by an uninsured defendant.[66]

---

[65]   See for instance the Dutch Wet Aansprakelijkheidsverzekering Motorrijtuigen, Stb 1963, 228 (WAM). A first-party traffic insurance can be found in, among other jurisdictions, Sweden. See also: Mary Kelly, Anne Kleffner and Maureen Tomlinson, 'First-Party Versus Third-Party Compensation for Automobile Accidents: Evidence From Canada' (2010) 13 Risk Management and Insurance Review.

[66]   Directive of the European Parliament and Council 2009/103/EC of 16 September 2009 relating to insurance against civil liability in respect of the use

This guarantees that the injured party is not confronted with the consequences of the defendant being uninsured by ensuring the compensation of the damage suffered.

A different type of compensation fund is found in the field of oil extraction and transport, specifically oil spills in case of an accident.[67] In response to an oil spill from an oil tanker at sea in 1967, a compensation fund, the IOPC Funds, was established.[68] The IOPC Funds pay for the damages caused by an oil spill, regardless of who was at fault.[69] All parties who receive more than a certain amount of oil through the sea transport of oil have to contribute to the fund.[70] The rationale behind this type of compensation fund lies in the dispersion of the risk of a certain activity – sea transport of oil – over those who benefit from it. The risk of an oil spill is relatively small, but its consequences can be very grave. In very severe cases one commercial party will typically not have the financial capacity to indemnify all those who suffered damage. The IOPC Funds place this burden on the entire sector that benefits from oil transport via the sea, thereby ensuring the damage to be compensated.

Like the IOPC Funds, similar compensation funds could be introduced for autonomous systems.[71] A compensation fund is particularly suitable for autonomous systems that are unlikely to cause any damage, but if they do, the consequences can be far-reaching. If the specific autonomous system would cause damage, despite its being designed to avoid harm, the injured party could be indemnified by the compensation fund. The injured party can directly claim damages from the compensation fund, not having to investigate which party might be liable. Thereby, the development risk, inherent to innovations, is borne by all those contributing to the compensation fund instead of being borne by just one party.

---

of motor vehicles, and the enforcement of the obligation to insure against such liability [2009] OJ L263/11, art 3.

[67] See for an economic perspective: Michael Faure and Wang Hui, 'Economic Analysis of Compensation for Oil Pollution Damage' (2006) 37 Journal of Maritime Law & Commerce.

[68] 'Funds Overview' (iopcfunds.org) <https://iopcfunds.org/about-us/> accessed 14 July 2021.

[69] International Convention on the Establishment of an International Fund for Compensation for Oil Pollution Damage (1992) 1110 UNTS 57, art 4.

[70] ibid, preamble.

[71] See in relation to autonomous vehicles: Nynke E Vellinga, 'Old Products, New Risks: The Findings of the New Technologies Formation and Automated Driving' (2022) 18 Illyrius – International Scientific Review.

Innovation and Incentives

A compensation fund can avoid the hindering of innovation though the chilling effect, just as insurance can put a halt to the chilling effect as described above. Insurance and compensation funds are both tools in ensuring compensation for the injured party, thereby serving the *compensation* function of tort law. From the perspective of compensation, one could even pose the question whether tort law is still necessary when insurance and compensation funds enable full compensation to be achieved.

For the answer to this question, one can turn to New Zealand, which has had a universal no-fault accident compensation scheme since 1974.[72] It covers everyone in New Zealand who has suffered a personal injury in an accident, regardless of the cause of the accident.[73] This Accident Compensation Scheme precludes (almost) all tort actions related to the accident.[74] Howell, Kavanagh and Marriott point out that as a consequence, the Accident Compensation Scheme has minimal incentives for the prevention of injuries.[75]

This puts the *prevention* function of tort law under pressure. Specifically in the Accident Compensation Scheme context, it seems unlikely that, although in theory there might be little incentive to avoid injury, this would lead to more careless behaviour. Simply because damage is covered, does not necessarily mean that there is no incentive or reason to avoid damage. Individuals will generally not want to miss out on school, work and social events because of a physical injury, for instance. Manufacturers, however, will not have these incentives.

Like the Accident Compensation Scheme, insurance and compensation funds can reduce the incentive for manufacturers to produce safer products or the incentive for defendants to act more carefully and take precautions. The defendant could become complacent, not striving for better conduct or safer products. By adhering to tort, the insurer that covered the damage of the injured party can seek redress from the defendant. That way, the defendant is still encouraged to design those safer products or

---

[72]   Simon Connell, 'Community Insurance versus Compulsory Insurance: Competing Paradigms of No-Fault Accident Compensation in New Zealand' (2019) 39 Legal Studies; Bronwyn Howell, Judy Kavanagh and Lisa Marriott, 'No-Fault Public Liability Insurance: Evidence from New Zealand' (2002) 9 Agenda: A Journal of Policy Analysis and Reform.

[73]   Accident Compensation Act 2001, section 20; Connell (n 72).

[74]   Accident Compensation Act 2001 (n 73), section 317. See also Connell (n 72); Howell, Kavanagh and Marriott (n 72) 141.

[75]   Howell, Kavanagh and Marriott (n 72) 146.

to take precautionary measures. Thereby the *prevention* function of tort law is maintained, while also providing the injured party with access to compensation.

Compensation funds and insurance alike should be carefully considered in light of the development of autonomous systems, taking into account both the incentives for the defendants to develop safer systems as well as to improve their conduct and the benefits in limiting the chilling effect. In striking the right balance between tort law and insurance mechanisms, both the *compensation* function and the *prevention* function of tort law can be served. A no-fault insurance scheme combined with the option for insures to seek redress could cater to both these functions, allowing for incentives to prevent damage caused by autonomous systems as well as providing compensation for the injured party.

FINAL REMARKS

A liability framework for autonomous systems cannot only ensure the injured party is compensated for damage caused by autonomous systems but can also encourage innovation and the development of ever safer products. The option of assigning legal personhood to autonomous systems does not do justice to the functions of tort law. Therefore, the attention is on other parties, such as the user of the autonomous system, the owner as well as the manufacturer of the autonomous system. Human (mis)conduct in relation to the damage is the pivotal point in establishing fault liability. This form of liability will therefore not be the focus in finding compensation for damage caused by autonomous systems, as these systems can cause damage independently from any human input. Strict liability will thereby gain in importance.

Tort, first- and third-party insurance and compensation funds are all tools that should be considered in finding the desired balance between the encouragement of innovation and the development of safer systems on the one hand and the compensation for damage suffered on the other hand. In finding that balance, the interest of the injured party is critical; having clear liability and compensation rules in place can encourage the acceptance by consumers of new developments such as more widespread adoption of autonomous systems.[76] A strict liability framework could lend

---

[76] See in relation to autonomous vehicles: Kareem Othman, 'Public Acceptance and Perception of Autonomous Vehicles: A Comprehensive Review' (2021) 1 AI and Ethics.

itself for this, as it does not place a burden of proof of fault on the injured party's shoulders. In addition, preventing damage caused by autonomous systems should be encouraged, stimulating manufacturers to develop safer autonomous systems and users of those systems of responsible use of autonomous systems.

LITERATURE

Bertolini A, 'Artificial Intelligence and Civil Liability' (study requested by the JURY Committee of the European Parliament, 2020).

Calabresi G, 'The Complexity of Torts – The Case of Punitive Damages' in M Stuart Madden (ed), *Exploring Tort Law* (Cambridge University Press 2005).

Cane P, *The Anatomy of Tort Law* (Hart Publishing 1997).

Chesterman S, 'Artificial Intelligence and the Limits of Legal Personality' (2020) 69 International & Comparative Law Quarterly.

Clark C and others, 'Can You Hear the Rivers Sing? Legal Personhood, Ontology, and the Nitty-Gritty of Governance' (2018) 45 Ecology Law Quarterly.

Connell S, 'Community Insurance versus Compulsory Insurance: Competing Paradigms of No-Fault Accident Compensation in New Zealand' (2019) 39 Legal Studies.

Faure M and Hui W, 'Economic Analysis of Compensation for Oil Pollution Damage' (2006) 37 Journal of Maritime and Commerce Law.

Fong TW and others, 'Autonomous Systems Taxonomy' (NASA Technical Reports Server 2018) <https://ntrs.nasa.gov/citations/20180003082> accessed 12 July 2021.

Förster C, 'BGB § 823 Schadensersatzpflicht' (*BeckOK BGB Hau/Poseck*, 58th edn, Beck online 2021).

Gates D, 'Q&A: What Led to Boeing's 737 MAX Crisis' (*The Seattle Times*, 22 November 2020) <https://www.seattletimes.com/business/boeing-aerospace/what-led-to-boeings-737-max-crisis-a-qa/> accessed 14 July 2021.

Gordon J, 'Artificial Moral and Legal Personhood' (2020) 36 AI & Society.

Horowitz MC, 'Why Words Matter: The Real World Consequences of Defining Autonomous Weapon Systems' (2016) 30 Temple International & Comparative Law Journal.

Howell B, Kavanagh J and Marriott L, 'No-Fault Public Liability Insurance: Evidence from New Zealand' (2002) 9 Agenda: A Journal of Policy Analysis and Reform.

Hubig C, 'Benefits and Limits of Autonomous Systems in Public Security' (2020) 5 European Journal for Security Research.

Kelly M, Kleffner A and Tomlinson M, 'First-Party versus Third-Party Compensation for Automobile Accidents: Evidence From Canada' (2010) 13 Risk Management and Insurance Review.

National Highway Traffic Safety Administration, 'ODI Resume: Investigation PE21-020' (US Department of Transportation, 13 August 2021) <https://static.nhtsa.gov/odi/inv/2021/INOA-PE21020-1893.PDF> accessed 1 December 2021.

Oldenhuis FT, 'GS Onrechtmatige daad: Afdeling 2 Boek 6 BW' (Wolters Kluwer 2021).

Othman K, 'Public Acceptance and Perception of Autonomous Vehicles: A Comprehensive Review' (2021) 1 AI and Ethics.

Pagallo U, 'Vital, Sophia, and Co.—The Quest for the Legal Personhood of Robots' (2018) 9 Information.

SAE International, 'Taxonomy and Definitions for Terms Related to Driving Automation Systems for On-Road Motor Vehicles, Standard J3016' (*SAE International*, April 2021).

Schellekens M, 'Self-driving Cars and the Chilling Effect of Liability Law' (2015) 31 Computer Law & Security Review.

Smith B, 'Legal Personality' (1928) 37 Yale Law Journal.

Solum LB, 'Legal Personhood for Artificial Intelligences' (1992) 70 North Carolina Law Review.

Van Dam C, *European Tort Law*, 2nd edn (Oxford University Press 2013).

Van den Hoven van Genderen R, 'Do We Need New Legal Personhood in the Age of Robots and AI?' in M Corrales, M Fenwick and N Forgó (eds), *Robotics, AI and the Future of Law* (Springer 2018).

Vellinga NE, 'Old Products, New Risks: The Findings of the New Technologies Formation and Automated Driving' (2022) 18 Illyrius – International Scientific Review.

Wagner G, 'Robot, Inc.: Personhood for Autonomous Systems?' (2019) 88 Fordham Law Review.

Wagner G, 'Vorbemerkung (Vor § 823)' (*Münchener Kommentar zum BGB*, 8th edn, Beck online 2021).

Yaacoub JA and others, 'Robotics Cyber Security: Vulnerabilities, Attacks, Countermeasures, and Recommendations' (2021) 21 International Journal of Information Security.

16. Autonomous Weapons Systems in warfare: is Meaningful Human Control enough?
Taís Fernanda Blauth

1. INTRODUCTION

In 2015, Artificial Intelligence (AI) experts, roboticists and relevant personalities from the industry endorsed an open letter calling for a ban of Autonomous Weapons Systems (AWS).[1] Later, in the Netherlands, an initiative calling for such a ban gathered more than 150 signatures from scientists in the field of AI and robotics.[2] A crucial ethical aspect of these discussions is whether the decision to kill a person should be entirely left to 'intelligent machines', and such a perspective has been widely criticised.[3] Nevertheless, proponents of the use of AWS highlight technological and operational factors that provide incentives for their development and use, such as reduced costs of military personnel.

The risks associated with the technology can cause extensive damages, with profound ethical, legal and socio-political implications. A pre-emptive ban on AWS is unlikely, given the lack of consensus towards implementing such a ban as a new protocol to the Convention on Certain

---

[1] 'Autonomous Weapons: An Open Letter from AI & Robotics Researchers' (*Future of Life Institute*, 2015) <https://futureoflife.org/open-letter-autonomous-weapons/> accessed 20 August 2021.

[2] 'Dutch Scientists Call for Ban on Killer Robots' (*PAX*, 30 November 2020) <https://paxforpeace.nl/news/overview/dutch-scientists-call-for-ban-on-killer-robots> accessed 29 July 2021.

[3] Denise Garcia, 'Lethal Artificial Intelligence and Change: The Future of International Peace and Security' (2018) 20 International Studies Review; Denise Garcia, 'Killer Robots: Why the US Should Lead the Ban' (2015) 6 Global Policy; Noel Sharkey, 'Staying in the Loop: Human Supervisory Control of Weapons' in Nehal Bhuta and others (eds), *Autonomous Weapons Systems: Law, Ethics, Policy* (Cambridge University Press 2016); 'The Campaign To Stop Killer Robots' (*Campaign To Stop Killer Robots*) <https://www.stopkillerrobots.org/> accessed 25 August 2020.

Conventional Weapons (CCW).[4] While some countries are still open to agreeing on a legal ban on AWS, a relevant key concept emerged from the negotiations within the United Nations framework. This 'second best moral option' stipulates that humans should be substantially involved in decisions with lethal consequences in military operations.[5] Article 36, a civil society organisation based in the United Kingdom, proposed 'Meaningful Human Control' (MHC) to represent this principle, which entails that a human should remain in control of decisions in such processes. This approach to MHC as a minimum requirement for the operation of AWS gained track through the support of scholars, NGOs and governments.[6] However, the meaning, components and practical implications of this principle are still contested and unclear. Also, it is not clear to what extent MHC can reduce the various risks posed by AWS.

This chapter starts by briefly exploring the concept of AWS and the current state of the technology. Subsequently, it examines the effects of developing and using AWS from four different perspectives: legal, political, technological and operational. Even though it does not provide an exhaustive list of pertinent issues, key arguments and considerations will be outlined. Within this analysis, it will be possible to engage with both the challenges and opportunities of using AI systems in warfare. On this basis it can be evaluated to what extent the principle of Meaningful Human Control (MHC) is able to mitigate the challenges posed by developing and using emerging technologies in the military realm.

2. AUTONOMOUS WEAPON SYSTEMS: DEFINITIONS AND CURRENT STATE OF DEVELOPMENT

One of the difficulties in the debate on the military use of AI systems is the lack of generally accepted definitions. Some authors adhere to

---

[4] 'The Convention on Certain Conventional Weapons' <https://www.un.org/disarmament/the-convention-on-certain-conventional-weapons/> accessed 28 June 2022.

[5] Christian Nikolaus Braun, 'LAWS and the *Mala in Se* Argument' (2021) 33 Peace Review, 245.

[6] Thompson Chengeta, 'Defining the Emerging Notion of "Meaningful Human Control" in Autonomous Weapon Systems (AWS)' (2017) 49 NYU Journal of International Law.

the term 'unmanned systems',[7] which refers to 'any form of military robotic hardware, be it remote-controlled or equipped with autonomous functions.'[8] In the scope of the ongoing discussions at the United Nations, such systems are referred to as Lethal Autonomous Weapons Systems (LAWS).[9] LAWS are the systems that, once activated, can track, identify and attack targets without further human action.[10] As lethality is not necessarily at the centre of the arguments of this chapter, the focus will be on AWS instead of LAWS.

It is noteworthy that the term 'autonomous weapons systems' is not ideal or precise. As Kirchschlaeger argues, the terminology is misleading, considering that machines lack both moral capability and autonomy.[11] However, given the complexity in finding agreement on the definition at the social, legal and political levels, a generally accepted definition helps to navigate the challenges posed by digital transformations in warfare. Thus, considering the broad understanding of the term, AWS will be used throughout this chapter to describe fully autonomous weapon systems, which are able to conduct a mission without human intervention.

Armed forces worldwide have been developing and integrating emerging technologies in weapon systems for a long time. Increased autonomy and reliance on technology have followed this trend, which means some semi-autonomous systems are already in use. In air defence, close-in weapons systems (CIWS) use radar to identify and track incoming threats; once

---

[7] Frank Sauer and Niklas Schörnig, 'Killer Drones: The "Silver Bullet" of Democratic Warfare?' (2012) 43 Security Dialogue; Anja Dahlmann and Marcel Dickow, 'Preventive Regulation of Autonomous Weapon Systems: Need for Action by Germany at Various Levels' (Stiftung Wissenschaft und Politik 2019).

[8] Dahlmann and Dickow (n 7) 7.

[9] 'Background on LAWS in the CCW' (*United Nations – Office for Disarmament Affairs*) <https://www.un.org/disarmament/the-convention-on-certain-conventio nal-weapons/background-on-laws-in-the-ccw/> accessed 20 June 2021.

[10] Sharkey (n 3) 23; Christof Heyns, 'Report of the Special Rapporteur on Extrajudicial, Summary or Arbitrary Executions' 1 <https://www.ohchr.org/ sites/default/files/Documents/HRBodies/HRCouncil/RegularSession/Session23/ A-HRC-23-47_en.pdf> accessed 4 May 2022; Christof Heyns, 'Autonomous Weapons Systems: Living a Dignified Life and Dying a Dignified Death' in Nehal Bhuta and others (eds), *Autonomous Weapons Systems: Law, Ethics, Policy* (Cambridge University Press 2016) 4.

[11] *Digital Transformation and Ethics: Ethical Considerations on the Robotization and Automation of Society and the Economy and the Use of Artificial Intelligence*, 1st edn (Nomos Verlagsgesellschaft mbH & Co KG 2021) 69–95 <https:// doi.org/10.5771/9783845285504>; 'Artificial Intelligence and the Complexity of Ethics' (2020) 14 Horizons.

detected, a computer-controlled fire system can select and autonomously attack them.[12] Two well-known examples of CIWSs are 'GoalKeeper' and 'Phalanx', used by the Netherlands and the United States, respectively.[13] They are set to defend a specific area, such as the zone around a military base, and can only operate in these simple and structured environments. Their functions are limited to if-then-else scenarios foreseen by the programmers during the design and development of the software.[14] They do not possess the ability to learn from experience, generalise scenarios and automatically adapt to new information and environments. Given X input, the automatic output will always be Y (unless there is a flaw, or the system fails).

The next step envisioned by many is developing and adopting fully autonomous weapons systems, which can track, identify and attack targets without further human action. These weapons would have the ability to operate in dynamic and complex environments. When given a series of inputs, the system would run probabilistic reasoning to evaluate the best course of action.[15] Unlike systems with automated functions, AWS can produce a wide range of outputs.

No public information regarding the offensive use of autonomous weapons was available until recently. However, a UN report released in March 2021 suggested that, in 2020, a drone airstrike in Libya was conducted by an AWS without human control.[16] The systems 'were programmed to attack targets without requiring data connectivity between the operator and the munition: in effect, a true "fire, forget and find" capability.'[17] It is not clear from the report whether the drones selected targets autonomously and if there were causalities resulting from the use

---

[12]   Vincent Boulanin and Maaike Verbruggen, *Mapping the Development of Autonomy in Weapon Systems* (SIPRI 2017) <https://www.sipri.org/sites/default/files/2017-11/siprireport_mapping_the_development_of_autonomy_in_weapon_systems_1117_1.pdf> accessed 24 February 2023.

[13]   Robert H Stoner, 'History and Technology – R2D2 with Attitude: The Story of the Phalanx Close-In Weapons – NavWeaps' (*NavWeaps*, 30 October 2009) <http://www.navweaps.com/index_tech/tech-103.php> accessed 10 June 2021; '30 Mm (1.2") Goalkeeper SGE-30' (*NavWeaps*) <http://www.navweaps.com/Weapons/WNNeth_30mm_Goalkeeper.php> accessed 10 June 2021.

[14]   ML Cummings, 'Artificial Intelligence and the Future of Warfare' (Chatham House 2017) 3.

[15]   ibid.

[16]   'Final Report of the Panel of Experts on Libya Established Pursuant to Security Council Resolution 1973 (2011)' (United Nations Security Council 2021) S/2021/229 <https://undocs.org/S/2021/229>.

[17]   ibid 17.

of these weapons. However, this report might be the first documented case of the use of AWS. Furthermore, during the early stages of the Russia–Ukraine War there were indications that AI-enabled weapons might have been used.[18] However, just as in the Libyan case, it remains unclear to which degree these weapons acted autonomously. The difficulties in determining the level of autonomy and whether a weapon is fully autonomous are among the many challenges that the discourse around AWS raises.

3.   MEANINGFUL HUMAN CONTROL

3.1   Early Categories of Human Oversight

The amount of control of humans over weapons has constantly changed as technology advanced.[19] While fighters with swords or guns might have almost complete control over the use of force in combat, modern remotely controlled weapons such as drones present a different scenario. As AWS become more common, the type (or lack) of control humans exercise is much debated. Despite the agreement that human oversight over such weapons should remain,[20] the extent, form or quality of control remains unclear. AI-enabled weapons tend to be divided into three main categories, according to the level of human involvement:[21]

- Human-in-the-loop (HITL): The weapon system can only select targets and perform an attack with a human command.
- Human-on-the-loop (HOTL): The weapon system can select targets and perform an attack under the oversight of a human operator, who can reject or cancel the autonomous decision.

---

[18]   Will Knight, 'Russia's Killer Drone in Ukraine Raises Fears about AI in Warfare' (*Wired*, 2022) <https://www.wired.com/story/ai-drones-russia-ukraine/> accessed 7 April 2022; Jeremy Kahn, 'A.I. is on the Front Lines of the War in Ukraine' (*Fortune*, 1 March 2022) <https://fortune.com/2022/03/01/russia-ukraine-invasion-war-a-i-artificial-intelligence/> accessed 7 April 2022.

[19]   Chengeta (n 6) 839–840.

[20]   CCW, 'Meeting of the High Contracting Parties to the Convention on Prohibitions or Restrictions on the Use of Certain Conventional Weapons which May Be Deemed to Be Excessively Injurious or to Have Indiscriminate Effects' (2019) CCW/MSP/2019/9 <https://undocs.org/CCW/MSP/2019/9> accessed 17 May 2022.

[21]   Bonnie Docherty, 'Losing Humanity: The Case against Killer Robots' (Human Rights Watch 2012) <https://www.hrw.org/report/2012/11/19/losing-humanity/case-against-killer-robots> accessed 15 March 2022; Sharkey (n 3).

- Human-out-of-the-loop (HOOTL): The weapon system can select targets and perform an attack without human interaction.

When discussing AWS, governments clarify that they will maintain human involvement in the deployment of AWS, and that no truly *autonomous* system will be used.[22] However, the often-mentioned 'human control' tends to refer to the HITL. Such level of autonomy is considered insufficient and generic.[23] 'A human simply pressing a "fire" button in response to indications from a computer, without cognitive clarity or awareness, is not sufficient to be considered 'human control' in a substantive sense.'[24]

3.2   Defining Meaningful Human Control

Given the inadequacy of previous concepts, non-profit organisation Article 36 proposed the principle of 'Meaningful Human Control' (MHC).[25] According to this principle, operators should possess sufficient information regarding the context and be capable of realistically *assessing* and, if necessary, *modifying* the actions proposed by the machine.[26] Santoni de Sio and van den Hoven identified two common and necessary conditions that should be satisfied for an AWS to be under MHC:

- **Tracking condition:** This condition establishes that 'a decision-making system should demonstrably and verifiably be *responsive* to the *human* moral reasons relevant in the circumstances – no matter how many system levels, models, software, or devices of whatever nature separate a human being from the ultimate effects in the world, some of which may be lethal. That is, decision-making systems should *track* (relevant) human moral reasons.'[27]

---

22   See Chengeta (n 6) 14–15.
23   Sharkey (n 3) 26; 'Key Areas for Debate on Autonomous Weapons Systems' <https://www.article36.org/wp-content/uploads/2014/05/A36-CCW-May-2014.pdf> accessed 7 April 2022.
24   Richard Moyes, 'Key Elements of Meaningful Human Control' (April 2016) <https://article36.org/wp-content/uploads/2016/04/MHC-2016-FINAL.pdf> accessed 24 February 2023.
25   It is noteworthy that HITL and HOTL might be components of MHC, but they are not equivalent.
26   Moyes (n 24).
27   Filippo Santoni de Sio and Jeroen van den Hoven, 'Meaningful Human Control over Autonomous Systems: A Philosophical Account' (2018) 5(15) Frontiers in Robotics and AI, 7.

- **Tracing condition:** The actions of a system 'should be traceable to a proper moral understanding on the part of one or more relevant human persons who design or interact with the system.'[28] This means that:
  a. There should be at least one individual involved in designing, programming, operating and deploying the system.
  b. Such individual(s) should understand what the system *can* do and the *consequences* it can cause when deployed.

When this condition is present, humans also exercise control by setting relevant parameters in the design phase of the algorithm. Such standards include, for example, 'system's predictability and reliability',[29] 'the ability for a human to intervene after the activation of the system',[30] 'limits on target type',[31] and 'fail-safe requirement'.[32]

In addition to these elements, two additional components can be found in reports published by civil society organisations:[33]

- **Operational condition:** Limits on *when* and *where* a weapons system can be deployed should be established, as well as *what* it can target.[34] The constraints include, for instance, 'exclude protected persons and objects' and creating 'exclusion zone, physical barriers, warnings'.[35]
- **Decision-making condition:** This condition aims to establish an adequate level of human oversight. Individuals responsible for controlling AWS should, for example, understand the operational environment (e.g., who and what is in a battlespace) and the weapons technology (e.g., what it could select and engage). Moreover, they should have enough time for deliberation, allowing operators

---

[28]   ibid 9.
[29]   'Key Elements of a Treaty on Fully Autonomous Weapons: Frequently Asked Questions' (Campaign to Stop Killer Robots 2020) 4 <https://www.stopkillerrobots.org/wp-content/uploads/2020/03/FAQ-Treaty-Elements.pdf> accessed 23 June 2022; Vincent Boulanin and others, 'Limits on Autonomy in Weapon Systems: Identifying Practical Elements of Human Control' (SIPRI and ICRC 2020).
[30]   'Key Elements of a Treaty on Fully Autonomous Weapons: Frequently Asked Questions' (n 29) 4.
[31]   Boulanin and others (n 29) 27.
[32]   ibid.
[33]   'Key Elements of a Treaty on Fully Autonomous Weapons: Frequently Asked Questions' (n 29).
[34]   ibid 4.
[35]   Boulanin and others (n 29) 27.

to make decisions in compliance with legal requirements (e.g., distinction and proportionality).[36]

MHC is a combination of these conditions, which complement each other. For a control that is truly meaningful, it is crucial to satisfy all these conditions, because, when deploying AWS, human beings would be carrying out the relevant humanitarian considerations instead of having them delegated to a system. AI-based weapons would be 'tools in the hands of humans.'[37] Due to the relevant role of the human agent, the question of whether humans retain control that is meaningful became the dividing line between acceptable and unacceptable behaviour.

The proposal for the principle gained traction with governments and governmental bodies. For instance, the European Parliament explicitly mentioned the principle in the resolution of 20 January 2021 titled 'Artificial Intelligence: questions of interpretation and application of international law'. Paragraph 3 of the resolution states that the Parliament 'considers that AI used in a military and a civil context must be subject to meaningful human control, so that at all times a human has the means to correct, halt or disable it in the event of unforeseen behaviour, accidental intervention, cyber-attacks or interference by third parties with AI-based technology or where third parties acquire such technology.'[38]

At the international level, the concept of MHC has prevailed in the negotiations within the framework of the Convention on Certain Conventional Weapons (CCW).[39] In 2019, the Meeting of the High Contracting Parties to the CCW adopted 11 guiding principles on emerging technologies in the area of LAWS. One of them states, 'human responsibility for the decisions on the use of weapons systems must be retained since accountability cannot be transferred to machines. This should be considered across the entire life cycle of the weapons system.'[40] The principle reflects the concerns of state parties regarding the accountability gap, an often-discussed legal challenge linked to AWS. Proper human oversight tends to be one of

---

[36]   'Key Elements of a Treaty on Fully Autonomous Weapons: Frequently Asked Questions' (n 29) 4.

[37]   Christof Heyns, 'Autonomous Weapons in Armed Conflict and the Right to a Dignified Life: An African Perspective' (2017) 33(1) South African Journal on Human Rights, 22.

[38]   European Parliament resolution of 20 January 2021 on artificial intelligence: questions of interpretation and application of international law in so far as the EU is affected in the areas of civil and military uses and of state authority outside the scope of criminal justice (2020/2013(INI)) 2021 (2021/C 456/04) C 456/37.

[39]   Dahlmann and Dickow (n 7) 17.

[40]   CCW (n 20) 10.

the ways to enable accountability when deploying AI-enabled weapons. The principle might represent, thus, an early indication that consensus could be reached for the establishment of MHC as a requirement for the deployment of autonomous weapons. Nonetheless, it is noteworthy that there is no official agreement in place nor a well-established and universally accepted description of MHC, its components and how it should be operationalised.

4.   AI IN WARFARE: CHALLENGES AND OPPORTUNITIES

When discussing safety frameworks for AI systems, especially for AWS, Isaac Asimov's three laws of robotics,[41] as well as the Zeroth Law introduced later,[42] are frequently being cited as a starting point:

0.   A robot may not harm humanity, or, by inaction, allow humanity to come to harm.
1.   A robot may not injure a human being or, through inaction, allow a human being to come to harm.
2.   A robot must obey the orders given by human beings, except where such orders would conflict with the First Law.
3.   A robot must protect its own existence as long as such protection does not conflict with the First or Second Law.

Asimov developed these rules to respond to fears of 'killer robots', a theme addressed throughout the short stories of the novel *I, Robot*.[43]

---

[41]   Isaac Asimov, *The Complete Robot* (Harper 1982).
[42]   Isaac Asimov, *Foundation and Earth* (Harper 1986).
[43]   Although the abovementioned rules are part of fiction literature, legal scholars have used them to develop general frameworks for the safety of AI systems. For instance, the European Parliament has incorporated Asimov's laws in a resolution. Regardless of its being part of fiction, these laws have been relevant in the ethical, legal and political debate about AWS. According to the resolution, Asimov's laws are 'directed at the designers, producers and operators of robots, including robots assigned with built-in autonomy and self-learning, since those laws cannot be converted into machine code', 'European Parliament Resolution of 16 February 2017 with Recommendations to the Commission on Civil Law Rules on Robotics (2015/2103(INL))' <https://eur-lex.europa.eu/legal-content/EN/TXT/PDF/?uri=CELEX:52017IP0051&from=EN> accessed 16 June 2021. However, the European Parliament has understood the laws as a guide that roboticists should follow instead of general principles that could be part of AI ethics.

If applied to a real-life context, the First Law would mean that AWS should be simply banned because a robot should not harm humans. Such harm should not happen in any scenario, not even in war. Even if a country were able to 'command' robots to kill an enemy, they would be forbidden to do so because that violates the 'not harming humanity' rule. These rules, especially the Second Law, provide an early indication of the importance of humans remaining in control of robots that, in science fiction, would be crucial towards avoiding the dystopian scenario of an AI taking over. In Asimov's world, the emphasis on human oversight stems from fears around the lack of control over machines that could, ultimately, threaten humanity.

Scholars have discussed at length the possible consequences to humanity of using AWS in war.[44] One of the well-known initiatives that resulted from such concerns is the campaign to ban 'killer robots'.[45] The reasoning behind initiatives aimed at limiting the use of robots in warfare is evidently not the fear of robots taking over. The debate is much more nuanced and complex.

The early discussions around the use of AI systems in warfare focused on the foundational ethics of AI as a military technology.[46] In particular, roboticist Ronald C. Arkin and computer scientist Noel Sharkey were the protagonists of early discussions. Arkin highlighted the advantages of autonomy in weapons, suggesting that robots 'can ultimately perform more ethically than human soldiers'.[47] In contrast, Sharkey emphasised the risks such weapons could pose in our society. He argued that, since robots could reduce the number of dead soldiers, there would be fewer

---

[44]   See Peter Asaro, 'On Banning Autonomous Weapon Systems: Human Rights, Automation, and the Dehumanization of Lethal Decision-Making' (2012) 94 International Review of the Red Cross; Elvira Rosert and Frank Sauer, 'Prohibiting Autonomous Weapons: Put Human Dignity First' (2019) 10 Global Policy; Heyns, 'Autonomous Weapons in Armed Conflict' (n 37); Robert Sparrow, 'Robots and Respect: Assessing the Case Against Autonomous Weapon Systems' (2016) 30 Ethics & International Affairs.

[45]   For instance, see 'The Campaign To Stop Killer Robots' (n 3).

[46]   Kate Crawford, *Atlas of AI: Power, Politics, and the Planetary Costs of Artificial Intelligence* (Yale University Press 2021) 191–192.

[47]   Ronald Arkin, 'The Case for Banning Killer Robots: Counterpoint' (2015) 58 Communications of the ACM, 46; see also Ronald Arkin, 'Lethal Autonomous Systems and the Plight of the Non-Combatant' in Ryan Kiggins (ed.), *The Political Economy of Robots: Prospects for Prosperity and Peace in the Automated 21st Century* (Palgrave Macmillan 2018).

disadvantages in waging wars. Reducing the 'body bag count' and, consequently, the costs of warfare would lead to more conflicts.[48]

Later, the debate around the use of AI systems in warfare focused on the possibilities AI presented in terms of accuracy and precision in weapon systems.[49] The ethical conundrums remained relevant, inseparable from technical discussions. Due to nuanced implications of the deployment of AWS, it is crucial to consider different perspectives and evaluate contrasting arguments. In this section, some of these perspectives will be discussed. They are summarised in the table below:

Table 16.1   Overview of perspectives and aspects under consideration

Perspective	Aspects under consideration	Remarks
Legal	Principles of discrimination and proportionality	Currently, there is no technical solution to incorporate IHL principles into algorithms.
Political	Offence–defence balance	Lower threshold for the use of force because of (1) fewer soldiers injured/killed, (2) reduced costs associated with AWS, and (3) swarming strategies favour offence.
Technological	Data sets and Machine Learning	Data sets might contain bias and not be representative, leading to errors and unpredicted negative consequences.
Operational	Automatic Reasoning	Although it helps to reduce the timeframe of certain decisions, there is a risk of automation and confirmation bias.

4.1   Legal Perspective

Relevant conditions established in International Humanitarian Law (IHL) need to be considered when deploying AWS.[50] One of them is

---

[48]   N Sharkey, 'Cassandra or False Prophet of Doom: AI Robots and War' (2008) 23 IEEE Intelligent Systems, 16.

[49]   Crawford (n 46) 192.

[50]   Other legal arguments are relevant in the LAWS debate, such as issues of accountability gaps and attribution. However, in this chapter, I focus on the principles of discrimination and proportionality for two main reasons: (1) a discourse framed around the indiscriminate nature of certain weapons was central to the development of new regulations in the past (e.g., landmines and cluster bombs); and (2) the fact that LAWS cannot distinguish between combatants and civilians is

the principle of distinction, which states that civilians and combatants should be differentiated in conflict: non-combatants must not be targeted. Any attack not directed at a military object is thus considered indiscriminate.[51] In particular, weapons considered indiscriminate by nature are prohibited (i.e., weapons that do not allow the abovementioned distinction, such as chemical weapons).[52] The other principle is proportionality, which entails that the use of force should not be exceeded beyond necessary.[53]

Some scholars advocate that AWS could ensure better compliance with the principles of distinction and proportionality compared with humans.[54] Arkin summarises the idea with the following rhetorical question: 'As robots are already faster, stronger, and in certain cases (e.g., Deep Blue, Watson) smarter than humans, is it really that difficult to believe they will be able to ultimately treat us more humanely in the battlefield than we do each other, given the persistent existence of atrocious behaviours by a significant subset of human warfighters?'[55] Proponents of this view argue that, because autonomous systems can be designed to avoid self-protection in specific scenarios (e.g., when self-defence could result in civilian harm), they would be more reliable in certain situations than humans. However, no technical solution has been developed yet for translating concepts of proportionality and discrimination into algorithms.[56] Distinguishing civilians from combatants is a highly complex and context-sensitive task, a type of activity that cannot, in principle, be translated into software.[57] Robots do not possess the ability to make moral assessments and

---

one of the strong arguments against autonomous weapons, especially in the framework of the Campaign to Stop Killer Robots.

[51]   Protocol additional to the Geneva Conventions of 12 August 1949, and relating to the Protection of Victims of International Armed Conflicts (opened for signature 8 June 1977, entered into force 7 December 1978) Art 51(4).

[52]   Rome Statute of the International Criminal Court (opened for signature 17 July 1998, entered into force 1 July 1992) Art 8(2)(b)(xx).

[53]   Protocol additional to the Geneva Conventions of 12 August 1949, and relating to the Protection of Victims of International Armed Conflicts (opened for signature 8 June 1977, entered into force 7 December 1978) Art 51(5)(b).

[54]   Ronald C Arkin, *Governing Lethal Behavior in Autonomous Robots* (CRC Press 2009) 29–30; Gary E Marchant and others, 'International Governance of Autonomous Military Robots' (2011) XII The Columbia Science and Technology Law Review, 279–280.

[55]   Arkin, 'Lethal Autonomous Systems' (n 47) 319.

[56]   Dahlmann and Dickow (n 7) 6.

[57]   Chantal Grut, 'The Challenge of Autonomous Lethal Robotics to International Humanitarian Law' (2013) 18 Journal of Conflict and Security Law, 11; Rosert and Sauer (n 44) 370.

understand social contexts, which, in principle, prevent them from making such distinctions.[58]

Due to the uncertainty regarding technical capabilities of developing AWS that can conform to IHL, designing robots that target only military objects (e.g., weapons and tanks), and not individuals, is the safest option. In this way, the probability of targeting civilians and using excessive force against human agents is reduced. This is one of the reasons why autonomy in systems used for defence purposes, such as the Goalkeeper and Phalanx, do not generate much concern.[59] They are specifically designed to attack military objects (e.g., incoming missiles). Due to their position, design and purpose, it is improbable that they will wrongly target civilian objects, even though it is still a risk.[60] Adjusting the target of AWS to only military objects might work well in some circumstances (e.g., defence systems located in specific areas), but it is not as simple for AWS operating in complex scenarios such as war zones among civilians.[61]

Given that it is not possible to translate abstract principles of discrimination and proportionality into algorithms at the moment, the machine by itself cannot comply with IHL. The safest option is to deploy AWS for defence, in specific and structured environments. If governments decide to develop and use such systems in the battlefield, the minimum requirement of MHC is necessary. Human control should be meaningful in the sense that the operator should be able to play the role of a 'fail-safe actor'.[62] The person exerting control must be capable of preventing malfunctions that could result in attacks against civilians or excessive use of force. In addition, the operator should have situational understanding.[63]

---

[58]   For a deeper analysis on this issue, see Heyns, 'Autonomous Weapons in Armed Conflict' (n 37) 6–12.

[59]   This does not mean that such systems should not be included in the discussions. There are lessons to be learned from past experiences with defence systems. For more on this, see Ingvild Bode and Tom FA Watts, 'Meaning-Less Human Control: Lessons from Air Defence Systems on Meaningful Human Control for the Debate on AWS' (Zenodo 2021) <https://dronewars.net/wp-content/uploads/2021/02/DW-Control-WEB.pdf> accessed 21 June 2022.

[60]   See Grut (n 57) 14–15.

[61]   ibid 12.

[62]   Daniele Amoroso and Guglielmo Tamburrini, 'Autonomous Weapons Systems and Meaningful Human Control: Ethical and Legal Issues' (2020) 1 Current Robotics Reports, 189.

[63]   It is noteworthy that previous experiences with air defence systems show that it is not easy for controllers to have a good understanding of the contextual factors. For the supervisor, it is difficult 'to question system outputs and make reasoned deliberations about selecting and engaging specific targets.' In Bode and Watts (n 59) 59.

4.2 Political Perspective

Among the issues under debate regarding the impact of the use of AI in military applications,[64] is the potential impacts on strategic stability.[65] Strategic stability is 'the condition that exists when two potential adversaries recognise that neither would gain an advantage if it were to begin a conflict with the other.'[66] A crucial element for stability is an offence–defence balance. According to offence–defence theory, 'international conflict and war are more likely when offense has the advantage, while peace and cooperation are more probable when defense has the advantage.'[67] Thus, it is critical to evaluate *if* and *how* the use of AWS might impact the offence–defence balance and, ultimately, strategic stability.

As technology evolves, new weapons are developed. Some of these might facilitate adopting an offensive or defensive strategy.[68] In the case of AWS, a common argument is that they could lead to a lower threshold for using force, favouring offensive strategies. Four main reasons support this argument:

1. States might be more susceptible to using AWS because fewer or no human lives will be at risk against the opponent on the battlefield.[69] In particular, Sauer and Schörnig identified that AWS seem more attractive to democracies than different types of weapons: citizens are more willing to support wars in which fewer of their soldiers are killed.[70]

---

[64] Other relevant discussions on this area were not included in this paper, such as the integration of AI in nuclear weapons systems and the consequences regarding the different stages of technology development between the global north and global south. For more on such topics, see James Johnson, 'The AI-Cyber Nexus: Implications for Military Escalation, Deterrence and Strategic Stability' (2019) 4 Journal of Cyber Policy.

[65] Jürgen Altmann and Frank Sauer, 'Autonomous Weapon Systems and Strategic Stability' (2017) 59 Survival.

[66] Steven A Hildreth and Amy F Woolf, 'Ballistic Missile Defense and Offensive Arms Reductions: A Review of the Historical Record' (Congressional Research Service 2010) R41251 4.

[67] Sean M Lynn-Jones, 'Offense–Defense Theory and Its Critics' (1995) 4 Security Studies, 660–661.

[68] ibid 691.

[69] Jean-Marc Rickli, 'Some Considerations of the Impact of LAWS on International Security: Strategic Stability, Non-State Actors and Future Prospects' (Meeting of Experts on Lethal Autonomous Weapons Systems Convention on Certain Conventional Weapons (CCW), Geneva, 16 April 2015) 1–2; Sharkey (n 48) 16.

[70] (n 7).

Thus, from the democratic peace theory viewpoint, greater public support could indicate a lower threshold for AWS use in democratic countries.

2.   Reduced costs associated with the use of AWS could lead to an increase in conflict.[71] It is expected that, with time, there will be fewer expenditures in, for example, aircraft, military personnel and training.

3.   As Heyns argued, humans have 'built-in constraints' that tend to prevent them from using force or going to war.[72] These include not wanting to get killed, losing loved ones, or killing. The deployment of AWS creates a physical and psychological distance from what is happening in the battlefield, from the human emotions that still permeate warfare. This distance can make military commanders use force more easily than before.

4.   According to Rickly, the offensive nature of some of the AWS, especially when considering swarming strategies, affects the offence-defence balance.[73] The coordinated and synchronised tactic consists of simultaneous attacks to overwhelm the adversary's defence. Such strategies negate the advantage of the defence and favour offence, which could lead to an increase in international conflict and war. Thus, considering that these factors favour offensive strategies, the development and use of AWS in warfare can lead to strategic instability.

As the level of autonomy in weapons systems increases, their responses and actions occur faster. At the same time, the behaviour of the systems can also become increasingly unpredictable if techniques such as machine learning are in place. Errors might lead to escalation, which can be difficult to correct or control at a later stage.[74] Given the dual-use nature of AI systems,[75] the potential for proliferation is high and difficult to control.

---

[71]   Leonard Kahn, 'Military Robots and the Likelihood of Armed Combat' in Patrick Lin, Keith Abney and Ryan Jenkins (eds), *Robot Ethics 2.0: From Autonomous Cars to Artificial Intelligence* (Oxford University Press 2017) 280–281; Ajey Lele, 'Debating Lethal Autonomous Weapon Systems' (2019) 13 Journal of Defence Studies, 57; Heyns, 'Report of the Special Rapporteur on Extrajudicial, Summary or Arbitrary Executions' (n 10) 11.

[72]   Heyns, 'Report of the Special Rapporteur on Extrajudicial, Summary or Arbitrary Executions' (n 10) 11.

[73]   Rickli (n 69) 1–2.

[74]   Altmann and Sauer (n 65) 117.

[75]   Dual-use technologies can be used both in commercial and military settings. In the case of AWS, 'defence and commercial enterprises compete for a virtually the same talent pool, and use similar infrastructure and hardware to support these

At the same time, if restrictions are too strong, they could also hamper technology development in general (civilian purposes included).

Guaranteeing MHC would, in principle, reduce the speed of actions and decisions, which could help mitigate the risks of escalation of conflict.[76] However, compliance with the principle does not considerably affect the offence–defence balance. The possession of such weapons could lower the restraints States have towards waging wars due to operational (e.g., fewer human lives at risk) and economic (e.g., fewer costs with military personnel) advantages. So, the fact that a given country has AWS and is willing to use them already favours an offensive strategy that could lead to international instability.

4.3   Technological Perspective

Technological aspects hold an important role in the discussions regarding human control.[77] The development of learning AI systems depends on large amounts of data to train the algorithms and systems. However, vast quantities of data do not necessarily lead to more predictable and adequate automated decision-making. The data sets used to train models are not always representative and might be biased, producing unpredictable or undesired results. The limitations and problems identified in civilian uses of machine learning systems,[78] can also represent a challenge in the military use of the technology.

The battlefield is an unstructured, complex and unpredictable environment. Designing software that can adapt to such ever-changing circumstances is not impossible, especially due to the advances in the field of machine learning. However, as Scharre cautioned in 2011, 'restraints on autonomous weapons to ensure ethical engagements are essential, but building autonomous weapons that *fail safely* is the harder task.'[79] In the face of unpredictable situations, the reactions of systems will also be unpredictable. As it is difficult (or even impossible) to anticipate every possible output of

---

efforts': James Johnson, 'Artificial Intelligence & Future Warfare: Implications for International Security' (2019) 35 Defense & Security Analysis, 162.

[76]   Dahlmann and Dickow (n 7) 15.

[77]   In addition to discussions on training data, other aspects such as the technical option to deactivate a system and the ability of a system to transmit important information to the human operator are relevant but were not included in this chapter. For more on the topic, see 'Areas of Alignment: Common Visions for a Killer Robots Treaty' (*Human Rights Watch*, 2 August 2021) <https://www.hrw.org/news/2021/08/02/areas-alignment> accessed 21 June 2022.

[78]   See Crawford (n 46) 123–149.

[79]   Paul Scharre, 'Why Unmanned' [2011] Joint Force Quarterly, 92.

an algorithm, it is also challenging to develop a system that will not have a glitch that could result in excessive use of force or harm to civilians.

Additionally, it remains unclear how militaries would generate data sets for learning systems that are both large and representative.[80] Civilian systems are often trained with available data originating from the internet, but these are hardly useful for military applications (if useful at all). Creating synthetic training data might be an option.[81] The possibility has been considered a good option in many civilian domains, especially to reduce privacy concerns. However, human-made data sets 'remain erroneous and incomplete, especially when it comes to unpredictable interactions in (real) conflict situations.'[82] Moreover, researchers have shown that synthetic data have a limited utility for several applications (e.g., to train predictive models).[83]

From the technological perspective, especially in relation to the quality of data sets, establishing the principle of MHC alone is not particularly helpful. Given that data are paramount for the development of AWS, legislation on the collection, treatment and use of military data sets could be a good starting point.[84]

4.4   Operational Perspective

The use of AWS is appealing from an operational point of view. As Schörnig explains,[85] drones and robots offer many advantages over combatants: they do not get emotionally affected or tired by the war, nor do they question 'orders'.[86] Johnson had a similar argument, stating that

---

[80]   Dahlmann and Dickow (n 7) 13.

[81]   Synthetically generated data are being increasingly used in machine learning. They can be used to (1) train models (e.g., computer vision); (2) increase real data sets, when hybrid data sets are more appropriate to train models; and (3) solve privacy and legal issues, when the real data cannot be used. In the case of AWS, they could be used to generate hybrid datasets. See Sergey I Nikolenko, *Synthetic Data for Deep Learning*, vol 174 (Springer International Publishing 2021) <https://link.springer.com/10.1007/978-3-030-75178-4> accessed 31 August 2021.

[82]   Dahlmann and Dickow (n 7) 13.

[83]   Oscar Giles and others, 'Faking Feature Importance: A Cautionary Tale on the Use of Differentially-Private Synthetic Data' (arXiv, 2 March 2022) <http://arxiv.org/abs/2203.01363> accessed 8 June 2022.

[84]   Dahlmann and Dickow (n 7) 13.

[85]   'Die Automatisierung des Krieges: der Vormarsch der Robotkrieger ist nicht mehr aufzuhalten und wirft einige Probleme auf' [2010] Peace Research Institute Frankfurt 5 <http://www.jstor.com/stable/resrep14321>.

[86]   Note that the increased autonomy in military weapons is not limited to drones. It also includes autonomous vessels, loitering munitions and hypersonic weapons, to name a few.

robots would 'do a better job than humans'.[87] In this context, Arkin laid down some of the primary motivators for using AWS:[88]

a.   'Force multiplication': fewer military personnel for a given mission.
b.   'Expand the battlespace': expands battlefield and war zones to larger areas.
c.   'Extending the war fighter's reach': enables soldiers to see or strike farther.
d.   'Casualty reduction': reduces the number of soldiers injured or killed during missions.

In addition to the abovementioned motivators, the possibility of reduced personnel can be analysed separately. With automation, many weapons might require only one supervisor, especially when acting in conjunction (e.g., swarming techniques). At first glance, this seems like a relevant advantage. However, due to the unpredictable circumstances of warfare, some problematic issues might arise.

One example is related to the reasoning processes of those supervising AWS. When supervisors make decisions regarding the necessity or legitimacy of an attack, their thinking processes can follow an automatic reasoning or controlled process (also known as the deliberative process).[89] Due to the nature of armed conflict, military personnel on the battlefield often do not have enough time to ponder the subsequent actions and must resort to automatic thinking. When decisions must be taken in a short time and scenarios of predictable events, automatic reasoning does offer an advantage over deliberative reasoning.[90] However, the dynamic warfare scenario is filled with unpredictable and contextual circumstances. These cannot be adequately considered via automatic reasoning by a supervisor working in a control room, distant from the situation and overseeing many different weapons.[91] Moreover, the speed of AI-based decision-making might overwhelm human capabilities. Autonomous systems may take

---

[87]   Tim Weiner, 'New Model Army SoldierRolls Closer to Battle' (*The New York Times*, 16 February 2005) <https://www.nytimes.com/2005/02/16/technology/new-model-army-soldierrolls-closer-to-battle.html> accessed 18 August 2021.
[88]   Arkin, *Governing Lethal Behavior in Autonomous Robots* (n 54) xii.
[89]   According to Sharkey (n 3) 30, 'automatic processing refers to fast responses that are always cued automatically, such as those required for playing tennis or riding a bicycle. Controlled refers to slower deliberative process that we need in order to make a thoughtful decision, such as determining the winner of a competition or judging a murder trial.'
[90]   ibid 32.
[91]   Grut (n 57) 11.

decisions too quickly, making them difficult for humans to follow. As there is usually a level of urgency in actions during military operations, the controller will not be able to properly evaluate the outputs of a system to make an informed decision. For this reason, 'having a single operator controlling multiple weapons systems, could be disastrous.'[92]

If automatic reasoning is used to select targets that must be later approved or vetoed by a human, a different challenge arises. Research has shown that when a computer system suggests an action based on automatic reasoning, it is likely that a human supervisor will accept such a suggestion. Known in the literature as automation bias, 'humans have a tendency to disregard or not search for contradictory information in light of a computer-generated solution that is accepted as correct.'[93] Since individuals attribute high value to automatically generated information, once an AI system suggests a target to be approved by human supervisors, they will most likely agree with this assessment. An associated phenomenon, confirmation bias, is the inclination to evaluate data with the tendency to confirm one's own beliefs. For instance, if someone seeks to confirm their belief that AWS are accurate, they will further affirm the validity of the automated decision – even when faced with inconsistent observations.[94] With increasing levels of autonomy in weapons, issues linked to automation and confirmation bias can lead to disastrous consequences.[95]

Operational aspects tend to fuel the discussions for AWS. Despite the arguments favouring such weapons systems, scholars are sceptical about the actual control a human can exercise far from the battlefield. In fact, an analysis of human–machine interaction in air defence systems demonstrated that the human decisions are frequently meaning*less*.[96] It is difficult to assess to what extent humans can employ control that is 'meaningful'. Grut argues that, 'as weapons systems are given increasing autonomy in order to respond to threats which humans may be too slow to respond to, in ways which are too complex for humans to control, it becomes even less realistic to expect human operators to exercise significant veto control over their operations.'[97] There is only an illusionary power given to controllers

---

[92]   Sharkey (n 3) 34.

[93]   Mary L Cummings, 'Automation and Accountability in Decision Support System Interface Design' (2006) 32 The Journal of Technology Studies, 25.

[94]   James Bridle, *New Dark Age: Technology and the End of the Future* (Verso 2019) 40.

[95]   For example, see the shooting down of Iran Air Flight 655 in Grut (n 57) 14–15.

[96]   Bode and Watts (n 59) 61.

[97]   Grut (n 57) 15.

if they are not given enough time and information for decision-making. Automation and confirmation bias are relevant aspects that are difficult to manage by human controllers.

5. IS MEANINGFUL HUMAN CONTROL (MHC) ENOUGH?

The principle of MHC can help mitigate some of the challenges posed by AWS – for instance, regarding the accountability gap.[98] When using AWS, it is not possible to hold a person accountable for violations of IHL, since the systems acts independently. Proper human oversight could close such a gap because the controller can be held responsible for wrongful actions taken by robots. However, other issues remain unsolved. For example, the use of AWS could lead to more asymmetric wars, in which the powerful leaders in the development of technology would be in possession of a considerable advantage. With the upper hand, it might become easier for certain countries to wage wars, leading to an increase in conflicts. Based on the aspects previously analysed from legal, political, technological and operational perspectives, three main challenges persist even if a human oversight requirement is established: namely, issues of control, verification and proliferation.[99]

5.1 Control

The demands of IHL can be difficult to implement in practice. Humans are not expected to be able to always comply with the principles of discrimination and proportionality, or to make only the 'right moves'. Such a standard seems unrealistically high when discussing decisions made during chaotic and dynamic circumstances, such as military operations. Algorithms, not different from humans, are also prone to mistakes. The issue is not that systems would fail, and humans would not. The problem lies in the different *consequences* of a human error and an

---

[98]   Heyns, 'Autonomous Weapons in Armed Conflict' (n 37) 11–12.

[99]   For more on these aspects, see Mark Gubrud and Jürgen Altmann, 'Compliance Measures for an Autonomous Weapons Convention' (International Committee for Robot Arms Control 2013) Working Paper #2. (on verification) and James Dawes, 'An Autonomous Robot May Have Already Killed People – Here's How the Weapons Could Be More Destabilizing than Nukes' (*The Conversation*, 29 September 2021) <http://theconversation.com/an-autonomous-robot-may-have-already-killed-people-heres-how-the-weapons-could-be-more-destabilizing-than-nukes-168049> accessed 18 May 2022 (on proliferation).

algorithmic error.[100] The outputs of autonomous weapons could result in faster attacks that can also be larger in terms of scale and scope. In a scenario where an algorithm-based system provides the human controller with wrong or inaccurate information, which is used to make a life-or-death decision, that could mean many avoidable fatalities.

5.2   Verification

The suspected use of AWS in the cases relating to Libya and in the Russia–Ukraine war also raises another crucial aspect: Is it possible to verify compliance with the principle of MHC after the fact? After using an AI-enabled weapon, it is challenging to prove the degree of autonomy of such weapons for three main reasons. The first is a well-known problem in civilian uses of AI systems – namely, opaque algorithms. Some complex models present results (outputs) that humans cannot interpret. If the algorithm gives the human responsible for oversight a wrong output that cannot be adequately understood, the entire decision-making chain might be compromised. Verification procedures become difficult because the reasoning behind the decision cannot be understood. The second involves the lack of standardisation regarding documentation of the actions. Verification is only possible if the State takes proper steps for evidence-keeping when using AWS. However, there is no agreement on what these should be. Finally, States might not always be willing to share such evidence – either out of guilt or because they do not want to share their intelligence data, methods or protocols. Invoking the need to protect classified information to avoid sharing evidence already happens, for instance, in international attribution of cyberattacks.[101]

Attempts to develop evidentiary standards include a tamper-proof system, as suggested by Gubrud and Altmann.[102] This could be possible 'by keeping the records of each engagement and making the records of specific engagements available to a Treaty Implementing Organization, on request, when sufficient evidence exists to support suspicious of illegal autonomous operation.'[103] Ensuring MHC is an essential step towards regulation on the topic, but the principle is insufficient. Best practices towards the development of explainable AI systems should be adopted

---

[100]   As Dawes illustrated, 'the difference between human error and algorithmic error is like the difference between mailing a letter and tweeting.' In Dawes (n 99).

[101]   See Kristen E Eichensehr, 'The Law and Politics of Cyberattack Attribution' [2020] U.C.L.A. Law Review 520, 569.

[102]   Gubrud and Altmann (n 99).

[103]   ibid 2.

by programmers. Additional provisions, specially drawn for the purpose of verification (e.g., necessary evidence that should be provided upon request),[104] are crucial for the effectiveness of a rule on human control.

5.3 Proliferation

Several countries have been investing large amounts of financial resources to research and develop their AI capabilities. Some governments are explicit about their goals of being frontrunners in what has been described as an arms race, while others wish to remain, at least, technologically competitive.[105] Similarly, the private sector has been investing in the implementation of machine learning to improve products and services, or to develop new ones. As a dual-use technology, civilian AI applications can be adapted and used in the military realm. As a result, the dynamic surrounding the development of AI systems is complex and scattered.

Algorithms, by their nature, cannot be easily controlled or contained in a physical closed space. The research and development of AI 'may be discreet (requiring little physical infrastructure), discrete (different components of an AI system may be designed without conscious coordination), diffuse (dozens of individuals in widely dispersed geographic locations can participate in an AI project), and opaque (outside observers may not be able to detect potentially harmful features of an AI system).'[106] One should not assume that militaries will be able to contain or control the development and use of AWS.

In general, preventing the proliferation of weapons is already a challenging task. As Dawes indicates, 'if the history of weapons technology has taught the world anything, it's this: Weapons spread.'[107] When it comes to

---

[104] As Gubrud and Altmann detailed, the 'evidence could include video and other data that was presented to the operator, plus a video view that includes the operator's hands on controls and the operator's view of the console. The data record would also include the commands as received by the console and codes for the identities of the accountable operator and accountable commander, which might be encrypted in physical keys which they are personally accountable for controlling at all times, and which are needed in order to operate the weapon.' In ibid 6.

[105] Justin Haner and Denise Garcia, 'The Artificial Intelligence Arms Race: Trends and World Leaders in Autonomous Weapons Development' (2019) 10 Global Policy.

[106] Matthew U Scherer, 'Regulating Artificial Intelligence Systems: Risks, Challenges, Competencies, and Strategies' [2015] SSRN Electronic Journal 356–357 <http://www.ssrn.com/abstract=2609777> accessed 3 March 2020.

[107] Dawes (n 99).

AI-based weapons, it can become even more difficult to prevent proliferation. Even if countries reach an international agreement on establishing the requirement of MHC when deploying AWS, malicious actors will most likely disregard the principle completely. This means that terrorist groups, for instance, could be using autonomous weapons in the future. In that case, malicious actors will not hold the same concerns and standards when it comes to targeting accuracy and compliance with IHL, for example.

6.   CONCLUSION

Considerations from different perspectives elucidate risks and challenges that might arise when autonomous systems can decide to kill a human. Undesirable results still predominate despite potential advantages such as fewer deaths and cost reduction. To avoid risks coming to fruition, human oversight is paramount. In fact, it can be considered a minimum requirement since a ban on AWS is unlikely. Especially within the UN framework, it is possible to identify consensus being built around the necessity for MHC. However, there need to be further discussions on what this concept entails, and how to operationalise the components into military practice.

In addition, it is necessary to explore how to guarantee a high-quality human–machine interaction. The individuals in charge of this control, making life and death decisions, are expected to adhere to IHL. To this end, they must be granted sufficient time and information, be well trained for this role, and be held accountable for their decisions. Human oversight should not be considered a simple 'press-the-button' task. For meaningful control, there must be a meaningful decision. However, as previously discussed, humans are prone to automation and confirmation biases. This means that the controller might not hold full cognitive capacity to evaluate the information in a short time. Such issues should be considered in the training process of controllers. More research on the topic is also welcome since machine and human teaming in a military context is still an underdeveloped concept. For now, it remains unclear how governments will operationalise a control that is 'meaningful'. Until we reach this point, the principle should not be codified as a component of international law on AWS.

Another relevant aspect that must be further developed is creating proper documentation standards that should be followed to allow verification. Without adequate evidence, it will not be possible to check if MHC was in place during a military operation. Software engineers have a crucial role and should focus on developing algorithms following best practices to achieve explainable AI systems. Finally, there is a need for collective effort when it comes to the issue of proliferation. We can be on a slippery slope with the development of weapons that should only be used with adequate human oversight but could also function without humans in the equation. If any AWS fall into the wrong hands, that could represent a global security threat. Guaranteeing MHC will most likely not be a concern when deploying AWS.

This study has analysed the challenges posed by AWS from many perspectives, which are by no means exhaustive. Discussions on other relevant aspects (e.g., accountability gap and ethical issues) were not included. Future research could investigate ways of mitigating the risks that the principle of MHC *per se* cannot address. For instance, the different forms of training and preparing military personnel who will exercise control over the weapon systems.

The lack of consensus in the discussions on AWS regulation, together with the rapid pace of advancements in the field of AI, is a daunting scenario. However, in the past similar apprehensions surrounded the use of biological and chemical weapons. The development of legal norms was possible in those cases, and constraints around using such weapons are in place today. Looking ahead, a consensus on one aspect, such as MHC, could help the negotiations to advance towards a broader agreement. Such an agreement should include provisions on verification, which are crucial for the success of any agreement regarding human control.

ACKNOWLEDGEMENTS

I thank the editors, Prof. Andrej Zwitter and Dr. Oskar Josef Gstrein, for valuable critical comments. I also thank Dr. Guangyu (Karin) Qiao-Franco and Dr. Christian Nikolaus Braun for providing helpful feedback on previous drafts of this chapter.

BIBLIOGRAPHY

'30 Mm (1.2") Goalkeeper SGE-30' (*NavWeaps*) <http://www.navweaps.com/Weapons/WNNeth_30mm_Goalkeeper.php> accessed 10 June 2021.
Altmann J and Sauer F, 'Autonomous Weapon Systems and Strategic Stability' (2017) 59 Survival.
Amoroso D and Tamburrini G, 'Autonomous Weapons Systems and Meaningful Human Control: Ethical and Legal Issues' (2020) 1 Current Robotics Reports.
'Areas of Alignment: Common Visions for a Killer Robots Treaty' (*Human Rights Watch*, 2 August 2021) <https://www.hrw.org/news/2021/08/02/areas-alignment> accessed 21 June 2022.

Arkin R, 'The Case for Banning Killer Robots: Counterpoint' (2015) 58 Communications of the ACM.

Arkin R, 'Lethal Autonomous Systems and the Plight of the Non-Combatant' in Ryan Kiggins (ed.), *The Political Economy of Robots: Prospects for Prosperity and Peace in the Automated 21st Century* (Palgrave Macmillan 2018).

Arkin RC, *Governing Lethal Behavior in Autonomous Robots* (CRC Press 2009).

Asaro P, 'On Banning Autonomous Weapon Systems: Human Rights, Automation, and the Dehumanization of Lethal Decision-Making' (2012) 94 International Review of the Red Cross.

Asimov I, *The Complete Robot* (Harper 1982).

Asimov I, *Foundation and Earth* (Harper 1986).

'Autonomous Weapons: An Open Letter from AI & Robotics Researchers' (*Future of Life Institute*, 2015) <https://futureoflife.org/open-letter-autonomous-weapons/> accessed 20 August 2021.

'Background on LAWS in the CCW' (*United Nations – Office for Disarmament Affairs*) <https://www.un.org/disarmament/the-convention-on-certain-conventional-weapons/background-on-laws-in-the-ccw/> accessed 20 June 2021.

Bode I and Watts TF, 'Meaning-Less Human Control: Lessons from Air Defence Systems on Meaningful Human Control for the Debate on AWS' (Zenodo 2021) <https://dronewars.net/wp-content/uploads/2021/02/DW-Control-WEB.pdf> accessed 21 June 2022.

Boulanin V and Verbruggen M, *Mapping the Development of Autonomy in Weapon Systems* (SIPRI 2017) <https://www.sipri.org/sites/default/files/2017-11/sipri report_mapping_the_development_of_autonomy_in_weapon_systems_1117_1.pdf> accessed 24 February 2023.

Boulanin V and others, 'Limits on Autonomy in Weapon Systems: Identifying Practical Elements of Human Control' (SIPRI and ICRC 2020).

Braun CN, 'LAWS and the *Mala in Se* Argument' (2021) 33 Peace Review.

Bridle J, *New Dark Age: Technology and the End of the Future* (Verso 2019).

CCW, 'Meeting of the High Contracting Parties to the Convention on Prohibitions or Restrictions on the Use of Certain Conventional Weapons which May Be Deemed to Be Excessively Injurious or to Have Indiscriminate Effects' (2019) CCW/MSP/2019/9 <https://undocs.org/CCW/MSP/2019/9> accessed 17 May 2022.

Chengeta T, 'Defining the Emerging Notion of "Meaningful Human Control" in Autonomous Weapon Systems (AWS)' (2017) 49 NYU Journal of International Law.

Crawford K, *Atlas of AI: Power, Politics, and the Planetary Costs of Artificial Intelligence* (Yale University Press 2021).

Cummings ML, 'Automation and Accountability in Decision Support System Interface Design' (2006) 32 The Journal of Technology Studies.

Cummings ML, 'Artificial Intelligence and the Future of Warfare' (Chatham House 2017).

Dahlmann A and Dickow M, 'Preventive Regulation of Autonomous Weapon Systems: Need for Action by Germany at Various Levels' (Stiftung Wissenschaft und Politik 2019).

Dawes J, 'An Autonomous Robot May Have Already Killed People – Here's How the Weapons Could Be More Destabilizing than Nukes' (*The Conversation*, 29 September 2021) <http://theconversation.com/an-autonomous-robot-may-have-already-killed-people-heres-how-the-weapons-could-be-more-destabilizing-than-nukes-168049> accessed 18 May 2022.

Docherty B, 'Losing Humanity: The Case against Killer Robots' (Human Rights Watch 2012) <https://www.hrw.org/report/2012/11/19/losing-humanity/case-against-killer-robots> accessed 15 March 2022.

'Dutch Scientists Call for Ban on Killer Robots' (*PAX*, 30 November 2020) <https://paxforpeace.nl/news/overview/dutch-scientists-call-for-ban-on-killer-robots> accessed 29 July 2021.

Eichensehr KE, 'The Law and Politics of Cyberattack Attribution' [2020] U.C.L.A. Law Review 520.

'European Parliament Resolution of 16 February 2017 with Recommendations to the Commission on Civil Law Rules on Robotics (2015/2103(INL))' <https://eur-lex.europa.eu/legal-content/EN/TXT/PDF/?uri=CELEX:52017IP0051&from=EN> accessed 16 June 2021.

European Parliament resolution of 20 January 2021 on artificial intelligence: questions of interpretation and application of international law in so far as the EU is affected in the areas of civil and military uses and of state authority outside the scope of criminal justice (2020/2013(INI)) 2021 (2021/C 456/04).

'Final Report of the Panel of Experts on Libya Established Pursuant to Security Council Resolution 1973 (2011)' (United Nations Security Council 2021) S/2021/229 <https://undocs.org/S/2021/229>.

Garcia D, 'Killer Robots: Why the US Should Lead the Ban' (2015) 6 Global Policy.

Garcia D, 'Lethal Artificial Intelligence and Change: The Future of International Peace and Security' (2018) 20 International Studies Review.

Giles O and others, 'Faking Feature Importance: A Cautionary Tale on the Use of Differentially-Private Synthetic Data' (arXiv, 2 March 2022) <http://arxiv.org/abs/2203.01363> accessed 8 June 2022.

Grut C, 'The Challenge of Autonomous Lethal Robotics to International Humanitarian Law' (2013) 18(5) Journal of Conflict and Security Law.

Gubrud M and Altmann J, 'Compliance Measures for an Autonomous Weapons Convention' (International Committee for Robot Arms Control 2013) Working Paper #2.

Haner J and Garcia D, 'The Artificial Intelligence Arms Race: Trends and World Leaders in Autonomous Weapons Development' (2019) 10 Global Policy.

Heyns C, 'Report of the Special Rapporteur on Extrajudicial, Summary or Arbitrary Executions' <https://www.ohchr.org/sites/default/files/Documents/HRBodies/HRCouncil/RegularSession/Session23/A-HRC-23-47_en.pdf> accessed 4 May 2022.

Heyns C, 'Autonomous Weapons Systems: Living a Dignified Life and Dying a Dignified Death' in Nehal Bhuta and others (eds), *Autonomous Weapons Systems: Law, Ethics, Policy* (Cambridge University Press 2016) .

Heyns C, 'Autonomous Weapons in Armed Conflict and the Right to a Dignified Life: An African Perspective' (2017) 33 South African Journal on Human Rights.

Hildreth SA and Woolf AF, 'Ballistic Missile Defense and Offensive Arms Reductions: A Review of the Historical Record' (Congressional Research Service 2010) R41251.

Johnson J, 'Artificial Intelligence & Future Warfare: Implications for International Security' (2019) 35 Defense & Security Analysis 147.

Johnson J, 'The AI-Cyber Nexus: Implications for Military Escalation, Deterrence and Strategic Stability' (2019) 4 Journal of Cyber Policy 442.

Kahn J, 'A.I. is on the Front Lines of the War in Ukraine' (*Fortune*, 1 March 2022) <https://fortune.com/2022/03/01/russia-ukraine-invasion-war-a-i-artificial-intelligence/> accessed 7 April 2022.

Kahn L, 'Military Robots and the Likelihood of Armed Combat' in Patrick Lin, Keith Abney and Ryan Jenkins (eds), *Robot Ethics 2.0: From Autonomous Cars to Artificial Intelligence* (Oxford University Press 2017).

'Key Areas for Debate on Autonomous Weapons Systems' <https://www.article36.org/wp-content/uploads/2014/05/A36-CCW-May-2014.pdf> accessed 7 April 2022.

'Key Elements of a Treaty on Fully Autonomous Weapons: Frequently Asked Questions' (Campaign to Stop Killer Robots 2020) <https://www.stopkillerrobots.org/wp-content/uploads/2020/03/FAQ-Treaty-Elements.pdf> accessed 23 June 2022.

Kirchschlaeger PG, 'Artificial Intelligence and the Complexity of Ethics' (2020) 14 Horizons.

Kirchschlaeger PG, *Digital Transformation and Ethics: Ethical Considerations on the Robotization and Automation of Society and the Economy and the Use of Artificial Intelligence*, 1st edn (Nomos Verlagsgesellschaft mbH & Co KG 2021) <https://doi.org/10.5771/9783845285504>.

Knight W, 'Russia's Killer Drone in Ukraine Raises Fears about AI in Warfare' [2022] *Wired* <https://www.wired.com/story/ai-drones-russia-ukraine/> accessed 7 April 2022.

Lele A, 'Debating Lethal Autonomous Weapon Systems' (2019) 13 Journal of Defence Studies 33.

Lynn-Jones SM, 'Offense–Defense Theory and Its Critics' (1995) 4 Security Studies.

Marchant GE and others, 'International Governance of Autonomous Military Robots' (2011) XII The Columbia Science and Technology Law Review.

Moyes R, 'Key Elements of Meaningful Human Control' (April 2016) <https://article36.org/wp-content/uploads/2016/04/MHC-2016-FINAL.pdf> accessed 24 February 2023.

Nikolenko SI, *Synthetic Data for Deep Learning*, vol 174 (Springer International Publishing 2021) <https://link.springer.com/10.1007/978-3-030-75178-4> accessed 31 August 2021.

Protocol additional to the Geneva Conventions of 12 August 1949, and relating to the Protection of Victims of International Armed Conflicts.

Rickli J-M, 'Some Considerations of the Impact of LAWS on International Security: Strategic Stability, Non-State Actors and Future Prospects' (Meeting of Experts on Lethal Autonomous Weapons Systems Convention on Certain Conventional Weapons (CCW), Geneva, 16 April 2015).

Rome Statute of the International Criminal Court.

Rosert E and Sauer F, 'Prohibiting Autonomous Weapons: Put Human Dignity First' (2019) 10 Global Policy.

Santoni de Sio F and van den Hoven J, 'Meaningful Human Control over Autonomous Systems: A Philosophical Account' (2018) 5(15) Frontiers in Robotics and AI.

Sauer F and Schörnig N, 'Killer Drones: The "Silver Bullet" of Democratic Warfare?' (2012) 43 Security Dialogue.

Scharre P, 'Why Unmanned' [2011] Joint Force Quarterly.

Scherer MU, 'Regulating Artificial Intelligence Systems: Risks, Challenges, Competencies, and Strategies' [2015] SSRN Electronic Journal <http://www.ssrn.com/abstract=2609777> accessed 3 March 2020.

Schörnig N, 'Die Automatisierung des Krieges: Der Vormarsch der Robotkrieger ist nicht mehr aufzuhalten und wirft einige Probleme auf' [2010] Peace Research Institute Frankfurt <http://www.jstor.com/stable/resrep14321> accessed 24 February 2023.

Sharkey N, 'Cassandra or False Prophet of Doom: AI Robots and War' (2008) 23 IEEE Intelligent Systems.

Sharkey N, 'Staying in the Loop: Human Supervisory Control of Weapons' in Nehal Bhuta and others (eds), *Autonomous Weapons Systems: Law, Ethics, Policy* (Cambridge University Press 2016).

Sparrow R, 'Robots and Respect: Assessing the Case Against Autonomous Weapon Systems' (2016) 30 Ethics & International Affairs.

Stoner RH, 'History and Technology – R2D2 with Attitude: The Story of the Phalanx Close-In Weapons – NavWeaps' (*NavWeaps*, 30 October 2009) <http://www.navweaps.com/index_tech/tech-103.php> accessed 10 June 2021.

'The Campaign To Stop Killer Robots' (*Campaign To Stop Killer Robots*) <https://www.stopkillerrobots.org/> accessed 25 August 2020.

'The Convention on Certain Conventional Weapons' <https://www.un.org/disarmament/the-convention-on-certain-conventional-weapons/> accessed 28 June 2022.

Weiner T, 'New Model Army SoldierRolls Closer to Battle' (*The New York Times*, 16 February 2005) <https://www.nytimes.com/2005/02/16/technology/new-model-army-soldierrolls-closer-to-battle.html> accessed 18 August 2021.

Index